D1175898

More OpenGL®
Game Programming

Dave Astle, Editor

THOMSON

COURSE TECHNOLOGY

Professional ■ Technical ■ Reference

ISBN: 1-59200-830-5
Library of Congress Catalog Card Number: 2004111224
Printed in the United States of America

06 07 08 09 10 PH 10 9 8 7 6 5 4 3 2

Publisher and General Manager, Thomson Course Technology PTR:
Stacy L. Hiquet

Associate Director of Marketing:
Sarah O'Donnell

Manager of Editorial Services:
Heather Talbot

Marketing Manager:
Cathleen Snyder

Senior Acquisitions Editor:
Emi Smith

Senior Editor:
Mark Garvey

Marketing Coordinator:
Jordan Casey

Project Editor:
Kate Shoup Welsh

Technical Reviewer:
Dave Astle

Thomson Course Technology PTR Editorial Services Coordinator:
Elizabeth Furbish

Copy Editor:
Anne Smith

Interior Layout Tech:
Jill Flores

Cover Designer:
Mike Tanamachi

Indexer:
Kelly Talbot

Proofreader:
Sara Gullion

THOMSON

COURSE TECHNOLOGY

Professional ■ Technical ■ Reference

Thomson Course Technology PTR,
a division of Thomson Course Technology
25 Thomson Place
Boston, MA 02210
http://www.courseptr.com

To Kevin Hawkins, for giving me the opportunity to strike out on my own with this book.

Acknowledgments

Any author will tell you that writing a book is a major undertaking that requires the support of your friends, family, and of course, your publisher. For me, this book has been particularly challenging, and I owe a debt of gratitude to a number of people who were instrumental in getting this book to finally see the light of day.

First and foremost, I want to thank my wife Melissa. She's been a book widow for almost five years now, but still supports me and complains surprisingly little. Likewise, I'm sure my five children are tired of hearing me tell them, "I can't right now, I've got to work on my book," so I'm glad that they haven't lynched me yet.

I want to thank all of the authors who contributed to this book. You've been a great group of people to work with, and I'm very happy with the results. James Ritts and Rob Jones also deserve special mention for their assistance with editing.

I've been working with Course Technology for so long that many of the people there seem like old friends, despite the fact that I see them only once or twice a year at conferences. They all deserve my thanks, especially Emi Smith, who bore the brunt of the numerous reschedules this book went through.

Finally, I want to thank my readers for buying my books and for giving me constructive feedback on how to make them better. I've tried my best to provide information that is accurate and useful, and I hope you'll be pleased with what you find herein.

ABOUT THE AUTHORS

DAVE ASTLE started programming games more than 20 years ago and has been programming games professionally for several years. In 2003, he joined QUALCOMM's Gaming and Graphics group, where he is currently a staff engineer and one of the lead OpenGL ES developers. He is the cofounder, Executive Vice President, and Executive Producer of GameDev.net, the leading online community for game developers. He coauthored *OpenGL ES Game Development, OpenGL Game Programming*, and *Beginning OpenGL Game Programming*, and has contributed to many other game-development books, both as an author and as an editor. He is a regular speaker at game industry conferences. He received his bachelor's degree in Computer Science from the University of Utah. When not hunched over his laptop, Dave enjoys weightlifting, mountain biking, listening to music, cooking, going to the beach, reading, collecting rhinos, and playing with his five kids. He lives in Temecula, CA. He can be reached at **dave@gamedev.net**.

PAUL BAKER has a first class degree in Mathematics from Oxford University, and a master's degree in Computing from Imperial College London. On leaving university, he spent some time working in the software division of a major silicon chip designer. He left to pursue his ambition of writing his own software. Paul's areas of interest include graphics, emulation, and operating systems. His Web site, showcasing several of his projects in these areas, can be found at **http://www.paulsprojects.net**.

DIMI CHRISTOPOULOS studied Computer Engineering and Informatics at the University of Patras, Greece, and holds a Master of Science (M.Sc.) in Virtual Reality and Computer Graphics from the University of Hull in Great Britain. He started game programming in the 1980s and has been using OpenGL since 1997. He currently works as a Virtual Reality and 3D Graphics Software Engineer, and spends time coding freeware games and demos and sharing his knowledge by writing tutorials. He contributed to the demo CD for *OpenGL Game Programming*, and has also written for NeHe (**http://nehe.gamedev.net**). For more information, visit his personal Web site at **http://vrbytes.port5.com**.

JASON CITRON graduated as valedictorian from Full Sail in 2004 with a Bachelor of Science in Game Design and Development. He focused his studies on the system architecture and people process issues present in game development. Currently, he is working at Stormfront Studios in California.

ANGUS DORBIE started out in 3D graphics modeling buildings for architects. He moved on to develop simulator graphics for Marconi, worked on virtual reality systems for Division, and worked at Silicon Graphics in the Reality Center, for the Applied Engineering group, and on the Performer development team in the Advanced Systems Division. He worked for Keyhole (now Google Earth) writing the first version of their global MIP map image processing tool chain, and created their client image overlay component. More recently, Angus helped develop graphics middleware for NOKIA, worked on an Xbox title for Atari, and currently helps design OpenGL ES graphics hardware as a systems engineer for QUALCOMM.

WAEL EL ORAIBY started programming at age 13. His love for electronics and software led him to an engineering diploma in computer and communication at the IUL Beirut, where he successfully built a low-cost 3D laser scanner with his friend. Later he went to France and obtained a master's degree in Computer Science from both Université de Haute Alsace and Université Louis Pasteur. You'll now find him earning a Ph.D. in computer science, pursuing algorithms that tackle k-sets, Delaunay, and Voronoi diagrams.

DAVID ELDER is a Ph.D. student at Boston University. His research focuses on neural network models of steering and obstacle avoidance, and on GPU-based neural network simulation techniques. His hobbies include graphics and games, and he plans to pursue a career in the graphics industry following the completion of his degree.

ANDREI GRADINARI is fifth-year student at the Technical University of Moldova. He studies Computer Science. Andrei has been programming computer graphics for four years. His professional activity in game programming started in 2004 when he joined the War of Clans development team. His major programming interests are graphics programming (OpenGL and Direct3D), in-game physics simulation, and networking. You can learn more about his projects at **http://www.glplanet3d.newmail.ru**.

LUKAS HEISE works for an international insurance company, which is based in Stockholm, Sweden. He develops new solutions to problems by approaching them from a unique perspective. During his free time he enjoys being with his friends or weightlifting at the gym. He believes in keeping both his mind and body in harmony.

ROBERT JONES is still alive; he considers this to be a good thing. Having been programming since the age of 12, when his friend showed him some BASIC code, he cut most of his programming teeth on an Atari STe using a 68000 Assembler. In 2000, at the age of 20, he discovered OpenGL and has been hooked ever since. Since first hearing of it, he has been a huge proponent of the OpenGL Shading Language, pushing it and the standard whenever he can.

BALDUR KARLSSON was born in Dundee, Scotland, in 1987. He got his first Amiga 500+ at the age of five. Six years later, the owner of a PC, he bought a book called *C: The Complete Reference* and has been programming ever since. At 14 he took an interest in OpenGL programming. He is just starting a Bachelor of Science degree in Computing Science and Mathematics at the University of Edinburgh.

JESSE LAEUCHLI is a self-taught programmer who is currently pursuing a degree at the University of Notre Dame. As a child of a Foreign Service officer, he has lived in foreign countries such as China, Taiwan, Africa, Saudi Arabia, and Hungary. He has written articles on graphics programming for several computer books and Web sites, including *Game Programming Gems 2*, *Graphics Programming Methods*, *ShaderX2*, and *ShaderX3*. He is an avid epee fencer.

JOSH PETRIE graduated from the DigiPen Institute of Technology with a Bachelor of Science in Real-Time Interactive Simulation. During his schooling he studied graphics programming, particularly non-photorealistic techniques. He currently works for Big Huge Games in Maryland.

LUKE PHILPOT is a student from Australia. He started learning C++ at the age of 11 and soon took an interest in OpenGL. He is a keen game developer and is always on the lookout for a good game idea.

A self-taught programmer, EVAN PIPHO has been using OpenGL since discovering GameDev.net in 2000. Now working in the mobile game industry, Evan continues to work with OpenGL and 3D graphics in his spare time. He also previously authored *Focus on 3D Models*, published in 2002 by Premier Press.

ANDRES REINOT is a graduate of Iowa State University, where he earned a degree in Computer Science and worked at the Virtual Reality Applications Center. A native Estonian, Andres now lives in Cedar Falls, Iowa, and is part owner of a start-up game studio called 8monkey Labs. His other interests include drawing, digital painting, 3D modeling, and of course computer graphics. You can see his work at **http://www.reinot.com**.

VLADIMIR REPCAK received a degree in Economics in 1999. After five years of working in that field while programming at night, he decided to switch industries and founded VladR Games, where he works on online and budget PC games to build up his portfolio and secure financing for a bigger game. He maintains a Web site at **http://www.avenger.sk**.

James Ritts received his Bachelor of Science in Computer Science in 2003 from the University of California, San Diego. Having no travel money following graduation, he immediately joined the OpenGL ES group at QUALCOMM, Inc., where he continues to work as an engineer. His interests include amateur astronomy, graphics programming, guitar pedal construction, and jazz.

Maciej Sawitus is a happy member of PeopleCanFly, where he's developing a next-generation 3D game engine for Xbox 360 and PlayStation 3. He graduated from Warsaw University in 2005 with an M.Sc. in Software Engineering. His main interests are general game engine development and modern 3D rendering techniques. One of his greatest successes is making his wife Małgorzata—who is not particularly interested in 3D graphics—distinguish shadow volumes from shadow mapping. He can be reached at **msawitus@gmail.com**.

Andrei Stoian will begin his first year of college at the Polytechnic University of Bucharest after finishing the IB diploma program in Norway. He is a self-taught programmer and will be studying Computer Science/Electrical Engineering in a four-year program. His computer interests include graphics, physics simulations, Web programming, geographic information systems, cryptography, and security.

Brian Story started programming at an early age and easily found it to be what he wanted to do with his life. With the "what" discovered, he has since spent his time trying to discover the "who" and "where." In 2002, Brian graduated from Full Sail with an Associate degree in game design and development, and started a small shareware company soon thereafter. Brian enjoys life with his wife Chandra and their two cats in Orlando, Florida.

Lee Thomason is a professional software architect who works in San Francisco. He is happily married, and enjoys rock climbing, swimming, photography, kites, and experimenting with software for graphics and video games. He is the creator and maintainer of several open source projects: the 3D game engine Lilith3D; Kyra, a sprite engine; an A* pathfinder called MicroPather; and the small and popular XML parser TinyXml. All of the projects can be accessed at SourceForge or from **http://www.grinninglizard.com**.

Joel Villagrana was born in 1978 in Guadalajara, Mexico, and has liked video games since he was a child. He pursued a bachelor's degree in Computer Science in his native city's university, where he hoped to learn how to create games; motivated by the lack of good CG courses in national universities and his interest in games, he went to the UK to pursue a master's degree in Virtual Environments. Currently he's back in Mexico working as a software engineer for IBM, but he looks forward to a career in the game industry. In his free time he enjoys being with his wife and one-year-old daughter, taking photographs, or programming.

Contents

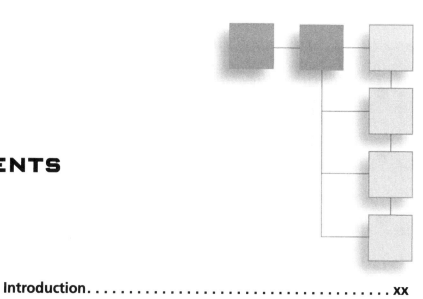

Chapter 4   The OpenGL Shading Language .79

BONUS REFERENCE APPENDIXES ON COMPANION WEB SITE

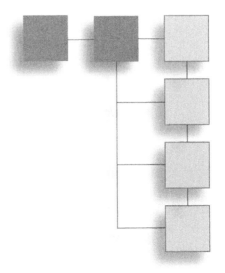

INTRODUCTION

Dave Astle

Welcome to *More OpenGL Game Programming*. This book provides a direct continuation of the topics covered in *Beginning OpenGL Game Programming*, as well as serving in many ways as a follow-up to *OpenGL Game Programming*. Within these pages, you'll learn about topics beyond the scope of many introductory game-programming texts. You'll also learn about the newest and most advanced features offered in OpenGL as of version 2.0 (as well as many things that are likely to appear in the next revision). As in the previous books, the focus will be on the graphical components of games.

This book is broken into three parts:

- In Part I, "Performance Tips and Hints," you'll learn about advanced OpenGL features, including buffer objects, shaders, occlusion queries, advanced texture mapping, advanced lighting, and more.
- In Part II, "Graphics Toolbox," you'll see how to use OpenGL to create special effects, render terrain, simulate natural effects, and more.
- In Part III, "Elements of a Game," you'll learn how to animate and render models, and how to efficiently manage the objects in your game.

Background

Unlike *Beginning OpenGL Game Programming* and *OpenGL Game Programming*, this book wasn't written by me and Kevin Hawkins. Instead, it was written by me and more than 20 other authors. I started working on this book more than two years ago, but I eventually came to the realization that in order to cover the topics I wanted to cover *and* get the book completed in a reasonable length of time, I'd have to work on this full time. Because that wasn't feasible, I instead decided to recruit a large group of people, each of whom could focus on a single topic (or in a few cases, a small number of topics).

However, unlike other multi-author books, this isn't a random collection of loosely related articles. Instead, I defined the topics that I felt would be important to a game or graphics programmer, organized them in a logical manner, and then found authors to write about each of those topics (as well as covering quite a few of them myself).

What We Will and Won't Cover

Like my previous books, this book focuses on using OpenGL to implement the graphical components of games. You'll be learning about OpenGL's advanced features, and then how to use them to implement some of the most popular elements used in games.

My intent with this book is to provide intermediate-level game programmers with a solid foundation in topics that you will likely find useful in your game development career. I have not attempted to cover these topics exhaustively; indeed, doing so in a text this size would be impossible. For example, the subject matter of Chapter 10, "Terrain," has had entire books devoted to it—and they still leave many topics untouched.

There are many good introductory game development books available, and there is a wealth of advanced material available in books, magazines, conference presentations, and online articles. But the amount of in-between material—that is, material that allows developers to more easily transition from beginning to advanced topics—is currently lacking. I see this book as helping to fill that gap, at least in the realm of OpenGL-based game graphics.

Because I'm focusing on graphics, the amount of non-graphics material will necessarily be limited. However, coverage of important related topics, such as loading and animating models and efficiently managing your scene, has been included.

What You Need to Know

As you should surmise from the title, this isn't a book for raw beginners. To get the most out of this book, you should already have a good understanding of OpenGL basics. If you have already read *Beginning OpenGL Game Programming* or *OpenGL Game Programming*, you're ready for this book. Alternatively, if you have read other OpenGL books and have at least some exposure to game programming, you should be able to understand and use the material presented here.

Like the previous two books, C++ will be used for sample programs, so you should have a solid understanding of C++. You don't need to be a C++ guru, however.

Most of the code samples included in the book will be platform-agnostic. However, because most of our readers use some flavor of Windows—and because Windows presents some unique challenges for OpenGL programmers—I'll be addressing a few Windows-specific issues. All sample programs will be available as Visual Studio projects with both Win32 and SDL versions.

Using This Book

If you don't read anything else in this introduction, read this section. It contains important information you'll need to get the most out of this book

Where's the CD?

I made the controversial decision to not include a CD with this book. Instead, I'll be providing the sample code and other supporting files via the book's Web site at **http://glbook.gamedev.net**. My reasoning for this is as follows:

- Including a CD adds to the production cost of the book, so by not including one, you're saving money.
- There are sure to be bugs in the code. By requiring you to get the code from the Web site, I'm ensuring that you're working with the latest and greatest.
- The Web site will also allow the other authors and me to release bonus material to supplement the book. In fact, if you extend our code, port it to other platforms, or do anything else that you'd like to share with other readers, feel free to contact us about putting it on the site.

The downside of this approach is that there are probably people out there who have limited or no Internet access. Even without the source code, however, the algorithms presented in the book will be valuable, and we've included the relevant source snippets where appropriate. We'll also keep the files on the Web site as small as possible, so if you have limited Internet access, you'll be able to quickly download everything you need.

Extensions

Because this book is using advanced OpenGL features, we'll be making extensive use of extensions. A solid knowledge of extensions will therefore be vital, especially for Windows programmers, where even core OpenGL features beyond version 1.1 are only available as extensions. If you've read *Beginning OpenGL Game Programming*, you already know everything you need to know. Otherwise, I recommend that you read an article I've written, available online at the following URL:

http://www.gamedev.net/reference/programming/features/openglext/

Throughout the book, whenever we discuss topics that require extensions or are only available as extensions under Windows, we'll provide a box with information about the extension to make it easier for you to use.

We'll again be using Ben Woodhouse's OpenGL Easy Extension library (GLee), which I introduced in *Beginning OpenGL Game Programming*, to manage extensions. You can find out more about GLee at **http://www.elf-stone.com/glee/**.

Function Names

Many OpenGL functions come in multiple versions to support different numbers and types of parameters. To avoid listing all the different variations of a function, we'll use the following convention:

```
glFunction{1234}{bsifd ubusui}(TYPE param);
```

```
glFunction{1234}{bsifd ubusui}v(TYPE *params);
```

This notation indicates that the function name will be followed by one of the numbers contained within the first set of curly braces and then one of the letters contained in the second set of curly braces. The letters stand for byte, short, integer, float, double, unsigned byte, unsigned short, and unsigned integer, respectively. `TYPE` is used as a placeholder for the specific data type accepted by the function. The second form varies from the first only in that it includes a `v`, which indicates that the function takes an array of values rather than a single value.

When referring to a function that has multiple forms within the text, we will generally refer to it as `glFunction()` without any parameter information.

Support Web Site

Finally, I'm maintaining a Web site at **http://glbook.gamedev.net** that we will use to provide support for this book (as well as my previous books). As mentioned, the source code and related files for all of the book's demos can be found on the Web site. You will also find color versions of the figures, and bonus material. I'll be updating this site regularly to post errata and updates to the sample programs as needed. Be sure to check it if you have any problems, and if you find any errors that made it past the editing, please let us know. You'll find contact information for us on the Web site.

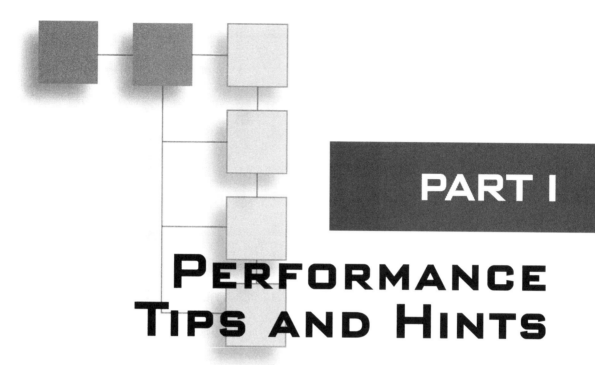

PART I

PERFORMANCE TIPS AND HINTS

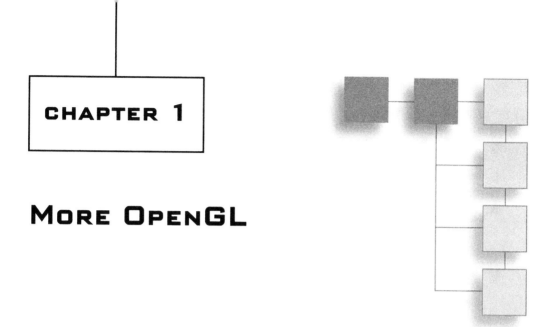

CHAPTER 1

MORE OPENGL

*B*eginning OpenGL Game Programming covered the most essential aspects of OpenGL for game developers. However, many of the more advanced topics were deferred to this volume. In addition, OpenGL has continued to evolve, most notably in updating the core specification to 2.0. Some important multivendor extensions have also been introduced.

These advanced and new features will be thoroughly covered in this book. Many of them will be discussed as needed later in the book as we cover general techniques. However, there are several topics that will be useful for many things covered in the later chapters, or that just don't fit well in other areas. You'll learn about them in this chapter. Specifically, you'll learn about:

- Vertex buffer objects
- Pixel buffer objects
- Framebuffer objects
- Multisampling
- Floating-point buffers
- Occlusion queries
- User clip planes
- Disabling Vsync

Vertex Buffer Objects

Dave Astle

extension
_____

Extension name: `ARB_vertex_buffer_object`

Name string: `GL_ARB_vertex_buffer_object`

Promoted to core: OpenGL 1.5

Function names: `glBindBufferARB`, `glGenBuffersARB`, `glDeleteBuffersARB`, `glBufferDataARB`, `glBufferSubDataARB`, `glMapBufferARB`, `glUnmapBufferARB`, `glGetBufferSubDaraARB`, `glGetBufferParameterivARB`, `glGetBufferPointervARB`

Tokens (partial list): `GL_ARRAY_BUFFER_ARB`, `GL_ELEMENT_ARRAY_BUFFER_ARB`, `GL_STREAM_DRAW_ARB`, `GL_STREAM_READ_ARB`, `GL_STREAM_COPY_ARB`, `GL_STATIC_DRAW_ARB`, `GL_STATIC_READ_ARB`, `GL_STATIC_COPY_ARB`, `GL_DYNAMIC_DRAW_ARB`, `GL_DYNAMIC_READ_ARB`, `GL_DYNAMIC_COPY_ARB`, `GL_READ_ONLY_ARB`, `GL_WRITE_ONLY_ARB`, `GL_READ_WRITE_ARB`
_____

In *Beginning OpenGL Game Programming,* you learned about vertex arrays, which provide a convenient way to render large amounts of geometry in a fairly efficient manner. You also learned about the compiled vertex array extension, which may allow the OpenGL implementation to cache some of your vertex data in video memory, allowing for faster rendering.

OpenGL 1.5 took this a step further by adding *vertex buffer objects* to the core specification. To fully understand the benefits of vertex buffer objects—or VBOs, as they're often called—let's take a moment to review how vertex arrays work.

With vertex arrays, you declare or allocate an array that is used to store the data representing the object you want to render. When you make a call to one of the `glPointer()` functions, you're telling OpenGL where that data is located in memory. Then, when you call `glDrawArrays()` or one of the other drawing functions, OpenGL retrieves the data from that memory location and processes it.

The important thing to note here is that the array exists in client memory, or more simply, the system memory on your computer. For your video card to access that data, it needs to be copied from client memory across a bus (usually AGP or PCI Express) and into video memory. Although they have improved in recent years, bus speeds have generally not kept up with processor and video-card speeds, so this process can be slow. Furthermore, the amount of data that can be transferred at one time (i.e., the bandwidth) is limited. Thus, when rendering even modestly sized data sets, the overhead involved with transferring data to the video card can become a bottleneck.

Vertex buffer objects solve this problem by allowing you to store frequently used vertex data in video memory. In the days when video cards had just enough memory for the framebuffer and a few textures, this wouldn't have been an option. But now, video cards with literally hundreds of megabytes of memory are becoming increasingly common, making this approach not only practical but prudent.

Unlike compiled vertex arrays, which only allow you to work with one set of arrays at a time and which provide you almost no control (they're really more of a hint), the APIs associated with vertex buffer objects enable you to manage many different sets of data with fairly detailed control of how they are used.

This section will fully explain how to create and use vertex buffer objects.

Creating Buffer Objects

Buffer objects are quite similar to other OpenGL objects, such as texture objects. To use them, you must first create the buffer object and associate it with a unique identifier—namely, an unsigned integer that acts as a name or handle. Each buffer object has a set of states and data associated with it.

Just as with texture objects, you can either create and manage unique identifiers yourself, or you can have OpenGL generate a range of unused identifiers for you. This is done with `glGenBuffers()`:

```
void glGenBuffers(GLsizei numBuffers, GLuint *buffers);
```

This will store `numBuffers` unique buffer names in `buffers`. The names are guaranteed to be unused, which means they haven't been bound (via `glBindBuffer()`) or generated by `glGenBuffers()` previously.

Calling `glGenBuffers()` doesn't actually do anything other than marking the names as used. The buffer objects associated with these names aren't created until a call to `glBindBuffer()` is made:

```
void glBindBuffer(GLenum target, GLuint buffer);
```

You must set `target` to `GL_ARRAY_BUFFER` or `GL_ELEMENT_ARRAY_BUFFER` (the latter will be covered in more detail in the "Using Buffers with Index Arrays" section later on), and `buffer` is the buffer name. Calling `glBindBuffer()` on a buffer that has already been created selects it as the currently active buffer, allowing you to make changes to it.

note

The value 0 is not a valid buffer name, but it does serve a special purpose. If you want to disable the use of vertex buffer objects and revert to using normal vertex arrays, simply bind buffer object zero.

Placing Data in Buffers

A buffer consists of a state vector and a data store. When a buffer is initially created, the data store is empty. To place data in the currently bound buffer, you will use the following API:

```
void glBufferData(GLenum target, GLsizeiptr size, const void *data, GLenum usage);
```

Again, target should be set to GL_ARRAY_BUFFER or GL_ELEMENT_ARRAY_BUFFER. The size parameter indicates the size, in machine units (generally bytes), of the desired data store. You use data to point to the client side memory that you want to have copied into the buffer; a NULL value will cause the data store to be allocated without initializing it. The usage parameter provides a hint to OpenGL as to the intended usage of the data, so that it can optimize for performance. Valid values for usage and their associated meanings are listed in Table 1.1. Keep in mind that these values are intended only as a hint; nothing (other than a possible performance penalty) will prevent you from using a buffer differently from the specified usage value.

Table 1.1 Buffer Usage Values

Value	Meaning
GL_STREAM_DRAW	The data for the buffer is provided once by the application and will be used infrequently by OpenGL drawing commands. An example of this would be model data that is animated every frame but used for only a single model.
GL_STATIC_DRAW	The data for the buffer is provided once by the application and will be used frequently by OpenGL drawing commands. This would be used for static objects, perhaps with many instances. This is generally the most common usage, as it offers the greatest benefit.
GL_DYNAMIC_DRAW	The data for the buffer is provided repeatedly by the application and will be used frequently by OpenGL drawing commands. This would be appropriate for model data that is animated every frame but shared by multiple instances or drawn repeatedly.
GL_STREAM_READ*	The data for the buffer is provided once by OpenGL and will be read infrequently by the application.
GL_STATIC_READ*	The data for the buffer is provided once by OpenGL and will be read frequently by the application.
GL_DYNAMIC_READ*	The data for the buffer is provided repeatedly by OpenGL and will be read frequently by the application.
GL_STREAM_COPY*	The data for the buffer is provided once by OpenGL and will be used infrequently by OpenGL drawing commands.
GL_STATIC_COPY*	The data for the buffer is provided once by OpenGL and will be used frequently by OpenGL drawing commands.
GL_DYNAMIC_COPY*	The data for the buffer is provided repeatedly by OpenGL and will be used frequently by OpenGL drawing commands.

*The _READ and _COPY variants of the usage values listed are not currently supported. They are intended for future use.

Calling glBufferData() on a buffer object that already contains data will cause the old data to be freed before the new data is copied. If you try to create a data store that is larger than the available video memory, the call will fail and the GL_OUT_OF_MEMORY error condition will be set.

OpenGL also offers the ability to update all or part of an existing data store. This can be useful for animation, or if you want to load a data store from more than one source. This is done using the following API:

```
void glBufferSubData(GLenum target, GLintptr offset, GLsizeiptr size, const void *data);
```

Once again, target should be GL_ARRAY_BUFFER or GL_ELEMENT_ARRAY_BUFFER. Both offset and size are used to indicate the section of data being updated, and data points to the new data.

When changing the entire contents of a data store without changing its size or usage, calling glBufferSubData() will tend to be more efficient than calling glBufferData(), since the latter will require that data be freed and reallocated.

Destroying Buffers

When you're done with your buffer objects, it's important to tell OpenGL to delete them to prevent a resource leak. This is done with the following:

```
void glDeleteBuffers(GLsizei numBuffers, GLuint *buffers);
```

Here, buffers is an array containing the numBuffers buffer names that you want to delete. After this call is made, each name in buffers is marked as unused, and the associated data is removed. If buffers contains bogus values (such as unused names or zero), they will simply be ignored without generating an error.

Using Buffers with Vertex Arrays

Now that you've learned how to create buffer objects, fill them with data, and destroy them when you're done, let's turn to how to use them. Buffer objects can be used as the data source for any vertex array attributes. When a nonzero vertex buffer is bound to GL_ARRAY_BUFFER, any subsequent calls to one of the gl*Pointer() functions will use the data in the vertex buffer as the source for that vertex attribute. Instead of treating the pointer parameter in the traditional way, it is used as an offset (representing the number of bytes) into the buffer object's data store. In this way, a single buffer object can be used to store multiple vertex attributes.

tip
_____

The VBO extension specification includes a macro that can be used to make sure that you correctly set offsets into VBOs. It'll also prevent compiler warnings that you'll get from passing an integer to a function that expects a pointer. It's defined as follows:

#define BUFFER_OFFSET(i) ((char *)NULL + (i))

i is simply the offset into the buffer, measured in bytes.
_____

To understand fully how this works, let's look at a simple example that renders a single triangle. For comparison, we'll first show the code using only vertex arrays:

```
// global
GLfloat vertices[] = {
   1.0f, -1.0f, 0.0f,
  -1.0f, -1.0f, 0.0f,
   0.0f,  1.0f, 0.0f
};

GLubyte colors[] = {
   255,  50, 160,
   180, 255,  70,
    90,  10, 255
};

...


// during rendering
glVertexPointer(3, GL_FLOAT, 0, vertices);
glColorPointer(3, GL_UNSIGNED_BYTE, 0, colors);
glDrawArrays(GL_TRIANGLES, 3);
```

Converting this code to use vertex buffers is straightforward:

```
// global
GLuint triangleBuffer;
...


// during initialization
GLfloat vertices[] = {
   1.0f, -1.0f, 0.0f,
  -1.0f, -1.0f, 0.0f,
   0.0f,  1.0f, 0.0f
};
```

```
GLubyte colors[] = {
  255, 50, 160,
  180, 255, 70,
  90, 10, 255
};

glGenBuffers(1, &triangleBuffer);

glBindBuffer(GL_ARRAY_BUFFER, triangleBuffer);
// Create a data store big enough for 9 floats and 9 bytes. Leave
// the data store uninitialized.
glBufferData(GL_ARRAY_BUFFER, 9 * (sizeof(GLfloat) + sizeof(GLubyte)),
             NULL, GL_STATIC_DRAW);

// load the position data
glBufferSubData(GL_ARRAY_BUFFER, 0, 9 * sizeof(GLfloat), vertices);

// followed by the color data
glBufferSubData(GL_ARRAY_BUFFER, 9 * sizeof(GLfloat), 9 * sizeof(GLubyte),
                colors);

...

// during rendering
glBindBufferARB(GL_ARRAY_BUFFER, triangleBuffer);
glVertexPointer(3, GL_FLOAT, 0, 0);
glColorPointer(3, GL_UNSIGNED_BYTE, 0, BUFFER_OFFSET(9 * sizeof(GLfloat)));

glDrawArrays(GL_TRIANGLES, 3);

...

// during shutdown
glDeleteBuffers(2, buffers);
```

The VBO version is considerably more complex than the vertex array version, and for this simple example, it is serious overkill. But for more complex objects, the additional effort is worth the performance gains offered by vertex buffer objects. It's worth noting that other than the setup, using vertex buffer objects is virtually identical to using vertex arrays.

Using Buffers with Index Arrays

Buffer objects can also be used to store the indices for glDrawElements(), glDrawRangeElements(), and glMultiDrawElements(), though the process for doing so is slightly different. When calling glBindBuffer(), glBufferData(), or glBufferSubData(), GL_ELEMENT_ARRAY_BUFFER is used instead of GL_ARRAY_BUFFER as the target parameter. When any of the variants of glDrawElements() is called, if a nonzero buffer is bound to GL_ELEMENT_ARRAY, it will be used for the source of vertex indices. The indices parameter acts as an offset (in bytes) into the indices in the buffer.

Mapping Buffers

Finally, OpenGL also allows you to map the contents of a buffer to client memory. This allows you to manipulate the data associated with the buffer object directly. An example of using this is writing animated vertex data directly to the data store, rather than writing to a temporary array and then copying the array into the data store. This functionality is exposed through glMapBuffer():

```
void *glMapBuffer();
```

If successful, glMapBuffer() will return a pointer to the currently bound buffer's data store. The pointer can't be used with any OpenGL functions that accept pointers. Attempting to do so may result in a crash or other unexpected behavior. But otherwise, you can use the pointer to read from or write to the buffer as you see fit.

note

Using the pointer returned by glMapBuffer() in a way that is inconsistent with the usage parameter for the vertex buffer object can result in performance degradation and instability, and is thus discouraged.

Before the data in the buffer can again be used by OpenGL, it has to be unmapped through a call to glUnmapBuffer():

```
GLboolean glUnmapBuffer();
```

If the value returned by glUnmapBuffer() is GL_FALSE, the contents of the buffer have been corrupted while the buffer was mapped, probably due to a windowing system event. Otherwise, the buffer is ready for use.

The benefit gained from mapping the buffer to client memory is highly dependent on the OpenGL implementation. With many current implementations, you probably won't see an improvement, and it's possible that performance may actually degrade due to synchronization and concurrency issues, so you should test and profile before making heavy use of this feature.

Vertex Buffer Object Examples

The source code for this chapter that is available on the book's website includes two example programs that use vertex buffer objects.

The first, SimpleVBO, renders a single triangle to illustrate the usage of VBOs as simply as possible.

The second, Marbles, takes the Marbles demo from *Beginning OpenGL Game Programming*, beefs up the triangle count, and allows you to toggle between immediate mode, vertex arrays, and vertex arrays with VBOs (the display list and compiled vertex array options have been removed for the sake of simplicity).

Many of the examples from later chapters will make use of VBOs as well.

Pixel Buffer Objects

Andrei Gradinari

extension

Extension name: ARB_pixel_buffer_object
Name string: GL_ARB_pixel_buffer_object
Tokens: GL_PIXEL_PACK_BUFFER_ARB, GL_PIXEL_UNPACK_BUFFER_ARB

Pixel buffer objects (PBOs) are built on the interface introduced for vertex buffer objects, so be sure you're familiar with the previous section before proceeding. This extension makes buffer objects capable of storing not only vertex array data, but also any kind of data you wish. Typically this feature is used for storing pixel data.

note

Don't confuse pixel buffer objects with pbuffers, which will be described in Chapter 5, "Advanced Texture Mapping."

Pixel buffer objects are created, deleted, bound, and filled with data in exactly the same way as vertex buffers, except that the target parameter for functions such as glBufferData() and glBindBuffer() will be one of the two values listed below:

GL_PIXEL_PACK_BUFFER_ARB: Used when writing into the bound buffer memory using functions such as glReadPixels().

GL_PIXEL_UNPACK_BUFFER_ARB: Used when using the data in the buffer as the source for operations such as glDrawPixels() or glTexImage().

Binding PBOs

When a buffer object is bound to one of the pixel targets, client-side functions work in buffer memory space instead of in application memory space. In other words, all OpenGL pixel operations will read from (for unpack) or write to (for pack) the buffer's data store whenever a nonzero buffer object is bound to the related pixel target. In this case, the pointer parameter of the operation in question is treated as an offset (in bytes) into the data store. For example, when a pixel buffer object is bound to GL_PIXEL_PACK_BUFFER_ARB, the following command will read from the framebuffer and write it to the buffer object's data store starting at the beginning (since the pixel parameter is NULL):

```
glReadPixels(0,0, 512, 512, GL_RGB, GL_UNSIGNED_BYTE, NULL);
```

For a complete list of commands that work with pixel buffer objects, see Table 1.2.

Table 1.2 Pixel Commands

Unpack	Pack
glBitmap()	glGetCompressedTexImage()
glColorSubTable()	glGetConvolutionFilter()
glColorTable()	glGetHistogram()
glCompressedTexImage1D()	glGetPixelMapfv()
glCompressedTexImage2D()	glGetPixelMapuiv()
glCompressedTexImage3D()	glGetPixelMapusv()
glCompressedTexSubImage1D()	glGetPolygonStipple()
glCompressedTexSubImage2D()	glGetSeparableFilter()
glCompressedTexSubImage3D()	glGetTexImage()
glConvolutionFilter1D()	glReadPixels()
glConvolutionFilter2D()	
glDrawPixels()	
glPixelMapfv()	
glPixelMapuiv()	
glPixelMapusv()	
glPolygonStipple()	
glSeparableFilter2D()	
glTexImage1D()	
glTexImage2D()	
glTexImage3D()	
glTexSubImage1D()	
glTexSubImage2D()	
glTexSubImage3D()	

Using Pixel Buffer Objects

To get a better idea of how PBOs work, let's take a look at using one to read from the back color buffer. The examples will read from a 512×512 area and copy data into the pixel buffer's memory.

Buffer Creation and Memory Allocation

The first step is to generate a buffer. This only needs to be done once, generally during program initialization.

```
GLuint m_iBuffer;
glGenBuffers(1, &m_iBuffer);
```

After the buffer is generated, it is bound to the GL_PIXEL_PACK_BUFFER_ARB target. Once it has been successfully bound, glReadPixels() and other OpenGL pack commands will write data into the bound buffer memory.

```
glBindBuffer(GL_PIXEL_PACK_BUFFER_EXT, m_iBuffer);
```

Once the buffer has been bound, you can allocate memory in its data store. In this case, 512×512×3 bytes are needed to store the image from the framebuffer. At this point, the memory is only being allocated, not initialized, so NULL is passed as the data parameter. Because the buffer will be updated frequently, GL_STREAM_DRAW is passed as the usage parameter.

```
glBufferData(GL_PIXEL_PACK_BUFFER_ARB, 512*512*3, NULL, GL_STREAM_DRAW);
```

After you have finished with memory allocation for the buffer, generally it is a good idea to unbind it from the target until it is ready to be used.

```
glBindBuffer(GL_PIXEL_PACK_BUFFER_ARB, 0);
```

To actually read from the back color buffer and write it into the pixel buffer object, you do the following:

```
glReadBuffer(GL_BACK); // specifies which color buffer to read from
glBindBuffer(GL_PIXEL_PACK_BUFFER_ARB, m_iBuffer);
glReadPixels(0,0, 512, 512, GL_RGB, GL_UNSIGNED_BYTE, NULL);
glBindBuffer(GL_PIXEL_PACK_BUFFER_ARB, 0);
```

Note the NULL parameter passed to glReadPixels() as a memory address. Because a buffer object is currently bound, glReadPixels() treats this as an offset into the PBO's memory. Since it is set to NULL, the command will start writing to the beginning of the buffer.

You can continue to reuse the buffer as many times you wish. Finally, when you don't need the buffer anymore, call `glDeleteBuffers()` to free the memory and other resources associated with it:

```
glDeleteBuffers(1, &m_iBuffer);
```

Mapping Buffer Memory Space to Application Memory Space

Just as with vertex buffer objects, you can map the data store of a pixel buffer object to client memory in order to be able to directly read or manipulate it. The following code shows how to do this using `glMapBuffer()`.

```
glBindBuffer(GL_PIXEL_PACK_BUFFER_ARB, m_iBuffer);
char *pBuffData = glMapBuffer(GL_PIXEL_PACK_BUFFER_ARB, GL_READ_WRITE);
...
// perform some operations on memory pointed to by pBuffData
...
glUnmapBuffer(GL_PIXEL_PACK_BUFFER_ARB);
glBindBuffer(GL_PIXEL_PACK_BUFFER_ARB, 0);
```

It's important to call `glUnmapBuffer()` as soon as you are done working with the data so that OpenGL can resume management of that memory.

Applications of PBOs

Now that you know how to use PBOs, let's look at a few examples of when they might help improve performance.

Render to Vertex Array

Internally, OpenGL views all buffer objects as an array of bytes, and the only differentiation between vertex and pixel buffer objects is in which targets they are bound to. Therefore, a buffer initially filled with vertex data can be bound to one of the pixel buffer targets and used for pixel operations, and vice versa. Among other things, this feature allows for a kind of *render to vertex array* technique. To do this, you would render an image using some shader (see Chapter 2, "Intro to Shaders," Chapter 3, "Low-Level Shaders," and Chapter 4, "The OpenGL Shading Language," for more information on shaders), read back the data from the color buffer into a PBO using `glReadPixels()`, and then use this buffer as a source for vertex data.

Asynchronously Read Pixels

If your application needs to read data back from a number of PBOs, there is a way to parallelize the reading process to make it faster. Take a look at the following piece of code:

```
glBindBuffer(GL_PIXEL_PACK_BUFFER_ARB, buff0);
glReadPixels(0, 0, width, height, GL_RGB, GL_UNSIGNED_BYTE, NULL);

glBindBuffer(GL_PIXEL_PACK_BUFFER_ARB, buff1);
glReadPixels(0, height/2, width, height, GL_RGB, GL_UNSIGNED_BYTE, NULL);
```

When a buffer is bound to GL_PIXEL_PACK_BUFFER_ARB target, glReadPixels()—which normally blocks until the data transfer operation finishes—returns control to the application immediately after the data transfer starts. So in this case the two data transfers most likely happen in parallel (depending on hardware capabilities and loading) and thus, in most cases, application performance increases.

Streaming Textures

If you have a texture that is being updated frequently, using PBOs will increase texture download performance. Here is a simple example:

```
glGenBuffers(1, &buffer);
glBindBuffer(GL_PIXEL_UNPACK_BUFFER_ARB, buffer);
glBufferData(GL_PIXEL_UNPACK_BUFFER_ARB, buffer, NULL, GL_STREAM_DRAW);

for(int i=0; i<N; i++)
{
  char *p = glMapBuffer(GL_PIXEL_UNPACK_BUFFER_ARB, GL_WRITE_ONLY);
  memcpy(p, texData[i], texDataSize);
  ...
  glUnmapBuffer(GL_PIXEL_UNPACK_BUFFER_ARB);
  TexSubImage2D(GL_TEXTURE_2D, 0, 0, 0, width, height, GL_RGB,
                GL_UNSIGNED_BYTE, NULL);
  // render textured geometry
  ...
}
```

note

As of OpenGL 2.0, pixel buffer objects are only available as an extension and are not yet widely supported. Although there is an ARB version of the extension, it is more commonly exposed as an EXT extension. From an application's perspective, there are no notable differences between the two versions.

Framebuffer Objects

Dave Astle

extension

Extension name: EXT_framebuffer_object

Name string: GL_EXT_framebuffer_object

Function names: glIsRenderbufferEXT, glBindRenderbufferEXT, glDeleteRenderbuffersEXT, glGenRenderbuffersEXT, glRenderbufferStorageEXT, glGetRenderbufferParameterivEXT, glIsFramebufferEXT, glBindFramebufferEXT, glDeleteFramebuffersEXT, glGenFramebuffersEXT, glCheckFramebufferStatusEXT, glFramebufferTexture1DEXT, glFramebufferTexture2DEXT, glFramebufferTexture3DEXT, glFramebufferRenderbufferEXT, glGetFramebufferAttachmentParameterivEXT, glGenerateMipmapEXT

Tokens: GL_FRAMEBUFFER_EXT, GL_RENDERBUFFER_EXT, GL_STENCIL_INDEX[1,4,8,16]_EXT, GL_RENDERBUFFER_WIDTH_EXT, GL_RENDERBUFFER_HEIGHT_EXT, GL_RENDERBUFFER_INTERNAL_FORMAT_EXT, GL_RENDERBUFFER_RED_SIZE_EXT, GL_RENDERBUFFER_GREEN_SIZE_EXT, GL_RENDERBUFFER_BLUE_SIZE_EXT, GL_RENDERBUFFER_ALPHA_SIZE_EXT, GL_RENDERBUFFER_DEPTH_SIZE_EXT, GL_RENDERBUFFER_STENCIL_SIZE_EXT, GL_FRAMEBUFFER_ATTACHMENT_OBJECT_TYPE_EXT, GL_FRAMEBUFFER_ATTACHMENT_OBJECT_NAME_EXT, GL_FRAMEBUFFER_ATTACHMENT_TEXTURE_LEVEL_EXT, GL_FRAMEBUFFER_ATTACHMENT_TEXTURE_CUBE_MAP_FACE_EXT, GL_FRAMEBUFFER_ATTACHMENT_TEXTURE_3D_ZOFFSET_EXT, GL_COLOR_ATTACHMENT[0-15]_EXT, GL_DEPTH_ATTACHMENT_EXT, GL_STENCIL_ATTACHMENT_EXT, GL_FRAMEBUFFER_COMPLETE_EXT, GL_FRAMEBUFFER_INCOMPLETE_ATTACHMENT_EXT, GL_FRAMEBUFFER_INCOMPLETE_MISSING_ATTACHMENT_EXT, GL_FRAMEBUFFER_INCOMPLETE_DUPLICATE_ATTACHMENT_EXT, GL_FRAMEBUFFER_INCOMPLETE_DIMENSIONS_EXT, GL_FRAMEBUFFER_INCOMPLETE_FORMATS_EXT, GL_FRAMEBUFFER_INCOMPLETE_DRAW_BUFFER_EXT, GL_FRAMEBUFFER_INCOMPLETE_READ_BUFFER_EXT, GL_FRAMEBUFFER_UNSUPPORTED_EXT, GL_FRAMEBUFFER_BINDING_EXT, GL_RENDERBUFFER_BINDING_EXT, GL_MAX_COLOR_ATTACHMENTS_EXT, GL_MAX_RENDERBUFFER_SIZE_EXT, GL_INVALID_FRAMEBUFFER_OPERATION_EXT

When OpenGL 2.0 was first proposed several years ago, one of the major features it included was the concept of *uberbuffers* (also known as superbuffers). The idea was to introduce generic blocks of memory that could be used for virtually any operation requiring large blocks of data in a highly optimized way. The vertex and pixel buffer objects described in the previous sections are somewhat specialized variations of this concept, though they aren't directly related to this effort.

The OpenGL ARB formed a workgroup to develop this uberbuffers concept. In early 2005, the workgroup released the EXT_framebuffer_object extension. Although it does not contain all of the functionality promised by uberbuffers, it does include much of it, most importantly a much-improved render-to-texture (see Chapter 5) capability. It also is designed to have additional functionality (e.g., rendering to vertex attributes) built on top of it.

Framebuffer Object Overview

So what exactly does the framebuffer object (FBO) extension entail? You'll recall that in OpenGL, the framebuffer is a collection of *logical buffers*, including the color, depth, stencil, and accumulation buffers. Although the framebuffer is the primary destination for rendering operations in OpenGL, it's managed by the windowing system, not by OpenGL itself.

The FBO extension allows you to create additional framebuffer objects that contain a similar set of logical buffers and associated state. Because these framebuffer objects are managed by OpenGL and not the windowing system, they provide a simple, efficient, and windowing-system-independent means of rendering to textures and offscreen surfaces.

For the sake of clarity, any references to "framebuffer object" in this section refer to application-defined framebuffers, and "default framebuffer" refers to the framebuffer provided by the windowing system.

Each logical buffer in a framebuffer object has an associated attachment point. Any *framebuffer-attachable image* can be attached to one of these points. These are simply 2D arrays of pixels, which can currently be either a texture image or a *renderbuffer*— another new object used for offscreen rendering.

Framebuffer objects don't replace the default framebuffer; you still need to use the latter ultimately to display the results of your rendering.

Advantages of Framebuffer Objects

As you'll learn in Chapter 5, existing render-to-texture methods carry some major draw-backs. As mentioned, the FBO extension presents a much better and more simplified method of rendering to texture. The advantages include:

- It only requires a single OpenGL context, so switching between framebuffers is faster than switching between pbuffers.
- It doesn't require the complex pixel format selection that pbuffers use, since the format of the framebuffer is determined by the texture or renderbuffer format. This puts the burden of finding compatible formats on developers.
- It's very similar to Direct3D's render target model, making porting code easier.

■ Renderbuffer images and texture images can be shared among framebuffers (for example, sharing a single depth buffer between multiple color targets), resulting in memory savings.

Using FBOs

This extension introduces two new objects to OpenGL. The first, framebuffer objects, consist of a collection of logical buffers and all of the associated state. The second, renderbuffer objects, can be rendered to but can't be used as texture images.

FBO Creation and Destruction

Managing FBOs (as well as renderbuffers) is similar to managing texture objects. They are created and deleted with the following functions:

```
void glGenFrameBuffersEXT(GLsizei n, GLuint *framebuffers);
void glDeleteFramebuffersEXT(GLsizei n, const GLuint *framebuffers);
```

The parameter n is the number of objects to be created or deleted, and framebuffers is an array that holds the names of the objects.

FBO Binding

As with most other OpenGL objects, you need to bind a framebuffer object to use it:

```
void glBindFramebufferEXT(GLenum target, GLuint framebuffer);
```

Presently, target can only be GL_FRAMEBUFFER_EXT, and framebuffer is the id of the FBO you want to bind. When an FBO is bound, its attached images become the source and destination for fragment operations. Binding an id of 0 causes the default framebuffer to be restored (i.e., rendering happens in the way you're used to).

note

Keep in mind that although binding a framebuffer id of 0 selects the default framebuffer, the default framebuffer does not act like a normal framebuffer object. Any operations that rely on having a valid FBO bound (such as attaching a texture image) will fail if the currently bound framebuffer is 0.

Attaching Texture Images to FBOs

Texture images can be attached to a framebuffer using one of the following:

```
void glFramebufferTexture1DEXT(GLenum target, GLenum attachment,
                                GLenum textarget, GLuint texture, GLint level);
void glFramebufferTexture2DEXT(GLenum target, GLenum attachment,
                                GLenum textarget, GLuint texture, GLint level);
```

```
void glFramebufferTexture3DEXT(GLenum target, GLenum attachment,
                               GLenum textarget, GLuint texture, GLint level,
                               GLint zoffset);
```

These functions allow you to attach images from a texture object to one of the logical buffers of the currently bound framebuffer. If no FBO is currently bound, using any of these functions will generate an error.

You should always set `target` to `GL_FRAMEBUFFER_EXT`, and `attachment` should be one of the values in Table 1.3.

If the value of `texture` is 0, then `textarget`, `level`, and `zoffset` are ignored, and any images attached to `attachment` are detached.

If `texture` is the name of a valid texture object, then valid values of `textarget` depend on which function is being called and (possibly) the current target of the texture object:

- When using `glFramebufferTexture1DEXT()`, `textarget` must be `GL_TEXTURE_1D`.
- When using `glFramebufferTexture2D()`, `textarget` must be `GL_TEXTURE_2D`, unless the texture object's current target is a cubemap, in which case `textarget` must name the cubemap face that you want to attach (i.e., `GL_TEXTURE_CUBE_MAP_POSITIVE_X`, `GL_TEXTURE_CUBE_MAP_NEGATIVE_X`, `GL_TEXTURE_CUBE_MAP_POSITIVE_Y`, `GL_TEXTURE_CUBE_MAP_NEGATIVE_Y`, `GL_TEXTURE_CUBE_MAP_POSITIVE_Z`, or `GL_TEXTURE_CUBE_MAP_NEGATIVE_Z`). If texture rectangles are supported (see Chapter 5), `textarget` can also be `GL_TEXTURE_RECTANGLE_ARB`.
- When using `glFramebufferTexture3DEXT()`, `textarget` must be `GL_TEXTURE_3D`.

Finally, `level` indicates which `mipmap` level to attach to.

Since the buffers in a framebuffer object are all 2D, when attaching the images from a 3D texture, the additional `zoffset` parameter is necessary to specify which plane in the z-direction the FBO should be attached to.

Once you've successfully attached the image to a framebuffer object, the texture image becomes the logical buffer indicated by the `attachment` parameter, so any rendering that modifies that buffer will update the texture.

Table 1.3 Framebuffer Attachment Values

Value	Meaning
GL_COLOR_ATTACHMENTi_EXT	Attach to color buffer *i*, where *i* ranges from 0 to GL_MAX_COLOR_ATTACHMENTS_EXT − 1.
GL_DEPTH_ATTACHMENT_EXT	Attach to the depth buffer.
GL_STENCIL_ATTACHMENT_EXT	Attach to the stencil buffer.

Generating Mipmaps

As you learned in *Beginning OpenGL Game Programming*, it's possible to enable automatic mipmap generation such that whenever the base mipmap level is updated, OpenGL automatically calculates and updates the rest of the levels.

When using the render-to-texture functionality of framebuffer objects, there is ambiguity in regards to what will trigger mipmap generation. Therefore, an additional function has been introduced to manually cause mipmap levels to be generated:

```
void glGenerateMipmapEXT(GLenum target);
```

Now target must be GL_TEXTURE_1D, GL_TEXTURE_2D, GL_TEXTURE_3D, or GL_TEXTURE_CUBE_MAP. The mipmap levels are generated for whichever texture object is bound to the indicated target for the active texture unit.

If you're using FBOs to render to texture and want to have OpenGL generate mipmaps for you, you should *always* use this function instead of enabling automatic mipmap generation. Doing the latter may result in unpredictable behavior and severe performance penalties.

note

You don't necessarily have to use glGenerateMipmapEXT() in conjunction with FBOs. You can use it to manually trigger mipmap generation at any time, for any complete texture.

Renderbuffers

Renderbuffers provide a general means to support efficient offscreen rendering. Among other things, they can be used when rendering to logical buffers that don't correspond to a texture format, such as the stencil buffer.

Renderbuffers are created and destroyed using the following:

```
void glGenRenderbuffersEXT(GLsizei n, GLuint *renderbuffers);
void glDeleteRenderbuffersEXT(GLsizei n, const GLuint *renderbuffers);
```

As with other object-management methods, n is the number of object names to create or destroy, and renderbuffers is an array to hold these names.

Renderbuffers also need to be bound:

```
void glBindRenderbufferEXT(GLenum target, GLuint renderbuffer);
```

Your target will always be GL_RENDERBUFFER_EXT, and renderbuffer is the id of the renderbuffer object. As usual, the id of 0 is reserved by OpenGL, but unlike framebuffer objects, there is no default renderbuffer. Binding a value of 0 simply unbinds the currently bound renderbuffer.

The first time a previously unused renderbuffer id is bound, it is initialized with default state and an empty image buffer. To specify the format and size of the image buffer, you use the following:

```
void glRenderbufferStorageEXT(GLenum target, GLenum internalformat,
                              GLsizei width, GLsizei height);
```

Again, `target` will be `GL_RENDERBUFFER_EXT`. For `internalformat`, you can use any of the following:

- `GL_RGB` or any of the sized formats `GL_R3_G3_B2`, `GL_RGB4`, `GL_RGB5`, `GL_RGB8`, `GL_RGB10`, `GL_RGB12`, or `GL_RGB16`.

- `GL_RGBA` or any of the sized formats `GL_RGBA2`, `GL_RGBA4`, `GL_RGB5_A1`, `GL_RGBA8`, `GL_RGB10_A2`, `GL_RGBA12`, or `GL_RGBA16`.

- `GL_DEPTH_COMPONENT` or any of the sized formats `GL_DEPTH_COMPONENT_16`, `GL_DEPTH_COMPONENT_24`, or `GL_DEPTH_COMPONENT_32`.

- `GL_STENCIL_INDEX` or any of the sized formats `GL_STENCIL_INDEX1_EXT`, `GL_STENCIL_INDEX4_EXT`, `GL_STENCIL_INDEX8_EXT`, or `GL_STENCIL_INDEX16_EXT`.

The `width` and `height` parameters are the dimensions of the renderbuffer image in pixels. You can query the maximum allowable values for these dimensions by passing `GL_MAX_RENDERBUFFER_SIZE_EXT` to `glGetIntegerv()`.

Even if one of the sized internal formats is used (and obviously, if no size is specified), the implementation will decide internally how many bits to use to represent each component. To learn how to find out which values were chosen, see the "Querying Information" section a little later on.

To attach a renderbuffer to a framebuffer object, you use the following:

```
void glFramebufferRenderbufferEXT(GLenum target, GLenum attachment,
                                  GLenum renderbuffertarget, GLuint renderbuffer);
```

The value for `target` must be `GL_FRAMEBUFFER_EXT`. The `attachment` parameter is any of the attachment points listed in Table 1.3. You must use `GL_RENDERBUFFER_EXT` for `renderbuffertarget`, and `renderbuffer` is the id of the renderbuffer that you want to attach. If `renderbuffer` is 0, then any renderbuffer attached to the indicated attachment point will be detached.

The contents of a renderbuffer can be read or written to using `glReadPixels()` and `glDrawPixels()`, or similar APIs. The renderbuffer will of course be written to as part of the normal rendering process when it is attached to a bound framebuffer object.

Setting the Read and Draw Buffer

Since a framebuffer object can have multiple color attachments, it may be necessary to specify which one should be updated during rendering commands, or should otherwise be the source of read operations or the destination for draw operations. This defaults to GL_COLOR_ATTACHMENT0_EXT, but you can change which attachment is used by passing the attachment name to glDrawBuffer() or glReadBuffer().

In order to render to only the depth and stencil buffers (for example, when using shadow volumes or shadow maps), you have to set the draw and read buffers to GL_NONE.

When multiple render targets (which you'll learn more about in Chapter 4) are available, you can set each target to write to a different color attachment using glDrawBuffers():

```
void glDrawBuffers(GLuint n, const GLenum *bufs);
```

You use n to specify the number of buffers you are setting, and when a framebuffer object is bound, bufs is an array of n values consisting of the color attachment constants (i.e., GL_COLOR_ATTACHMENTi_EXT).

Querying Information

Like any other OpenGL objects, framebuffer objects and renderbuffers come with a number of APIs that allow you to query information about them.

```
GLboolean glIsFramebufferEXT(GLuint framebuffer);
GLboolean glIsRenderbufferEXT(GLuint renderbuffer);
```

These functions will return GL_TRUE if the id passed in is, respectively, a valid framebuffer or renderbuffer object, and GL_FALSE otherwise. Both object types are considered valid from the time they are first bound until they are deleted.

To query information about a framebuffer object's attachments, use:

```
void glGetFramebufferAttachmentParameterivEXT(GLenum target, GLenum attachment,
                                              GLenum pname, GLint *params);
```

For target, you must use GL_FRAMEBUFFER_EXT; attachment can be any of the values in Table 1.3. For pname, you must use one of the values in Table 1.4, and the value of the parameter is returned in params.

To query information about a renderbuffer, use:

```
void glGetRenderbufferParameterivEXT(GLenum target, GLenum pname,
                                     GLint *params);
```

Here target must be GL_RENDERBUFFER_EXT, and pname must be one of the values in Table 1.5. The value of the parameter is returned in params.

Table 1.4 Framebuffer Attachment Parameters

Value	Meaning
GL_FRAMEBUFFER_ATTACHMENT_OBJECT_TYPE_EXT	Will return the type of the attachment, which can be GL_NONE (no attachment), GL_TEXTURE (a texture image), or GL_RENDERBUFFER_EXT (a renderbuffer).
GL_FRAMEBUFFER_ATTACHMENT_OBJECT_NAME_EXT	Will return the name of the texture object (if a texture is attached) or name of the renderbuffer object (if a renderbuffer is attached). Otherwise an error is generated.
GL_FRAMEBUFFER_ATTACHMENT_TEXTURE_LEVEL_EXT	Will return the mipmap level of the texture that is attached (only valid if a texture is attached).
GL_FRAMEBUFFER_ATTACHMENT_CUBE_MAP_FACE_EXT	Will return the cubemap face (e.g. GL_TEXTURE_CUBE_MAP_POSITIVE_X) that is attached (only valid if a cubemap texture is attached).
GL_FRAMEBUFFER_ATTACHMENT_TEXTURE_3D_OFFSET_EXT	Will return the z-offset of the 2D image of the 3D texture that is attached (only valid if a 3D texture is attached).

Table 1.5 Renderbuffer Parameters

Value	Meaning
GL_RENDERBUFFER_WIDTH_EXT	Width of the renderbuffer in pixels.
GL_RENDERBUFFER_HEIGHT_EXT	Height of the renderbuffer in pixels.
GL_RENDERBUFFER_INTERNAL_FORMAT_EXT	Internal format of the renderbuffer as specified with glRenderbufferStorateEXT().
GL_RENDERBUFFER_RED_SIZE_EXT	Size in bits of the red components.*
GL_RENDERBUFFER_GREEN_SIZE_EXT	Size in bits of the green components.*
GL_RENDERBUFFER_BLUE_SIZE_EXT	Size in bits of the blue components.*
GL_RENDERBUFFER_ALPHA_SIZE_EXT	Size in bits of the alpha components.*
GL_RENDERBUFFER_DEPTH_SIZE_EXT	Size in bits of the depth components.*
GL_RENDERBUFFER_STENCIL_SIZE_EXT	Size in bits of the stencil components.*

*These values are the actual resolutions, not the values specified when the image storage was created.

You can also get the currently bound framebuffer object or renderbuffer by passing `GL_FRAMEBUFFER_BINDING_EXT` or `GL_RENDERBUFFER_BINDING_EXT` to `glGetIntegerv()`.

FBO Completeness

Similar to textures, framebuffers define a "completeness" that must be satisfied when rendering in order to work properly. A framebuffer is considered complete if the following conditions are met:

- The texture format makes sense for attachment points (e.g., don't try to attach a depth texture to a color attachment).
- There is at least one image attached.
- No images are attached more than once.
- All attached images have the same width and height.
- All images attached to `COLOR_ATTACHMENTi_EXT` must have the same format.
- The combination of all the attached images is allowed by the implementation.

There are additional conditions that are required for a framebuffer to be considered complete, but they are less likely to come up. See the extension specification for details.

Since completeness can be implementation dependent, the extension includes the ability to check the framebuffer status via `glCheckFramebufferStatusEXT()`:

```
GLenum glCheckFramebufferStatusEXT(GLenum target);
```

The value for `target` must again be `GL_FRAMEBUFFER_EXT`. If the return value is `GL_FRAME-BUFFER_COMPLETE_EXT`, then the currently bound FBO is complete. If it is incomplete, an error code will indicate why (see the specification for a complete list). If the return value is `GL_FRAMEBUFFER_UNSUPPORTED_EXT`, you should keep trying different format combinations until you find one that works.

Performance Tips

To get optimal performance when using framebuffer objects, keep the following tips in mind:

- Don't create and destroy them every frame (this is true for other objects, but the penalty with FBOs is much worse).
- Try to avoid modifying textures used as rendering destinations using `glTexImage()`, `glCopyTexImage()`, and the like.

- When using multiple rendering destinations, there are several ways to switch between them. The following are listed in order of increasing performance. Note that these may vary by platform, and because the extension is very immature, these may change over time.

  1. Use multiple FBOs, with a separate FBO for each texture, and switch between them using `glBindFramebufferEXT()`. This is the most straightforward approach, and it is at least twice as fast as having to switch contexts.

  2. Use a single FBO with multiple texture attachments. This requires that the textures have the same format and dimensions. You can switch between textures using `glFramebufferTexture()`. This is slightly more lightweight than using multiple FBOs, so it may be faster.

  3. Use a single FBO with multiple texture attachments and attach the textures to different color attachments. Use `glDrawBuffer()` to switch between the attachments.

Conclusion

Framebuffer objects are still fairly new, and are only available as an EXT extension, but as they are used and the design is proven, they will almost certainly be promoted to ARB status and then to the core.

As mentioned in the introduction, this extension also establishes a framework upon which additional functionality will likely be built. Some of the possibilities include:

- Render to vertex attribute (similar to using vertex buffer objects with pixel buffer objects). This would be useful for particle systems and other applications. This functionality will likely be built on top of renderbuffers.

- The addition of *format groups*. Similar to pixel formats, these define groups of formats that work together for a given implementation.

- Multisampling and accumulation buffer support (both of which are missing from the extension currently).

Several later chapters include demo programs that make use of framebuffer objects, in particular Chapter 4 and the render-to-texture section in Chapter 5. See the code for these demos for further information.

Multisampling

Dave Astle

extension

Extension name: `ARB_multisample`

Name string: `GL_ARB_multisample`

Promoted to core: `OpenGL 1.3`

Function names: `glSampleCoverageARB`

Tokens: `GL_MULTISAMPLE_ARB`, `GL_SAMPLE_ALPHA_TO_COVERAGE_ARB`, `GL_SAMPLE_ALPHA_TO_ONE_ARB`, `GL_SAMPLE_COVERAGE_ARB`, `WGL_SAMPLE_BUFFERS_ARB`, `WGL_SAMPLES_ARB`

Multisampling is a common method used for full-screen anti-aliasing. To fully understand it, we'll first review how rasterization works.

During rasterization, a geometric description of a triangle is translated into pixels. Pixels are typically thought of as being infinitely small points, but in reality, each pixel is a small square or rectangle on the screen. Any given pixel may be wholly or partially covered by a given triangle. Or it may be partially covered by multiple triangles. This is illustrated in Figures 1.1 and 1.2.

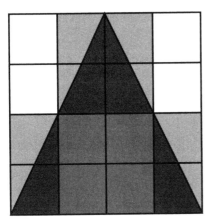

Figure 1.1 Four pixels are completely covered by the triangle, and four pixels aren't covered by the triangle at all. The remaining eight pixels are only partially covered.

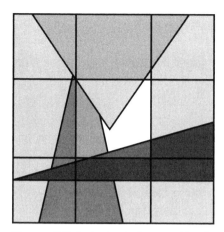

Figure 1.2 A single pixel covered by three different triangles.

The determination of how to color a pixel that is fully covered by a triangle is simple and obvious. It is not so obvious for pixels that are only partially covered by a triangle, or that are partially covered by many triangles. The technique used by modern rasterizers is to use the pixel's center to determine whether or not a primitive affects the pixel. This is known as *point sampling*.

There are a number of problems with this approach. One is that the color at the pixel center might not accurately represent the value of the entire pixel. Another is that in an animated scene (e.g., any game) even small movements will change which triangles cover pixel centers, leading to very noticeable aliasing artifacts at boundaries.

An ideal solution would be to determine the percentage of a pixel's area covered by each triangle, and use that information to blend together fragments from each triangle to determine the pixel's color. This is known as *area sampling*.

Multisampling is essentially a compromise between these approaches. Instead of sampling a single point, several points within a pixel are sampled, and the results are averaged to determine the final color. This requires the use of an additional buffer called the *multisampling buffer*.

The following sections will explain how to take advantage of OpenGL's multisampling support.

Using Multisampling

Using multisampling in OpenGL is straightforward, since all of the work is done by OpenGL. The only challenge is in making sure that you request a rendering context that includes a multisampling buffer. The multisampling buffer includes a color buffer as well as depth and stencil buffers. There are no separate depth and stencil buffers for formats that support a multisampling buffer.

Once you have a multisampling buffer, using multisampling is simply a matter of enabling it and optionally controlling how samples are generated.

Adding a Multisample Buffer

Support for multisampling must be requested as part of the rendering context. Since this functionality is handled by the windowing API rather than OpenGL itself, requesting a multisample buffer generally requires platform-specific code. Since Windows has been the primary target platform, we'll first look at how this is done using WGL, and then we'll look at how SDL allows us to do this in a platform-independent way.

Multisampling with WGL

The existing WGL functions for context creation don't include multisampling support, so the use of a WGL extension is needed. `WGL_ARB_pixel_format` defines new entry points that let you find and choose pixel formats. Unlike the previous functions, which include a `PIXELFORMATDESCRIPTOR` structure to specify the pixel format you want, the new functions use lists of attributes so that the types of attributes can be easily extended.

e x t e n s i o n

Extension name: `WGL_ARB_pixel_format`

Name string: `WGL_ARB_pixel_format`

Function names: `wglGetPixelFormatAttribivARB`, `wglGetPixelFormatAttribfvARB`, `wglChoosePixelFormatARB`

Because the functions needed to choose a pixel format with multisampling are only available via extensions, you must first create a window with a hardware accelerated context. Then you can retrieve the function pointers, destroy the window, and create a new window with multisampling support.

In order to find the appropriate pixel format, you use the following:

```
BOOL wglChoosePixelFormatARB(HDC hdc, const int *piAttribIList,
                             const FLOAT *pfAttribFList, UINT nMaxFormats,
                             int *piFormats, UINT *nNumFormats);
```

The `hdc` parameter is the handle to your device context. The `piAttribIList` and `pifAttribFList` parameters are pointers to arrays of attribute pairs of types and values. Table 1.6 lists the types and their most frequently used associated valid values (for a complete list, refer to the extension specification). The lists are terminated with a pair of zeros. You use `nMaxFormats` to indicate the maximum number of pixel formats that you want to retrieve. The identifiers for these formats are returned in piFormats—an array that you must allocate and that must be big enough to hold nMaxFormats identifiers. Finally, nNumFormats will contain the number of matching formats that were found.

note

If wglChoosePixelFormatARB() returns true, it does not necessarily mean that it was able to find a matching pixel format. You should check the value of nNumFormats to make sure that it is not zero.

When you call wglChoosePixelFormatARB(), OpenGL will examine all of the pixel formats available and attempt to find those that match the attributes that you specify. It will assume that you don't care about any attributes that aren't listed, and won't take those into account when determining whether an existing format matches your request. The pixel formats are stored in piFormats in an order that is based on how closely they match the attributes you specify and how well the hardware can support them. Typically, you'll use the first format returned.

Since the pixel formats returned may not exactly match what you requested, you can query the attributes of a given pixel format using one of the following:

```
BOOL wglGetPixelFormatAttribivARB(HDC hdc, int iPixelFormat, int iLayerPlane,
                                  UINT nAttributes, const int *piAttributes,
                                  int *piValues);
BOOL wglGetPixelFormatAttribfvARB(HDC hdc, int iPixelFormat, int iLayerPlane,
                                  UINT nAttributes, const int *piAttributes,
                                  FLOAT *pfValues);
```

Again, hdc is a handle to the device context. Next, iPixelFormat is the identifier for the pixel format you are querying. You should set iLayerPlane to 0. The parameter nAttributes is the number of attributes listed in piAttributes, which contains types from Table 1.6. Make sure piValues or pfValues is the same size as piAttributes, as they will be used to store the values associated with the types you specified.

The following code shows how to use all of this to request a pixel format that supports a multisample buffer. For a more complete example of setting up a multisampling buffer, see the demo for this section on the book's website.

Table 1.6 Pixel Format Attributes

Value	Meaning
WGL_ACCELERATION_ARB	Whether or not the pixel format is supported in hardware. Valid values are WGL_NO_ACCELERATION_ARB, WGL_GENERIC_ACCELERATION_ARB, and WGL_FULL_ACCELERATION_ARB.
WGL_DRAW_TO_WINDOW_ARB	Whether or not the format can be used with a window. Values can be GL_TRUE or GL_FALSE.
WGL_DRAW_TO_BITMAP_ARB	Whether or not the format can be used with a memory bitmap. Values can be GL_TRUE or GL_FALSE.
WGL_SWAP_METHOD_ARB	Used with a back buffer to control how the buffers are swapped. If the value is WGL_SWAP_EXCHANGE_ARB, the front and back buffer contents are exchanged. If it is WGL_SWAP_COPY_ARB, the back buffer is copied to the front buffer. If it is WGL_SWAP_UNDEFINED_ARB, the back buffer is copied to the front buffer, but after the copy, the contents of the back buffer are undefined.
WGL_SUPPORT_GDI_ARB	Whether or not drawing with GDI is supported. Values can be GL_TRUE or GL_FALSE.
WGL_SUPPORT_OPENGL_ARB	Whether or not OpenGL is supported. Values can be GL_TRUE or GL_FALSE.
WGL_DOUBLE_BUFFER_ARB	Whether or not double buffering is supported. Values can be GL_TRUE or GL_FALSE.
WGL_PIXEL_TYPE_ARB	The type of pixel data. Values can be WGL_TYPE_RGBA_ARB or WGL_TYPE_COLORINDEX_ARB.
WGL_COLOR_BITS_ARB	The number of bits for the color buffer, including alpha.
WGL_DEPTH_BITS_ARB	The number of bits for the depth buffer.
WGL_STENCIL_BITS_ARB	The number of bits for the stencil buffer.
WGL_ACCUM_BITS_ARB	The number of bits for the accumulation buffer.
WGL_SAMPLE_BUFFERS_ARB	The number of multisample buffers. The value should either be 0 or 1.
WGL_SAMPLES_ARB	The number of samples per pixel. Valid values depend on the implementation.

```
int    pixelFormat;
UINT   numFormats;
int    attributes[] = {
  WGL_DOUBLE_BUFFER_ARB, TRUE,
  WGL_ACCELERATION_ARB, WGL_FULL_ACCELERATION_ARB,
  WGL_SAMPLE_BUFFERS_ARB, 1,
  WGL_SAMPLES_ARB, 4, // requests at least 4 samples per pixel
  0, 0 };
```

```
wglChoosePixelFormatARB(hdc, attributes, NULL, 1, &pixelFormat, &numFormats);
if (numFormats == 0)
{
  // unable to get a pixel format with multisampling support
}
```

Multisampling with SDL

One of the nice things about SDL is that it greatly simplifies application setup, and this is especially true when it comes to multisampling. When setting the OpenGL attributes prior to setting the video mode, you merely need to include the following:

```
SDL_GL_SetAttribute( SDL_GL_MULTISAMPLEBUFFERS, 1 );
SDL_GL_SetAttribute( SDL_GL_MULTISAMPLESAMPLES, numSamples);
```

Here, numSamples is the number of samples you would like per pixel. If the implementation doesn't support the number of samples you request, the call to set the video mode will succeed, but multisampling support will not be included. You can use SDL_GL_GetAttribute() to query SDL_GL_MULTISAMPLEBUFFERS and SDL_GL_MULTISAMPLESAMPLES to see whether they were set to your requested values. If not, you can reduce the number of samples and try setting the video mode again.

Enabling Multisampling

Once you have a multisample buffer, using multisampling is easy. You can turn it on or off as needed by passing GL_MULTISAMPLE to glEnable() or glDisable().

Multisampling works best with triangles and other polygons. It is easier to use and produces better results than enabling GL_POLYGON_SMOOTH. However, it doesn't work as well with points and lines, so for anti-aliasing those, you'll get better results using GL_POINT_SMOOTH and GL_LINE_SMOOTH.

You should be aware that using multisampling isn't free. It requires more video memory and it burns additional fill rate. However, it can add considerable visual quality, and modern hardware can handle it without too much of a performance hit.

Controlling Coverage

When multisampling is enabled, each sample includes a coverage value indicating how much of a pixel the fragment covers. This coverage value doesn't take the alpha value into account, which is typically fine. However, for some advanced effects, you may want to take greater control of how the coverage value is calculated. OpenGL offers this control through three special modes that you can enable or disable as desired. All three are disabled by default, and they can stay that way if you just want "normal" anti-aliasing.

If you enable GL_SAMPLE_ALPHA_TO_COVERAGE, then the alpha value of the fragment will be logically ANDed with the coverage value to determine the final coverage value.

If you enable GL_SAMPLE_ALPHA_TO_ONE, the fragment alpha value is set to one after the coverage value is calculated.

If you enable GL_SAMPLE_COVERAGE, then you can specify an additional value using glSampleCoverage() that will be logically ANDed with the results of the other coverage calculations to produce the final coverage value. If the invert parameter is set to GL_TRUE, then the inverse of the value is used instead. The following is the definition for glSampleCoverage() :

```
void glSampleCoverage(GLclampf value, GLboolean invert);
```

Floating-Point Buffers

Dave Astle

extension

Extension name: ARB_color_buffer_float
Name strings: GL_ARB_color_buffer_float, WGL_ARB_pixel_format_float, GLX_ARB_fbconfig_float
Function names: glClampColorARB
Tokens (partial): GL_RGBA_FLOAT_MODE_ARB, GL_CLAMP_VERTEX_COLOR_ARB, GL_CLAMP_FRAGMENT_COLOR_ARB, GL_CLAMP_READ_COLOR_ARB, GL_FIXED_ONLY_ARB, WGL_TYPE_RGBA_FLOAT_ARB, GLX_RGBA_FLOAT_TYPE_ARB, GLX_RGBA_FLOAT_BIT_ARB

The traditional OpenGL pipeline is based around a fixed-point model. Although colors can be passed in as floating-point and represented as such throughout the pipeline, eventually they'll be converted to fixed-point and clamped to the [0, 1] range, and ultimately they will be written to a fixed-point color buffer.

This extension allows you to create color buffers supporting true floating-point values. It also gives you control over the way color values are clamped.

At the time of writing, this extension is not yet widely supported, but I'm including coverage of it because several techniques presented later in the book (notably, the "High Dynamic Range Lighting and Rendering" section in Chapter 6, "Advanced Lighting and Shading") work optimally when floating-point buffers are available. In addition, the use of floating-point color buffers will undoubtedly become much more common in the future, so it is likely that this extension will eventually be promoted to the OpenGL core.

Creating Floating-Point Buffers

Creating a floating-point buffer is handled by the windowing system, as you would expect, so the method for creation depends on the windowing system being used. I'll again use WGL as an example.

In the previous section, you learned about the wglChoosePixelFormatARB() function that provides a more extensible method for selecting a pixel format. To request a floating-point color buffer, you just need to request a pixel format that has WGL_PIXEL_TYPE_ARB set to WGL_TYPE_RGBA_FLOAT_ARB:

```
int    pixelFormat;
UINT   numFormats;
int    attributes[] = {
  WGL_DOUBLE_BUFFER_ARB, TRUE,
  WGL_ACCELERATION_ARB, WGL_FULL_ACCELERATION_ARB,
  WGL_PIXEL_TYPE_ARB, WGL_TYPE_RGBA_FLOAT_ARB,
  0, 0 };
wglChoosePixelFormatARB(hdc, attributes, NULL, 1, &pixelFormat, &numFormats);
if (numFormats == 0)
{
  // unable to get a pixel format with a floating point color buffer
}
```

Color Clamp Control

In OpenGL, color clamping happens in two primary places: when the final vertex color is calculated, and before a fragment is written into the color buffer. This extension includes a new function that allows you to modify this behavior:

```
void glClampColorARB(GLenum target, GLenum clamp);
```

To modify vertex color clamping, target should be set to GL_CLAMP_VERTEX_COLOR_ARB. To modify fragment color clamping, target should be GL_CLAMP_FRAGMENT_COLOR_ARB. You can set clamp to GL_TRUE (clamping is enabled), GL_FALSE (clamping is disabled), or GL_FIXED_ONLY_ARB (clamping is enabled if there are no enabled floating-point color buffers, and disabled otherwise).

Vertex color clamping is enabled by default, and fragment color clamping defaults to GL_FIXED_ONLY_ARB.

Clamping also occurs when reading from the color buffer with glReadPixels(). This can be modified by setting target to GL_CLAMP_READ_COLOR.

Occlusion Queries

Dave Astle

extension

Extension name: ARB_occlusion_query

Name string: GL_ARB_occlusion_query

Promoted to core: OpenGL 1.5

Function names: glGenQueriesARB, glDeleteQueriesARB, glIsQueryARB, glBeginQueryARB, glEndQueryARB, glGetQueryivARB, glGetQueryObjectivARB, glGetQueryObjectuivARB

Tokens: GL_SAMPLES_PASSED_ARB, GL_QUERY_COUNTER_BITS_ARB, GL_CURRENT_QUERY_ARB, GL_QUERY_RESULT_ARB, GL_QUERY_RESULT_AVAILABLE.

A simple rule in graphics for improving performance is "don't draw what you can't see." In *Beginning OpenGL Game Programming*, you learned how to avoid sending objects to OpenGL when they aren't visible by using frustum culling. Frustum culling offers cheap and simple removal of objects that are positioned outside the currently viewable area, but it does nothing for objects that are inside the view frustum but completely hidden by other objects.

OpenGL provides a generic mechanism to determine whether or not an object is visible. Through *occlusion queries*, you can render any set of geometry and then determine how many fragments are visible. This in and of itself does nothing to improve performance, since you're still drawing the object regardless of whether or not it's visible. The general idea (though greatly simplified) is to do the following:

- First, draw large objects that may occlude other objects.
- Next, draw bounding volumes for the objects that you want to test for occlusion, using occlusion queries to test whether any part of the bounding volume is visible.
- If the occlusion query indicates that one or more fragments is visible, draw the full object.

The following sections will go into greater detail about how to take advantage of occlusion queries to improve performance. But first, we'll describe the APIs you'll need to use them.

Creating and Destroying Queries

Occlusion queries make use of query objects, which are similar to other objects in OpenGL such as texture objects or buffer objects. To make use of query objects, you first call the following function:

```
void glGenQueries(GLsizei n, GLuint *ids);
```

The parameter n is the number of query objects that you want, and ids is an array that will hold the names of the query objects returned by the function.

When you have finished using your query objects, you need to destroy them to free the resources associated with them. This is done using:

```
void glDeleteQueries(GLsizei n, const GLuint *ids);
```

The usage of n and ids is the same as with glGenQueries(). If ids contains 0 or any unused query object name, the values are simply ignored without generating an error.

Using Queries

In order to start using a query, you make a call to:

```
void glBeginQuery(GLenum target, GLuint id);
```

Here, target should always be GL_SAMPLES_PASSED, and id is the name of the query object that will be used. When the call to glBeginQuery() is made, the count associated with the query object is reset to 0.

After calling glBeginQuery(), you can draw the geometry that you want to test. While the query is active, a count is kept of all the fragments (or samples, if you're using anti-aliasing) that pass the depth test. Typically, you do not want the bounding volumes to affect the framebuffer in any way, so writes to the color and depth buffers are disabled (via glColorMask() and glDepthMask(), respectively). Because the query counts the number of fragments (or samples, if you're using multisampling) that pass the depth test, be sure to have depth testing enabled. Otherwise, you can turn off most rendering states, such as texturing and shading, to make rendering as inexpensive as possible.

When you have finished rendering the geometry that you want to test—and before beginning another query—you'll need to end the current query by calling:

```
void glEndQuery(GLenum target);
```

Again, target should be GL_SAMPLES_PASSED.

To determine how many fragments passed the depth test, you use one of the following APIs:

```
void glGetQueryObjectiv(GLuint id, GLenum pname, GLint *params);
void glGetQueryObjectuiv(GLuint id, GLenum pname, GLuint *params);
```

Once again, id is the name of the query object you are asking about. To retrieve the number of fragments that passed, pname should be set to GL_QUERY_RESULT, in which case the result is returned in params.

Occlusion queries operate asynchronously, so the results may not be available when you ask for them. If that's the case, the pipeline will stall until your query has finished processing. This is obviously bad for performance. Instead, you can find out whether or not the results are ready by passing GL_QUERY_RESULT_AVAILABLE to glGetQueryObject(). If this returns a value of GL_TRUE, you know you can safely retrieve the results. If not, you can do other things in your program—including issuing additional rendering commands—and check again later. This is illustrated in the following pseudocode snippet.

```
glBeginQuery(GL_SAMPLES_PASSED, query);
// render object
glEndQuery(GL_SAMPLES_PASSED);

// do other things
GLint resultAvailable = GL_FALSE, result;

while (!resultAvailable)
{
  glGetQueryObjectiv(query, GL_QUERY_RESULT_AVAILABLE, &resultAvailable);
  if (resultAvailable)
  {
    glGetQueryObjectiv(query, GL_QUERY_RESULT, &result);
  }
  else
  {
    // do other stuff
  }
}
```

For optimal performance, you should use multiple query objects, issue them all sequentially, and then do other tasks (e.g., processing AI or physics) before checking to see if the queries have completed. You should strive for the highest degree of parallelism between the GPU and CPU whenever possible.

tip

Queries are executed in order, so if you issue several queries, and you determine that the last query has completed, you know that *all* queries have completed.

Occlusion queries aren't going to magically improve your performance. In fact, if used naïvely, they usually have the opposite effect. Consider the following when deciding whether or not to use occlusion queries.

- They help most when you're trying to reduce the amount of geometry sent down the OpenGL pipeline. If your game is fill-rate limited, they may hurt performance instead.

- Because occlusion queries are a general-purpose solution, they may not perform as well as solutions that can take advantage of special knowledge you may have about your game world.

- Never request the results of a query unless you know they are available. If they aren't, you'll stall both the CPU and GPU.

- They work best when it's likely that a large number of objects with complex geometry will be occluded by other objects. If that doesn't describe your game, they may not be for you.

The main point to understand is that the benefit you get from occlusion queries is dependent on the exact nature of your game and how smart you are about using them. They are another tool to be added to your programmer's toolbox. Now that you know how they work, it's up to you to determine how to best use them.

tip

Although we're primarily looking at occlusion queries as a means to avoid drawing objects that aren't visible, they can be used for other things. Because the query returns the number of pixels that were drawn, and not just whether any pixels were drawn, you can use the query results to make other decisions about the scene. For example, you might use the information if you have an extremely bright object in the scene (e.g., the sun) and you want to simulate an overexposure effect based on how much of the object is visible. Or if you are using multiple levels of detail, you could use this information to select the appropriate level.

Occlusion Query Example

A simple demo application has been included on the book's website that illustrates the basic functionality of occlusion queries. The demo, shown in Figure 1.3, uses an occlusion query to test how much of the sun is visible, and it overexposes the scene based on this result.

Figure 1.3 Occlusion query demo.

User Clip Planes

Andrei Gradinari

When you specify the projection matrix, you create a view frustum consisting of six planes. As geometry is rendered, it is clipped against these planes by OpenGL to avoid processing geometry that is not visible. OpenGL also allows applications to define additional clip planes. This allows the programmer to clip geometry as shown in Figure 1.4.

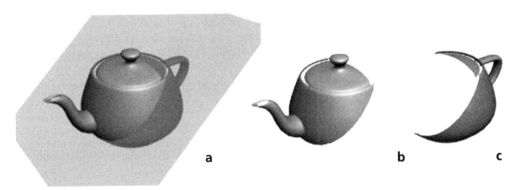

a   b   c

Figure 1.4 A teapot (a)

Figure 1.4a shows a teapot crossed by a plane. The teapot is divided by this plane into two parts, as shown in Figures 1.4b and 1.4c. This kind of clipping can be done in real time using *user clip planes.*

User clip planes are used in various rendering techniques. They are especially useful when doing planar reflections or refractions.

You can add your own clip planes by calling the following:

```
void glClipPlane(GLenum p, GLdouble eqn[4]);
```

Here, p takes a constant of the form GL_CLIP_PLANE*n*, where n is a value between 0 and GL_MAX_CLIP_PLANES − 1. The value of GL_MAX_CLIP_PLANES can be determined by calling glGetIntegerv(). It is guaranteed to be at least 6. The parameter eqn contains the four coefficients of the plane equation in object coordinates. The inverse of the modelview matrix (at the time glClipPlane() is called) is applied to these coefficients to transform them to eye-space coordinates, where calculations are performed.

Each clip plane can be individually enabled or disabled as needed. This is done by passing GL_CLIP_PLANE*n* to glEnable() or glDisable().

tip

Enabling many clip planes can result in performance degradation. Don't enable more clip planes than you need.

How to Find a Plane Equation

You learned about the plane equation in *Beginning OpenGL Game Programming*, but a quick review is in order. The plane equation looks like this:

$$A^*x + B^*y + C^*z + D = 0$$

A, B, C and D are plane equation coefficients. Each set of them defines some plane in 3D space. If you place the x-, y-, and z-coordinates of any point into this equation and the equation remains true, then the point lies on the plane.

The A, B and C coefficients define the normal to the plane. So if you have the normal to the plane and any point on the plane, you can determine the plane equation. Often, you won't immediately have the normal, but you'll have three noncollinear points on the plane that you can use to calculate the normal, as shown in Figure 1.5.

As shown, you use the three points to determine two vectors. You then take the cross product of these vectors to find the normal. Using the normal and any of the three points, you can rearrange the plane equation and solve for D to get the final coefficient, as follows:

$$D = -(A^*x + B^*y + C^*z)$$

The demo for this section (which you'll find on the book's website) includes a function that calculates the plane coefficients using three points as input.

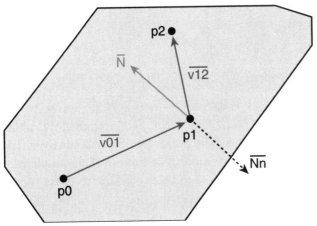

Figure 1.5 Finding a plane from three points.

Specifying the Half Space to Cut

Any plane cuts the world into two half spaces. The positive half space is the side that the plane's normal points toward, and the negative half space is thus the other side. Since the direction of a normal calculated via cross product depends on the order of the input vectors, care should be taken when calculating your plane normal to be sure that you get the half space you want. In Figure 1.6, the arrow on the left is the positive normal, and the one on the right is the negative normal. The OpenGL clipping mechanism will cut the half space on the negative side of the plane and keep everything on the positive side.

Figure 1.6 Selecting the half space.

Clip Planes and Planar Reflections

Clipping planes become absolutely necessary when rendering planar reflections. Take the situation shown in Figure 1.7 as an example.

Figure 1.7 Visualizing planar reflections using clip planes.

Here we have a box, a sphere, and a mirror. The box is in front of the mirror and the sphere is behind it. The following pseudocode is a first attempt at rendering this (for simplicity, the mirror lies in the xz-plane).

```
// Load mirror mask to stencil buffer
// Set up stencil test appropriately
glPushMatrix();
  glScalef(1.0, 1.0, -1.0); // set up reflection transformation
  RenderGeometry();         // render sphere and box
glPopMatrix();

// Render mirror mesh to depth buffer
RenderGeometry(); // Rendering geometry itself
```

Figure 1.8 shows the results of this. Notice that a piece of the sphere appears reflected in the mirror, which is wrong.

Figure 1.8 The reflection incorrectly includes the sphere.

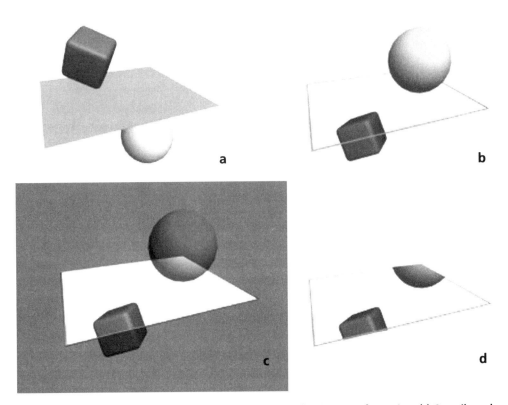

Figure 1.9 (a) Our scene. (b) The scene after applying reflection transformation. (c) Stencil mask. (d) Final reflection image after applying stencil mask.

Figure 1.9 illustrates what went wrong. After setting up the reflection transformation, all objects that had been in front of the mirror are behind it, and vice versa. Before applying the reflection transformation, the sphere had been behind the mirror. After applying the transformation, it appears to be in front of the mirror and gets rendered as part of the reflection image. Obviously, what we need to do before rendering the reflection image is set up a single clip plane so that it clips all geometry in front of the mirror. The correct rendering pseudocode is as follows:

```
// Load mirror mask to stencil buffer
// Set up stencil test appropriately
GLfloat mirror_plane[4];
get_plane_equation(vec3(0,0,1), vec3(0,0,0), vec3(1,0,0), mirror_plane);
// pay attention, positive normal specified by these 3 points will be
// (0, -1, 0). This is exactly what I want, because in this case we need to
// clip geometry above xz-plane
```

```
glEnable(GL_CLIP_PLANE0);
glClipPlane(GL_CLIP_PLANE0, mirror_plane);
glPushMatrix();
  glScalef(1.0, 1.0, -1.0); // set up reflection transformation
  RenderGeometry();          // render sphere and box
glPopMatrix();
// Render mirror mesh to depth buffer
RenderGeometry(); // Rendering geometry itself
```

Figure 1.10 illustrates these steps graphically, and Figure 1.11 shows the correctly rendered results.

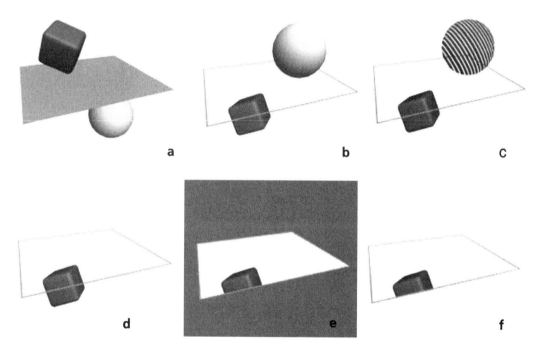

Figure 1.10 (a) Our scene. (b) The scene after applying reflection transformation. (c) Clipping extra geometry; sphere gets clipped here. (d) Scene after clipping. (e) Stencil mask. (f) Final reflection image after applying stencil mask.

Figure 1.11 The correctly rendered reflection.

Advanced Clipping Technique

If you look back at Figure 1.4c, you'll notice that there is no clip edge. In other words, where the clip plane intersected the geometry, there is simply nothing. Since the model is hollow, you don't see the cross-section you'd expect to see when cutting a real-world object. If you want to create a cross-section using OpenGL, you'll have to do some additional work. I've written an article explaining how to do this, which is included on the book's website as bonus material. Figure 1.12 shows a screenshot from the demo created using this technique.

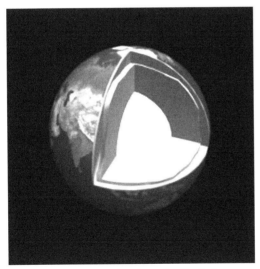

Figure 1.12 Screenshot from the Earth demo.

Disabling Vsync

Dave Astle

Normally, the rate at which OpenGL can update the framebuffer is limited to the monitor's refresh rate. This process is known as vertical sync, or vsync. This is done to prevent an artifact known as *tearing*, which is caused by updating the display while the monitor is in the middle of drawing to it. At times, it can be useful to disable this behavior and have display updates happen as soon as OpenGL is ready. For example, you might do this when optimizing to determine how your improvements affect the frame rate.

Controlling this behavior is outside the scope of OpenGL's functionality. Instead, it is handled through the windowing system. I'll look at how WGL handles this.

Support for controlling buffer swapping is included as an extension to WGL. The name of the extension is WGL_EXT_swap_control.

extension

Extension name: WGL_EXT_swap_control
Name string: WGL_EXT_swap_control
Function names: wglSwapIntervalEXT, wglGetSwapIntervalEXT

The extension adds a new entry point that lets you control the swap interval, which is how many frames the driver will wait before swapping the front and back buffers. The function you use is wglSwapIntervalEXT():

```
BOOL wglSwapIntervalEXT(int interval);
```

The value passed to interval determines how may frames the driver will wait before performing a swap. If you set the interval to 0, swaps will happen as soon as you call wglSwapBuffers(). The default value is 1. You can query the current swap interval using the following:

```
GLint wglGetSwapIntervalEXT();
```

note

Disabling vsync is treated as a request by the OpenGL driver. Video card drivers typically have an option for users to have vsync always enabled, always disabled, or controlled by the application. Unless they have the last option selected (which is the default), your request will be ignored. It's common practice to allow the user to control whether or not your game disables vsync in the game's settings.

Summary

In this chapter, you've learned about some of the most important new features in OpenGL, some of which are part of the core, and some of which are available as extensions. You've seen how vertex buffer objects provide a vital tool in improving performance by storing geometric data on the GPU, and how pixel buffer objects provide similar functionality for pixel data. You've seen how to use the new framebuffer objects. You now know how to enable OpenGL's built-in full-screen anti-aliasing support via multisampling. You also know how to create a floating-point color buffer.

You've been introduced to the occlusion query APIs and seen some ways in which they can be used to help improve performance. You also know how to specify clip planes to enable OpenGL to clip away geometry that you don't want. Finally, you've seen how to disable vertical sync to allow your application to run at the maximum possible frame rate.

The most important new additions to OpenGL are yet to come. In the next three chapters, you'll be learning about shaders.

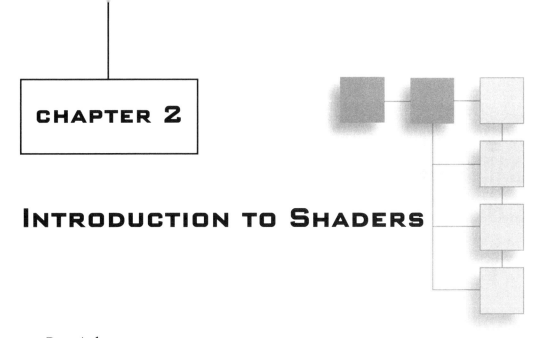

CHAPTER 2

INTRODUCTION TO SHADERS

Dave Astle

For years, OpenGL operated using a fixed-function pipeline. In other words, the operations that happen at each stage of the pipeline are predetermined. An OpenGL developer could adjust parameters but ultimately had relatively little control over how geometry was processed and rendered. This was fully intentional; the fixed-function pipeline allowed hardware vendors to create graphics hardware that could perform these operations very quickly. The smaller the number of parameters that could be adjusted, the more the hardware could be optimized.

As graphics hardware evolved and the needs of developers—particularly game developers—changed, greater flexibility was exposed. This was done through the extension mechanism. Dozens of extensions were added to give developers a greater degree of control over what happens in the graphics pipeline, in particular at the fragment and vertex stages.

Typically, two to three years pass from the time a graphics chip is first designed until it ships in a consumer product. Changes made late in this process can be extremely expensive, and yet the highly competitive nature of the graphics business sometimes requires them. To cope with this, graphics-hardware vendors began to introduce *programmability* in their hardware. This allowed them to create microcode programs that would control how the hardware functions at various stages. That way, they could make fairly large changes not only late in the development cycle, but even after the product had shipped, via driver updates.

Not surprisingly, developers wanted access to this level of control as well, and in 2001, they got it, when DirectX 8 was released with support for *shaders*—small programs that can be loaded dynamically to control processing at certain stages of the graphics pipeline. The same functionality appeared as extensions to OpenGL soon thereafter.

Shaders have drastically changed the way games and graphics applications are developed. You'll be learning more about them in the next several chapters, and many applications of them appear throughout the remainder of the book. First, a more detailed introduction to them is in order, so that's what this chapter will focus on. In this chapter, you'll learn about

- The history of shaders
- What a shader is
- What types of shaders are currently available in OpenGL
- An overview of the primary ways in which you can write and use shaders

A Brief History of Shaders

Although shaders have only (relatively) recently become available in consumer graphics hardware, the idea is nothing new. Table 2.1 lists some of the most important milestones in the evolution of shaders and programmable graphics hardware.

Table 2.1 Programmability Evolution

Year	Milestone
1988	Renderman, Pixar
1998	Pixelflow, University of North Carolina
2001	Real Time Shading Language (RTSL), Stanford
2001	DirectX 8 assembly, Microsoft
2002	`ARB_vertex_program`, `ARB_fragment_program`
2002	Cg/HLSL, NVIDIA/Microsoft
2004	OpenGL Shading Language, OpenGL ARB
2004	Sh, University of Waterloo

Renderman, developed by Pixar, is considered by many to be the father of modern shading languages. It's a software-based rendering engine used primarily in film. Unlike the shading languages used by OpenGL and DirectX, it uses shaders throughout the pipeline, giving its users a huge amount of control over how things get drawn. Renderman is still widely used today, and many people writing shaders in other languages use Renderman shaders as inspiration.

Pixelflow is a dedicated, customized hardware and software system developed at the University of North Carolina. It offers a high degree of programmability at many stages in the pipeline and can render in real- time. Pixelflow was never commercially successful, but it helped lay some of the foundation for future programmable hardware.

The Real Time Shading Language (or RTSL) was developed at Stanford University. It offers programmability by acting as an abstraction layer over fixed-function consumer hardware. It works by combining whatever features are available in the hardware with multiple rendering passes. RTSL isn't really used commercially, but it has provided valuable research.

Undeniably the most exciting feature of DirectX 8 was the addition of low-level vertex and pixel shaders. For the first time, developers had total control over what happens at these critical stages in the pipeline. Initially, the instruction set and amount of space available for shaders was limited, and there were incompatibility issues between hardware vendors. Fortunately, the language and hardware capabilities evolved quickly.

Varying degrees of programmability had been appearing in OpenGL as vendor-specific extensions. These finally converged in the `ARB_vertex_program` and `ARB_fragment_program` extensions. The low-level shading language defined by these extensions is similar to what's available in DirectX, though it's slightly more high level (you don't have to manage registers, and OpenGL state can be accessed through global structures). You'll learn more about these extensions in Chapter 3, "Low-Level Shaders."

The low-level shaders were naturally followed by high-level shading languages. NVIDIA and Microsoft worked closely to develop Cg and HLSL. Cg (short for "C for graphics") is available on several platforms and works with both OpenGL and DirectX. HLSL is essentially the same language, but it is only available for DirectX.

Around the same time, 3DLabs launched an initiative to significantly update OpenGL for version 2.0. The core of this update would be the addition of a high-level shading language. Members of the OpenGL Architecture Review Board refined and polished this language for almost two years. The final product, the OpenGL Shading Language, was released as part of the OpenGL 2.0 core at SIGGRAPH 2004. You'll learn more about the OpenGL Shading Language in Chapter 4, "The OpenGL Shading Language."

What Is a Shader?

It's time to take a closer look at what shaders really are and how they fit into the graphics pipeline. To do that, a review of the OpenGL pipeline is in order.

As you probably know, the OpenGL pipeline takes geometry specified as vertices and pixel data as input, and produces pixels in the framebuffer as output. As geometric data travels down the pipeline, it goes through a series of conceptual stages that process the data. A simplified representation of these stages is shown in Figure 2.1.

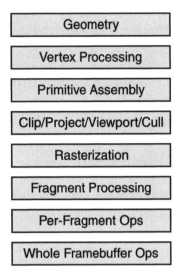

Figure 2.1 Simplification of the fixed-function pipeline.

As stated in the introduction, in the traditional fixed-function pipeline, the operations that happen at each stage, as well as the inputs and outputs, are well- defined, though the programmer has a limited degree of control through changing various state settings.

With the introduction of shaders, some of these pipeline stages become programmable. Currently, these stages are the vertex and fragment processing stages, as shown in Figure 2.2. With programmable hardware, the programmer can write code that will run at these stages in place of the predefined operations. This code is called a vertex or fragment shader (or sometimes, a vertex or fragment program).

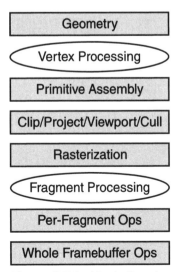

Figure 2.2 In this pipeline, the vertex and fragment stages are programmable.

The following is a sample fragment shader written using the OpenGL Shading Language. This shader calculates lighting on a per-pixel basis. At this point, this shader is intended to give you a taste of what's to come; you're not expected to fully understand it yet.

```
varying vec4 position;
varying vec3 normal;

uniform vec3 globalAmbient;
uniform vec3 lightColor;
uniform vec3 lightPosition;
uniform vec3 eyePosition;
uniform vec3 materialEmissive;
uniform vec3 materialAmbient;
uniform vec3 materialDiffuse;
uniform vec3 materialSpecular;
uniform vec3 materialShininess;

void main(void)
{
  vec3 P = position.xyz;
  vec3 N = normalize(normal);

  vec3 emmisive = materialEmmisive;

  vec3 ambient = materialAmbient * globalAmbient;

  vec3 L = normalize(lightPosition - P);
  float diffuseLight = max(dot(N, L), 0);
  vec3 diffuse = materialDiffuse * lightColor * diffuseLight;

  vec3 V = normalize(eyePosition - P);
  vec3 H = normalize(L + V);
  float specularLight = pow(max(dot(N, H), 0), materialShininess);
  if (diffuseLight <= 0) specularLight = 0;
  vec3 specular = materialSpecular * lightColor * specularLight;

  gl_FragColor = vec4(materialEmissive + ambient + diffuse + specular, 1.0);
}
```

note

Although only the vertex and fragment stages are currently programmable, other stages may become programmable in the future. Whether or not this happens and which stages become programmable depends on the potential utility of this feature.

Shader Input and Output

In order for the shader to work properly with the rest of the pipeline, it has to meet certain constraints in regard to the handling of input and output. Figure 2.3 diagrams the data flow through vertex and fragment shaders.

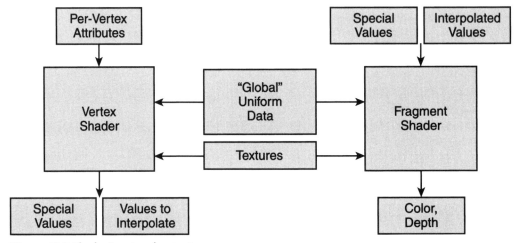

Figure 2.3 Shader input and output.

The input into the vertex shader consists of per-vertex *attributes*, such as positions, normals, vertex colors, and so on. Vertex shaders output *varying* values that are interpolated between vertices, and these values then become input sources for the fragment shader. The "special values" referenced in the diagram are values that must be written for the pipeline to work correctly, such as the vertex position in clip space. The fragment shader ultimately produces one or more color values and perhaps a depth value as well.

Both vertex and fragment shaders have access to *uniform* data. Uniform values include built-in variables holding all relevant OpenGL state settings, as well as user-defined values that change on a per-primitive or per-object basis. Fragment shaders can also read from textures, and vertex shaders may be able to as well.

note

It's important to note that shaders operate on a single element at a time. In other words, vertex shaders handle a single vertex, and fragment shaders handle a single fragment. Within a shader, you have no knowledge of neighboring vertices or fragments. This limitation allows for high-performance parallel processing.

Because shaders replace portions of the pipeline, it's important to know what functionality you lost—and thus may have to replicate—if you enable shaders, so let's look at that next.

Vertex Shaders

When using a vertex shader, the following fixed-function pipeline steps are bypassed:

- Matrix application (modelview, projection, texture)
- Normal transformation, rescale, and normalization
- Texture coordinate generation
- Per-vertex lighting
- Point-size distance attenuation

Fragment Shaders

When using a fragment shader, the following fixed-function pipeline steps are bypassed:

- Texture application (including texture environment). The texture fetch (including filtering) is still handled by the fixed-function pipeline.
- Fog
- Color sum

Applications of Shaders

You now have a general idea of what a shader is, but you may be wondering why you'd want to use them. After all, if you're getting good results out of the fixed-function pipeline, it may not be immediately obvious why you'd want to throw that out and handle everything yourself. The following list presents some of the ways shaders can help improve your games:

- **Greater control.** Maybe OpenGL's lighting model isn't realistic enough for you. Or maybe you want to generate an effect that OpenGL just wasn't designed to handle. With shaders, you can do exactly what you want in order to produce nearly any desired effect.

- **Offloading work to the GPU.** GPUs are often more powerful than the CPUs they are used with, and they are generally much better at operating on vectors. If your game is bottlenecked on the CPU, moving work (animation, for example) to the GPU through shaders can improve overall performance.

- **Speed.** In reality, modern GPUs no longer have fixed-function pipelines at the vertex and fragment stages. If you're not explicitly using shaders yourself, the driver provides shaders that mimic the fixed-function pipeline. By providing your own shaders, you can ensure that you're only paying for things that you actually use.

- **Reuse.** A well-written shader, just like any other piece of well-designed code, can be used in many applications, thus speeding up development time.

These are just some general benefits that shaders provide. You'll see many more specific examples throughout the book.

Summary

Now that you know what shaders are and have a high-level overview of how they work, it's time to dig into the details. In the next two chapters, you'll learn about the two primary shading languages available in OpenGL. Both of these chapters—and in fact, much of the rest of the book—will include numerous examples of how shaders can be used to enhance your games.

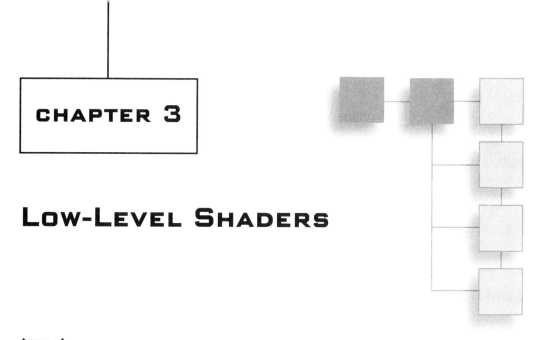

CHAPTER 3

Low-Level Shaders

This chapter will explain how to use OpenGL's low-level shading languages. These are covered by the ARB-approved extensions ARB_vertex_program and ARB_fragment_program. The languages are "low-level" because they resemble assembly language rather than a high-level language like C++. However, as assembly languages go, they are very simple, having only 27 and 33 instructions respectively and no support for branching or looping. The languages also deal with only a single data type: floating-point vectors with four components.

ARB_vertex_program

Paul Baker

As you read in the previous chapter, if vertex programming is enabled, a vertex program will be run for every vertex that you pass to OpenGL (using `glVertex3f()`, `glDrawArrays()`, etc.). OpenGL's fixed-function transform and lighting operations are bypassed, and the vertex program is responsible for carrying out these operations.

Data Vectors

As mentioned, all data used by an ARB_vertex_program are comprised of four component vectors. The four components can be referenced by "x," "y," "z," and "w," respectively.

These vectors are of four different types:

- **Attributes.** Properties of the vertex being operated on. These include the object-space vertex position, the vertex's color, and the vertex's normal.

- **Parameters.** Constants that remain the same through several invocations of the vertex program. These can be OpenGL state variables, such as the current modelview matrix, or can be vectors passed explicitly to the program.

- **Temporaries.** Vectors that are used for temporary storage within the program.
- **Outputs.** Properties of the vertex that are sent forward for further processing. These include the clip-space vertex position, the vertex's final color, and the vertex's texture coordinates.

Appendix A, "Assembly Shading Reference," found on this book's companion Web site, gives a comprehensive list of the attributes, OpenGL state parameters, and outputs available to a vertex program.

Generally, these vectors are given names by the programmer and are declared before use. However, it is possible to use attributes, parameters, and results inline, without naming them first. It is also possible to use write constant vectors inline.

Instructions

These vectors are operated on by instructions that take the form:

```
OP dest, src1[, src2[, src3]];
```

That is, the operation OP is applied to source vectors, of which there can be between 1 and 3, and the result is written into a destination vector. Unlike some other low-level shading languages, there are no restrictions on how many of each type of vector can be used in each instruction. For a more concrete example, the instruction DP4 performs a four-dimensional dot product between its two source vectors and writes the scalar result into all four components of the destination vector. So the operation

```
DP4 dest, src1, src2;
```

yields

```
dest.x = src1.x*src2.x + src1.y*src2.y + src1.z*src2.z + src1.w*src2.w;
dest.y = src1.x*src2.x + src1.y*src2.y + src1.z*src2.z + src1.w*src2.w;
dest.z = src1.x*src2.x + src1.y*src2.y + src1.z*src2.z + src1.w*src2.w;
dest.w = src1.x*src2.x + src1.y*src2.y + src1.z*src2.z + src1.w*src2.w;
```

Appendix A also lists all of the instructions available to a vertex program, giving an explanation of what each instruction does.

Write Masking

It is possible to restrict which components of a destination vector are updated by an operation. This is done by adding a suffix to the destination vector's name in the instruction. This suffix comprises a period (.) followed by any combination of the destination vector's components. For example, dest.xz would restrict the writing of a result to the x and z components of a destination vector only. Thus

```
DP4 dest.xz, src1, src2;
```

gives

```
dest.x = src1.x*src2.x + src1.y*src2.y + src1.z*src2.z + src1.w*src2.w;
dest.z = src1.x*src2.x + src1.y*src2.y + src1.z*src2.z + src1.w*src2.w;
```

and dest.y and dest.w are untouched and retain their previous values.

Example 1: Vertex Program

Here is a simple example of a vertex program:

```
!!ARBvp1.0

ATTRIB iPos = vertex.position;
ATTRIB iCol = vertex.color;


PARAM mvp[4] = {state.matrix.mvp};

OUTPUT oPos = result.position;
OUTPUT oCol = result.color;

# Transform vertex position to clip coords
DP4 oPos.x, mvp[0], iPos;
DP4 oPos.y, mvp[1], iPos;
DP4 oPos.z, mvp[2], iPos;
DP4 oPos.w, mvp[3], iPos;

# Pass through the vertex color
MOV oCol, iCol;


END
```

First, notice that the vertex program begins with a token that identifies it as an ARB vertex program, version 1.0.

The attribute vectors to be used in this program are declared next. These have the type ATTRIB, and in this program we are asking for the object-space position of the vertex we are dealing with to be placed in iPos and for the color of the vertex to be placed in iCol.

This program uses a single parameter that will hold the combined modelview and projection matrix. This is the matrix that transforms object-space coordinates into eye-space coordinates. The array notation is used to place this in mvp[0] to mvp[3]; mvp[0] will contain the first row of the matrix, and mvp[3] the last row.

The program will produce two outputs: the position of the vertex (in clip coordinates) and the vertex's color. To calculate the vertex's clip-space position, it is necessary to multiply its object-space position by the modelview-projection matrix. This is done by the four DP4 instructions, each of which calculates one component of the result by performing a single row's part of the matrix-vector multiplication.

In this program, the vertex's final color after the vertex program has executed is the same as its initial color. This is accomplished by using the MOV instruction, which simply copies its source vector into its destination vector.

The program finishes with an END statement, which is used to confirm to OpenGL that the end of the program has been reached.

OpenGL Functions for ARB_vertex_program

Now that we have a string of text that represents a vertex program, we need to load the program into OpenGL and ask for it to be executed for each vertex.

Vertex programs are handled using objects that are very similar to texture objects. The function

```
void glGenProgramsARB(GLsizei n, GLuint *programs);
```

generates n unused, unsigned integer program-object "handles" and writes them to the array programs. This is similar to the function glGenTextures().

A vertex program object can be made current by using the function

```
void glBindProgramARB(GLenum target, GLuint program);
```

Like glBindTexture(), this associates a given program object with a given target. For ARB vertex programs, the target is GL_VERTEX_PROGRAM_ARB.

To initialize the current vertex program object with a vertex program, the following function is used:

```
void glProgramStringARB(GLenum target, GLenum format, GLsizei len,
                  const GLvoid *string);
```

Again, the target is GL_VERTEX_PROGRAM_ARB. The format parameter should be GL_PROGRAM_FORMAT_ASCII_ARB, len should be the length of the program string, excluding any null terminator, and string should point to the program string itself.

Loading a vertex program may fail for several reasons. If it does, calling

```
glGetIntegerv(GL_PROGRAM_ERROR_POSITION_ARB, &err);
```

will set err to the character offset within the program at which an error was detected. If there is no error, err will contain −1. In the case of an error, calling:

```
glGetString(GL_PROGRAM_ERROR_STRING_ARB);
```

will return a string describing the error.

The command

```
glGetProgramivARB(GL_ PROGRAM_UNDER_NATIVE_LIMITS_ARB, &native);
```

will set `native` to false if the vertex program exceeds limits (for example, a maximum instruction count) defined by the current OpenGL implementation. On a hardware accelerated implementation, this may mean that rendering using the vertex program cannot be performed on the hardware and a (typically considerably slower) software fallback will be used.

Once the program object has been initialized by a program string, it is ready to use. In order to do this, simply enable it as follows before rendering any geometry:

```
glEnable(GL_VERTEX_PROGRAM_ARB);
```

The vertex program will then be run on every vertex rendered, until it is disabled with:

```
glDisable(GL_VERTEX_PROGRAM_ARB);
```

Explicit Program Parameters

The previous vertex program used a single parameter: the current modelview-projection matrix. In addition to using OpenGL state as program parameters, it is possible to pass any values from your main program into the vertex program. There are two types of such explicit parameters. *Program environment parameters* are shared between all programs using a particular target, whereas *program local parameters* are unique to the currently bound program. These parameters are sent using the following functions.

To set program environment parameters:

```
void glProgramEnvParameter4{fd}[v]ARB(GLenum target, GLuint index, TYPE coords);
```

To set program local parameters:

```
void glProgramLocalParameter4{fd}[v]ARB(GLenum target, GLuint index,
                                        TYPE coords);
```

In all cases, the target parameter should be `GL_VERTEX_PROGRAM_ARB` and `index` is the number by which the parameter can be referenced from within the vertex program. The `coords` are four floating-point values (or a pointer to four values) which are then accessible as a vector from within the vertex program using the `program.env[n]` or `program.local[n]` parameters.

Source-Vector Modifications

The input vectors to instructions can have their components reordered prior to the operation taking place. This is known as *swizzling* and is activated by adding a suffix to the source vector's name in the instruction. This suffix comprises a "." followed by any combination of four of the destination vector's components. The four components named are used in order, rather than the default of using x, y, z, and w.

For example, the ADD instruction adds its two source vectors component-wise. The instruction

```
ADD dest, src1, src2;
```

thus performs

```
dest.x = src1.x + src2.x;
dest.y = src1.y + src2.y;
dest.z = src1.z + src2.z;
dest.w = src1.w + src2.w;
```

whereas

```
ADD dest, src1.zzyw, src2.yxzx;
```

performs

```
dest.x = src1.z + src2.y;
dest.y = src1.z + src2.x;
dest.z = src1.y + src2.z;
dest.w = src1.w + src2.x;
```

The suffixes .x, .y, .z, and .w are also legal. When an operation requires a scalar input, these suffixes select a single component of a vector. When used with operations requiring vector inputs, these suffixes represent .xxxx, .yyyy, .zzzz, and .wwww respectively.

Source vectors can also be negated before being used in operations. This is performed by prefixing the name by "-". For example, to subtract v2 from v1 and place the result in v0, both of the following are valid syntaxes:

```
SUB v0, v1, v2;
ADD v0, v1, -v2;
```

Example 2: Vertex Interpolation

For the next example, a vertex program will be used to perform a quadratic interpolation between the vertex positions of three fixed models. This will result in a smooth animation.

The inputs to the vertex program will include three vertex positions, and these will be combined to produce a final position. As in the simple vertex program above, the output color for the vertex will be the same as the input color—no lighting will be performed. In order to make the results of the vertex program clear, the example will draw the model in wireframe. Figure 3.1 shows an image of this example in action.

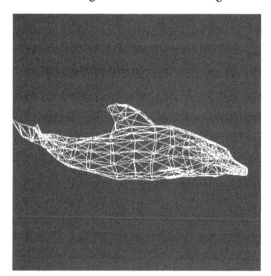

Figure 3.1 A wireframe model animated by interpolating vertex positions.

The vertex program used is the following:

```
!!ARBvp1.0
ATTRIB iPos1 = vertex.position;
ATTRIB iPos2 = vertex.texcoord[0];
ATTRIB iPos3 = vertex.texcoord[1];
ATTRIB iCol  = vertex.color;
PARAM mvp[4] = {state.matrix.mvp};
PARAM t      = program.local[0];        #(t, 1-t, 0, 0)
TEMP tFactors, objPos;
OUTPUT oPos  = result.position;
OUTPUT oCol  = result.color;

# Calculate the object-space position (= (1-t)*(1-t)*p1 + 2*(1-t)*t*p2 + t*t*p3)
MUL tFactors, t.yyxz, t.yxxz;
MUL tFactors.y, tFactors.y, 2.0;
MUL objPos, iPos1, tFactors.x;
MAD objPos, iPos2, tFactors.y, objPos;
MAD objPos, iPos3, tFactors.z, objPos;
```

```
# Transform the vertex position to clip coords
DP4 oPos.x, mvp[0], objPos;
DP4 oPos.y, mvp[1], objPos;
DP4 oPos.z, mvp[2], objPos;
DP4 oPos.w, mvp[3], objPos;

# Pass through the vertex color
MOV oCol, iCol;


END
```

Since we need to pass in three vertex positions in order to perform the interpolation between them and there is only one vertex.position attribute, we pass in the other two vertex positions as texture coordinates. There is no obligation for texture-coordinate attributes to actually hold texture coordinates, and since these have the required range, they seem a good place to send this extra vertex data into the vertex program. We also pass in the incoming vertex color.

As before, we require the combined modelview-projection matrix as a parameter from the OpenGL state. This time, we also pass in an explicit parameter, which contains (t, 1-t, 0, 0), where t is the interpolation factor between the frames of animation (t is in [0, 1]).

The vertex program calculates the object-space position of the vertex by interpolating between the object-space vertex positions passed in. The interpolation is performed using:

```
V = (1-t)*(1-t)*V1 + 2*(1-t)*t*V2 + t*t*V3
```

Note the use of swizzling to efficiently calculate the interpolation factors (in the temporary vector tFactors) using only two MUL instructions, and the use of MAD to accumulate the final position in objPos. The interpolated position is then transformed to clip space as in the previous example.

The output color of the vertex is simply copied from the input color to complete the processing performed by the vertex program.

Generic Vertex Attributes and Matrices

In addition to the vertex attributes that correspond directly to standard OpenGL vertex-specification commands (e.g., vertex.position, vertex.normal), generic vertex attributes are available. These are 16 or more four-component vectors that can be used to pass any per-vertex information into the vertex program.

In immediate mode, the commands used to do this are of the form:

```
GLvoid glVertexAttrib{1234}{sfd}ARB(GLuint index, T coords);
GLvoid glVertexAttrib{123}{sfd}vARB(GLuint index, T coords);
```

```
GLvoid glVertexAttrib4{bsifd ubusui}vARB(GLuint index, T coords);
GLvoid VertexAttrib4NubARB(GLuint index, T coords)
GLvoid VertexAttrib4N{bsifd ubusui}vARB(GLuint index, T coords);
```

The index parameter contains the index of the generic attribute vector that is being set. This is filled with the coordinates specified. If an "N" is given in the function name, the specified values are normalized to lie in the range $[0, 1]$ or $[-1, 1]$.

Arrays of generic vertex attributes are also supported. The source data is specified using the command:

```
GLvoid glVertexAttribPointerARB(GLuint index, GLint size, GLenum type,
                                GLboolean normalized, GLsizei stride,
                                const GLvoid *pointer);
```

Again, index tells OpenGL which generic vertex attribute is to be filled with the data from this array. The parameter normalized is equivalent to the N in the immediate mode commands; if normalized is true, then data values are normalized to lie in the range $[0, 1]$ or $[-1, 1]$. The parameters size, type, stride, and pointer are exactly the same as for standard array pointer commands, such as glVertexPointer().

These arrays are enabled and disabled using the following commands:

```
GLvoid glEnableVertexAttribArrayARB(GLuint index);
```

```
GLvoid glDisableVertexAttribArrayARB(GLuint index);
```

These generic attributes are accessed from within the vertex program using the vertex.attrib[n] attribute vectors.

Generic vertex attributes may or may not be aliased with conventional vertex attributes. That is, setting a generic vertex attribute might also set a corresponding conventional vertex attribute, depending on your implementation of OpenGL. In order to avoid problems, consider a conventional vertex attribute to be undefined if the corresponding generic attribute is set, and vice versa. The mapping between generic and conventional vertex attributes is shown in Table 3.1.

Note that even if all conventional vertex attributes are in use, generic attributes 6 and 7 are still available if more per-vertex data is required.

In a similar vein to generic vertex attributes, generic program matrices are also available. The token

```
GL_MATRIXn_ARB
```

(where n is between 0 and 31) can be used as an argument to glMatrixMode(). Any operations on the current matrix (glTranslate(), glLoadMatrix(), etc.) will then act upon the program matrix.

Table 3.1 Generic-to-Conventional Attribute Mapping

Generic Attribute Number	Conventional Attribute
0	Vertex position
1	Weights 0–3
2	Normal
3	Primary color
4	Secondary color
5	Fog coordinate
6	None
7	None
8–15	Texture coordinate set 0–7

The values of the program matrices will have no effect upon the OpenGL fixed-function pipeline. When vertex programming is enabled, the matrices can be accessed from within vertex programs using the `state.matrix.program[n]` parameters.

Lighting

When vertex programming is enabled, the standard OpenGL lighting calculations are bypassed. To add lighting to the previous example, the lighting calculations need to be added to the vertex program.

Lighting calculations, of course, require normals. The normal passed into OpenGL using `glNormal*()` is accessible as an attribute called `vertex.normal`. If further normals are required, these can be passed in using texture coordinates, as were used for vertex positions in the previous example, or they can be passed as generic attributes.

The normals are, by default, in object space when passed into the vertex program. OpenGL performs its internal lighting calculations in eye space. To transform normals from object space to eye space, it is necessary to transform them by the inverse-transpose of the modelview matrix, rather than by the unaltered modelview matrix, as would be used for transforming vertex positions. This is necessary to obtain correct results in the presence of nonuniform scaling.

It is also necessary to know the position of the light in eye space in order to perform lighting. This can be used along with the eye-space position of the vertex to calculate a normalized vector from the vertex to the light. The diffuse lighting intensity is then calculated by a simple dot product of this vector with the eye-space normal.

Since the eye lies, by definition, at the origin of eye space, a vector from the vertex to the eye can easily be calculated in a vertex program. This eye vector can be combined with the normal and the light vector to calculate a specular brightness.

Fog

If `ARB_vertex_program` is enabled, OpenGL fog calculations do not work as they normally do. This is because the standard fog interpolation factors are calculated using the eye-space z-coordinate—which is not calculated automatically when vertex programming is enabled. Instead, the output `result.fogcoord.z` can be written to, and this value will be used in fog calculations. This is a generalization of the fog coordinate feature introduced by the `EXT_fog_coord` OpenGL extension.

Example 3: Vertex Interpolation with Lighting and Fog

This chapter's second example will add lighting and fog to the previous example. The vertex program requires three positions and three normals to interpolate. Rather than use four sets of texture coordinates to pass these, generic vertex attributes will be used. The vertex's color is also passed as an attribute, but in this program the output color is computed via lighting calculations rather than being a simple pass-through. Figure 3.2 shows the improvement made to the previous example by adding lighting and fog.

Figure 3.2 Lighting and fog add atmosphere to the animated model.

The vertex program used for this example is:

```
!!ARBvp1.0
ATTRIB iPos1  = vertex.position;
ATTRIB iPos2  = vertex.attrib[6];
ATTRIB iPos3  = vertex.attrib[7];
ATTRIB iCol   = vertex.color;
ATTRIB iNorm1 = vertex.normal;
```

```
ATTRIB iNorm2 = vertex.attrib[8];
ATTRIB iNorm3 = vertex.attrib[9];
PARAM modelview[4]   = {state.matrix.modelview};
PARAM itModelview[4] = {state.matrix.modelview.invtrans};
PARAM mvp[4]  = {state.matrix.mvp};
PARAM t         = program.local[0];    #(t, 1-t, 0, 0)
PARAM eyeLightPos     = program.local[1];
TEMP tFactors, objPos, eyePos, objNorm, eyeNorm, eyeLight, lighting;
OUTPUT oPos   = result.position;
OUTPUT oCol   = result.color;
OUTPUT oFog   = result.fogcoord;

# Calculate the object-space position (= (1-t)*(1-t)*p1 + 2*(1-t)*t*p2 + t*t*p3)
MUL tFactors, t.yyxz, t.yxxz;
MUL tFactors.y, tFactors.y, 2.0;
MUL objPos, iPos1, tFactors.x;
MAD objPos, iPos2, tFactors.y, objPos;
MAD objPos, iPos3, tFactors.z, objPos;

# Transform the vertex position to eye coords
DP4 eyePos.x, modelview[0], objPos;
DP4 eyePos.y, modelview[1], objPos;
DP4 eyePos.z, modelview[2], objPos;
DP4 eyePos.w, modelview[3], objPos;
# Transform vertex position to clip coords
DP4 oPos.x, mvp[0], objPos;
DP4 oPos.y, mvp[1], objPos;
DP4 oPos.z, mvp[2], objPos;
DP4 oPos.w, mvp[3], objPos;

# Similarly calculate the object-space normal
MUL objNorm, iNorm1, tFactors.x;
MAD objNorm, iNorm2, tFactors.y, objNorm;
MAD objNorm, iNorm3, tFactors.z, objNorm;

# Renormalize the normal
DP3 objNorm.w, objNorm, objNorm;
RSQ objNorm.w, objNorm.w;
MUL objNorm, objNorm.w, objNorm;

# Transform normal to eye coords
DP4 eyeNorm.x, itModelview[0], objNorm;
DP4 eyeNorm.y, itModelview[1], objNorm;
```

```
DP4 eyeNorm.z, itModelview[2], objNorm;
DP4 eyeNorm.w, itModelview[3], objNorm;

# Calculate normalized eye-space light vector
SUB eyeLight, eyeLightPos, eyePos;
DP3 eyeLight.w, eyeLight, eyeLight;
RSQ eyeLight.w, eyeLight.w;
MUL eyeLight, eyeLight.w, eyeLight;

# Calculate N.L
DP3 lighting.x, eyeNorm, eyeLight;

# Modulate the vertex color by the diffuse component
MUL oCol, iCol, lighting.x;

# Use the eye-space -Z as the fog coordinate
MOV oFog, -eyePos.z;

END
```

The parameters required by this vertex program include those used in the last example, and add the modelview and inverse-transpose modelview matrices that are necessary to transform positions and normals to eye space for lighting calculations. The position of the light in eye space is also required.

The outputs from the vertex program include the clip-space position and color as before, and also a fog coordinate.

The first operations carried out by the program are calculating the object-space position via interpolation and transforming this both to eye space for lighting calculations and to clip space for the final position. Interpolation is used again to calculate the object-space normal, which is then renormalized and converted to eye space.

The eye-space light vector—that is, the vector from the vertex to the light—is then calculated and normalized. The diffuse lighting brightness is calculated in the standard manner: by performing N.L in eye space. This is then modulated by the incoming vertex color to give the output color.

Finally, the (negated) z-coordinate of the eye-space position is output as the fog coordinate so that fog calculations are performed as for the fixed-function pipeline.

Program Options

The `ARB_vertex_program` extension also supports an `OPTION` command. This can be used to specify any special processing that the program requires.

The position invariant option is the only one supported by `ARB_vertex_program` as standard. There is no guarantee that clip-space positions generated by a transformation using the modelview-projection matrix in a vertex program will produce exactly the same results as a transformation by the fixed-function pipeline, because the two generation methods differ in terms of precision. The position invariant option allows a program to ask that the clip-space position be calculated using the fixed-function pipeline while the rest of the vertex program is executed. This option is specified using

```
OPTION ARB_position_invariant;
```
If this option is used, a vertex program must not write to result.position itself.

Relative Addressing

`ARB_vertex_program` also supports `ADDRESS` variables. These are integer (rather than the standard floating-point) vectors in which only the x component is accessible. An address variable is declared using the following syntax:

```
ADDRESS addr;
```

A value is loaded into the address register using the ARL instruction. This value can then be used as a relative offset into an array of vectors. For example:

```
PARAM colors = {{1.0, 0.0, 0.0, 0.0}, {0.0, 1.0, 0.0, 0.0}, {0.0, 0.0, 1.0, 0.0}};
ARL addr.x, temp.x;
MOV oCol, colors[addr.x+1];
```

ARB_fragment_program

If `ARB_fragment_program` is enabled, a fragment program will be run for every fragment generated. In this case, standard OpenGL texturing, color sum, and fog application operations are replaced by a user-defined fragment program.

The language of `ARB_fragment_program` is similar to that of `ARB_vertex_program`. As before, the data handled by the program are all four-component vectors, and the types of vectors are the same as for `ARB_vertex_program`. The exact attributes and results of a fragment program are different from those for a vertex program, however, and these are listed in Appendix A. Unlike `ARB_vertex_program`, fragment programs have no generic attributes available, but the generic program matrices are still accessible.

Since the vectors in a fragment program may just as easily represent colors as Cartesian coordinates, in addition to being able to access the components of a vector as x, y, z, w, they may be accessed as r, g, b, a, respectively.

The ARB_vertex_program LOG and EXP instructions are removed from the instruction set for ARB_fragment_program, but several new instructions are added. Again, Appendix A lists the instructions available in the low-level shading languages and specifies which subset of these is available to ARB_fragment_program. The other major difference between the fragment and vertex programming language is that ARB_fragment_program has no support for an address register.

ARB_fragment_program supports a saturation modifier that can be applied to any instruction by simply suffixing the instruction mnemonic with _SAT. This will clamp each component of the result of the operation to [0, 1]. This is useful for colors, since RGBA components of a color displayed on a standard framebuffer must lie in the range 0 to 1. It can also be helpful in other situations, as can be seen later in the chapter.

For example, the instruction

```
ADD tmp, {0.0, 1.0, 0.5, 0.25}, {2.0, -2.0, 0.5, 0.25};
```

will leave tmp holding {2.0, -1.0, 1.0, 0.5}, as expected, whereas, if the _SAT modifier is used

```
ADD_SAT tmp, {0.0, 1.0, 0.5, 0.25}, {2.0, -2.0, 0.5, 0.25};
```

tmp will hold {1.0, 0.0, 1.0, 0.5}.

The same OpenGL functions are used for handling fragment-program objects as for vertex-program objects. The target parameter for a fragment program is GL_FRAGMENT_PROGRAM_ARB. Thus, to enable fragment programming, call:

```
glEnable(GL_FRAGMENT_PROGRAM_ARB);
```

Example 4: Procedural Shading

One of the many uses of ARB_fragment_program is to perform procedural shading. This first example will draw a teapot with a star on either side. The planes making up the sides of the star are passed into the fragment program as local parameters. For each fragment, a calculation is performed to see whether or not the fragment lies within the star. This result is used to decide between two different material colors for the fragment. Standard Phong-model lighting calculations are then performed using this material color. The result is shown in Figure 3.3.

Figure 3.3 A teapot displaying a star generated by procedural shading.

The fragment program used is:

```
!!ARBfp1.0

ATTRIB iObjPos      = fragment.texcoord[0];
ATTRIB iEyeNorm     = fragment.texcoord[1];

PARAM itModelview[] = { state.matrix.modelview.invtrans};
PARAM modelview[]   = { state.matrix.modelview};
PARAM plane0        = program.local[0];
PARAM plane1        = program.local[1];
PARAM plane2        = program.local[2];
PARAM plane3        = program.local[3];
PARAM plane4        = program.local[4];
PARAM eyeLightPos   = program.local[5];
PARAM purple        = {0.8, 0.0, 0.6, 0.0};
PARAM yellow        = {1.0, 1.0, 0.0, 0.0};

TEMP distPlane1, distPlane2, classPlane1, classPlane2, inStar, materialColor;
TEMP eyePosition, eyeLight, normEyeLight, normNormal, lighting, reflection, eyeView;

OUTPUT oCol         = result.color;

# Calculate the distance of the fragment from each plane
DP4 distPlane1.x, iObjPos, plane0;
DP4 distPlane1.y, iObjPos, plane1;
```

```
DP4 distPlane1.z, iObjPos, plane2;
DP4 distPlane1.w, iObjPos, plane3;
DP4 distPlane2.x, iObjPos, plane4;

#Classify the fragment by each plane
SGE classPlane1, distPlane1, 0.0;
SGE classPlane2, distPlane2, 0.0;

#Calculate whether the fragment is in the star
DP4 inStar, classPlane1, 1.0;
ADD inStar, inStar, classPlane2.x;
SUB_SAT inStar, inStar, 3.0;

#If so, the base color is yellow, otherwise purple
LRP materialColor, inStar, yellow, purple;

# Calculate the eye-space position
DP4 eyePosition.x, modelview[0], iObjPos;
DP4 eyePosition.y, modelview[1], iObjPos;
DP4 eyePosition.z, modelview[2], iObjPos;
DP4 eyePosition.w, modelview[3], iObjPos;

# Calculate the eye-space light vector
SUB eyeLight, eyeLightPos, eyePosition;

# Calculate a normalized light vector
DP3 normEyeLight.w, eyeLight, eyeLight;
RSQ normEyeLight.w, normEyeLight.w;
MUL normEyeLight.xyz, normEyeLight.w, eyeLight;

# Normalize the normal
DP3 normNormal.w, iEyeNorm, iEyeNorm;
RSQ normNormal.w, normNormal.w;
MUL normNormal.xyz, normNormal.w, iEyeNorm;

# Calculate N.L
DP3 lighting.x, normNormal, normEyeLight;

# Calculate the reflection vector, R = 2(N.L)N-L
MUL reflection, lighting.x, 2.0;
MUL reflection, reflection, normNormal;
SUB reflection, reflection, normEyeLight;
```

```
# Calculate the normalized eye-space view vector
DP3 eyeView.w, eyePosition, eyePosition;
RSQ eyeView.w, eyeView.w;
MUL eyeView.xyz, eyeView.w, -eyePosition;

# Calculate R.V
DP3 lighting.y, reflection, eyeView;

# Specular exponent 32
MOV lighting.w, 32.0;

# Calculate lighting coefficients
LIT lighting, lighting;

# Add the ambient brightness to the diffuse
ADD lighting.y, lighting.y, 0.1;

# Calculate the final color
MAD oCol, materialColor, lighting.y, lighting.z;

END
```

First, notice that the initial token identifying a fragment program is !!ARBfp1.0. As before, the program concludes with an END token.

The only per-fragment inputs to the program are the eye-space normal and the object-space position. Both of these are specified per-vertex and interpolated to give the per-fragment values. The only result generated by this program is the final fragment color.

The object-space coordinates of the planes delimiting the star are given in five local parameters. These define the position of the star as shown in Figure 3.4. The first operation performed by the fragment program is to calculate the signed distance from the fragment's object space position to each of the five planes. This distance is positive if the fragment is in front of the plane and negative if it is behind the plane. The SGE instruction is then used to convert this distance into a classification of the fragment relative to each plane—each component of the classPlane vectors is 0.0 if the fragment is behind the plane and 1.0 if the fragment is in front of the plane.

From Figure 3.4, it is clear that the fragment is inside the star if it is in front of at least four of the five planes. By summing the classifications, then subtracting 3 and clamping (via the SAT instruction modifier) to [0, 1], the vector inStar holds 0.0 in all components if the fragment is outside the star, and 1.0 in all components if the fragment is within the star. Note the use of the DP4 instruction, with a second source parameter of (1.0, 1.0, 1.0, 1.0) to add the four components of classPlane1 in a single instruction.

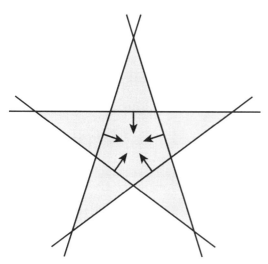

Figure 3.4 The planes used to delimit the star on the teapot.

The inStar vector is then used to linearly interpolate between the basic colors used outside and inside the star. The vector materialColor thus contains the material color to be used in lighting calculations.

Phong lighting is then performed for each fragment. As in the second ARB_vertex_program example, lighting is performed in eye space. The eye-space fragment position is used to calculate a normalized vector from the fragment to the light (L). The eye-space normal (N) is passed into the fragment program, and once this has been renormalized (since it will have become non-unit-length as it is interpolated across the polygons), a dot product yields the diffuse lighting component.

The light vector is also reflected about the normal to produce a reflection vector (R), as shown in Figure 3.5. This is used in a dot product with a normalized vector from the fragment to the eye (V), to give the specular brightness. The LIT instruction is then used to combine these two dot products, along with a specular exponent, in a lighting vector whose y-component holds the diffuse brightness and whose z-component holds the specular brightness. After adding a little ambient light to the diffuse brightness, these are combined with the material color produced in the first half of the fragment program to produce a final fragment color.

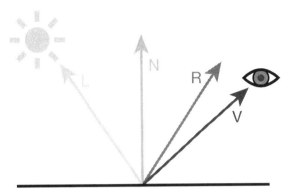

Figure 3.5 Vectors required to perform Phong lighting calculations.

Texture Sampling

The TEX instruction available in ARB_fragment_program performs a texture lookup, given a vector supplying texture coordinates, a texture unit, and a texture target. For example, to place the (r, g, b ,a) result of a lookup in the 2D-texture bound to texture unit 0 in the vector col, using the (s, t, r) texture coordinates in the first three components of coords, the following command is used:

```
TEX col, coords, texture[0], 2D;
```

Five texture targets are available, reflecting the five texture targets that are available in fixed-function OpenGL. These are shown in Table 3.2.

Table 3.2 Texture Targets

TEX texture target – Fixed function texture target	
1D	GL_TEXTURE_1D
2D	GL_TEXTURE_2D
3D	GL_TEXTURE_3D
CUBE	GL_TEXTURE_CUBE_MAP
RECT	GL_TEXTURE_RECTANGLE

When ARB_fragment_program is enabled, the fixed-function texture enables are ignored. The texture target supplied to a TEX instruction is accessed regardless of whether that target is enabled for the given texture unit. However, only one texture target can be accessed per texture unit in each fragment program.

There are two other texture-sampling instructions available. The TXB instruction performs a texture lookup using the first three parameters of the coordinate vector unaltered and interprets the fourth parameter as a level-of-detail bias to be used in selecting mipmaps.

The TXP instruction is used for projective texturing—the vector of texture coordinates (s, t, r, q) undergoes perspective division before being used. The texture lookup is performed with the coordinates (s/q, t/q, r/q).

Example 5: Per-Pixel Reflection

The final example in this chapter shows texture accesses in a fragment program. It uses a technique called a "dependent texture read" in which a first texture sampling is performed, and the resulting color is used as texture coordinates to look up in a second texture. This example uses this technique to perform per-fragment bump-mapped reflection. This produces the effect shown in Figure 3.6.

note

For more on bump-mapping and other texturing techniques mentioned in this chapter, see Chapter 5, "Advanced Texture Mapping."

Figure 3.6 A torus shaded using per-fragment reflection.

The fragment program used in this example is:

```
!!ARBfp1.0

ATTRIB iPos         = fragment.texcoord[0];
ATTRIB istn0        = fragment.texcoord[1];
ATTRIB istn1        = fragment.texcoord[2];
ATTRIB istn2        = fragment.texcoord[3];
ATTRIB iTexCoord    = fragment.texcoord[4];
PARAM  itModelview[] = { state.matrix.modelview.invtrans};
```

```
PARAM modelview[]   = { state.matrix.modelview};
TEMP fragNorm, objNorm, eyeNorm, eyePos, nDotV, reflection;
OUTPUT oCol         = result.color;

#Read the fragment normal from 2d texture 0
TEX fragNorm, iTexCoord, texture[0], 2D;

#Expand each component to [-1, 1]
MAD fragNorm, fragNorm, {2.0, 2.0, 2.0, 0.0}, {-1.0, -1.0, -1.0, 0.0};

#Transform the normal to object space
DP3 objNorm.x, istn0, fragNorm;
DP3 objNorm.y, istn1, fragNorm;
DP3 objNorm.z, istn2, fragNorm;

#Transform the normal to eye space
DP3 eyeNorm.x, itModelview[0], objNorm;
DP3 eyeNorm.y, itModelview[1], objNorm;
DP3 eyeNorm.z, itModelview[2], objNorm;

#Transform the fragment position to eye space
DP4 eyePos.x, modelview[0], iPos;
DP4 eyePos.y, modelview[1], iPos;
DP4 eyePos.z, modelview[2], iPos;
DP4 eyePos.w, modelview[3], iPos;

#Reflect the vector from the fragment position to the eye about the normal
#R = 2(N.-V)N+V
DP3 nDotV, eyeNorm, -eyePos;
MUL reflection, nDotV, 2.0;
MUL reflection, reflection, eyeNorm;
ADD reflection, reflection, eyePos;

#Use this to look up in the environment map
TEX oCol, reflection, texture[1], CUBE;

END
```

The very first operation performed by the fragment program is a texture lookup—this time into the 2D-texture bound to texture unit 0. This yields the tangent-space normal at the fragment. This normal been packed into [0, 1] in order to be placed in an RGB texture, so is expanded to [−1, 1].

The tangent-space normal is then multiplied by the matrix whose columns are the interpolated s-tangent, t-tangent, and normal at the fragment—since these are the vectors that define tangent space, this transforms the normal into object space. Notice that these three vectors are passed into the program using texture coordinate parameters—there are no generic attributes available to fragment programs. The normal is then transformed into eye space by multiplying by the inverse-transpose modelview matrix.

The object-space position is transformed to eye space by multiplying it by the modelview matrix. Given this position, the vector from the fragment to the eye is simply the negation of this vector, since the eye lies at the origin in eye space. This vector is then reflected about the eye-space normal, yielding an eye-space reflection vector.

The reflection vector is then used in another TEX instruction as a set of texture coordinates, to look up into the cubic environment map bound to texture unit 1. The result of this texture lookup is the fragment's final color.

KIL: Kill Fragment Instruction

ARB_fragment_program supports an instruction that can be used to immediately discard a fragment at any point. This can be useful when drawing objects with transparent parts— any fragment lying in a transparent region can easily be killed. The KIL instruction takes a single vector parameter and determines whether any of the four components are negative; if so, further processing is prevented.

Depth Output

Both of the fragment program examples we have seen only produce a final color for a fragment. Fragment programs can also affect fragments by altering a fragment's depth. This is performed by writing a value between 0.0 and 1.0 to the z component of result.depth. If the fragment program does not write to this value, OpenGL will calculate the depth value normally. ARB_fragment_program does not allow a fragment program to alter the x- and y-coordinates of the fragment's position.

Summary

This chapter explained how to use OpenGL's low-level shading languages. Both languages use the same data type and have similar inputs, outputs, and instruction sets. `ARB_vertex_program` was used to animate and color vertices, and `ARB_fragment_program` was used for shading, lighting, and performing reflection calculations on a per-fragment basis.

These languages are low-level, and using them is similar to programming in assembly language. The next chapter will look at the high-level shading language introduced by the OpenGL Shading Language. Using this language is a lot more like programming in C or C++.

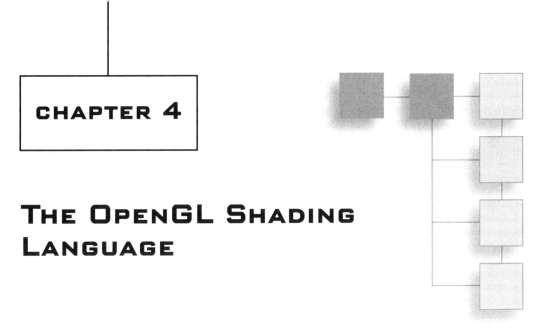

CHAPTER 4

THE OPENGL SHADING LANGUAGE

Rob Jones

Introduction

In the previous two chapters you were given an introduction to what shaders are—how they fit into the graphics pipeline and what you can do with low-level shaders. In this chapter you will

- Learn about the OpenGL Shading Language
- Learn about the associated C API for working with it
- See some examples of how to use the OpenGL Shading Language
- Find a few tips to help you with your development

What is the OpenGL Shading Language?

extension
_____

Extension name: ARB_shading_language_100, ARB_vertex_shader, ARB_fragment_shader, ARB_shader_objects
Name string: GL_ARB_shading_language_100, GL_ARB_vertex_shader, GL_ARB_fragment_shader, GL_ARB_shader_objects
Promoted to core: OpenGL 2.0
_____

The OpenGL Shading Language (GLSL) is what's known as a high-level shading language. That means the language is similar to ANSI C and not to the low-level shading language you have seen thus far. While a lot of the functionality of C has been used in the language, it also borrows some aspects of C++. For that reason, many of the aspects of GLSL, such as keywords, program layout, and general syntax, will look familiar to those with a background in C-based languages (including C++ or C# as well as C itself). Despite the similarities, there are also many differences between C and GLSL. These will be covered as we encounter them.

An example of a typical shader is below; in this instance it's a vertex shader. For now just look at the structure of the program; by the end of the chapter you'll understand what it all means.

```
/* A GLSL vertex program to perform setup for normal mapping */
#version 110
varying vec3 LightDir;
varying vec3 EyeDir;
uniform vec3 LightPosition;     // in world space!

attribute vec3 Tangent;
void main(void)
{
  // transforms EyeDir into eye-space
  EyeDir = vec3(gl_ModelViewMatrix * gl_Vertex);
  // transforms LightPosition into eye-space
  vec3 LightPos = vec3(gl_ModelViewMatrix * vec4(LightPosition,1.0));
  gl_Position = ftransform();
  gl_TexCoord[0] = gl_MultiTexCoord0;

  vec3 n = normalize(gl_NormalMatrix * gl_Normal);
  vec3 t = normalize(gl_NormalMatrix * Tangent);
  vec3 b = cross(n,t);

  vec3 v;
  // Convert the vectors to tangent space
  vec3 tmp = LightPos - EyeDir;
  v.x = dot(tmp,t);
  v.y = dot(tmp,b);
  v.z = dot(tmp,n);
  LightDir = normalize(v);

  v.x = dot(EyeDir,t);
  v.y = dot(EyeDir,b);
  v.z = dot(EyeDir,n);
  EyeDir = normalize(v);
}
```

As with C, the program execution begins in a "main" function and terminates once the program exits that function at the bottom. Comments can be made using either the // or /*...*/ styles, and statements are terminated using a semicolon, just as in C or C++.

Like any other program, this one has both inputs and outputs, some of which are user defined and some of which are built-in. Later in the chapter we will cover how the data gets in and out of shaders.

The example also shows how some built-in functions are used. These exist to help speed up development and perform commonly used functionality.

As with the `ARB_vertex_program` and `ARB_fragment_program` extensions, OpenGL Shading Language–based shaders are broken up into two parts: a vertex shader, which operates per vertex, and a fragment shader, which operates per fragment. However, unlike the afore-mentioned extensions, in order to use the shaders you must link them together to form a program object that can then be bound (like a texture) in order to be activated for use. The precise way this is done will be covered later; for now just keep it in mind.

Variables and Data Types

The most fundamental part of any language after its syntax is the data types available to use, and GLSL is no exception to this rule. It has a number of data types, all of which are built upon a small group of three scalar types.

These types are used to declare and define variables for the programs to use as input, output, or temporary values during the execution of the program. You'll see many examples of this in the coming pages.

Variables are also subject to the same scope and declaration rules as they are in C++, which differ somewhat from C. The term scope refers to the visibility of a variable within a block of code. In C++ a block is defined inside a pair of curly braces ({...}); anything declared inside that block is visible from its declaration point until the closing curly brace is reached. Variables can exist at varying levels of scope.

- Program scope
- Shader scope
- Function scope

Variables that exist at program scope are visible in both vertex and fragment shaders. User-defined varying variables and uniform variables can exist at this scope, depending on their type. (The concept of varying and uniform variables will be explained later.)

A variable that is visible only at shader scope can be seen only in a vertex or a fragment shader. Data passed to a vertex shader per vertex is data that falls into this scope.

Finally, function-scope variables exist only while the function they are in is running and are visible only to that function.

As in C++, there is no restriction on when you can declare a variable for use. As soon as it is declared it is available until it goes out of scope.

Like C++, GLSL is type safe, but unlike C++, there are no implicit type casts. That means that types must match when being assigned, and there is no automatic promotion from one type to another. The shader writer can, however, explicitly cast from one type to another. This system simplifies the language by removing ambiguities such as which version of an overloaded function to call.

Finally, when defining your variable names, keep in mind that there are numerous reserved names you can't use.

- Anything that is of the form gl_<name>GL is reserved for future OpenGL use, as is anything with a double underscore (__<name>).
- Vendors also have the option to extend the OpenGL Shading Language, so there are various reserved names for them. These follow the form gl_<name>*VEN* and __<name>*VEN*, where *VEN* is series of letters representing a vendor and can be any of the following: SGI, HP, IBM, APPLE, SUN, NV, MESA, ATI, or I3D. In addition to vendor names, *VEN* can also be a multivendor acronym such as EXT, OML, OES, or simply ARB for ARB-approved extensions.

Scalars

The three scalar types available are

- **float.** Declares a floating-point number
- **int.** Declares a single integer
- **bool.** Declares a single Boolean value

You use these types to declare variables the same way you would in a C or C++ program, as shown in the following example:

```
float f;
float myVar, myotherVar = 3.14;
int i = 7;
bool somestatement = false;
```

Floating-point values are best used to express things such as color and position within a shader.

Whereas floating-point operations and values work much like they do in C, the integer values do not. You are guaranteed at least 16 bits of precision and a sign bit, which allows for variables in at least the range of $[-65535, 65535]$, but there is no requirement for it to be fixed at 16 bits, so under- and overflow due to arithmetic is undefined and bit-wise operations such as left-shift (<<) and "and" (&) are not supported.

Boolean variables act like the bool type in C++ in that they can only hold a value of true or false. Relationship operators such as less than (<) and logical operators like logical "and" (&&) always return a value of type bool. Unlike C++, in which almost any value can be used as part of a flow-control statement (such as if-else), the OpenGL Shading Language requires the use of a variable of type bool.

Literal values can also be used in programs for all of the above types. For bool values, the literals true and false are supplied. Floating-point values are used in much the same way as their C counterparts; however, as there is only one floating-point type, there is no need to use a suffix to indicate precision. Some examples of floating-point literals would be

```
3.14
0.7
.768
4.4e10
0.7E-7
```

While integers aren't as flexible in GLSL as they are in C or C++, they still have their uses. As literal types they can be used to express the size of arrays and structures and the end condition of fixed-length loops. As variable values they can be used as an index into an array; to dynamically determine the end of a loop; and as counters for loops. They can be declared using any of the following number systems:

```
42    // a decimal literal
052   // an octal literal
0x2a  // a hexadecimal literal
```

Vectors

While scalars are the basis of all the variable types in the GLSL, they aren't the most useful of types in computer graphics. As you might have noticed while using OpenGL, data tends to consist of more than one value linked to a variable (x, y, and z for position, red, green, blue, and alpha for color, and so on). For this reason, GLSL has native support for vectors of floating-point, integer, and Boolean values.

> vec2: Vector of two floating-point numbers
>
> vec3: Vector of three floating-point numbers
>
> vec4: Vector of four floating-point numbers
>
> ivec2: Vector of two integer numbers
>
> ivec3: Vector of three integer numbers
>
> ivec4: Vector of four integer numbers

bvec2: Vector of two Booleans

bvec3: Vector of three Booleans

bvec4: Vector of four Booleans

As you can see, vectors can store two, three, or four values in one variable. This makes them very useful for representing values such as vertex positions, colors, texture coordinates, or anything else that requires multiple values. Built-in variables are vector types more often than not, and built-in functions also make extensive use of these types for passing parameters.

You can access vectors as you would an array or via field selection much as you would a structure, as shown in the following example:

```
vec3 foo;
float x = foo.x
float bar = foo[0];
```

Because foo.x and foo[0] both reference the same value, x and bar would be equivalent.

The following names can be used to access the components of a vector:

x,y,z,w—Accesses the vector as if it were a position or direction

r,g,b,a—Accesses the vector as if it were a color

s,t,p,q—Accesses the vector as if it were a texture coordinate

As far as GLSL is concerned, a vector doesn't represent anything more than a collection of values, so these named access methods exist only to improve the readability of the code and do not cause the vector they are used with to be changed in any way. The only checking that is performed at compile time is to ensure that the vector is big enough to allow access to the value you requested (for example, you can't access the w component of a vec3). Also, you cannot mix letters from different groups within a single statement.

```
vec3 foo.xyz;    // legal
vec3 foo.xr;     // illegal
vec3 foo.xyzw;   // illegal, too many names referenced
```

When accessing vectors as arrays, the indices are zero-based just as in C and C++. The indices don't have to be literals, but if variables are used they must be of the integer type. At compile time all literal indices are checked to make sure that they are within the allowed range for the vector type.

```
vec3 foo[2];    // legal
vec3 foo[3];    // illegal, only values 0 to 2 are allowed for a vec3
vec4 foo[3];    // legal
```

Matrices

While vectors and scalars are available in `float`, `int` and `bool` types, matrices are only available as floats. The following matrix types are supported:

> `mat2`: A matrix of floating-point values, 2×2 in size
>
> `mat3`: A matrix of floating-point values, 3×3 in size
>
> `mat4`: A matrix of floating-point values, 4×4 in size

Although the matrix types are most often used to store matrices you're familiar with (such as the modelview matrix), they can also be used to store any other data appropriate for a two-dimensional array, such as an image filter. Values of these types are treated like matrices and can have arithmetic operations performed on them. When combined with vectors, the proper linear-algebraic rules are applied to the arithmetic in question. You'll learn more about vector and matrix arithmetic later in the chapter.

In OpenGL, matrices are considered to be column major, and where appropriate, GLSL treats them in the same manner. This is particularly relevant when it comes to accessing members of the matrix. When doing so, GLSL treats the matrix like an array of column vectors.

```
mat3 foo;
vec3 bar = foo[1]; // as before, the index is zero based
```

This would access the second column of the matrix `foo`, and the resulting type would be a `vec3`. Because the returned type is a vector, you can directly access it in the same way as was shown above.

```
float x = foo[1][2];
```

This would access the third component of the second column of the matrix `foo`. This allows you to treat matrices almost as if they were 2D arrays of floats. However, keep in mind that the first value selects the column and the second selects the row.

As with vectors, variable indices can be used, and literal indices are checked to make sure they are within range for the type of matrix you are accessing.

Structures

The OpenGL Shading Language allows you to define your own composite types by using C-like structures.

```
struct vert
{
  vec4 position;
  vec3 color;
}
```

This would define a new type called `vert` that contains two `vec3s` named `position` and `color`. Once defined this type can be used to define variables of type `vert` in the same way the built-in types are used, and these variables can be accessed the same way as C or C++ structures.

```
vert myVert;
myVert.position;   // access the vec4 position
myVert.color;      // access the vec3 color
```

Structures can be nested and embedded, with embedded structures obeying the C scoping rules on name visibility. Structure members can also be arrays of other types. In keeping with the lack of bit-wise operator support, bitfields are not supported. Anonymous embedded structures are not supported either, so all embedded structures must have a name associated with them.

Arrays

Arrays operate in much the same way as their C counterparts. You can declare an array of any type you want.

```
vec4 foo[10];   // declares an array called 'foo' of 10 vec4s
mat3 foo[5];    // declares an array called 'foo' of 5 mat3s
vert foo[10];   // declares an array called 'foo' of 10 vert structures
```

As with vectors and matrices, all indices are zero based. Because the language lacks pointers, all vectors must be defined by the square-bracket method; however, you don't have to declare the array's size, so a declaration such as

```
vec4 foo[];
```

is perfectly legal. However, before using an array declared this way, you must either redeclare it with a fixed size or use static indices so that the compiler can determine how large the array is meant to be.

To fix the size of the array via the redeclaration method, you just declare the array again, this time with a size inside the brackets.

```
vec4 foo[];     // foo is an unsized array
vec4 foo[10];   // foo is now an array with 10 elements
```

Once an array's size is declared, it cannot be changed.

```
vec4 foo[];     // foo is an unsized array
vec4 foo[10];   // foo is now an array with 10 elements
vec4 foo[15];   // this is illegal
vec4 foo[];     // as is this
```

If the above were used in a shader it would cause the compiler to report an error on the line trying to resize foo to 15 elements as well as on the line trying to reset it to an unsized array.

The other way to size an array is to use compile-time constants to index it. The compiler will determine the largest index accessed and automatically set the array to that size. This feature allows the compiler to allocate no more resources than required by any given array.

```
vec4  foo[];                        // foo is an unsized array
foo[3] = vec4(1.0,1.0,1.0,1.0);  // foo is now an array of 4 elements
foo[9] = vec4(3.0,3.0,3.0,3.0);  // foo is now an array of 10 elements
```

Shaders sharing the same array can each define it to be a different size; the linker stage will correctly resize the array to the largest size required.

Samplers

One of the most common operations performed in a fragment shader is a texture lookup. This is where samplers come in. Samplers are used to indicate what to use as the source of the texture lookup. GLSL doesn't care if you are sampling from a texture unit or some other hardware system; it relies on the driver to sort the details out. So the sampler acts as a higher-level opaque handle to a texture.

Samplers come in a number of forms.

sampler1D: Used to access a 1D texture

sampler2D: Used to access a 2D texture

sampler3D: Used to access a 3D texture

samplerCube: Used to access a cube-mapped texture

sampler1DShadow: Used to access a 1D shadow map

sampler2DShadow: Used to access a 2D shadow map

The sampler types are initialized by the application and cannot be changed in any way by the shader. They are strictly a read-only attribute (details on how the application can set up this data will be covered later in the chapter).

```
uniform sampler2D source;   // declare a 2D texture sampler called "source"
vec2 texcoords(0.5,0.5);     // declare a 2D vector and initialize it to hold the
                            // value (0.5,0.5)
vec4 color = texture2D(source, texcoords); // sample from the 2D texture from
                                           // the position held in texcoords and
                                           // assign it to the variable "color"
```

As you can see from the example above, sampling a texture is straightforward (though this will be covered in greater detail later). The GLSL compiler and the OpenGL API will together ensure that only correct values for the declared sampler type will be assigned to each texture sampler. The texture-sampling functions will be covered later in the chapter.

Void

The final type to cover is void. This type is used to indicate that a function doesn't return a value, an example of which would be the main() function in the first example you saw in this chapter. Beyond that, void serves no useful purpose.

Type Qualifiers

Type qualifiers can be prefixed to any variable to modify the variable in some manner. The available qualifiers are listed in Table 4.1.

Table 4.1 Type Qualifiers

Qualifier	Description
default	A local variable that can be both written to and read from. Also used with input parameters to functions.
const	Declares that the variable is a compile-time constant. Also declares that the variable passed into a function is read-only.
attribute	Declares that the variable is a per-vertex attribute. The value in this variable is updated automatically with per-vertex information. This is one method of passing data into a vertex shader from the calling program.
uniform	A variable that doesn't change as often as an attribute variable; quite often it changes per object instead of per vertex. This is another method of passing data into a vertex shader from the calling program.
varying	A variable used to pass information between the vertex and fragment shaders. This value is then interpolated to form the final value passed to the fragment shader per fragment.
in	Declares that the variable is an input variable into a function and can only be read from within a function.
out	Declares that the variable is an output variable from a function and can only be written to within a function.
inout	Declares that the variable is both an input and an output from a function and as such can be both written to and read from inside the function.

When using qualifiers you need to keep the following rules in mind:

- Global variables are only able to use const, attribute, uniform, and varying qualifiers.
- Local variables are only able to use the const qualifier.
- Function definitions are only allowed to use the in, out, inout, and const qualifiers.
- Values in structures cannot use qualifiers.
- Return types from functions cannot use qualifiers.

In this section you will learn about the first five qualifiers. The final three will be left for the section on functions, as they are most relevant there.

The Default Qualifier

A variable without a qualifier acts as you would expect a normal variable to act, by providing a section of read/write memory in which you can store temporary values used during vertex- or fragment-program calculations.

Variables without qualifiers can be declared both inside functions and outside of them in global scope. The variables and their values only exist while the program is running; as soon as the program exits, the values cease to exist. Trying to use a global variable to pass information between different runs of the same type of shader will fail.

Fragment and vertex shaders both have their own space for placing globally declared variables that don't use qualifiers, which means that they can't share data in this manner (see the discussion of varying and uniform qualifiers later in this section for methods of sharing data). It also means that you can use global variables with the same name in both the vertex shader and the fragment shader without causing errors, even if the variables are of different types.

```
// vertex shader
uniform vec4 foo;
uniform mat3 bar;


// fragment shader
uniform vec4 foo;   // OK
uniform vec3 bar;   // OK
```

The const Qualifier

The const qualifier is used to provide a compile-time constant variable or to show that a function parameter is read-only. This qualifier can be applied to any of the basic types as well as structures. In all cases the variable must be initialized with data when declared.

```
const vec4 foo = vec4(1.0,1.0,2.0,3.0); // OK
const vec4 bar;                          // error
```

You can initialize const variables with other constant variables, literal values, or an expression of any of these (i.e., any values that can be determined at compile time). However, you can't initialize a variable from a function's parameters

```
void someFunc(const vec3 foo)
{
  const vec3 bar = foo;  // error
}
```

nor from a function's return value

```
const vec4 foo = someotherFunc();  // error
```

The attribute *Qualifier*

The attribute qualifier is used to pass per-vertex information, such as color or position, to the vertex shader. It can't be used as part of a fragment shader. The variables are effectively read-only, so any attempt to write to them will cause a compiler error. They must also be in global scope (outside any function definitions). The attribute qualifier is only valid on the floating-point data types (floats, vectors, and matrices) and cannot be used with arrays or structures of data.

```
attribute vec4 position;
attribute float time;
attribute mat3 someMatrix;
```

Values are placed into these variables by OpenGL via either an immediate mode function or from a vertex-array stream of data.

Currently GPUs have limited space for attributes (for example, the ATI Radeon X800XT has space for 32), so you must be careful when declaring them, as using too many will cause an error when you compile or link your shader (the shader-compilation process is covered later in the chapter).

When declaring attributes, keep in mind that a vec4 and a float both use up one attribute slot, so it might be worthwhile packing floats into a vec4 if you need a number of them. Matrices use up the same number of attribute slots as they have columns, so a mat3 will take three attribute slots. Attributes that are declared but not used in the shader will not count towards the final attribute count for the shader.

Accessible from within the shader are a number of built-in attributes that map to standard OpenGL vertex attributes. These are covered in the section on built-in variables later in the chapter. When counting the number of attribute slots used by the shader, the total is the number of user-defined variables added to the number of built-in variables, only counting those that are actually used by the shader.

The uniform *Qualifier*

Variables declared as uniform are variables that are expected to remain the same for an extended period of time, unlike attribute variables, which are expected to change with every vertex processed. Like attributes, these values are read-only and can be declared only in global scope. Unlike attributes, uniforms aren't just restricted to simple floating-point types—they can be any of the types discussed earlier in the chapter and can also be declared as arrays of those types.

```
uniform vec4 foo;       // a vec4 uniform variable
uniform vec3 bar[10];   // an array of 10 vec3 uniform variables
struct vert
{
```

```
  vec4 position;
  vec3 color;
}
uniform vert myVert;    // a "vert" structure uniform variable
```

Uniform data can be passed to both fragment and vertex shaders. The names for these variables are shared between the two shader types, so when fragment and vertex shaders are linked, any variables that use the same name must be of the same type.

```
// vertex shader
uniform vec4 foo;
uniform mat3 bar;

// fragment shader
uniform vec4 foo;   // OK, types match
uniform vec3 bar;   // error, types do not match
```

As with attributes, there are a limited number of spaces for uniform variables. However, the limit is often much higher for uniform variables than for attributes (for example, an ATI Radeon X800XT has space for 4,096 uniform variables). There are also built-in uniform variables maintained by OpenGL. All built-in and user-defined uniform variables that are used count toward the final uniform usage.

An important point to keep in mind with uniform variables is that, in terms of performance, they can be quite expensive to change, so they should be left the same for as long as possible during rendering.

The varying Qualifier

The final qualifier is the varying qualifier. Variables marked as varying are used to pass values from the vertex shader to the fragment shader. This is the only way to pass information from one part of the pipeline to the other. These variables are set per vertex and then interpolated across the primitive and passed to the fragment shader. They can be both read from and written to in the vertex shader but are read-only in the fragment shader. In the vertex shader, reading from a varying variable that has not yet been written to results in an undefined value.

As with uniforms, the types for varying variables of the same name must match in both the vertex and fragment shaders.

```
// vertex shader
varying vec4 foo;
varying mat3 bar;
```

```
// fragment shader
varying vec4 foo;   // OK, types match
varying vec3 bar;   // error, types do not match
```

Like attribute variables, varying variables can only be of floating-point types (floats, vectors, and matrices) and cannot be structures. However, you can use arrays.

```
varying vec4 foo;       // OK, a vec4 varying variable
varying vec3 bar[10];   // OK, an array of 10 vec3 varying variables
struct vert
{
  vec4 position;
  vec3 color;
}
varying vert myVert;   // error, structures cannot be used as varying types
```

As with attribute and uniform variables, the number of varying variables you can declare and use is limited (again, in the case of the ATI Radeon X800XT, the number of varying floats you can use is 44).

Varying variables also must be declared at global scope. If a varying variable isn't read from in a fragment shader, then the vertex shader doesn't have to write to it. Because vertex and fragment shaders can be used with the fixed-function pipeline, there are a number of built-in varying variables that can be read from or written to. If you are using just a vertex shader, then you must write to these variables to allow the fixed-function pipeline to render correctly. If you are using just a fragment shader, then the OpenGL fixed-function pipeline will calculate the values and place them into the built-in varying variables for you to use.

To ensure that the correct values are present in the fragment shader, all varying variables are interpolated in perspective-correct manner across the primitive. That way the values change correctly across edges introduced by surface subdivision.

Constructors

Constructors have a dual purpose in the OpenGL Shading Language: they provide a method to initialize variables and a method to convert from one type to another. For those coming from a C++ background, the usage of constructors should be familiar. Those coming from a C background can think of constructors as functions that set the initial values of a variable before use.

Constructors as Scalar Type Converters

As previously mentioned, there is no automatic conversion between types in the OpenGL Shading Language, but that doesn't mean that you can't convert variables from one type to another. You just have to be explicit about it, which is where constructors come in.

```
int(bool)   // converts a Boolean value to an integer
int(float)  // converts a floating-point value to an integer
float(bool) // converts a Boolean value to a floating-point value
float(int)  // converts an integer value to a floating-point value
bool(int)   // converts an integer value to a Boolean value
bool(float) // converts a floating-point value to a Boolean value
```

When this conversion is applied, certain rules are used to convert the values correctly. When floats are converted to ints, the fractional part is simply dropped.

```
float pi = 3.14;
int roundpi = int(pi);   // roundpi = 3
```

Conversion of a float or an int to a bool follows the same basic rules as C++. Values that are zero are converted to false, and nonzero values are converted to true. When converting from a bool to a float or int, values of false are converted to 0.0 for floats and 0 for ints; true is converted to 1.0 for floats and 1 for ints.

Scalar constructors can also be used with nonscalar types, in which case the constructor uses the first element in the nonscalar provided. This is a simple way to convert from a vector or matrix to a scalar type.

```
vec3 myVec = vec3(1.0,2.0,3.0);
int myInt = int(myVec);   // myInt = 1
```

Vector Constructors

Vector constructors are used both to initialize a vector from a group of supplied scalar values and to shrink vectors.

The first thing to note is that if a type supplied doesn't match the type of the vector, then it is converted using the conversion rules from the previous section. This allows you to construct, for example, a vector of floats from a couple of int values.

```
vec2 foo(1,2);   // foo holds 1.0 and 2.0
```

If you require a vector to hold multiple copies of the same value, then instead of specifying that value more than once you can supply the vector's constructor with the value once and it will apply it multiple times to the vector. So if you want to initialize the vec3 foo with the value 1.0, you would do the following:

```
vec3 foo(1.0);
```

Now foo holds three copies of the value 1.0, which can be read back using any of the access methods covered earlier.

You aren't limited to just supplying scalar values to the constructors of vectors; you can supply other vectors as well. When this is done the values are taken from left to right in the source vector and applied in the same manner to the destination vector.

```
vec3 foo(1,2,3);
vec3 bar(foo);
```

After this operation is complete, bar holds the same values as foo in the same locations.

A vector's constructor can also be used to shrink a vector from one size to another.

```
vec3 foo(1.0,2.0,3.0);
vec2 bar(foo);    // bar contains 1.0 and 2.0
```

Multiple source vectors can be used in constructors and are accessed in the same left-to-right manner to fill up the destination vector. For example:

```
vec2 foo(1,2);
vec2 bar(3,4);
vec4 foobar(foo,bar); // foobar.x = foo.x, foobar.y = foo.y,
                      // foobar.z = bar.x and foobar.w = bar.y
```

As you can see, the left-to-right order still holds. The two vectors supplied do not have be the same size as the destination vector; when totaled, they can be larger than the destination, in which case the trailing values are ignored.

```
vec2 foo(1,2);
vec3 bar(3,4,5);
vec4 foobar(foo,bar); // foobar.x = foo.x, foobar.y = foo.y,
                      // foobar.z = bar.x and foobar.w = bar.y
```

The only difference between this example and the previous one is that bar.z is ignored as it would overflow the vec4 type.

Scalars and vectors can also be mixed when constructing a vector.

```
vec3 foo(1,2,3);
vec4 bar(foo,4);
// or
vec4 bar(4,foo);
```

The main point to remember with constructors is that you must supply the correct number of values to fully construct the vector. While the constructor can deal with too many values when vectors are supplied, it is an error to supply too many values when using scalars. The following shows a number of legal and illegal constructors, providing a summary of the rules given in this section. In each case, the underlined values are added to the destination vector.

```
vec4(1.0);                          // OK
vec4(1.0,2.0);                      // error, too few parameters
vec4(1.0,2.0,3.0);                  // error, too few parameters
vec4(1.0,2.0,3.0,4.0);              // OK
vec4(1.0,2.0,3.0,4.0,5.0);          // error, too many parameters
vec4(vec3(1.0,2.0,3.0),4.0);        // OK
vec4(vec3(1.0,2.0,3.0),vec2(4.0,5.0)); // OK, part of the second vector ignored
vec4(vec3(1.0,2.0,3.0),4.0,5.0);    // error, too many parameters
```

Matrix Constructors

The constructors for matrices are much the same as the vector constructors. The biggest difference is that you cannot construct a matrix from another matrix (this possibility is reserved for future use by the ARB, however).

```
mat2(mat3(1.0)); // not allowed
```

The other real difference is that supplying a single value to a constructor doesn't initialize all the values; it only initializes the diagonal values of the matrix and sets all other values to zero.

```
mat3 foo(1.0);   // initializes the matrix so that its diagonal values are all
                 // 1.0, the same as the identity matrix
```

Aside from that, the rules for matrix construction are the same as for vectors. Make sure you supply enough arguments to the constructor to construct the matrix in question. You must also keep in mind that matrices are filled in column major order. The layout of the following scalar-constructor examples should help you visualize this.

```
mat2( float, float,
      float, float);

mat3( float, float, float,
      float, float, float,
      float, float, float );

mat4( float, float, float, float,
      float, float, float, float,
      float, float, float, float );
```

Vectors can also be used to construct matrices.

```
mat2( vec2, vec2 );
mat3( vec3, vec3, vec3 );
mat4( vec4, vec4, vec4 );
```

You can of course also mix scalars and vectors in constructors, as long the correct number of values is present.

```
mat4( vec3, float,
      vec3, float,
      vec3, float,
      vec3, float );
```

Other combinations are possible, but this should be enough to give you the basic idea.

Structure Constructors

The constructors for structures are the easiest ones to deal with. Once you define a structure, the name given to it can be used as a constructor, just as with the built-in types. When using the constructor, the arguments must be in the order in which they are declared in the structure and they must be of the same type.

```
struct
{
  float intensity;
  vec4 position;
  vec3 color;
} light;
light lightvar = light(0.9,vec4(1.0,2.0,3.0,4.0),vec3(1.0,2.0,3.0));
// or
vec3 foo(1.0,2.0,3.0);
vec4 bar(1.0,2.0,3.0,4.0);
light lightvar = light(0.9,bar,foo);
```

Operators

Up until this point you've seen a lot of talk of types and constructors but haven't seen how to manipulate data. This is where operators come in.

Standard Operators

The standard operators work in the same way as their C or C++ counterparts. Table 4.2 shows their precedence and provides a basic summery of what they perform. Operators marked as reserved are not in use but are reserved for future language use and thus shouldn't be used as of the time of this writing.

When using the basic operators add (+), subtract (-), multiply (*), and divide (/), you must follow a couple of rules and keep a few things in mind.

Table 4.2 Operator Precendence

Precedence	Operator Class	Operators	Associativity
1 (Highest)	parenthetical grouping	( )	N/A
2	array subscript, function call and constructor structure, field selector, swizzle, postfix increment and decrement	[] () . ++ --	Left to Right
3	prefix increment and decrement, unary (tilde is reserved)	++ -- + - ~ !	Right to Left
4	multiplicative (modulus reserved)	* / %	Left to Right
5	additive	+ -	Left to Right
6	bit-wise shift (reserved)	<< >>	Left to Right
7	relational	< > <= >=	Left to Right
8	equality	== !=	Left to Right
9	bit-wise and (reserved)	&	Left to Right
10	bit-wise exclusive or (reserved)	^	Left to Right
11	bit-wise inclusive or (reserved)	|	Left to Right
12	logical and	&&	Left to Right
13	logical exclusive or	^^	Left to Right
14	logical inclusive or	||	Left to Right
15	selection	? :	Right to Left
16	assignment, arithmetic assignment (modulus, shift, and bit-wise are reserved)	= += -= *= /*%= < <= >>= &= ^= |=	Right to Left
17 (lowest)	sequence	,	Left to Right

First, while these operators can work on both floating-point and integer values, when used in an expression both values must be of the same basic type. For example, you can multiply a floating-point value by another floating-point value (be it a float, a vector, or a matrix) and you can multiply an integer by another integer (or an int with an integer vector), but you can't mix and match the types (e.g., you can't multiply a floating-point vector by an integer).

Second, with one important exception, these operators either work like their C and C++ counterparts or perform their action component-wise. An example of this would be

```
vec3 v, u, w;
w = u + v;
```

which would be the same as

```
w.x = u.x + v.x
w.y = u.y + v.y
w.z = u.z + v.z
```

For operators involving two vectors, the vectors must match in size.

When you perform a basic operation and one of the values is a scalar and the other is either a vector or a matrix, the scalar is applied to each component of the vector or matrix. So if you were to multiply a vector by a scalar, the effect would be as follows:

```
vec4 foo(1.0,2.0,3.0,4.0);
vec4 bar = 2 * foo;    // bar = (2.0,4.0,6.0,8.0)
```

The same idea applies to a scalar and a matrix.

There is an exception to the component-wise rule above: when you multiply a vector by a matrix or a matrix by a matrix, the operation is performed according to the rules of linear algebra. If you need to perform a component-wise matrix-matrix multiply, you would use a built-in function that is covered later.

The logical operators not (!), and (&&), or (||), and exclusive or (^^) only operate on scalar Boolean values and always result in a scalar Boolean value. These operators act as they do in C: the right-hand operand of && is not evaluated if the left-hand side is false; the right-hand operand of || isn't evaluated if the left-hand side is true; and both sides of ^^ are always evaluated. While these operators don't work on vectors, there is a built-in function to perform a logical not (!) on a vector of Booleans.

The relational operators (<, >, <=, and >=) only operate on floating-point and integer scalars and result in a scalar Boolean value. Built-in functions exist to perform these operations component-wise on vectors of floats and ints.

Unlike the relational and logical operators, the equality operators (== and !=) can be applied to all types except arrays. When applied they compare all the components of a type or all members of a structure, returning a scalar Boolean value. Two values are equal if they are of the same type and all of their components and/or members are equal. It is possible to perform a component-wise comparison between two vectors by using built-in functions.

When you use the assignment operator (=), both operands must have the same type. This is required because, as noted before, values are not automatically promoted from one type to another. Like the equality operators, the assignment operator can be applied to any type other than arrays.

The arithmetic assignment operators (+=, -=, *=, and /=) work much like their C and C++ counterparts with the simple rule that when expanded out they must make sense and the result of the operation must have the same type as the left-hand value. For example,

```
a *= b;
```

expands to

```
a = a * b;
```

In order for this operation to be valid a * b must be a valid operation as explained earlier.

The final two operators are the ternary-selection operator (?:) and the sequence operator (,), both of which act the same way as they do in C or C++.

The ternary operator evaluates one expression and, based on the result, selects one of the following expressions to evaluate and return the value of:

```
value = exp1 ? exp2 : exp3;
```

The result of exp1 must be a Boolean scalar value. If this scalar Boolean is true, then exp2 is evaluated and the result is placed in value. Otherwise exp3 is evaluated and the result is placed in value. It's possible for exp2 and exp3 to result in any nonarray type, but they must be the same type (and value must also be of that type).

```
float value = true ? 1.0 : 2.0;
float value = false ? 1.0 : 2.0;
```

The foregoing is a simple example of the ternary operator in use. In the first instance, value is assigned 1.0. In the second instance, value is assigned 2.0.

The sequence operator isn't used very often. It allows you to carry out a series of operations and only return the value of the rightmost operation. For example:

```
float a = 1.0;
float b = ++a,++a,++a;
```

In this example, the list of ++as is evaluated from left to right and the resulting value of 4 is placed in the variable b.

Swizzling

Swizzling gives you the ability to select and rearrange the components of a vector by selecting them by name as shown in the section on vectors. This allows you to extract certain values from a vector and even duplicate values from one vector to another.

Some examples of how swizzling works are shown below.

```
vec4 v;
v.rgba;  // same as a normal vec4
v.rgb;   // is a vec3
v.b;     // is a float
v.xy;    // is a vec2
v.xgba;  // illegal—all names must be from the same group (see vector section)
```

The names of the components can also be out of order; this allows you to rearrange data from one vector to another.

```
vec4 foo(1.0,2.0,3.0,4.0);
vec4 swizzled = foo.wxzy    // swizzled = (4.0,1.0,3.0,2.0)
vec4 duplicated = foo.xxww // duplicated = (1.0,1.0,4.0,4.0)
```

For any given swizzle you can use up to four names as either the source or destination. Source names can be duplicated, in which case the data is duplicated in the destination vector. Destination names, however, must be unique.

```
vec4 foo(1.0,2.0,3.0,4.0);
foo.xy = vec2(3.0,5.0);  // pos = (3.0,5.0,3.0,4.0);
foo.wx = vec2(6.0,7.0);  // pos = (7.0,5.0,3.0,6.0);
foo.ww = vec2(1.0,1.0);  // illegal—duplicate destination names are not allowed
```

Swizzling can also be done on any function that returns a vector. For example, to extract the red and blue colors of a texture lookup, you could do the following:

```
vec2 color = texture2D(sampler, coord).rb;
```

This selects the r and b values from the `vec4` that `texture2D()` returns and assigns them to `color`.

Program Statements and Structures

In this section you'll learn in greater detail about how shaders are arranged and how you can control the execution of a shader and its outputs.

Flow Control

Program flow control works very much like a C or C++ program, with the execution beginning at the top of a `main()` function and ending when the `main()` function exits. However, since a GLSL program is made up of both vertex and fragment shaders, it in fact has two `main()` functions, one for the vertex program and one for the fragment program. Before a `main()` function is entered, any global variables are initialized so that they are ready for use as soon as the program starts.

Once the program is running, its flow can be adjusted, as in a C or C++ program, by calling another function, looping, or using conditional branching and selection.

Looping is done via the `for`, `while`, and `do-while` keywords. These work like their C++ counterparts, including the ability to declare variables inside the `for` and `while` statements that are only in scope for the duration of the loop.

```
for(int i = 0; i < 42; i++)
{
  // do something here
}
// at this point any attempt to use the variable "i" is invalid
```

As in C and C++ you have access to the break and continue keywords.

Conditional branching can be achieved via the if and if-else keywords, which operate as they do in C++ except that you cannot declare a variable in an if statement.

```
if(somecondition)  // legal
{
  // do something
}
if(boolean foo = somecondition)  // illegal
{
  // do something
}
```

As described in the "Operators" section, you can also select based on the ternary operator (?:).

The type supplied to an if or a while statement and the termination condition of a for statement must be a scalar Boolean value. This is often the result of a comparison of some sort.

```
float foo;
float bar;
while(foo == bar)
{
  // do something
}
```

There is also a special branch statement, discard. This statement is only valid in fragment shaders and allows you to stop processing the current fragment without altering the frame-buffer. While this may improve performance in future hardware, currently most hardware that supports shaders will continue to execute the shader but won't produce any output.

The final way to adjust program flow is to call user-defined functions. Like everything else in GLSL, these functions work very much like their C or C++ counterparts. Before a function can be used it must be declared or defined within the correct scope.

```
void someFunc();   // a declaration
void someFunc()    // a definition
{
  // do something
}
```

You may have multiple declarations of a function but only a single definition.

The other thing GLSL functions share with C++ is that you can overload a function based on its parameter types, a feature that is used to great effect for the built-in functions, as you will see shortly. When overloading, parameter types must match precisely, because as previously mentioned, no automatic type conversions are performed on variables. This type matching also extends to the number of elements in an array, which must be given when you declare the function.

```
void someFunc(vec4 values[]);    // illegal
void someFunc(vec4 values[2]);   // legal, matches when the function is supplied
                                 // with an array of vec4s of size 2
```

The above is also a good example of the types in a function call needing to match. The valid declaration of someFunc() will only be called if it is called with an array of vec4s of size 2. If the array is bigger or smaller or the type isn't a vec4, the compiler will fail to match it and report an error. If a function is declared with an empty parameter list, then the function doesn't take any variables and thus any attempt to supply it with some will result in an error.

User-defined functions can also return values, the type of which is declared before the function's name. Any type but arrays may be used, including structures. As with the rest of the language, the value returned by the function must match the declared type. To return a value, you use the return keyword followed by the value to return. Functions declared as void can still use the return keyword, but they must not be followed by a value. It is also valid to use return in the main() function; however, doing so before setting all the output variables could cause unexpected results.

An important point about using functions is that you may not call them recursively, either directly or indirectly. Any attempt to do so will result in an error at compile time.

Understanding the calling convention of functions is also important. The calling convention used by the OpenGL Shading Language is known as "call by value-return." The "by value" part works the same as in C and C++: the value passed is copied into the function's local variable, and any changes to it won't affect the original variables. The "return" part of the calling convention, however, allows values to be copied back out of the function and into the variable in the calling function. This is somewhat like using references in functions in C++. There are also variables that are for output only, so when you call the function you supply a variable to take the value that is assigned in the function.

To achieve this, three keywords are included to let the compiler know what you want to do with the variables.

in: Copy the value in but don't copy back out. The variable can still be written to in the function.

out: Only copy the value out into this variable. When the function is called, the content of this variable is undefined.

inout: Copy both in and out.

So if you only want to pass a value into a function but not copy its value back out, you would use the in qualifier, which is also implicitly used when you don't specify a qualifier. To retrieve a value into a variable, you would use the out qualifier; when the function is finished any value in this variable is copied back out to the variable used to call the function. Finally, inout allows you to pass variables both into and out of a function. These three qualifiers are shown in the following examples:

```
void someFunc(float f); // The floating-point value "f" is copied in. It may be
                        // used in the function; however, any changes won't be
                        // returned

void someFunc(in float f); // this is the same as the above
void otherFunc(out float f)
{
  f = 1.0;   // upon exit the value of "f" (in this case 1.0) will be
             // copied back out to whatever variable was supplied for it
}

void lastFunc(inout float f)
{
  f *= 2.0;
}
float foo = 2.0;
lastFunc(foo);   // on return foo = 4.0
```

You can also apply the const qualifier, which was discussed earlier, to function parameters. In this instance, instead of referring to a compile-time constant, the usage of const means that the variable cannot be written to in the function, unlike normal in qualified variables, which can be written to but not returned. Variables qualified with out or inout cannot be qualified as const, as that would make no sense with regard to the usage requested.

```
void someFunc(const in float f)
{
  f = 2.0;  // this isn't allowed, as "f" has been declared const
}
```

The Preprocessor

The final part of the language's syntax to cover is the preprocessor. As in C and C++, the preprocessor in GLSL runs before the code is compiled. This allows you to make changes to the source code, using things such as macros and short names for built-in variables (you'll soon see just how useful this is).

The complete list of current preprocessor directives is

```
#define
#undef
#if
#ifdef
#ifndef
#else
#elif
#endif
#error
#pragma
#line
#version
#extension
```

The directives #define, #undef, #if, #ifdef, #ifndef, #else, #elif and #endif all work in GLSL as in C and C++. These are complemented by the defined operator, which also works just as it does in the C and C++ preprocessors.

The directives #define and #undef can be used to create macros that operate just before the code is compiled. As in C++, these macros can take parameters. There are three built-in macros for your use.

```
__LINE__
__FILE__
__VERSION__
```

__LINE__ is replaced by an integer constant that is one more than the number of new-line characters that precede it in the current source string.

__FILE__ is replaced by an integer constant that indicates which source string is currently being processed. This number can be different from the __LINE__ number because a single line can have multiple new-line characters and each shader can be made up of multiple lines. This will become clearer once we cover the C API and show you how to load shaders.

Finally, __VERSION__ is replaced by an integer that represents the version of the OpenGL Shading Language currently in use. The original pre-OpenGL2.0 version was returned as 100. The most recent version, 1.10—which is standard with an OpenGL2.0 compliant implementation—will be replaced with 110.

It should be noted that all macros beginning with a double underscore (__) are reserved for future predefined macros, and as such you shouldn't use them. Macros beginning with GL_ are also reserved.

The #define directive can also be used to form short names for longer built-in variables, such as the following:

```
#define MVIT gl_ModelViewMatrixInverseTranspose
```

Using this system in your code you can use MVIT instead of gl_ModelViewMatrix-InverseTranspose, which cuts down on typing and can make the code a little clearer. When the shader is compiled, the compiler will replace all occurrences of MVIT with gl_ModelViewMatrixInverseTranspose.

The preprocessor also has a number of operators that can be used in expressions; these appear in Table 4.3. These operators match those in the C and C++ preprocessors.

note

Note that unlike C and C++ preprocessors, the GLSL preprocessor doesn't include any support for strings, since strings aren't present in GLSL. This includes the hash (#, ##, etc.) operators.

The directive #error allows you to signal an error condition and add a message to the shader's info log. Its usage is "#error message". The message can be any length up to the first new-line character. The following example uses this directive:

```
#error Something has gone wrong!
```

When the compiler encounters an #error directive, it will treat the shader as ill-formed and refuse to compile it.

Table 4.3 Preprocessor Operators

Operator	Description
+ - ~ !	unary
* / %	multiplicative
+ -	additive
<< >>	bit-wise shift
< > <= =>	relational
== !=	equality
& ^ |	bit-wise
&& ||	logical

The directive #pragma is used to supply implementation-specific instructions to the compiler. If the implementation doesn't understand or support the tokens that follow the #pragma statement, it will ignore it. There are a number of built-in #pragma directives supplied in the language.

```
#pragma optimize(on)
#pragma optimize(off)
```

The optimize #pragma allows you to request that the compiler enable or disable optimizations. By default optimizations are on; however, turning them off can aid in debugging. This #pragma can only be used outside of function definitions.

```
#pragma debug(on)
#pragma debug(off)
```

The debug #pragma causes debugging information and annotation to be added when compiling. This information can be used with a debugger. This directive can only be used outside of functions, and it is off by default.

The preprocessor directive #line is used to reset the line number that is reported when errors and such are encountered. The directive can take two forms.

```
#line line
#line line source-string-number
```

The first form just resets the line number. Once it is executed, all lines are numbered sequentially from *line*+1 until the compiler encounters another #line directive. The second form also changes the source-string number reported, both in the logs and when using __FILE__.

When writing a shader you should declare which shader version the shader was written for. This can allow future compilers to make adjustments to how they compile the source or declare an error if the version isn't supported. This declaration can be achieved via the #version directive.

```
#version number
```

The value for *number* follows the same convention as the __VERSION__ macro above. Currently this number must be 110. Any number less than 110 will cause a compiler error, and any number greater than the number the compiler supports will also cause an error. Version 1.10 of the OpenGL Shading Language does not require that you specify a version, and if it doesn't find a version number, it will act as if #version 110 is defined.

The #version directive must occur before any lines of code in a shader, but it can be preceded by comments and white space.

By default, when a shader is compiled, it is compiled with strict compliance to the specification, as indicated by the #version number, and will issue errors for anything that doesn't match (be it syntax or grammatical or semantic errors in the code). However, in keeping with the rest of OpenGL, the OpenGL Shading Language can also be extended by vendors, and when used, any such extensions must be requested. This is achieved by the #extension directive.

```
#extension name : behavior
```

Here *name* is the name of the extension. If *name* is *all*, then the requested behavior applies to all extensions supported by the compiler. For *behavior* , you must use one of the values listed in Table 4.4.

Table 4.4 Behavior Values

Behavior	Effect
require	Behave as specified by the extension name. Give an error on the #extension if the extension name is not supported or if all is specified.
enable	Behave as specified by the extension name. Warn on the #extension if the extension name is not supported. Give an error on the #extension if all is specified.
warn	Behave as specified by the extension name, except issue warnings on any detectable use of that extension that is not supported by other enabled or required extensions. If all is specified, then warn on all detectable uses of any extension used. Warn on the #extension if the extension name is not supported.
disable	Behave (including issuing errors and warnings) as if the extension name is not part of the language definition. If all is specified, then behavior must revert back to that of the nonextended core version of the language being compiled for. Warn on the #extension if the extension name is not supported.

When used, #extension doesn't check to see if enabling the extension requested makes sense when it is enabled with any other extensions; that detail must be handled elsewhere. The ordering of #extension directives matters, as directives issued later in the source code can override those issued earlier. If all is used as the name, then it overrides all previously issued directives; however, as Table 4.4 indicates, the only valid behaviors for all are warn and disable, and attempts to use the others will result in an error.

By default all extensions are disabled as if the directive

```
#extension all : disable
```

had been issued at the top of the shader.

Built-in Variables

Up until this point we have only covered user-defined variables and built-in types. In this section, you'll learn about the built-in variables supplied by the OpenGL Shading Language.

Vertex Shader Built-in Variables

The first built-in variable for vertex shaders is the gl_Position variable. This variable indicates the position of the vertex after it has been processed. This value should be in clip space (see the OpenGL Programming Guide for a discussion on the different "spaces" used with OpenGL) and the variable *must* be written to in order to ensure proper program execution. It is possible that the compiler could report that gl_Position hasn't been written to, but this isn't guaranteed, and the compiler might not always get it right.

The next variable is gl_PointSize. This variable is used to indicate the size of the point that should be drawn and represents its size in pixels.

The final vertex-shader-only variable is gl_ClipVertex. This allows the OpenGL Shading Language to interact with the standard OpenGL user clip planes described in Chapter 1, "More OpenGL." User clipping occurs after the vertex program has executed, so in order to use user clipping with a GLSL vertex program you must write out the vertex position to this variable. The value written must be in the same space as the clip planes.

Because these variables have global scope, each may be written to or read from at any time during vertex-shader execution. However, reading from one of these variables before it has been written to results in an undefined value. It is possible to write to all the variables multiple times, but only the last value written will be passed on to the rest of the pipeline.

The vertex-shader-only variables are defined as follows:

```
vec4  gl_Position;
float gl_PointSize;
vec4  gl_ClipVertex;
```

Vertex shaders also have access to a set of built-in attributes that allow you to provide the shader with information provided using the standard OpenGL fixed-function APIs. These variables are defined as follows:

```
attribute vec4  gl_Color;
attribute vec4  gl_SecondaryColor;
attribute vec3  gl_Normal;
attribute vec4  gl_Vertex;
attribute vec4  gl_MultiTexCoord0;
attribute vec4  gl_MultiTexCoord1;
attribute vec4  gl_MultiTexCoord2;
attribute vec4  gl_MultiTexCoord3;
attribute vec4  gl_MultiTexCoord4;
attribute vec4  gl_MultiTexCoord5;
attribute vec4  gl_MultiTexCoord6;
attribute vec4  gl_MultiTexCoord7;
attribute float gl_FogCoord;
```

The data held in each of these variables is set per vertex using either immediate mode functionality or the corresponding vertex array functions.

Fragment Shader Built-in Variables

The fragment shader has two types of built-in variables: input and output.

The first input variable is gl_FragCoord. This is a read-only variable that holds the current fragment's window-relative coordinate (x,y,z,1/w). This value is the output from the hardware that interpolates values for primitives after the vertex-processing stage has been completed for a primitive. The value contained in the z-coordinate is adjusted by the polygon-offset calculation.

The second input variable is gl_FrontFacing. This variable indicates whether or not a fragment belongs to a front-facing primitive. This can allow you to apply different shading depending on the direction of the primitive you are rendering or even emulate two-sided lighting.

The remaining three variables are output variables. The first one we are going to cover is gl_FragDepth. This variable allows you to override the depth value calculated by the fixed-function pipeline. If gl_FragDepth isn't written to in your fragment program, then the z value from gl_FragCoord is written to the depth buffer instead. The value in this variable is clamped to the range [0, 1] once the shader exits.

tip

If you have a fragment program that uses branching and writes to gl_FragDepth, care must be taken to ensure that it is written to in all paths. If a path is taken that results in gl_FragDepth not being written to, the value from gl_FragCoord won't be written to the depth buffer.

The remaining two output variables, gl_FragColor and gl_FragData, are similar in that they both allow color output to be written. The difference between the two is that gl_FragData is an array of variables.

Data written to gl_FragColor is used as the color data for the rest of the fixed-function pipeline. If this value isn't written to, then the color used by the remainder of the pipeline is undefined. The normal destination for data written to gl_FragColor is the buffer specified as the draw buffer using glDrawBuffer().

Data written to gl_FragData is also used by the rest of the fixed-function pipeline; however, you can have *n* sets of this data, all going to different final locations. This functionality enables you to render different data to different render targets all in the same pass. To do so, you must use the GL_ARB_draw_buffers extension (which is present in any OpenGL 2.0–compliant driver). Don't worry if you don't understand how this all works right now; it will be covered in an example later in this chapter.

If a shader assigns any value to gl_FragColor, then it must not assign data to gl_FragData, and vice versa. If the discard keyword is issued during fragment-shader evaluation, then the values of gl_FragColor, gl_FragData[], and gl_FragDepth become irrelevant because the framebuffer isn't going to be updated.

The five fragment-shader built-in variables are defined as follows:

```
vec4   gl_FragCoord;
bool   gl_FrontFacing;
vec4   gl_FragColor;
vec4   gl_FragData[gl_MaxDrawBuffers];
float  gl_FragDepth;
```

Built-in Uniform Variables

The OpenGL Shading Language also provides a set of built-in uniform variables you can access in either vertex or fragment shaders. A complete list of the built-in uniform variables can be found in Appendix B, "GLSL Shading Reference" (found on this book's companion Web site), but the following is an overview of what is available.

- Access to all the matrix states, including the matrix for each texture unit on the card
- Access to the inverse, transpose, and inverse transpose of the same matrices
- Information on all enabled lights that have been set up using `glLight()`
- Information about the global lighting-model settings
- Front and back material information
- Texture-environment details
- User clip planes
- Fog parameters
- Point-parameters details
- The depth-buffer range
- Rescaling information for normals

As you can see, a lot of the OpenGL state is available to you to use. These values will be automatically updated and maintained by the OpenGL driver; all you have to do is reference them in your code. Keep in mind that when you reference a built-in uniform variable, it counts toward your total uniform-variable count.

Built-in Varying Variables

There is also a set of built-in varying variables for you to use. Unlike varying variables you declare yourself, the built-in ones do not share a name between the vertex and fragment shaders. Instead, the driver takes care of mapping the information written by the vertex shader into the correct varying name for the fragment shader. It is done this way so that you can use the fixed functionality of the hardware for vertex or fragment processing and control the other stage yourself via shaders. To do this you must write to or read from these variables to produce output for or acquire input from the fixed-function hardware.

The varying variables defined for the vertex shader to write to are as follows:

```
varying vec4  gl_FrontColor;
varying vec4  gl_BackColor;
varying vec4  gl_FrontSecondaryColor;
varying vec4  gl_BackSecondaryColor;
varying vec4  gl_TexCoord[];  // will be at most gl_MaxTextureCoord in size
varying float gl_FogFragCoord;
```

So if a fragment shader or the fixed-function pipeline depends on any of the data represented by these variables, you *must* write to the corresponding variable or the results are undefined.

When you use the gl_TexCoord[] array for output, the normal rules for arrays apply. You must either write to it with a constant index number so that the compiler can determine how large it needs to make the array, or you must redeclare it at the top of your shader so the compiler explicitly knows how large to make it.

```
varying vec4 gl_TexCoord[5];  // we are writing five sets of texture coordinates

// or in a function
void someFunc()
{
  gl_TexCoord[4] = vec2(1.0,1.0);
  gl_TexCoord[5] = vec2(1.0,1.0);
}
```

In the second example just given, the compiler will automatically size the array to 6.

In the fragment shader, the following varying variables are available as input:

```
varying vec4  gl_Color;
varying vec4  gl_SecondaryColor;
varying vec4  gl_TexCoord[]; // will be at most gl_MaxTextureCoord in size
varying float gl_FogFragCoord;
```

You might have noticed that the variables gl_Color and gl_SecondaryColor have the same names as the attributes passed to a vertex shader. This doesn't cause a name clash, because the two variables are only visible in their respective shaders.

The values passed to gl_Color and gl_SecondaryColor will be automatically selected from the values written to gl_FrontColor, gl_FrontSecondaryColor, gl_BackColor, and gl_BackSecondaryColor by the vertex shader based on which face is visible for the current fragment at the time of processing.

The values held in gl_TexCoord[] are the interpolated values supplied by the vertex shaders that were run for the current primitive. As before, you must either redeclare the size of the gl_TexCoord[] array or access it via constant indices so that the compiler can calculate the correct size of the array at compile time.

The value used in gl_FogFragCoord is used to pass the values used in fog calculations to the fragment shader. This is produced by either the fixed-function pipeline or a shader (the fog examples later use this variable).

Built-in Constant Variables

The final set of built-in variables is a group of constants that indicate various implementation-dependent limits. The values in the examples below are the minimums you can expect to find; actual values could be higher.

```
const int gl_MaxLights = 8;                            // OpenGL 1.0
const int gl_MaxClipPlanes = 6;                        // OpenGL 1.0
const int gl_MaxTextureUnits = 2;                      // OpenGL 1.3
const int gl_MaxTextureCoords = 2;                     // ARB_fragment_program
const int gl_MaxVertexAttribs = 16;                    // ARB_vertex_shader
const int gl_MaxVertexUniformComponents = 512;  // ARB_vertex_shader
const int gl_MaxVaryingFloats = 32;                    // ARB_vertex_shader
const int gl_MaxVertexTextureImageUnits = 0;     // ARB_vertex_shader
const int gl_MaxCombinedTextureImageUnits = 2;  // ARB_vertex_shader
const int gl_MaxTextureImageUnits = 2;                // ARB_fragment_shader
const int gl_MaxFragmentUniformComponents = 64; // ARB_fragment_shader
const int gl_MaxDrawBuffers = 1;                       // ARB_draw_buffers
```

The comments after each variable indicate which OpenGL version or extension is required for each variable to be valid.

While most of the constants are self-explanatory, there are a couple that might require some more explanation.

Unlike the ARB_vertex_program extension, the OpenGL Shading Language allows you to sample a texture in the vertex shader (as long as the hardware allows it). To this end, the constant gl_MaxVertexTextureImageUnits is supplied; it tells you the number of texture units you can sample in the vertex shader. This isn't the only way to find this information, as you'll discover later in the chapter; however, at run time, the existence of this variable makes it easy to detect the number of units available.

The gl_MaxCombinedTextureUnits constant indicates the maximum number of texture units you can access from both the vertex and fragment shaders. Accessing the same texture unit from the vertex shader and the fragment shader counts as two texture units. A vertex-and-fragment-shader pair can not exceed the limit imposed by gl_MaxCombinedTextureUnits.

The final constant is gl_MaxDrawBuffers. This value is part of the ARB_draw_buffers extension, which enables you to draw to multiple color buffers at once (via the gl_FragData[] array mentioned earlier in the section on fragment-program built-in variables). The gl_MaxDrawBuffers value indicates the maximum number of buffers you can write to. This value must be at least 1 so that you can write to a color buffer as normal (the buffer in question being set by a call to glDrawBuffer()). See the Multiple Render Target example at the end of the chapter for more on this feature.

Built-in Functions

The OpenGL Shading Language has a number of built-in functions for operations on predominately vector and scalar types of data. The majority of these functions can be used in both vertex and fragment shaders; however, a few are specifically for one shader, as they are designed to interact with hardware features.

If you've read Chapter 3, these functions might seem trivial; however, they exist for a number of good reasons. The functions presented in this section broadly fall into one of three categories.

1. Functions that expose specific hardware functionality. Texture-access functions fall into this category.

2. Functions that are very commonly used and might have hardware support to speed up the operation. This enables the implementation writer to use hardware-specific instructions, something that wouldn't be possible if you wrote the function yourself.

3. Functions that are expected to gain hardware support in the near future. Trigono-metric operations such as sine and cosine fall into this category.

Many of the function names will be familiar if you've used the C or C++ math libraries. The main difference with these functions is that most of them operate on both vectors and scalars.

While it is possible for you to write your own version of many of these functions, it is strongly recommended that you use the built-in functionality, which is likely to perform better because it takes advantage of hardware support. You could write your own routine to calculate sine, for example, but it would likely be much slower than the built-in function, which on some cards can be executed in a single cycle.

It is possible for you to redefine the built-in functions using your own code. This is done by declaring a function with the same name and taking the same types as the function you wish to replace. Once you have done that, all calls to that function will call your code, and the built-in function will be hidden. Again, this should be avoided most of the time as you could be hiding hardware-supported functionality and thus negatively affecting the speed of your shader's execution.

The built-in functions can be arranged into nine groups.

1. Angle and trigonometric functions
2. Exponential functions
3. Common functions
4. Geometric functions
5. Matrix functions
6. Vector relational functions
7. Texture-lookup functions
8. Fragment-processing functions
9. Noise functions

When reading the following sections, keep in mind that a function's input arguments and return value must be of the same type. For functions where the input arguments can be float, vec2, vec3, or vec4, the placeholder *genType* is used in the function arguments and the return-type definition. Functions using *mat* for the input parameters and return type can be used on matrices of any size.

Angle and Trigonometric functions

The functions in Table 4.5 define operations on angles and trigonometric functions. The input to the sin(), cos(), and tan() functions are expected to be in radians. All of these functions operate on their inputs component-wise, so all descriptions are based on this.

Exponential Functions

Like the angle and trigonometric functions, all the functions in Table 4.6 operate component-wise on their inputs, so all the descriptions are based on this.

Common Functions

Again like the previous two groups, the functions in Table 4.7 all operate component-wise on their inputs, and all descriptions are based on this.

Geometric Functions

Unlike the previous three groups, the functions in Table 4.8 operate on their inputs as vectors, and all descriptions are based on this. This group also has the first of the functions that are valid in one shader type only, namely the ftransform() function, which is used to transform vertex positions.

Table 4.5 Trigonometric Functions

Syntax	Description
`genType radians(genType degrees)`	Converts degrees to radians and returns the result, i.e., result = [pi]/180 * degrees.
`genType degrees(genType radians)`	Converts radians to degrees and returns the result, i.e., result = 180/[pi] * radians.
`genType sin(genType angle)`	The standard trigonometric sine function.
`genType cos(genType angle)`	The standard trigonometric cosine function.
`genType tan(genType angle)`	The standard trigonometric tangent.
`genType asin(genType x)`	Arc sine. Returns an angle whose sine is x. The range of values returned by this function is [−[pi]/2, [pi]/2]. Results are undefined if |x| > 1.
`genType acos(genType x)`	Arc cosine. Returns an angle whose cosine is x. The range of values returned by this function is [0, [pi]]. Results are undefined if |x| > 1.
`genType atan(genType y, genType x)`	Arc tangent. Returns an angle whose tangent is y/x. The signs of x and y are used to determine what quadrant the angle is in. The range of values returned by this function is [−[pi], [pi]]. Results are undefined if x and y are both 0.
`genType atan(genType y_over_x)`	Arc tangent. Returns an angle whose tangent is y_over_x. The range of values returned by this function is [−[pi]/2, [pi]/2].

Table 4.6 Exponential Functions

Syntax	Description
`genType pow(genType x, genType y)`	Returns x raised to the y power, i.e., x^y. Results are undefined if x < 0. Results are undefined if x = 0 and y <= 0.
`genType exp(genType x)`	Returns the natural exponentiation of x, i.e., e^x.
`genType log(genType x)`	Returns the natural logarithm of x, i.e., returns the value y that satisfies the equation $x = e^y$. Results are undefined if x <= 0.
`genType exp2(genType x)`	Returns 2 raised to the x power, i.e., 2^x.
`genType log2(genType x)`	Returns the base 2 logarithm of x, i.e., returns the value y that satisfies the equation $x = 2^y$. Results are undefined if x <= 0.
`genType sqrt(genType x)`	Returns the positive square root of x. Results are undefined if x < 0.
`genType inversesqrt(genType x)`	Returns the reciprocal of the positive square root of x. Results are undefined if x <= 0.

Table 4.7 Common Functions

Syntax	Description
`genType abs(genType x)`	Returns x if x >= 0, otherwise it returns −x.
`genType sign(genType x)`	Returns 1.0 if x > 0, 0.0 if x = 0, or −1.0 if x < 0.
`genType floor(genType x)`	Returns a value equal to the nearest integer that is less than or equal to x.
`genType ceil(genType x)`	Returns a value equal to the nearest integer that is greater than or equal to x.
`genType fract(genType x)`	Returns x − floor(x).
`genType mod(genType x, float y)`	Modulus. Returns x − y * floor(x/y).
`genType mod(genType x, genType y)`	Modulus. Returns x − y * floor(x/y).
`genType min(genType x, genType y)`	Return y if y < x, otherwise it returns x.
`genType min(genType x, float y)`	
`genType max(genType x, genType y)`	Return y if x < y, otherwise it returns x.
`genType max(genType x, float y)`	
`genType clamp(genType x, genType minVal, genType maxVal)`	Return min(max(x, minVal), maxVal). Note that colors and depths written by fragment shaders will be clamped by the implementation after the fragment shader runs.
`genType clamp(genType x, float minVal, float maxVal)`	
`genType mix(genType x, genType y, genType a)`	Return x * (1 − a) + y * a, i.e., the linear blend of x and y.
`genType mix(genType x, genType y, float a)`	
`genType step(genType edge, genType x)`	Return 0.0 if x < edge; otherwise it returns 1.0.
`genType step(float edge, genType x)`	
`genType smoothstep (genType edge0, genType edge1,genType x)`	Return 0.0 if x <= edge0 and 1.0 if x >= edge1 and performs smooth Hermite interpolation between 0 and 1 when edge0 < x < edge1. This is useful in cases where you would want a threshold function with a smooth transition. This is equivalent to: `genType t; t = clamp ((x − edge0) / (edge1 − edge0), 0, 1); return t * t * (3 − 2 * t);`.
`genType smoothstep(float edge0, float edge1,genType x)`	

Table 4.8 Geometric Functions

Syntax	Description
`float length(genType x)`	Returns the length of vector x, i.e., sqrt(x[0] * x[0] + x[1] * x[1] + ...).
`float distance(genType p0, genType p1)`	Returns the distance between p0 and p1, i.e. length(p0 − p1).
`float dot(genType x, genType y)`	Returns the dot product of x and y, i.e., result = x[0] * y[0] + x[1] * y[1] + ...
`vec3 cross (vec3 x, vec3 y)`	Returns the cross product of x and y, i.e., result.0 = x[1] * y[2] − y[1] * x[2] result.1 = x[2] * y[0] − y[2] * x[0] result.2 = x[0] * y[1] − y[0] * x[1].
`genType normalize (genType x)`	Returns a vector in the same direction as x but with a length of 1.
`vec4 ftransform()`	For vertex shaders only. This function ensures that the incoming vertex value will be transformed in a way that produces exactly the same result as would be produced by OpenGL's fixed-functionality transform. It is intended to be used to compute gl_Position, e.g., gl_Position = ftransform(). This function should be used, for example, when an application is rendering the same geometry in separate passes, one using the fixed-functionality path to render and the other using programmable shaders.
`genType faceforward(genType N, genType I, genType Nref)`	If dot(Nref, I) < 0 return N; otherwise return −N.

Matrix Functions

At present, there is only one matrix function, `MatrixCompMult()`. It performs a component-wise multiplication between two matrices of the same size. The full function definition is

```
mat MatrixCompMult(mat x, mat y);
```

where `mat` is a matrix of any size. All inputs and outputs must be the same size. The operation performed on the matrix is a component-wise multiplication, i.e., result[i][j] = x[i][j] * y[i][j]. If you require a linear-algebraic multiplication, then just multiply the two matrices together using the multiplication operator as described earlier.

Vector Relational Functions

The standard relational operators (!=, ==, >=, <=, <, and >) are defined (or reserved) so that they return a scalar Boolean result (see the "Operators" section for details) based on a comparison of a vector to a vector. However, sometimes you need to compare a vector of values together as a group of scalars, not as a vector. The vector relational functions exist for this reason. In the functions listed in Table 4.9, bvec is a placeholder for a Boolean vector (bvec2, bvec3, or bvec4), ivec is a placeholder for an integer vector (ivec2, ivec3, or ivec4), and vec is a placeholder for a floating-point vector (either vec2, vec3, or vec4). As with the other functions, the input and output vector sizes must match.

Table 4.9 Vector Relational Functions

Syntax	Description
bvec lessThan(vec x, vec y)	Return the component-wise compare of x < y.
bvec lessThan(ivec x, ivec y)	
bvec lessThanEqual(vec x, vec y)	Return the component-wise compare of x <= y.
bvec lessThanEqual(ivec x, ivec y)	
bvec greaterThan(vec x, vec y)	Return the component-wise compare of x > y.
bvec greaterThan(ivec x, ivec y)	
bvec greaterThanEqual(vec x, vec y)	Return the component-wise compare of x >= y.
bvec greaterThanEqual(ivec x, ivec y)	
bvec equal(vec x, vec y)	Return the component-wise compare of x == y.
bvec equal(ivec x, ivec y)	
bvec equal(bvec x, bvec y)	
bvec notEqual(vec x, vec y)	Return the component-wise compare of x != y.
bvec notEqual(ivec x, ivec y)	
bvec notEqual(bvec x, bvec y)	
bool any(bvec x)	Returns true if any component of x is true.
bool all(bvec x)	Returns true only if all components of x are true.
bvec not(bvec x)	Returns the component-wise logical complement of x.

Texture-Lookup Functions

As previously noted, texture lookups can be performed in both vertex and fragment shaders, and the OpenGL Shading Language provides built-in functions to facilitate them. The functions listed in Table 4.10 allow you to access textures via samplers that are set up via the OpenGL API. There is no provision for accessing or setting details such as texture size, pixel format, number of dimensions, filtering method, number of mipmap levels, depth compare, or other texture functions. These must all be set in the normal manner via the OpenGL API. However, the functions take them all into account when accessing a sampler to retrieve texture data.

There are a couple of things you should be aware of when using these functions.

If the texture you are accessing via a sampler has mipmap levels defined, a level-of-detail value is automatically calculated so that the texture-lookup function can sample from the correct mipmaps. Many of the texture functions have a `bias` parameter. This parameter (which is only valid for fragment shaders) allows you to adjust the calculated bias, which in turn affects which mipmap level the lookup function samples from. This parameter is not accepted in a vertex program and will cause an error if you try to compile a shader using it. If the texture doesn't have mipmap levels, then the default base level is sampled and the bias parameter is ignored.

In a vertex program, the mipmap level can be chosen using one of the functions ending with "`Lod`", which are only available in vertex programs. The value of `lod` specifies which mipmap level is used. This is the only way for a level other than the base texture to be used in a vertex program. Non-`Lod` functions access only the base texture.

Finally, the shadow-access functions are provided for use with depth textures. If a shader performs a shadowing sample on a texture unit without a depth texture bound or without the depth-compare function being set, the results are undefined. Likewise, if a non-shadow-texture access is performed on a depth texture with comparisons enabled, the result is undefined.

Table 4.10 Texture-Lookup Functions

Syntax	Description
vec4 texture1D(sampler1D sampler the ,float coord [, float bias])	Use the texture coordinate `coord` to do a texture lookup in 1D texture currently bound to `sampler`. For the projective ("Proj") versions, the texture coordinate `coord.s` is divided by the last component of `coord`.
vec4 texture1DProj(sampler1D sampler,vec2 coord [, float bias])	
vec4 texture1DProj(sampler1D sampler,vec4 coord [, float bias])	
vec4 texture1DLod(sampler1D sampler,float coord, float lod)	
vec4 texture1DProjLod(sampler1D sampler, vec2 coord, float lod)	
vec4 texture1DProjLod(sampler1D sampler,vec4 coord, float lod)	
vec4 texture2D(sampler2D sampler ,vec2 coord [, float bias])	Use the texture coordinate `coord` to do a texture lookup in the 2D texture currently bound to `sampler`. For the projective ("Proj") versions, the texture coordinate (`coord.s`, `coord.t`) is divided by the last component of `coord`. The third component of `coord` is ignored for the vec4 `coord` variant.

continued

vec4 texture2DProj(sampler2D sampler,vec3 coord [, float bias])	
vec4 texture2DProj(sampler2D sampler,vec4 coord [, float bias])	
vec4 texture2DLod(sampler2D sampler,vec2 coord, float lod)	
vec4 texture2DProjLod(sampler2D sampler,vec3 coord, float lod)	
vec4 texture2DProjLod(sampler2D sampler,vec4 coord, float lod)	
vec4 texture3D(sampler3D sampler, the vec3 coord [, float bias])	Use the texture coordinate coord to do a texture lookup in 3D texture currently bound to sampler. For the projective ("Proj") versions, the texture coordinate is divided by coord.q.
vec4 texture3DProj(sampler3D sampler,vec4 coord [,float bias])	
vec4 texture3DLod(sampler3D sampler,vec3 coord, float lod)	
vec4 texture3DProjLod(sampler3D s ampler,vec4 coord, float lod)	
vec4 textureCube(samplerCube sampler,vec3 coord [, float bias])	Use the texture coordinate coord to do a texture lookup in the cube-map texture currently bound to sampler. The direction of coord is used to select which face to do a 2D-texture lookup in.
vec4 textureCubeLod(samplerCube sampler,vec3 coord, float lod)	
vec4 shadow1D(sampler1DShadow sampler,vec3 coord [, float bias])	Use texture coordinate coord to do a depth comparison lookup on the depth texture bound to sampler. The third component of coord (coord.p) is used as the R value. The texture bound to sampler must be a depth texture, or results are undefined. For the projective ("Proj") version of each function, the texture coordinate is divided by coord.q, giving a depth value R of coord.p/coord.q. The second component of coord is ignored for the "1D" variants.
vec4 shadow2D(sampler2DShadow sampler, vec3 coord [, float bias])	
vec4 shadow1DProj(sampler1DShadow sampler, vec4 coord [, float bias])	
vec4 shadow2DProj(sampler2DShadow sampler, vec4 coord [, float bias])	
vec4 shadow1DLod(sampler1DShadow sampler, vec3 coord, float lod)	
vec4 shadow2DProjLod(sampler2DShadow sampler, vec4 coord, float lod)	
vec4 shadow1DProjLod(sampler1DShadow sampler, vec4 coord, float lod)	
vec4 shadow2DLod(sampler2DShadow sampler, vec3 coord, float lod)	

Fragment-Processing Functions

The OpenGL Shading Language provides three functions that are specifically for fragment processing only. These three functions, shown in Table 4.11, allow you to evaluate the rate of change of per-vertex variables that are interpolated per fragment.

Table 4.11 Fragment-Processing Functions

Syntax	Description
genType dFdx(genType p)	Returns the derivative in x using local differencing for the input argument p.
genType dFdy(genType p)	Returns the derivative in y using local differencing for the input argument p.
genType fwidth(genType p)	Returns the sum of the absolute derivative in x and y using local differencing for the input argument p, i.e., `return = abs(dFdx (p)) + abs(dFdy (p));`.

Noise Functions

The noise functions in Table 4.12 are available in both vertex and fragment programs. The values returned by these functions are not truly random, but they are random enough to be useful in increasing the apparent rendering complexity and to generate complex textures such as marble and other natural forms.

Table 4.12 Noise Functions

Syntax	Description
float noise1(genType x)	Returns a 1D noise value based on the input value x.
vec2 noise2(genType x)	Returns a 2D noise value based on the input value x.
vec3 noise3(genType x)	Returns a 3D noise value based on the input value x.
vec4 noise4(genType x)	Returns a 4D noise value based on the input value x.

As noted the values returned are not truly random. Instead they fit into the following rules:

- The return value(s) are always in the range $[-1.0, 1.0]$ and cover at least the range $[-0.6, 0.6]$, with a Gaussian-like distribution.
- The return values have an overall average of 0.0.
- They are repeatable in that a particular input value will always produce the same return value.
- They are statistically invariant under rotation (i.e., no matter how the domain is rotated, it has the same statistical character).

- They have a statistical invariance under translation (i.e., no matter how the domain is translated, it has the same statistical character).
- They typically give different results under translation.
- The spatial frequency is narrowly concentrated, centered somewhere between 0.5 and 1.0.
- They are C-continuous everywhere (i.e., the first derivative is continuous).

The OpenGL Shading Language C API

Now that you've seen what you have to work with, I'm sure you are ready to start using the OpenGL Shading Language in your own programs. However, first you'll need to know how to pass these shaders to OpenGL and bind them for use. This is where the OpenGL Shading Language C API comes in.

The process of getting a shader program to a usable state isn't that hard.

1. Create a shader object.
2. Load the shader code into the object.
3. Compile the code for that object.
4. Repeat as needed for other shaders (vertex and fragment).
5. Create a program object.
6. Attach all the relevant shader objects to the program object.
7. Ask OpenGL to link the program object.

Once these steps have been successfully completed, you have a shader program linked and ready to use.

Those are the basics behind using shaders. Now let's look into the details.

Vertex- and Fragment-Shader Setup

The steps to set up and load a shader into a vertex- or fragment-shader object are virtually identical, so we'll look at them together, pointing out the differences as we come across them.

The first thing to do is create a *shader object* to represent our shader code once it's loaded in. These shader objects are similar to texture objects and vertex-buffer objects: you ask OpenGL to create one and it returns a handle to it, which you can then use to operate on the object.

Creation is handled by a call to glCreateShader(). When you call this function, you specify which shader type you want to create (vertex and fragment are the only types available currently, but it is possible that, as hardware evolves, new shader types could appear) and it returns a handle to the shader object.

```
GLuint glCreateShader(GLenum type);
```

Here type must be either GL_VERTEX_SHADER or GL_FRAGMENT_SHADER, depending on the type of shader the object will hold. Once successfully created, the function will return a handle. If the value returned is 0, then the function failed and you should query glGetError() to find out what the problem was.

Once the shader object has been created, it's time to load a shader into the object. This is done using the function glShaderSource(), which takes an array of strings representing the shader and makes a copy of it to store in the shader object. Note that shaders are loaded as strings and not from files. This is because, like the rest of OpenGL, the API doesn't do more work than it has to. It's up to you to load the shader into memory to pass to the shader object.

```
void glShaderSource(GLuint shader, GLuint nstrings, const GLchar **strings,
                    GLint *lengths);
```

Here shader is the shader object you are working with; nstrings indicates the number of strings that will be passed in the following parameter; strings is a pointer to an array of strings; and lengths is a pointer to an array that holds the lengths of the strings pointed to in the strings parameter. Finally, lengths should be the same length as strings, and lengths[n] is the length of strings[n]. If lengths is NULL, then each string in strings is assumed to be a null terminated string, and the length of each will be determined by OpenGL.

At this point it is worth revisiting the __LINE__ and __FILE__ preprocessor directives. You just learned, however, that the OpenGL Shading Language does not handle files. So the concept of a file as related to the __FILE__ directive refers to an individual string within strings. Every time a new line character is encountered in the string it counts as a line, which is what __LINE__ refers to.

You know now how to load a shader, so the next step is to compile it. This is handled by the glCompileShader() function.

```
void glCompileShader(GLuint shader);
```

When invoked, the OpenGL implementation will attempt to compile the shader attached to the shader object shader. The function is nonblocking, so the shader may not yet be compiled when control is returned to the caller. However, any functions that rely on a shader being compiled (suck as glLinkProgram()) will block until the compilation process is finished if needed.

You might notice that the function doesn't indicate whether the compilation was successful or not. This shouldn't come as a surprise, considering that the compilation may not be complete when the function returns. Instead, it is possible to query the status of a shader with glGetShaderiv(). You can also retrieve a log containing errors and other information from OpenGL using glGetShaderInfoLog(). Both of these functions will be explained in greater detail later in the chapter.

Shader Programs

Once you've loaded and compiled a set of shaders, you need to attach them to a program and perform a link operation so that you can bind them as the active shaders. However, before you do that, you have to create a program object to attach the shaders to. This can be accomplished by the following function:

```
GLuint glCreateProgram();
```

Like glCreateShader(), this function also returns a handle to an object, in this case a program object. This handle is used with other functions that work on program objects.

Once you have created a program object, the next task is to attach shaders to the program so that you can use them. This is accomplished with the glAttachShader() function.

```
void glAttachShader(GLuint program, GLuint shader);
```

This function attaches the shader indicated by shader to the program indicated by program. A program can have more than one shader object attached to it at any given time. Generally, programs will have two shader objects attached (one vertex and one fragment), though it is possible to have more than one shader object of either type attached as well. The linking stage sorts out how they connect.

Linking is done by calling the function glLinkProgram(). This will attempt to link the attached shader objects into a working shader program that can then be used.

```
void glLinkProgram(GLuint program);
```

It is possible for the link operation to fail for a number of reasons. The status of the linking is stored as part of the program object's state and can be queried via the function glGetProgramiv(), which will be covered later. There are a number of reasons that a program can fail to link.

- The program exceeds the number of attributes supported by the implementation.
- The program exceeds the number of uniform variables supported by the implementation.
- The function main() is missing from either a vertex or fragment shader (or possibly both).
- The user-defined varying variables in the fragment and vertex shaders don't match (either the types are different or the variables are missing completely).
- There is an unresolved reference to a variable or function name.

- There has been a conflict with a shader variable; either it has been declared as two different types or it has been initialized to two different values.
- One or more of the attached shader objects hasn't been successfully compiled.

If the link operation is successful, then user-defined uniform variables are initialized to zero, and they will be assigned a location so that they can be set by the relevant OpenGL functions (which will be covered shortly). Also, vertex attributes that are not already bound to a location are bound in this stage so that they can be given values per vertex.

As already noted, a shader object only requires a minimum of one shader of either type attached in order to link it. If a vertex shader is present but there is no fragment shader, then the vertex shader is linked against the standard fixed-function attributes and varying variables for fragment processing as discussed earlier. If a fragment shader is present without a vertex shader, then it is linked against the standard fixed-function attributes and varying variables for vertex processing, also as discussed earlier.

As with the `glCompileShader()` function, the implementation doesn't have to wait for the link operation to complete before returning control to the program. However, any functions that require the linking to be complete will wait for the process to finish before continuing. Any information about the state of the shader program after it has been linked can be retrieved with the function `glGetProgramInfoLog()`, which will be covered later. It should be noted that when you link a group of shaders into a working program, you will lose any information the information log contained previously, whether or not the link is successful.

Once a linking operation has completed you can modify attached shader objects, detach them, and even attach new ones without changing either the compiled program or the information log that goes with it. The only operation that adjusts the log and the state of the executable program is the link operation.

Once a program has been successfully linked, it is time to install it for usage. This is where the function `glUseProgram()` comes in.

```
void glUseProgram(GLuint program);
```

This function installs the program associated with `program` as the active program for the current context. This program will run whenever a drawing command is executed until it is uninstalled and a new one replaces it or the fixed-function pipeline is switched back on. If `program` is 0, then shader processing is disabled and fixed functionality takes over for all drawing operations. If the program installed only has a vertex shader, then the fixed-function fragment processing remains active to process fragments. Likewise, if the program installed only has a fragment shader, then the fixed-function vertex processing remains active to process vertices.

Once a program is in use, you are free to modify, detach and recompile, or delete attached shader objects, as well as attach new objects and even delete the program itself without affecting the program at all. However, a call to glLinkProgram() will affect the program, and upon a successful relinking, the program will be reinstalled as the active program. If you make the active program inactive and you have requested its deletion, then at this point it will be deleted (see next section for more details). You can also use standard OpenGL function calls to update the various fixed-function states as you require. This won't affect the current program and will only come into effect once fixed-function processing is reinstalled.

Shader and Program Management

You now know how to create and use shader and program objects. In this section, you'll learn how to delete them, detach shaders from program objects, and query information about both object types.

Object Deletion

Once you are done with a shader or a program, you can ask the OpenGL implementation to delete it. This is accomplished by the following two functions:

```
void glDeleteShader(GLuint shader);
void glDeleteProgram(GLuint program);
```

These two functions request that the OpenGL implementation delete either the shader or program requested. If the program requested is the current shader, it won't be deleted immediately but will be tagged for deletion once it becomes inactive, at which point any attached shaders that aren't flagged for deletion are detached and the program is deleted. If you request the deletion of a shader that is still attached to a program, the shader will be tagged for deletion as well and deleted once it has been detached from all the programs it is attached to.

The deletion state of a shader or program can be queried with glGetShaderiv() and glGetProgramiv() respectively.

Detaching Shaders

You can detach a shader object from a program at any time by calling the function glDetachShader().

```
void glDetachShader(GLuint program, GLuint shader);
```

This function detaches the shader object shader from the program object program. If the shader has been flagged for deletion and it isn't attached to any other program object, the shader is deleted immediately.

Determining an Object's Type

You might have noticed that although the handles are all `GLuint` values, certain objects must be called with the correct functions. For example, calling a function designed for a shader on a program will result in an error at best and a crash at worst. However, there are two functions that allow you to query the type of object associated with a handle.

```
GLboolean glIsShader(GLuint handle);
GLboolean glIsProgram(GLuint handle);
```

These functions will return `GL_TRUE` if the handle is associated with the indicated object, or `GL_FALSE` otherwise. So a shader handle passed to `glIsProgram()` would return `GL_FALSE`, but when passed to `glIsShader()`, it would return `GL_TRUE`.

Retrieving Shader Source

Normally when you pass the shader string to a shader object using `glShaderSource()` you would delete the source string from memory because the OpenGL implementation makes an internal copy of it. However, there are times when you might want to read the string back again. The function `glGetShaderSource()` allows you to do this.

```
void glGetShaderSource(GLuint shader, GLsizei bufSize, GLsizei *length,
                       GLchar *source);
```

For this function, `shader` is the shader object that you want to retrieve the source from, and `bufSize` indicates how many characters can be stored in `source`, which should point to a block of memory to store a copy of the shader in. When the function returns, `length` will hold the number of characters (including the null terminator) that were copied into `source`. This value can be less than or equal to `bufsize` but never larger. Rather than allocating an excessively large block of memory to store the source, you can query the size of the source code held by shader object by using `glGetShaderiv()`, which is explained later.

Program Validation

The final management function is `glValidateProgram()`, which is more of a debugging tool than a true management tool.

```
void glValidateProgram(GLuint program);
```

This function checks to see if the program specified by the handle `program` can be run in its current state. Any information relating to this validation process can be stored in the program's information log; however, this is implementation dependent and might not produce any information at all. The validation phase also checks things such as the correct binding of samplers and other related states. The final validation state is stored as part of the program state and can be accessed via the `glGetProgramiv()` function, as explained later.

Keep in mind that validation is a slow process, so it is generally only performed during debugging and initial program development. You won't want to call this in your main game loop at all because it will hinder your frame rate and take up a great deal of CPU time.

Supplying Shaders with Information

You have seen how to create shader and program objects, how to combine them and install them as the active program, and how to remove them and delete them. However, a program is no good without information to act upon, so in this section you'll learn how to supply it.

The data that programs act upon can be broken into two groups.

- Per vertex (attributes)
- Per polygon or more (uniform)

The per-vertex attributes are of course those variables marked as `attributes` in the shader. The other group of variables, which use the `uniform` qualifier, are changed at most per polygon, simply because they can't be changed more often than that. Typically these values are only changed per object or per group of objects.

Specifying Per-Vertex Data

As with normal OpenGL drawing operations, there are two methods of providing per-vertex data—via immediate mode, or via vertex arrays—both of which work on *generic attributes* as well as the named ones you are used to (vertex, color, texture coordinates, etc.).

When working with the standard OpenGL vertex attributes, you don't have to do any extra work. Just call the functions you're used to, and the OpenGL implementation will deal with feeding that data to the vertex shader. Table 4.13 shows how the built-in vertex attributes map to their vertex-shader counterparts.

Table 4.13 Vertex Attribute to Shader Variable Mapping

OpenGL Function	Built-in shader variable
`glVertex(...)`	`gl_Vertex`
`glColor(...)`	`gl_Color`
`glNormal(...)`	`gl_Normal`
`gl_SecondaryColor(...)`	`gl_SecondaryColor`
`glFogCoord(...)`	`gl_FogCoord`
`glMultiTexCoord(n*,...)`	`gl_MultiTexCoord`n

*n can range from 2 to the maximum number of vertex coordinates allowed.

These mappings apply both to immediate mode and to the corresponding vertex arrays. Using these variables, you can quickly write shaders that you can drop into current code without having to worry about setting up attributes for them. You can also stick with the functions you are already familiar with, which is useful during prototyping stages.

Generic Attributes

The other method for passing data to a vertex program is to use *generic attributes.* While it can be handy to use the built-in types for some data, there are times when the data you are specifying won't fit into the types indicated by standard OpenGL function calls. This is where generic attributes come into play, as they allow you to use any arbitrary vertex attributes in your vertex program and send data to them without indicating any type information beyond their being per-vertex data.

So how do generic attributes work? The answer lies in the attribute slots mentioned earlier. If you recall, we said that an OpenGL implementation has a set number of slots to allocate for vertex attributes (each slot being a vec4). Each of these slots has a number from zero to the maximum number of slots minus one. So if an implementation supports 16 slots, they are numbered 0 to 15. To pass data to OpenGL, we need to get a slot number to insert the data into. You can do this in either of two ways.

- Let the GLSL compiler assign the slots when it links the program and then ask it for the slot for each attribute by name.
- Before linking, tell the OpenGL implementation where you want each attribute assigned.

Using GLSL Assigned Slots

To use GLSL assigned slots, we have to ask the OpenGL implementation which slot the attribute we are after is assigned to. This action is performed by glGetAttribLocation(), which returns the slot number if successful, or -1 to indicate failure.

```
GLint glGetAttribLocation(GLuint program, const GLchar *name);
```

In this function, program is the program object that you wish to query for the location of the attribute. This program doesn't have to be the current one, but it needs to have undergone at least one successful linking for the attributes to have been assigned slots. Alternatively, the name could have been allocated by hand. The parameter name is the name of the attribute you are finding the location for, and it should precisely match the attribute's name as given in the shader.

If the name specified is that of a matrix, then the index maps to the first column of the matrix. The rest of the columns are automatically mapped to index+1 (mat2), index+2 (mat3), and index+3 (mat4), as required.

Assigning Slots Yourself

Using `glGetAttribLocation()` is the easiest and quickest way to get attribute locations, but sometimes you'll want to assign attributes to certain slots, perhaps to fit some uniform numbering system in your own program. In this case, you need to use the function `glBindAttribLocation()` to bind the locations yourself.

```
void glBindAttribLocation(GLuint program, GLuint index, const GLchar *name);
```

As with `glGetAttribLocation()`, `program` refers to the program object you wish to bind an attribute for, and `name` is the name of the attribute. The additional parameter `index` holds the slot number to which you wish to bind the attribute given by `name`. This value must be within the range of valid slots for the current implementation. The value 0 is considered a special value. While it can still be bound, it has a special meaning, which I will cover in a moment. Table 4.14 shows how you can potentially bind an index to any given name.

Table 4.14 Binding an Index

Attribute Details	Example Shader-Variable Name
glVertexAttrib(0,...)	gl_Vertex or myVertex
glVertexAttrib(1,...)	Foo
glVertexAttrib(2,...)	Bar
glVertexAttrib(n,...)	(unused)

As with `glGetAttribLocation()`, if the name specified is a matrix, then the first column is mapped to `index`, and all the remaining columns are mapped to `index+1`, `index+2`, and `index+3` as required.

Any attempt to bind a predefined OpenGL attribute name to an index will fail. These attributes are automatically set up as required by the compiler and linker and cannot be changed.

You can't bind the same attribute to more than one slot. Any attempt to do so will just redefine the slot for that name. However, it is possible to have more than one name bound to a slot through *attribute aliasing*. This is allowed if only one of the attributes aliased to a single slot is accessed in the compiled program. For example, if you have two attribute names aliased to the same slot and try to use both attribute names in the program, an error will occur at link time. If you are using aliasing you have to be careful as optimizations performed by the compiler and linker are free to assume that no aliasing of attributes is taking place, thus potentially breaking your code (this is because, by default, you can't bind the built-in attribute names, and so cannot alias them; therefore the compiler is free to assume this will always be the case). You should use this feature with care.

As mentioned earlier, the attribute slot 0 (zero) has special meaning. This slot is the one to which the vertex data submitted via glVertex() is sent, and this is considered special because once the vertex position is specified, it is considered to be the end of the vertex definition. If you use generic attributes you must take care to either submit data via glVertex() (or use the related vertex array) or write to the attribute bound to 0 in order to let OpenGL know the vertex is complete.

The final important note about specifying your own attribute slots is that you must specify them before a link operation in order for them to take effect. Any changes made after a program object has been linked won't take effect until after a subsequent link. It is fine to bind attributes for program objects that don't yet have a vertex shader bound to them, and it's also legal to bind attributes that are never used in the program.

Assigning Data to Generic Attribute Slots

Once you have a slot number, either requested or specified, you can place data into it. As mentioned, the two traditional ways of sending data to the GPU are used to send both generic attributes and the built-in types. This means we have two sets of functions, one relating to immediate mode and one to vertex arrays.

Generic Attributes and Immediate Mode

Immediate mode works in the manner you're used to, with data for a vertex being specified inside a glBegin()/glEnd() block and finished with a call to glVertex() or by writing to the attribute bound to slot 0.

The first group of per-vertex functions is as follows:

```
void glVertexAttrib1{sfd}(GLuint index, TYPE v);
void glVertexAttrib2{sfd}(GLuint index, TYPE v1, TYPE v2);
void glVertexAttrib3{sfd}(GLuint index, TYPE v1, TYPE v2, TYPE v3);
void glVertexAttrib4{sfd}(GLuint index, TYPE v1, TYPE v2, TYPE v3, TYPE v4);
void glVertexAttrib{123}{sfd}v(GLuint index, const TYPE *v);
void glVertexAttrib4{bsifd ubusui}v(GLuint index, const TYPE *v);
```

All of the above functions pass data into the generic attribute slot indicated by index, but each of them does so in a slightly different way.

The first four functions allow you to specify each piece of data in a separate variable. So, for example, the following code snippet would pass three floating-point values to the attribute assigned to slot 1:

```
glVertexAttrib3f(1, 1.0, 2.0, 3.0);
```

The fifth function in the group above lets you specify a pointer to a group of data to pass to OpenGL. The following code snippet is functionally equivalent to the previous example:

```
GLfloat attrib[] = {1.0, 2.0, 3.0};
glVertexAttrib3fv(1, attrib);
```

For any of the first five glVertexAttrib() functions, if the second or third components are not specified they are assumed to be zero, and if the fourth component isn't specified it is assumed to be one.

The final function listed above differs from the others in that it comes in versions supporting a larger range of data types. However, when using this variation, you must specify all four components.

All values passed using these functions are converted to floating-point values for internal use by OpenGL, so doubles and floats are mapped as expected and all integer types gain a decimal point (e.g., a value of 42 would become 42.0).

There are two final functions for passing per-vertex data via immediate mode. They are used to pass normalized data to OpenGL.

```
void glVertexAttrib4Nub(GLuint index, GLubyte v1, GLubyte v2, GLubyte v3,
                        GLubyte v4 );
void glVertexAttrib4N{bsifd ubusui}v(GLuint index, TYPE v );
```

The first form of the function allows you to pass in four unsigned bytes of data. The second form accepts a broad range of types in vector format.

When called, both of these functions normalize the data that is passed in. For floats and doubles this has no effect, but for integer types the values are mapped into a normalized range depending on the variable type. Unsigned types are mapped into the range $[0, 1]$ where 1 maps to the highest value the type can hold (e.g., in the case of a GLubyte, the value 255 is mapped to 1 and 127 is mapped to 0.5). For signed types, the range is $[-1, 1]$ with the most positive value being mapped to 1 and the most negative value being mapped to -1.

As mentioned earlier, attributes can also be matrix types, and for each column of a matrix, a slot is required. To demonstrate this, assume a mat3 called filter has been declared and used in a vertex shader. The code to fill it would be as follows:

```
GLint slot = glGetAttribLocation(program, "filter");
glVertexAttrib3f(slot, 1.0, 2.0, 3.0);
glVertexAttrib3f(slot+1, 4.0, 5.0, 6.0);
glVertexAttrib3f(slot+2, 7.0, 8.0, 9.0);
```

The resulting filter matrix would look like this.

```
mat3 filter = [ 1.0, 4.0, 7.0,
                2.0, 5.0, 8.0,
                3.0, 6.0, 9.0]
```

Generic Attributes and Vertex Arrays

We'll now move on to the vertex-array method of passing generic attribute data. This method is the same as working with normal vertex arrays. You tell OpenGL where it can find the data and what format it is in, and then before drawing, enable the attribute array so that it is accessed when you issue a drawing command such as `glDrawArrays()`.

Like other `gl*Pointer()` functions such as `glTexCoordPointer()` or `glColorPointer()`, `glVertexAttribPointer()` tells OpenGL the location and format of the data you wish to specify per vertex.

```
void glVertexAttribPointer(GLuint index, GLint size, GLenum type,
                           GLboolean normalized, GLsizei stride,
                           const GLvoid *pointer);
```

Most of the parameters are similar to the `gl*Pointer()` functions that you're familiar with, with `size` indicating the number of components (which must be between one and four) and `type` indicating the type of data stored in the array. For `type`, you can use `GL_BYTE`, `GL_UNSIGNED_BYTE`, `GL_SHORT`, `GL_UNSIGNED_SHORT`, `GL_INT`, `GL_UNSIGNED_INT`, `GL_FLOAT`, or `GL_DOUBLE`.

The value of `stride` indicates the number of bytes between one set of values and the next, which allows you to interleave the values as you can with a normal vertex array. Finally, `pointer` points to the memory containing the data that will be accessed per vertex.

The two parameters that are new are `index` and `normalized`. As you might expect, `index` is the slot number the per-vertex attributes are to be streamed into when the vertex array is accessed during drawing. The Boolean variable `normalized` indicates whether the data should be normalized as it is passed into the hardware. The normalization process performed is the same as indicated above for the `glVertexAttrib4N()` and functions.

Once the vertex-array pointer has been set up, you need to enable the vertex array so that it will be used when drawing. Rather than using the existing glEnableClientState()/ glDisableClientState() entry points, GLSL uses two new functions.

```
void glEnableVertexAttribArray(GLuint index);
void glDisableVertexAttribArray(GLuint index);
```

These two functions enable or disable accessing of the vertex array bound to the attribute slot indicated by the value in `index`.

Assuming that we have a pointer to some unnormalized data we wish to send to OpenGL for processing via a vertex array, this is how we would set it up.

```
glVertexAttribPointer(1, 4, GL_BYTE, GL_FALSE, 0, pointer);
glEnableVertexAttribArray(1);
// perform drawing with glDrawArrays(), glDrawElements(), etc.
glDisableVertexAttribArray(1);
```

Active Attributes

When a shader program has been linked, the attributes that are used in the program are known as *active attributes*. These are the only attributes you can query for a slot location using `glGetAttribLocation()`. If other attributes exist that aren't used in the program, any attempts to query for them will result in a return value of −1, indicating that no slot has been assigned. You can query the names of the active attributes using the function `glGetActiveAttrib()`. This can be handy in situations where shader development is separate from application development, because it allows shader developers to use a set of agreed-upon names for attributes that the program can then query for and bind only the data that the shader requires.

```
void glGetActiveAttrib(GLuint program, GLuint index, GLsizei maxLength,
                       GLsizei *length, GLint *size, GLenum *type, GLchar *name);
```

The `usage` of program and `index` should be obvious by now. The `name` parameter is a pointer to a block of memory to hold the name of the active attribute. The size of this block is passed in `maxLength`. It is possible to query the maximum length of an active attribute for a given program by using `glGetProgramiv()`, which will be covered later.

The other three parameters return information about the attribute bound to slot `index`. The `length` parameter holds the actual length of the string written to `name`, which is a null terminated string. The `type` parameter holds the type of the attribute; it will be one of the constants from Table 4.15. Upon return, `size` will hold the size of the attribute in type units.

The function above must be called after a link operation has been completed (even if the link wasn't successful). Without a link operation, the attributes won't be defined as active, so `glGetActiveAttrib()` can't retrieve information about them. The function will attempt to retrieve as much information as it can, but if it can't retrieve anything—due to the link operation failing, for example—then the value returned in `length` will be 0 and `name` will be blank.

Table 4.15 Attribute Types

Enum Value	Description
GL_FLOAT	A `float` attribute
GL_FLOAT_VEC2	A vec2 attribute
GL_FLOAT_VEC3	A vec3 attribute
GL_FLOAT_VEC4	A vec4 attribute
GL_FLOAT_MAT2	A mat2 attribute
GL_FLOAT_MAT3	A mat3 attribute
GL_FLOAT_MAT4	A mat4 attribute

The number of active attributes in a program can be queried with `glProgramiv()`, which again will be covered later. The indices of all active attributes range from 0 (for the first one) to the total number of active attributes minus one (for the last one). For example, assuming the variable `maxSlots` holds the number of slots in use as returned by `glProgramiv()`, then the following would query all the active attributes for a given program object.

```
GLchar names[MAX_NAME_LENGTH];   // sized to some length that is assumed to be
                                 //long enough to hold the longest attribute name
GLsizei length;
GLint size;
GLenum type;
for (int i = 0; i < maxSlots; ++i)
{
  glGetActiveAttrib(program, i, MAX_NAME_LENGTH, &length, &size, &type, names);
  // perform some processing and save the details somewhere
}
```

Querying Generic Attribute State

OpenGL provides several functions that allow you to query various states for generic attributes. The first of these are as follows:

```
void glGetVertexAttribfv(GLuint index, GLenum pname, GLfloat *params);
void glGetVertexAttribiv(GLuint index, GLenum pname, GLint *params);
void glGetVertexAttribdv(GLuint index, GLenum pname, GLdouble *params);
```

You indicate the slot you wish to query for details using index, and the queried value is returned in params. You indicate which information you're interested in using pname, which must be one of the values in Table 4.16. With the exception of GL_CURRENT_VERTEX_ATTRIB, the information returned is client-side.

In addition to these states, you can also retrieve the pointer to the data that is being used for a given attribute (which was previously set with glVertexAttribPointer()).

```
void glGetVertexAttribPointer(GLuint index, GLenum pname, GLvoid **pointer);
```

As before, index indicates the slot you are interested in. You must set pname to GL_VERTEX_ATTRIB_ARRAY_POINTER. Upon return, pointer will hold the address of the data being used for this slot.

Expanding upon the previous vertex-array example:

```
glVertexAttribPointer(1, 4, GL_BYTE, GL_FALSE, 0, pointer);
glEnableVertexAttribArray(1);
// perform drawing with glDrawArrays(), glDrawElements(), etc.
glDisableVertexAttribArray(1);
GLvoid *datapointer;
glGetVertexAttribPointer(1, GL_VERTEX_ATTRIB_ARRAY_POINTER, &datapointer);
```

Once the call to glGetVertexAttribPointer() is completed, the address held in datapointer will be the same as the one held in pointer.

Table 4.16 Attribute States

Name	Description
GL_VERTEX_ATTRIB_ARRAY_ENABLED	params returns a single nonzero (true) value if the vertex attribute array for index is enabled and 0 (false) if it is disabled. The initial value is GL_FALSE.
GL_VERTEX_ATTRIB_ARRAY_SIZE	params returns a single value, the size of the vertex attribute array for index. The size is the number of values—1, 2, 3, or 4—for each element of the vertex attribute array. The initial value is 4.
GL_VERTEX_ATTRIB_ARRAY_STRIDE	params returns a single value, the array stride for (number of bytes between successive elements in) the vertex attribute array for index. A value of 0 indicates that the array elements are stored sequentially in memory. The initial value is 0.
GL_VERTEX_ATTRIB_ARRAY_TYPE	params returns a single value, a symbolic constant indicating the array type for the vertex-attribute array for index. Possible values are GL_BYTE, GL_UNSIGNED_BYTE, GL_SHORT,GL_UNSIGNED_SHORT, GL_INT, GL_UNSIGNED_INT, GL_FLOAT, and GL_DOUBLE. The initial value is GL_FLOAT.
GL_VERTEX_ATTRIB_ARRAY_NORMALIZED	params returns a single nonzero (true) value if fixed-point data types for the vertex-attribute array indicated by index are normalized when they are converted to floating point and 0 (false) otherwise. The initial value is GL_FALSE.
GL_CURRENT_VERTEX_ATTRIB	params returns four values that represent the current value for the generic vertex attribute specified by index. Generic vertex attribute 0 is unique in that it has no current state, so an error will be generated if index is 0. The initial value for all other generic vertex attributes is (0,0,0,1).

Specifying Uniform Data

You've seen how to specify data that changes every vertex, but what about data that changes less often and tends to be constant over the life of a whole object or even a group of objects? Well, this is where uniform data comes into play.

As mentioned earlier, the OpenGL Shading Language supplies a number of built-in uniform variables that allow you to access information that is set via standard OpenGL state-management functions, such as glLight() and functions that manipulate material information. The full list of these built-in uniform functions can be found in Appendix

B. When a program object is loaded as the current object, any built-in uniform variables are automatically initialized with the correct information based on the current OpenGL state, and their data is updated automatically if the state changes while the program is active.

However, as with per-vertex attributes, you may need uniform data beyond that which is provided by OpenGL, and thus mechanisms are in place for you to define your own uniform data.

Getting Uniform Locations

Passing uniform data is a little different from passing per-vertex attribute values. You can't tell OpenGL how you want each uniform to be linked to a certain slot. Instead, it defines these automatically during linking. The practical upshot of this is that you must query the program object using the function `glGetUniformLocation()` for the locations of the uniform variables you need. This needs to be performed after each link operation, as the locations can change.

```
GLuint glGetUniformLocation(GLuint program, const GLchar *name);
```

Much like `glGetAttribLocation()`, the above function returns the slot number for the uniform named `name` for the program object in `program`.

As uniform data can be arrays or structures in addition to plain types, the string for `name` can include the field selection operator (`.`) and the element operator (`[]`) so that you can select the locations of array elements and fields of structures. When looking up the first element in an array, you can use either just the name or the name with a "[0]" postfix. However, the result of looking up a name *must not* be another structure, another array of structures, or a component of a vector or matrix.

For example, given the following structure

```
struct
{
  float a;
  struct
  {
    vec2 b;
    vec2 c[10];
  } d[5];
  vec4 e;
} uniform f;
```

the following calls to `glGetUniformLocation()` would be valid:

```
glGetUniformLocation(program, "f.a");
glGetUniformLocation(program, "f.d[0].b");
glGetUniformLocation(program, "f.d[1].c");
glGetUniformLocation(program, "f.e");
glGetUniformLocation(program, "f.d[0].c");
glGetUniformLocation(program, "f.d[0].c[0] ");   // the same as the line above
```

The following calls, however, would *not* be valid:

```
glGetUniformLocation(program, "f.d[0]");        // references a struct
glGetUniformLocation(program, "f.d[0].b[2]"); // references a vector component
```

If the named uniform is not found then -1 is returned. This value is also returned if the string held in name has the prefix "gl_", because this is reserved for internal usage only (note that all the built-in uniforms have this prefix).

The value returned by glGetUniformLocation() is valid *only* for the location you requested. It isn't possible to use offsets from this location to get the location of the next or previous element in an array, for example. If you require access to those array elements you must query their locations. For example, if the following is defined in a vertex shader

```
uniform float foo[10];
```

then in the application code the following isn't legal where noted:

```
GLint bar = glGetUniformLocation( program, "foo");  // bar  holds location of
                                                    // foo[0]
bar++;    // bar is now no longer valid and doesn't point to foo[1] as you
          // might have expected
```

Any attempt to use uniform locations in this manner will not work. This is because uniform locations don't have to map to memory locations and don't have to be contiguous, and thus the OpenGL implementation is free to assign the locations as it sees fit.

Writing to Uniforms

Once you have successfully acquired the location of a uniform variable you can write the data. There are three groups of functions to do this. One sets a single group of values, one sets multiple groups of values, and one sets matrices.

The first group we'll look at sets up a single uniform value per call.

```
void glUniform1i(GLuint location, GLint v);
void glUniform2i(GLuint location, GLint v1, GLint v2);
void glUniform3i(GLuint location, GLint v1, GLint v2, GLint v3);
void glUniform4i(GLuint location, GLint v1, GLint v2, GLint v3, GLint v4);
void glUniform1f(GLuint location, GLfloat v);
```

```
void glUniform2f(GLuint location, GLfloat v1, GLfloat v2);
void glUniform3f(GLuint location, GLfloat v1, GLfloat v2, GLfloat v3);
void glUniform4f(GLuint location, GLfloat v1, GLfloat v2, GLfloat v3,
                 GLfloat v4);
```

The location to be set is passed in location and the values are passed in the remaining parameters. There are no separate functions for Boolean uniforms, but those can be set using any of the functions above, using the standard convention that zero is false and any other value is true.

The number of values passed to glUniform() must match the number of components in the uniform being set. For example, glUniform1() must be used with float, int, or bool uniforms, and glUniform3() must be used with vec3, ivec3, or bvec3 uniforms.

The second method, setting a group of variables, is designed to allow you to quickly pass data to an array.

```
void glUniform1iv(GLuint location, GLuint count, const GLint *v);
void glUniform2iv(GLuint location, GLuint count, const GLint *v);
void glUniform3iv(GLuint location, GLuint count, const GLint *v);
void glUniform4iv(GLuint location, GLuint count, const GLint *v);
void glUniform1fv(GLuint location, GLuint count, const GLfloat *v);
void glUniform2fv(GLuint location, GLuint count, const GLfloat *v);
void glUniform3fv(GLuint location, GLuint count, const GLfloat *v);
void glUniform4fv(GLuint location, GLuint count, const GLfloat *v);
```

Again, location is the location of the uniform. Unlike the previous functions, a vector of data is passed in v; count is the number of elements in v.

A count value of 1 indicates that it should only update a single value and works much the same as the functions above. A count greater than 1 indicates that it is updating an array of values. The number in the function once again indicates the number of components in each value, which must match the uniform being modified (e.g., the glUniform2() variants would be used to modify vec2s, ivec2s, or bvec2s).

The usage of these functions is best illustrated with an example. Assume we have defined the following uniform in a shader.

```
vec3 foo[3];
```

To modify it, we must first get a location and then write to it as follows:

```
GLuint bar = glGetUniformLocation(someprogram, "foo");
GLfloat data[] = { 1.0,2.0,3.0,
                   4.0,5.0,6.0,
                   7.0,8.0,9.0};
glUniform3fv(bar,3,data);
```

This will cause the values in data to be written to the uniform variable foo. Each row of the data above will be written to a different vec3 (the rows are only split up to illustrate how it would be written; you can place your own data on one row if you like).

The final set of functions for writing to uniform variables is for use with matrices.

```
void glUniformMatrix2fv(GLuint location, GLuint count, GLboolean transpose,
                        const GLfloat *values);
void glUniformMatrix3fv(GLuint location, GLuint count, GLboolean transpose,
                        const GLfloat *values);
void glUniformMatrix4fv(GLuint location, GLuint count, GLboolean transpose,
                        const GLfloat *values);
```

These functions serve to set a single matrix uniform or to set an array of matrices. Of course, location is the location of the matrix (or first matrix in an array of matrices), and the count variable indicates how many matrices should be updated using the data in values.

The Boolean parameter transpose indicates whether the data needs to be transposed. A value of GL_TRUE indicates that the data is in row major order and a value of GL_FALSE indicates that the data is in column major order.

The number in these function names indicates the size of the matrix it is meant to operate on, e.g. glUniformMatrix4fv() is for 4×4 matrices.

All variations of these glUniform() functions can fail for any of the following reasons.

- There is no current program object.
- location is an invalid location for the current program.
- The number of values indicated by count is greater than the location pointed to by location, either by exceeding the array size or the type size.
- The type and size of the uniform variable doesn't match the type and size indicated by the function being used to set it.

Active Uniforms

Uniform variables that can be used are referred to as *active uniforms*. As with vertex attributes, any uniform variable that is declared but isn't used isn't activated by the compiler/linker and as such doesn't have any space allocated to it. You can query which uniforms are active and retrieve details about them using glGetActiveUniform().

```
void glGetActiveUniform(GLuint program, GLuint index, GLsizei maxLength,
                        GLsizei *length, GLint *size, GLenum *type,
                        GLchar *name);
```

This function works much the same way as its attribute counterpart. It retrieves information about the uniform in the slot indicated by index in the program indicated by program. This function can retrieve information about both user-defined and built-in (i.e., those prefixed with "gl_") uniforms, but it should not be called until the program has been linked, since that's when locations for these uniforms are assigned.

The maxLength parameter indicates the maximum length of the string that can be stored in name. The name of the longest active uniform can be queried by using glGetProgramiv(), as explained later.

Upon execution of this function and a successful retrieval of the data for a given uniform, the name of the uniform is copied into name and the length of this string is placed in the length (unless NULL is passed, in which case the length is discarded).

The type of the uniform is held in type. It can be any of the following symbolic constants: GL_FLOAT, GL_FLOAT_VEC2, GL_FLOAT_VEC3, GL_FLOAT_VEC4, GL_FLOAT_MAT2, GL_FLOAT_MAT3, GL_FLOAT_MAT4, GL_INT, GL_INT_VEC2, GL_INT_VEC3, GL_INT_VEC4, GL_BOOL, GL_BOOL_VEC2, GL_BOOL_VEC3, or GL_BOOL_VEC4.

The value returned in size is the size of the uniform variable. For arrays, the value returned is the number of elements in the array; for anything else, this value will be 1 (structures will be explained momentarily).

It is also possible to query the number of active uniforms in a program using glProgramiv(), as described later. As with glGetActiveAttrib(), if an index of zero is passed, then the first uniform is queried, and if the value is the number of active uniforms minus one, then the last uniform is queried.

The glGetActiveUniform() function will attempt to return as much information as it can, but if it can't return anything, then length returns zero and name will be blank. This is most likely to occur after a link operation that failed.

Uniform Structure Name and Size

Let's return to the subject of structures in the context of the size parameter used with glGetActiveUniform(). As you've seen, structures are handled differently from other uniforms (e.g., having to set the members of a struct separately rather than being able to directly set all values of the struct at once). When querying data from a uniform structure, the name returned is the fully qualified name of the components of the structure. For example, let's say you have a uniform using the following structure:

```
struct
{
  vec2 a;
  struct
```

```
   {
     vec3 b;
     vec4 c;
   } d[2];
} e;
```

If you were to query data for the members of this structure, the names for the data would show as follows:

```
e.a
e.d[0].b
e.d[0].c
e.d[1].b
e.d[1].c
```

Notice how each array element is accessed and how each member of the nested struct is fully qualified based on the array index. As the structure is reduced to its component parts each part of the structure is given a location and thus takes up one slot. Using the structure in this example would take up five uniform slots.

Another important point is that even if you access only one element of an array, the whole array is considered to be active. In the above example, even if we only used e.d[0], the rest of the elements of the array would be activated as well. This is an important point to keep in mind when using arrays, as you could quickly eat into your uniform space in this manner.

Querying Uniform Values

The final uniform-related functions are for querying the current value of a uniform variable. This allows you to retrieve the last set of data you wrote to it or that was set using the OpenGL API. As uniform variables are read-only in a shader, you can't use this as a method to pass data back from a shader to the running executable.

```
void glGetUniformfv(GLuint program, GLuint location, GLfloat *params);
void glGetUniformiv(GLuint program, GLuint location, GLint *params);
```

These functions both return data from the uniform variable indicated by location in the program object indicated by program.

If the uniform variable pointed to by location is a scalar data type (such as float or bool) then only one value will be returned. If it's a vector type, multiple values will be returned: three for a vec3, 4 for a vec4, and so on. If it's a matrix, then the data is returned in column major order.

When it comes to arrays, if you wish to retrieve the data from every element, then you must call the function once for each index of the array you wish to read back. When it comes to structures, you need to call the function once for each element of the structure you are interested in reading back. As stated earlier, structures and arrays are not mapped to a single location or set of contiguous locations; instead they are broken down into their component parts, and each part has its own unique slot for data to be placed in.

Shader and Program Object Information Query Functions

There are times when you will need to query shader or program objects for information, to view logs when debugging a shader, for example, or to check the details of attribute or uniform usage. The OpenGL Shading Language API provides a number of functions to allow you to read back this information. I have referred to these functions many times throughout the chapter, and now it's time for you to learn about them.

Querying Shaders

The first function we'll look at is `glGetShaderiv()`, which allows you to get information from a shader object.

```
void glGetShaderiv(GLuint shader, GLenum pname, GLint *params);
```

When this function is called it queries the `shader` indicated by the parameter shader for information relating to `pname`, which must be one of the values in Table 4.17. If successfully retrieved, the data is copied into `params`.

Table 4.17 Shader Parameters

Token	Description
GL_SHADER_TYPE	`params` returns GL_VERTEX_SHADER if `shader` is a vertex-shader object, and GL_FRAGMENT_SHADER if `shader` is a fragment-shader object.
GL_DELETE_STATUS	`params` returns GL_TRUE if `shader` is currently flagged for deletion, and GL_FALSE otherwise.
GL_COMPILE_STATUS	`params` returns GL_TRUE if the last compile operation on shader was successful, and GL_FALSE otherwise.
GL_INFO_LOG_LENGTH	`params` returns the number of characters in the information log for `shader`, including the null termination character (i.e., the size of the character buffer required to store the information log). If `shader` has no information log, a value of 0 is returned.
GL_SHADER_SOURCE_LENGTH	`params` returns the length of the concatenation of the source strings that make up the shader source for the `shader`, including the null termination character. (i.e., the size of the character buffer required to store the shader source). If no source code exists, 0 is returned.

To query a shader object's info log length, you would do the following:

```
GLuint length;
glGetShaderiv(shaderobject, GL_INFO_LOG_LENGTH, &length);
```

Querying Programs

The function for querying information from program objects is similar to that for shader objects.

```
void glGetProgramiv(GLuint program, GLenum pname, GLint *params);
```

In this function, program is the handle to the program object you are retrieving information about, and pname is the parameter you are querying, which must be one of the values in Table 4.18. Upon completion, the value will be placed in params.

Table 4.18 Program Parameters

Token	Description
GL_DELETE_STATUS	params returns GL_TRUE if program is currently flagged for deletion, and GL_FALSE otherwise.
GL_LINK_STATUS	params returns GL_TRUE if the last link operation on program was successful, and GL_FALSE otherwise.
GL_VALIDATE_STATUS	params returns GL_TRUE if the last validation operation on program was successful, and GL_FALSE otherwise.
GL_INFO_LOG_LENGTH	params returns the number of characters in the information log for program, including the null termination character (i.e., the size of the character buffer required to store the information log). If program has no information log, a value of 0 is returned.
GL_ATTACHED_SHADERS	params returns the number of shader objects attached to program.
GL_ACTIVE_ATTRIBUTES	params returns the number of active attribute variables for program.
GL_ACTIVE_ATTRIBUTE_MAX_LENGTH	params returns the length of the longest active attribute name for program, including the null termination character (i.e., the size of the character buffer required to store the longest attribute name). If no active attributes exist, 0 is returned.
GL_ACTIVE_UNIFORMS	params returns the number of active uniform variables for program.
GL_ACTIVE_UNIFORM_MAX_LENGTH	params returns the length of the longest active uniform variable name for program, including the null termination character (i.e., the size of the character buffer required to store the longest uniform variable name). If no active uniform variables exist, 0 is returned.

For example, to retrieve the length of the longest uniform name, you would use the following:

```
GLint length;
glGetProgramiv(someprogram, GL_ACTIVE_UNIFORM_MAX_LENGTH, &length);
```

Provided the program someprogram has undergone a successful link operation, this will store the length of the longest active uniform name in length.

Retrieving Attached Shaders

There are times when, having attached a number of shader objects to a program object, you need to retrieve their handles. You can track this information yourself, but sometimes it's convenient to query this information from the program object.

```
void glGetAttachedShaders(GLuint program, GLsizei maxCount, GLsizei *count,
                          GLuint *shaders);
```

The program parameter indicates the program you wish to query, and maxCount is the maximum number of handles that can be held in shaders (i.e., the size of the array). Upon return, count will hold the actual number of handles that are returned. You can determine the total number of attached shaders in advance using glGetProgramiv() and allocate an array accordingly. If you don't need to know how many shader handles are written into shaders, then you can pass NULL to count instead.

Retrieving Information Logs

The final two OpenGL Shading Language API functions deal with the retrieval of the information log that is generated at compile and link times. This log can provide vital details when you're debugging shaders. Unfortunately, the format of the logs is implementation dependent, so relying on them for anything other than debugging reasons isn't practical.

```
void glGetProgramInfoLog(GLuint program, GLsizei maxLength, GLsizei *length,
                         GLchar *infoLog);
void glGetShaderInfoLog(GLuint shader, GLsizei maxLength, GLsizei *length,
                        GLchar *infoLog);
```

As you can see, the two functions are virtually identical, with the only difference being the type of object they query.

These functions copy the info log from the object identified in the first parameter into infoLog. The maxLength parameter indicates the size of this buffer, while length will be used to return how much data was actually written. If you don't care about the length, you can pass NULL for this parameter. The log is returned as a null terminated string. Again, if you want to determine the size of the log in advance, you can do so using glGetProgramiv() or glGetShaderiv().

To retrieve the info log for a shader object, you would do the following:

```
GLint loglength;
glGetShaderiv(someshader, GL_INFO_LOG_LENGTH, &loglength);
GLchar *infolog = new char[loglength];
GLint writtenlength;
glGetShaderInfoLog(someshader, loglength, &writtenlength, infolog);
```

Upon return, the info log for the shader `someshader` will have been copied into `infolog`, and the length of the log will be in `writtenlength`.

Retrieving Implementation Details

Finally, you can use the existing OpenGL glGet() APIs to retrieve information about the OpenGL Shading Language implementation. The values that can be queried are listed in Table 4.19.

Table 4.19 Values That Can Be Queried

Variable	Description
GL_MAX_VERTEX_ATTRIBS	Defines the number of active vertex attributes that are available. The minimum value allowed is 16.
GL_MAX_VERTEX_UNIFORM_COMPONENTS*	Defines the number of components of type "floating point" that are available for vertex shaders. The minimum value allowed is 512.
GL_MAX_VARYING_FLOATS*	Defines the number of floating-point variables available for varying values. The minimum value allowed is 32.
GL_MAX_VERTEX_TEXTURE_IMAGE_UNITS	Defines the number of hardware units that can be used to access texture data in a vertex shader. The minimum value allowed is 0.
GL_MAX_COMBINED_TEXTURE_IMAGE_UNITS	Defines the total number of hardware units that can be used to access texture data from the vertex and fragment shaders combined. The minimum value allowed is 2.
GL_MAX_TEXTURE_IMAGE_UNITS	Defines the number of hardware units that can be used to access texture data from the fragment shader. The minimum value allowed is 2.
GL_MAX_TEXTURE_COORDS	Defines the number of texture coordinate sets (gl_MultiTexCoord*n*) that are available. The minimum value allowed is 2.
GL_MAX_FRAGMENT_UNIFORM_COMPONENTS*	Defines the number of components of type "floating point" that are available for fragment shaders. The minimum allowed value is 64.

*Note: these are allocated in groups of vec4.

Using the OpenGL Shading Language

You now know everything you need to start writing OpenGL Shading Language shaders and including them in your own programs. In this last section, you'll see several examples of exactly that. But first, you'll be introduced to a couple of C++ classes provided in order to assist in working with shaders and programs.

Shader Management Classes

The classes in question will be used throughout the examples in this chapter and are used to make program and shader objects real C++ objects. They provide methods for working with the objects as well as some lifetime management and optimization functionality.

The two classes are named GLSLShader and GLSLProgram. GLSLShader classes are used to hold shaders, and they can then be attached to GLSLProgram objects so that you can link them together to form a valid OpenGL Shading Language program.

GLSLShader

The class GLSLShader has the simplest interface, so let's look at it first. GLSLShader has the following public methods:

```
GLSLShader(const std::string &filename, GLenum shaderType = GL_VERTEX_SHADER);
GLSLShader(GLenum shaderType = GL_VERTEX_SHADER );
~GLSLShader();
void compile();
bool isCompiled() const;
void getShaderLog(std::string &log) const;
void getShaderSource(std::string &shader) const;
void setShaderSource(std::string &code);
GLuint getHandle() const;
void getParameter(GLenum param, GLint *data) const;
```

The first two functions are used when the shader object is first constructed. The first form allows you to specify a file to read from and to specify the shader type. The second form just creates an empty shader object of the type specified (in both cases the default type is a vertex shader).

The third function is used when the object is deleted. When this occurs, it automatically asks the OpenGL implementation to delete the shader object.

With compile(), you can request that the shader object be compiled, and isCompiled() allows you to check to see if the compilation was successful. The details of any compilation errors will be available in the shader's log, which can be accessed using getShaderLog().

With `getShaderSource()` and `setShaderSource()`, you can retrieve the shader source and replace it with a different source as you wish. This can be useful when debugging your shaders, so you can read back, replace, and recompile them on the fly.

If for any reason you need the handle that this object manages, you can get it using `getHandle()`. You probably won't require access to this all that often, but it's a handy function to have.

Finally, `getParameter()` allows you to query the shader for information, as covered in the "Querying Shaders" section earlier.

GLSLProgram

The class `GLSLProgram` is a little more complex to explain, as it has a slightly larger interface to reflect the added functionality of program objects. The public functions are as follows:

```
GLSLProgram();
GLSLProgram(const std::string &shader,
             unsigned int shaderType=GL_VERTEX_SHADER_ARB);
GLSLProgram(const std::string &vertexShader, const std::string &fragmentShader);
~GLSLProgram();

void attach(GLSLShader &shader);
void attach(GLSLShader *shader);
void detach(GLSLShader &shader);
void detach(GLSLShader *shader);

void link();
void use() const;
void disable() const;

void sendUniform(const std::string &name, float x);
void sendUniform(const std::string &name, float x, float y);
void sendUniform(const std::string &name, float x, float y, float z);
void sendUniform(const std::string &name, float x, float y, float z, float w);
void sendUniform(const std::string &name, int x);
void sendUniform(const std::string &name, int x, int y);
void sendUniform(const std::string &name, int x, int y, int z);
void sendUniform(const std::string &name, int x, int y, int z, int w);
void sendUniform(const std::string &name, float *m, bool transp=false,
                 int size=4);

void sendUniform(GLuint location, float x);
void sendUniform(GLuint location, float x, float y);
```

```
void sendUniform(GLuint location, float x, float y, float z);
void sendUniform(GLuint location, float x, float y, float z, float w);
void sendUniform(GLuint location, int x);
void sendUniform(GLuint location, int x, int y);
void sendUniform(GLuint location, int x, int y, int z);
void sendUniform(GLuint location, int x, int y, int z, int w);
void sendUniform(GLuint location, float *m, bool transp=false, int size=4);

GLuint getUniformLocation(const std::string &name) const;
void setAttributeLocation(const std::string &name, GLuint location);
GLuint getAttributeLocation(const std::string &name) const;

void GetProgramLog(std::string &log) const;
GLuint getHandle() const;
void getParameter(GLenum param, GLint *data) const;
void validate() const;
bool IsValidProgram() const;
void getAttributeInfo(GLuint location, std::string &name, GLenum &type,
                      GLint &size) const;
void getUniformInfo(GLuint location, std::string &name, GLenum &datatype,
                    GLint &size) const;
void getAttachedShaders(std::vector<GLuint> &shaderhandles);
void getAttachedShaders(std::vector<GLSLShader> &shaders);
```

The first three functions are used when the GLSLProgram object is constructed. The first form creates an empty program and just generates a handle for it. The second and third forms are convenience functions that automatically load the files specified, compile them, and link the shaders ready for use. When programming simple shaders and examples, this form can be the easiest to use.

The fourth function, ~GLSLProgram(), is called when the GLSLProgram object is deleted. If you used either of the convenience constructors, the function will delete any shader objects attached and then ask the OpenGL implementation to delete the program object.

The next four functions allow you to attach or detach shaders from a program object. An important point here is that the GLSLProgram object doesn't take ownership of the GLSLShader objects passed; it just attaches them by handle and returns. So if you later delete the GLSLShader object you passed, it'll be lost (however, you can create another GLSLShader object containing the handle, as covered later).

The three functions after that control the state of the GLSLProgram object. The first links all attached shaders, the second installs the program as the active OpenGL Shading Language program, and the final one disables the program and returns control to the fixed-function pipeline.

Next there are a number of functions for setting uniform variables. The first group takes the name of a uniform, determines which slot the uniform is bound to, and then writes the data to it. Since constantly querying a program object for uniform locations is a relatively slow process, these functions use a caching system, so you only incur the cost the first time or after a relink. If the uniform name can't be found, then an exception of std::logic_error() is thrown with the details of which uniform couldn't be found.

The next block of uniform functions are virtually the same, but they take the slot location rather than the name. When using these functions, it is up to you to ensure the slot numbers are correct. These functions are included to allow for direct setting of uniform locations without having to pass a name around all the time.

Because it returns the location of a uniform for the program object (or -1 if it can't be found), getUniformLocation() relates directly to the above. Working as a pair, setAttributeLocation() and getAttributeLocation() allow you to set and retrieve the location of attributes associated with the program. Remember that locations that are set do not take effect until the next link operation is performed.

The functions getProgramLog(), getHandle(), and getParameter() work in the same way as their GLSLShader counterparts.

The next two functions are related to validating the program. You use validate() to ask the OpenGL implementation to validate the shader, as described in the "Program Validation" section. The function IsValidProgram() returns a Boolean value indicating whether the program is valid or not.

The following two functions retrieve information about attribute or uniform values and return the information in the supplied variables.

The final functions allow you to discover which shaders are attached to the program. Both of these functions require an std::vector as a parameter to return the information in. The first version only returns the handles of the shader objects. The second returns a vector of GLSLShader objects that wrap the handles.

With that in mind, let's get into some examples of how you can use these shaders yourself. We'll start simple so you can get the hang of using them before moving on to some more complex examples that you might find useful when writing games. Keep in mind when looking at these examples that we assume that any textures have been successfully loaded; we are concentrating here only on the OpenGL Shading Language aspect of the code.

Texturing

One of the simplest shaders is one that applies a texture to a primitive, so that's where we are going to start. From there you'll learn how to adjust the texture data once you've read it into the shader.

Example 1: Simple Texturing

Let's start with the vertex shader. In this instance it's a very simple shader as it only trans-forms the vertex into clip space and passes the texture coordinates down to the fragment shader using the built-in varying variables.

```
// A simple vertex shader
#version 110
void main()
{
  gl_TexCoord[0] = gl_MultiTexCoord0;
  gl_Position = ftransform();
}
```

The first line defines the main() function for the shader, which is where execution begins. The third line sets the built-in varying variable gl_TexCoord[0] to the value passed in via the OpenGL API function glTexCoord(). Finally, the fourth line of the shader performs the transformation of the vertex position from object coordinates to clip coordinates. This line could also be written as

```
gl_Position = gl_ModelViewProjectionMatrix * gl_Vertex;
```

However, the usage of ftransform() allows you to mix shaders with the fixed-function pipeline, thus I prefer to use it where I can.

Next we need a fragment shader to sample the texture and apply the color to the fragment that is currently being processed.

```
// A simple fragment shader
#version 110
uniform sampler2D tex;

void main()
{
  gl_FragColor = texture2D(tex, gl_TexCoord[0].st);
}
```

Again, this is a very simple shader. The first line after the comment and version declares the sampler we will be using to retrieve the texture data. As with the vertex shader, a main() function is defined to control where execution begins. The only line of code sets the out-put variable, gl_FragColor, to the result of the texture lookup performed on the sampler tex using the texture coordinates held in the built-in varying variable gl_TexCoord[0]. Note how swizzling is used to select only the s and t components of the vector.

Remember that since gl_TexCoord[0] is a varying variable, the value it holds is the result of an interpolation across the face of the polygon in question. This ensures that the correct location in the texture is sampled with respect to the per-vertex texture coordinates.

Now that you have your shaders, the next step is to use them in a program. To start with, you have to load the shaders into the program, compile them, attach them to a program object, and link them. Thanks to the shader classes introduced earlier, this is a breeze.

```
GLSLShader simplevert("simple.vs");
GLSLShader simplefrag("simple.fs", GL_FRAGMENT_SHADER);
GLSLProgram simpleprog;
simpleprog.attach(simplevert);
simpleprog.attach(simplefrag);
simpleprog.link();
```

The code above loads in the two specified shader files from the current working directory and compiles them as part of the loading process. The shaders are then attached to a program object that is linked to produce the final executable.

Now that we have the program linked together, we need to process some geometry so that the program has something to run on. For this example we'll use a simple textured quad.

```
void GLDrawScene()
{
  // Clear the screen and the depth buffer
  glClear(GL_COLOR_BUFFER_BIT | GL_DEPTH_BUFFER_BIT);
  // Reset The View
  glLoadIdentity();
  simpleprog.use();
  glActiveTexture(GL_TEXTURE0);
  glBindTexture(GL_TEXTURE_2D, tex);
  simpleprog.sendUniform("tex", 0);
  // Now we draw the quad
  glBegin(GL_QUADS);
  glTexCoord2f(0.0f, 1.0f); glVertex3f(-1.0f, 1.0f, -5.0f); // top left
  glTexCoord2f(0.0f, 0.0f); glVertex3f(1.0f, 1.0, -5.0f);   // top right
  glTexCoord2f(1.0f, 0.0f); glVertex3f(1.0, -1.0, -5.0f);   // bottom right
  glTexCoord2f(1.0f, 1.0f); glVertex3f(-1.0, -1.0f, -5.0f); // bottom left
  glEnd();
  simpleprog.disable();
}
```

The GLSLProgram class does hide a number of implementation details from you, but since it increases code clarity, that is certainly a good thing.

So how does this code connect to the vertex and fragment shaders? First we have to ensure the texture we wish to sample is loaded into the correct texture unit. This is achieved via the standard OpenGL multitexturing functions, which you should be familiar with. The main difference is that you don't have to enable texturing on the texture unit, just activate it and bind the texture to it. After that you have to tell the fragment shader which texture sampler to use. If you recall, we declared a uniform variable called `tex` in the fragment shader. It is into this variable we send the number of the texture *unit* to sample from. Unit is emphasized because this is an important concept that can confuse people. You don't pass the texture object handle to GLSL, instead you pass the texture unit that the texture is bound to.

That takes care of the uniform data, so the next step is sending the primitive data to your shaders. This example makes use of the built-in attribute variables, so the values passed via `glTexCoord2f()` end up in the variable `gl_MultiTexCoord0` in the vertex shader. As we saw earlier, this value is then copied into varying variable `gl_TexCoord[0]` which is interpolated across the quad. The values passed in via `glVertex3f()` are transformed by the `ftransform()` function in the vertex shader, and these transformed locations are stored as the output position for the primitive in clip space.

In the fragment shader, the interpolated value in `gl_MultiTexCoord0` is read and used to sample the texture at the right point. This value in this case will be somewhere between (0, 0) and (1, 1), depending on where on the primitive the fragment is. This mode of texturing is equivalent to the OpenGL `GL_REPLACE` mode.

The results of this example are shown in Figure 4.1

Figure 4.1 A single texture on a quad.

Example 2: Multitexturing

Applying one texture to a primitive is good as a building block, but for modern games it's very primitive, so for the next step we'll introduce multitexturing GLSL style.

The first version will use the same vertex program as the first example, as we'll only be supplying one set of texture coordinates. The fragment program is a little different, however.

```
// A simple multitexturing fragment shader
#version 110
uniform sampler2D tex;
uniform sampler2D tex2;
void main()
{
  vec4 texcolor = texture2D(tex, gl_TexCoord[0].st);
  vec4 tex2color = texture2D(tex2, gl_TexCoord[0].st);

  gl_FragColor = texcolor + tex2color;
}
```

As you can see, this program is a little longer than before. This time we are sampling from two texture samplers using the same texture coordinates on both samplers. The resulting colors are stored in two variables and then added together to provide the final output color. It's easy to vary the output this shader gives just by changing the way the two colors are combined.

The program to use this shader is very much like the first one, with only minor differences.

```
GLSLShader simplevert("simple.vs");
GLSLShader simpleMTfrag("simpleMT.fs", GL_FRAGMENT_SHADER);
GLSLProgram simpleprog;
simpleprog.attach(simplevert);
simpleprog.attach(simpleMTfrag);
simpleprog.link();
```

First, notice that the original "simple.vs" shader from the previous example is being reused. This is a very basic example of the reusability of shaders. Apart from the name of the fragment shader and the shader file loaded in, everything here is the same as before, so let's look at how we use this slightly different fragment shader in the program.

```
void GLDrawScene()
{
  // Clear the screen and the depth buffer
  glClear(GL_COLOR_BUFFER_BIT | GL_DEPTH_BUFFER_BIT);
  // Reset The View
  glLoadIdentity();
  simpleprog.use();
  glActiveTexture(GL_TEXTURE0);
  glBindTexture(GL_TEXTURE_2D, tex);
```

```
glActiveTexture(GL_TEXTURE1);
glBindTexture(GL_TEXTURE_2D, tex2);
simpleprog.sendUniform("tex", 0);
simpleprog.sendUniform("tex2", 1);
// Now we draw the quad
glBegin(GL_QUADS);
glTexCoord2f(0.0f, 1.0f); glVertex3f(-1.0f, 1.0f, -5.0f); // top left
glTexCoord2f(0.0f, 0.0f); glVertex3f(1.0f, 1.0, -5.0f);   // top right
glTexCoord2f(1.0f, 0.0f); glVertex3f(1.0, -1.0, -5.0f);   // bottom right
glTexCoord2f(1.0f, 1.0f); glVertex3f(-1.0, -1.0f, -5.0f); // bottom left
glEnd();
simpleprog.disable();
}
```

This program is very much like the last. The additions are shown in bold type and consist of binding the second texture to texture unit one and telling the GLSL program where to sample from. The rest of the data works as before, with the texture coordinates and the vertex coordinates being passed via built-in variables. Figure 4.2 shows the results of this example.

Figure 4.2 A simple multitexturing example.

Example 3: Texture Interpolation, Method 1

A common operation when multitexturing is to perform interpolation between two or more textures based on some other input variable, so the next three examples will build on the multitexturing example from before and demonstrate a simple two-texture interpolation. The first will use a per-primitive value passed as a uniform, the second will operate per vertex using the built-in OpenGL color functions, and the third will use custom per-vertex attributes and varying variables.

For the first example there is again nothing to change for the vertex program. The fragment program we used earlier needs only a few small changes.

```
// A linearly interpolating multitexturing fragment shader
#version 110
uniform sampler2D tex;
uniform sampler2D tex2;
uniform float alpha;
void main()
{
  vec4 texcolor = texture2D(tex,gl_TexCoord[0].st);
  vec4 tex2color = texture2D(tex2,gl_TexCoord[0].st);

  gl_FragColor = texcolor * alpha + tex2color * (1.0 - alpha);
}
```

The first thing to note here is the addition of an alpha uniform. This is used to control how much of each texture is used in the interpolation. The other change is from a simple addition of the colors to a linear interpolation between the two, based on the value of alpha (this is the same as OpenGL's texture combiner GL_INTERPOLATE mode).

As before, we have to load and bind the shaders to a program.

```
GLSLShader simplevert("simple.vs");
GLSLShader simpleMTfrag("simpleMTinterpolate.fs", GL_FRAGMENT_SHADER);
GLSLProgram simpleprog;
simpleprog.attach(simplevert);
simpleprog.attach(simpleMTfrag);
simpleprog.link();
```

Finally, the rendering loop has to be adjusted to pass the alpha value we wish to use to the shader before it is executed. As before, changes are shown in bold type.

```
void GLDrawScene()
{
  // Clear the screen and the depth buffer
  glClear(GL_COLOR_BUFFER_BIT | GL_DEPTH_BUFFER_BIT);
  // Reset The View
  glLoadIdentity();
  simpleprog.use();
  glActiveTexture(GL_TEXTURE0);
```

```
glBindTexture(GL_TEXTURE_2D, tex);
glActiveTexture(GL_TEXTURE1);
glBindTexture(GL_TEXTURE_2D, tex2);
simpleprog.sendUniform("tex", 0);
simpleprog.sendUniform("tex2", 1);
simpleprog.sendUniform("alpha", 0.5f);
// Now we draw the quad
glBegin(GL_QUADS);
glTexCoord2f(0.0f, 1.0f); glVertex3f(-1.0f, 1.0f, -5.0f); // top left
glTexCoord2f(0.0f, 0.0f); glVertex3f(1.0f, 1.0, -5.0f);   // top right
glTexCoord2f(1.0f, 0.0f); glVertex3f(1.0, -1.0, -5.0f);   // bottom right
glTexCoord2f(1.0f, 1.0f); glVertex3f(-1.0, -1.0f, -5.0f); // bottom left
glEnd();
simpleprog.disable();
}
```

The only change from "simpleMT.fs" is the addition of the line to set the alpha value to 0.5, which means you will see the textures combined with 50 percent of each texture. The output of this shader can be seen in Figure 4.3.

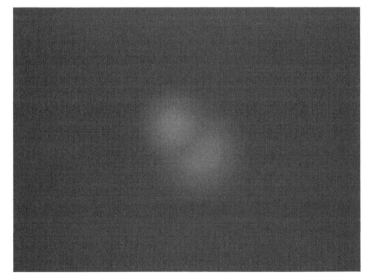

Figure 4.3 A uniform alpha-based texture interpolation.

Example 4: Texture Interpolation, Method 2

The next method uses OpenGL's built-in variables to pass alpha values in. This allows you to produce a smooth change across the primitive from one texture to another by setting the alpha value of the OpenGL per-vertex color accordingly. To archive this we first have to adjust our vertex shader so that it passes the per-vertex color information on to be interpolated and sent to the fragment shader.

```
// A simple vertex shader that passes color information
#version 110
void main()
{
  gl_TexCoord[0] = gl_MultiTexCoord0;
  gl_FrontColor = gl_Color;
  gl_Position = ftransform();
}
```

We are only setting the front color since in this simple example, we shouldn't see any back-facing polygons anyway. Depending on your scene you might want to deal with back-facing polygons as well.

Next up is the fragment shader. This will be pretty much the same as the previous example, but instead of getting our alpha value from a uniform we will be using the built-in color varying.

```
// A linearly interpolating multitexturing fragment shader
#version 110
uniform sampler2D tex;
uniform sampler2D tex2;
void main()
{
  vec4 texcolor = texture2D(tex, gl_TexCoord[0].st);
  vec4 tex2color = texture2D(tex2, gl_TexCoord[0].st);

  gl_FragColor = texcolor * gl_Color.a + tex2color * (1.0 - gl_Color.a);
}
```

Notice how the field selector operator is used to retrieve only the alpha value from the color variable. The remaining three values could be used to color the output somehow, or they could also be used to interpolate more textures into the mix. For example, if you had three textures, you could use three values to select a certain percentage of each texture to contribute to the final output color as follows:

```
gl_FragColor = texcolor * gl_Color.r + tex2color * gl_Color.g +
                  tex3color * gl_Color.b;
As before, we have to load, compile, and link the shaders.
GLSLShader vert("vertexcolorMTinterpolate.vs");
GLSLShader frag("vertexcolorMTinterpolate.fs", GL_FRAGMENT_SHADER);
GLSLProgram prog;
```

```
prog.attach(vert);
prog.attach(frag);
prog.link();
```

Finally, some changes need to be made to the rendering function to supply the color information to the vertex shader.

```
void GLDrawScene()
{
  // Clear the screen and the depth buffer
  glClear(GL_COLOR_BUFFER_BIT | GL_DEPTH_BUFFER_BIT);
  // Reset The View
  glLoadIdentity();
  prog.use();
  glActiveTexture(GL_TEXTURE0);
  glBindTexture(GL_TEXTURE_2D, tex);
  glActiveTexture(GL_TEXTURE1);
  glBindTexture(GL_TEXTURE_2D, tex2);
  prog.sendUniform("tex", 0);
  prog.sendUniform("tex2", 1);
  // Now we draw the quad
  glBegin(GL_QUADS);
  glColor4f(0.0f, 0.0f, 0.0f, 1.0f);
  glTexCoord2f(0.0f, 1.0f); glVertex3f(-1.0f, 1.0f, -5.0f); // top left
  glColor4f(0.0f, 0.0f, 0.0f, 0.0f);
  glTexCoord2f(0.0f, 0.0f); glVertex3f(1.0f, 1.0, -5.0f);   // top right
  glColor4f(0.0f, 0.0f, 0.0f, 0.0f);
  glTexCoord2f(1.0f, 0.0f); glVertex3f(1.0, -1.0, -5.0f);   // bottom right
  glColor4f(0.0f, 0.0f, 0.0f, 1.0f);
  glTexCoord2f(1.0f, 1.0f); glVertex3f(-1.0, -1.0f, -5.0f); // bottom left
  glEnd();
  prog.disable();
}
```

The changes this time are again minor. We've removed the setting of the `alpha` uniform and instead added four calls to `glColor4f()` to set the alpha value (in this example, the rest of the color components are set to 0, but they can be set to any valid value without changing the output). The output from this program can be seen in Figure 4.4.

Figure 4.4 A glColor()-based alpha texture interpolation.

Example 5: Texture Interpolation, Method 3

The final example uses a custom attribute to send the alpha value to the vertex shader and thus the fragment shader. As before, we need to make a slight change to the vertex shader to allow this to happen.

```
// A simple vertex shader that passes color information
// using a custom attribute and varying variable
#version 110
attribute float alpha;
varying float out_alpha;
void main()
{
  gl_TexCoord[0] = gl_MultiTexCoord0;
  out_alpha = alpha;
  gl_Position = ftransform();
}
```

Like the example using the built-in variables, this vertex shader passes the alpha value through to be interpolated across the polygon and fed to the fragment shader.

The fragment shader is similar to what it was before. However, instead of built-in varying variables, the custom one is used.

```
// A linearly interpolating multitexturing fragment shader
#version 110
uniform sampler2D tex;
```

```
uniform sampler2D tex2;
varying float out_alpha;
void main()
{
  vec4 texcolor = texture2D(tex,gl_TexCoord[0].st);
  vec4 tex2color = texture2D(tex2,gl_TexCoord[0].st);

  gl_FragColor = texcolor * out_alpha + tex2color * (1.0 - out_alpha);
}
```

Now that the shaders have been updated, the next step is to load, compile, and link them. Since we are using a custom attribute, we have to make a choice about how we are going to access it. We can either let the linker decide on a location for it, or we can specify one ourselves. In this case we will be using the default linker-assigned location as there is no good reason not to.

```
GLSLShader vert("customattribMTinterpolate.vs");
GLSLShader frag("customattribMTinterpolate.fs", GL_FRAGMENT_SHADER);
GLSLProgram prog;
prog.attach(vert);
prog.attach(frag);
prog.link();
GLuint alphaloc = prog.getAttributeLocation("alpha");
```

The only change here from before is the additional line to retrieve the location of the alpha attribute from the shader program for later use in the rendering stage.

```
void GLDrawScene()
{
  // Clear the screen and the depth buffer
  glClear(GL_COLOR_BUFFER_BIT | GL_DEPTH_BUFFER_BIT);
  // Reset The View
  glLoadIdentity();
  prog.use();
  glActiveTexture(GL_TEXTURE0);
  glBindTexture(GL_TEXTURE_2D, tex);
  glActiveTexture(GL_TEXTURE1);
  glBindTexture(GL_TEXTURE_2D, tex2);
  prog.sendUniform("tex", 0);
  prog.sendUniform("tex2", 1);
  // Now we draw the quad
  glBegin(GL_QUADS);
  glVertexAttrib1f(alphaloc, 1.0f);
  glTexCoord2f(0.0f, 1.0f); glVertex3f(-1.0f, 1.0f, -5.0f);  // top left
```

```
glVertexAttrib1f(alphaloc, 1.0f);
glTexCoord2f(0.0f, 0.0f); glVertex3f(1.0f, 1.0, -5.0f);    // top right
glVertexAttrib1f(alphaloc, 0.0f);
glTexCoord2f(1.0f, 0.0f); glVertex3f(1.0, -1.0, -5.0f);    // bottom right
glVertexAttrib1f(alphaloc, 0.0f);
glTexCoord2f(1.0f, 1.0f); glVertex3f(-1.0, -1.0f, -5.0f);  // bottom left
glEnd();
prog.disable();
}
```

Once more, we only have a small change to the rendering loop, this time the addition of a glVertexAttrib1f() call to set the value at the location held in alphaloc so that we can read from it in the vertex shader and pass it down to the fragment shader. Figure 4.5 shows the output from this example.

Figure 4.5 A custom-attribute-based texture interpolation.

These few examples are just the start of the effects you can create with texturing. If you want to produce effects like those allowed by OpenGL standard multitexturing, it is a simple matter to map the formulas used to GLSL code.

Lighting and Fog

Texturing is one of the most important elements of creating a realistic world, but by itself it can lead to a flat look without depth cueing from changes in light, which is where the following examples come in. While the examples won't form a complex lighting system (as that is outside of the scope of this chapter) they should give you some ideas about how lighting can be achieved. This section will also touch on fog, as this is an important visual cue when it comes to helping the user judge distances in the world.

The examples here are just the start of what you can achieve and are very primitive lighting systems that don't take into account ambient light or the material properties of the object the light is striking. However, as lighting can take up a whole book on its own, we will stick with some simple examples to give you an idea of how it's done.

Example 6: Vertex Lighting

The first example is a simple vertex lighting system, where the color value is calculated per vertex and then interpolated between vertices to light a polygon. The majority of the work for this shader is done in the vertex shader, which is defined as follows:

```
#version 110
const float specAmount = 0.1;
const float diffuseAmount = 1.0 - specAmount;

void main(void)
{
  vec4 ecPos = vec3(gl_ModelViewMatrix * gl_Vertex);
  vec3 norm = normalize(gl_NormalMatrix * gl_Normal);
  vec3 lightVec = vec3(normalize(gl_LightSource[0].position - ecPos));
  vec3 reflectVec = reflect(-lightVec, norm);
  vec3 viewVec = vec3(normalize(-ecPos));

  float specValue = clamp(dot(reflectVec, viewVec), 0.0, 1.0);
  specValue = pow(specValue, 6.0);

  gl_FrontColor =
    (gl_LightSource[0].diffuse * diffuseAmount * max(dot(lightVec,norm), 0.0)) +
    (gl_LightSource[0].specular * specAmount * specValue);

  gl_Position = ftransform();
}
```

This vertex shader does quite a bit more work than the examples you've seen so far, so let's walk through it. The two constants at the top define how much the diffuse and specular color components are going to contribute to the final color. After that we hit the main shader, and this is where the real work begins.

Because lighting calculations are done in eye coordinates, the first thing we need to do is transform the vertex position from world space to eye space. After that we also need to transform the normal by the normal matrix (which is just the inverse transpose of the top left 3×3 of the modelview matrix) so that it is transformed correctly into eye space.

After that we need to find a few vectors for the lighting equations later on. These are the vector from the vertex position in eye space to the light's location, the reflection vector about the vertex's normal, and the vector from the camera to the vertex. All of these vectors are represented in eye coordinates.

After the required amount of specular highlighting is calculated, the pow() function allows you to increase or decrease the size of the specular highlight (6.0 is used in the example, but this will vary based on the material).

Finally, the output color at this vertex is determined by adding together the diffuse color of the light and the specular color of the light (using the built-in light variables to give us the diffuse and specular color values) and writing to the built-in gl_FrontColor variable so it can be interpolated across the primitive. The final operation to be performed is the transformation of the vertex position from object space to clip space.

The fragment program for this particular form of lighting is pretty simple.

```
#version 110
void main(void)
{
    gl_FragColor = vec4(gl_Color.rgb, 1.0);
}
```

This is where we output the interpolated color value to the screen. Note that we force the alpha value to 1.0 since gl_FragColor requires a four-component vector, and we're not doing anything interesting with alpha anyway.

The next step is to load, compile, and link the shaders as usual.

```
GLSLShader vert("vertexlighting.vs");
GLSLShader frag("vertexlighting.fs", GL_FRAGMENT_SHADER);
GLSLProgram prog;
prog.attach(vert);
prog.attach(frag);
prog.link();
```

Next we need a scene to light. We are going to progress slightly from the previous examples' fixed quad and move on to the ever popular spinning cube, which should give us a decent idea about how the lighting changes as the object rotates. Because this code is a bit longer than the previous examples, I won't include it all here. Instead you'll want to look at the source code (available on the book's website) to see how it all works.

However, a snippet of the cube-drawing code follows.

```
// Front Face
glNormal3f( 0.0f, 0.0f, 1.0f);
glVertex3f(-1.0f, -1.0f, 1.0f);
glVertex3f( 1.0f, -1.0f, 1.0f);
glVertex3f( 1.0f, 1.0f, 1.0f);
glVertex3f(-1.0f, 1.0f, 1.0f);
```

As you can see, we only supply face normals. This is because all the normals will be pointing in the same direction for each face on the cube, thus constantly resupplying them would be redundant. The values passed via glNormal3f() are the ones we are working with when we use gl_Normal in the vertex shader.

The only other details to set up are those for the light. Since we don't have any attenuation in our lighting calculations, we are restricted to using directional lights as our light source. Because we used the OpenGL Shading Language's built-in variables to read the light values, we will be using OpenGL's built-in functions to set up and position the light source as follows:

```
void SetUpLighting()
{
  // Set up lighting
  GLfloat lightpos[] = { 1.0f, 1.0f, 1.0f, 0.0f};
  glLightfv(GL_LIGHT0, GL_POSITION, lightpos);
  GLfloat lightcolor[] = {1.0f, 0.0f, 0.0f, 1.0f};
  glLightfv(GL_LIGHT0, GL_DIFFUSE, lightcolor);
  GLfloat lightspeccolor[] = {1.0f, 1.0f, 1.0f, 1.0f};
  glLightfv(GL_LIGHT0, GL_SPECULAR, lightspeccolor);
}
```

As you can see, we have specified the light's diffuse and specular colors, as these are the ones read by the vertex shader. The camera and light source won't be moving, so we have also specified their positions.

The final rendering code is as follows:

```
void GLDrawScene()
{
  // Clear the screen and the depth buffer
  glClear(GL_COLOR_BUFFER_BIT | GL_DEPTH_BUFFER_BIT);
  // Reset The View
  glLoadIdentity();
  prog.use();
  DrawCube(xrot, yrot);
  prog.disable();
```

```
  xrot+=xspeed;
  yrot+=yspeed;
}
```

The results of this example are shown in Figure 4.6. While fast, the lighting quality is fairly poor. In the next example we are going to improve the lighting slightly by changing from per-vertex to per-fragment lighting, which is one of the major uses of shaders.

Figure 4.6 A simple vertex lighting example.

Example 7: Fragment Lighting

A simple per-fragment lighting system isn't that different from the per-vertex code you saw in the previous example. The main change is that the light values are calculated every fragment instead of every vertex. One of the things you have to watch with per-fragment shaders is the amount of work you are doing per fragment, as this can significantly slow down your rendering. The trick is to balance it with the vertex shader, so that the vertex shader does any work that only needs to be done per vertex, leaving the remainder of the work to the fragment shader.

As before, the first thing we need to do is produce a vertex shader. For this example we are going to calculate the various vectors we'll need and pass them on as varying variables. This allows us to perform some reasonably costly work in the vertex shader and use the results in the fragment shader.

```
#version 110
varying vec3 normal;
varying vec3 lightVec;
varying vec3 viewVec;
```

```
void main(void)
{
  vec4 ecPos = gl_ModelViewMatrix * gl_Vertex;
  normal = normalize(gl_NormalMatrix * gl_Normal);
  lightVec = vec3(normalize(gl_LightSource[0].position - ecPos));
  viewVec = vec3(normalize(-ecPos));

  gl_Position = ftransform();
}
```

As you can see, shifting of lighting from the vertex shader to the fragment shader has made the vertex shader a little less complex. Instead of calculating the vertex color, we only determine the normal, light vector, and view vector for later use by the fragment shader, which follows:

```
#version 110
varying vec3 normal;
varying vec3 lightVec;
varying vec3 viewVec;

void main(void)
{
  vec3 nnormal = normalize(normal);
  vec3 nlightVec = normalize(lightVec);
  vec3 nviewVec = normalize(viewVec);
  vec3 reflectVec = reflect(-nlightVec, nnormal);

  float specValue = clamp(dot(reflectVec,nviewVec),0.0,1.0);
  specValue = pow(specValue, 6.0);

  gl_FragColor = vec4(gl_LightSource[0].diffuse * diffuseAmount *
                      max(dot(nlightVec,nnormal),0.0)) +
                  (gl_LightSource[0].specular * specAmount * specValue).rgb,1.0);
}
```

As you can see, the fragment shader is a little more complex than it was before, but it's using the same basic lighting equation as the vertex shader in the previous example. The difference is that the color values are now being calculated per fragment, which can increase the quality of the output when compared to the per-vertex solution, particularly when it comes to specular highlights. Note that the incoming varying variables have been normalized at the start of the shader. This is because the interpolation process can cause these vectors to become non-unit length.

These two shaders can be used with the same basic program as before as they require the same rendering code and setup. The only difference is the shaders which are loaded.

```
GLSLShader vert("vertexandfragmentlighting.vs");
GLSLShader frag("vertexandfragmentlighting.fs", GL_FRAGMENT_SHADER);
GLSLProgram prog;
prog.attach(vert);
prog.attach(frag);
prog.link();
```

Figure 4.7 shows the output of this shader.

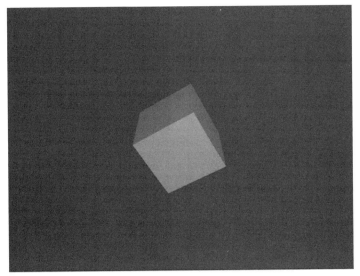

Figure 4.7 A simple per-fragment lighting example.

This simple lighting system can be further improved by doing practically all the work in the fragment shader. This will give much better results (within the limits of this lighting equation) but will also put more of a burden on the fragment-shader stage of the pipeline. However, as this involves a couple of slightly more advanced concepts, it is beyond the scope of this chapter. The sections on bump mapping in Chapter 5, "Advanced Texturing," will further expand on the concepts introduced here.

Example 8: Fog

As mentioned at the start of this section, while lighting is important for showing depth information in a scene, applying fog also helps give a sense of depth and distance.

To give you an idea of how to use fog in your own shaders we'll recreate the three built-in OpenGL fog modes (i.e., linear and the two exponential methods).

When using fog, you need to know how much fog to apply to a given vertex or fragment. There are two general ways to determine this. The first is using the built-in vertex attribute gl_FogCoord to access application-supplied values. The second is to take the absolute value of the depth of the vertex's position in eye space.

The interaction with OpenGL's built-in fog system occurs through glFog(). The type of fog selected adjusts the values, which are precalculated for you. These are covered as we discuss each method of fogging.

The simplest method of producing fog is to use the linear fog system, which is selected by using the GL_LINEAR constant. The fog factor is calculated as follows:

```
fog = (fog_end - z) / (fog_end - fog_start)
```

The fog's start and end points are specified via glFog(). When this fog function is in use, the divisor part of the equation can be precalculated as it doesn't depend on any per-vertex or per-fragment results. So the value 1.0/(fog_end – fog_start) is placed in the built-in variable gl_Fog.scale. This can then be used to calculate the fog value as shown in the vertex shader below.

```
#version 110
uniform bool fogCoordsPresent;
varying float fogValue;
void main(void)
{
  if(fogCoordsPresent)
    gl_FogFragCoord = gl_FogCoord;
  else
  {
    vec4 ecPos = gl_ModelViewMatrix * gl_Vertex;
    gl_FogFragCoord = abs(ecPos.z);
  }

  fogValue = (gl_Fog.end - gl_FogFragCoord) * gl_Fog.scale;
  fogValue = clamp(fogValue, 0.0, 1.0);

  gl_FrontColor = gl_Color;
  gl_Position = ftransform();
}
```

You'll notice that fogValue is clamped to the [0.0, 1.0] range, which OpenGL requires.

The two exponential fog functions have similar equations and produce results that are more realistic. Either of the following two equations could be dropped into the shader above to change the fog's effect.

```
// GL_EXP fog : fog value = e^-(density dot z)
fogValue = exp2(-gl_Fog.density * gl_FogFragCood * (1.0/log(2.0)));
// GL_EXP2 fog : fog value = e^(-(density dot z)^2)
fogValue = exp2(-gl_Fog.density * gl_Fog.density * gl_FogFragCood *
                gl_FogFragCood * (1.0/log(2.0)));
```

Both of these functions can easily be sped up with two optimizations. The first is to replace `1.0/log(2.0)` with:

```
const float LOG2E = 1.442695
```

The second is to replace `-gl_Fog.density * LOG2E` and `-gl_Fog.density * gl_Fog.density * LOG2E` with a user-defined uniform, since the fog density won't change per vertex.

To use the above shader in a program you would need a fragment shader to apply the fogging factor to the output color. A simple example of this would be

```
#version 110
varying float fogValue;
void main(void)
{
  gl_FragColor = mix(vec4(gl_Fog.color), gl_Color, fogValue);
}
```

This shader blends between the supplied interpolated color and the fog color using `fogValue` as the blend factor. As with lighting, it's possible to perform the entire fog calculation on a per-fragment basis for improved quality. However, unless you have large polygons that cover a large span in the z direction, the quality gained by this approach is generally not worth the expense. The output from this example is shown in Figure 4.8.

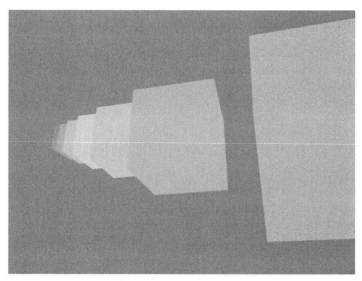

Figure 4.8 A simple fog example.

Using Multiple Render Targets

Earlier in the chapter I mentioned that it is possible to output to multiple color buffers at once. This section will cover how to do exactly that.

extension

Extension name: ARB_draw_buffers
Name string: GL_ARB_draw_buffers
Promoted to core: OpenGL 2.0
Function names: glDrawBuffersARB
Tokens: GL_MAX_DRAW_BUFFERS_ARB, GL_DRAW_BUFFERn_ARB

Unlike the previous examples, this one requires two stages. The first stage draws the output to a number of color buffers, and the second draws a screen-aligned quad using the output of the other drawing operations as textures.

For this example, we will use a new test scene. Instead of a single spinning cube, we'll now have eight of them. This example also uses a framebuffer object (FBO) manager class for handling the render-to-texture operations. FBOs were covered in Chapter 1, and render-to-texture will be covered in greater detail in Chapter 5.

We will start by defining a simple vertex shader. This one simply does the transformation of the vertex position and passes down a set of texture coordinates and the vertex color.

```
#version 110
void main(void)
{
  gl_Position = ftransform();
  gl_TexCoord[0] = gl_MultiTexCoord0;
  gl_FrontColor = gl_Color;
}
```

The simple nature of this shader allows us to use it for both the fragment shaders we'll be producing.

The first fragment shader writes to multiple color buffers. While there are many effects you could produce by writing to multiple color buffers, we are just going to split the output so that each color channel is drawn to a separate render-target..

```
#version 110
#extension GL_ARB_draw_buffers : require
uniform sampler2D tex;
void main(void)
{
  vec4 color = texture2D(tex, gl_TexCoord[0].st);

  gl_FragData[0] = vec4(color.r, 0.0, 0.0, 1.0);
  gl_FragData[1] = vec4(color.g, 0.0, 0.0, 1.0);
  gl_FragData[2] = vec4(color.b, 0.0, 0.0, 1.0);
}
```

The last three lines of the shader are the important ones in this operation. They take the color we read from the texture and send one component to each of the color buffers. You should also note the inclusion of the #extension line. This is required because while gl_FragData[] is built into the language, the ability to write to different color buffers at the same time is an extension to the OpenGL Shading Language, so you must request that it be activated to use it.

The second fragment shader is a little more complex. We are going to read back the colors and then, depending on the values they store, adjust the output colors.

```
#version 110
const vec3 lumCoeff = vec3(0.2125, 0.7154, 0.0721);
uniform sampler2D rsrc;
uniform sampler2D gsrc;
uniform sampler2D bsrc;

void main()
{
```

```
    float basered = texture2D(rsrc, gl_TexCoord[0].st).r;

    if(basered > 0.7)
        gl_FragColor = vec4(1.0, 0.0, 0.0, 1.0);
    else
    {
        float basegreen = texture2D(gsrc,gl_TexCoord[0].st).r;
        float baseblue = texture2D(bsrc,gl_TexCoord[0].st).r;
        float color = dot(vec3(basered,basegreen,baseblue),lumCoeff);
        if(color > 0.5)
            gl_FragColor = vec4(1.0,1.0,1.0,1.0);
        else
        {
            if(color  < 0.2)
                gl_FragColor = vec4(0.2,0.2,0.2,1.0);
            else
                gl_FragColor = vec4(vec3(color),1.0);
        }
    }
}
```

This fragment shader is the biggest one you've seen so far. It demonstrates a few functions that were covered in the language introduction but haven't been mentioned since, so let's take a look at this in detail.

First of all, the constant vector lumCoeff is defined. This is used to convert a RGB color into its luminance value, which is a single float. Next, the three samplers are all defined to point to the textures we rendered to in the previous shader.

In the shader itself, the first thing we do is sample the texture holding the red data. As we only stored one value in the textures, we convert the value to a float by using the field selector on the vec4 returned by texture2D(). If this value is above a certain threshold (0.7 in this case), then pure red is written to the color buffer; otherwise we move on to the next part of the if statement.

The first thing we do in this section is read in the final two color components. We then determine the luminance of all the texture components by performing a dot product between the three color components and lumCoeff.

This value is first compared to 0.5, and if it's greater than 0.5, white is written to the color buffer (1.0 in all four color channels). The luminance value is then compared to the value 0.2, and if it's less, then 0.2 is written. This acts as a kind of clamp to prevent values from going to black. If the value is between 0.2 and 0.5 then the luminance values are used to build a color to write out, which produces a gray-scale effect.

Having written our two shaders, the next thing we need to do is load them in and create the shader objects.

```
GLSLShader simplevert("mrtsimplevertex.vs");
GLSLShader mrtfrag("mrtfrag.fs", GL_FRAGMENT_SHADER);
GLSLShader outputfrag("mrtoutputfrag.fs", GL_FRAGMENT_SHADER);
GLSLProgram firstprog;
GLSLProgram secondprog;
firstprog.attach(simplevert);
firstprog.attach(mrtfrag);
firstprog.link();
secondprog.attach(simplevert);
secondprog.attach(outputfrag);
secondprog.link();
```

Note that the same vertex shader is used with both fragment shaders.

The final thing to cover is the main rendering loop. The rendering loop is effectively split into two sections. The first renders the three color channels to the three textures; the second uses these three textures to produce the final output.

```
void GLDrawScene()
{
  // first section
  fbo.activate();
  fbo.attachRenderTarget(texred,0);
  fbo.attachRenderTarget(texgreen,1);
  fbo.attachRenderTarget(texblue,2);
  glDrawBuffers(3,mrtdrawbuffs);
  glViewport(0,0,RTT_SIZE_WIDTH,RTT_SIZE_HEIGHT);
  {
    glClear(GL_COLOR_BUFFER_BIT | GL_DEPTH_BUFFER_BIT);
    glLoadIdentity();
    glTranslatef(0.0f,0.0f,-5.0f);
    firstprog.use();
    Scene.Draw();
    firstprog.disable();
  }
  fbo.deactivate();
  glDrawBuffer(GL_BACK);

  // second section
  secondprog.use();
  secondprog.sendUniform("rsrc",0);
```

```
  secondprog.sendUniform("gsrc",1);
  secondprog.sendUniform("bsrc",2);
  glActiveTexture(GL_TEXTURE0);
  glBindTexture(GL_TEXTURE_2D,texred);
  glActiveTexture(GL_TEXTURE1);
  glBindTexture(GL_TEXTURE_2D,texgreen);
  glActiveTexture(GL_TEXTURE2);
  glBindTexture(GL_TEXTURE_2D,texblue);

  glClear(GL_COLOR_BUFFER_BIT | GL_DEPTH_BUFFER_BIT);
  DrawQuad(RTT_SIZE_WIDTH,RTT_SIZE_HEIGHT,RTT_SIZE_WIDTH,RTT_SIZE_HEIGHT);
  secondprog.disable();
}
```

The first section of rendering code performs the initial split of the color into three different color buffers. The second section produces the final output.

At the start of the first section is the first piece of code you won't recognize. The `fbo` object is used to interface with the framebuffer-object extension to control render-to-texture operations, so once it's activated it becomes the target for all drawing operations. After that we attach three textures to the framebuffer object as color buffers so that we can write to them in the shader code. We then tell OpenGL that it has three buffers to draw to via the `glDrawBuffers()` function. Then we resize the viewport to the same size as the textures (`RTT_SIZE_WIDTH` and `RTT_SIZE_HEIGHT` are constants that hold the size of the textures to render to).

After that the rendering code should look more familiar. We clear the buffer, reset the camera position, move it back a bit, activate the shader program, draw the scene, and then deactivate the shader (since we're using another shader in the next section, this isn't strictly needed, as binding a new shader program will automatically remove the old one). Once the drawing operations are complete, we deactivate the FBO as the target and reset the output to the back buffer for the next stage.

The next stage should be easy for you to follow by now. First we activate the program, and then we tell it where it can find the three textures to sample from. After that we activate each texture unit in turn and bind a texture to each one for the fragment shader to sample.

Once that is complete we clear the buffer and draw a quad the same size as the textures we rendered to on the screen. The `DrawQuad()` function provides the shader with vertex positions and a single set of texture coordinates. It also takes care of switching from projected to orthographic drawing modes. After that the buffers are swapped, and you should see the output shown in Figure 4.9.

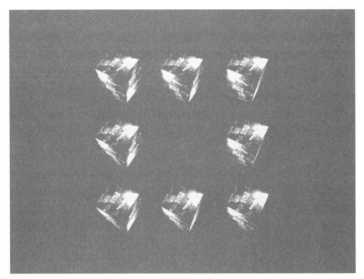

Figure 4.9 An example of using multiple render targets.

Performance Tips and Hints

Before wrapping up this chapter, I'll provide a few tips and hints gleaned from working with the OpenGL Shading Language. Using these tips should help you produce better shaders and faster programs.

1. Write Clear Code

This is an important tip both from a maintenance standpoint and for helping the compiler make the best of your code. From a purely maintenance standpoint, writing clear code allows you to come back to your code later and understand easily what you were trying to achieve with it. From the compiler's point of view, the clearer the code, the easier it is to work out the programmer's intent and the better the final programs produced. Try to avoid nesting too many statements together, because this can make it much harder for the compiler to do its job.

2. Do as Much as You Can as Early as You Can

If you can get away with performing an operation per vertex, then do so. While each generation of hardware has more pixel pipelines than the last, it will always be cheaper to execute things once per vertex, because there are typically far fewer vertices than fragments for any given object. Sometimes you can even offload simple per-object calculations to the CPU, which can gain you some speed, as the calculations only have to be performed once and the result can be cached between each rendering.

3. Prefer ALU Operations to Texture Fetches

While the bandwidth on graphics cards is increasing, it still requires a lot of resources to fetch information from a texture. Fetching from a single texture can consume 32GB/sec of bandwidth, so you really want to try to perform calculations on the GPU instead of fetching them from a texture (which was a very common method of dealing with things when instruction counts were much lower than they are now).

4. Minimize Array Sizes

While arrays are very useful in some programs, you'll want to try to minimize their size because they can consume a lot of resources on the GPU pretty quickly if they get too big.

5. Avoid Using Vectors to Store Scalars

This might seem obvious, but people do it. If you want a scalar type, then use one; doing otherwise can waste resources and make the compiler's life harder as it will try to maintain the contents of the rest of the vector at all times.

6. Use Compile-Time Constants Where Possible

The compiler can make very efficient use of constants when compiling your shaders. The fog examples earlier made good use of compile-time constants for values that don't change during a shader's execution.

7. Use Uniforms Carefully

Uniforms require some work when changing since they have to be optimized as they are set. Therefore, you should avoid setting them too often. Also, constantly querying a program for its uniform locations isn't a good idea as this is also time consuming. Instead, you should maintain a cache of the locations and only requery when something happens to cause a possible change in the locations (such as relinking). The GLSLProgram class has a basic caching system in place as an example of how to perform this kind of operation.

8. Try to Perform Vector Operations

Due to the nature of the operations they perform, GPUs are inherently parallel devices. By explicitly performing vector-based operations, you can help the compiler produce better code. Using vector operations also reliably uses hardware-specialized functions to get the best performance from your code.

9. Avoid Unnecessary State Changes

As you should know, state changes are expensive, so you should try to minimize them. The most expensive state changes are changing shaders or switching between the programmable and fixed-function pipeline. Batching your geometry based on state settings will help avoid unnecessary state changes during your drawing routines.

This also applies to remapping of samplers (i.e., setting their sampler number via glUniform()), as the driver has to perform a lookup to determine if the sampler type matches the texture type bound to that texture unit. This can be a lot of work, so you should only change it when you need to.

10. Be Careful of Ubershaders

While it might be tempting to produce one big shader that uses uniforms to change the program flow to handle multiple effects, you might be better off specializing shaders to a certain task and switching between them. This is something you'll need to test, and on later hardware the usage of so-called ubershaders might become more viable. For now, however, you should be careful when using them.

Summary

In this chapter, you've learned about the OpenGL Shading Language itself and the OpenGL APIs available for working with it. You've also seen numerous examples of how GLSL shaders can be used. As the book progresses from here, you'll learn about many advanced effects that can be implemented using the OpenGL Shading Language, so be sure that you're comfortable with it before moving on.

References

3Dlabs OpenGL Shading Language API Man Pages. **http://developer.3dlabs.com/documents/glslmanpage_index.htm.**

GDC 2005 ATI and NV OpenGL Shading Language Presentation. **http://www.ati.com/developer/gdc/GDC2005_OpenGL_Shading_Language.pdf.**

GDC 2005 ATI and NV OpenGL Performance Tuning Presentation. **http://www.ati.com/developer/gdc/GDC2005_OpenGL_Performance.pdf.**

OpenGL Shading Language v1.10 Specification. **http://oss.sgi.com/projects/ogl-sample/registry/ARB/GLSLangSpec.Full.1.10.59.pdf.**

Rost, Randi J. *OpenGL Shading Language*. Boston: Addison-Wesley, 2004.

Shreiner, David, Mason Woo, Jackie Neider, and Tom Davis. *OpenGL Programming Guide*, 4th ed. Addison-Wesley, 2003.

Thanks go to Abdul "Java Cool Dude" Bezrati for his FrameBuffer Object class and some testing work related to the MRT examples (**http://www.realityflux.com/abba/**).

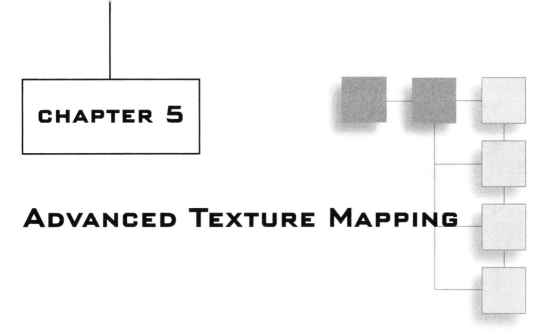

CHAPTER 5

ADVANCED TEXTURE MAPPING

In *Beginning OpenGL Game Programming*, you spent two chapters learning the details of OpenGL's texturing system and some of the things that can be done with it. In this chapter, you'll continue your education. You'll learn about some of the more advanced features offered by OpenGL for texture mapping support via core features and common extensions, and you'll learn about how to accomplish advanced texture-related effects.

The topics that you'll learn about include:

- Anisotropic filtering
- Compressed textures
- Non-power-of-two textures
- Floating-point texture formats
- Depth textures
- Bump mapping
- Displacement mapping
- Parallax mapping
- Detail texturing
- Projective textures
- Render-to-texture

Anisotropic Filtering

Dave Astle

Normally, OpenGL samples textures *isotropically*, meaning that both directions are sampled equally. This works well with roughly screen-aligned surfaces, but can cause blurriness when the surface is nearly perpendicular to the screen and one direction is changing much more rapidly than the other. Figure 5.1 shows an example of this. *Anisotropic filtering* remedies this situation by taking more samples in the rapidly changing direction.

Figure 5.1 The texture looks fine on the left, but when rotated away from the camera, as on the right, it becomes blurry.

OpenGL does not include anisotropic filtering as a core feature, but most implementations support it through the EXT_texture_anisotropic extension. This extension adds a per-texture object attribute that controls the level of anisotropy. This can be set as follows:

```
glTexParameteri(GL_TEXTURE_2D, GL_TEXTURE_MAX_ANISOTROPY_EXT, max);
```

The value for max, the maximum number of samples to take in the direction of greatest change, can range from 1.0—which is equivalent to isotropic filtering—to the maximum value supported by the implementation. The maximum can be determined by passing GL_MAX_TEXTURE_MAX_ANISOTROPY_EXT to glGetFloatv().

Maximum anisotropy is set independently of the texture filtering modes, so it can be used with any of them.

Although enabling a high level of anisotropic filtering can greatly improve visual quality, keep in mind that it doesn't come free. Although this is becoming less of an issue as hardware evolves, increasing the number of samples per texel can affect performance. The extent of this impact depends on your existing bottlenecks, but I recommend that you selectively use this feature and carefully profile when you choose to use it. You can also reduce the performance impact by setting the maximum anisotropy level to a value that is lower than the maximum supported by the implementation.

This book's website includes a demo, Anisotropic Road, that shows you how to set up an anisotropic filter. The demo also allows you to use the spacebar to toggle between mipmapping with and without anisotropic filtering so that you can appreciate the quality improvement that it offers. Figure 5.2 shows this in action.

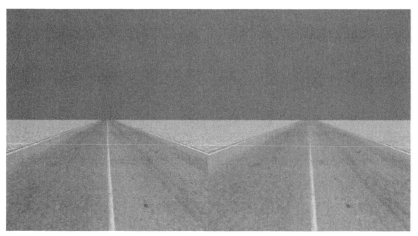

Figure 5.2 Anisotropic Road demo. The left side shows rendering with a maximum anisotropy level of 16, and the right shows the same scene without anisotropic filtering.

Compressed Textures

Dave Astle

extension

Extension name: ARB_texture_compression

Name string: GL_ARB_texture_compression

Promoted to core: OpenGL 1.3

Function names: glCompressedTexImage3DARB, glCompressedTexImage2DARB, glCompressedTexImage1DARB, glCompressedTexSubImage3DARB, glCompressedTexSubImage2DARB, glCompressedTexSubImage1DARB, glGetCompressedImage3DARB

Tokens (partial list): GL_COMPRESSED_ALPHA_ARB, GL_COMPRESSED_LUMINANCE_ARB, GL_COMPRESSED_LUMINANCE_ALPHA_ARB, GL_COMPRESSED_INTENSITY_ARB, GL_COMPRESSED_RGB_ARB, GL_COMPRESSED_RGBA_ARB, GL_TEXTURE_COMPRESSION_HINT_ARB, GL_TEXTURE_COMPRESSED_IMAGE_SIZE_ARB, GL_TEXTURE_COMPRESSED_ARB, GL_NUM_COMPRESSED_TEXTURE_FORMATS_ARB, GL_COMPRESSED_TEXTURE_FORMATS_ARB

Modern video cards have a lot of memory, but this memory isn't unlimited. Video-card memory is shared between the framebuffer, buffer objects, and textures. Textures are usually the most demanding, with sizes of up to 2,048×2,048 or 4,096×4,096, and cubemaps and 3D textures consuming far more memory. Games tend to use a lot of textures, especially because of multitexturing effects, so it's quite possible to run out of video memory. When this happens, textures get swapped out to the memory on your PC and then swapped back in when needed. This, of course, results in a performance hit. In *Beginning OpenGL Game Programming*, you learned how to set texture priorities to keep the most important textures in memory. In this section, you'll learn how to use OpenGL's compressed texture support to make the most of your video memory. In addition to allowing you to fit more textures on your video card—and thus make it less likely that the textures will need to be swapped out—the smaller size of the compressed textures means that if they do need to be swapped out, they will be transferred more quickly.

OpenGL provides two main options for working with compressed textures. First, it can compress textures for you at run time. Second, it allows you to directly load textures from images that are already compressed.

Automatic Texture Compression

Asking OpenGL to compress your textures when you load them is quite simple. When using any of the `glTexImage()` functions, instead of the `internalformat` parameter that you'd normally use, you pass one of the values in Table 5.1.

Table 5.1 Compressed Texture Formats

Generic Compressed Format	Base Internal Format
GL_COMPRESSED_ALPHA	GL_ALPHA
GL_COMPRESSED_LUMINANCE	GL_LUMINANCE
GL_COMPRESSED_LUMINANCE_ALPHA	GL_LUMINANCE_ALPHA
GL_COMPRESSED_INTENSITY	GL_INTENSITY
GL_COMPRESSED_RGB	GL_RGB
GL_COMPRESSED_RGBA	GL_RGBA

When you use compression in this way, the texture load may incur a bit more overhead than normal because of the time required to compress the texture.

After loading your texture, you can check to see whether it was successfully compressed using `glGetTexLevelParameter()`, which you learned about in *Beginning OpenGL Game Programming*. As a reminder, this function's prototype is as follows:

```
void glGetTexLevelParameteriv(GLenum target, Glint level, GLenum pname,
                              GLfloat *params)
```

To find out whether OpenGL compressed your texture, just pass `GL_TEXTURE_COMPRESSED` as `pname`. If the compression failed, the texture will be stored in the corresponding base format from Table 5.1.

You'll notice that the compressed formats in Table 5.1 are labeled *Generic*. This is because the OpenGL specification doesn't mandate any particular compression method. When you pass one of these generic values, the implementation decides internally which method to use.

You can find out how many compressed texture formats are supported by the implementation by passing `GL_NUM_COMPRESSED_TEXTURE_FORMATS` to `glGetTexLevelParameteriv()`. The values of the formats can be retrieved using `GL_COMPRESSED_TEXTURE_FORMATS`.

Any specific compression method used must be exposed through an extension. By far the most common texture compression extension is `EXT_texture_compression_s3tc`. This extension defines the four new internal formats listed in Table 5.2. The major difference between the four formats is the way alpha is handled, which is described in the table.

Table 5.2 S3TC Formats

Compressed format	Internal format	Description
GL_COMPRESSED_RGB_DXT1_EXT	GL_RGB	Alpha is always 1.0
GL_COMPRESSED_RGBA_DXT1_EXT	GL_RGBA	Alpha is either 0.0 or 1.0
GL_COMPRESSED_RGBA_DXT3_EXT	GL_RGBA	Alpha is stored as 4 bits.
GL_COMPRESSED_RGBA_DXT5_EXT	GL_RGBA	Alpha is a weighted average of 8-bit values.

Note: These formats are only supported for 2D textures.

If the implementation supports this extension, the values in Table 5.2 can be used as the `internalformat` parameter in any `glTexImage()` function.

Since multiple compression methods may be supported, you can influence which one is used through the `glHint()` mechanism. If you want the compression to be performed as quickly as possible, perhaps because you frequently load textures, you'd use:

```
glHint(GL_TEXTURE_COMPRESSION_HINT, GL_FASTEST);
```

Otherwise, you can use the following to take advantage of the highest-quality compression (which is what you'd want if you're reading the texture back):

```
glHint(GL_TEXTURE_COMPRESSION_HINT, GL_NICEST);
```

Loading Precompressed Textures

Instead of having OpenGL compress textures for you at load time, you can directly load images that are already compressed. To support this, OpenGL includes six functions:

```
void glCompressedTexImage1D(GLenum target, GLint level, GLenum internalformat,
                            GLsizei width, GLint border, GLsizei size,
                            const void *data);
void glCompressedTexImage2D(GLenum target, GLint level, GLenum internalformat,
                            GLsizei width, GLsizei height, GLint border,
                            GLsizei size, const void *data);
void glCompressedTexImage3D(GLenum target, GLint level, GLenum internalformat,
                            GLsizei width, GLsizei height, GLsizei depth,
                            GLint border, GLsizei size, const void *data);
void glCompressedTexSubImage1D(GLenum target, GLint level, GLint xoffset,
                            GLsizei width, GLenum format, GLsizei size,
                            const void *data);
void glCompressedTexSubImage2D(GLenum target, GLint level, GLint xoffset,
                            GLint yoffset, GLsizei width, glsizei height,
                            GLenum format, GLsizei size, const void *data);
void glCompressedTexSubImage3D(GLenum target, GLint level, GLint xoffset,
                            GLint yoffset, GLint zoffset, GLsizei width,
                            glsizei height, GLsizei depth, GLenum format,
                            GLsizei size, const void *data);
```

These functions are very similar to their `glTexImage()` and `glTexSubImage()` equivalents, except for a couple of differences. First, `internalformat` parameter (or the `format` parameter for the subimage functions) must be one of the extension-defined compressed formats, such as one of the S3TC values from Table 5.2. This is the format that the `data` must be in. You cannot use one of the generic compressed texture values for this purpose. The second difference is the `size` parameter, which is used to specify the size of the compressed image, in bytes.

There are tools freely available to convert texture images to the most popular compressed formats. Alternatively, you can use OpenGL to perform the conversion for you. The steps to accomplish this are as follows:

1. Load an uncompressed image.
2. Pass it to `glTexImage()`, but use one of the generic compression formats described in the previous section. The texture compression hint should be set to `GL_NICEST`.
3. Verify that the texture has been compressed. If it has, read it back using `glGetCompressedTexImage()`.

4. Save the image to disk. You'll also want to save the width, height, format, and size, since you'll need them when loading the image.

Your game could do this the first time the user plays it, and then in subsequent executions, it could use the compressed textures instead. This would eliminate the overhead of having to compress your textures every time they are loaded, as well as prevent you from having to worry about providing specific compressed texture formats with your game.

The prototype for `glGetCompressedTexImage()` is as follows:

```
void glGetCompressedTexImage(GLenum target, GLint level, void *data)
```

This will store the compressed data stored in mip-level `level` of the currently bound texture object in `data`. To determine how much memory to allocate for `data`, you can pass `GL_TEXTURE_COMPRESSED_IMAGE_SIZE` to `glGetTexLevelParameteriv()`, which will return the size in bytes.

This book's website includes a demo for this section that implements the method just described.

Floating-Point Textures and Buffers

Dave Astle

extension

Extension name: `ARB_texture_float`

Name string: `GL_ARB_texture_float`

Tokens: `GL_RGBA32F_ARB`, `GL_RGB32F_ARB`, `GL_ALPHA32F_ARB`, `GL_INTENSITY32F_ARB`, `GL_LUMINANCE32F_ARB`, `GL_LUMINANCE_ALPHA32F_ARB`, `GL_RGBA16F_ARB`, `GL_RGB16F_ARB`, `GL_ALPHA16F_ARB`, `GL_INTENSITY16F_ARB`, `GL_LUMINANCE16F_ARB`, `GL_LUMINANCE_ALPHA16F_ARB`, `GL_TEXTURE_RED_TYPE_ARB`, `GL_TEXTURE_GREEN_TYPE_ARB`, `GL_TEXTURE_BLUE_TYPE_ARB`, `GL_TEXTURE_ALPHA_TYPE_ARB`, `GL_TEXTURE_LUMINANCE_TYPE_ARB`, `GL_TEXTURE_INTENSITY_TYPE_ARB`, `GL_TEXTURE_DEPTH_TYPE_ARB`, `GL_UNSIGNED_NORMALIZED_ARB`

In Chapter 1, "More OpenGL," you learned about creating floating-point color buffers using the `ARB_color_buffer_float` extension. There is a similar extension, `ARB_texture_float`, which adds the ability to use textures represented with 32- or 16-bit floating-point values per component. Like `ARB_color_buffer_float`, this extension is not yet widely supported, but it has many practical applications, so support for it will soon be more common.

This extension introduces a number of new floating-point internal formats that can be passed as the `internalformat` parameter for `glTexImage1D()`, `glTexImage2D()`, or `glTexImage3D()`. These formats are listed in Table 5.3.

Table 5.3 Floating-Point Texture Formats

Sized Internal Format	Base Internal Format	Description
GL_RGBA32F_ARB	GL_RGBA	32-bit floating point RGBA texture
GL_RGB32F_ARB	GL_RGB	32-bit floating point RGB texture
GL_ALPHA32F_ARB	GL_ALPHA	32-bit floating point alpha texture
GL_INTENSITY32F_ARB	GL_INTENSITY	32-bit floating-point intensity texture
GL_LUMINANCE32F_ARB	GL_LUMINANCE	32-bit floating-point luminance texture
GL_LUMINANCE_ALPHA32F_ARB	GL_LUMINANCE_ALPHA	32-bit floating-point luminance-alpha texture
GL_RGBA16F_ARB	GL_RGBA	16-bit floating-point RGBA texture
GL_RGB16F_ARB	GL_RGB	16-bit floating-point RGB texture
GL_ALPHA16F_ARB	GL_ALPHA	16-bit floating-point alpha texture
GL_INTENSITY16F_ARB	GL_INTENSITY	16-bit floating-point intensity texture
GL_LUMINANCE16F_ARB	GL_LUMINANCE	16-bit floating-point luminance texture
GL_LUMINANCE_ALPHA16F_ARB	GL_LUMINANCE_ALPHA	16-bit floating-point luminance-alpha texture

Loading an RGBA image stored as 32-bit floats per component would be done as follows:

```
glTexImage2D(GL_TEXTURE_2D, 0, GL_RGBA32_ARB, image.width, image.height, 0,
             GL_RGBA, GL_FLOAT, image.data);
```

When using a floating-point texture, the texel values are not clamped during the texture filtering process. If you are using the fixed-function pipeline, then the texture color will be clamped to [0, 1] before it is used in the texture environment application. This behavior can be changed using glClampColorARB() as described in Chapter 1. If you are using a fragment shader, the texture color will not be clamped.

Querying Texture Component Types

Since this extension makes it possible for texture image data to either be integers or floating-point values, it also includes the ability to query the type of each component of a texture image. This is done by passing GL_TEXTURE_RED_TYPE_ARB, GL_TEXTURE_GREEN_TYPE_ARB, GL_TEXTURE_BLUE_TYPE_ARB, GL_TEXTURE_ALPHA_TYPE_ARB, GL_TEXTURE_LUMINANCE_TYPE_ARB, GL_TEXTURE_INTENSITY_TYPE_ARB, or GL_TEXTURE_DEPTH_TYPE_ARB as the value parameter to glGetTexLevelParameter(). The value returned will be GL_NONE, GL_FIXED, or GL_UNSIGNED_NORMALIZED_ARB.

Half Floats

e x t e n s i o n

Extension name: ARB_half_float_pixel
Name string: GL_ARB_half_float_pixel
Tokens: GL_HALF_FLOAT_ARB
Types: GLhalfARB

ARB_texture_float doesn't include enumerants that would allow you to pass in a texture that is already represented using 16-bit floats. It only allows you to request that the texture be stored internally using 16 bits rather than 32 bits.

To be able to pass 16-bit floating point images to OpenGL, you'll need an additional extension, ARB_half_float_pixel, which defines the half precision float type GLhalfARB. This extension also defines a single new token, GL_HALF_FLOAT_ARB, which can be used as the type parameter for any of the glTexImage() or glTexSubImage() functions, as well as for glDrawPixels(), glReadPixels(), and functions in the imaging subset.

Since no native programming language supports 16-bit floats, GLhalfARB is defined as an unsigned short with 1 sign bit, 5 exponent bits, and 10 mantissa bits.

ARB_half_float_pixel only adds support for 16-bit floating-point values for pixel data. Half floats can't be used for vertex data.

Non-Power-of-Two Textures and Texture Rectangles

Dave Astle

A long-standing restriction in OpenGL has been that texture dimensions have to be in powers of two (e.g., 512×512, 1,024×1,024). This restriction allows for simpler and faster texturing hardware. A few years ago, a couple of extensions were introduced that modified this restriction. One, ARB_texture_non_power_of_two, simply removes the restriction without requiring any additional changes. It was promoted to the core in OpenGL 2.0. The other extension, ARB_texture_rectangle, adds a new texture target with a number of significant limitations. Because hardware support is not yet widespread for either, both will be covered here. I'll also suggest some alternatives for cases when neither extension is present.

Non-Power-of-Two Textures

e x t e n s i o n

Extension name: `ARB_texture_non_power_of_two`

Name string: `GL_ARB_texture_non_power_of_two`

Promoted to core: OpenGL 2.0

Function names: None

Tokens: None

As long as the implementation you're using supports OpenGL version 2.0 or higher, or supports the `ARB_texture_non_power_of_two` extension, using non-power-of-two (NPOT) textures becomes trivial. All you have to do is load the texture using any of the `glTexImage()` functions—and that's it.

You can use NPOT textures with 1D, 2D, and 3D texture targets, and even with cubemaps—though the cubemap textures still have to be square. Any texture wrapping and filtering modes can be used, including mipmapping and automatic mipmap generation. Texture coordinates are normalized (i.e. range from 0 to 1) just like power-of-two textures.

Texture Rectangles

e x t e n s i o n

Extension name: `ARB_texture_rectangle`

Name string: `GL_ARB_texture_rectangle`

Promoted to core: N/A

Function names: None

Tokens: `GL_TEXTURE_RECTANGLE_ARB`, `GL_TEXTURE_BINDING_RECTANGLE_ARB`, `GL_PROXY_TEXTURE_RECTANGLE_ARB`, `GL_MAX_ RECTANGLE_TEXTURE_SIZE_ARB`

Texture rectangles are considerably different and much more limited than the non-power-of-two support just described. Although they are not part of the core, at the time of writing they are more widely supported than general NPOT textures, so they are worth devoting a little space to.

This extension introduces a new texture target, `GL_TEXTURE_RECTANGLE_ARB`, which can be used with most of the existing texture functions. This target has a priority that is higher than `GL_TEXTURE_2D` but lower than `GL_TEXTURE_3D` and `GL_TEXTURE_CUBE_MAP`. To use a texture rectangle, it has to be enabled just like any other texture target:

```
glEnable(GL_TEXTURE_RECTANGLE_ARB);
```

In most ways, texture rectangles work like normal 2D textures. They are loaded using the variants of `glTexImage2D()` with `target` set to `GL_TEXTURE_RECTANGLE_ARB`, and they are typically accessed using two texture coordinates. However, this brings up one of the first important differences: texture rectangle texture coordinates are nonnormalized. In other words, rather than ranging from $[0...1]$, $[0...1]$, they range from $[0...w]$, $[0...h]$, where w and h are the width and height of the texture, respectively.

Texture rectangles also carry a number of limitations:

- They don't support mipmapping. The default filter is `GL_LINEAR`.
- They only support the `GL_CLAMP`, `GL_CLAMP_TO_BORDER`, and `GL_CLAP_TO_EDGE` (default) wrapping modes.
- Texture borders are not supported.

The maximum texture dimensions supported can be queried using `GL_MAX_RECTANGLE_TEXTURE_SIZE_ARB`:

```
GLint maxSize;
glGetIntegerv(GL_MAX_RECTANGLE_TEXTURE_SIZE_ARB, &maxSize);
```

Alternative Approaches

If neither of the extensions described in the previous sections are supported, you still have a number of options.

- Rescale your image in your image-editing tool of choice to have power-of-two dimensions. This gives you the greatest control over the appearance of the rescaled image.
- Use your favorite image-editing tool to place the image inside a larger image with power-of-two dimensions, and adjust texture coordinates accordingly. This approach may result in artifacts at the edge, and wastes texture memory.
- Use `gluBuild2DMipmaps()` or `gluScaleImage()` to rescale the image to a power-of-two at run time. The downside of this approach is that the filtering method used may not produce acceptable results.

For the sake of portability, and to avoid some potential performance issues, you may want to use these even if the extensions are supported. Of course, your best bet is to try to stick with textures that have power-of-two dimensions in the first place.

Bump Mapping

David Elder

Many real-world materials, such as brick, rusted metal, stucco, and stone, are rough or bumpy. The small-scale structure of their surfaces is responsible for their rough appearance.

You could render a bumpy surface using a highly detailed polygonal model with texture maps, lighting, and so forth. For performance reasons, large models are usually not practical for real-time rendering, so you should try another approach. Fortunately, several techniques allow you to approximate bumpy and rough surfaces without increasing the geometric complexity of your models. The basic approach is called *bump mapping*, and it typically involves perturbing the surface normal per pixel across a polygon to mimic a bumpy or rough material. Bump mapping can greatly improve the visual quality of a scene, making it appear to have much more geometric detail than it actually does. You can also apply different bump maps to the same model and radically change its appearance without actually modifying the geometry. Various bump-mapping techniques are discussed by Akenine-Möller and Haines' *Real-Time Rendering*, along with a wide variety of other rendering topics.

Working in Texture Space

A variety of coordinate systems are used in 3D graphics, including object space, world space, and image space. Bump mapping relies on another coordinate system, called *texture space*, which is related to the texture coordinates associated with each vertex in a polygonal model. A surface normal is by definition orthogonal to a polygonal surface at a vertex. Let's denote a surface normal by $N = (N_x, N_y, N_z)$, and let's suppose you want to build a new coordinate system with N as one of its axes. You can build another axis by finding a vector $T = (T_x, T_y, T_z)$, called the *tangent*, that is perpendicular to N and that follows the texture coordinate s. The final axis $B = (B_x, B_y, B_z)$ is called the *binormal* and is found by computing the cross product $B = N \times T$. The three axes N, B, and T define a 3D coordinate system, the texture space. The axes T and B together define a 2D coordinate system which is parallel (or tangent) to the polygonal model's surface at a particular vertex and whose axes should point along the texture axes s and t. The texture-space axes for a sphere are illustrated in Figure 5.3.

Binormal vs. Bitangent

It has been argued that referring to the third vector in the texture space basis as *binormal* isn't mathematically correct, and that it should instead be called *bitangent*. There is actually mathematical justification for both terms, and the authors of this book discussed them at length in deciding which term to use. Ultimately, the decision to use *binormal* was made for pragmatic reasons: the overwhelming majority of the existing literature related to bump mapping uses the term *binormal*, so to avoid confusion, that's the term that is used throughout the book.

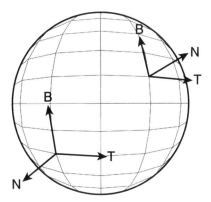

Figure 5.3 The texture-space
coordinate system on a sphere.

Most diffuse lighting models use a light direction vector L, which is the normalized direction of a light source from a given vertex. The light direction vector L is specified in object space, but bump-mapping techniques need to recompute L in texture space. This can be achieved by constructing a basis matrix using the coordinate axes N, B, and T:

$$M = \begin{pmatrix} T_x & T_y & T_z & 0 \\ B_x & B_y & B_z & 0 \\ N_x & N_y & N_z & 0 \\ 0 & 0 & 0 & 1 \end{pmatrix}$$

Multiplying L by this matrix rotates the light direction vector into texture space.

In practice, the tangent vector should be precom-puted and supplied along with normal vector for each vertex. OpenGL has methods for supplying per-vertex surface normals, but no direct support for supplying tangent vectors. The solution is to supply the tangent vector as an additional texture coordinate using `glMultiTexCoord3f()`. The binormal vector can be computed in a vertex shader using the cross product. A useful method for computing the tangent vector, given a polygonal model with normals and 2D texture coordinates, is described by Eric Lengyel in *Mathematics for 3D Game Programming and Computer Graphics*.

Now that most of the math is out of the way, let's take a look at some techniques for bump mapping.

Emboss Mapping

Before I discuss the main bump-mapping technique in use today, I want to briefly mention an older method, called *emboss mapping* (or sometimes *forward-differencing*). Figure 5.4 shows an example of an emboss-mapped polygon. As you can see, this method gives a chiseled or carved look to a surface. Emboss mapping begins with a *height map*, which is a texture map storing the height of the surface at each texel. A height map can be stored efficiently in OpenGL using a single-channel texture format, such as `GL_LUMINANCE`. Given a height map and a diffuse color for a surface, the multipass emboss-mapping algorithm is:

1. Disable lighting. Render the surface using the height map as a color texture.

2. Shift the texture coordinates (s, t) at each vertex in the direction of the light.

3. Rerender the surface with height map again applied as a color texture, using the shifted texture coordinates. Subtract the new values from the old values rendered in step 1.

4. Enable lighting. Render the surface a final time smooth-shaded with the diffuse color and add the results to the image produced in step 3.

Note that shifting the texture coordinates toward the light in step two is equivalent to shifting the second-pass height map away from the light.

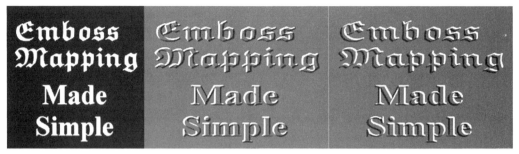

Figure 5.4 The emboss-map height field (left); embossed image illuminated from the upper left (center); image illuminated from the upper right (right).

The tricky part of the emboss-mapping algorithm is determining how much to shift the texture coordinates in step 2. This is where texture space comes in handy. Given a light direction vector L in object space, we compute the texture space vector L' using the basis matrix described earlier. If $L' = (L_x', L_y', L_z')$, then L_x' and L_y' give the direction of the light along the T and B axes, respectively. (The third coordinate, L_z', gives the direction of the light along the normal N, which we don't need here.) The values L_x' and L_y' are multiplied by some scale value and added to the original texture coordinates to produce the shifted coordinates (s', t'). You wanted to shift the height map by one texel in the direction of the light, so you should normalize the shift direction (L_x', L_y') and set the shift multiplier to $1/N$, where N is the resolution of the height map. This is illustrated in Figure 5.5.

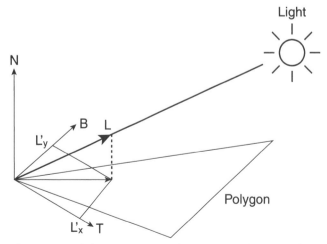

Figure 5.5 Shifting texture coordinates in the direction of the light.

Emboss mapping has some significant problems and is not widely used today. The technique works reasonably well with one light in a scene, but it doesn't scale well to scenes with multiple lights. It also can't easily render bumps facing away from a light.

Normal Mapping

You might have noticed that the emboss mapping algorithm doesn't really change the surface normal on a per-pixel basis; instead, it approximates the effects of changing the surface normal by shifting the height map. Rather than working directly with the bump heights, we could simply store the surface normal at each texel in a *normal map*. This is the technique that is commonly used in many recent games. It allows us to simply look up a perturbed surface normal for every rendered pixel in a bump-mapped surface. Conceptually, normal mapping is much simpler than emboss mapping, and it produces much better results. In a nutshell, the normal-mapping algorithm computes the light direction and half-angle vectors in texture space, reads a surface normal from the normal map, and then, using the texture-space lighting vectors and surface normal, applies a lighting equation to determine the color at each pixel. Figure 5.6 compares a normal-mapped torus with a torus using per-vertex normals. The mathematics of the torus are simple enough that the texture-space coordinate system can be computed using analytical equations, as described by Fernando and Kilgard's *Cg Tutorial.*

Figure 5.6 The left image shows a torus illuminated with per-vertex surface normals. The right image shows the torus illuminated with a normal map.

An important consideration is how to store the normal map in a texture. The (x, y, z) coordinates of the normal will be stored in the RGB values of the texture map, but the x, y, and z values are in the range $[-1, 1]$, where as the RGB values are normally clipped to the range $[0, 1]$, assuming fixed-point GL_FLOAT storage. Floating-point texture formats such as GL_RGBA32F_ARB don't have this limitation. However, certain floating-point texture formats require rectangular texture formats, which do not have normalized texture coordinates. For simplicity, let's assume that ordinary fixed-point GL_FLOAT textures will be used. To pack a surface normal (x, y, z) into the RGB color channels of a texture, we compress the range using the following formulas:

$$R = 0.5 * (x + 1.0)$$

$$G = 0.5 * (y + 1.0)$$

$$B = 0.5 * (z + 1.0)$$

To retrieve the surface normal from a packed RGB color—for instance, in a GLSL fragment program—we use the following formulas:

$$x = 2.0 * R - 1.0$$
$$y = 2.0 * G - 1.0$$
$$z = 2.0 * B - 1.0$$

Normal Mapping with GLSL

Normal mapping has a simple and elegant implementation using GLSL vertex and fragment shaders. The vertex processing algorithm is:

1. Compute and normalize the object-space light direction vector L and the eye direction vector E (for specular highlights).
2. Construct the texture-space basis matrix by computing the binormal $B = N \times T$ and building the matrix as done previously.
3. Rotate the vectors L and E into texture space using the basis matrix.
4. Compute and normalize the half-angle vector $H = L + E$ in texture space.
5. Compute the new vertex position using the modelview-projection matrix and send the vertex position, texture coordinates, and texture-space lighting vectors L' and H' to the fragment processor.

To determine the color at a fragment, you'll use the surface normal stored in the normal map as well as the lighting vectors from the vertex program. You'll also need to know the specular and ambient lighting colors and the diffuse color of the surface. You can specify the diffuse color using an ordinary RGB texture map. The other lighting colors can be passed to the fragment program using uniform parameters. The fragment processing algorithm is:

1. Read the surface normal N from the normal map. Expand the range-compressed normal using the formulas given earlier.

2. Compute the diffuse and specular lighting coefficients using the surface normal and the lighting vectors L and H passed in from the vertex program. The diffuse coefficient is `max(dot(N, L), 0)`, and the specular coefficient is `max(dot(N, H), 0)`. The specular coefficient is raised to some integer power to control the shininess of the surface.

3. Optionally, compute per-pixel distance-based attenuation for the light source.

4. Look up the diffuse color in an ordinary texture map.

5. Determine the fragment color using the standard lighting equations, incorporating the ambient, diffuse, and specular lighting values. If necessary, scale the ambient and diffuse contributions by the attenuation value.

The vertex program outlined above passes the lighting vectors L and H to the fragment program. These vectors are normalized in the vertex program and are interpolated across the screen-space polygon by the rasterizer. In certain cases, interpolation can mess up the lengths of these vectors, which can have bad effects when computing the diffuse and specular lighting coefficients. You might want to move the normalization of L and H to the fragment program. Normalization, of course, involves computing the reciprocal square root of the length of a vector, which could be an expensive operation in terms of run time. If you normalize in the fragment program, you'll have to compute a reciprocal square root for hundreds or thousands of individual vectors on a per-pixel basis, potentially leading to a performance bottleneck. Fortunately, you can avoid the cost of all these reciprocal square roots by using a *normalization cubemap*. A cubemap is a texture map with six square faces corresponding to the six faces of a cube. A cubemap is sampled using a 3D texture coordinate, specifying a vector from the center of the cube. An RGB value is read from the cube map by determining the point of intersection of the vector with one of the cubemap faces. You can store a normalized version of a vector in the texels of a cubemap (range-compressed, as above), so that sampling the cubemap with an arbitrary 3D vector returns the normalized version of that vector. Since texture-access operations are fast in the fragment processor, using a normalization cubemap can be significantly faster than computing reciprocal square roots at every pixel. The demo source code shows how to build a normalization cubemap.

As you can see, the normal-mapping algorithm has a straightforward implementation on a programmable GPU. Here is a GLSL vertex shader implementing normal mapping:

```
varying vec3 halfAngle;
varying vec3 lightDirection;

void main(void)
{
```

```
    vec3 normal = gl_Normal;
    vec3 tangent = gl_MultiTexCoord1.xyz;
    vec2 texcoord = gl_MultiTexCoord0.st;

    // compute lighting
    vec4 position = gl_ModelViewMatrix * gl_Vertex;
    normal  = gl_NormalMatrix * normalize(normal);
    tangent = gl_NormalMatrix * normalize(tangent);
    vec3 binormal = cross(normal, tangent);
    mat3 textureSpaceMatrix = mat3(tangent, binormal, normal);

    vec3 lightPosition = gl_LightSource[0].position.xyz;
    vec3 eyeDirection = textureSpaceMatrix * normalize(-position.xyz);
    lightDirection = textureSpaceMatrix * normalize(lightPosition - position.xyz);
    halfAngle = normalize(eyeDirection + lightDirection);

    // required outputs
    gl_Position = gl_ModelViewProjectionMatrix * gl_Vertex;
    gl_TexCoord[0].st = texcoord * vec2(1.0, -2.0);
}
```

And here is the corresponding fragment shader:

```
uniform float ambient;
uniform sampler2D normalMap;
uniform sampler2D textureMap;
uniform sampler2D glossMap;

varying vec3 halfAngle;
varying vec3 lightDirection;

void main(void)
{
  vec3 normal = texture2D(normalMap, gl_TexCoord[0].st).xyz;
  normal = vec3(2.0) * (normal - vec3(0.5));

  float diffuse = smoothstep(0.0, 1.0, dot(normal, lightDirection));
  float specular = smoothstep(0.0, 1.0, dot(normal, halfAngle));
  float pF = pow(specular, 16.0);

  vec4 diffuseColor = texture2D(textureMap, gl_TexCoord[0].st);
  vec4 glossColor = texture2D(glossMap, gl_TexCoord[0].st);
  gl_FragColor = (ambient + diffuse) * diffuseColor + glossColor * pF;
}
```

Normal Mapping with OpenGL Extensions

It's possible to implement normal mapping on a graphics card that doesn't support GLSL. OpenGL 1.3 promoted the GL_ARB_texture_env_combine and GL_ARB_texture_env_dot3 extensions to the core. These extensions provide several new texture environment functions. Texture environment functions control how textures are applied to surfaces. For example, a texture could simply replace the underlying surface color, or it could blend with or modulate the original color. For the purposes of normal mapping, the combine and dot3 texture environments allow you to perform arithmetic and dot products on operands, which can be texture-map colors, vertex colors, or the results of the previous texture environment. In other words, you can add, subtract, multiply, and take dot products of different texture maps or per-vertex interpolated values such as surface normals or light direction vectors. In GLSL, you can compute the texture-space lighting vectors L and H in a vertex program; however, when you implement normal mapping using these texture functions, you have to do the texture-space calculations in your application, outside OpenGL.

Implementing a complete normal-mapping algorithm, including specular highlights and normalization cubemaps, with texture environment functions is pretty complicated. I'll outline the basic steps needed for normal mapping with diffuse lighting. A complete example with specular highlights and cubemaps is on this book's website. The following code snippet shows how to configure the textures stages to compute the diffuse lighting with dot(N, L):

```
// set up stage 0 to compute dot(N,L)
glActiveTexture(GL_TEXTURE0);
glEnable(GL_TEXTURE_2D);
glBindTexture (GL_TEXTURE_2D, normalMapId);


// enable dot3 texture environment function...
glTexEnvf(GL_TEXTURE_ENV, GL_TEXTURE_ENV_MODE, GL_COMBINE);
glTexEnvf(GL_TEXTURE_ENV, GL_COMBINE_RGB, GL_DOT3_RGB);
// with the normal map as operand0...
glTexEnvf(GL_TEXTURE_ENV, GL_SOURCE0_RGB, GL_TEXTURE);
glTexEnvf(GL_TEXTURE_ENV, GL_OPERAND0_RGB, GL_SRC_COLOR);
// and the light direction vector L as operand1
glTexEnvf(GL_TEXTURE_ENV, GL_SOURCE1_RGB, GL_PRIMARY_COLOR);
glTexEnvf(GL_TEXTURE_ENV, GL_OPERAND1_RGB, GL_SRC_COLOR);


// set up stage 1 to modulate the diffuse texture with dot(N,L)
glActiveTexture(GL_TEXTURE1);
glBindTexture (GL_TEXTURE_2D, diffuseTexId);
```

```
// enable modulation texture environment function...
glTexEnvf(GL_TEXTURE_ENV, GL_TEXTURE_ENV_MODE, GL_COMBINE);
glTexEnvf(GL_TEXTURE_ENV, GL_COMBINE_RGB, GL_MODULATE);
// with previously computed dot(N,L) as operand0...
glTexEnvf(GL_TEXTURE_ENV, GL_SOURCE0_RGB, GL_PREVIOUS);
glTexEnvf(GL_TEXTURE_ENV, GL_OPERAND0_RGB, GL_SRC_COLOR);
// and the diffuse texture as operand1
glTexEnvf(GL_TEXTURE_ENV, GL_SOURCE1_RGB, GL_TEXTURE);
glTexEnvf(GL_TEXTURE_ENV, GL_OPERAND1_RGB, GL_SRC_COLOR);

// now draw the geometry
glBegin(GL_TRIANGLE);
for(int i = 0; i < 3; i++) {
  // compute texture space matrix and compute texture space
  // light direction vector L
  // ...

  // pass L as primary color
  glColor3f(L.x, L.y, L.z);
  // pass vertex positions and texture coordinates
  glVertex3f(vert[i].x, vert[i].y, vert[i].z);
  glMultiTexCoord2f(GL_TEXTURE0, tc[i].s, tc[i].t);
  glMultiTexCoord2f(GL_TEXTURE1, tc[i].s, tc[i].t);
}
glEnd();
```

The key to implementing an algorithm like normal mapping with these texture operations is understanding how to hook the various texture stages together and which texture environment functions to use. Adding a normalization cubemap and specular highlighting to the above code requires a few more texture stages, but the essential method is the same. By the way, if you were wondering, the GL_DOT3_RGB operation used above automatically unpacks range-compressed normals stored in a texture map.

Computing a Normal Map

You can build a normal map from a height field. Suppose $h_{i,j}$ is the value of the height field at a given texel (i, j), $h_{i+1,j}$ is the height of the neighboring texel on the right, and $h_{i+1,j}$ is the height of the neighboring texel above the given texel. Then the surface normal is given by the following formula:

$$normal = \frac{(h_{i,j} - h_{i,j+1},\ h_{i,j} - h_{i+1,j},\ 1)}{\sqrt{(h_{i,j} - h_{i,j+1})^2 + (h_{i,j} - h_{i+1,j})^2 + 1}}.$$

Note that the denominator of this equation is a vector, and the numerator is the length of that vector, so the surface normal is normalized. There are other methods for generating a normal map from a height field, but this method usually suffices.

A more sophisticated method for building a normal map is based on ray tracing. Recall that the whole point of bump mapping is to produce the illusion of high geometric complexity. Suppose you have a low-polygon model containing several hundred to a few thousand polygons. If you have a high-polygon version of the same model containing perhaps several hundred thousand polygons, you could trace rays from the low-polygon model to the high-polygon model. At each intersection point on the high-polygon model, you would compute the surface normal and store it in a normal map. In fact, there are commercial software tools for doing exactly this.

Final Thoughts

Bump mapping provides a method for increasing the apparent geometric complexity of a polygonal model by making fine-scale adjustments to the surface normal. Normal mapping is simple to implement in GLSL and produces compelling results. Other methods, such as parallax mapping and per-pixel displacement mapping, improve upon the basic normal-mapping paradigm (see documents by Walsh and Donnelly for additional information on these other methods). Any game developed now or in the near future will surely use some version of bump mapping to produce high-quality graphics.

References

Akenine-Möller, Tomas, and Eric Haines. *Real-Time Rendering*, 2nd ed. Natick, MA: A. K. Peters, 2002.

Donnelly, William . "Per-pixel displacement mapping with distance functions." In *GPU Gems 2*, 123–142. Upper Saddle River, NJ: Addison-Wesley, 2005.

Fernando, Randima, and Mark J. Kilgard. *The Cg Tutorial*. Boston: Addison-Wesley, 2003.

Lengyel, Eric. *Mathematics for 3D Game Programming and Computer Graphics*, 2nd ed. Hingham, MA: Charles River Media, 2003.

Walsh, Terry. "Parallax mapping with offset limiting: A per-pixel approximation of uneven surfaces." **http://www.infiscape.com/doc/parallax_mapping.pdf**. 2004.

Parallax Mapping

James Ritts

Imagine you are holding an aerial photograph of a mountain. Rather than having been printed on a piece of paper, however, the photograph is silk-screened onto a thin sheet of rubber, which can be stretched, distorting the image in the process. Now visualize sticking a pin in the rubber sheet, right on the peak of the mountain, and tugging it towards one edge, warping the photograph in such a way that the mountain appears as if it is being viewed from an angle—as though you have flown some distance beyond the summit. This scenario captures the idea behind a per-pixel technique known as *parallax mapping*, in which the texture coordinate at each pixel fragment is perturbed by a small amount in order to simulate the parallax effect caused by a changing viewing angle over surface relief. Since the effect takes the location of the viewer into account and simulates the relative motion of small features at different heights on a rough surface, it complements other techniques that only affect lighting. Particularly when combined with bump mapping, parallax mapping can produce a highly convincing illusion of surface complexity.

Figure 5.7 depicts the identity scenario, in which the eye vector is aligned with the surface normal and the texture coordinate under the viewer does not need adjustment. As the view angle changes, areas of high relief are effectively shifted away from the viewer, as in Figure 5.8. Note that the illustrations are approximate; in reality, the texture coordinate is modified independently for each fragment, and each fragment has its own interpolated value of the view vector.

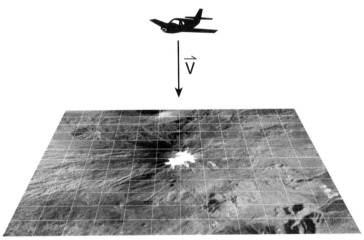

Figure 5.7 Since most textures represent an overhead image of a real surface, the texture coordinate for the point on the polygon directly underneath the eye does not need to be adjusted.

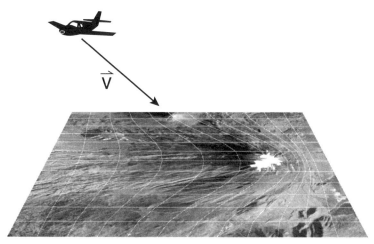

Figure 5.8 As the eye moves away from perpendicular, the texture coordinates for areas of high relief are nudged toward the eye, which correspondingly causes those same parts of texture itself to retreat from the eye.

Methodology

On top of what is already required for standard texture mapping, two additional pieces of input are needed by a pixel shader that implements parallax mapping: a height function, which specifies the contour of the surface being simulated by the material; and the location of the viewer or camera. The height function is nearly always represented by a texture map (henceforth the *height map*), and can be provided to the shader within the alpha channel of the material's color or normal textures. The view vector, however, requires somewhat more thought, as it must be expressed to the shader in the context of a surface-aligned coordinate system known as *tangent space.*

A more thorough treatment of tangent space can be found within the previous section on bump mapping. In brief terms, tangent space at any arbitrary point on a mesh's surface is defined by a vector basis that includes the normal vector at that point, along with two other precalculated vectors (called the *tangent* and *binormal vectors*) that are both orthogonal to the normal as well as to each other, and which define the tangent plane at that point. So for any vector in tangent space, its z component represents a perpendicular distance from the surface, and its x and y components represent tangential distances across the surface. Since vertex normal data is usually already provided for any given mesh, and the binormal can be obtained with a cross product, all that remains to precalculate for each vertex is the tangent vector. In a game implementation, the tangent vectors for a mesh's vertices are typically generated either by an external tool, or at load time within the engine, and then stored within a buffer object. The calculations that subsequently compute the view vector and transform it into tangent space are carried out by a vertex shader, which passes the vector to the pixel shader as an interpolated variable.

The equation we will use to model the parallax effect of an uneven surface is shown below and illustrated in Figure 5.9. In the equation, *To* and *Tn* are the original and adjusted texture coordinates, respectively. *V* is the tangent-space view vector. The coefficient h' is a scaled version of a sampled value from the height map, and will be discussed in more detail presently.

$$T_n = T_o + h' * \frac{V_{\{x,y\}}}{V_{\{z\}}}$$

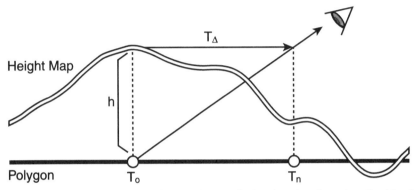

Figure 5.9 Depicted is the polygon, along with the virtual surface described by the height function. In parallax mapping, a texture coordinate offset, T∆, is calculated for every pixel from the tangential component of the tangent-space view vector.

Geometrically, the parallax equation couldn't be simpler. The division of the view vector's x and y components by its z component is nothing more than a slope calculation. Since the height value, h', constitutes a *rise* along the z, or normal, axis, the product of h' and the view vector's slope yields a proportional, tangential *run* across the model's surface. This tangential offset is then added to the original texture coordinate, nudging it in the direction of the eye to a location that more closely approximates the intersection of the view vector with the height map.

To understand how a movement along the view vector can be employed as a texture-coordinate offset, recall that the view vector is represented within a coordinate system that follows the contour of the model's surface. The same can be said of the more familiar two-dimensional coordinate system in which texture coordinates are expressed. In fact, the transformation matrices that delineate tangent space are typically calculated directly from how texture coordinates are oriented across a mesh, such that for any point on the mesh's surface, the tangent-space x-axis is roughly aligned with texture U, and the y-axis with texture V. Thus, a distance along *Vx* or *Vy* amounts to an offset in *Tu* or *Tv*, respectively.

Like the view vector, the height coefficient needs some massaging before it can be used in the parallax calculation. Texel lookups within a pixel shader return floating-point numbers that range from 0.0 to 1.0. If sampled values from the height map were left in this range when used for the height coefficient in the parallax equation, the resulting texture coordinates would be massively overcorrected, producing a shimmering mess of pixels. Instead, the value returned by the texture sampler must be transformed into a more reasonable range using constant scale and bias values, as in the following equation:

$$h' = (h * s) + b$$

The values of s and b are arbitrary and tunable. Nonetheless, for any individual material, a scale value should ideally be chosen that best represents the range of depth of the surface being represented in the texture. For example, if a material's texture is a photograph of a square-foot section of cobblestone road, and the physical difference in height between the tops of the stones and the underlying mortar is 1/2", then an appropriate scale factor would be (1/2" *deep* / 12" *across*), or 0.042. Once the scaling factor is determined, a bias value is usually chosen that centers the range of the height coefficient about 0. For the cobblestone texture, a good bias value would therefore be −0.021, or more generally:

$$b = \frac{-s}{2}$$

The Bad News

Of course, parallax mapping is still just a loose approximation. While convincing on surfaces that are viewed close to face-on, the technique tends to deteriorate at acute viewing angles, for several reasons. The first reason is that, as with bump mapping, we are not actually modifying the underlying geometry or creating new geometry; thus, the low polygonal detail of the surface is revealed when seen in profile. Additionally, parallax mapping cannot address situations in which one area of a texture is occluded by another, taller foreground feature on the same texture. Perhaps its biggest failure is the problem posed by high-frequency information in the height map. That is, at low viewing angles, steep gradients in the height map can cause ugly visual artifacts collectively called *texture swim*, where the adjusted texture coordinates appear overcorrected or discontinuous.

The biggest source of texture swim is illustrated in the surface diagram in Figure 5.9: notice how the "corrected" texture coordinate significantly overshoots the actual intersection point of the view vector with the height function, the point on the texture the viewer *should* see at that angle. The parallax equation only takes the height of the surface at the original texture coordinate into account and ignores the surface's overall shape. Put another way, it effectively assumes that every point on the surface is at the same displacement from the underlying polygon! This assumption allows for a fast shader implementation without any branch operations, but is physically wrong. Nonetheless, there exist effective and efficient ways to mitigate swim artifacts.

Offset Limiting

By virtue of its simplicity, one of the most common ways to reduce texture swim is the simple removal of the 1/z term in the parallax equation, resulting in the modified equation below.

$$T_n = T_o + h'^* \ V_{\{x,y\}}$$

Taking out the z division limits the texture offset to a maximum of h' in both the U and V directions, which goes a long way towards reducing artifacts from overcorrection. If the view vector is normalized, then at steep viewing angles, the modified function approximates the original, more physically correct equation, since the value of z is close to 1.0. As the view angle approaches 0, each fragment's calculated texture-coordinate offset approaches, but does not exceed, the scaled height-map value for that fragment. Limiting the offset in this manner predictably results in a conspicuous "flattening" effect that destroys the parallax illusion at glancing angles, but it turns out to be far less visually disturbing than texture swim.

It's worth noting that in the original parallax equation, the view vector was used to calculate slopes, and so the magnitude of the vector didn't matter. With the 1/z term removed, the x and y components of the view vector instead become scaling factors, and therefore must be prenormalized. Fortunately, the extra cost of the normalization operation is at least partially compensated for by the removal of the z division. Depending on your normalization method (or whether your shader already requires a normalized view vector for other calculations), this may be more or less efficient overall.

Also note that another side effect of removing the z division is that the equation now forces an orientation upon the view vector. In this case, the vector is assumed to point away from the surface, towards the eye. If the opposite is the case in your implementation, simply reverse the sign of h'.

Self-Shadowing

Particularly on video accelerators that implement Shader Model 3.0, which provides branching support in its instruction set, it is efficient and possible to implement rudimentary ray casting in hardware. While it is, strictly speaking, beyond the topic of this section, one pertinent application of ray casting is to compute self-shadowing at a subtriangle level, using the same height map that was used for parallax mapping.

Figure 5.10 illustrates a method for determining whether a fragment is in shadow. We begin at the point on the virtual surface directly above the parallax-adjusted texture coordinate, and march a ray along the light vector, pausing every step to check whether the z component of the ray is greater or less than the height-map value at that location.

If we are still above the virtual surface, we continue marching. If, on the other hand, we have dipped underneath it, our original point is therefore in shadow, and the fragment color is darkened.

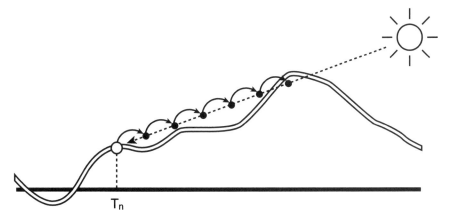

T_n

Figure 5.10 Starting at a fragment's texture coordinate, a ray is marched along the light vector and repeatedly tested for intersection with the height map. In the above diagram, the ray intersects the height map upon the sixth iteration, placing *Tn* in shadow.

A well-tuned and commented vertex and pixel shader implementation that supports normal mapping, parallax mapping, and self-shadowing can be found on the book's website. For clarity, pseudocode of the self-shadowing algorithm is listed below. As input, the algorithm takes the height map, light vector, starting texture coordinate, and a floating-point step value representing a small vertical distance, and returns TRUE if the fragment is in shadow. Note that a small value is added to RayHeight upon initialization to avoid errors due to rounding.

```
function SelfShadow( texture HeightMap,
                     vector3 LightVector,
                     vector2 TexCoord,
                     float   Step )
{
  float SurfaceHeight = HeightMap. At( TexCoord );
  float RayHeight = SurfaceHeight + _;

  vector2 TexCoordDelta = Step * LightVector. XY / LightVector. Z;

  while( RayHeight > SurfaceHeight && RayHeight < 1. 0 )
  {
    RayHeight += Step;
    TexCoord += TexCoordDelta;
```

```
    SurfaceHeight = HeightMap. At( TexCoord );
  }

  return( RayHeight < SurfaceHeight );
}
```

Figures 5.11 to 5.13 show some screenshots that illustrate the benefit of parallax mapping. Figure 5.11 is rendered with normal mapping alone. Figure 5.12 adds parallax mapping, and Figure 5.13 enables self-shadowing.

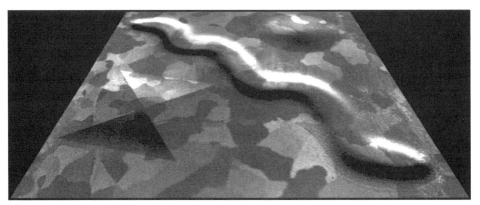

Figure 5.11 Image rendered with normal mapping.

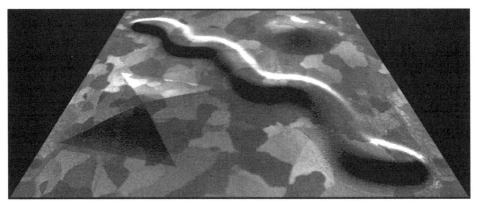

Figure 5.12 Image rendered with normal mapping and parallax mapping.

Figure 5.13 Image rendered with normal mapping, parallax mapping, and self-shadowing.

References

Walsh, Terry. Parallax Mapping with Offset Limiting: A Per-Pixel Approximation of Uneven Surfaces. **http://www.infiscape.com/doc/parallax_mapping.pdf**.

McGuire, Morgan, and Max McGuire. Steep Parallax Mapping. **http://graphics.cs.brown.edu/games/SteepParallax/index.html**.

Displacement Mapping

James Ritts

Most pixel-shader-based techniques for increasing the apparent detail of a model, such as bump mapping and parallax mapping, have inherent shortcomings, particularly when it comes to accurately rendering the profiles of objects. Since they don't modify the vertices that make up a surface, and instead, in the interest of efficiency, focus on manipulating texture or lighting calculations, mesh edges tend to look smooth and flat, revealing the relative lack of underlying geometrical detail. In recent times, however, memory bandwidth and graphics hardware performance have been approaching an important threshold, where vertex processing is fast enough that the detail simulated by techniques such as bump mapping can be conveyed by actual geometry at real-time speeds. As a result, another image-based technique known as *displacement mapping* is quickly becoming a method of choice for adding surface detail to a model. Rather than modifying the colors of pixels within triangle boundaries, displacement mapping uses a height map to form the actual geometrical contour of a model at run time.

Methodology

Generally speaking, displacement mapping begins with a low-frequency, or *smooth*, yet high-polygon base mesh, and then nudges each vertex in the mesh along its normal vector by an amount that is queried from an image. Expressed mathematically, the fundamental operation in displacement mapping—the translation of a vertex along its normal—is the simple summation:

$$\vec{V_n} = \vec{V_o} + s * h * \vec{N}$$

In the equation, Vo and Vn are the original and adjusted positions of the current vertex, respectively. The vector N is the vertex normal. The scalar value h is the texture sample at the current texture coordinate. Finally, the constant s is a simple scale value, applied to the offsets of all vertices, that controls the overall amount of displacement. The texture is known as the *height map* or *displacement map*, and needs to have only one color component per pixel. Provided the base mesh contains sufficiently dense and numerous vertices to convey the detail in the height map, the information contained in the height map is thus accurately "textured" onto the geometry itself. Figure 5.14 illustrates the effect.

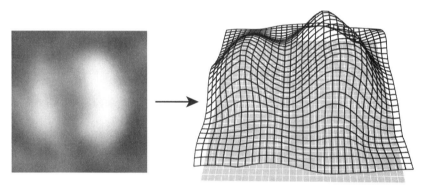

Figure 5.14 Through displacement mapping, the height map on the left may be "textured" onto a flat surface, resulting in the more detailed and contoured mesh on the right.

Tessellation

The concept of displacement mapping is by no means new. Implemented in software, it has long been used in commercial modeling packages. It has also been popular in game engines as a method for simulating water and for rendering dynamically generated or deformed terrain. More recently, displacement mapping has been used to efficiently add fine geometrical detail to models. Common to most applications of displacement mapping is a front-end component that subdivides, or *tessellates*, the model where geometrical detail is needed most, prior to vertex displacement.

As of this writing, the major players in graphics hardware have yet to manufacture a consumer-level video card that can procedurally generate new vertices in hardware, so real-time polygonal tessellation must still be performed by the CPU. There are numerous, differing techniques for tessellating a model, many of them geared towards specific applications of displacement mapping. For instance, terrain engines often tessellate using patch-based (see Wagner's "Terrain Geomorphing in the Vertex Shader") or tile-based (see Snook's "Simplified Terrain Using Interlocking Tiles") techniques that optimize for the more gradually varying geometry that is typical of terrain. Displacement mapping for arbitrary meshes requires a more generalized tessellation algorithm, such as N-Patches (see Akenine-Möller and Haines), or Moule and McCool's adaptive tessellation method. Most tessellation algorithms used in displacement-mapping implementations scale the amount of subdivision (for any particular point on a mesh) using a heuristic that combines several factors that may include distance, visibility, and the amount of height-map curvature at that point. The end result is, ideally, a mesh with just enough geometric resolution to convey all of the detail in the desired height map.

Implementation

While tessellation must still be carried out by the CPU, with the arrival of video accelerators that support Vertex Shader Model 3.0, the displacement operation itself can now be accelerated in hardware. In particular, the new vertex shader architecture adds the TXL instruction, which allows vertex shaders to arbitrarily fetch texel values from a small set of restricted texture types. This provides major performance gains for image-based geometrical effects: vertex data need not be recalculated whenever the displacement map is updated, which can avoid a costly copy operation into and out of video memory. Also, the graphics processor's efficient SIMD architecture can displace large amounts of vertex data very quickly, offloading the task from the CPU. Best of all, adding displacement-mapping functionality to a vertex shader often has virtually no overall performance impact; within the rendering pipeline, most games are bottlenecked in pixel operations, leaving headroom for additional complexity in vertex processing.

A demo application that can perform displacement mapping equivalently in both software and hardware can be downloaded from the website for this book. A simple OpenGL assembly vertex shader that implements displacement mapping is listed below.

The first line of the vertex shader simply provides versioning information to OpenGL, and denotes that the text that follows it is a vertex program conforming to the GL_ARB_vertex_program extension. The second line is a compile-time option that enables Shader Model 3.0 support on NVIDIA hardware; without it, OpenGL's shader assembler will balk at the TXL instruction discussed below.

note

> At present, only some NVIDIA products support the complete Shader Model 3.0 feature set, which is required to accelerate displacement mapping in hardware. ATI is not far behind, however, and many other devices will support version 3.0 functionality in the near future; check your video hardware manufacturer's developer website to see if your device supports the GL_NV_vertex_program3 extension.

```
!!ARBvp1.0
OPTION NV_vertex_program3;
```

The following three lines declare the variables we will use in the vertex shader. The first PARAM statement defines a read-only variable that acts as a reference to the current modelview-projection matrix. The second PARAM statement defines a constant scale value to be applied to the amount of displacement; a value of 5.0 means that each vertex can move a maximum distance of five object-space units from its original position. The third line declares mutable, temporary storage to hold intermediate values in our calculations.

```
PARAM MVP[4] = { state.matrix.mvp };
PARAM HEIGHT_SCALE = { 5.0 };
TEMP temp_position, displace_texel;
```

The next instruction is what allows us to accelerate displacement mapping on the GPU; it performs a 2D-texel lookup on an actively bound texture. Since we are reading from a luminance texture, only a single floating-point value will be sampled and stored in the red component of the destination register. That is, after the TXL instruction executes, displace_texel.x will contain our height value.

```
TXL displace_texel, vertex.texcoord, texture[0], 2D;
```

Next, we scale up the displacement value.

```
MUL displace_texel.x, displace_texel.x, HEIGHT_SCALE;
```

The following two instructions are what actually displace the vertex. The scaled height value stored in displace_texel.x is multiplied by the vertex normal, and the product is added to the original vertex position. This new location of the vertex is then written to one of the temporary registers we declared above. The w component of the new position is then set to 1.0 to prepare it for its transformation into clip space.

```
MAD temp_position.xyz, vertex.normal, displace_texel.x, vertex.position;
MOV temp_position.w, 1.0;
```

The next four lines perform the calculation required of most vertex shaders: take an object-space vertex position and transform it into clip space (sometimes called projection space), using the concatenated modelview-projection matrix. This is accomplished with a matrix-vector multiplication, implemented as four dot products.

```
DP4 result.position.x, MVP[0], temp_position;
DP4 result.position.y, MVP[1], temp_position;
DP4 result.position.z, MVP[2], temp_position;
DP4 result.position.w, MVP[3], temp_position;
```

Finally, the last line denotes the end of the vertex shader.

```
END
```

References

Akenine-Möller, Tomas, and Eric Haines. "Bézier Triangles and N-Patches." Gamasutra, **http://www.gamasutra.com/features/20020715/mollerhaines_01.htm**.

Moule, Kevin, and Michael D. McCool. "Efficient Bounded Adaptive Tessellation of Displacement Maps." University of Waterloo. **http://www.cgl.uwaterloo.ca/~krmoule/dmap_gi2002.pdf**.

Snook, Greg. "Simplified Terrain Using Interlocking Tiles." *In Game Programming Gems 2*, 377–83. Hingham: Charles River Media, 2001.

Wagner, Daniel. "Terrain Geomorphing in the Vertex Shader." *In ShaderX2: Shader Programming Tips and Tricks with DirectX 9.0*, 18–32, ed. Wolfgang F. Engel. Plano: Wordware Publishing, 2003.

Detail Texturing

Luke Philpot

Low-resolution textures, when stretched onto a surface, have the tendency to pixelate and lose detail (especially when filtered). This means that a single texel is shared across a number of pixels, resulting in an unrealistic scene (especially when a base texture is stretched over a large terrain mesh).

You could use large (2,048×2,048 or even higher) textures to increase the amount of detail, but this greatly increases the memory requirements. The benefits of doing this often aren't worth the memory and bandwidth cost, since this added detail tends to be viewed only infrequently.

A viable alternative is to use a technique known as *detail texturing* to give the illusion that there is more detail on the surface. A single detail texture is tiled several times over the base texture. As shown in Figure 5.15, detail textures tend to contain high-frequency information that repeats in a fairly uniform manner across the surface. They are typically represented as medium resolution (256×256 to 512×512 pixels) grayscale images. Because of these characteristics, detail textures allow you gain detail at a much lower memory cost than using high-resolution versions of your base textures. Figure 5.16 illustrates the visual impact detail textures can make on terrain rendering.

Detail texturing is most commonly used in terrain renderers, but it provides the same effect for any kind of geometry.

Detail texturing is achieved by tiling the detail texture over a surface a few times, generally repeating at a higher frequency than the base texture. This is shown in Figure 5.17. The detail texture is usually modulated with the base texture, though it can be additively blended. The example presented here uses modulation.

Figure 5.15 An example detail texture.

Figure 5.16 Side-by-side comparison of a terrain with and without detail texturing.

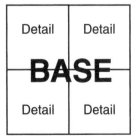

Figure 5.17 Detail-texturing diagram.

Detail texturing can be implemented with OpenGL in a single pass by using multitexturing, fragment shaders (via either `ARB_fragment_program`, the OpenGL Shading Language, or vendor-specific extensions) or by using a dual-pass approach (rendering the scene with the base texture first, then rerendering it with the detail texture and blending the result together). Unfortunately, the dual-pass method can be expensive, as each detail-textured polygon needs to be drawn twice, whereas with multitexturing or fragment shaders the draw can be done in a single pass. We'll be using multitexturing, since it will provide a viable solution on a very broad range of hardware, but the method presented here can be easily adapted to fragment shaders.

Multitexturing

Using multitexturing to perform detail texturing is very easy. The first step is to bind your base texture to texture unit 0 and your detail texture to texture unit 1.

To tile the detail texture on top of the base texture, first use normal texture coordinates for texture unit 0. For unit 1, however, the texture coordinates need to repeat at a different frequency. We can achieve this by multiplying our texture coordinates for the detail texture unit by the amount of times we want it to tile. For example, if our original coordinates were (1.0f, 1.0f) and we wanted it to tile three times, the coordinates would become (3.0f, 3.0f).

tip

Ideally, the detail texture should only be rendered when the base texture is being magnified. Unfortunately, determining whether or not this is the case requires nontrivial calculations. Instead, a similar effect can be achieved if the average value of all texels in the detail map is 0.5. When using bilinear filtering (or even better, mipmapping), the detail texture will blur and effectively disappear as it becomes minified.

There is one last thing to do in order to have the detail texture show up correctly. As mentioned earlier, we'll be modulating the detail texture with the base texture. Modulating has a darkening effect, since we're multiplying the base color by a value between 0.0 and 1.0. We'd like to have the detail texture both darken and lighten the base texture. We can accomplish this by using a texture combiner to scale the detail texture value by 2 before it is used:

```
glTexEnvi(GL_TEXTURE_ENV, GL_TEXTURE_ENV_MODE, GL_COMBINE_ARB);
glTexEnvi(GL_TEXTURE_ENV, GL_RGB_SCALE_ARB, 2);
```

When using this method for terrain height maps (with a large color map stretched over the entire terrain), you can generally get away with tiling the detail texture once across each polygon rather than tiling it three or four times. The following code was used to generate the image shown in Figure 5.15.

```
glMultiTexCoord2fARB(GL_TEXTURE0_ARB, 1.0f, 1.0f);
glMultiTexCoord2fARB(GL_TEXTURE1_ARB, 4.0f, 4.0f);
glVertex3f(10.0f, -1.5f, -40.0f);

glMultiTexCoord2fARB(GL_TEXTURE0_ARB, 0.0f, 1.0f);
glMultiTexCoord2fARB(GL_TEXTURE1_ARB, 0.0f, 4.0f);
glVertex3f(-10.0f, -1.5f, -40.0f);

glMultiTexCoord2fARB(GL_TEXTURE0_ARB, 0.0f, 0.0f);
glMultiTexCoord2fARB(GL_TEXTURE1_ARB, 0.0f, 0.0f);
glVertex3f(-10.0f, -1.5f, 0.0f);

glMultiTexCoord2fARB(GL_TEXTURE0_ARB, 1.0f, 0.0f);
glMultiTexCoord2fARB(GL_TEXTURE1_ARB, 4.0f, 0.0f);
glVertex3f(10.0f, -1.5f, 0.0f);
```

Conclusion

Detail mapping is a cheap and easy way of making your scenes a bit more realistic. So long as you have a free multitexture unit, you can implement it with a minimal effect on performance.

This method is best used when rendering large height maps with a single color map texture stretched over it. It makes your terrain textures look higher-resolution than they really are, and combined with effects like lighting can make your terrains look very realistic.

The demo, which can be downloaded from the website, illustrates the topics covered here and allows you to modify different parameters to better understand how detail textures work.

Projective Textures

Andrei Gradinari

Imagine a situation where you want an image to be projected onto your scene as if by a slide projector. For example, you might be programming a game in which you need to implement a flashlight, a spotlight, car headlights, or moonlight coming through a window. The technique for accomplishing this sort of effect is *projective texture mapping*. As you might expect, a projective texture is simply an image projected onto your scene's geometry. There are two kinds of projective textures: parallel and perspective.

In the left-hand image in Figure 5.18, a texture is projected onto a surface by a directional source—typically something effectively located at infinity, such as the sun or moon. With parallel projection, all projection rays emanating from the light source are parallel to each other, aimed in a single direction. In real life, parallel projection can be seen, for example, when inside a church, with sunlight shining through a stained-glass window and onto the floor. In a simulation of such a scene, the projected texture would be a simple, "flat" image of the window itself; a specific procedure is then followed to apply the texture to the geometry comprising the floor.

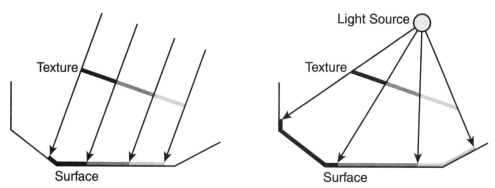

Figure 5.18 Parallel projective texturing (left) and perspective projective texturing (right).

The right-hand image in Figure 5.18 illustrates how perspective projective texturing works. In this case, light is emitted by a light source that is within or close to the scene, and thus the projection rays diverge from each other, forming a cone that spreads outward as distance from the light increases. An example of such a projection in real life is a slide projector; the projected texture is equivalent to the film inserted into the slide projector, and the light source is the lamp inside of it.

This section will concentrate more heavily on perspective projective texturing, since it is used more widely in practice. Implementing parallel projective texturing is similar, and the differences between the two methods will be covered later.

note

In this article I will use the terms *projector view matrix, and projector projection matrix*, in addition to *view matrix*, and *projection matrix*. Be careful not to confuse them, as their meanings are distinct. The term *projection matrix* refers to the OpenGL projection matrix used to transform vertices from view space into clip space; projector projection matrix, on the other hand, is a *projection matrix* belonging to a particular projector in a scene.

When dealing with projective textures, the most important mathematical concepts to grasp are the texture's *view* and *projection* matrices. These matrices should be generated for each projector in a scene, such that they accomplish the following:

- The p*rojector view matrix* transforms global-space vertex coordinates into the projector's local space (known as projector-view space).

- The projector *projection matrix* transforms vertices from the projector's local space to the projector's clip space (see Figure 5.19).

Together, these matrices define the following function, which takes a global-space vertex position as an argument and evaluates to the vertex's projective texture coordinate.

$$
(1) \quad \begin{bmatrix} S \\ T \\ R \\ Q \end{bmatrix} = P_p * V_p * \begin{bmatrix} X \\ Y \\ Z \\ W \end{bmatrix}_g
$$

Vp — Projector's *view* matrix.

Pp — Projector's *projection* matrix.

[X, Y, Z, W]g — Global-space vertex position.

[S, T, R, Q] — Resulting vertex texture coordinates.

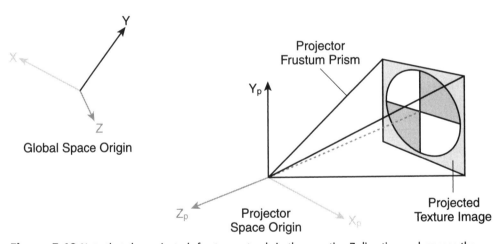

Figure 5.19 Note that the projector's frustum extends in the negative-Z direction and crosses the projected texture image at its center point.

Q Coordinate Division

As usual, the resulting texture coordinates are linearly interpolated over the triangle face and passed through the graphics pipeline to be rasterized. However, there still remains one operation to be performed for each pixel's interpolated texture coordinate before it may be used in a texel lookup: each pixel's texture coordinate's S and T values must be divided by the Q value. This is known as *perspective division*.

It might surprise you to know that OpenGL performs this division by Q for each pixel, even when you do not ask it to. It does this in order to make textures scale correctly with distance from the viewer—that is, to be *perspective correct*. Perspective-correct texturing is itself a fairly complicated topic, and beyond the scope of this section. But it is important to keep in mind that this operation will always take place. In most cases (for example, when simply applying a 2D texture to a mesh), the client-side Q value for each texture coordinate is equal to one, and thus dividing by Q has no impact on the values of S and T. In projective texturing, however, this division by Q becomes very useful. The effect of the Q coordinate can be seen in Figure 5.20.

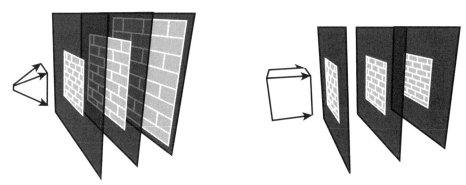

Figure 5.20 In the image on the right, the Q coordinate is set to 1.0 for all vertices. In contrast, the image on the left depicts the effect of scaling Q according to the vertex's distance from the projector.

To set up projective texture mapping, you first generate the projector's view and projection matrices. Building these matrices manually can be complicated; fortunately, the GLU library provides a set of useful functions for matrix creation and manipulation, and we will use them to build our projector matrices.

- `gluLookAt()` can be used to generate a projector's view matrix.
- `gluPerspective()` can be used to generate a projector's projection matrix.

The demo for this section on the book's website contains a class implementation called `CProjector`. This class provides basic functionality needed to work with projective texturing; specifically, it can build projector's matrices as well as set up the OpenGL pipeline for rendering with projective textures.

Below are two routines: the first generates the projector's view matrix, and the second generates the projector's projection matrix.

```
void CProjector :: LookAt(vec3 pos, vec3 at, vec3 v_up) {
  glMatrixMode(GL_MODELVIEW);
  glPushMatrix();
  glLoadIdentity();
```

```
    gluLookAt(pos.x, pos.y, pos.z,  at.x, at.y, at.z,
              v_up.x, v_up.y, v_up.z);
    glGetFloatv(GL_MODELVIEW_MATRIX, (GLfloat*)&mat4_view);
    glPopMatrix();
}
void CProjector :: SetProjection(float aspect_ratio_xy, float fovy) {
    glMatrixMode(GL_PROJECTION);
    glPushMatrix();
    glLoadIdentity();
    gluPerspective(fovy, aspect_ratio_xy, 1, 100);
    glGetFloatv(GL_PROJECTION_MATRIX, (GLfloat*)&mat4_projection);
    glPopMatrix();
    glMatrixMode(GL_MODELVIEW);
}
```

The matrix-setup routines are very simple. They simply push a new "scratch" matrix onto the stack to protect the existing data, generate the projector matrix, save the matrix to a class variable, and then pop the temporary matrix. It is important to note that OpenGL processes matrices in column major order. Thus, any matrix returned by glGetFloatv() will come in column major order—in other words, transposed.

The key operations in both function calls are highlighted in bold. The projector's view matrix is created by a call to gluLookAt() with the projector's position, look-at point, and up direction. The projector's projection matrix is created by gluPerspective() with the projector's x-to-y aspect ratio and y-axis field-of-view angle. An aspect ratio of 1.0 is typically chosen for projective textures, but any may be used. Note that z_near and z_far can be set to any value, since depth information is neither calculated nor required by projective texturing.

Parallel Texture Projections

The changes required to perform parallel projection instead of perspective are very simple. When generating the projector's projection matrix, use glOrtho() instead of gluPerspective(). The glOrtho() function creates a projection matrix that, when used in equation 1, generates texture coordinates whose Q values are always equal to 1.0. Thus, Q coordinate division does not incur any texture scaling, and the projection appears parallel.

Fixed-Function Projective Texturing

Projective texturing can be implemented using OpenGL's standard texture-coordinate-generation facility. If you have ever implemented cube environment mapping, the glTexGen() functions may be familiar. When texture generation (texgen) is enabled, OpenGL will ignore the user-specified per-vertex texture coordinates and substitute them with procedurally generated data, calculated internally according to the current texgen matrix and texgen function. There are several kinds of texgen functions that are relevant to various applications, such as GL_EYE_LINEAR, GL_OBJECT_LINEAR, and GL_SPHERE_MAP; the most useful mode for projective texturing is GL_EYE_LINEAR. When this function is selected, OpenGL will generate texture coordinates according to the following equation:

$$(2) \quad \begin{bmatrix} S \\ T \\ R \\ Q \end{bmatrix} = TG * MV_i * \begin{bmatrix} X \\ Y \\ Z \\ W \end{bmatrix}_v$$

[X Y Z W]v — Vertex coordinates in view (also known as eye) space.

[S T R Q] — Generated texture coordinates.

TG — Texgen matrix, the product of the projector's view and projection matrices.

MVi — Current modelview matrix inverse.

Note that *MVi* is the current value of the modelview matrix at the time that glTexGenfv() is called. As a result, texture coordinate generation should be set up immediately after the scene's camera (using gluLookAt(), for instance), but before specifying any model or other transformations. That is, MVi in the above equation should contain the inverse of only the view transformations. That way, the view-space vertex positions will be placed back into global space prior to the calculation of the final texture coordinate.

The operation of the OpenGL fixed-function pipeline with and without texgen enabled is shown in Figure 5.21.

Now that the theory has been covered, here are the basic steps in implementing projective texturing using the fixed-function pipeline:

1. Render a basic first pass of the entire scene.
2. Set up scene's camera.
3. Set appropriate texgen modes.
4. Generate the projector's view and projection matrices, and set their product as the texgen matrix.
5. Render a second pass with texturing enabled, along with additive blending.

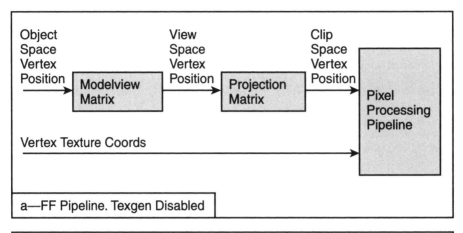

a—FF Pipeline. Texgen Disabled

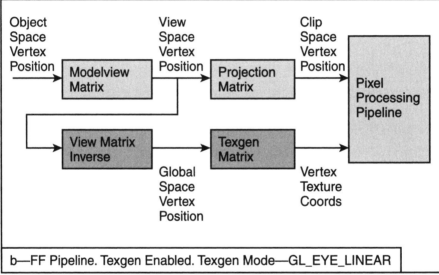

b—FF Pipeline. Texgen Enabled. Texgen Mode—GL_EYE_LINEAR

Figure 5.21 This figure illustrates the differences within the OpenGL pipeline when operating with and without the texgen facility enabled.

The following code snippet illustrates steps 2 through 5:

```
// setting up scene's camera
LookAt(5,-5,4, 0,0,1, 0,0,1);
...
m_Projector.LookAt(pos, pos+dir, up);
m_Projector.SetProjection(1, 60);
m_Projector.SetupTexGen();
...
void CProjector :: SetupTexGen() {
```

```
float offset[16] = { 0.5, 0,   0,   0,
                     0,   0.5, 0,   0,
                     0,   0,   0,   0,
                     0.5, 0.5, 0,   1 };
mat4 m_offset = mat4(offset);
mat4 m_result = (m_offset * mat4_projection * mat4_view).transpose();

glTexGenfv(GL_S, GL_EYE_PLANE, (GLfloat*)&m_result.mat[0]);
glTexGenfv(GL_T, GL_EYE_PLANE, (GLfloat*)&m_result.mat[4]);
glTexGenfv(GL_R, GL_EYE_PLANE, (GLfloat*)&m_result.mat[8]);
glTexGenfv(GL_Q, GL_EYE_PLANE, (GLfloat*)&m_result.mat[12]);

glTexGeni(GL_S, GL_TEXTURE_GEN_MODE, GL_EYE_LINEAR);
glTexGeni(GL_T, GL_TEXTURE_GEN_MODE, GL_EYE_LINEAR);
glTexGeni(GL_R, GL_TEXTURE_GEN_MODE, GL_EYE_LINEAR);
glTexGeni(GL_Q, GL_TEXTURE_GEN_MODE, GL_EYE_LINEAR);

glEnable(GL_TEXTURE_GEN_S);    glEnable(GL_TEXTURE_GEN_T);
glEnable(GL_TEXTURE_GEN_R); glEnable(GL_TEXTURE_GEN_Q);
}
```

Note the presence of an extra matrix: the offset matrix. Without the offset matrix, the resulting texture coordinates would be in the range [−1, 1], akin to projection-space coordinates. The offset matrix places these coordinates into the range [0, 1], which is more appropriate for texturing.

Also note that the product of the projector matrices is transposed before being passed to glTexGenfv(). This is necessary because all three matrices store data in column major order. After transposing, the result is in row major order, which is what glTexGenfv() expects.

Figure 5.22 shows the results of implementing projective texturing as discussed thus far.

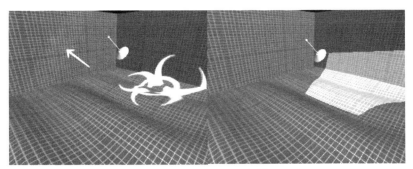

Figure 5.22 A texture projected onto a scene (left) and the projection prism intersecting with the scene geometry (right). The result is fairly satisfying, but there are still some problems.

Eliminating Unwanted Artifacts

Notice the green area (at which the arrow is pointing) in Figure 5.22. This artifact appears in areas where a pixel's texture Q coordinate has a very small value in the region outside of the projection prism. There is a simple way to eliminate this artifact: just disable mip-mapping, using the GL_LINEAR minification filter instead of GL_LINEAR_MIPMAP_LINEAR, as in:

```
glTexParameterf(GL_TEXTURE_2D, GL_TEXTURE_MIN_FILTER, GL_LINEAR);
```

Another common artifact is *reverse projection*, which is a byproduct of the mathematics of projective texturing. Figure 5.23 illustrates reverse projection.

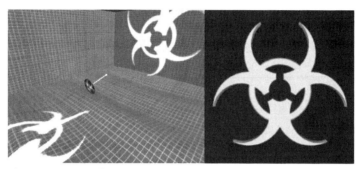

Figure 5.23 The first image (left) depicts reverse projection. The second image shows the texture.

Reverse projection can be eliminated with multitexturing in the following way. Suppose your projection texture is bound to the first texture unit. The second texture unit should be bound to a one-dimensional grayscale texture, as in the image below, and given a wrap mode of GL_CLAMP.

The texgen facility should then be set up for the second texture unit such that primitives with Q coordinates less than 0.0 have negative texture coordinates, and vice versa. Thus, primitives with negative Q coordinates will be mapped with a black color, and the reverse projection will disappear.

Fixed-function projective texturing is rarely used nowadays, and in the future likely won't be used at all. A much more flexible and convenient way to implement projective textures is to use shaders. Most importantly, shaders allow you to perform projective texturing in a single pass with a single set of shader programs.

Projective-Texture Implementation Using Shaders

Projective-texture implementation using shaders is very similar to a fixed-function implementation. The essential idea is to generate the projected texture coordinates in the vertex shader and then perform the Q division in the pixel shader. The main benefit of using shaders is the elimination of a costly extra rendering pass. It also tends to allow for a far more readable, elegant, and unified effect architecture, because shaders are easy to manage, and many different kinds of effects can be combined into a single shader (projective texturing with bump mapping and shadow casting, and so on). Note that you may avoid using a fragment shader to perform Q division and just allow the fixed pipeline to handle it; however, using a fragment shader allows you to more easily eliminate reverse projection.

Here are GLSL implementations of shaders, taken from the demo on the website accompanying this book, that perform projective texturing:

Vertex Shader: proj.vert

```
uniform mat4 mat4_view_inv; // matrix view inverse
void main()
{
  gl_Position = gl_ModelViewMatrix * gl_Vertex;
  vec4 pos_global = mat4_view_inv * gl_Position;

  gl_TexCoord[0] = gl_TextureMatrix[0] * pos_global;

  // ftransform() = gl_ModelViewProjectionMatrix * gl_Vertex
  gl_Position = ftransform();
}
```

Note the presence of the uniform variable mat4_view_inv. Unfortunately, OpenGL does not maintain a copy of the inverse view matrix itself. Rather than blindly combining view and model transformations, you will have to independently keep track of the view transformation yourself. In the demo, the application tracks the view matrix in the following way: after setting up the camera transform using the gluLookAt() function, but before concatenating the model transformations, it saves the current modelview matrix into a local buffer. Once saved, the inverse of the matrix is calculated and later passed into the shader.

The very first instruction in the shader transforms the vertex position from object space into view (also known as pre-projection) space. Next, the vertex position is multiplied with the inverse view matrix, which takes it from view space into global space.

```
gl_Position = gl_ModelViewMatrix * gl_Vertex;  // OBJ space to VIEW space
vec4 pos_global = mat4_view_inv * gl_Position; // VIEW space to GLOBAL space
```

The next instruction, listed below, generates the projective texture coordinate for the vertex by multiplying the calculated global-space vertex position by the texture matrix. The texture matrix should have been set up in exactly the same manner as the texgen matrix in the fixed-function implementation. That is, it should contain the product of the offset, projector view, and projector projection matrices. The value of the texture matrix need only be updated when the projector moves within the scene.

```
gl_TexCoord[0] = gl_TextureMatrix[0] * pos_global;
```

The final instruction is typical of most vertex shaders, and simply transforms the vertex position into clip space.

```
gl_Position = ftransform();
```

Fragment Shader: proj.frag

```
uniform sampler2D tex_unit_0;
void main()
{
  vec3 color = vec3(0,0,0);

  // eliminate reverse projection
  if(gl_TexCoord[0].w > 0.0)
    color = texture2DProj( tex_unit_0, gl_TexCoord[0] ).rgb;

  gl_FragColor = vec4(color, 1.0);
}
```

The first instruction in the fragment shader defines a temporary variable that will hold our final pixel color. Note that it is initialized to black, which we will take advantage of when eliminating reverse projection later on.

```
vec3 color = vec3(0,0,0);
```

The next few statements eliminate reverse projection artifacts by *only* fetching a texel from the projector's texture if the texture coordinate's Q value is positive. To be clear, `gl_TexCoord[0]` contains the projective texture coordinate previously calculated in the vertex shader. In shader notation, dereferencing a vector's w component yields the vector's fourth component; since the vector in question is a texture coordinate, `gl_TexCoord[0].w` gives the value of Q. If the value of Q is less than or equal to zero, no texel fetch occurs, and the pixel color remains black.

```
if(gl_TexCoord[0].w > 0.0)
  color = texture2DProj( tex_unit_0, gl_TexCoord[0] ).rgb;
```

Finally, the computed color value is stored in the pixel.

```
gl_FragColor = vec4(color, 1.0);
```

Dynamic Texturing

James Ritts

Dynamic texturing (also known as render-to-texture, or RTT) is a simple yet very powerful technique that allows an animated, rendered image to be used as an object's texture. Some of its more common applications are

- **Dynamic environment mapping.** Reflections on objects that change in real time along with the surrounding scene.

- **Imposters.** Billboarded sprites that are rerendered on the fly as the viewer moves in relation to them.

- **Dynamic displacement- or normal-map generation.** Hardware-accelerated creation of small geometrical details, such as bullet holes, skid marks, and contact impressions.

- **Motion blur, FSAA, depth of field.** Efficiently allows for various kinds of multipass effects.

- **Glow effects.** Adds a hazy, glowing, or overexposed quality to brightly lit surfaces.

- **Portals, security cameras, television screens, 3D HUD elements.** Generic texturing of a secondary scene onto an object in the primary scene. For such applications, dynamic textures can often be used in place of traditional and sometimes less efficient stencil-based techniques.

The basic procedure for using a dynamic texture is to first render an image, then somehow create a texture from that image and use it as you would any other. In any application of dynamic texturing, the two most important points of consideration are the following: the exact location to which to render the image, and how to get the resulting image into an OpenGL texture.

As for the question of choosing a render destination, one can either render directly to the window buffer or instead use some form of offscreen render target, such as a pixel buffer (henceforth pbuffer), or a framebuffer object (henceforth FBO). Despite how comparatively simple it may be to implement, it is often undesirable to render the image to be textured directly to the window buffer itself. For one, you're stuck with just one rendering context, requiring the management of possibly many state changes when switching between rendering the texture and rendering the actual scene. It also means that the resolution and pixel format of the texture are limited to the size and format of the window itself, which may not be sufficient for every application.

In the future, the best way to render to an offscreen surface will be to use an FBO. FBOs are superior to pbuffers for two major reasons. First, they use a more intuitive and coherent API than pbuffers, and consequently tend to be easier to work with and debug. Perhaps more importantly, FBOs are provided as a generic OpenGL extension, unlike pbuffers, which are implemented differently on different platforms. An application that uses pbuffers and must run in both Windows and Linux, for instance, will have to contain an interface that abstracts both the WGL and glX pbuffer extensions, which is a lot of extra work. Nevertheless, pbuffers are far more widely supported than FBOs on current hardware, and thus will be covered below. See Chapter 1 for a detailed description of FBOs.

Offscreen Rendering with pbuffers

Rendering to a pbuffer in Microsoft Windows requires the extensions WGL_ARB_pbuffer and WGL_ARB_pixel_format to be supported, and consists of the following basic steps. Note that the first and last steps need only be performed once for each pbuffer used by an application.

1. Initialize the pbuffer and related state variables.

2. Set the pbuffer's rendering context as current.

3. Issue OpenGL drawing commands.

4. Release the pbuffer and related state variables.

Creating a pbuffer is a fairly involved process. First, you query for the active device context. Note that, alternatively, the Win32 function GetDC() may be used to obtain the main window's device context if none has been made current through WGL.

```
HDC hPrimaryDevCtx = wglGetCurrentDC();
```

Next, you define the minimum requirements you have for the pbuffer, and you ask WGL to choose a pixel format based on those requirements. This is done by first filling out a zero-terminated array of integers with name-value pairs that denote the parameters.

```
int pBufRequirements[] = {
    WGL_DRAW_TO_PBUFFER_ARB, TRUE,        // Enable rendering to buffer
    WGL_BIND_TO_TEXTURE_RGBA_ARB, TRUE,   // Usable as a texture
    WGL_SUPPORT_OPENGL_ARB, TRUE,         // Associate with OpenGL
    WGL_DOUBLE_BUFFER_ARB, FALSE,         // Single-buffered
    WGL_RED_BITS_ARB, 8,                  // 8 bits of red minimum
    WGL_GREEN_BITS_ARB, 8,                // 8 bits of green minimum
    WGL_BLUE_BITS_ARB, 8,                 // 8 bits of blue minimum
    WGL_DEPTH_BITS_ARB, 16,               // 16 bits for depth minimum
    0 };                                  // End of list
```

This parameter list is then passed to wglChoosePixelFormatARB(), which will output a list of pixel format identifiers that meet the requests.

```
wglChoosePixelFormatARB(
    hPrimaryDevCtx,                 // Device context to query
    (const int*) pBufRequirements, // List of integer parameters
    NULL,                          // List of float parameters
    1,                             // Number of formats to return
    &iPixelFormat,                 // The outputted pixel format
    &iFormatCount );               // Number of outputted formats
```

Now that you have a device context and a pixel format, you can create the pbuffer. Note that a similar name-value parameter list is also accepted by wglCreatePbufferARB(), but for now you will pass nothing.

```
HPBUFFERARB hPBuffer = wglCreatePbufferARB(
  hPrimaryDevCtx,                    // Window device context
  iPixelFormat,                      // Chosen pixel format
  iWidth,                            // pbuffer width
  iHeight,                           // pbuffer height
  NULL );                            // No extra attributes
```

You also need to keep track of the pbuffer's own device context, as well as create an OpenGL rendering context for the pbuffer to store all of its associated render state.

```
HDC hPBufferDevCtx = wglGetPbufferDCARB( hPBuffer );
HGLRC hPBufferRenderCtx = wglCreateContext( hPBufferDevCtx );
```

Now that the pbuffer has been created, it may be used as a render target. To allow the pbuffer to begin accepting render calls, you "make current" on its context handles.

```
wglMakeCurrent( hPBufferDevCtx, hPBufferRenderCtx );
```

With the pbuffer bound as the current render surface, any subsequent OpenGL drawing commands will output to it rather than to the window.

Finally, when finished with the pbuffer, you must release all resources associated with it.

```
wglDeleteContext( hPBufferRenderCtx );
wglReleasePbufferDCARB( hPBuffer, hPBufferDevCtx );
wglDestroyPbufferARB( hPBuffer );
```

Now that the choice of render target has been addressed, the next step is to determine how to initialize an OpenGL texture from the rendered image. There are four primary methods for accomplishing this, detailed in the following sections.

RTT Method 1: glReadPixels()

One of the simplest to implement, yet by far the slowest and most archaic way to render to a texture, is to use glReadPixels() to copy the framebuffer contents to client memory, and then glTexImage2D() to populate a texture from the copy. On current hardware, this method is at least several times slower than Method 2, described next, and thus has become obsolete in practice. The only reason to use glReadPixels() to perform dynamic texturing is if you're procedurally manipulating the image or if the platform does not support the sharing of textures among multiple render contexts.

Procedure:

1. Render image.
2. Read framebuffer with glReadPixels(bufptr).
3. Copy to texture with glTexImage2D(bufptr).

Pros:

- Compatible and portable.
- No need to share contexts if rendering offscreen.

Cons:

- Requires two slow copies across AGP or PCI bus.
- High memory overhead.

RTT Method 2: `glCopyTexSubImage()`

This method represents the quickest way to get a render-to-texture implementation up and running. Its performance characteristics are fairly good, requiring only one copy in video memory per update. It also uses only native OpenGL functions and is supported on any device with OpenGL version 1.1 or later. Note that either `glCopyTexSubImage2D()` or `glCopyTexImage2D()` may be used; however, `glCopyTexImage2D()` reinitializes (and possibly reallocates) the texture each time it is called, and therefore may be slower on some hardware.

When combined with offscreen rendering using pbuffers, a small bit of additional setup is required to get this RTT method to work. Since the pbuffer and the primary window are associated with different rendering contexts, textures and other resources are not shared between them by default. In other words, before you can call `glCopyTexSubImage2D()` to copy a pbuffer's contents to a texture that can be used to render the main scene, you need to tell OpenGL that you intend to share textures between contexts. In Windows, this is accomplished by making the following call after having initialized the pbuffer, passing to it both the pbuffer's and the window's rendering contexts.

```
BOOL wglShareLists( HGLRC renderContext1, HGLRC renderContext2 );
```

Procedure:

1. Render.
2. Copy rendered image to a texture with `glCopyTexSubImage2D()`.

Pros:

- Much faster than Method 1.
- Compatible and portable.
- Needs only one video memory copy.

Cons:

- Still requires a copy.
- Must share contexts if rendering offscreen.

RTT Method 3: `WGL_ARB_render_texture`

On Windows-based platforms that support the extension `WGL_ARB_render_texture`, it is possible to render to a texture with almost no performance overhead. With this extension, instead of copying the color information from the pbuffer into the texture, the pbuffer is "bound" to a texture and used directly.

This method has a few ramifications for how you initialize the pbuffer. Specifically, OpenGL needs to know what sort of texture you intend to bind the pbuffer to. This information is passed to OpenGL in the attributes list parameter of the call to `wglCreatePbufferARB()`. Referring back to the code listing for pbuffers, creating the pbuffer would instead look like the following:

```
int pBufRequirements [] = {
  // pbuffer will bind to a 2D texture
  WGL_TEXTURE_TARGET_ARB, WGL_TEXTURE_2D_ARB,
  // pbuffer will bind to a texture with format RGBA
  WGL_TEXTURE_FORMAT_ARB, WGL_TEXTURE_RGBA_ARB,
  0 };


HPBUFFERARB hPBuffer = wglCreatePbufferARB(
hPrimaryDevCtx,              // Window device context
iPixelFormat,               // Chosen pixel format
iWidth,                     // pbuffer width
iHeight,                    // pbuffer height
pBufRequirements );         // Extra buffer attributes
```

Extra steps are also required when rendering to bind the pbuffer to a texture. After having rendered to the pbuffer and subsequently "made current" on the window's rendering context to prepare for rendering the main scene, you bind the texture ID we wish to use for the dynamic texture.

```
glBindTexture( GL_TEXTURE_2D, dynamicTextureID );
```

Next, you bind the pbuffer containing the rendered image to the active texture. Assuming a single-buffered, monoscopic pbuffer, you pass `WGL_FRONT_LEFT_ARB` as the second parameter.

```
wglBindTexImageARB( hPBuffer, WGL_FRONT_LEFT_ARB );
```

Drawing commands can now be issued on the window surface that utilizes the dynamic texture. Finally, after the primary scene is rendered, but before you can render to the pbuffer once again, you must first unbind the pbuffer from the active texture.

```
wglReleaseTexImageARB( hPBuffer, WGL_FRONT_LEFT_ARB );
```

Procedure:

1. Make pbuffer context current.

2. Render to pbuffer.

3. Make window context current.

4. Bind pbuffer to a texture.

5. Render scene.

6. Release pbuffer from texture.

Pros:

- Very fast; usually no copying.
- Compatible with most hardware.
- Pixel format and resolution are flexible.

Cons:

- Complex and bug-prone.
- Platform-specific extensions.
- No Linux supports.
- Switching between contexts can be expensive.

RTT Method 4: `GL_EXT_framebuffer_object`

When developing for new video hardware, FBOs are the ideal method for dynamic texturing, as they have all of the performance benefits of using pbuffers with Method 3, but without all of the portability and implementation headaches. Refer to Chapter 1 for a complete reference on the framebuffer object extension. Additionally, working demos of all four render-to-texture methods can be found on the book's website.

Procedure:

1. Bind FBO for rendering.

2. Attach texture to FBO's color buffer.

3. Render to FBO.

4. Bind primary window for rendering.

5. Render scene.

Pros:

- Optimally fast.
- Unified OpenGL extension.
- Single rendering context.

Cons:

- Not yet supported in all hardware.

Summary

As you've seen from this chapter, OpenGL supports a great deal of powerful functionality related to textures. This functionality allows you to accomplish a wide range of effects and dramatically improve visual quality. This chapter provides only a small sampling of the things you can do with texturing, but as you can see, the possibilities are nearly endless, especially combined with the power of programmability.

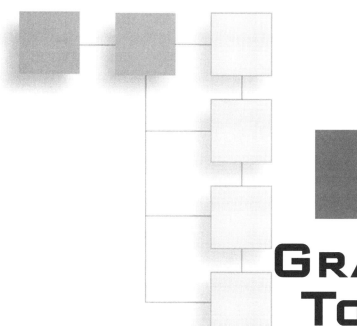

PART II

GRAPHICS TOOLBOX

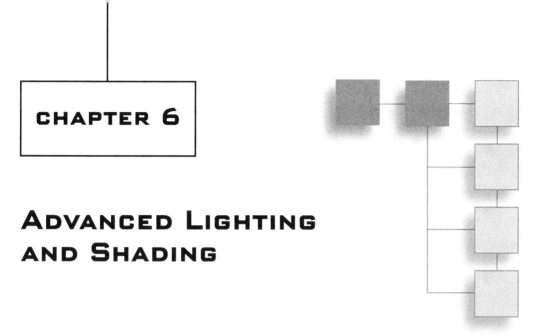

CHAPTER 6

ADVANCED LIGHTING AND SHADING

The shading languages covered in Chapter 3, "Low-Level Shaders," and Chapter 4, "The OpenGL Shading Language," enable developers to take much greater control of the visual effects in their games. One of the most common applications of this is to replace the basic manner in which OpenGL performs lighting and shading with more advanced approaches. This includes coming up with more accurate models of reality, but it also includes nontraditional approaches that may not be realistic at all.

This chapter focuses on some of the more common and interesting advanced lighting and shading techniques, including:

- Advanced lighting and materials using alternative lighting models
- Deferred shading
- High dynamic-range lighting and rendering
- Non-photorealistic rendering

Advanced Lighting and Materials

David Elder

The OpenGL fixed-function pipeline allows you to set up hardware-accelerated lighting to improve the realism of the scene. OpenGL's built-in lighting model supports global ambient illumination, diffuse light reflections, and specular highlights, based on properties of the light source itself and of the material associated with a polygonal surface. Changing the lighting and material properties can give you greater control over the appearance of illuminated surfaces, and you can approximate the look of a wide range of materials this way. However, there is really only one lighting model in OpenGL, and that model does not accurately describe how every type of surface interacts with the light. Out in the real world, the physical, fine-grained characteristics of a material determine how it interacts with light, and the light-material interaction in turn determines the visual appearance of the material under different lighting conditions. Through OpenGL's programmable graphics pipeline, you can implement realistic physically based lighting and material models to more accurately render many different types of materials. In this section, I will point out some of the deficiencies of the standard OpenGL lighting model and show you how to construct new lighting models based on physical and geometric principles.

Review of the OpenGL Lighting Model

The OpenGL lighting model is based on elements of Gouraud and Phong shading. Gouraud shading is a technique for approximating a smooth surface using per-vertex surface normals. Given a surface normal at each vertex of a polygon, Gouraud shading linearly interpolates the surface normals across the interior of the polygon. Gouraud shading is activated in OpenGL using glShadeModel(GL_SMOOTH). The major problem with Gouraud shading is that, even if unit-length surface normals are specified at the vertices, the interpolated normals in the polygon interior will not be unit length. As you'll see, this can have important consequences for the lighting model. Phong shading is a term that is indiscriminately applied to both an interpolation method and a lighting model. The interpolation method is identical to the Gouraud method, except that the surface normals are renormalized to unit length per-pixel. In other words, Gouraud shading works at the vertex level, and Phong shading works at the pixel level. Clearly, Phong shading is more computationally expensive, and it is not supported in the OpenGL fixed-function pipeline. You can, however, implement Phong shading in GLSL by renormalizing the surface normal in the fragment shader.

The OpenGL lighting equation is a *phenomenological* model, meaning it produces results that look correct but are not physically accurate. It is based on the Blinn-Phong lighting model, discussed below (see also McReynolds and Blythe's *Advanced Graphics Programming Using OpenGL*). The equation computes the final pixel color by taking into account ambient light, diffuse and specular reflections, and material color emission:

$$Color_{pixel} = Ambient_{Mat} \times Ambient_{Scene}$$
$$+ \; Ambient_{Mat} \times Ambient_{Light}$$
$$+ \; \max(\mathbf{L} \cdot \mathbf{N}, 0) \times Diffuse_{Mat} \times Diffuse_{Light}$$
$$+ \; \max(\mathbf{L} + \mathbf{E} \cdot \mathbf{N}, 0)^{Shininess} \times Specular_{Mat} \times Specular_{Light}$$

where N is the surface normal, L is the light direction vector, and E is the eye direction vector. The term L + E is called the *half-angle vector* and is denoted E. All the vectors should be normalized to unit length, including the half-angle vector. The light's ambient, diffuse, and specular contributions can be optionally scaled by a distance-based attenuation factor

$$atten = \frac{1}{k_c + k_l d + k_q d^2}$$

where d is the distance from the light to the surface, and k_c, k_l, and k_q are the constant-, linear-, and quadratic-attenuation parameters, respectively. Additional effects such as spot-light attenuation and cutoff can be added to the lighting equation.

The Blinn-Phong lighting model is a local model that takes into account light emitted directly from a light source and ignores indirect ambient illumination. The basic equation takes into account diffuse and specular reflections:

$$BlinnPhong(\mathbf{L}, \mathbf{E}; \mathbf{N}) = \mathbf{L} \cdot \mathbf{N} \times Diffuse_{Light}$$
$$+ \mathbf{H} \cdot \mathbf{N} \times Specular_{Light}$$

The pixel color is determined by

$$Color_{Pixel} = Color_{Mat} \times BlinnPhong(\mathbf{L}, \mathbf{E}; \mathbf{N})$$

The OpenGL lighting model modifies the Blinn-Phong model by adding ambient illumination, distance-based attenuation, material emission, and separate diffuse and specular material colors. For reference, Figure 6.1 shows a sample scene illuminated with the standard OpenGL lighting model.

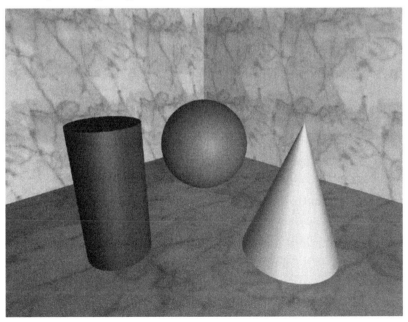

Figure 6.1 Reference scene illuminated with the OpenGL lighting model.

BRDFs

The Blinn-Phong lighting equation is an example of what's known as a *bidirectional reflectance distribution function* (BRDF). Given a surface normal N, a BRDF computes the amount of light reflected in direction E toward the eye due to light arriving at the surface from direction L. Direction E is called the *reflected* light direction, and L is called the *incident* light direction. You can denote a BRDF by *BRDF(**L, E; N**, params)*, where *params* is an optional set of additional lighting and material parameters such as shininess, surface color, and light color. Note that there is a more sophisticated way to write a BRDF in terms of differential surface area and solid angles, but that formulation is not particularly useful for real-time graphics, so I'll skip it. (For more information, see *Physically Based Modeling* by Matt Pharr and Greg Humphreys.) The geometry of a BRDF is shown in Figure 6.2.

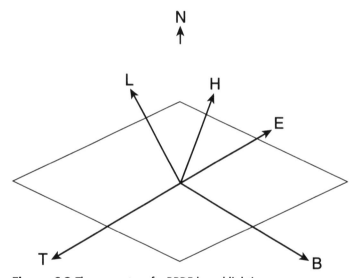

Figure 6.2 The geometry of a BRDF-based lighting.

A physically based BRDF obeys two additional constraints:

1. **Reciprocity:** The BRDF remains the same if you swap the incident and reflected light directions. In other words, *BRDF(**L, E; N**) = BRDF(**E, L; N**)*.

2. **Energy conservation:** The amount of light reflected by the surface must be no greater than the amount of light arriving at the surface. A surface could absorb and transmit some light, so the energy conservation constraint could be written

   Incident Light = Reflected Light + Absorbed Light + Transmitted Light

   In general, it requires some mathematical effort to verify that a BRDF is energy conserving.

Although it may not be obvious, the Blinn-Phong lighting model described above is neither reciprocal nor energy conserving. If you rewrite the Blinn-Phong equation, omitting the L·N factor in the diffuse term, and constrain $Diffuse_{light} = 1 - Specular_{light}$, then the model becomes reciprocal and energy conserving (this is explained in Robert Lewis's article listed below).

The diffuse term in the OpenGL and Blinn-Phong lighting equations models a *Lambertian* surface. A Lambertian surface is perfectly matte and reflects diffuse light according to the cosine of the angle between the light and the surface normal. You might recall from linear algebra that for unit vectors v_1 and $v_2, v_1 \cdot v_2 = \cos(\Theta)$, where Θ is the angle between v_1 and v_2.

So far, I have described the geometry of a BRDF in terms of vectors. An alternative representation is in terms of four angles Θ_i, Θ_r, ϕ_i, and ϕ_r, as illustrated in Figure 6.3. The angles Θ_i and Θ_r are the angles between the vectors L and E and the surface normal N. The angles ϕ_i and ϕ_r are the angles formed by L and E in the tangent plane TB. Essentially, this representation stores the vectors L and E in spherical coordinates.

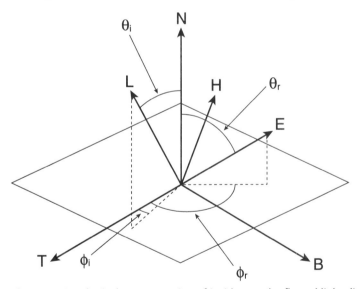

Figure 6.3 Spherical representation of incident and reflected light directions.

Microfacet Models

Several interesting BRDFs model light reflection by considering a surface composed of tiny polygons called *microfacets* (see Figure 6.4). Microfacets are light-reflecting polygons, but they are much smaller than the surface details that can be modeled with bump mapping techniques. Rather than simulate light interactions with individual microfacets, which would be prohibitively expensive, some models compute light reflections using statistical properties of the underlying microfacet distribution. Microfacets can have complicated interactions with incoming light, including interreflection, shadowing of other facets, and masking of reflected light, as illustrated in Figure 6.5. A microfacet lighting model will typically aggregate the effects of interreflection, self-shadowing, and masking into a single mathematical expression.

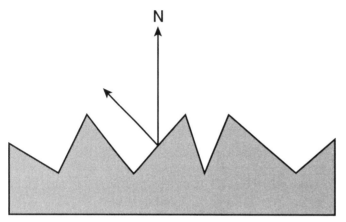

Figure 6.4 Structure of a microfaceted surface.

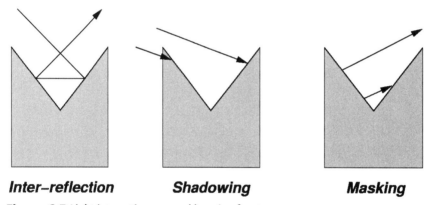

Inter–reflection   ***Shadowing***   ***Masking***

Figure 6.5 Light interactions caused by microfacets.

The derivation of a microfacet model usually involves some heavy math, which I'll omit for clarity in the discussions below.

Oren-Nayar Model

The Oren-Nayar model was derived by taking measurements of the light reflected from a variety of real-world materials. This model accounts only for diffuse light reflection, ignoring specular highlights. The diffuse reflectance properties are modeled by assuming that the surface is composed of V-shaped microgrooves, the surfaces of which are Lambertian reflectors. The model includes a statistical isotropic Gaussian distribution of microfacet orientations with mean $M = 0$ and slope variance Σ, and it has a geometric attenuation factor accounting for microfacet light interactions. The actual model is an integral equation, but it can be simplified into a qualitative model controlled by three parameters: P for the surface roughness, Σ for the width of the microfacet slope distribution, and E0 for the intensity of the light source:

$$OrenNayar(\theta_r, \theta_i, \varphi_r, \varphi_i) = \frac{\rho}{\pi}\ E_0 \cos\theta_i(A + B\max[0,\ \cos(\varphi_r - \varphi_i)]\sin\alpha\ \tan\beta)$$

$$A = 1.0 - 0.5\ \frac{\sigma^2}{\sigma^2 + 0.33}$$

$$B = 0.45\ \frac{\sigma^2}{\sigma^2 + 0.09}$$

$$\alpha = \max(\theta_r, \theta_i)$$

$$\beta = \min(\theta_r, \theta_i)$$

This model may look intimidating, but it can be implemented easily in a GLSL fragment shader. For a particular set of parameters P, Σ, and E_0, you can precompute A, B, and R = P/Σ·E_0. Here is a GLSL fragment shader for the Oren-Nayar model:

```
uniform float R;
uniform float A;
uniform float B;

varying vec3 position3;
varying vec3 normal3;

void main(void)
{
  vec3 lightDir = vec3(gl_LightSource[0].position) - position3;
  lightDir = normalize(lightDir);
  vec3 eyeDir = normalize(-position3);
  normal3 = normalize(normal3);

  float nDotL = dot(normal3, lightDir);
  float nDotE = dot(normal3, eyeDir);

  float sinT_r = length(cross(eyeDir, normal3));
  float cosT_r = clamp(nDotE, 0.0001, 1.0);
  float sinT_i = length(cross(lightDir, normal3));
  float cosT_i = clamp(nDotL, 0.0001, 1.0);
```

```
    float tanT_i = sinT_i / cosT_i;
    float tanT_r = sinT_r / cosT_r;

    float3 E_p = normalize(eyeDir - nDotE * normal3);
    float3 L_p = normalize(lightDir - nDotL * normal3);
    float cosPhi = dot(E_p, L_p);

    float I = R * cosT_i * (A + B*max(0.0, cosPhi)*
            max(sinT_r, sinT_i)*min(tanT_i,tanT_r));

    gl_FragColor = vec4(I) * gl_FrontMaterial.diffuse;
}
```

Figure 6.6 shows the scene rendered with the Oren-Nayar model, using parameters $P = 0.458105$, $\Sigma = 1.057673$, and $E_0 = 0.998868$. Note that the term R could be very small, resulting in a dimly lit scene. You might want to scale this value up to get better results. These parameters are for the material Stones from the CURET database, which contains Oren-Nayar parameters for 61 real-world materials. The materials in this database are natural materials such as limestone, skin, brick, bread, paper, and grass that do not have strong specular reflections. Since the Oren-Nayar model only accounts for diffuse illumination, it won't work well for shiny materials such as metal or glossy paint.

Figure 6.6 Scene illuminated with Oren-Nayar diffuse lighting.

Cook-Torrance Model

The Cook-Torrance model is a specular microfacet model for simulating shiny metal and plastic surfaces. Similar to the Oren-Nayar model, the Cook-Torrance model includes a statistical distribution of microfacet orientations and a geometric attenuation factor. It also introduces a Fresnel reflection term. The model is given by the equation

$$CookTorrance(\mathbf{L}, \mathbf{E}; \mathbf{N}) = \frac{F_\lambda(\mathbf{L}, \mathbf{N})}{\pi} \frac{D_{Beckmann}}{\mathbf{L} \cdot \mathbf{N}} \frac{G}{\mathbf{E} \cdot \mathbf{N}}$$

$$F_\lambda = (1.0 + \mathbf{E} \cdot \mathbf{N})^\lambda$$

$$D_{Beckmann} = \frac{1}{4m^2(\mathbf{H} \cdot \mathbf{N})^4} e^{-\frac{\tan^2\alpha}{m^2}}$$

$$G = \min\left[1.0, \max\left[0.0, \max\left[\frac{2(\mathbf{H} \cdot \mathbf{N})(\mathbf{E} \cdot \mathbf{N})}{\mathbf{H} \cdot \mathbf{E}}, \frac{2(\mathbf{H} \cdot \mathbf{N})(\mathbf{L} \cdot \mathbf{N})}{\mathbf{H} \cdot \mathbf{E}}\right]\right]\right]$$

where F is the Fresnel term, $D_{Beckmann}$ is the Beckmann distribution, G is the geometric attenuation term, and _ is the angle between $\mathbf{H}$ and $\mathbf{N}$ (see McReynolds and Blythe). The parameters _ and m control the Fresnel effect and the width of the Beckmann distribution, respectively. Note that the term $\tan^2$_ can be computed with the trigonometric identity

$$\tan^2\alpha = \frac{1 - \cos^2\alpha}{\cos^2\alpha} = \frac{1 - (\mathbf{H} \cdot \mathbf{N})^2}{(\mathbf{H} \cdot \mathbf{N})^2}$$

The Cook-Torrance model can be implemented in a GLSL fragment shader:

```
uniform float lambda;
uniform float m;

varying vec3 position3;
varying vec3 normal3;
varying vec3 tangent3;

const float ONE_OVER_PI = 0.31831;
const float e = 2.718282;

float Beckmann(vec3 H, vec3 N, float m)
{
  float nDotH = max(0.001, dot(N, H));
  float nDotH2 = nDotH * nDotH;
  float nDotH4 = nDotH2 * nDotH2;
```

```
  float tan2a = (nDotH2-1.0)/nDotH2;

  return (1.0/(4*m*m*nDotH4)) * pow(e, tan2a/(m*m));
}


float Gatten(vec3 L, vec3 E, vec3 H, vec3 N)
{
  float nDotH = dot(N, H);
  float nDotE = dot(N, E);
  float nDotL = dot(N, L);
  float hDotE = max(0.001, dot(H, E));

  float X = 2.0*nDotH/hDotE;

  return min(1.0, max(0.0, max(X * nDotE, X * nDotL)));
}


float Fresnel(vec3 E, vec3 N, float lambda)
{
  return pow(1.0 + dot(E, N), lambda);
}


void main(void)
{
  vec3 N = normalize(normal3);
  vec3 L = normalize(gl_LightSource[0].position.xyz - position3);
  vec3 E = normalize(-position3);
  vec3 H = normalize(L + E);

  float F = ONE_OVER_PI * Fresnel(E, N, lambda);
  float D = Beckmann(H, N, m) / max(0.001, dot(L, N));
  float G = Gatten(L, E, H, N) / max(0.001, dot(E, N));

  float CT = F * D * G;

  vec4 diffuse = max(0.0, dot(N,L)) * gl_FrontMaterial.diffuse;
  vec4 specular = max(0.0, CT) * gl_FrontMaterial.specular;

  gl_FragColor = diffuse + specular;
}
```

Figure 6.7 shows the scene rendered with the Cook-Torrance Model, using parameters _ = 0.75 and m = 0.3. Note that m controls the roughness, so increasing m causes the specular highlight to diminish, and vice versa. The diffuse reflectance is Lambertian, although it could have been computed with Oren-Nayar.

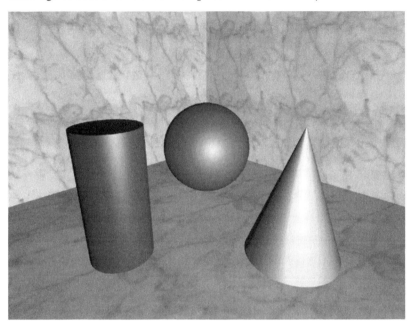

Figure 6.7 Scene rendered with the Cook-Torrance Model.

Ashikhmin Model

Both of the preceding models have been isotropic, meaning that the reflectance is not skewed along a particular axis. However, some materials exhibit anisotropic reflectance with specular highlights stretched in some direction. Brushed metal is an anisotropic material, and it has highlights perpendicular to the brush stroke direction. Neither of the previous models can handle anisotropic materials, but the Ashikhmin model was developed with this in mind. This model contains both diffuse and specular BRDFs, and it maintains physical reciprocity and energy conservation in both parts. The anisotropy is controlled by parameters nu and nv, which scale the amounts of anisotropy along the tangent and binormal vectors, respectively. The model equations are

$$S(\mathbf{L}, \mathbf{E}; \mathbf{N}) = \frac{\sqrt{(nu+1)(nv+1)}}{8\pi} \, \frac{(\mathbf{N} \cdot \mathbf{H})^{\frac{(nu(\mathbf{H_x})^2 + nv(\mathbf{H_y})^2)}{1 - (\mathbf{H_z})^2}}}{(\mathbf{L} \cdot \mathbf{H})\max((\mathbf{L} \cdot \mathbf{H}), (\mathbf{E} \cdot \mathbf{H}))} \, F(\mathbf{L} \cdot \mathbf{H})$$

$$D(\mathbf{L}, \mathbf{E}; \mathbf{N}) = \frac{28R_d}{23\pi} \, (1 - R_s)\left[1 - \left(1 - \frac{\mathbf{N} \cdot \mathbf{L}}{2}\right)^5\right]\left[1 - \left(1 - \frac{\mathbf{N} \cdot \mathbf{E}}{2}\right)^5\right]$$

$$F(\mathbf{L} \cdot \mathbf{H}) = R_s + (1 - R_d)(1 - (\mathbf{L} \cdot \mathbf{H})^5)$$

where $S(\mathbf{L}, \mathbf{E}; \mathbf{N})$ is the specular term, $D(\mathbf{L}, \mathbf{E}; \mathbf{N})$ is the diffuse term, and F is the Fresnel reflection factor (for a full explanation, see Ashikhmin and Shirley's article, listed among the references at the end of this section). A GLSL shader for Ashikhmin's model is here:

```glsl
uniform float spec_coeff;
uniform float diff_coeff;
uniform float nu, nv;

varying vec3 position3;
varying vec3 normal3;
varying vec3 tangent3;

vec4 pow5(vec4 f)
{
  vec4 t = f * f;
  return t * t * f;
}

vec4 Fresnel(vec4 refl, vec4 kh)
{
  return refl + (vec4(1.0) - refl) * pow5(vec4(1.0) - kh);
}

vec4 mclamp(vec4 v)
{
  return max(v, vec4(0.01));
}

vec4 ash_specular(float nu, float nv, vec3 n, vec3 h, vec3 light, vec3 eye,
                  vec3 u, vec3 v, vec4 spec)
{
```

```
  vec3 k = light;
  vec4 nDotH = mclamp(vec4(dot(h, n)));
  vec4 nDotK = mclamp(vec4(dot(k, n)));
  vec4 nDotL = mclamp(vec4(dot(light, n)));
  vec4 nDotE = mclamp(vec4(dot(eye, n)));
  vec4 kDotH = mclamp(vec4(dot(k, h)));
  vec4 hDotU = vec4(dot(h, u));
  vec4 hDotV = vec4(dot(h, v));

  vec4 exponent = (vec4(nu)*hDotU*hDotU +
                     vec4(nv)*hDotV*hDotV)/(vec4(1.0) - nDotH*nDotH);
  vec4 Gatten = pow(nDotH, exponent)/(nDotK * max(nDotL, nDotE));

  return Gatten * Fresnel(spec, kDotH);
}


vec4 ash_diffuse(vec3 normal, vec3 light, vec3 viewer, vec4 spec, vec4 diffuse)
{
  vec4 scale = diffuse * (vec4(1.0) - spec);
  vec4 v = vec4(1.0) - pow5(vec4(1.0 - max(dot(normal, light), 0.0)/2.0));
  vec4 l = vec4(1.0) - pow5(vec4(1.0 - max(dot(normal, viewer), 0.0)/2.0));
  return scale * v * l;
}


void main(void)
{
  vec3 k1 = normalize(gl_LightSource[0].position.xyz - position3);
  vec3 k2 = normalize(-position3);

  vec3 n = normalize(normal3);
  vec3 u = normalize(tangent3);
  vec3 v = normalize(cross(normal3, u));

  vec3 h = normalize(k1 + k2);

  vec4 Rs = gl_LightSource[0].specular;
  vec4 Rd = gl_LightSource[0].diffuse;
  vec4 Ms = gl_FrontMaterial.specular;
  vec4 Md = gl_FrontMaterial.diffuse;

  gl_FragColor = Ms * spec_coeff * ash_specular(nu, nv, n, h, k1, k2, u, v, Rs)+
    Md * diff_coeff * ash_diffuse(n, k1, k2, Rs, Rd);
}
```

Figure 6.8 shows the scene rendered with the Ashikhmin shader, parameters $nu = 10$ and $nv = 100$. Note how the specular highlights are stretched; this is the anisotropy.

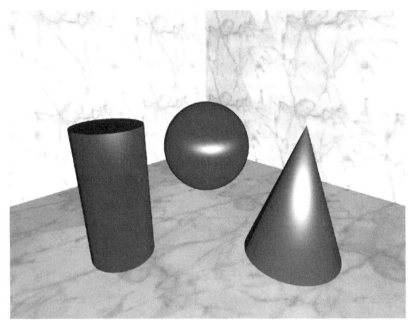

Figure 6.8 Scene rendered with Ashikhmin's model.

Conclusion

Rendering realistic scenes requires you to model the interaction between lights and materials. BRDFs express the way a particular material reflects light, and they can incorporate sophisticated physical interactions in a compact way. There are other BRDF models besides the ones presented here. Lafortune's model is notable. It consists of a Lambertian diffuse term and a sum of multiple Phong-like specular lobes. This model is useful for representing complex BRDFs obtained from data measurements. Another interesting approach to BRDF-based illumination is the concept of a spatial BRDF. You can store different BRDF parameters in a texture map and load the parameters in a fragment shader. This allows you to render very complicated materials like patterned fabrics in an efficient manner. As always, the best way to understand advanced lighting concepts is to experiment with different BRDFs and parameters. You can even try creating your own BRDFs for custom lighting effects.

References

Ashikhmin, Michael, and Peter Shirley. "An Anisotropic Phong BRDF Model." *Journal of Graphics Tools* 5 (2000): 25–32.

Columbia-Utrecht Reflectance and Texture (CURET) Database. **http://www1.cs.columbia.edu/CAVE/curet/**.

Cook, R. L., and K. E. Torrance. "A Reflectance Model for Computer Graphics." *Computer Graphics* 15 (1981): 307–16.

Lewis, Robert R. "Making Shaders More Physically Plausible." *Computer Graphics Forum* 13 (1994): 109–120.

McReynolds, Tom, and David Blythe. *Advanced Graphics Programming Using OpenGL*. San Francisco: Morgan-Kaufmann, 2005.

Oren, M., and S. K. Nayar. "Generalization of Lambert's Reflectance Model." In *Proceedings of SIGGRAPH 1994*, ed. A. Glassner, 239–46.Computer Graphics Proceedings, Annual Conference Series, vol. 28. ACM Press: New York, 1994.

Pharr, Matt, and Greg Humphreys. *Physically Based Rendering*. San Francisco: Morgan-Kaufmann, 2004.

Deferred Shading

David Elder

As graphics hardware evolves, game designers are creating more and more visually complicated game environments. Rendering a realistic visual environment is really all about lighting (and its complement, shadowing). Programmable GPUs allow designers to build sophisticated per-pixel illumination models, but designing a system that can efficiently handle many light sources is a major challenge. For example, most current graphics cards can handle a maximum of eight hardware accelerated lights at once. But suppose your scene needs 10 or 20 lights, or the number of lights changes at run time. How can you design a system that is efficient and general enough to adaptively handle all of these potential lighting scenarios? The standard OpenGL rendering methodology, called forward shading, really only offers two options:

1. **Single-pass.** For each object, include all light sources in a single monolithic shading pass.

2. **Multi-pass.** For each light, render all illuminated objects and accumulate results into framebuffer.

As I'll discuss, these approaches have significant drawbacks in complicated illumination environments. Fortunately, there is a third way: *deferred shading*. Deferred shading is a two-pass rendering algorithm. In the first pass, the geometry and surface color information needed for lighting is drawn into a *G-buffer*. In the second pass, lighting is applied as an image-space postprocess, using the per-pixel geometry and color information stored in the G-buffer. This technique is called deferred shading because you defer the shading (or lighting) computations until after all of the scene geometry has been processed and you have determined the relevant surface properties for shading at every pixel. Deferred shading has only recently become practical as a real-time rendering methodology. It is currently an active area of research, and there is not a universally "correct" way of doing it. I will discuss the advantages of deferred shading and provide an overview of how to implement the basic components of a deferred-shading system in OpenGL. The references at the end of this section list other discussions of deferred shading; see Shishkovtsov; Hargreaves and Harris; Hargreaves; and Geldrich, Pritchard, and Brooks.

Limitations of Forward Shading

To justify the use of deferred shading, you should understand some of the problems with the forward-shading algorithm. Recall that real-time lighting in OpenGL uses three types of light sources. *Spot lights* cast a cone of light onto surfaces; *point lights* radiate light in all directions; and *directional lights* illuminate surfaces from a fixed direction, approximating infinitely distant light sources. A game environment may contain many polygonal models illuminated by different combinations of light sources. Some light sources, such as the sun or a ceiling light, will be statically baked into the scene. Others, such as explosions, flashlights, or headlights, will be dynamically moving and possibly exist for a period of time. The point is that the illumination environment for a game level can be quite complicated.

The single-pass approach renders each visible object sequentially, applying all the relevant lighting in a single shader. To make this work, you must determine exactly which lights affect each object and shade the object using only those lights. Different combinations of light types will require different shaders, and you could potentially need hundreds of shaders to handle all the lighting combinations in your game. Even if you found a way to manage this combinatorial problem efficiently, you would still find that you are unnecessarily shading partially or fully occluded polygons. Spatial management schemes such as BSP trees or portal systems (see Chapter 12, "Scene Management") can help you reduce the number of occluded polygons you draw, but some amount of pixel overdraw is inevitable in a dynamic 3D environment. You would prefer to not execute an expensive lighting shader on all those pixels that will be eventually overdrawn. Finally, processing several lights simultaneously will make it very tough to generate dynamic shadows using the stencil buffer or projective shadow maps.

The multi-pass approach avoids some of the problems with single-pass lighting, but it introduces some new problems of its own. Multi-pass lighting looks at each light sequentially and renders only the illuminated geometry for each light. To do this, each light will need a bounding volume that describes the light's region of influence. Only the objects contained within the bounding volume will be rendered on each pass. Since each pass involves only a single light, the lighting shaders will be cheaper, individually, than the shaders invoked by the single-pass method. However, since an object could fall within several bounding volumes, the total number of shading instructions per illuminated pixel will be similar to the single-pass method. Multi-pass rendering suffers from the same pixel overdraw problems as the single-pass method. On the other hand, both stencil shadows and projective shadow maps have straightforward implementations in multi-pass rendering. The major bottleneck in a multi-pass algorithm is the need to retransform the geometry and resample texture maps for objects in each lighting volume. This means the algorithm is potentially repeating the same work over and over again on each lighting pass.

You might think, given the preceding discussion, that forward-pass algorithms have crippling handicaps. That's not necessarily true, so let me briefly highlight a few of their advantages. First, forward shading is conceptually simple and is the "natural" shading architecture in OpenGL. This means that a forward-shading system can be fairly easy to implement. Single-pass lighting works very well in scenes with a small number of lights, particularly outdoor scenes illuminated by the sun. Multi-pass lighting can work well if you can partition the scene geometry along light boundaries so that you reduce the number of times each object is transformed and drawn. Certain rendering effects and tweaks are easier to do in a forward-shading system. Finally, virtually every major 3D game written to date has used forward shading.

Nevertheless, deferred shading bypasses some of the trickier problems mentioned above. The remainder of this section discusses the basic components of a deferred shading system and provides pointers on how to implement them in OpenGL.

Deferred Shading Overview

Deferred shading cleanly divides the rendering algorithm into separate geometry-processing and lighting phases. Conceptually, this is a two-pass algorithm. The first pass renders all the scene geometry but does not apply lighting. The scene geometry is stored in the above-mentioned G-buffer, a fat framebuffer that holds (typically) the 3D position, surface normal, diffuse color, and a few other parameters needed for lighting. The G-buffer is actually a collection of three or four color buffers, each storing a different parameter for lighting. Lighting is computed in the second pass by rendering the bounding volume for each light into the framebuffer and applying the lighting equation per-pixel using the geometry and color information stored in the G-buffer. If the scene to be rendered has M objects and N lights, then deferred shading has a theoretical algorithmic complexity of $O(M + N)$, much better than the worst-case $O(M * N)$ for the forward-shading methods described above.

What OpenGL features are needed to implement deferred shading? Ideally, your OpenGL implementation would support the following:

- **Multiple render targets (MRTs).** MRTs allow a fragment shader to output up to four RGBA color values simultaneously. If you have MRTs, you can fill the G-buffer in one pass.

- **Floating-point textures.** This texture format allows you to store true 16- or 32-bit floating-point values in texture maps, which is needed for storing the vertex position and surface normal in the G-buffer.

- **Texture rectangles.** Usually the screen dimensions in a game are not powers of two, and texture rectangles allow you to create a G-buffer whose dimensions match exactly the dimensions of the game screen.

- **Offscreen pbuffers.** You can allocate a new OpenGL rendering context offscreen, called a pbuffer, with its own framebuffer. Rendering intermediate passes offscreen can be significantly cheaper than rendering onscreen, although switching contexts can be somewhat costly.

- **Render-to-texture (RTT).** RTT lets you render directly into a texture map, essentially using the contents of a buffer as an input texture for a subsequent texture-mapping operation. Using this feature can give a significant performance increase over functions like `glCopyTexImage2D()`.

- **Programmable pipeline.** GLSL or assembly-language shaders are used to process vertices, write outputs to the G-buffer, and compute per-pixel lighting.

Only recent graphics cards support all of these features. In principle you could implement deferred shading on a card that lacked all of these features, but that would require some sophisticated and nonintuitive trickery with multitexturing and texture combiners. To keep this discussion simple, I will assume that your graphics card is modern and supports the full feature set listed above.

Working with the G-Buffer

A G-buffer works best if you can allocate an offscreen pbuffer supporting a floating-point pixel format, multiple color buffers (MRTs), rectangular dimensions, and render-to-texture. At a low level, OpenGL always interacts with the underlying graphics system of your OS, though the details are typically hidden from view by GLUT and other auxiliary libraries. There are groups of OpenGL extensions, prefixed by WGL in Microsoft Windows and GLX in X Window, that give you some low-level control over several things, including the creation and management of offscreen pbuffers. Unfortunately, the WGL and GLX extensions are some of the more esoteric parts of OpenGL. Also, the details of how to create a pbuffer with the required features differ somewhat on ATI and NVIDIA hardware. In fact, the best place to learn about pbuffers in WGL and GLX is in the developer SDKs provided by ATI and NVIDIA. Both SDKs wrap the WGL and GLX pbuffer mechanisms into a C++ class, and they give you an easy way to control the attributes and format of the pbuffer. Below I've outlined the basic steps needed to set up an offscreen pbuffer with WGL extensions.

PBuffer Creation

To create an offscreen pbuffer, you need to specify the desired pixel format for the buffer and the type of buffer you want. The following code snippet sets the pixel and buffer formats and creates the buffer.

```
int pixel_format[] = {
  WGL_DRAW_TO_PBUFFER_ARB, 1,
  WGL_SUPPORT_OPENGL_ARB,  1,
  WGL_PIXEL_TYPE_ARB,        WGL_TYPE_RGBA_ARB,
  WGL_DEPTH_BITS_ARB,      24,
  WGL_STENCIL_BITS_ARB,     8,
  WGL_FLOAT_COMPONENTS_NV, 1,
  WGL_AUX_BUFFERS_ARB,      4,
  WGL_BIND_TO_TEXTURE_RECTANGLE_FLOAT_RGBA_NV, 1,
  WGL_RED_BITS_ARB,          32,
  WGL_GREEN_BITS_ARB,        32,
  WGL_BLUE_BITS_ARB,         32,
  WGL_ALPHA_BITS_ARB,        32,
  0};
int buffer_format[] = {
  WGL_PBUFFER_LARGEST_ARB, 1,
  WGL_TEXTURE_TARGET_ARB,  WGL_TEXTURE_RECTANGLE_NV,
  WGL_TEXTURE_FORMAT_ARB,  WGL_TEXTURE_FLOAT_RGBA_NV,
  0};

// Get current device and rendering contexts
HDC win_dc = wglGetCurrentDC();
HGLRC win_glrc = wglGetCurrentContext();
HPBUFFERARB pbuffer;
int best_format = 0;

best_format = GetPixelFormat(win_dc);
unsigned int num_formats;

wglChoosePixelFormatARB(win_dc, pixel_format, NULL, 1, &best_format,
                        &num_formats);

pbuffer = wglCreatePbufferARB(win_dc, format, width, height, buffer_format);

HDC buffer_dc = wglGetPbufferDCARB(pbuffer);
HGLRC buffer_rc = win_rc;
// That assumes we are sharing the rendering context between the pbuffer and the
```

```
// window. If not, create a HGLRC for the pbuffer with:
// HGLRC buffer_rc = wglCreateContext(buffer_dc);

// If we are sharing gl objects between the pbuffer and
// the window, we need to set that up:
// wglShareLists(win_rc, buffer_rc);
```

Note that the pixel and buffer attributes chosen above are for NVIDIA hardware. Different values need to be used for ATI hardware. This code creates an offscreen pbuffer with 32-bit floating-point RGBA pixels, rectangular dimensions, and auxiliary color buffers; this code also specifies that the buffer is to be used as a texture-rendering target (RTT). Pbuffer creation should occur *after* you have created the main rendering window.

PBuffer Destruction

When you are done with the pbuffer, you should destroy it with the following code:

```
// If we created a rendering context for the pbuffer, destroy that too:
// wglDeleteContext(buffer_rc);
wglReleasePbufferDCARB(pbuffer, buffer_dc);
wglDestroyPbufferARB(pbuffer);
```

If you are sharing contexts between the pbuffer and the window, don't delete the pbuffer's rendering context, as you'll kill the context for the window as well!

PBuffer Activation and Deactivation

When you are rendering into the offscreen pbuffer, you need to activate its rendering context:

```
wglMakeCurrent(buffer_dc, buffer_rc);
```

To deactivate the pbuffer and activate the original rendering window, do the same thing with the window's contexts:

```
wglMakeCurrent(win_dc, win_rc);
```

Binding an Offscreen Buffer as a Texture

The pbuffer is actually a collection of color buffers and stencil, depth, and accumulation buffers (optionally). To bind a color buffer (e.g., WGL_AUX0_ARB) as a texture in texture unit 0, call these functions:

```
glActiveTextureARB(GL_TEXTURE0);
wglBindTexImageARB(pbuffer, WGL_AUX0_ARB);
```

Before you can draw into WGL_AUX0_ARB again, you must release it:

```
wglReleaseTexImageARB(buffer, WGL_AUX0_ARB);
```

You can have several buffers bound to textures simultaneously. You can specify which texture unit to use by activating the appropriate texture unit before binding the buffer.

G-Buffer Configurations

The hard part about setting up your G-buffer is creating and configuring the underlying offscreen pbuffer. Once you have a pbuffer that supports MRTs, RTT, floating-point textures, and texture rectangles, you have to decide what geometric and chromatic properties to store in it. Current OpenGL implementations support single-pass rendering into a maximum of four color buffers. However, certain NVIDIA cards, notably the GeForce 6800 series, have a performance bottleneck when using four MRTs (see Hargreaves and Harris), so for maximum cross-vendor performance, you should try to store your G-buffer in three color buffers. Using three RGBA color buffers, your G-buffer can store 12 floating-point values per pixel. The basic G-buffer layout is shown in Table 6.1.

Table 6.1 G-Buffer Layout

Buffer	Red	Green	Blue	Alpha
Buffer 0	Position.x	Position.y	Position.z	Specular
Buffer 1	Normal.x	Normal.y	Normal.z	Emissive
Buffer 2	Diffuse.r	Diffuse.g	Diffuse.b	Material ID

Most of these parameters should be obvious, except perhaps the material ID in the buffer 2 alpha channel. You might want to apply a different lighting model depending on the type of material at each pixel, and the material ID could be used as a switch in your lighting shader. Alternatively, certain surfaces, notably the skybox, do not need to have lighting applied, and you could use the material ID to disable lighting on skybox pixels. While we're on the topic of skyboxes, if you are using deferred shading in an outdoor scene, the skybox will occupy approximately 20 to 40 percent of the scene at any particular moment. You can speed up the filling of the G-buffer by disabling depth-buffer writes and MRTs and drawing the diffuse color and material ID only into a single buffer when rendering the skybox. If you draw the skybox first, with depth-buffer writing disabled, then you can be sure that you won't accidentally draw any of your scene geometry "behind" the skybox.

If you want to use normal mapping with the G-buffer, you will need to convert the normals read from the normal map into eye-space coordinates. During the G-buffer phase of deferred shading, you don't know anything about the position and direction of the lights, so you can't compute the light direction vector in texture space, as you would in a forward-shading system. To convert the normals into eye space, first rotate the per-vertex normal and tangent into eye space with gl_NormalMatrix. Then construct the texture-space matrix in the fragment shader, using the eye-space normal and tangent. Finally, read the normal from the normal map and multiply it by the texture-space matrix to get the normal into eye-space coordinates.

This is certainly not the only way you could structure your G-buffer. You should design your G-buffer layout around your lighting and material model. If you wanted additional material parameters—for example, a separate specular color—you would need to find some additional space in the G-buffer. Since each "pixel" in the G-buffer corresponds to exactly one pixel in the image, you know the screen-space coordinates of each G-buffer pixel. You could represent position using a single float (rather than three as above) by simply storing the distance along a ray through the given pixel. Then in your lighting shader, you could reconstruct the original 3D position in world coordinates. This would save you two floats in the G-buffer. You could play a similar sort of trick with your surface normal, storing only the x- and y-coordinates and reconstructing the z-coordinate with the Pythagorean theorem in your lighting shader.

There is yet another option for configuring the G-buffer. Rather than store specular and emissive color information directly in the G-buffer, you could store these colors in a separate set of textures, effectively creating a material palette. In the G-buffer, you would simply store an index into the material palette at each pixel. Your lighting shader would then read the appropriate material parameters from the palette in the lighting phase of the renderer. For texture-mapped objects, you would still need per-pixel diffuse color information in the G-buffer.

To actually get values into the G-buffer, you use a GLSL program and multiple render targets. MRTs are activated with a call to glDrawBuffers() like this:

```
GLenum buffers[] = {GL_AUX0, GL_AUX1, GL_AUX2};
glDrawBuffers(3, buffers);
```

GLSL fragment shaders write output into the registers gl_FragData[0] ... gl_FragData[n] instead of gl_FragColor when using MRTs. It is an error to write to both gl_FragColor and gl_FragData[i] in the same fragment shader. In the example above, gl_FragData[0] corresponds to the buffer GL_AUX0 and so on.

Here is an example vertex shader for filling the G-buffer. The first texture coordinate holds the actual texture coordinates for the polygon, the second texture coordinate holds the per-vertex tangent, and the third texture coordinate holds specularity, emission, and material ID values.

```
varying vec3 position3;
varying vec3 normal;
varying vec3 tangent;
varying vec4 color;
```

```
// Specularity, emission, material id
varying vec3 sem;

void main(void)
{
  gl_Position = gl_ModelViewProjectionMatrix * gl_Vertex;
  gl_TexCoord[0] = gl_MultiTexCoord0;

  vec4 position = gl_ModelViewMatrix * gl_Vertex;
  position3 = (vec3(position)) / position.w;
  normal = gl_NormalMatrix * gl_Normal;
  tangent = gl_NormalMatrix * gl_MultiTexCoord1.xyz;
  color = gl_Color;
  sem = gl_MultiTexCoord2.xyz;
}
```

Here is a sample fragment shader for filling the G-buffer.

```
uniform sampler2D diffuseTex;
uniform sampler2D normalMap;
uniform samplerCube normalizationCubeMap;

varying vec3 position3;
varying vec3 normal3;
varying vec3 tangent3;
varying vec4 color;
varying vec3 sem;

void main(void)
{
  normal3  = vec3(2.0) *
    textureCube(normalizationCubeMap,  normal3).xyz - vec3(1.0);
  tangent3 = vec3(2.0) *
    textureCube(normalizationCubeMap, tangent3).xyz - vec3(1.0);

  // Construct the texture-space matrix and rotate the normal into eye space
  vec3 binormal3 = cross(normal3, tangent3);
  mat3 rotMat = mat3(tangent3, binormal3, normal3);
  vec3 vnormal = texture2D(normalMap, gl_TexCoord[0].st).xyz;
  vnormal = vec3(2.0) * vnormal - vec3(1.0);
  vec3 snormal = rotMat * vnormal;
  snormal = vec3(2.0) *
    textureCube(normalizationCubeMap, snormal).xyz - vec3(1.0);
```

```
gl_FragData[0] = vec4(position3, sem.x);
gl_FragData[1] = vec4(snormal, sem.y);
gl_FragData[2] = vec4(color.rgb*texture2D(diffuseTex, gl_TexCoord[0].st).rgb,
                      sem.z);
}
```

Figures 6.9 to 6.11 show the contents of the G-buffer for a sample scene.

Figure 6.9 Depth values.

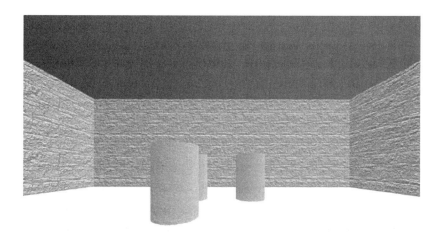

Figure 6.10 Eye-space surface normals.

Figure 6.11 Diffuse color values.

Image-Space Lighting

Lighting is applied as an image-space operation, using the G-buffer as input. You create a 3D polygonal model representing the volume illuminated by each light. When you render this lighting volume, pixels that are "drawn" correspond to pixels in the G-buffer that (potentially) need to be illuminated by the given light. For example, the bounding volume for a spot light would be a cone, and the bounding volume for a point light would be a sphere. Directional lights, such as the sun, could be handled with a full-screen quad. You could of course construct more complicated bounding volumes for different light types—for example, cylindrical light sources. The illumination effects of each individual light are blended together in the framebuffer to create the final output image. Figure 6.12 shows the final illuminated image and the light volume for a conical spot light.

Figure 6.12 Illuminated scene containing a global point light and a local conical spot light.

The naïve lighting algorithm just described has the potential to overilluminate the scene by incorrectly illuminating pixels outside the lighting volume for a particular light source. Suppose a portion of the light volume contains no illuminated objects. The light volume's geometry will still cover many pixels in the background that fall outside the volume and should not be illuminated. The basic problem is determining whether a particular pixel in the G-buffer actually lies within the light volume, given that the pixel is occluded by the light volume's geometry in screen space. Since you are storing the 3D position at each pixel, you could use a distance test to determine per-pixel light-volume containment. This method could become quite expensive, especially if you have multiple large lights in a scene. The problem is illustrated in Figure 6.13. Fortunately, you can simplify the containment test using the stencil buffer.

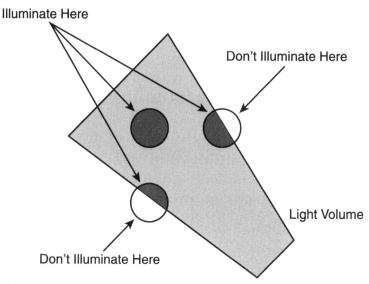

Figure 6.13 How to limit lighting to the region enclosed by the lighting volume.

The stencil-test algorithm uses two passes per light, but only the second pass applies the full lighting shader. The algorithm is:

1. **Fill stencil buffer.** First clear the stencil buffer with 0x0 and disable color and depth writes. Then

   (a) render the light-volume back faces with depth test GL_GREATER, stencil function GL_ALWAYS, stencil z-fail GL_REPLACE, and other stencil ops GL_KEEP; and

   (b) render the light-volume front faces with stencil- and depth-pass op GL_REPLACE and other stencil ops GL_KEEP.

2. **Compute illumination.** Enable color writes, but keep depth writes disabled. Set the stencil function to GL_NOTEQUAL and all stencil ops to GL_KEEP. If the light volume contains the eye point, render the back faces. Otherwise render the front faces.

Stencil pass 1(a) tags all the pixels behind the light volume, and pass 1(b) tags the pixels in front of the volume. In the illumination pass, using stencil function GL_NOTEQUAL culls all the fragments we just tagged and passes the remaining fragments, which are all within the light volume. Here is a code example for implementing the stencil test:

```
// Set up stencil buffer/test
glDepthMask(GL_FALSE);
glColorMask(GL_FALSE, GL_FALSE, GL_FALSE, GL_FALSE);
```

```
glEnable(GL_DEPTH_TEST);
glEnable(GL_STENCIL_TEST);
glClearStencil(0x0);
glClear(GL_STENCIL_BUFFER_BIT);

// Draw light volume back faces
// Tag pixels behind volume
glCullFace(GL_FRONT);
glDepthTest(GL_GREATER);
glStencilFunc(GL_ALWAYS, 0x1, 0x1);
glStencilOp(GL_KEEP, GL_REPLACE, GL_KEEP);

drawLightVolume();

// Draw light volume front faces
// Tag pixels in front of volume
glCullFace(GL_BACK);
glStencilFunc(GL_ALWAYS, 0x1, 0x1);
glStencilOp(GL_KEEP, GL_KEEP, GL_REPLACE);

drawLightVolume();

// Lighting phase

// Set up stencil buffer/test
glDepthMask(GL_FALSE);
glColorMask(GL_TRUE, GL_TRUE, GL_TRUE, GL_TRUE);
glEnable(GL_DEPTH_TEST);
glDepthFunc(GL_ALWAYS);
glEnable(GL_STENCIL_TEST);
glStencilFunc(GL_NOTEQUAL, 0x1, 0x1);
glStencilOp(GL_KEEP, GL_KEEP, GL_KEEP);

// See if light volume contains eye point and set appropriate culling state
if(contains(volume, eye))
  glCullFace(GL_FRONT);
else
  glCullFace(GL_BACK);

// Activate lighting program, set up parameters
glUseProgramObjectARB(lighting_program);
setupLightParameters();
```

```
drawLightVolume();

// Restore state
glEnable(GL_CULL_FACE);
glCullFace(GL_BACK);
glDepthMask(GL_TRUE);
glDisable(GL_STENCIL_TEST);
glDisable(GL_LIGHTING);
glDisable(GL_LIGHT0);
```

The stencil buffer trick allows us to illuminate only the pixels falling within a particular light volume, but how do we actually compute the illumination per pixel? The lighting shader simply reads the position, normal, shininess (specularity), and diffuse color from the G-buffer and applies the standard Blinn-Phong lighting formula.

The GLSL vertex shader for a light source simply transforms the position of the light-volume vertices. The fragment shader samples the G-buffer and performs the lighting calculations. You can pass in the lighting parameters using uniform variables or through the OpenGL lighting functions. Here is an example fragment shader for a point-light source:

```
// G-buffer components
uniform samplerRect positionTex;
uniform samplerRect normalTex;
uniform samplerRect diffuseTex;

uniform vec3 eyePos;

void main(void)
{
  vec4 ambient  = vec4(0.0);
  vec4 diffuse  = vec4(0.0);
  vec4 specular = vec4(0.0);

  // Sample the G-buffer
  vec2 texcoord = gl_FragCoord.xy;
  vec4 position4 = texture2DRect(positionTex, texcoord);
  vec4 normal4 = texture2DRect(normalTex, texcoord);
  vec4 diffuse4 = texture2DRect(diffuseTex, texcoord);

  vec3 position3 = position4.xyz;
  vec3 normal3 = normal4.xyz;
  vec3 diffuse3 = diffuse4.xyz;
```

```
vec3 sem = vec3(position4.w, normal4.w, diffuse4.w);
vec4 emission = sem.yyyy;
float shininess = sem.x;

// Perform lighting calculations
vec3 lightDir = vec3(gl_LightSource[0].position.xyz -position3);

float d = length(lightDir);
lightDir = normalize(lightDir);

float attenuation = 1.0/(gl_LightSource[0].constantAttenuation +
                         gl_LightSource[0].linearAttenuation * d +
                         gl_LightSource[0].quadraticAttenuation * d * d);

vec3 halfAngle = normalize(lightDir + eye);

float nDotLD = max(0.0, dot(normal3, lightDir));
float nDotHA = max(0.0, dot(normal3, halfAngle));

float spec_power;
if(nDotLD == 0.0)
  spec_power = 0.0;
else
  spec_power = pow(nDotHA, shininess);

ambient = gl_LightSource[0].ambient;
diffuse = gl_LightSource[0].diffuse * nDotLD * attenuation;
specular += gl_LightSource[0].specular * spec_power * attenuation;

vec4 color = vec4(diffuse3, 1.0);
gl_FragColor = (emission + ambient + diffuse)*color + specular;
}
```

The shaders for spot and directional lights are similar (see Rost for implementations).

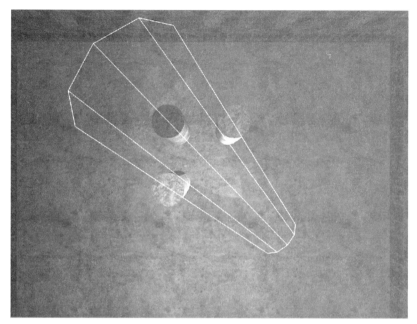

Figure 6.14 A top-down view of the scene, showing the lighting volume. The cylinders and floor are clipped to the lighting volume using the stencil buffer.

Your G-buffer format will probably have floating-point pixels, but the rendering window will use the standard fixed-point pixel format. One important limitation of floating-point pbuffers is that blending is not allowed. This is because certain blend operations only make sense if the source and destination fragments are clamped to [0, 1]. To get around this problem, you should deactivate the pbuffer and switch to the onscreen rendering context after filling the G-buffer. You will need to copy the pbuffer's depth buffer to the onscreen depth buffer with glReadPixels() and glDrawPixels(). Enable blending, and you can start drawing the lighting volumes in the onscreen rendering context.

Shadows

Shadows are easily incorporated in a deferred-shading system. You can use either the standard stencil-shadowing or projective shadow-mapping techniques for directional or spot lights. Point lights are a bit trickier. Shishkovtsov discusses a couple of techniques for dealing with shadow-casting point lights. The technique he recommends is to treat the point light as six separate spot lights for the purposes of shadow generation. Other possibilities include casting shadows into a cubemap, or unrolling a cubemap into a 2D texture, and then using a cubemap to look up the 2D texture coordinates.

Shadow-casting techniques usually require retransforming a portion of the scene geometry to render the scene from the point of view of a shadow-casting light. Fortunately, shadow generation does not involve complicated per-pixel calculations, so the cost of retransforming the scene for each shadow-casting light is relatively small compared to the cost of illuminating the scene. Nevertheless, in practice you should attempt to limit the number of shadow-casting lights in your scene to improve performance.

Transparency and Anti-aliasing

Drawing transparent surfaces and performing anti-aliasing are very difficult in a deferred shading system. Transparent surfaces can only be handled by rerendering the transparent objects after the main deferred-shading passes and blending them into the scene. If you retain the original depth buffer, you can forward shade the transparent surfaces last. This is also true for other blended effects like particles or explosions.

Hardware-accelerated anti-aliasing is not compatible with a deferred-shading system. Aliasing artifacts are most apparent at edges caused by depth discontinuities and creases (surface-normal discontinuities). Shishkovtsov describes a simple image-space technique for blurring these types of edges and creases. Because the G-buffer stores position and surface normal per-pixel, you can run an image-space edge detection filter over the G-buffer to find discontinuities in depth and surface orientation. Once you find such an edge, you can resample the illuminated scene image to blur the edges and reduce aliasing artifacts. As a side note, the edge-detection filter could also be used for special effects like cartoon shading.

Conclusion

Deferred shading offers better theoretical performance than forward-shading systems. In principle, each surface is illuminated by only the lights affecting it and only after its visibility has been determined at each pixel. In practice, however, many factors can affect your decision to use deferred shading. If you are working on a scene that has lots of large lights, such as a daytime outdoor scene, deferred shading won't perform so well. On the other hand, indoor scenes and nighttime scenes with lots of small, dynamical lights will work well with deferred shading. The ability to implement deferred shading in real time is relatively new, so the best way to evaluate the technique is to try it out and perform your own experiments in actual game situations.

References

ATI Developer SDK. **http://www.ati.com/developer/radeonSDK.html**.

Geldrich, Rich, Matt Pritchard, and John Brooks. "Deferred Lighting and Shading." Presentation at Game Developers Conference, San Jose, CA, March 2004. http://www.gdconf.com/archives/2004/pritchard_matt.ppt. 2004.

Hargreaves, Shawn, and Mark Harris. "Deferred Shading." Presentation at NVIDIA's 6800 Leagues under the Sea, June 28–29, 2004. **http://download.nvidia.com/ developer/presentations/2004/6800_Leagues/6800_Leagues_Deferred_Shading.pdf**.

Hargreaves, Shawn. "Deferred Shading." Presentation at Game Developers Conference, San Jose, CA, March 2004. **http://www.talula.demon.co.uk/DeferredShading.pdf**.

NVIDIA Developer SDK. **http://developer.nvidia.com/object/sdk_home.html**.

Rost, Randi J. *OpenGL Shading Language*. Boston: Addison-Wesley, 2004.

Shishkovtsov, Oles. "Deferred Shading in S.T.A.L.K.E.R." In *GPU Gems 2*, 143–166, ed. Matt Pharr. Upper Saddle Creek, NJ: Addison-Wesley, 2005.

High Dynamic Range Lighting and Rendering

Andres Reinot

High Dynamic Range Imaging (HDRI) is a standard technique used in film and computer graphics. *Dynamic range* is a general engineering term that refers to the range of values some parameter is capable of representing. In this case, dynamic range refers to the number of distinct shades of color an image can contain. In a typical digital image, a pixel is represented by 32 bits, 8 bits per color component (red, green, blue, alpha). Eight bits per component allows for 2^8 or 256 distinct shades of each color component. That means 32-bit color has a dynamic range of 0 to 255, which is considered fairly low, hence Low Dynamic Range (LDR). An image in which each color component is represented by a floating-point number ups the dynamic range to about -10^{50} to 10^{50}, which is considered High Dynamic Range (HDR).

The only real difference between HDR and LDR is color accuracy. For the most part, LDR color is accurate enough to represent standard images to an acceptable degree. The reason for this depends partly on the limits of human perception and partly on display hardware. There is a limit to how small a step in luminance the human eye can detect before that step appears as a smooth gradient to the mind, and display hardware exploits this phenomenon. Consumer-level display technology has a relatively low dynamic range, meaning the range of luminance that current displays can emit is limited. In this small range, 256 distinct steps appear smooth enough, and there is no real reason to display color more accurately. However, when manipulating and filtering an image, HDR imaging becomes important. Many postprocessing effects run strenuous algorithms on each pixel, causing errors and artifacts to accumulate if the image lacks color precision. Many graphics effects benefit from the use of accurate HDR color; there are even a few new tricks that are not possible without certain properties of HDR.

Superbright Pixels

A great benefit of HDR imaging is the ability to store more information than will ultimately be displayed on the screen. A very useful example of this is storing *superbright pixels*, or values "brighter" than white, in an image. For instance, in a floating-point pixel format the value 0.0 could represent black, 0.5 a middle grey, and 1.0 pure white. But floating-point lets us go much further: a very bright pixel could be represented by 2.0 or 3.0 or even 10.040 without a problem. This is illustrated in Figure 6.15. In fact, this is such a useful property of HDR imaging that over the years the phrase "High Dynamic Range" has become synonymous with this exact use of HDR color in computer graphics.

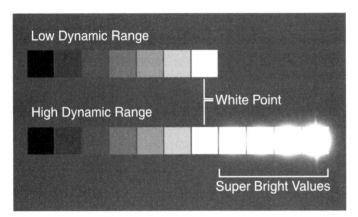

Figure 6.15 Gradients in LDR vs. HDR.

In Figure 6.15, the seventh value in the gradient was selected to represent the value of flat white color; anything below it is grey and not quite white, and anything above it is super-white and considered to be luminous. For the sake of clarity we will refer to this point on the color gradient as the *white point*. Superbright pixels allow us to store the true luminance of bright objects in an image. As an example, consider a photo of a lit 100-watt light bulb and the sun. The sun needs to appear millions of times brighter than the light bulb, but LDR color does not allow for that. Both objects cannot be accurately represented at the same time within the limited color range of LDR; HDR is needed.

The real benefit of using superbright pixels becomes apparent when the data has to be scaled or shifted on the color gradient in order to allow for data that was previously above the white point to enter the gray area below the white point. This brings information previously hidden above the white point to a visible range, and new details in the image become visible. As an example, consider an environment map reflecting off of a semireflective surface such as marble. Marble reflects only a small percentage of incoming light, so every environment-map pixel reflected off the marble surface is modulated by some fraction less than 1. When superbright pixels are modulated by this fraction they still remain fairly bright, whereas dim pixels may all but disappear in the reflection. In addition, some superbright pixels will fall below the white point after modulation, whereas others will not, and new details in the environment map are revealed. When LDR data is used, superbright pixels have already been clamped at the white point, and as a result, detail is lost. Also, all pixels are going to fall below the white point after modulation, and bright areas of the environment appear too dim and faded in the reflection, as illustrated in Figure 6.16. Modulation of superbright pixels is a key component of HDR data's usefulness. Understanding this concept is an important step in learning to take full advantage of HDR in computer graphics.

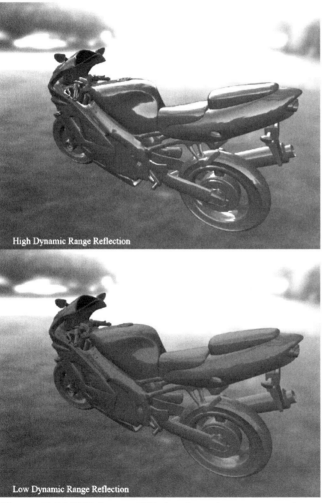

Figure 6.16 HDR data vs. LDR data in environment mapping.

Another example is accurate fogging. Fog is yet another parameter that modulates the color of objects in the scene, so it is a natural candidate for HDR benefits. The fog modulation will automatically take superbright values into account so that light sources, objects with bright highlights, and objects with bright HDR reflections will all fade into the fog more slowly and farther from the eye than dimmer objects. It is a subtle but important detail that can bring quite a bit of photorealism to the scene.

Common screen-aligned effects and filters also benefit from HDR. Take, for instance, a simple Gaussian blur effect. To blur an image, at each pixel we sample some neighboring pixels and average their color values together. Mathematically it is easy to see why an HDR image would blur differently than an LDR image. If a pixel with a luminance value of 1,000,000 is averaged together with its neighboring pixels of luminance around 1, the result is still much larger than 1 because the extremely bright pixel outweighs its dim neighbors considerably. Visually, blurring an HDR image results in bright areas blooming or glowing more than dim areas. This is an effect that can be observed in photography and is emulated in many games by adding glow sprites to bright objects or using other bloom tricks. With an HDR framebuffer, the entire frame can be copied, Gaussian blurred, and drawn as an overlay for accurate, beautiful-looking glow.

Tone Mapping

The process of fitting some range of luminance values from the HDR image to be represented in an LDR image is generally called *tone mapping* but is also sometimes referred to as *re-exposing* the image. This is in reference to photography, where the photographer carefully adjusts exposure settings on the camera to control how much light is allowed to accumulate on the film. In essence, the camera is mapping HDR light from the world to LDR color on the film. Tone mapping involves picking a range of values from the HDR image. All information outside this range is discarded and clamped, and the highest value in the range becomes the new white point. The values in the range are then shifted, scaled, and quantized to fit the LDR image. Tone mapping is illustrated in Figure 6.17.

When tone mapping the light-bulb-and-sun image, the sun will invariably have to be clamped to the white point, or the light bulb will disappear from the image completely. If there are other dimmer details in the image, the light bulb may also need to be clamped. Now both the light bulb and the sun appear as the same value of white in the LDR image, and no distinction between pixels of the two objects can be made. The true luminance ratio is lost.

Tone mapping to LDR inevitably causes information loss in the image. The loss may be minimized by picking a good range and white point, but the losses are still permanent and the resulting image may be unsuitable for some purposes. For an HDR image to be

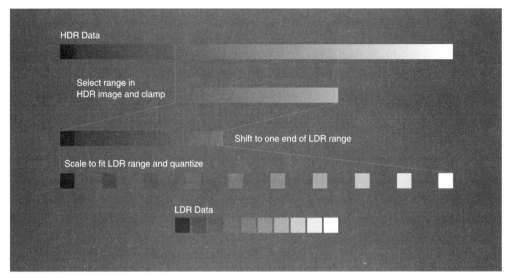

Figure 6.17 Tone mapping.

displayed on an LDR computer screen, it still needs to be tone mapped to fit into the limited color range. The difference, however, lies in where information is discarded, and keeping HDR information around as long as possible is useful in many ways.

Real-Time Tone Mapping

Programs such as PhotoShop and offline raytracers may use quite complex algorithms for tone mapping, but for real-time applications we are looking for a simple, fast approach. Typically, when an HDR image is tone mapped, it is scaled and shifted beforehand to set the white point at 255 when using an 8-bit integer-based pixel format, or 1.0 when using a float-based pixel format. OpenGL ultimately clamps all color at 255 or 1.0 respectively, so the white point in the HDR image must correspond to that.

Dynamic Tone Mapping

Like a camera, the human eye has exposure settings of a kind. The eye is capable of adapting to a huge range of luminance values, from pitch-black rooms at night to bright sunlit areas in daytime, and it is capable of adapting fairly quickly. In a matter of seconds the eye can adjust to completely different lighting conditions. This adaptation can be thought of as *dynamic tone mapping*. The re-exposure multiplier is dynamic, based on how much light is hitting the eye, so in a well-lit room the multiplier is small to tone down the image, whereas in a dark room the multiplier is high to brighten it.

Implementing dynamic tone mapping in real time is fairly straightforward, provided the rendering pipeline keeps HDR data around. Each rendered frame must be re-exposed based on the eye's exposure level. For instance, if the entire frame is rendered to an HDR pixel format, each resulting pixel could be re-exposed by the exposure multiplier. An even easier approach would be to scale the contributions from all light sources, including dynamic light sources and lightmaps, before any lighting calculations are done, again provided the lighting properties and lightmaps are stored as HDR data. It should be noted that standard diffuse and specular properties such as texture and color do not need to be changed, as they only represent the fraction of light reflected back from the surface. Only the actual lighting information needs to be scaled for proper re-exposure, and only the lighting information is then required to be HDR data.

The challenge in implementing dynamic tone mapping is how to figure out what the eye's exposure level should be. A simple approach would be to tag sections of the world as dim or bright. Caves could be marked as extremely dark, lit rooms moderately so, and outdoor areas as extremely bright. Moving from one area to another would then result in a slow fade between exposure levels. The downside to this approach is that an entire room or area is marked with one exposure level, but in reality, the exposure varies only with what's being viewed. Looking at the ground in an outdoor environment would result in a different exposure level than staring straight at the sun; similarly, looking out the window inside a room should result in a different exposure level than staring at a dark corner. To solve this problem, we need to set the exposure level based on the average brightness of the pixels in the frame. One approach would be to render the frame to a mipmapped texture, resulting in mipmap levels all the way down to 1×1. The one pixel in the deepest mipmap level could be sampled in a shader in a second pass or in the next frame, and its brightness used to come up with an acceptable exposure level and proper multiplier for the tone mapping.

HDR Lighting

Developing an HDR pipeline for standard dot-product lighting is not hard, because the nature of lighting algorithms does not change with the use of HDR data. For instance, when using the Gouraud or Blinn shading model, the diffuse component of the surface color is still calculated by the dot product between the light direction and surface normal, modulated by the light luminosity and the surface color. Except in an HDR lighting model the light luminosity can be very high and defined very precisely. The dot product still represents the percentage of light scattered off the surface to the observer's eye and can still be in the range of 0 to 1. It should be noted again that material properties such as diffuse or specular color should never be above 1.0. These properties represent the percentage of red, green, and blue light reflected by the surface, so a value above 100 percent would be meaningless; the same is true for diffuse and specular textures. However, it may still be desirable to store these parameters and textures as HDR data simply for higher color precision.

Image-Based Lighting and Rendering

An HDR environment map can be used to define light emitted by the entire environment around an object. This is a technique invented by Gregory Ward, popularized by Paul Debevec, and used widely in the film industry when compositing computer graphics with real footage. An environment map of the movie set is captured by photographing a mirror ball, such as a polished ball bearing. The reflection on the mirror ball actually contains a near-360-degree panorama of the entire environment at that exact point. Several photos of the ball are taken at different exposure rates and the results are combined into one HDR image on the computer. The result is an HDR environment map from the point at which the mirror ball was located. Because the image is HDR, the amount of light received from each pixel is stored accurately. This technique for lighting is crucial for compositing computer graphics with real film footage and can be used to define complex and realistic lighting in games as well.

Diffuse Irradiance Maps

The environment map can be thought of as a set of light sources. Each texel in the map is a directional light pointing to the center, allowing arbitrarily complex lighting situations to be defined. In real-time computer graphics, contributions from every light source cannot be calculated fast enough trivially (there is research into doing this through spherical harmonics; however, that topic is outside the scope of this chapter). Instead, contributions from every light source for any given normal can be precalculated and stored in a different cubemap. This process is sometimes referred to as *diffuse convolution*, and the resulting cubemap is called the *diffuse irradiance map* (DIM).

Essentially, the total diffuse light at any given point on the surface of the model can be obtained by performing a texture lookup into the DIM using the surface normal for the coordinates. In situations with additional dynamic light sources, this illumination value can be considered the ambient component of the lighting equation, and additional illumination results can be added on top of it. Because of the nature of the DIM, it should also be kept as an HDR image, as light sources may be super bright.

The diffuse convolution algorithm goes as follows:

```
for( every possible normal N )
{
  illum = 0;
  for( every environment map texel T in the hemisphere around the normal )
  {
    // light direction defined by the texture coordinate for this texel
    L = -T.texCoord;

    // accumulate diffuse light contributions from every texel for this normal
```

```
        illum += dot3( L, N ) * T.color;
    }
    //store illumination under texture coordinates equal to N
    diffuseIrradianceMap.store( illumination, N );
}
```

Typically, diffuse irradiance maps are relatively small, say around 64×64 pixels per cubemap face. One reason for this is that our brute force diffuse convolution algorithm is very expensive to compute. However, diffuse irradiance maps resulting from the convolution are very smooth and gradated; there are no sharp transitions between colors, so a small map with linear texture filtering works just fine. Another nice property of a DIM is that it doesn't change dramatically with model location. Since the effect of a DIM is rather subtle, DIMs could be generated from a few key places around the world and interpolated between. Outdoor scenes are even more forgiving, as the main light-emitting objects in the scene are going to be the sun, the sky, and the ground (emitting reflected light), all of which change insignificantly with respect to model position. It is entirely reasonable to use one DIM for an entire outdoor scene and achieve acceptable results. This frees up quite a bit of texture memory and opens doors for other tricks. Several DIMs could be stored for different times of day and interpolated between for very nice sunrise and sunset effects. The scene could even contain two DIMs, one for direct sunlight and one for shadowed objects. Since the sun is a major player in the lighting environment, turning it off will have major consequences for the DIM. Objects in shadow should not receive direct sunlight but would still be lit by light bouncing off of the ground and nearby objects.

Specular Convolution

An algorithm similar to diffuse convolution can be used to precompute the specular contribution from the environment as well; it is aptly called *specular convolution* and results in a *specular irradiance map* (SIM). Specular convolution is dependent on the specularity or shininess of the surface material, which means every material could potentially require a unique SIM. SIMs are used for materials that are rough but still shiny, such as brushed metal and frosted glass. Really a mirror can be thought of as a material with infinitely high specularity so the environment reflects off of it perfectly. Anything less than a mirror surface reflects the environment back slightly blurred. A SIM stores the environment map blurred to some degree. The specular highlight, as it is known in common shading models like Blinn-Phong, is a crude approximation of this blurred environment reflection. The assumption in these models is that typically only bright light sources show up in the reflection as point highlights, which can be approximated using a dot product and a specular exponent. An HDR SIM allows for true specular reflections from the environment, resulting in a much more realistic look and allowing for potentially infinite light sources.

Ambient Occlusion

Another common step in using DIMs is to multiply the resulting illumination by the *ambient occlusion* term. Ambient occlusion is a precalculated term that defines the "accessibility" of a point on a surface by environment lighting. It defines what percentage of the surrounding environment is visible to the point on the surface, and what percentage of it is occluded by the model itself. Figure 6.18 illustrates occluded and unoccluded points on a surface. Ambient occlusion makes dents and crevasses in models look shadowed and occluded, whereas flat and exposed areas appear bright and unoccluded, as shown in Figure 6.19.

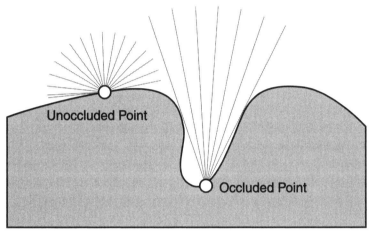

Figure 6.18 Occluded vs. unoccluded points.

Multiplying the diffuse irradiance lookup by the ambient occlusion term limits the contribution from the environment in places where the model should receive little ambient light, resulting in a very realistic appearance of soft self-shadowing. Calculating dynamic ambient occlusion in real time is not trivial, nor is it practical on current graphics hardware, so it is usually precalculated for every model (usually in a modeling package such as Maya) and stored either per vertex or as a texture. The downside to precalculated ambient occlusion is of course that it is static. Animated meshes would need an animated ambient occlusion dataset because the term changes as the shape of the mesh changes. Ambient occlusion represents a percentage of occlusion, so there is little need to store it as HDR data; however, it is still a vital component in HDR image-based lighting and should not be neglected.

Figure 6.19 Ambient occlusion applied to a model.

Bent Normals

An inaccuracy arises when using the standard surface normal to sample a DIM. When the normal is used to sample the DIM, the normal ray may in fact be occluded from the environment by other parts of the model. This is usually the case in creases and crevasses, as illustrated by Figure 6.20. In reality, the ambient lighting that will reach such areas in the crevasse is closer to the ray in Figure 6.20 labeled "bent normal." This ray is the average of all the unoccluded rays emanating from the point, as illustrated in the figure, and is referred to as the *bent normal*. It is the surface normal at the point, "bent" toward the area of least occlusion in the crevasse, and it leads to a more accurate illumination value sampled from the DIM. This term is also precomputed, usually along with ambient occlusion as many of the same calculations need to be performed on the geometry.

When you implement bent normal DIM lookups, however, you will discover that their results sometimes cause light to pool in crevasses as if light rays were naturally bouncing around in them. Some developers deliberately leave this side effect in because at times the results resemble global illumination; however, this is merely an illusion. What's actually happening is that the bent normal samples the DIM, but the resulting illumination value was calculated assuming that the normal used for sampling is the true surface normal. In essence, during the diffuse convolution, lights summed at the sampled DIM texel are assumed to hit the surface head on, but instead they are grazing the surface at an angle. Each light hits the surface at a slightly different angle, but the average of all the angles is

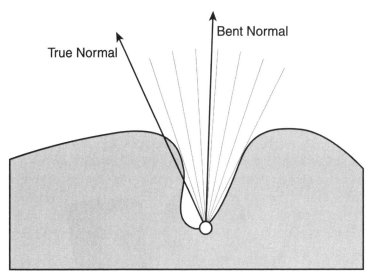

Figure 6.20 Bending normals.

approximately equal to the angle between the true normal and the bent normal. This means the illumination sampled from the DIM is brighter than it should be in areas where the bent normal differs from the true normal significantly, and light appears to pool in occluded crevasses. This can be accounted for by multiplying the sampled illumination value by the dot product between the true and bent normals. The resulting lighting equation, complete with ambient occlusion, a DIM sampled with a bent normal, and the bent-normal adjustment, ends up as

```
Ill = DIM.sample( bentNormal ) * AmbientOcc * dot3(normal, bentNormal)
```

The result is still not 100 percent accurate, but it is close. For true results, diffuse convolution needs to consider only the area of the environment map visible to the point on the surface, so only the unoccluded rays that escape the crevasse should be considered in the convolution. This, however, links the convolution algorithm to mesh topology, and no universal DIM that works for every model can be generated. In short, the colors in the DIM should be slightly different and the illumination slightly dimmer, but bent normals get us close enough, and that's what real-time computer graphics are all about.

OpenGL Limitations

OpenGL imposes a few limitations on HDR lighting. First of all, between the vertex and fragment stage, vertex color values are clamped to the 0 to 1 range. This is undesirable because vertex-based lighting results get stored in vertex colors and any HDR lighting information gets discarded. The vertex stage does allow for high-precision floating-point calculations, even in the fixed-function lighting model. Superbright values can be passed in to all the OpenGL lighting and material functions and are used correctly in the vertex stage. This means standard OpenGL lighting can be made HDR easily by just passing superbright values to certain functions. For instance, a light can be assigned the diffuse color <1000, 1000, 1000> without problems, and if it illuminates an object with the diffuse color <0.0005, 0.0005, 0.0005>, the result is still grey, smooth shading on the object. If nothing further is done with the lighting calculations, the clamping is acceptable. Problems arise, however, when the results of the lighting calculations are needed in the fragment stage for things like texture modulation. Using clamped lighting values for texture modulation results in bright highlights appearing too dim and washed out. Vertex color gets clamped even in the programmable pipeline, and the only way to avoid this clamping is by not using vertex color to pass information to the fragment stage. Instead, the results of per-vertex lighting calculations should be transferred to the fragment stage using texture coordinates, which pass through unclamped, and then a fragment shader interprets the coordinates as colors again.

The fixed-function fragment stage is even more stringent. It only operates with very coarse floating-point values in the 0 to 1 range. Even if a floating-point texture is sampled, superbright texels are immediately clamped before any other operations are done on them. To use HDR textures, you must use the programmable pipeline. The ARB fragment program and GLSL fragment shader extensions both guarantee true floating-point precision at the fragment level, so using a fragment shader automatically enables us to sample and use HDR data.

Hardware Limitations

Current graphics hardware imposes additional limitations on HDR data and textures. Partial support for floating-point textures has been around for a few years now. ATI cards have supported 24-bit floating-point textures and cubemaps for some time. However, these textures are severely limited. They cannot be mipmapped or filtered in any way. NVIDIA GeForce FX series and up have supported 32-bit and 16-bit floating-point (also known as half-float) textures and cubemaps, also without texture filtering or mipmapping support. The recent GeForce 6 series of graphics cards boasts support for filtering of floating-point textures and cubemaps, but still at quite a performance hit, especially with cubemaps. ATI cards also support a 16-bit integer texture format (Int16 format), which allows for a range of 0 to 65,535 per color component instead of 0 to 255, which is sufficient dynamic range for most HDR effects. It should also be noted that all floating-point textures, when sampled in a fragment program, are capable of returning arbitrary float values, but Int16 textures will always return values between 0 and 1. However, the 16 bits of precision are still present, so 65,535 distinct values can be represented between 0 and 1. This can make implementing an HDR pipeline with Int16 and floating-point texture support quite a headache. Int16 textures have to be scaled right so the white point matches up with the floating-point textures.

These hardware and driver shortcomings will of course disappear in time as graphics cards improve, but a problem that won't just go away is memory footprint. An 8-bit LDR texture uses 24 or 32 bits of texture memory per pixel, but a 32-bit floating-point texture uses that much just per color component! That means a floating-point texture is three to four times the size of an LDR texture—96 or 128 bits per pixel. Both the half-float format and the 16-bit integer formats cut the memory footprint in half, but HDR textures still create quite a large overhead and should be used sparingly.

Yet another, more theoretical problem with HDR color buffers lies in anti-aliasing. Traditional anti-aliasing techniques such as supersampling and multisampling do not work with superbright pixels, and for the very same reasons HDR blurring is so special. A superbright pixel averaged with a dim pixel can still lead to a superbright value that will ultimately get clamped to white. This causes edges of very bright polygons on dark backgrounds to remain aliased unless the color is clamped to LDR before the anti-aliasing step. This is a problem with HDR color buffers in general, as reliable anti-aliasing cannot be performed without discarding the HDR information.

Image-Based Lighting Example

Let's look at the demo included with this chapter for a hands-on example of image-based lighting. The demo features a motorcycle model with a precomputed ambient occlusion term, lit by a diffuse irradiance map, and a semireflective surface material that reflects an HDR environment map. There are many environments to cycle through, each with its own background and lighting environment as defined by the reflection map and DIM.

The environment maps used for the demo are all from Paul Debevec's website. The original images are used as reflection maps, and DIMs are generated from them using HDR Shop's diffuse-convolution feature. Both the reflection maps and the DIMs are stored as vertical cross images representing the six faces of a cubemap unwrapped, as shown in Figure 6.21. The vertical-cross configuration wastes a lot of disk-space because half of the image is black and unused, but it is convenient for content management, as you don't have to worry about cutting faces into separate images. Instead, the cubemap faces are separated out in code as part of the cubemap assembly. The vertical cross images are stored in a floating-point format, and the cubemaps will be floating-point cubemaps (16-, 24-, or 32-bit floating-point, depending on hardware).

The model itself is separated into four pieces. Each piece has vertex normals, one set of texture coordinates, and an LDR ambient occlusion texture to go with it. The texture coordinates and the ambient occlusion texture were both precomputed for each piece using standard modeling software such as 3D Studio Max or Maya. The modeling software generates texture coordinates in such a way that each polygon of the model occupies a unique area in texture space and there is no tiling of the texture. The results of the ambient occlusion calculations are then stored in a 2D image based on this texture mapping.

Figure 6.21 Bending normals.

This type of precalculation process is commonly referred to as "baking" and results in images similar to Figure 6.22. The model was first split into four pieces for resolution considerations in the baking process. Resolution is a precious commodity when it comes to baked textures, so any such model splitting should be done at the artist's discretion. It can even help to edit the generated texture coordinates before the rendering step to maximize the use of surface area in each texture.

Figure 6.22 A baked ambient occlusion map.

The demo does not require a vertex shader; everything is achieved through the fixed-function vertex pipeline through the use of texture-coordinate generation. The following code segment sets up texture-coordinate generation to make texture coordinates of texture unit 1 be the vertex normals and texture coordinates of texture unit 2 the reflection vectors from standard OpenGL reflection mapping.

```
glActiveTexture( GL_TEXTURE1 );
glTexGeni(GL_S, GL_TEXTURE_GEN_MODE, GL_NORMAL_MAP );
glTexGeni(GL_T, GL_TEXTURE_GEN_MODE, GL_NORMAL_MAP );
glTexGeni(GL_R, GL_TEXTURE_GEN_MODE, GL_NORMAL_MAP );
glEnable(GL_TEXTURE_GEN_S);
glEnable(GL_TEXTURE_GEN_T);
glEnable(GL_TEXTURE_GEN_R);

glActiveTexture( GL_TEXTURE2 );
glTexGeni(GL_S, GL_TEXTURE_GEN_MODE, GL_REFLECTION_MAP );
```

```
glTexGeni(GL_T, GL_TEXTURE_GEN_MODE, GL_REFLECTION_MAP );
glTexGeni(GL_R, GL_TEXTURE_GEN_MODE, GL_REFLECTION_MAP );
glEnable(GL_TEXTURE_GEN_S);
glEnable(GL_TEXTURE_GEN_T);
glEnable(GL_TEXTURE_GEN_R);
glActiveTexture( GL_TEXTURE0 );
```

One problem remains: these texture coordinates will be generated in eye space, but for this demo we would like them in world space instead. To fix this, we transform the texture coordinates to world space using texture matrices. The following code segment loads the inverse of the modelview matrix into texture matrices of texture units 1 and 2 through the camera's `setupInverseRotation()` function. Texture coordinates generated by the fixed-function pipeline are then multiplied through by the appropriate texture matrices, and we get world-space coordinates.

```
glMatrixMode( GL_TEXTURE );
glActiveTexture( GL_TEXTURE2 );
glLoadIdentity();
mCamera.setupInverseRotation();

glActiveTexture( GL_TEXTURE1 );
glLoadIdentity();
mCamera.setupInverseRotation();

glActiveTexture( GL_TEXTURE0 );
glMatrixMode( GL_MODELVIEW );
```

We do, however, need a fragment shader in order to avoid texture clamping. The fragment shader samples the ambient occlusion texture, the DIM, and the reflection map, with the appropriate texture coordinates. The reflection term is then modulated by the reflectivity of the material, as stored in the vertex color. The diffuse irradiance term is modulated by the ambient occlusion term and added to the reflection term. Finally, the results are modulated by the exposure scale, passed in as a uniform shader attribute, and output to the screen. The ARB fragment program is as follows:

```
!!ARBfp1.0
PARAM exposure = program.env[0];

TEMP diff, refl;
TEX occ,  fragment.texcoord[0], texture[0], 2D;
TEX diff, fragment.texcoord[1], texture[1], CUBE;
TEX refl, fragment.texcoord[2], texture[2], CUBE;

MUL refl, refl, fragment.color;
```

```
MUL diff, diff, occ;
ADD diff, refl, diff;

MUL result.color, diff, exposure;
END
```

And the C++ code to pass in the uniform exposure parameter is as follows:

```
glProgramEnvParameter4fvARB(GL_FRAGMENT_PROGRAM_ARB, 0, mExposure);
```

The result looks quite impressive. The image-based lighting really helps the model fit into each environment naturally. The demo also includes a simulated LDR version of the shader above, where every TEX instruction has been replaced by TEX_SAT. TEX_SAT clamps, or saturates, the results of the texture lookup to the 0-to-1 range as the fixed-function pipeline would. The difference is very noticeable as all the bright reflection highlights disappear and the DIM also gets clamped, resulting in grey blobs in brighter spots.

Conclusion

The benefits of High Dynamic Range imaging can seem subtle at first, but HDR can be quite powerful when used effectively. We have covered the basics of HDR imaging and just a few of the effects and tricks that are possible through HDR color. Many old graphics techniques such as fog, reflection, and motion blur improve in quality and accuracy. A few new tricks such as dynamic tone mapping and image-based lighting have become possible only through the use of HDR. And as graphics hardware continues to improve, use of high-precision, HDR color will undoubtedly become standard practice in real-time computer graphics.

References

Akenine-Möller, Tomas, and Eric Haines. "Advanced Lighting and Shading." *In Real-Time Rendering*, 2nd ed., 181–288. Natick, MA: A. K. Peters, 2002.

Bunnell, Michael. "Dynamic Ambient Occlusion and Indirect Lighting." In *GPU Gems 2*, 223–234. Upper Saddle River, NJ: Addison-Wesley, 2005.

Cohen, Johnathan, Chris Tchou, Tim Hawkins, and Paul Debevec. "Real-Time High Dynamic Range Texture Mapping." Eurographics Rendering Workshop 2001. London: 2001.

Debevec, Paul, and Jitendra Malik. "Recovering High Dynamic Range Radiance Maps from Photographs." In *Proceedings of SIGGRAPH 1997*, 369–378. Computer Graphics Proceedings, Annual Conference Series. Addison-Wesley: Los Angeles, 1997.

King, Gary. "Real-Time Computation of Dynamic Irradiance Environment Maps." In *GPU Gems 2*, 167–176. Upper Saddle River, NJ: Addison-Wesley, 2005.

Environment maps courtesy of Paul Debevec, **http://www.debevec.org/probes/**.

Non-Photorealistic Rendering

Josh Petrie

As you've seen so far in this chapter, computer graphics techniques are typically concerned with achieving renderings of photorealistic quality. Such images are generally produced by approximating the physical interactions of light with a scene. These approximations can range from the crude to the complex, depending on accuracy and speed requirements, but ultimately the aim of such a rendering method is to mimic reality as closely as possible.

In contrast, the purpose of non-photorealistic techniques is to communicate a concept as effectively as possible. Where photorealistic techniques try to pack as much information as they can reasonably compute in a sixtieth of a second into the scene, non-photorealistic techniques often aim to reduce the amount of information presented, to eliminate redundancy. Displaying a scene in this manner allows the scene to present a concept or an idea rather than a verbatim copy of reality. The human visual processor is very good at extracting information from incomplete data such as those of the more artistic imagery produced by non-photorealistic rendering. Consider Figure 6.23. No triangle appears, explicitly, in the image; however, the eye readily picks up on the missing sections of the circles and interprets the empty space as a triangle.

Figure 6.23 An image suggesting the idea of a triangle.

This is a simple example of the eye/brain system's ability to recognize the *idea* presented in the image (a triangle) instead of just the presentation itself (some circles with wedges cut out of them). This is the kind of expression non-photorealistic rendering offers to the graphics programmer: the ability to *show* viewers something rather than to directly *tell* them what they are seeing.

The primary motivation for choosing to use non-photorealistic rendering in a game is this: many games are about fictional, often surreal or stylized worlds—why should such a universe look and feel exactly like our own? Applying some kind of artistic technique to the scenes of your game can give it that extra visual kick that catches the attention of your players, pulls them in, and helps make your game world feel that much more authentic. There are additional benefits: game play can be accentuated by stylized techniques that serve to emphasize important aspects of a level or a character, and techniques designed to assist an artist in the process of content creation can be leveraged to streamline the asset pipeline.

Non-photorealistic rendering techniques come in many flavors, such as the simulation of artistic depiction methods, automatic generation of technical diagrams and blueprints, or the aforementioned algorithms to assist an artist. In this chapter, we will explore some techniques that fall into the first category, because they are the most directly applicable to game development. It is important to remember that computer graphics—at least as far as general real-time techniques suitable for game development are concerned—is not an exact science, and non-photorealistic techniques are certainly no exception. Exploration is highly encouraged!

The Model Format

The techniques discussed below do not make reference to a specific model format so as to be as general as possible. However, they do refer to certain properties and data sets that the model is assumed to have:

- A list of vertices.
- A list of triangles; a triangle is a 3-tuple of vertex indices.
- A list of per-vertex normals.
- A list of per-triangle normals.

This data can be provided by any means—it can be stored directly in the file format itself, precalculated during model load, or generated on the fly each frame by the animation controller—as long as it is available and current every time the model is to be rendered.

Edge Rendering

The process of extracting and rendering various types of edges is often used to complement other more robust styles of non-photorealistic rendering. The so-called feature edges of a model (its contours, creases, and surface boundaries) are often on their own enough information for the eye to process and recognize an object; occasionally edge rendering is used on its own as a complete technique.

The three types of edges have the following definitions:

- Contours are edges shared between a front-facing triangle and a back-facing triangle as determined by their normal vectors and the view vector. In Figure 6.24, the contour edge is marked A. Silhouette edges are those contours that lie between the object and the background.

- Crease edges are those between two front-facing triangles whose dihedral angle is above some arbitrary threshold. Figure 6.24 shows a "valley crease" (marked B) and a "ridge crease" (marked C).

- Surface boundaries are edges on a triangle that are not shared with another triangle—they only occur on nonclosed models. Border edges occur as locations D and E in Figure 6.24.

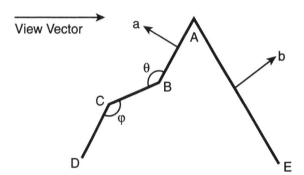

Figure 6.24 A side-view slice of a 3D model showing the feature edges and the properties used to determine them.

Feature edges can be detected in either image space or object space, and there are many techniques for doing this detection (a survey of such methods can be found in Gooch and Gooch's book *Non-Photorealistic Rendering,* listed among the references at the end of this section). Image-space techniques benefit from the fact that nothing needs to be known about an object's surface representation—generally only a depth-buffer rendering of the object is required. However, limitations arise due to the resolution of the depth buffer, and some image-space techniques require multiple render passes and costly buffer read-back operations. Geometric, object-space techniques avoid those drawbacks, but are typically more complex in nature.

Unfortunately, like the rest of the non-photorealistic rendering field, feature-edge detection is not a solved problem; there is no one algorithm or approach that is better in all cases—the onus is on the programmer to select a method that best suits the needs of the project. This chapter will present three methods. The first two are simple and operate in image space. The last is more powerful and operates in object space.

Image-Space Approaches to Feature-Edge Detection

The silhouettes (e.g., the outline of the object) can be rendered easily in five passes. In the first four passes, the object is rendered with a different viewport each time—offset one pixel to the left, then offset one pixel to the right, and so on. For these passes, the depth buffer is not utilized. In the final pass, the depth buffer is enabled and the object is rendered normally or all in white.

note

If you are going to render the model in a single flat color, as is presented here, then during the fifth pass you don't actually need to re-enable the depth test. However, you should re-enable the depth test if you are going to render the model normally during the final pass.

```
int vp_x,vp_y,vp_w,vp_h;     // X, Y, width and height of viewport
glColor3f(0.0f,0.0f,0.0f);   // Black outlines
glDisable(GL_DEPTH_TEST);

// Displace viewport and render; do this four times
glViewport(vp_x - 1,vp_y,vp_w - 1,vp_h);
RenderModel();
glViewport(vp_x + 1,vp_y,vp_w + 1,vp_h);
RenderModel();
glViewport(vp_x,vp_y - 1,vp_w,vp_h - 1);
RenderModel();
glViewport(vp_x,vp_y + 1,vp_w,vp_h + 1);
RenderModel();

// Render final pass in white with the depth test on again
glEnable(GL_DEPTH_TEST):
glClear(GL_DEPTH_BUFFER_BIT);
glColor3f(1.0f,1.0f,1.0f);
RenderModel();
```

The output of this algorithm is shown in Figure 6.25. This algorithm is rather undesirable, however: it requires *five* passes, and the output of those five passes isn't even very good. It cannot render interior contours, for example, and the viewport offset (which determines the thickness of the edges) cannot be very large, or highly noticeable gaps will appear where the model has acute corners (see Figure 6.26).

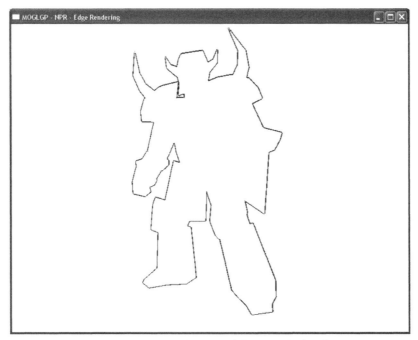

Figure 6.25 Rendering only the silhouettes (object outline) in five passes.

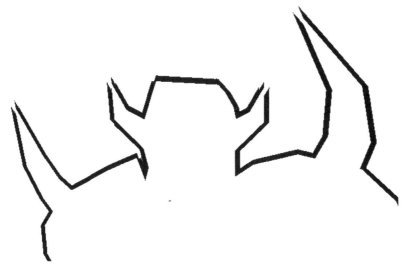

Figure 6.26 The five-pass technique generates gaps at acute corners when the line thickness is too high (note the horns in particular).

A better to way to render the contours of an object is to exploit the depth buffer and depth testing mechanisms of the graphics pipeline. Contour edges occur along edges where the surface changes from front- to back-facing; in other words, the set of all contours edges is the intersection of the set of front-facing triangles closest to the eye and the set of all other triangles. We can compute that intersection implicitly using a *two*-pass rendering algorithm.

```
// Step 1: Enable back-face culling, set depth function to "less than."
glCullFace(GL_BACK);
glDepthFunc(GL_LESS);

// Render the model with the background color (here we use white).
glColor3f(1.0f,1.0f,1.0f);
RenderModel();

// Enable front-face culling, set depth function to "less than or equal."
// Draw model in wireframe, in desired edge color.
glCullFace(GL_FRONT);
glDepthFunc(GL_LEQUAL);
glPolygonMode(GL_BACK,GL_LINE);
glColor3f(0.0f,0.0f,0.0f);
RenderModel();
```

Let's take a look at the algorithm in detail. In the first pass, we have disabled writes to the color buffer and so are just priming the depth buffer with the z-values of the front-most triangles of the model. This establishes the set of "closest front-facing polygons." In the second pass, we are using front-face culling since we want to find where back faces intersect the already-drawn front faces. The depth test is relaxed to "less than or equal," so that fragments along contour edges (which will have the same depth value as that of the shared front-facing triangle previously rasterized) are drawn.

This technique is only slightly more complex than the last, and it takes much less work. Unfortunately, it too has a number of drawbacks:

- The mesh must be closed (e.g., can have no unshared boundary edges, because those edges will not be rendered).
- Triangles must not intersect the interior area of other triangles, because the edges formed by those intersections will not be rendered.
- The eye point must not be allowed to penetrate the object.
- The thickness of the strokes is still difficult to control. Depth-buffer-precision issues can cause some pixels to be missed in such a way that some edge lines will have gaps and some may appear thicker than others (the nature of the triangles in the model itself can also contribute to this problem). This is illustrated in Figure 6.27. Use of glPolygonOffset() may alleviate this problem.

Figure 6.27 Depth buffer precision can cause holes in the edges.

Additionally, both algorithms discussed so far share a common defect: it is not possible to render stylized strokes—wavy or brushlike strokes, for example—using them. To do so requires the ability to provide a texture parameterization for the stroke, so that textures can be mapped onto its length. This in turn implies that the lines we are currently rendering need to be expanded to quads; in short, we need a more robust technique.

A Geometric Approach to Feature-Edge Detection

We want to generate thick lines that can be textured with simple stroke textures. The obvious way to do this is to generate an oriented quadrilateral for each edge, and apply a texture to it. In order to do this, we will require some information about the edges in the mesh. In their article "Hardware-Determined Feature Edges," M. McGuire and J. F. Hughes present a structure called the edge mesh—a list of edge properties built from a mesh during a preprocessing stage. We can use those properties to generate the required geometry and create texture-mapped edge strokes.

note

The algorithm we present here, which is similar to the one discussed in McGuire and Hughes's article, has two serious drawbacks: it requires a large amount of data to be sent to the GPU, and it requires a branch-heavy vertex program that may result in increased render times on some GPUs. Both of these issues, however, are problems of scale that will be lessened by the advances of next generation GPUs.

Each "vertex" of the edge mesh describes a single edge. These vertices are sent in a certain order to the GPU, where the vertex program turns them into edges when appropriate. For an edge between vertices v0 and v1, an edge vertex is defined to be the set of properties { v0, v1, v2, v3, n0, n1, i } where the first four fields are the vertices of the triangles sharing the edge such that triangle A is formed by { v0, v1, v2 } and triangle B is formed by { v1, v0, v3 }. The vertex normals of v0 and v1 are n0 and n1, respectively, and i is an integer from 0 to 3 that is used to differentiate between the inside, outside, start, and stop ends of an edge. Figure 6.28 provides a visual definition of some of the aforementioned properties.

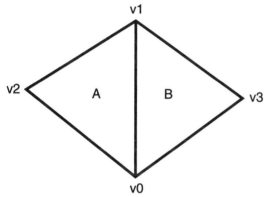

Figure 6.28 The triangles share the edge from v0 to v1.

The edge mesh for a model is built as a preprocessing step in two parts.

Step 1: Triangle Adjacency

Given an edge defined by its two vertices, we will need to know something about the two triangles that share that edge. We will also eventually want a simple means to ensure we only process a given edge once later in the construction process. It is therefore to our benefit to construct a triangle-adjacency table, which is a list of integer 3-tuples. Each index in the list corresponds to the triangle with the same index in the original mesh's triangle list; the 3-tuple at that index contains the indices of the three adjacent triangles. We use the special value −1 to indicate that there is no triangle sharing that edge.

When we talk about the edges of a triangle, we number them using the lower of the two vertex numbers that form the edge. In other words, a triangle with vertices { v0, v1, v2 } has three edges:

```
Edge 0 is the edge from v0 to v1.
Edge 1 is the edge from v1 to v2.
Edge 2 is the edge from v2 to v0.
```

We can represent an adjacency table entry with the following simple structure.

```
struct Adjacency
{
  int neighbor[3];
};
```

Inside our model, we simply store an array of Adjacency elements the same size as the number of triangles in the model. When the model is loaded, we allocate the appropriate amount of storage and build the triangle adjacency table.

We initially assume the entire adjacency table is degenerate (i.e., nothing is adjacent anything—every entry contains { −1, −1, −1 }). Then for each edge of each triangle, we search every other triangle for the matching edge. If the edge is found, we store the index to the triangle it was found on in the appropriate field of the tuple for the original triangle; otherwise we do nothing and the field remains −1, indicating a boundary edge. On a given pair of adjacent triangles, an edge on one that looks like { p0, p1 } will appear on the other in reverse order ({ p1, p0 }). This is the condition we look for when trying to find matching edges.

tip

It is generally safe to search for matching vertex indices, rather than directly looking for matching vertices. Indices, being integers, are not susceptible to the floating-point precision issues that could arise when trying to compare vertex components directly.

```
void ComputeAdjacency(Model *m)
{
  // adj is an appropriately-sized array of Adjacency structures
  // (one entry per triangle in the model).
  Adjacency *adj = m->GetAdjacencyList();

  // For each triangle...
  for(int i = 0; i < m->GetTriangleCount(); ++i)
  {
    // Initially assume all edges are unshared.
    adj[i].neighbor[0] = adj[i].neighbor[1] = adj[i].neighbor[2] = -1;

    // Then, for each edge...
    for(int j = 0; j < 3; ++j)
    {
      // A triangle contains the indices of the three vertices that
      // form it, in counterclockwise order.
      Triangle  ti = m->GetTriangle(i);
```

```
      // The edge is from p0 to p1; on the neighboring triangle it will appear
      // as p1 to p0, so scan every other triangle for such an edge.
      int   p0 = ti.vertex[j];
      int   p1 = ti.vertex[(j + 1) % 3];

      for(int k = 0; k < m->GetTriangleCount(); ++k)
      {
        Triangle  tk = m->GetTriangle(k);

        // For each edge...
        for(int l = 0; l < 3; ++l)
        {
          // If the edge is built from the same vertices but in opposite
          // order, we've found our neighbor triangle, so store it.
          if(p0 == tk.vertex[(l + 1) % 3] &&
             p1 == tk.vertex[l])
            adj[i].neighbor[j] = k;
        }
      }
    }
  }
}
```

Step 2: Building the Edges

Since our model object contains most of the information we need for an edge mesh already, there is no sense is duplicating it in the edge mesh itself; we will simply reference the appropriate parts of the model. For example, instead of storing the components of each vertex, we will store the index of the vertex inside the model's vertex list. This reduces the overall size of the edge mesh.

caution

Be aware that in representing the edge mesh in this fashion, we can't use high-performance methods of geometry specification such as vertex arrays or vertex-buffer objects. The demos for this chapter, in fact, use the simple-but-slow immediate mode calls to specify vertex attributes. This approach is clearer, but not well suited to production code.

We represent an edge mesh vertex with the following structure:

```
struct EdgeInfo
{
  int    v0; // Index of v0.
  int    v1; // Index of v1.
  int    v2; // Index of v2.
```

```
   int     v3; // Index of v3.
   int     a;  // Index of triangle A, which is (v0,v1,v2).
   int     b;  // Index of triangle B, which is (v1,v0,v3).
   int     i;  // Edge vertex type.
};
```

To build the edge mesh, we must search through all edges of the model, without repeating an edge. Fortunately, we can use the triangle-adjacency table to ensure we don't process an edge more than once. To process each edge, we can search through every triangle and process any edges that we haven't seen before. After we process an edge, we mark it as "seen" so that we will skip it the next time we come across it.

The easiest (although nearly the slowest) method to mark an edge is to keep a set of 2-tuples, where the elements of the tuple are the start and end vertex indices:

```
std::set< std::pair< int, int > >  seenEdges;
```

When looking for, or marking, an edge, we must take into account the fact that the edge may appear with the start and end vertices swapped. So, for an edge with vertex indices v0 and v1, we construct the pairs { v0,v1 } and { v1,v0 }. The existence of either of these pairs in the marked-edges set indicates that the edge has been previously processed and should not be processed again.

```
typedef std::vector< EdgeInfo >  EdgeMesh;

EdgeMesh BuildEdgeMesh(const Model &m)
{
   EdgeMesh                           edges;
   std::set< std::pair< int,int > >  seenEdges;

   // For each triangle...
   for(int i = 0; i < source.GetTriangleCount(); ++i)
   {
      Triangle   t = source.GetTriangle(i);
      Adjacency  a = source.GetTriangleAdj(i);

      // For each edge...
      for(int j = 0; j < 3; ++j)
      {
         // Find the index of the edge on the triangle adjacent to this one.
         Triangle  ta      = source.GetTriangle(a.neighbor[j]);
         unsigned short    p0     = t.vtxIdx[j];
         unsigned short    p1     = t.vtxIdx[(j + 1) % 3];
         int               adjIdx = -1;
```

```
// On the adjacent triangle, the first vertex of the edge will be p1,
// not p0, so the index at which p1 appears is the index of the edge.
for(int k = 0; k < 3; ++k)
  if(p1 == ta.vtxIdx[k])
    adjIdx = k;

// See if the edge from p0 to p1, or the other way around, has been seen
// already or not. If neither form of the edge exists in the map, we have
// not yet seen this edge.
std::pair< int,int >  edge0 = std::make_pair(p0,p1);
std::pair< int,int >  edge1 = std::make_pair(p1,p0);

if(seenEdges.find(edge0) == seenEdges.end() &&
   seenEdges.find(edge1) == seenEdges.end())
{
  EdgeInfo  e;

  // v0 and v1 are the indices of the actual edge vertices.
  e.v0 = p0;
  e.v1 = p1;

  // v2 is on triangle t.
  e.v2 = t.vtxIdx[(j + 2) % 3];

  // v3 is on triangle ta.
  e.v3 = t.vtxIdx[(adjIdx + 2) % 3];

  // a and b are indices of the main and adjacent triangle.
  e.a = i;
  e.b = a.neighbor[j];

  // Add the edge. The edge is added four times, each of which is
  // identical except for the value of i, which ranges from 0 to 3.
  e.i = 0;
  edges.push_back(e);
  e.i = 1;
  edges.push_back(e);
  e.i = 2;
  edges.push_back(e);
  e.i = 3;
  edges.push_back(e);
```

```
      // Insert both edges into the map to ensure we don't add this
      // edge to the edge mesh again.
      seenEdges.insert(edge0);
      seenEdges.insert(edge1);
    }
  }
 }
 return (edges);
}
```

Drawing the Edges

Simple Edges

The technique presented here for building edges allows for thick texture-mapped strokes. However, it is also possible to render thin, untextured strokes. This method requires only half of the original edge mesh data; instead of inserting an edge into the mesh four times, the edge is inserted only twice. The vertex program logic required is also simpler, which makes for a more streamlined shader.

Using `GL_LINES` mode, the edge-mesh vertices are drawn in the following order: { 0,1,4,5,8,9… }. This will result in pairs of edge vertices being sent to the GPU that are identical except for the value of i, which will be either 0 or 1. To render an edge, the vertex program simply transforms either v0 or v1, depending on the value of i. The feature-edge determination and discard techniques used in the more complicated thick-edge rendering routine still apply to this simplified algorithm. This will result in thin strokes and actually only requires half the edge-mesh geometry, which can reduce the storage overhead of the technique if thin edges will suffice.

During the render process, we will need to discard vertices for edges that are not actually feature edges. The information stored in our edge mesh allows us to easily determine whether or not an edge is a contour, crease, or border edge.

- Contour-edge determination is the most involved. Given that nA and nB are the face normals of the triangles sharing the edge, and v is a vector from the first vertex of the edge to the eye point, if either one (but not both) of dot(nA,v) < 0 or dot(nB,v) < 0, is true, the edge is a contour.

- An edge is a ridge or valley crease edge if the dot product of the face normals is greater than the cosine of the desired crease threshold.

- An edge is a border or marked edge if v0 is the same as v3 (this is an arbitrary condition that must be enforced during the construction of the edge mesh).

The ridge and valley thresholds must be chosen and either fixed in the vertex program or passed in as uniforms. The view point is easily computable within the vertex program itself. All other data is available within the edge mesh.

Edges that do not pass at least one of the above conditions should not be drawn. Since it is not actually possible to discard geometry in the vertex program, we will do the next best thing and transform all the vertices of a nonfeature edge to the point { 0,0,−1,1 }, which is beyond the far clip plane and will be discarded by the hardware during the clip phase.

Using GL_QUADS mode, every vertex in the edge mesh is drawn sequentially. Recall that the edge mesh contains four duplicates of an edge vertex, each with increasing values of i. We can use i to determine which direction to "push" the input vertex in order to end up with a quad (Figure 6.29).

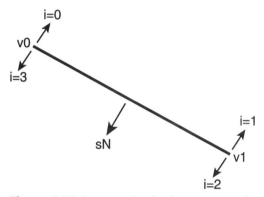

Figure 6.29 A geometric edge between v0 and v1, and how the vertices should be transformed to create a quad for that edge.

Note that our "push" is actually displacing the vertex along the positive or negative (as appropriate) screen-space normal; the first step in our vertex program will be to compute the screen-space positions of the input vertices v0 and v1 by multiplying them with the modelview-projection matrix and dividing by the resulting w-coordinates. We'll call these screen-space coordinates s0 and s1, respectively.

n o t e

The output of a vertex program should be coordinates in homogeneous clip space, which will be transformed to coordinates in screen space (all components in the range [−1, 1]) by the hardware via division by the w-component. By outputting a value of 1 in the w-coordinate, we can effectively skip that step and output screen-space coordinates directly. We utilize this fact during our edge-extraction step.

We can compute the normal to the edge vector, sN, as:

```
vec2  sN = normalize(vec2(s0.y - s1.y,s1.x - s0.x));
```

There is one other problem, namely that sN is in screen space and will need to be scaled down in order to produce strokes that are of reasonable thickness (using sN without scaling will result in lines as thick as half the screen, in many cases). The x and y components of sN must be scaled independently, by a factor of k / w and k / h, respectively (w and h are the half-width and half-height of the viewport). Varying k allows us to vary the stroke width (scaling sN in this fashion will produce a k-pixel-thick line).

The next step of this phase is to actually perform the transformation, using the value of i to tell us which corner of the quad we are creating, and discarding the vertex if none of the feature-edge-determination tests passed. The relevant portion of the vertex program looks like:

```
// Scale sN to provide a k-pixel-thick stroke.
sN.x = sN.x * (k / halfW);
sN.y = sN.y * (k / halfH);

vec2  q0 = (s0 - sN);
vec2  q1 = (s1 - sN);
vec2  q2 = (s1 + sN);
vec2  q3 = (s0 + sN);

// If the vertex is on a feature edge...
if(is_contour || is_ridge || is_valley || is_border)
{
  // Write the appropriate corner of the quad.
  if(i == 0.0)
    gl_Position = vec4(q0.x,q0.y,0,1);
  else if(i == 1.0)
    gl_Position = vec4(q1.x,q1.y,0,1);
  else if(i == 2.0)
    gl_Position = vec4(q2.x,q2.y,0,1);
  else
    gl_Position = vec4(q3.x,q3.y,0,1);
}
else
{
  // Not a feature edge; output a point that will be clipped.
  gl_Position = vec4(0,0,-1,1);
}
```

The last step in the render process is to apply texture coordinates to the quad so that stroke textures can be applied. We can safely set the v-coordinates to 0 and 1 for the inside and outside stroke vertices. The only trick is the assignment of the u-coordinates, which must be flipped in certain cases to prevent the stroke texture from flipping. This flip occurs when the screen-space projection of a vertex normal (labeled m) faces a different direction than the screen-space projection of the stroke perpendicular. This can be determined via a dot product between m and sN.

Adjusting the u-coordinates in this fashion will prevent the strokes from jumping around, but it must be noted that this texture parameterization is still far from perfect—it is quite difficult to achieve perfect texture parameterizations, as noted by McGuire and Hughes. The style of the applied texture can widely influence the aesthetic appeal of the resulting image. Figures 6.30 and 6.31 both show results of this algorithm.

Figure 6.30 Results of the thick-edge rendering to detect contour edges without attempting to discard back-facing edges.

Figure 6.31 Results of the thick-edge rendering process detecting contour edges, removing obscured edges, and drawing texture-mapped strokes.

Cartoon Shading

One of the most common NPR techniques is known as cel or "toon" shading, because it attempts to mimic the style of hand-drawn animation such as one might see on a Saturday morning cartoon or in Japanese anime. In the traditional technique, the image is drawn or painted onto the back of a piece of plastic (usually acetate—this is where the term cel, short for celluloid, originates). The paint is applied to the back of the plastic so that brush strokes are not apparent. Since a single cel often represents a single frame of animation, and many thousands of frames of animation are needed for even a short film, animators did not have the luxury of blending a wide array of tones. Doing so would have vastly increased production time and cost, not to mention the increased difficultly of creating frame-to-frame coherency in the regions of complex color blending.

Consequently, cel shading is characterized by its high degree of color quantization—often each color uses only two or three tones—and the use of outlining to emphasize the boundaries and creases of an object. Armed with this observation, we can develop an algorithm for rendering a scene in this fashion.

We can utilize the edge-rendering techniques discussed in the above section to outline our objects however we wish. The important part of the cel-shading algorithm is the method used to obtain the color quantization effect. We want two tones per color—a shadow tone and a light tone. The obvious way to determine which tone should be used is the illumination coefficient (henceforth labeled ki) produced by a lighting equation. Any lighting model will suffice, but for simplicity we will select the simple "n-dot-l" diffuse-lighting equation.

There are a number of ways we could go about the actual process of color quantization. We could do it mathematically by using ki as the input to some series of scales, translations, floors, or ceilings that eventually yielded some quantized value. A function of that nature that yields the desired result is likely to be complicated and certainly won't be easy to tweak. A better solution would be to test ki explicitly in the shader program and modify the output color appropriately.

```
if(ki >= 0.33) {
  // output "light" color
} else {
  // output "shadow" color
}
```

This allows us to easily control the locations of breaks in the color quantization, and it lets us extend the method up to an arbitrary number of color buckets (limited of course by the branching capabilities of the target GPU). However, chances are the color-break control is something that will be left to an artist, and most artists will be slightly less than pleased to hear they must edit source code to alter the appearance of their models. Worse, the artists may want the shadow tone to vary smoothly from dark to light, and the light tone to be broken up into two discrete buckets—or something equally convoluted. Plus, if your game must run on machines with older graphics cards, the requisite branching functionality might not be available to you—or you might need to use it for something else.

Fortunately, there is a better way: ki is in the range [0, 1]. We can use that value directly as a texture coordinate that is used to read a one-dimensional texture (or a two-dimensional texture where the second texture-coordinate component is fixed at some constant, such as 0). This texture, which we will call the *light-map* texture, can be easily created in any painting program, and allows for an arbitrarily large set of tone buckets without the need to resort to branching (see Figure 6.32). The style of each bucket can be fully customized as well. As an added bonus, it keeps the artists in their painting suites and out of the IDEs, which usually makes for happier artists.

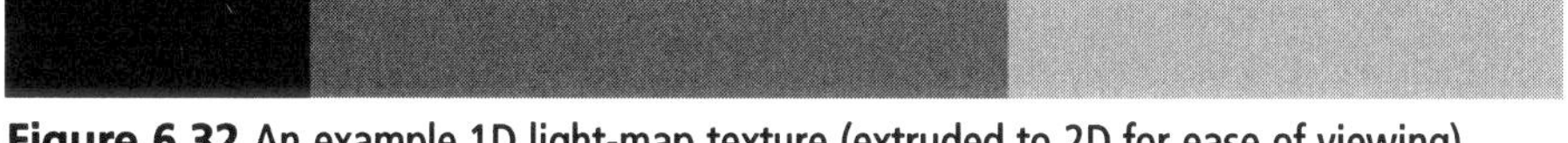

Figure 6.32 An example 1D light-map texture (extruded to 2D for ease of viewing).

The algorithm for our basic cel shader is quite simple. The vertex program looks like:

```
void main(void)
{
  // Bring input data to view space.
  vec4   viewVtx   = gl_ModelViewMatrix * gl_Vertex;
  vec3   viewNrm   = gl_NormalMatrix * gl_Normal;
  vec4   viewLight = gl_ModelViewMatrix * gl_LightSource[0].position;

  // Compute a vector from the vertex to the light.
  vec3   lightDir = vec3(viewLight.xyz) - vec3(viewVtx.xyz);

  // Compute illumination method factor and store it in a texcoord.
  // For this example we will use simple diffuse lighting.
  gl_TexCoord[0].x = max(0.0,dot(viewNrm,normalize(lightDir)));
  gl_TexCoord[0].y = 0.0;

  // Bring view-space position to clip space for output.
  gl_Position = gl_ProjectionMatrix * viewVtx;
}
```

Then, the fragment program simply uses ki to read from the light-map texture:

```
uniform sampler2D  lightMap;

void main(void)
{
  gl_FragColor = texture2D(lightMap,gl_TexCoord[1]);
}
```

The output of the simple cel shader is shown in Figure 6.33.

While we can see that we've achieved the color quantization effect, the resulting image on the whole is a little boring. This is because we've done away with the textures that provided the object's visual details. The human brain is great at extrapolating based on insufficient data, but it seems in this case we've left a little too much up to the imagination. What we need to do is restore some of that color data—just enough that the different regions of the object become recognizable again.

note

Once again, in the non-photorealistic realm, it is entirely possible that a given solution to a problem may suit one particular project quite well but be completely useless in another. The problem of color-region identification is one such solution. The demos for this chapter, for instance, use the MD2 file format, which means they have only one PCX texture file for the entire model, making it somewhat difficult to compute effective color regions procedurally. It is important to remember that non-photorealistic rendering techniques are often highly tailored to a given problem domain.

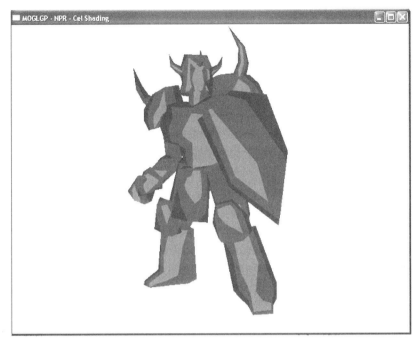

Figure 6.33 Output from the simple cel shader.

We're going to resort to getting color information from a texture, as usual. However, we're still going to use our light-map texture for the illumination of the colors retrieved from the texture, so we will modify our light-map texture so that it is monochromatic, and consider only a single channel (for example, the red channel) from it. In other words, our light-map is going to give us a scalar in the range [0, 1] just like the original ki.

Given a texture such as that in Figure 6.34, we want to give each distinct region its own meaningful color. The most straightforward way is simply to paint those colors in manually using a painting program. This offers the advantage of fine control—for example, the eyes and mouth could be painted in using a suitable art style. An automated algorithm like the one outlined below will ignore those details. The downside is, of course, the effort required to manually repaint each texture and to ensure that the paint does not "bleed" into parts of the texture that map onto completely different portions of the model. This is easy to do by accident, and annoying to correct.

Alternatively, an automatic approach can be used. This option is a lot less work in the long run, but it provides much less artistic control. Every triangle in the model maps to some region of the texture. The texture coordinates in each vertex of the triangle can be used to calculate the actual pixel coordinates of the triangle's mapping within the texture. From there, the average color of the triangle can be determined and the region can be filled with that color.

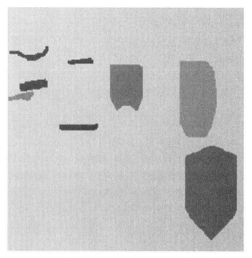

Figure 6.34 A texture (from the pknight MD2 file) containing color data, and the manually edited version for use with the cel shader.

tip

An alternative automatic approach to providing color data could be to pass the averaged color through some set of filtering criteria to yield another color, so that "mostly red" colors all ended up a uniform red, for example.

An approximation to the average color of the triangle can be found by taking a suitable number of random samples within the triangle (see the sidebar "Triangle Point Picking"). A better approach is to implement a scan-line triangle "rasterizer" that reads the color at each point, rather than writing a color. The scan-line rasterizer can be used to fill the triangle region with the appropriate final color as well. Software scan-line rasterization is outside the scope of this book, but is covered in great detail in J. D.Foley et al.'s *Computer Graphics: Principals and Practice in C.*

Figure 6.35 displays the results of enhancing the cel shader with a texture.

Triangle Point Picking

Given a triangle defined by three points { p0, p1, p2 }, a random point within the triangle can be found by x = p0 + a1 * v1 + a2 * v2, where a1 and a2 are random scalars in the range [0, 1] and v1 and v2 are p1 − p0 and p2 − p0, respectively. This actually yields a random point in the quadrilateral shown in Figure 6.36; points outside the triangle can be discarded. For more information, see E. W. Weisstein's "Triangle Point Picking" and "Triangle Interior," both listed in the references at the end of this section.

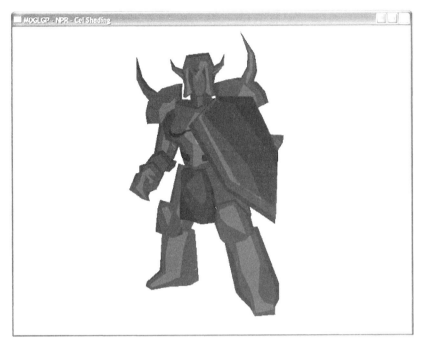

Figure 6.35 Output from the texture-enhanced cel shader.

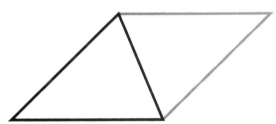

Figure 6.36 A triangle (in black) and the quadrilateral (in grey) used to select a random point inside that triangle.

Other Techniques

Entire books can be (and have been: see for example Gooch and Gooch's aforementioned *Non-Photorealistic Rendering* as well as Strothotte and Schlechtweg's *Non-Photorealistic Computer Graphics: Modeling, Rendering and Animation*) written about non-photorealistic rendering techniques. This last section will provide a brief overview of some of the more complex techniques that comprise the current state of the art.

Crosshatching

Hatching illustrates the form and tone of an object via collections of short strokes. The density of the strokes serves to illustrate the tone, and the direction and curve of the strokes provide a sense of shape. To increase the tonal range, crosshatching—a technique whereby additional strokes are placed across the existing hatch strokes—is employed. Since the number of strokes required to suitably crosshatch a single object is quite large, the strokes are drawn using textures (individually rendering the strokes is certainly possible, but would not make for a real-time technique). Varying levels of stroke density are drawn into a series of textures, and the illumination coefficient of a given vertex is used to blend between the two closest texture levels.

There are two pitfalls to crosshatching: determining the direction of the strokes and maintaining consistent stroke size as an object's distance from the eye varies. The latter problem is typically solved by exploiting the mipmapping feature of the GPU: additional mip levels of the stroke textures are provided, but they are constructed in such a way that all strokes are the same pixel width in all levels (the small levels simply have fewer strokes).

The problem is that stroke direction is trickier. In "Real-Time Hatching," E. Praun et al. suggest using the *lapped texture* technique, described in Praun, Finkelstein, and Hoppe's "Lapped Textures," to grow triangle patches on the surface of the model. Since each patch is grown so that it has a parameterization, that parameterization is used to orient the stroke texture. A simpler but less effective method would be to orient the stroke texture along the principal direction of curvature of the mesh for a given triangle.

Charcoal Rendering

Charcoal is a very evocative medium. A common method for accomplishing charcoal rendering is to employ a contrast-enhanced noise texture to render a model in "grainy" shades of grey. The contrast enhancement helps capture the limited dynamic range of charcoal. Typically a paper texture—an embossing effect—is applied to the entire render surface as well to illustrate the texture of the paper and add believability to the graininess of the charcoal-filled areas. Majumder and Gopi's "Hardware Accelerated Real-Time Charcoal Rendering" describes a hardware-based technique for charcoal rendering.

Charcoal techniques sometimes cause very slight swimming effects when models animate, which can be distracting. Additionally, in the complex scenes that often appear in games, the limited range of charcoal may make the scene too difficult to view. Art style and level layout should be given careful consideration when employing a charcoal-like rendering scheme.

Pencil Rendering

When speaking of pencil rendering we refer specifically to the technique of A. Girshick and V. Interrante's "Real-Time Principal Direction Line Drawings of Arbitrary 3D Surfaces," which traces strokes over a vector field determined by an estimation of the surfaces' directions of principal curvature. The directions were jittered randomly to enhance the hand-drawn appearance, and the result is a very sparingly rendered image that looks loosely sketched. The effect works best on models with relatively consistent curvatures.

Painterly Rendering

Painterly rendering is difficult to do in real time in a suitable manner. One existing technique is described in Sperl's *Realtime Painterly Rendering for Animation*, which decomposes geometry into a collection of particles on the surface of the geometry and transforms those particles into quadrilaterals in the vertex program (not unlike our technique used to generate edge strokes, discussed above). The quadrilaterals are textured with brush-stroke images, colored based on a reference-color render of the scene, and depth-sorted based on a reference-depth render of the scene. The technique is suitable for real-time application, but it suffers some drawbacks: strokes at the edge of the object can pop into view abruptly, and precision issues can further that effect. It's also very difficult to get the effect of variable-length strokes with this effect, so scenes rendered in this fashion tend to look like pointillist paintings.

The difficulty in doing real-time painterly rendering lies primarily in generating suitable-looking brush strokes quickly enough, and preventing the "shower-door effect" caused by a lack of frame-to-frame coherence in the strokes (image-space-based painting techniques tend to exhibit the shower-door effect quite noticeably when applied to an animating scene).

References

Foley, J. D., A. van Dam, S. K. Feiner, and J. F. Hughes. *Computer Graphics: Principals and Practice in C. Reading*, MA: Addison-Wesley, 1995.

Girshick, A., and V. Interrante. "Real-Time Principal Direction Line Drawings of Arbitrary 3D Surfaces." In *ACM SIGGRAPH 1999*, 271. New York: ACM Press, 1999.

Gooch, B., and A. Gooch. *Non-Photorealistic Rendering*. Natick, MA: A. K. Peters, 2001.

Majumder, A., and M. Gopi. "Hardware Accelerated Real-Time Charcoal Rendering." In *NPAR 2002*, 59–66. New York: ACM Press, 2002.

McGuire, M., and J. F. Hughes. "Hardware-Determined Feature Edges." In *NPAR 2004*, 35–47. New York, ACM Press, 2004.

Praun, E., A. Finkelstein, and E. Hoppe. "Lapped Textures." In *ACM SIGGRAPH 2000*, 465–70. New York: ACM Press, 2000.

Praun, E., E. Hoppe, M. Webb, and A. Finkelstein. "Real-Time Hatching." In *ACM SIGGRAPH 2001*, 581–6. New York: ACM Press, 2001.

Raskar, R., and M. Cohen. "Image Precision Silhouette Edges." In *ACM SIGGRAPH 1999*, 135–40. New York: ACM Press, 1999.

Sperl, D. *Realtime Painterly Rendering for Animation*. Austria: Hagenberg College of Information Technology, 2001

Strothotte, T., and S. Schlechtweg. *Non-Photorealistic Computer Graphics: Modeling, Rendering and Animation*. San Francisco: Morgan-Kaufmann, 2002.

Van Verth, J., and L. Bishop. *Essential Mathematics for Games and Interactive Applications*. San Francisco: Morgan-Kaufmann, 2004.

Weisstein, E. W. "Triangle Interior." From MathWorld—A Wolfram Web Resource, http://mathworld.wolfram.com/TriangleInterior.html.

Weisstein, E. W. "Triangle Point Picking." From MathWorld—A Wolfram Web Resource, http://mathworld.wolfram.com/TrianglePointPicking.html.

Summary

In this chapter, you've seen some of the most common ways in which shaders and other advanced OpenGL features can be used to enhance the lighting and shading used in your games. You've seen various lighting algorithms that can replace OpenGL's limited model, and you've learned about improving performance with deferred shading. You've learned about High Dynamic Range rendering and lighting and how it can be used to more accurately capture natural lighting effects. Finally, you learned about a number of non-photorealistic rendering methods that can add flavor and a unique visual style. We've really only scratched the surface, but you should now have a better idea of the number of possibilities available to you.

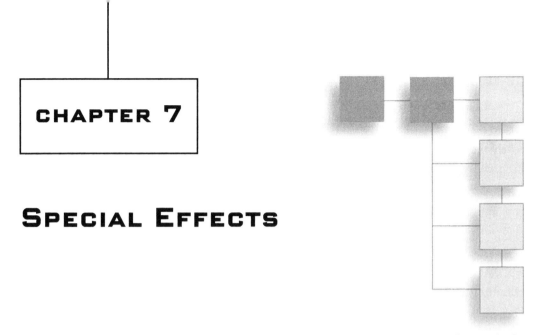

CHAPTER 7

SPECIAL EFFECTS

U p to this point, we've discussed a variety of graphics techniques that will provide the foundation of your games. Now it's time to fill your programming toolbox with techniques to add flash and spice to your games. It's time to learn some special effects. After all, what's a game without eye candy?

"Special effects" is a fairly broad topic, and we can't cover nearly as many effects as we'd like to, but we'll explain some of the most common ones here. In this chapter, you'll read about

- Using billboarding to reduce the polygon count
- Creating a particle system for a variety of effects, from fountains to fireballs
- Using particle systems to implement explosions and fire
- Simulating a glow effect
- Adding reflections and refractions to flat surfaces
- Adding multiple levels of reflections
- Creating shadows

No matter what effect you want to achieve, there are usually several commonly known ways to achieve it, each with varying degrees of quality, realism, and performance. Because this is a game-programming book, we'll focus on techniques that can be done at interactive rates.

Billboards

Lee Thomason

Billboards are a geometry-reduction technique. A 3D model is replaced with a 2D image. When the billboard is far away and viewed from the correct angle, it is a good visual approximation of the model itself. From a polygon-reduction standpoint, it is hard to do better than a billboard; any number of polygons becomes a single textured quad.

Imagine you are walking downtown and see a tree at the end of the street, just before you turn the corner. Now, was that a real tree or a life-size cutout picture of a tree? Probably a tree, because a life-size cutout would be absurd. But what if some urban artist was running around putting up life-size tree pictures? Which did you see?

Without going back and looking more closely, it's hard to say. That's how billboards work. Your eye doesn't see complex shapes and shadows at a distance unless you look closely.

Trees are symmetric around their up (y-) axis. Trees tend to have lots of polygons, and outdoor scenes tend to have lots of trees. A rendering pipeline can quickly become consumed by nothing but trees and foliage.

The discussion below focuses on trees as an example, but there are many objects that can be replaced with billboards. Space scenes can be overwhelmed by stars, planets, and galaxies, city scenes by the street details of lampposts, signs, statuary, and fixtures. All of these objects are candidates for the billboard treatment.

There are plenty of ways to use billboards and variations on them, and there is a spectrum from billboards to particles. Your billboard and particle engines may or may not use the same code. In a space scene, for example, the stars might be particles and the galaxies billboards. Specifying the difference between a particle and a billboard is problematic—for this section, we focus on a billboard as a LOD technique and assume that particles are used for complete effects, not geometry reduction.

Radial Symmetry

We'll start with a very simple tree, shown in Figure 7.1.

As a first approximation, this tree is the same viewed from any angle in its plane. Since it is radially symmetric, we can replace any side view with one billboard. A billboard of the tree is always aligned with the tree's up axis and turned to face the camera. It is possible to move the camera to see the top of an axially aligned billboard, but never the side.

To place the billboard we need to:

1. Create a 2D image of the model.
2. Place the 2D image in the world.

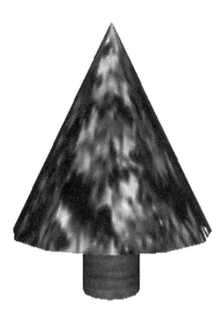

Figure 7.1 A simple tree model.

Using a single texture and a quad rather than the full model is clearly a huge savings in polygon count. But what are the drawbacks of using billboards?

- **Angle of view.** Viewing the tree billboard at its level (at approximately the same y coordinate) will be quite convincing. But as the camera flies over the billboard, the 2D nature of the image will become obvious.
- **Lighting.** A subtle problem with billboards is that the lighting varies across the scene. When using low directional lights, such the sun at daybreak or sunset, and strong light sources in space, lighting inconsistencies can be very obvious.

There are workarounds to these issues, discussed below.

Creating a 2D Image of the 3D Model

Of course, before you can put the billboard in the scene, you need to generate the billboard.

Billboards can often be quite small: 16×6 to 64×64. They don't need to be any bigger than the objects they are replacing, which are often far from the viewer. You may want to render the billboard with the more accurate texture parameter GL_LINEAR_MIPMAP_LINEAR rather than the default GL_NEAREST_MIPMAP_LINEAR, so that you get a smoother billboard.

Drawing a billboard seems straightforward—just a miniature version of what a rendering engine does—but can be tricky. Rendering the billboard texture has a couple of twists compared to the camera transformation used by your rendering engine. The billboard texture should fill the entire texture square since it will be stretched back to the proper aspect ratio when the billboard is put in the scene. Another subtle point is that you may want to use an orthographic projection so that the billboard image isn't biased from any particular distance. One approach (of many) is to set the projection matrix to be a unit cube, and transform your model to that space:

1. Save the current OpenGL state by pushing a new projection and modelview matrix and recording the current viewport, background color, and so on.

2. Use `glViewport()` to set your output area to be the texture size you want to use.

3. Use `glOrtho()` to set the projection matrix to a unit cube from [0,0,0] to [1,1,1].

4. Choose a modelview matrix that places your model to fit the unit cube.

5. Render the model.

6. Restore the OpenGL state.

7. Query the pixels from the color buffer to the texture.

This general process should be familiar if you've read the render-to-texture section in Chapter 5, "Advanced Texture Mapping."

A billboard generated in this way is a cutout: a combination of opaque texels and fully transparent ones. The billboard texture has the same problem as all cutouts, namely *ghosting* caused by mixing the correct foreground color of the billboard image with an incorrectly colored neighboring transparent background pixel. A possible workaround is to use an "average" color of the billboard as a transparent background color when the billboard is rendered.

Rendering the Billboard to the Scene

Since the billboard is axially symmetric, it is drawn preserving its up axis, but rotated towards the camera. This greatly simplifies placement in the scene. The dimensions of the billboard quad are specified from the origin of the model. The y-max and y-min of the quad are the y-max and y-min of the axis-aligned bounding box of the object, and the width of the quad is the width of the model. This is illustrated in Figure 7.2.

Since the billboard is rotated towards the camera, the normal N is the normal from the model origin (P) to the camera. The up vector is the same as that used by the world geometry.

The up vector and the normal are readily available. The right vector is the cross product of the up and normal vectors. From there, working out the four corners of the quad is straightforward. The vectors in question are shown in Figure 7.3.

You will need to turn on alpha testing (enable `GL_ALPHA_TEST`) in order to render the cutout. An alpha function of "greater" with a cutoff of 0.4 seems to work well:

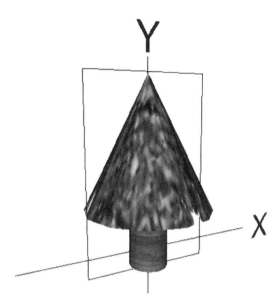

Figure 7.2 Determining the x and y extents of the quad.

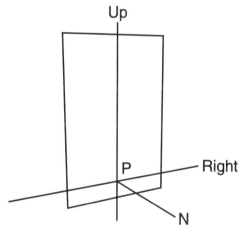

Figure 7.3 Basis for the billboard's orientation.

```
glAlphaFunc ( GL_GREATER, 0.4f )
```

Since the billboard texture doesn't repeat, be sure to turn on texture clamping, or else the edges of the billboard will wrap to the other side.

Transitioning between Billboard and Model

With a billboard, we have a nice looking 2-poly model that looks great in the far field, but what about the billboard-to-model transition? As it gets closer, you need to replace the flat image with a better representation.

The simplest thing to do is just switch the billboard to the model at some threshold distance. Obviously, this is going to cause visible popping in most cases. However, if the threshold distance is far enough away, it may not be noticeable. (It is often surprising how well the truly cheap solutions work.)

The obvious way to avoid popping is to alpha blend from the billboard to the model. The obvious answer is by no means a simple answer. An object that is sometimes alpha composited and sometimes opaque needs to go into the color and depth buffers at the correct time, or else you will get rendering artifacts. Depending on the features of your engine, that can be easy or a lot of work to render correctly.

You also need to decide between alpha functions. Figure 7.4 provides a graphical representation of two options.

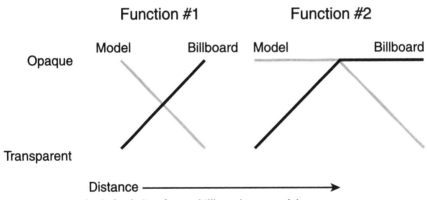

Figure 7.4 Methods for fading from a billboard to a model.

The first approach cross-fades the model and billboard alphas. This gives good performance, but often creates (more) alpha artifacts. Midway through the fade you have about 25 percent alpha through a solid object. The second approach blends the model to fully opaque before blending out the billboard. This avoids some of the alpha blending artifacts, and there is never an awkward point where you can see through a solid object. But a longer transition means more polygons being sent to the GPU.

Using alpha blending conflicts with the alpha test used to create the cutout. Since the alpha test is performed after the blend function is applied, your entire texture could awkwardly disappear, thereby ruining the subtle alpha blend. It is easy to overcome this behavior by reducing the alpha cutoff value, but that tends to result in a slightly less appealing transition. (Translucency always brings to mind the old adage "There is no free lunch.")

There is no correct solution except what looks best.

A less obvious approach is to use stippling. With this approach, the billboard fades out with an increasingly dense stipple pattern while the model fades in with the inverse pattern. Stippling suffers from the general problem of "shimmering" when used to replace alpha, since pixels (in screen space) are switched between two objects. Stippling can work surprisingly well for billboards, because you are blending something to an approximation of itself, which tends to minimize the shimmer. Additionally, it completely avoids the z-buffer and sorting issues that plague alpha blends, since each pixel is written by either the model or the billboard but not both.

In any case, the blend from billboard to model definitely involves the art of computer programming more than the science. Take some time to play with the best solution for your application.

An Extra Dimension

As mentioned earlier, the main drawbacks of using billboards are issues with the angle of view and lighting. Either of these cases can be addressed nicely with a 3D texture. In fact, a 3D texture seems perfect for this problem. Take the angle-of-view case. Imagine a 16×16 texture, encoded at 16 view angles. By mapping the view angle to texture depth, you can create a very convincing billboard that is mipmapped and gracefully interpolates as the angle of view changes.

It looks great, and billboard sizes are often very practical for 3D textures. Billboard perfection!

Sadly, this is not the case. You generally can't solve both problems at the same time. As an added complication, 3D-texture support varies wildly in performance across graphics cards. But given that you have accelerated 3D textures and you only need to solve one of the issues, it can be a great solution.

Asymmetrical Objects

The tree we've been using so far is almost completely symmetrical, which allows it to be easily converted to a billboard. What about a less symmetrical model of a tree? What about much less symmetrical objects?

The general approach is to switch from a billboard that always faces the camera to multiple billboards that are aligned to the object. Take, for example, a stop sign in a cityscape. Although it may be a three-dimensional model, it can easily be modeled as a single billboard picture of a stop sign that is in the plane of the sign itself.

Since most real-world objects aren't flat, using two billboards oriented at right-angle planes is more appropriate, as shown in Figure 7.5

Figure 7.5 Using two billboards to represent an asymmetrical object.

For this to work, you need to create four billboard textures—one from each view direction (north, south, east, and west). The billboard is named for the direction it is viewed from—so in the case of the north billboard, the camera is at $-Z'$ looking at the object positioned at the origin.

At draw time, the camera can see two of the billboards at any given time: one of the north-south and one of the east-west. (If viewed from exactly the correct angle, the camera can only see one billboard, but that case is extremely subtle, so passing it probably isn't worth optimizing for.) The billboards are easy to render as they are the same size as the axis-aligned bounding box for the object and only need to be positioned at the origin of the model.

Choosing the correct billboard of the east-west and north-south pair becomes a matter of taking the dot product of the camera to object vector (Q) and the normal of the north $(-Z')$ or east (X') billboard. A billboard with a negative dot product of its normal and Q is facing the camera. In Figure 7.6, $Q \cdot Z$ is negative, so the camera can see the south billboard. $Q \cdot X'$ is positive, and therefore the west billboard is used. Note that Q does not need to be normalized, which can save a step.

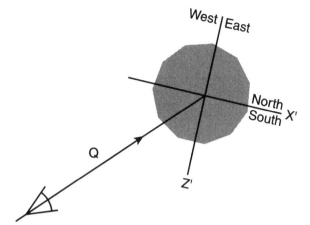

Figure 7.6 Determining the correct billboard to render.

Although simple in theory and practice, the choice of which billboard to render involves quite a few more lines of code than a single billboard that always faces the camera, and you are sending double the number of quads to the GPU. However, it can yield great visual results when rendering objects that are somewhat symmetrical, and it can do a much better job of fooling the eye.

Transitions—and all the trickiness hidden in them—are the same as with standard billboards.

Obviously, you are thinking, "If two billboards are so useful, can't we easily generalize to three billboards to address the angle of view issue?" Indeed it is. In practice, it can be harder to visually blend between three billboards than two, but for fast flyovers it may be a good solution. Again it comes down to the art of programming graphics and what looks good in your application.

This section only covers a couple of specific applications of a powerful technique. Once you start using billboards, you may be surprised at how generally useful they are.

Introduction to Particle Systems

Dave Astle

A *particle system* is a collection of a number of individual elements, or *particles*. Each particle has individual attributes, such as velocity, color, and life span. Each particle acts mostly autonomously—that is, it doesn't care about what other particles are doing. The particles within a given particle system generally share a common set of attributes, so that even though the individual particles act independently, together they create a common effect. An easy-to-visualize example of a particle system is a shower of sparks coming from fireworks, where each spark is an individual particle. Through the clever use of textures and other properties, particle systems can also be used to create effects like fire, smoke, explosions, liquid (such as water or blood) spraying, snow, star fields, and vapor trails. Clearly, you want to create a powerful and versatile system capable of simulating any of these effects.

Because of the self-contained nature of the elements of particle systems, they lend themselves to an object-oriented design. Two alternatives using C++ classes are (1) you can create a base particle system class and then derive a new child class for each type of particle system you want (for example, a smoke particle system, a fire particle system, and so on), or (2) you can create a single generic particle system class with a set of attributes that you can change to determine the particle system type. Which you choose is really a matter of personal preference. In this section, we'll be taking the first approach for the sake of simplicity. Later, the "Enhanced Particle Systems" section will take the second approach, using scripting for optimal flexibility.

Before we get into implementation specifics, let's look at each component of the particle system and discuss the methods and attributes each one could possess.

Particles

We'll start at the most basic element: the individual particle. To begin, you need to decide what attributes a particle should posses. Possible attributes include

- Position
- Velocity
- Life span
- Size
- Weight
- Representation
- Color
- Owner

note

This list provides examples of fairly typical particle attributes, but you may find that you need more or fewer attributes for your purposes. As always, feel free to experiment and find what works best for you.

Position

You need to know where the particle is in 3D space so that you can render it correctly. Position is an attribute that will almost certainly belong to the particle, not the particle system. You may also want to track the particle's last position to achieve effects such as trails. Note that the particle's position will be affected by the particle's velocity.

Velocity

Your particles are probably going to be moving, so you need to store their velocity. It's most convenient to store this as a vector representing both speed and direction, so that you can use this value to update the position.

Velocity will likely be affected by such factors as wind and gravity, which we'll discuss later in this chapter in the "Forces" subsection under "Particle Systems." If the particle is capable of accelerating itself, that could affect the velocity as well, and you'd want to create an additional attribute to store the acceleration. More often, though, factors that affect the velocity of a particle are external.

Life Span

For most effects, particles are going to be emitted from their source and, after some period of time, are going to disappear. For this reason, you need to either keep track of how long a particle has been alive or how long it has left to live (the latter can be thought of as the amount of energy left in the particle). The life span may affect other attributes, because a particle will often grow, shrink, fade, and so on, over time.

Size

Size is an attribute that may not need to be handled by individual particles. In fact, unless the size of a particle changes over its life span or there is variation in the sizes of particles within a system, there is no need to store size with the particle. However, in practice, you'll probably find that there are many situations in which you will want variation in particle sizes, so you may want to include it as a particle attribute. You may also want to have another attribute to store how the size should change over time.

Mass

Mass is a lot like size in terms of whether it should be included as a particle attribute or particle system attribute. It determines how much of an effect external forces will have on the particle.

Representation

To have the particles produce some kind of effect, you're going to have to be able to see them. The question is, how are you going to represent them on the screen? There are three commonly used alternatives:

- **Points** can be used for a number of effects, especially those that aren't viewed closely. Each particle is simply a 3D point.
- **Lines** can be used to create a trailing effect, which is often useful. The line connects the particle's current position with its last position.
- **Texture-mapped quads** offer the greatest flexibility, and are thus probably the most widely used. The particle itself is a quad or pair of triangles, upon which a texture is drawn, usually with some degree of alpha blending. One example of this would to be to use an image of an actual spark as the texture for a spark particle.

note

If quads are used, you'll probably want to use billboarding so that they always face the user, as we discussed in the first section of this chapter.

In most cases, all the particles within a system will share the same representation, including the same texture if quads are used, so this is something you'll likely want to handle on the particle system level.

Color

If you choose the point or line representation discussed in the preceding section, you'll also want to give each particle a color. Even if you're using texture-mapped quads, there may be times when you want to blend the color of the particle with the texture (such as in a multicolored spark shower). Color is something that may change over time, so a color delta attribute may be used—for example, to have the particle fade out as it ages.

Owner

Each particle might need to know which particle system it belongs to so that it can access methods in the particle system class.

Methods

In addition to attributes, your particle class is going to need some methods. As it turns out, the only method your particle class needs in this case is a method to update its attributes. This method will take as a parameter the amount of time that has passed since the last call. Other operations on particles (such as initialization or shutdown) will be handled directly by the particle system.

Particle Systems

Each particle system will control a set of particles that act autonomously but share some common attributes. It is the job of the particle system to assign these attributes in such a way that, collectively, the particles create the desired effect. Some of the things a particle system should handle include

- Particle list
- Position
- Emission rate
- Forces
- Default particle attributes and ranges
- Current state
- Blending
- Representation

Particle List

First and foremost, the particle system needs to be able to access the particles it's managing, so it needs a list of all of them. It should also know the maximum number of particles it's allowed to generate.

Position

The particle system must be located somewhere to determine where particles start. Although this is usually modeled as a single point in space, it doesn't have to be. You could represent it as a two-dimensional rectangle, and then emit particles from random positions within the rectangle. This would be useful for a snow particle system, where the rectangle is some region in the sky from which snow is falling. Three-dimensional shapes could be used as the origin as well.

note

If the particle system can move, then you may want to include a velocity vector as well, rather than modifying the position directly from your program.

Emission Rate

The emission rate determines how often a new particle is created. To maintain a regular emission rate, the particle system will also need to keep track of how much time has elapsed since the last particle was emitted, and reset that value each time a new particle is emitted.

tip

The emission rate will have to interact with the maximum number of particles, and thus the average life span of particles. If particles are living for too long, you'll reach the maximum number of particles—when you try to emit a new one, you won't be able to, creating a spurting effect. (Of course, a spurting effect may be what you're after, but if not, then you'll either have to better balance the emission rate and life span, or possibly kill old particles prematurely when it's time to emit new ones.)

note

Not all particle systems will require an emission rate. An explosion, for example, might emit all its particles in a single burst.

Forces

Adding one or more external forces acting on a particle system can create a greater degree of realism, so you'll want at least one force vector as part of your particle system. It's preferable to assign a unique force vector to each particle system instead of assigning a single value shared by all particle systems in your world.

Default Particle Attributes and Ranges

When the system creates a new particle, it will initialize the values within the particle, so the system needs to know which values are valid. Some particles have attributes that change over time, so the system will need to know both the initial and final values.

When initializing particles, you'll also want to introduce some variation in these default attributes so that your particles don't all look and act the same. To achieve this, include a variable for each value that holds the maximum acceptable variation from the default value. When creating the particle, you'll multiply this value by a random floating-point value ranging between −1 and 1, and add the result to the default value to set the particle's attributes.

note

Some of the default values tracked by the particle system may not directly correspond to a particle attribute. For example, particles have a velocity, but you'll store the speed and direction separately in the particle system, because both can have variation, and it's thus easier to handle them separately.

Current State

You may want your particle system to change its behavior over time; in the system we're building, that change simply involves turning the system on or off. There are a couple of cases in which you'll want to do this—one is when the particle system involves a limited-time effect, such as an explosion. After a while, you'll want the system to stop emitting new particles. Another is if the system is temporarily outside the viewing frustum; there's no point in updating the particles every frame if the player can't see them.

When the particle system is turned off, you may want the system to stop emitting new particles but let existing particles live out their normal life span, or you may want to kill them all immediately. To be able to do all this and to invoke any other changes beyond simply turning the system on or off, you'll need to include a variable to track which state the particle system is in.

Blending

Most particle systems use some form of alpha blending. Because the exact form of blending will likely be specific to the system, you need to include the source and destination blend settings to pass to OpenGL's blend function.

Representation

In most cases, all particles within a system are going to be represented in the same way, whether that be points, lines, or texture-mapped quads. You can store information about that representation within the particle system itself. For example, if you're using texture maps, you can store the name of the texture in the particle system class rather than in each particle.

note

> Here you must make a design decision: Do you make a general-purpose particle system class that can support points, lines, or quads, which you can specify through function calls? Or do you create a base particle system class and then derive new classes that differ in the form of representation? For that matter, do you even need all three representations, or are you using only one? There's no right answer, because everyone has his own preferences and needs. For the particle system you're implementing here, however, you'll use the base-class-with-inheritance approach, primarily because it leaves room to add alternative representations easily.

Methods

The particle system will have to do things. The following is a list of some of the functions you'll need:

- **Initialize.** You'll need to set up the particle system to produce a desired effect; you do this by setting the properties listed previously with an initialize function. Because there are numerous parameters, you might want to pass them all to the function in a single structure containing all the values rather than passing them individually.

- **Update.** This function will use a time delta to update the particles managed in the system. It will also determine whether it's time to release one or more new particles.

- **Render.** The particle system knows how its particles are represented, so this function will just need to loop through its particles and use their position, size, and color to render them.

- **Move.** Even if you have set up the particle system on its own, there may be times when you want to explicitly relocate it in your world. This is done with a move function. You'll also add a function that returns the system's current position.

- **Change state.** This function simply changes the system's state, as mentioned previously. A corresponding function to determine the current state will be helpful as well.

- **Get/set force.** You'll use these to modify the force acting on the system, because it may change over time, and because the particles themselves will need to access this information when they update themselves.

As always, you may want to add or remove functions to fit your needs.

Particle System Managers

So you have individual particles, which mostly handle themselves, and you have particle systems, which generate, update, and kill particles, and which can move and otherwise change themselves. If you have multiple particle systems within a game, which is usually the case, you might consider adding another layer that is to particle systems what particle systems are to particles: a *particle-system manager*. A particle system manager could do things like move particle systems around; change the forces acting on particle systems, which would be influenced by some global values, such as wind; and create and kill particle systems, either as they are generated by happenings in the game world or as they move beyond the field of view of the player(s).

Particle system managers can be fairly application specific, and for that reason, we're not going to provide an implementation here. However, the ideas suggested here and the implementation of the particles and particle systems should provide the bases you need to write your own.

Implementation

So far we've been focusing on design issues involved with the creation of a particle system. It's very important to think about the design, because you want your particle system to be as flexible and powerful as possible. To that end, the approach you'll take will be to first create a set of base classes that provide a bare minimum of the functionality common to any type of particle effect you want to create. These classes are not intended to be used directly for particle effects; instead, you'll derive new classes from them, each new class implementing a specific type of effect.

First let's look at the individual-particle class. Because you only have data members that will be accessed directly, you'll make it a struct:

```
struct Particle
{
  Vector3  m_pos;              // current position of the particle
  Vector3  m_prevPos;         // last position of the particle
  Vector3  m_velocity;        // direction and speed
  Vector3  m_acceleration;    // acceleration

  float    m_energy;              // determines how long the particle is alive

  float    m_size;               // size of particle
  float    m_sizeDelta;          // amount to change the size over time

  float    m_weight;             // determines how gravity affects the particle
  float    m_weightDelta;        // change over time

  float    m_color[4];           // current color of the particle
  float    m_colorDelta[4];      // how the color changes with time
};
```

You'll notice that this implementation doesn't include many of the attributes discussed earlier. That's because this is a base class. You want to include only those attributes that will be useful in most particle effects. The alternative, which is to include all the attributes you think you'll ever need, has the advantage that you likely won't have to ever derive a new particle class. However, it also means that you'll have a lot of wasted memory, because for any given effect, at least a few fields will go unused. When dealing with effects that use thousands of particles, the wasted space can add up, so we'll take a minimalist approach here.

You've probably also noticed that this class has no methods. There's no need for anything other than the default constructor or destructor; the particle system will handle initializing the particles' attributes because some fields are dependent on values known only to the particle system. Also, although we discussed having a function that updates the particles' attributes based on a time delta, there is no such function. Again, the particle system will handle this. We decided to do this because the particle system needs to be fast, and since there is some overhead involved in every function call, we wanted to avoid calling an update function possibly thousands of times every frame.

Moving on, you have the particle system itself:

```cpp
class ParticleSystem
{
public:
  ParticleSystem(int maxParticles, Vector3 origin);

  // abstract functions
  virtual void  Update(float elapsedTime)    = 0;
  virtual void  Render()                      = 0;

  virtual int   Emit(int numParticles);

  virtual void  InitializeSystem();
  virtual void  KillSystem();

protected:
  virtual void  InitializeParticle(int index) = 0;
  Particle    *m_particleList;     // particles for this emitter
  int          m_maxParticles;     // maximum number of particles in total
  int          m_numParticles;     // indices of all free particles
  Vector3      m_origin;           // center of the particle system

  float        m_accumulatedTime;  // used to track how long since the last
                                   // particle was emitted

  Vector3      m_force;            // force acting on the particle system
};

// Particles.cpp
ParticleSystem::ParticleSystem(int maxParticles, Vector3 origin)
{
  m_maxParticles = maxParticles;
  m_origin = origin;
  m_particleList = NULL;
}

int ParticleSystem::Emit(int numParticles)
{
  // create numParticles new particles (if there's room)
  while (numParticles && (m_numParticles < m_maxParticles))
  {
    // initialize the current particle and increase the count
```

```
      InitializeParticle(m_numParticles++);
      --numParticles;
   }
   return numParticles;
}


void ParticleSystem::InitializeSystem()
{
   // if this is just a reset, free the memory
   if (m_particleList)
   {
      delete[] m_particleList;
      m_particleList = NULL;
   }

   // allocate the maximum number of particles
   m_particleList = new Particle[m_maxParticles];

   // reset the number of particles and accumulated time
   m_numParticles = 0;
   m_accumulatedTime = 0.0f;
}


void ParticleSystem::KillSystem()
{
   if (m_particleList)
   {
      delete[] m_particleList;
      m_particleList = NULL;
   }

   m_numParticles = 0;
}
```

This is an abstract base class, so it can't be used directly, but it provides a common framework from which you can easily create a new particle class. It provides functions to initialize and kill the system, which are responsible for allocating and deleting an array large enough to hold the maximum number of particles. From 0 to (m_numParticles − 1), this array contains active particles, and m_numParticles to (m_maxParticles −1) contains particles that the Emit() function helps manage in this array.

Particle System Effects

With a base particle system implemented, you can now derive new particle systems from it to create specific effects. The trick is in knowing what attributes and behaviors to add to simulate a particular effect. As it turns out, it usually takes a bit of work and experimentation to get the effect you're after. You'll see several examples throughout the book that should give you some ideas, but coming up with the effect you want will take some thought and experimentation, and possibly applying some real physics. Also, searching the Internet to see what others have done may inspire you.

Example: Snowstorm

A discussion of particle systems wouldn't be complete without a program demonstrating some effects, so I put together an example, which you'll find on the book's website in the directory for this chapter.

This example is a simple snowstorm effect, shown in Figure 7.7. The class derived for this effect, CSnowstorm, uses textured quads to represent individual snowflakes, and emits the particles from a rectangular area (the "sky"). Refer to the code on the website for implementation details.

Figure 7.7 Snow on a foggy terrain.

Enhanced Particle Systems

Joel Villagrana

Now that you have a foundation in the basics of particle systems from the previous section, it's time to look at how to improve them and make them more efficient. Specifically, I'm going to discuss the possibility of using scripting to make a more flexible system, as well as improving particle systems with the use of the GPU.

I'll start by making some modifications to the approach used in the previous section. The main modification is that we'll take out some attributes of the particle system class and include them in the new `PSystemEmitter` class. This will allow a particle system to have more than one emitter, which will allow, for example, a particle system with emitters that have different textures, representation, or emission rates, for a combined effect.

For the scripting part, I'll create a very basic language to create the scripts for custom particle systems. For this I'll need a few more classes. The `ParticleSystem_Scripted` class will be derived from the base particle system class; this class will allow us to change properties of the system, emitter, and particles at run time by executing events at specific times. This class will have a member variable of type `PSystemScript`, which will parse the script. Each emitter will store a list of events of type `PSystemEvent` that have information for all property changes.

Finally, I'll review Lutz Latta's article "Building a Million Particles" and see how to incorporate the scripting into his approach.

Before starting with the scripting, let's look at improving particle systems by using point sprites to represent particles.

Point Sprites

The previous section used texture-mapped quads to represent the particles. In this section, you'll see how you can represent them with *point sprites*. Point sprites were introduced to OpenGL as an extension (initially the vendor-specific `NV_point_sprite`, and then `ARB_point_sprite`), and they were promoted to a core feature in OpenGL 2.0.

extension

Extension name: `ARB_point_sprite`

Name string: `GL_ARB_point_sprite`

Promoted to core: OpenGL 2.0

Tokens: `GL_POINT_SPRITE_ARB`, `GL_COORD_REPLACE_ARB`, `GL_POINT_SPRITE_COORD_ORIGIN_ARB`, `GL_LOWER_LEFT_ARB`, `GL_UPPER_LEFT_ARB`

What Are Point Sprites?

Point sprites are basically hardware-accelerated billboards capable of being textured. Rather than specifying a texture-mapped quad, which requires four vertices and all of their relevant attributes, you specify particles as a single point, which greatly reduces the amount of geometry sent to the graphics card. For each point, OpenGL will automatically calculate a billboard and apply any enabled textures to it.

Using Point Sprites

It takes a few steps to render your particle system with point sprites. First you need to verify that the implementation supports them. This is true if the OpenGL version is 2.0 or higher, or if the ARB_point_sprite extension is present. If your card doesn't support point sprites, you can switch back to rendering particles as texture-mapped quads.

```
// Init Particle System
bool CParticleSystem_Snow::Init()
{
  // Use GLee to check if point sprites are supported
  if((GLEE_VERSION_2_0) ||
     ((GLEE_ARB_point_sprite)&&(GLEE_ARB_point_parameters))
  {
    m_usePointSprites = true;
    m_minPointSize = 1.0f;
    m_fadeSize = 5.0f;
    glGetFloatv(GL_POINT_SIZE_MAX_ARB, &m_maxPointSize);
  }
}
```

Since point sprites are rendered as points, their properties can be adjusted by using the existing point functions. The point size is thus set using glPointSize(), and glPointParameter() is used to specify how the distance from the viewer will affect the point sprite size (GL_POINT_DISTANCE_ATTENUATION), the minimum and maximum point size the graphics card should use (GL_POINT_SIZE_MIN and GL_POINT_SIZE_MAX), and the threshold at which the point sprites will start to fade (GL_POINT_FADE_THRESHOLD_SIZE).

Since points consist of a single vertex, they normally only have a single texture coordinate. Since this would result in a single texel being used for every pixel in a point sprite, OpenGL can automatically generate texture coordinates that range from (0,0) to (1,1) across the point sprite. The following line enables this behavior:

```
glTexEnvf(GL_POINT_SPRITE, GL_COORD_REPLACE, GL_TRUE);
```

Passing GL_FALSE disables texture-coordinate generation. When using multitexturing, you'll have to do this for every texture unit.

For the purposes of texture-coordinate generation, by default the upper left corner of the point sprite is considered the origin. However, because of vendor-specific issues and to ease porting from DirectX, it's possible to change the origin to the lower left, as follows:

```
glPointParameterf(GL_POINT_SPRITE_COORD_ORIGIN, GL_LOWER_LEFT);
```

Use GL_UPPER_LEFT to restore the default behavior.

note

The ability to change the texture-coordinate origin was added to the point-sprite mechanism when it was promoted to the core in OpenGL 2.0. If you're using an older OpenGL implementation, this functionality won't be present.

tip

If you use point sprites with pixel buffers or frame buffer objects, you need to set GL_POINT_SPRITE_COORD_ORIGIN to GL_LOWER_LEFT for fully hardware-accelerated rendering on NVIDIA hardware (this is more fully explained in NVIDIA's OpenGL support documentation).

Before rendering your particles, you need to enable point sprites by calling:

```
glEnable(GL_POINT_SPRITE);
```

Finally, you can render your particles as GL_POINTS, using textures and any other rendering states that you desire. Be sure to disable point sprites when you're done.

The following code illustrates the preceding steps.

```
// render using point sprites
void CParticleSystem_Snow::Render()
{
  GLfloat att_param[]={ 0.0, 0.1, 0.0 };

  // enable blending, texturing, vertex arrays...

  if((m_usePointSprites)&&(GLEE_VERSION_2_0))
  {
    // set point size
    glPointSize(m_pointSize);

    // how distance from the viewer will affect point sprite size
    glPointParameterfv(GL_POINT_DISTANCE_ATTENUATION, att_param);

    // minimum and maximum point sprite the hardware should use
```

```
    glPointParameterf(GL_POINT_SIZE_MIN, m_minPointSize);
    glPointParameterf(GL_POINT_SIZE_MAX, m_maxPointSize);

    // the hardware should do the texture-coordinate generation
    glTexEnvf(GL_POINT_SPRITE, GL_COORD_REPLACE, GL_TRUE);

    // specify at what size the point sprite will start to fade
    glPointParameterf (GL_POINT_FADE_THRESHOLD_SIZE, m_fadeSize);

    // enable point sprites
    glEnable(GL_POINT_SPRITE);

    // render with vertex arrays
    // (you could also call glVertex3f for each particle with GL_POINTS)
    glDrawArrays(GL_POINTS, 0, m_numParticles);

    // disable point sprites
    glDisable(GL_POINT_SPRITE);
  }
  else if((m_usePointSprites)&&( GLEE_ARB_point_sprite))
  { //... }
  else // point sprites not supported, render as quads
  { //... }
} // end Render()
```

Note the code above shows how to render point sprites using OpenGL 2.0. If only ARB_point_sprite is available, the code differs only in adding the ARB suffix for the new tokens.

Point Sprites vs. Texture-Mapped Quads

Even though point sprites are fairly new and they have a number of advantages, there are still some reasons you might continue using texture-mapped quads:

- Since point sprites are transformed in the pipeline as points, they are clipped by their center vertex position. This will mean particles disappear suddenly around the edges of the screen when the center vertex goes off the screen.
- You cannot rotate a point; you would need to rotate the associated texture coordinates in a fragment shader.
- Point sprites are not supported in older cards.
- Point-sprite size is dependent on the available OpenGL point sizes.
- You get only one vertex in vertex and fragment shaders.

- You cannot call `glPointSize()` inside `glBegin()`/`glEnd()` (though you could pass the point size as a generic vertex attribute using a vertex shader).
- Some old graphics-card drivers seem to have issues with point sprites.

Adding Basic Scripting to the Particle System

Scripting allows you to make your particle system more flexible. It makes it possible for you to change the behavior of the particle system without requiring recompilation of the game. In turn, this allows you—or, if you're working as part of a team, the artists and level designers—to quickly and easily modify the particle system to create more interesting effects.

Scripting can also allow you to define more complex behavior than a hard-coded particle system. Let's suppose you want to change some properties over time. With a hard-coded particle system, you could have start and end values and interpolate between them. With a scripted particle system, you could allow the properties to have many values over the particle system's life. You can set events to trigger changes in system, emitter, or particle properties (such as velocity, color, size, texture, emit rate, and batch size) after a specific amount of time elapses.

In order to do all this you'll need a simple scripting language. Existing scripting languages such Lua or Python work well for this, but since I don't have space to cover these languages, I'll use a simple custom language to get you started. This scripting system won't generate bytecode or create a virtual machine for executing the scripts, but it will parse the scripts to make sure they're valid (lexical and syntax analysis), create a particle system with the properties defined in the script, and then create a series of events that will interpret the property changes at run time.

Since the scripts will only have instructions of the type "property = value" and a few keywords, features common in almost every language, such as conditionals, variables, and loops, won't be supported. An example of how you could incorporate simple loops can be found in Mason McCuskey's *Special Effects Game Programming with DirectX*. For the particle properties, you'll have two different instructions, one that completely replaces the current property value and another that fades the current value to another over a specific time. These fade events can only be associated with certain properties; they won't allow for fade events for properties like life or position, but they'll allow fade events for other properties like color or size.

Script Structure

The three main sections of a script will be

- **SystemProperties section.** SystemProperties is where initial system values are specified, such as max particles and global forces.

- **Emitter section.** The Emitter section is where you'll define the emitter properties such as emitter position, emitter type, particle representation, texture, emission rate, batch size, blending modes, shader, size range, and life range.

- **Event_at section.** Event_at is where you'll specify properties changes for the system, emitters, or particles.

Figure 7.8 shows an example of what one of our scripts would look like.

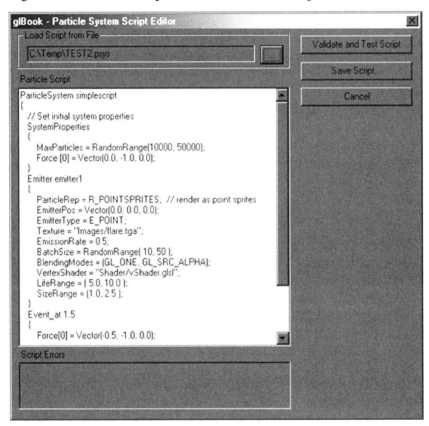

Figure 7.8 The script editor and a sample script.

Using BNF to Define the Scripting Language

We'll use Backus Naur Form (BNF) to define our language. BNF is a notation to describe languages and their rules. By defining the language, we'll be able to decide what's valid and what isn't when parsing the scripts.

There are three main parts in BNF:

- **Terminal symbols.** Terminal symbols need no further definition; they should appear in the script as they are.

- **Nonterminal.** Nonterminals are enclosed in <> and are defined in terms of other nonterminals and terminals.
- **Productions.** Productions are the rules that describe how each nonterminal is constructed.

The main BNF symbols are as follows:

- '_' means "or"
- '::=' means "defined as"
- '{ }' means zero or more occurrences of the terminal or nonterminal to which it is attached
- '< >' means a nonterminal
- '[ ]' means optional

Let's start with the definition of the particle system.

```
<Particle_System> ::= ParticleSystem <Identifier> "{"
                      <SystemProperties> <Emitters> {<Event>} "}"
```

Following the ::= symbol, ParticleSystem, "{", and "}" are terminal symbols and <Identifier>, <SystemProperties>, <Emitters>, and <Event> are nonterminal symbols.

This means that <Particle_System> is defined as the keyword ParticleSystem followed by an <Identifier> and an opening bracket, then <SystemProperties>, <Emitters>, and zero or more <Event>s followed by a closing bracket.

This leaves a few nonterminals to define: <Identifier>, <SystemProperties>, <Emitters>, and <Event>. We need to define each one until we have all nonterminals defined in our grammar. Let's see more definitions:

```
<SystemProperties> ::= SystemProperties "{" {<SystemProperty>} "}"
<Emitters> ::= <Emitter> {<Emitter>}
<Emitter> ::= Emitter <Identifier> "{" {<EmitterProperty>} "}"
<Event> ::= Event_At <SysProp_Num> "{" {<EmitterPropertyChg> |
                      <SystemPropertyChg>} "}"
```

If I continue defining the nonterminal symbols you'll see, for example, that <Identifier> is a combination of alphabetic characters and digits, but it must begin with an alphabetic character or underscore. <SysProp_Num> can be a specific numerical value or a random number in a specified range.

Now that you've seen how BNF definitions are constructed, let's finish constructing the language. Here's the full definition of the grammar:

```
<Particle_System> ::= ParticleSystem <Identifier> "{"
  <SystemProperties> <Emitters> {<Event>} "}"


<SystemProperties> ::= SystemProperties "{" {<SystemProperty>} "}"
<Emitters>::= <Emitter> {<Emitter>}
<Emitter> ::= Emitter <Identifier> "{" {<EmitterProperty>} "}"
  <Event> ::= Event_At <SysProp_Num> "{" {<EmitterPropertyChg> | <SystemPropertyChg>}
"}"


<SystemProperty> ::= <SYSP_MaxParticles> | <SYSP_Force>
<SystemPropertyChg> ::= <SYSP_Force>
<SYSP_MaxParticles> ::= MaxParticles = <SysProp_Num>;
<SYSP_Force> ::= Force [<Number>] = <Vector>;


<EMP_EmitterPos> ::= EmitterPos = <Vector>;
<EMP_EmitterType> ::= EmitterType = E_LINE|E_POINT|E_SPHERE|E_BEAM|E_RING;
<EMP_ParticleRep> ::= ParticleRep = <Representation>;
<EMP_MaxParticles> ::= MaxParticles = <SysProp_Num>;
<EMP_Texture> ::= Texture = <Literal>;
<EMP_EmissionRate> ::= EmissionRate = <SysProp_Num>;
<EMP_BatchSize> ::= BatchSize = <SysProp_Num>;
<EMP_BlendingM> ::= BlendingModes ( <Blending_mode> , <Blending_mode> );
<EMP_VertexShader> ::= VertexShader = <Literal>;
<EMP_PixelShader> ::= PixelShader = <Literal>;
<EMP_Force> ::= Force [<Number>] = <Vector> at pos <Vector> dst <Number>;
<EMP_SizeRange> ::= SizeRange = ( <SysProp_Num>, <SysProp_Num> );
<EMP_LifeRange> ::= LifeRange = ( <SysProp_Num>, <SysProp_Num> );
<EMP_State> ::= EmitterON | EmitterOFF
<EmitterProperty> ::= <EMP_ParticleRep> | <EMP_MaxParticles> |
                      <EMP_EmitterPos> | <EMP_Texture> | <EMP_EmissionRate> |
                      <EMP_BatchSize> | <EMP_BlendingM> | <EMP_VertexShader> |
                      <EMP_PixelShader> | <EMP_SizeRange> | <EMP_LifeRange> |
                      <EMP_Force> | <EMP_State>
<EmitterPropertyChg> ::= For Emitter <Identifier>
                         "{" {<EMP_EmitterPos> | <EMP_Texture> |
                         <EMP_EmissionRate> | <EMP_BatchSize> | <EMP_BlendingM> |
                         <EMP_VertexShader> | <EMP_PixelShader> | <EMP_State> |
                         <EMP_Force> | <ParticlePropertyChg>} "}"


<PartP_color> ::= ParticleColor = <Color>;
<PartP_size> ::= ParticleSize = <SysProp_Num>;
<ParticleProperty> ::= <PartP_color> | <PartP_size>
```

```
<PartP_fadeTimeRange> ::= FadeFromNow to <SysProp_Num> <ParticleProperty>
<ParticlePropertyChg> ::= <ParticleProperty> | <PartP_fadeTimeRange>

<Blending_mode> ::= GL_ZERO | GL_ONE | GL_DST_COLOR | GL_SRC_COLOR |
                    GL_ONE_MINUS_DST_COLOR | GL_ONE_MINUS_SRC_COLOR |
                    GL_SRC_ALPHA | GL_ONE_MINUS_SRC_ALPHA | GL_DST_ALPHA |
                    GL_ONE_MINUS_DST_ALPHA | GL_SRC_ALPHA_SATURATE
<Representation> ::= R_POINTS | R_QUADS | R_POINTSPRITES | R_LINES
<Vector> ::=  Vector ( <SysProp_Num>, <SysProp_Num>, <SysProp_Num> )
<Color> ::= RGBA (<SysProp_Num>, <SysProp_Num>, <SysProp_Num>, <SysProp_Num>)
<Comment> ::= //<Any_char>
<Identifier> ::= <Allowed_char> {<Allowed_char>|<Digit>}
<Literal> ::= " {<Allowed_char>|;|,|/|.|<Digit>} "
<Allowed_char> ::= a|b|c|d|e|f|g|h|i|j|k|l|m|n|o|p|q|r|s|t|u|v|w|x|y|z|_
<SysProp_Num> ::= <Sys_number> | <Random_range>
<Random_range> ::= RandomRange ( <Sys_number> , <Sys_number> )
<Sys_number> ::= [-] <Number> [.<Number>]
<Number> ::= <Digit> {<Digit>}
<Digit> ::= 0_1_2_3_4_5_6_7_8_9
```

note

> Note that forces are defined both at the system properties and at the emitter level; this means that there are forces that affect all emitters in a system and forces that affect only the associated emitter. This will provide a basic implementation of a second-order particle system, as explained in Ilmonen and Kontkanen.

Parsing the Script

Now that the grammar has been defined, you need to see how to parse the scripts. The first step is to create a list of *tokens* (each "word" in the script). Each token has a type; it can be a number, a bracket, a keyword, and so on (tokens for comments or spaces won't be created). After all the tokens are in a list, they can be checked according to the BNF rules.

Creating the Tokens

In order to get the tokens, you'll use a small finite state machine (FSM); a FSM is a *model of behavior* composed of states, transitions, and actions.

To help you visualize this, Figure 7.9 shows an FSM that recognizes only series of letters and numbers separated by spaces.

As you can see in the figure, the initial *state* is "start." From there, the FSM checks the next character of the input string:

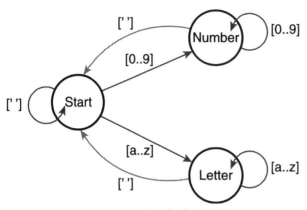

Figure 7.9 A simple example of a finite state machine.

- If it's (a..z), a *transition* occurs to state "letter."
- If it's (0..9), a transition occurs to state "number."
- If it's ' ', no transition occurs and it stays at "start."

Once in state "number":

- If the next character is (0..9), no transition occurs and it stays at "number."
- If the next character is ' ', it does an *action* (saves the current token) and a transition to "start" occurs.

Once in state "letter":

- If the next character is (a..z), no transition occurs and it stays at "letter."
- If the next character is ' ', it does an action (saves the current token) and a transition to "start" occurs.

This task will be performed by the CPSystemScript::TokenizeScript( ) method. Figure 7.10 shows the FSM used by our scripting system.

Checking the Syntax

Checking the syntax is very easy. You simply need to create a function to process each of the grammar rules, starting at <Particle_System>, which would look a bit like this:

```
bool CPSystemScript::Parse_ParticleSystem()
{
  m_tokenIterator = m_tokenList.begin();
  //...

  // first token should be ParticleSystem keyword
  if((*m_tokenIterator)->GetTokenType() != KEYWORD_PARTICLESYSTEM)
  { //error... }
```

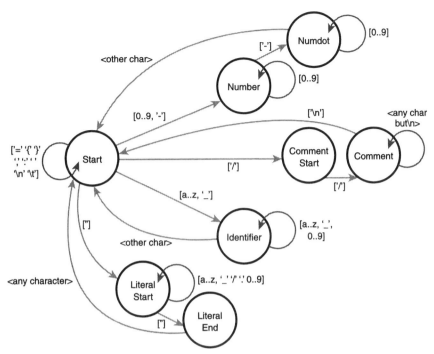

Figure 7.10 FSM for the scripting system.

```
// get next token...

// this token should be the system identifier
if((*m_tokenIterator)->GetTokenType() != IDENTIFIER)
{ //error... }

// get next token...

// this token should be '{'
if((*m_tokenIterator)->GetTokenType() != BRACKET_OPEN)
{ //error... }

// get next token...

// this should be 'SystemProperties'
if((*m_tokenIterator)->GetTokenType() == KEYWORD_SYSTEMPROPERTIES)
  continueParsing = ParseSystemProperties();
else
  { //error... }
}
```

Processing the Script

Once you have validated the script, you'll process each script block to assign all values to the particle system properties, emitters, particles, and events. Below is the code that processes the system properties block.

```cpp
void CParticleSystem_Scripted::AddSystemProperties()
{
  m_script.SetIterator_SysP();

  while(m_script.MoreSystemProperties())
  {
    propertyType = m_script.Get_PropType();

    if(propertyType==SYSP_MAXPARTICLES)
    {
      int maxP;
      m_script.Get_IntValues(&maxP, 1);
      Set_SysMaxParticles(maxP);
    }
    else if(propertyType==SYSP_FORCE)
    {
      int index;
      float force[3];
      m_script.Get_IntValues(&index, 1);
      m_script.Get_FloatValues(force, 3);
      Set_SysForce(index, force);
    }
  }
}
```

Also, you'll need to modify the particle system's Update() function to check for any events that need to be processed depending on the current time and delta time.

```cpp
void CParticleSystem_Scripted::Update(float deltaTime)
{
  //...
  m_eventIterator = m_eventList.begin();
  while(m_eventIterator != m_eventList.end())
  {
    if(!((*m_eventIterator)->AlreadyProcessed())
    {
      (*m_eventIterator)->ProcessIfNeeded(deltaTime);
    }
```

```
        m_eventIterator++;
    }
}
```

Figure 7.11 shows a particle system created with a script. You can find the full implementation of the scripting system on this book's website.

Figure 7.11 An example particle effect created using scripting.

Improving Particle Systems with the GPU

Particle systems present some performance challenges. It can take tens of thousands of particles to create realistic effects, and a game may have numerous particle systems active at any given time. As the total number of particles increases (over 100,000, for example), performance will degrade, mostly because of the CPU-to-GPU bandwidth you're using. However, modern GPU features offer several alternatives to address this problem.

You could use the GPU to implement a `stateless` particle system. This means the particle's position and velocity are calculated in the GPU based only on a few factors such as time of birth, acceleration, actual time, and defined forces. An example of a vertex program for a stateless particle system can be found in Randima and Kilgard's *Cg Tutorial*.

A more flexible way to avoid sending all the particle data each frame would be to do the simulation and rendering on the GPU (refer to Kipfer, Segal, and Westermann's "Uberflow: A GPU-Based Particle Engine," and Kolb, Latta, and Rezk-Salama's "Hardware-Based Simulation and Collision Detection for Large Particle Systems"). In this approach, you store all particle data in the GPU at initialization and then update the data in a fragment shader, rendering that updated data without copying it to the CPU again. This is called a *state-preserving particle* system because all the particle data is kept in the GPU.

As I mentioned earlier in this chapter, this section is based on the "Building a Million Particle System" paper by Lutz Latta. Because I don't have space to discuss this technique in depth, I'll only cover it at a high level and propose how to incorporate scripting into it so you can update some properties at run time.

A State-Preserving Particle System

The implementation of a state-preserving particle system needs functionality that is only available in the last generation of graphics cards, specifically a floating-point pixel pipeline and data communication between pixel and vertex memory.

Floating-Point Pixel Pipeline

The vertex pipeline already has support for floating-point data types, but it's new for the pixel pipeline. Previously, only fixed-point support was available, and these values were clamped to ranges like $[0, 1]$ or $[-1, 1]$.

This functionality is available through the following OpenGL extensions:

- `NV_float_buffer` (vendor specific)
- `ATI_pixel_format_float` (vendor specific)
- `ATI_texture_float` (vendor specific)
- `ARB_texture_float` (ARB)

Data Communication from Pixel to Vertex Memory

You'll need to be able to allocate a block of GPU memory that you can write to in a fragment shader and then read from in the vertex shader. At the time of writing, this functionality is only available for OpenGL through the following extensions:

- `NV_pixel_data_range` (vendor specific)
- `NV_pixel_buffer_objects` (vendor specific)
- `EXT_pixel_buffer_objects` (multivendor)
- `ARB_pixel_buffer_objects` (ARB)

Storing the Particle Information on the GPU

In order to keep all the particle information on the GPU, we will store it in textures. Each texel of the texture will represent a particle, so we'll treat the components of each texel as an (x,y,z) vector (position of the particle) instead of (r,g,b,a). Since the (x,y,z) components of the position or velocity are not integers, we need a floating-point texture.

The most important particle properties are position and velocity, so we need a texture for each of those and another texture for storing static properties such as time of birth; it's in this last texture that we'll store the system and emitter properties that can change with the events defined in our scripts.

Particle Simulation on the GPU

There are basically six tasks required to do the simulation on the GPU each frame.

Creating and Destroying Particles

The allocation of particles cannot be done in parallel; therefore, the CPU must handle this task using some kind of list that stores the indices used. The deallocation is handled separately in the CPU and GPU. In the CPU, the index needs to be marked as available; in the GPU, the position of the particle needs to be moved to some point out of view.

Updating the Particle Velocities

This is the first part of the simulation. In this rendering pass, the velocity texture is updated in a fragment shader. Since a texture cannot be read and updated at the same time, two velocity and two position textures are needed; one texture is used as a render target, and the other is used to read the values from the previous iteration.

Updating the Particles Positions

In this rendering pass, the position texture is updated in a fragment shader using either Euler or Verlet integration with the velocities computed in the first rendering pass.

Sorting Particles

If the particles are rendered with blending enabled, it is a good idea to sort the particles in order to avoid artifacts. In this case a sorting algorithm that can be done in parallel (such as odd-even merge sort) needs to be used. Since the number of elements to sort will be quite high, the sorting is expensive and needs to be distributed over a few frames.

Transfer Pixel Data to Vertex Data

The position texture needs to be interpreted as vertex data, so the texture is transferred to a vertex buffer.

Rendering

The rendering is done in the normal way using `glDrawArrays()` or `glDrawElements()`. Since only one vertex (position) of the particles is stored in the texture, it's convenient to render the particles as point sprites to avoid extra work in the vertex unit.

Uploading Script Changes to GPU with FBOs

To incorporate scripting we have two options: whenever we process an event, we can send the system/emitter properties as parameters to the shaders or store them in another texture in the GPU. Since we already have a texture for storing some static properties, we'll store the other properties there as well.

Since the textures used can only store floating-point values, we won't be able to store non-numeric properties like blending modes. Therefore, we'll store only the following properties in the texture: emitter position, emission rate, batch size, emitter state, and forces.

Every time we need to update these properties we'll do a render-to-texture. We could use Latta's original approach (using the `ARB_pbuffers` and `ARB_render_texture` extensions) for rendering to the texture, but instead we will use the new `EXT_framebuffer_object` extension because it's easier to use and more efficient. Also, using the combination of `ARB_pbuffers` and `ARB_render_texture` requires creating another GL context and therefore a context change to make the pbuffer's rendering context active, and this operation can be expensive.

See Chapter 1, "More OpenGL," for more information on using framebuffer objects.

The following code shows what you need to set up render-to-texture with this extension.

```
void CParticleSystem_Scripted::UpdatePropsTexture()
{
  GLuint frameBuffer; // framebuffer object
  GLenum status;      // status of the fbo

  // check for support
  if(GLEE_EXT_framebuffer_object)
  {
    // generate framebuffer
    glGenFramebuffersEXT(1, &frameBuffer);

    // bind framebuffer to currentcontext
    glBindFramebufferEXT(GL_FRAMEBUFFER_EXT, frameBuffer);

    // bind texture
    glBindTexture(GL_TEXTURE_2D, prop_tex);

    // attach texture to frameBuffer's color buffer
    glFramebufferTexture2DEXT(GL_FRAMEBUFFER_EXT,
                              GL_COLOR_ATTACHMENT0_EXT,
                              GL_TEXTURE_2D, prop_tex, 0);
```

```
    status = glCheckFramebufferStatusEXT(GL_FRAMEBUFFER_EXT);
    if(status!=GL_FRAMEBUFFER_COMPLETE_EXT)
    { //error... }

    glBindTexture(GL_TEXTURE_2D, 0);
    glBindFramebufferEXT(GL_FRAMEBUFFER_EXT, frameBuffer);

    // render...

    // enable rendering to the windowing system's framebuffer again
    glBindFramebufferEXT(GL_FRAMEBUFFER_EXT, 0);

    // delete framebuffer
    glDeleteFrameBuffersEXT(1, &frameBuffer);
  }
}
```

References

Aho, Alfred V., Ravi Sethi, and Jeffrey D. Ullman. *Compiler: Principles, Techniques, and Tools.* Boston: Addison Wesley Longman, 1998.

Astle, Dave, and Kevin Hawkins. *OpenGL Game Programming.* Roseville, CA: Thomson Course Technology, 2002.

Fernando, Randima, and Mark J. Kilgard. *The Cg Tutorial.* Boston: Addison-Wesley, 2003.

Greß, Alexander, and Gabriel Zachmann. "Object-Space Interference Detection on Programmable Graphics Hardware." Institut für Informatik II, Universität Bonn, *Computer Graphics Technical Reports 2004.*

Harris, Kevin. "Scripting Particle Systems." From Torque Game Engine Tutorials, **http://www.codesampler.com/torque.htm** .

Ilmonen, Tommi, and Janne Kontkanen. "The Second Order Particle System." Helsinki University of Technology, **http://wscg.zcu.cz/wscg2003/Papers_2003/J11.pdf**.

Kipfer, Peter, Mark Segal, and Rudiger Westermann. "Uberflow: A GPU-Based Particle Engine." Computer Graphics and Visualization, Technische Universitat Munchen, ATI Research 2004.

Kolb, A., Lutz Latta, and C. Rezk-Salama. "Hardware-Based Simulation and Collision Detection for Large Particle Systems." **http://www.2ld.de/gh2004/**

Latta, Lutz. "Building a Million Particle System." **http://www.2ld.de/gdc2004/** .

McAllister, David K. "Particle System API." **http://www.cs.unc.edu/~davemc/Particle/**. 2001.

McCuskey, Mason. *Special Effects Game Programming with DirectX*. Roseville, CA: Premier Press, 2002.

NVIDIA OpenGL 2.0 Support. **http://developer.nvidia.com/object/nv_ogl2_support.html**.

"Particles in the Unreal Engine." From Unreal Wiki: The Unreal Engine Documentation Site, **http://wiki.beyondunreal.com/wiki/Particle_System**.

"Particle Scripts." **http://www.ogre3d.org/docs/manual/manual_22.html**.

Van der Burg, John. "Building an Advanced Particle System." *Game Developer Magazine*, March 2000: 44–50.

Glow

Andrei Gradinari

Adding a glow effect can provide an added degree of realism to objects that are burning or otherwise emitting light, as shown in Figure 7.12. Glow can be used for lava, metallic surfaces, LEDs, and many other things.

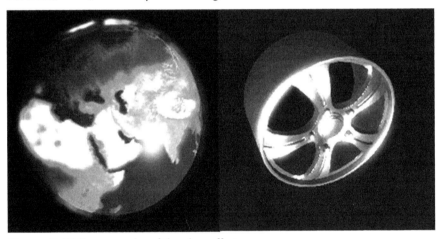

Figure 7.12 Two examples of the glow effect.

A glow effect can be implemented fairly easily in real time using postprocessing and multiple passes. The steps involved in this approach are as follows:

1. Render your scene as usual to the frame buffer.
2. Render the same scene to a texture.
3. Blur this texture *N* times (the larger the value of *N*, the better the final image quality).
4. Render the texture to the frame buffer using additive blending.

This process will be explained in detail using the demo behind the Earth image in Figure 7.12 as an example. This version will use a *diffuse-color-based* approach. The alternative is a *specular-component-based* approach, which is what the demo for the chrome wheel from Figure 7.12 uses. The implementation differences between the two approaches are minor, so the specular approach will be explained after we discuss the Earth demo.

Implementation Details

For our render-to-texture needs, we'll be using pbuffers. We'll also require two shaders written in GLSL. The first shader will handle the texture blurring. It will be used with two pbuffers to perform multiple blurring passes while avoiding `glCopyTexSubImage()` calls. The second shader will handle the rendering of the final blurred texture into the frame buffer, adding some contrast in the process.

Let's go through the rendering sequence steps in order.

1. **Render your scene as normal to the frame buffer.** To do this, the demo sets up lighting and binds a simple Blinn-Phong per-fragment lighting shader. This will light the Earth model nicely, as shown in Figure 7.13.

2. **Render the same scene to a texture.** Actually, we won't be using exactly the same scene. We'll be rendering without any shader, using only the diffuse color. This texture, shown in Figure 7.14, will be used to create the glow effect.

Since the first step should be very straightforward, we'll focus on the second step. We'll be primarily discussing the algorithms, but you can reference the demo source code for implementation details.

PBuffer Initialization

The first step is to create two pbuffers and initialize them. The pbuffers should be set up to support 2D RGB textures, and they should share context data and objects with the current OpenGL context. We'll be using 256×256 pbuffers, but even 128×128 pbuffers should be big enough for this effect.

Rendering to Texture

The next step is to render the scene to one of the two pbuffers. The geometry is rendered without lighting and is then scaled to be slightly larger than normal. The latter step isn't strictly necessary, but it will make the glow effect more noticeable.

Blurring the Texture

Now that we have our texture, it's time to blur it. The idea is pretty simple: for every pixel in the destination, we'll take four texels from the source texture and average them. The results of a single blurring pass are shown in Figure 7.15. This process is repeated N times. In this particular demo, the value of N is 5, which results in a good final image quality.

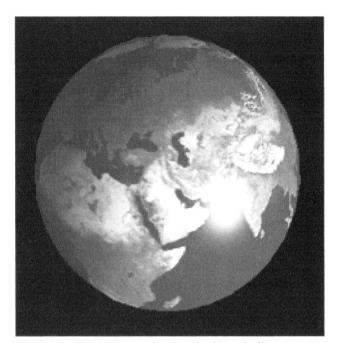

Figure 7.13 Scene as rendered to the frame buffer.

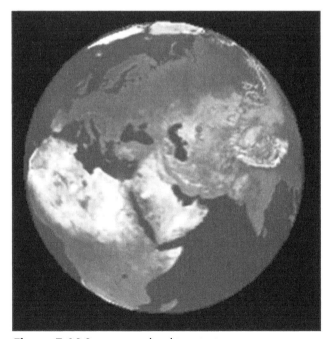

Figure 7.14 Scene as rendered to a texture.

Figure 7.15 The original image (left) and the image after a single blurring pass (right).

The Blur Shaders

The vertex shader used to accomplish blurring is as follows:

```
uniform float radius_x, radius_y;
void main()
{
  gl_TexCoord[0] = gl_MultiTexCoord0 - vec4(-radius_x, 0.0, 0.0, 0.0);
  gl_TexCoord[1] = gl_MultiTexCoord0 - vec4(radius_x, 0.0, 0.0, 0.0);
  gl_TexCoord[2] = gl_MultiTexCoord0 - vec4(0.0, -radius_y, 0.0, 0.0);
  gl_TexCoord[3] = gl_MultiTexCoord0 - vec4(0.0, radius_y, 0.0, 0.0);
  gl_Position = ftransform();
}
```

The uniform values `radius_x` and `radius_y` are blur radiuses along corresponding axes. Typically their values are set to `1.0/pbuffer_width` and `1.0/pbuffer_height` respectively. This results in a 1-pixel radius blur.

This is used in conjunction with the following fragment shader.

```
uniform sampler2D tex_unit_0; // texture from previous blurring stage
void main()
{
  vec4 sample[4];
  sample[0] = texture2D(tex_unit_0, gl_TexCoord[0].st);
  sample[1] = texture2D(tex_unit_0, gl_TexCoord[1].st);
  sample[2] = texture2D(tex_unit_0, gl_TexCoord[2].st);
  sample[3] = texture2D(tex_unit_0, gl_TexCoord[3].st);
  gl_FragColor = (sample[0] + sample[1] + sample[2] + sample[3]) / 4.0;
}
```

Within the main rendering code, we need to set the uniform values `radius_x` and `radius_y`, bind the source texture to texture unit 0, and render a screen-aligned textured quad, as follows:

```
glBegin(GL_QUADS);
  glTexCoord2d(0, 0); glVertex3d(0, 0, -1);
  glTexCoord2d(1, 0); glVertex3d(1, 0, -1);
```

```
  glTexCoord2d(1, 1); glVertex3d(1, 1, -1);
  glTexCoord2d(0, 1); glVertex3d(0, 1, -1);
glEnd();
```

This assumes that the modelview matrix is set to identity and the projection matrix is created using

```
glOrtho(0, 1, 0, 1, 0.01, 100);
```

Using Two PBuffers

If we only needed to render texture to the screen using the blur shader, we would just bind the blur shader and render a textured quad. But what we need is to blur our texture, then blur it again, and then blur it again, and so on, *N* times. This can be easily accomplished using two pbuffers as shown in the following pseudocode:

```
render the scene to pbuffer1
bind the blur shader
for (int i = 0; i < N; ++i)
{
  if (i is even)
  {
    bind pbuffer1 as a texture
    set pbuffer2 as the render target
  }
  else // i is odd
  {
    bind pbuffer1 as a texture
    set pbuffer2 as the render target
  }
  render a screen-aligned textured quad
}
```

Figure 7.16 shows the Earth texture from Figure 7.14 after five blurring passes.

The Glow Shaders

Once we've produced the blurred texture, we'll render it to the scene using shaders to achieve the final glow affect. This shader will just add some contrast to the blurred texture while rendering it to color buffer.

The vertex shader used simply passes on the texture coordinates and transforms the vertex positions into clip space:

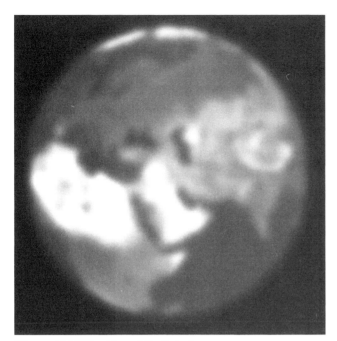

Figure 7.16 The blurred Earth texture.

```
void main()
{
  gl_TexCoord[0] = gl_MultiTexCoord0;
  gl_Position = ftransform();

}
```

The fragment shader just reads from the texture and applies contrast to it. The contrast results in the blurred texture used to produce the output shown in Figure 7.17.

```
uniform sampler2D tex_unit_0; // blurred screen space texture
void main()
{
  vec3 sample = texture2D(tex_unit_0, gl_TexCoord[0].st).rgb;
  sample = (pow(sample, vec3(2.0))- vec3(0.0, 0.2, 0.2) )*3.0;
  gl_FragColor = vec4(sample, 1.0);
}
```

Setting Up Blending

Finally, we just need to enable additive blending to add the glow to the existing scene:

```
glEnable(GL_BLEND);
glBlendFunc(GL_ONE, GL_ONE);
```

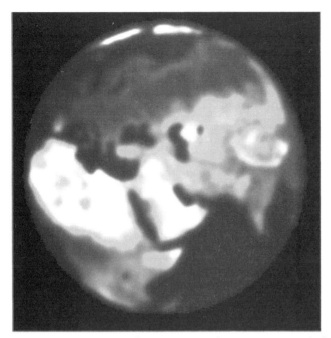

Figure 7.17 The blurred Earth texture after contrast is applied.

After we've bound the blurred earth image to texture unit 0 and bound the glow shader, we once again render a screen-aligned quad.

```
glBindTexture(GL_TEXTURE_2D, m_iRenderTexture);
pbuffer[buff_index]->Bind(WGL_FRONT_LEFT_ARB);
glUseProgramObject(m_iGlowShader);
```

And, finally, render the screen-space blurred texture quad to the color buffer. This is what produced the image on the left in Figure 7.12.

Specular-Component-Based Glow

The approach described so far bases the glow effect entirely on the model's diffuse color, without using lighting at all. An alternative is to create a glow effect based on the specular contribution. This is the method that was used on the chrome wheel from Figure 7.12.

The only difference between these two approaches is that with the diffuse method, while rendering the scene to a pbuffer, lighting is disabled. For the specular method, lighting is enabled and set so that only the specular component makes a contribution to the image rendered to the pbuffer. To do this, simply set all the nonspecular material properties to 0, or use a shader that only calculates the specular component.

Because all other steps are identical to the diffuse method, they won't be covered in detail. 7.18 shows the primary stages of the specular method.

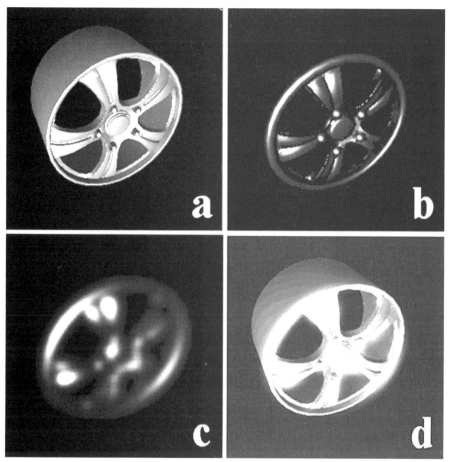

Figure 7.18 Content of the color buffer after rendering the scene with diffuse and specular lighting (a); pbuffer content after rendering the scene with specular lighting only (b); the pbuffer after five blurring passes (c); and the final image (d).

For the best results, use the diffuse-based glow to create the effect of something literally glowing, and use specular-based glow to create the effect of something shining.

Planar Reflections and Refractions

Andrei Gradinari

Reflections and refractions are among the most popular special effects used in 3D graphics. Both add complexity and realism to your games, and they are easy to implement.

Reflections

There are several ways to implement reflections. In *Beginning OpenGL Game Programming*, you learned how to implement them using environment mapping. This section will explain how to render planar reflections, which provide an attractive alternative in many situations.

Figure 7.19 illustrates the difference that reflections can make in a simple scene. The version with reflections looks better and more realistic than the one without. Notice how the reflections transmit spatial relationships between objects. Figure 7.19a makes it clear that the dice and pencil are on the desk, whereas Figure 7.19b creates the impression that objects are floating above it.

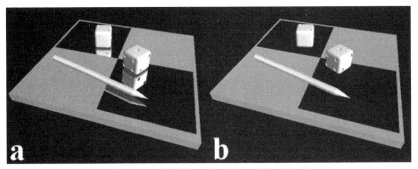

Figure 7.19 A simple scene with (a) and without (b) reflections.

Figure 7.20 shows the elements used to create Figure 7.19a. As you can see, implementing the reflection effect is a matter of generating the reflection image and combining it with the source scene image.

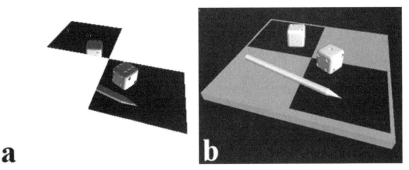

Figure 7.20 The reflection image (a) and the source scene image (b).

There are two major approaches to implementing planar reflections. They differ mainly in the way they generate the reflected image and combine it with the scene. One approach uses the stencil buffer, and the other uses screen-space textures.

The steps involved in the stencil-buffer approach are

1. Set up the mirror clipping plane, but don't enable it yet.
2. Render the geometry representing the mirror to the stencil buffer.
3. Set up a reflected camera transformation.
4. Set up reflected lighting.
5. Enable the clipping plane and stencil buffer and render the scene.
6. Restore the initial camera transformation.
7. Render the mirror to the depth buffer.
8. Set up lighting.
9. Render the scene normally.

The steps involved in the screen-space texture approach are

1. Set up the mirror clipping plane, but don't enable it yet.
2. Set up a reflected camera transformation.
3. Set up reflected lighting.
4. Enable the clipping plane and render the scene to a reflection texture.
5. Restore the initial camera transformation.
6. Render the mirror mesh with the reflection texture projected on it.
7. Set up lighting.
8. Render the scene normally.

The advantages and disadvantages of each of these approaches are summarized in Table 7.1.

Table 7.1 Planar Reflection Method Pros and Cons

	Stencil Buffer	**Screen-Space Texture**
Advantages	Fast.	Easy to implement many mirrors at once.
	Resolution of reflection is the same as the frame buffer.	Easy to implement semitransparent mirrors.
Disadvantages	Hard to implement many mirrors at once.	Resolution of reflection is usually lower than final scene.
	Impossible to implement semitransparent mirrors (e.g., glass).	Higher texture resolutions result in lower rendering speeds.

In this section I'll concentrate on stencil-buffer reflections. Once you understand how to do them, it will be easy for you to implement screen-space texture reflections. As you can see, their implementations are very similar and differ only in a few rendering steps.

Stencil-Buffer Reflections

Now that you've had an overview of the two primary planar reflection techniques, let's look at the steps involved in implementing stencil-buffer reflections in detail.

Setting Up the Clipping Plane

As you learned back in Chapter 1, clipping planes are essential in correctly rendering reflections. The mirror clipping plane should be set up before applying the reflection transformation. If you reverse these steps, you'll have to multiply the plane normal by -1 before passing the plane equation to OpenGL.

The code for setting up the clipping plane is as follows:

```
vec3 a, b, c, n;
GLdouble eq[4];
// any triangle in the mirror's mesh can be used to define the plane
if(m_pMesh[0]->nVertices > 2 && m_pMesh[0]->nTriangles > 1) {
   int ai = m_pMesh[0]->pIdx[0],
       bi = m_pMesh[0]->pIdx[1],
       ci = m_pMesh[0]->pIdx[2];

     a = vec3(& m_pMesh[0]->pVert[ai*3]);
     b = vec3(& m_pMesh[0]->pVert[bi*3]);
     c = vec3(& m_pMesh[0]->pVert[ci*3]);

     get_plane_equation(c, b, a, eq);
     n = vec3(eq[0], eq[1], eq[2]);
}
// set up clipping plane, but leave it disabled
glClipPlane(GL_CLIP_PLANE0, eq);
```

Here I take the first triangle in the mirror's mesh (any face can be used since they all lie in a single plane). I use get_plane_equation(c, b, a, eq), which takes three points and returns the plane equation in eq. Notice the order of the arguments passed to the function. The order is important, since it determines which half space will be cut by the clipping plane during reflection image rendering.

Rendering the Mirror Mesh to the Stencil Buffer

Before rendering the reflected scene to the color buffer, you need to tell OpenGL what area of the final image will be occupied by the reflection image. You'll use the stencil buffer to mask this area. The idea is to render the mirror mesh to the stencil buffer and then use the stencil-buffer contents as a mask for rendering the reflected image.

```
// render the mirror mesh to the stencil buffer
glDepthMask(GL_FALSE); // disable writing to depth buffer
glColorMask(GL_FALSE, GL_FALSE, GL_FALSE, GL_FALSE); // and to color buffer

glEnable(GL_STENCIL_TEST);
glStencilMask(1); // enable writing to stencil buffer 1st bit plane
glStencilFunc(GL_ALWAYS, 1, 1); // tell stencil test always to pass
// tell OpenGL to replace stencil-buffer value each time stencil test passes
glStencilOp(GL_KEEP, GL_KEEP, GL_REPLACE);

m_pMesh[0]->Draw(); // render mirror mesh

// enable writing to color and depth buffers
glDepthMask(GL_TRUE);
glColorMask(GL_TRUE, GL_TRUE, GL_TRUE, GL_TRUE);
glDisable(GL_STENCIL_TEST);
```

After you render the mirror mesh to the stencil buffer, it will contain the mask shown in Figure 7.21. The image is white where the stencil-buffer values are 1, and black where values are 0.

Figure 7.21 Stencil mask created by the mirror mesh.

Setting Up Reflected Camera Transformation

Specially for this demo, I wrote a camera class (see "CCamera.h" and "CCamera.cpp" included with the demo). This class implements some handy utility functions for camera positioning and reflecting about arbitrary planes.

The only member of this class is an array of four points (vec3 p[4]). This array stores camera transformation data, so that in camera space

```
x-axis = vec3(p[0], p[1]) -- normalized right vector
y-axis = vec3(p[0], p[2]) -- normalized up vector
z-axis = vec3(p[0], p[3]) -- normalized vector to viewer
```

The up, right, and vector-to-viewer vectors could be stored as separate members, but when stored this way, it is easier to reflect the camera.

The methods of this class are as follows:

- **LookAt(vec3 pos, vec3 at, vec3 v_up).** Positions camera according to position (pos), the point being looked at (at), and the up vector (v_up). This method just computes v_up, v_right, and v_view, and loads p array values.

- **Apply(vec3 A, vec3 N).** Applies the camera transformation. In other words, it multiplies the current matrix by the camera transformation matrix. The camera transformation matrix is generated based on the camera's position and v_right, v_up, and v_view vectors.

- **Reflect(vec3 A, vec3 N).** Reflects the camera about a plane. The plane is defined by an arbitrary point belonging to it (A), and a normal vector (N).

Let's take a closer look at the last function.

```
void CCamera :: Reflect(vec3 A, vec3 N)
{
  for(int i=0; i<4; i++)
    p[i] = reflect_point_about_plane(p[i], A, N);
}
```

All this does is call reflect_point_about_plane() for each of four points, so let's look at this function as well.

```
// reflects point P about plane defined by arbitrary point belonging to it (A)
// and its normal vector (N).
inline vec3 reflect_point_about_plane(vec3 P, vec3 A, vec3 N)
{
  vec3 ret;
  N.normalize();
  vec3 PA(P, A);
  vec3 PA_proj_N = N * dot(PA, N); // PA projected on N
  ret = P + PA_proj_N * 2.0f;
  return ret;
}
```

Figure 7.22a illustrates what this function does.

The easiest way to reflect a point about a plane is to:

1. Project the point onto the plane. The result of projection is point P_{proj}.
2. Build vector(P, P_{proj}) = PA_proj_N — this is a projection of vector PA onto vector N.
3. Calculate the reflected point P' using P' = P + 2 * PA_proj_N.

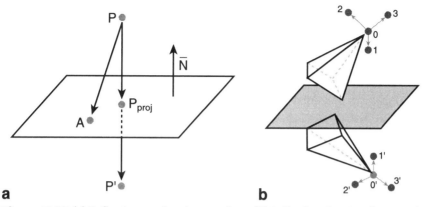

Figure 7.22 (a) Reflecting a point about a plane. (b) Reflecting the view frustum about a plane.

So looking at the code again, first it normalizes N and builds the vector PA. It then finds PA_proj_N by scaling N by the dot product of PA and N. This vector is thus perpendicular to the plane and has a length equal to the distance of point P from the plane. So the final step just doubles this vector's length and adds it to the original point P to find the reflected point P'.

Figure 7.22b shows the view frustum before and after calling CCamera::Reflect(), which is used as follows:

```
CCamera cam_refl = cam; // cam is our initial camera
// plane equation evaluation
cam_refl.Reflect(a, n); // reflecting camera about the plane
...
glPushMatrix();    // save the modelview matrix
glLoadIdentity();
cam_refl.Apply(); // apply camera before rendering reflection image
glPushMatrix();    // restore the modelview matrix
```

Adjusting Polygonal Winding

OpenGL normally uses a left-handed coordinate system (i.e., x = v_right, y = v_up, z = v_view). In a left-handed coordinate system, front faces are those which, after being projected onto the screen, have a counterclockwise vertex order. After reflection, the coordinate system becomes right-handed, as does our camera space. This causes front faces to become back faces, and vice versa. In order for culling to work correctly when rendering the reflected scene, you need to tell OpenGL to treat vertices in clockwise order as front-facing:

```
glPushAttrib(GL_POLYGON_BIT);  // push front face order
glLoadIdentity();
cam_refl.Apply();              // apply reflection transform
```

```
glFrontFace(GL_CW);              // change front face vertex order
... // render reflected image
glPushAttrib(GL_POLYGON_BIT);    // restore front face order
```

Lighting Setup

Since OpenGL stores lights' positions in view space, and you define lighting positions in global space, each time you change the camera transformation, you need to reset each light's position (using `glLight()`). This will cause OpenGL to position lights correctly according to the current modelview matrix.

Render the Reflected Scene

It's now time to render the reflected scene. Figure 7.23a shows what you would get if you rendered the scene without enabling the stencil test. To get the desired result instead (Figure 7.23b), you need to mask this image by the image shown in Figure 7.21.

To do this, you enable the stencil test and set up the stencil operation so that it passes only when the value in the stencil buffer is 1. You also need to enable the clipping plane at this point. Using the stencil buffer and clipping plane, the image in Figure 7.23b will be produced.

Figure 7.23 Rendering the reflected image without (left) and with (right) the stencil buffer.

Restore Initial Camera Transformation

At this point, the reflected scene has been rendered, and you're ready to start rendering the rest of the scene. Before you do so, the original camera transformation matrix needs to be restored. This is generally just a matter of calling `glPopMatrix()`. As mentioned before, since the camera transformation has changed, you need to be sure to reset your lighting.

Render Mirror Mesh to Depth Buffer

In order to avoid depth artifacts in your scene, before rendering the rest of the scene, you should render the mirror mesh to just the depth buffer:

```
glColorMask(GL_FALSE, GL_FALSE, GL_FALSE, GL_FALSE);
m_pMesh[0]->Draw();
glColorMask(GL_TRUE, GL_TRUE, GL_TRUE, GL_TRUE);
```

Render Scene

You can now render the scene normally. The end result of all these steps as performed in the demo is shown in Figure 7.19a.

note

Let me reiterate that this discussion has been about planar reflections. This implies that the mesh representing the mirror needs to have all of its vertices in a single plane. If the mesh doesn't meet this requirement, rendering artifacts will appear.

Refractions

In the scene in Figure 7.24, you can see a pencil and a die immersed in some transparent liquid. Notice the difference between the objects immersed and those not immersed in the liquid. The ones that are immersed seem to be "scaled." This is what you see in real life when you put something into water. Also, the pool seems to be very shallow—perhaps one-third of the platform's height. In reality, it's almost as deep as the platform is high. Both of these effects are created by refraction.

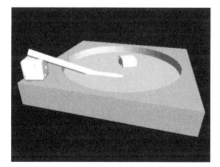

Figure 7.24 A simple scene using refraction.

Implementing planar refraction is very similar to planar reflection, but there are a few differences between them. They are:

1. Instead of setting up a reflection transform, you should set up refraction transform for your camera. In the demo, CCamera::Refract(vec3 A, vec3 N, float index_of_refraction) implements this camera transformation. It scales camera points along the plane's normal depending on index_of_refraction. When index_of_refraction is 1.0, the camera transform doesn't change. The bigger the

index of refraction, the more the camera approaches the plane after this method is called. Applying the refraction transformation does not change which half space the points fall in (Figure 7.25).

2. The refracted coordinate system remains left-handed, and thus, you don't need to change polygonal winding.

3. When you deal with refractions, you deal with an *index of refraction* coefficient, which is effectively a scaling factor. The value of this coefficient depends on the materials on each side of the plane. For example, for air-water interfaces (i.e., viewer is in air looking at the water surface) it is approximately 1.3. The bigger this coefficient, the more noticeable the refraction effect is. In the demo for this section, it is equal to 2.0.

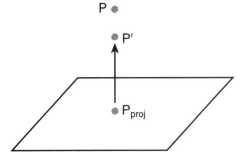

Figure 7.25 P′ is P after refraction.

It is often useful to mix reflected and refracted images, as when rendering water. For a more detailed discussion, see the section "Rendering Water" in Chapter 8, "Rendering Nature".

Robust Multilevel Reflections

Maciej Sawitus

Imagine a room with two mirrors placed opposite each other. As you stand between them and look into one, you will see a potentially infinite recursive interreflection chain, where on each of the reflections each side of your body will appear in turns. Such recursive reflections of reflections, or, as I will call them, *multilevel reflections*, add another level of realism and complexity to the scene. However, they come at a cost that has to be carefully considered. The goal of this section is to show you how to render planar multilevel reflections correctly and effectively using OpenGL. Because this visual effect is recursive in nature, its implementation requires an appropriate graphics-pipeline design and therefore will be discussed with this in mind. It's assumed that you are familiar with standard frustum construction and culling (described in *Beginning OpenGL Game Programming*) and have a good understanding of rendering single planar reflections using stencil-buffer masking as described in the previous section, "Planar Reflections and Refractions."

Introduction

Rendering multilevel reflections requires recursive rendering, so one natural limitation you have to consider is the maximum reflection recursion depth. Before I go into implementation details, it's worth realizing that given n mirrors and maximum recursion depth r, the total number of rendering passes required to render the scene in the worst case scenario is:

$$1 + n + n(n-1) + n(n-1)^2 + \ldots + n(n-1)^{r-1} = 1 + n\sum_{i-0}^{r-1}(n-1)^i$$

Don't be scared by these numbers; in practice they'll be much lower. To achieve acceptable performance in scenes with multiple reflective surfaces, you have to make clever use of multiple optimization techniques, all having basically the same goals—minimizing the amount of geometry being rendered and minimizing fill rate (i.e., the number of pixels drawn per frame). The main optimizations are frustum culling and scissor tests. The first minimizes the amount of geometry rendered, while the second helps minimize fill rate. There are more optimization techniques available, but these two are definitely the most important ones.

Multilevel Reflections in Game Engines

Quite a few modern game engines, such as *Doom 3*'s, are capable of rendering multilevel reflections, but achieving this kind of visual effect can be expensive. As a result, level designers avoid creating game worlds with multiple reflective surfaces that are within each other's line of sight—either because it could result in undesired visual effect (e.g., the graphics engine is capable of rendering single reflections only) or because of the potentially high cost of rendering interreflections (due to the large amount of geometry to render and high fill rate). However, this doesn't have to be the case.

Note that multilevel reflections are not the kind of special effect you can just add to an existing graphics engine. To be appropriately handled, interreflections within a complex graphics engine need to be considered at an early design stage. This is due to the recursive nature of reflections, which has a great impact on the order of rendering operations; put simply, the scene would need to be rendered as reflected in mirrors first, and then rendered as seen directly. You should be aware that rendering multilevel reflections turns the whole rendering process into a recursive tree-like operation in which tree nodes correspond to reflective surfaces visible to the viewer at successive reflection levels. For each reflective surface visible at some reflection level, separate geometry culling and drawing is needed.

Figure 7.26 shows screenshots from a simple map (included with the demo source) designed to try out *Doom 3*'s capability of rendering multilevel mirrors. As you can see, Doom 3 uses the simple *depth-covering method* (described later) to render reflections, but it has one serious drawback I will discuss in a moment. One of the reasons *Doom 3* doesn't use the *stencil-buffer-masking* method (described earlier in this chapter) is its intensive use of stencil buffers for shadow volumes. Later you'll learn how to handle both methods at the same time.

Figure 7.26 A *Doom 3* room with one mirror on each of its four walls (left), and the same room seen from below (with Doom's *no clipping* mode enabled; right). Dashed lines show bounding mirrors' rectangles used to define scissor test rectangles.

Available Techniques

When using OpenGL for rendering multilevel reflections on today's GPUs, you have two general techniques to consider. The first renders the reflected scene directly to the color buffer with the help of the stencil buffer, and the second makes use of additional render textures (also called render targets) to which to render the reflected scene. While the first method is well suited for planar nondeformed reflections, the latter can simulate per-pixel deformed reflections on arbitrarily shaped surfaces by using either a single additional texture or a cube texture. In this section, I'll cover how to implement planar multilevel reflections using stencil-buffer masking. An approach based on using additional render textures will not be discussed here, but the general idea stays the same for both methods, especially as far as geometry culling is concerned. The second method is slightly more complex and expensive, though.

There is also another method that is often used for planar multilevel reflections, mainly for its simplicity—I will call it the *depth-covering* method. It doesn't use stencil masking; instead it simply renders the reflected scene, clears the depth buffer, and then, with alpha blending enabled, renders the mirror surface to write appropriate depth values to the z-buffer. All implementation details of this method can be found in the *OpenGL Technical FAQ*. The main reason I won't describe it here is because it cannot render overlapping mirrors correctly, a serious limitation. Rendering multiple mirrors in a scene can over-write previously rendered mirrors, resulting in incorrect reflections. There are ways to minimize these issues, but they can't be avoided.

The use of the stencil buffer allows for per-pixel control of which pixels are drawn to and thus of which are arbitrarily placed, meaning overlapping mirrors in the scene can be properly handled. Stencil masking comes at some extra expense, though—an additional three passes over the mirror surface are required, increasing fill rate.

Rendering Stencil Multilevel Reflections

From now on, when talking about reflections, I will always mean planar reflections. At the beginning, I will also make an assumption that every mirror surface in the scene consists of nonoverlapping and coplanar polygons, so planar reflection for such surfaces makes sense. *Mirror portal* refers to the bounding polygon of the mirror. For the best performance as well as simplicity, I will always use quadrilateral portals, which can be a good enough approximation of any polygon.

First I will show how the stencil buffer will be used, and then I will present two main optimizations: recursive frustum intersecting and recursive scissor rectangle intersecting. Several C++-like code snippets based on the demo source code will help you understand crucial implementation details, but bear in mind that for readability, some sections of the code are omitted because they aren't really necessary to explain the idea being presented.

Stencil-Buffer Usage

To correctly render multilevel reflections, you will make use of `glStencilOp()` to set `GL_INCR` (increase) and `GL_DECR` (decrease) operations on the stencil buffer. Before rendering the scene, the stencil buffer is cleared to 0. As you render a mirror, you "tag" mirror pixels by increasing by the stencil-buffer value by 1 for fragments that pass the depth test. The reflected scene is then rendered, but only to tagged pixels; the same tagged pixels' stencil values are then decreased by 1. Finally, the alpha-blended mirror mesh is rendered over the reflected parts of the scene. This stencil masking algorithm avoids overwriting any previously rendered geometry, including other mirrors, and also saves fill rate by not drawing pixels outside the mirror surface.

Recursive Frustum Intersection

The method described here makes heavy use of a custom software-implemented frustum-culling test to cull away invisible geometry. In order to determine the geometry potentially visible at a certain reflection level, you will need to perform the frustum test for the whole scene. Using hierarchical spatial structures designed especially for culling (e.g., quadtrees or octrees), recursive frustum intersection can be a highly optimized operation when additionally combined with occlusion culling, even though a big part is done in software.

With each successive reflection level on the recursive call stack, you will reflect (using a reflection matrix calculated from the mirror's plane) frustum planes so they will appropriately cull geometry visible in the mirror reflection. This is illustrated in Figure 7.27.

To enhance culling efficiency in cases where a mirror is only partially visible, you can calculate the approximate geometrical intersection between the current frustum and the frustum constructed based on the mirror portal. The new frustum will then be used for successive frustum tests and, if needed, intersected again with other frustums. This way, the frustum becomes tighter with each successive mirror portal you visit on the recursive rendering path.

This kind of approach in general is reminiscent of portal-based scene design where sectors (e.g., rooms and corridors) are connected through portals (e.g., windows and doors). Often, special mirror portals are used as well to achieve a planar reflection effect, possibly with some additional image distortion. All of these portals, whether they are regular portals connecting sectors or mirror portals, are used to incorporate the recursive frustum culling scheme. Figure 7.27 illustrates a few steps of frustum intersection for successive mirror portal intersections.

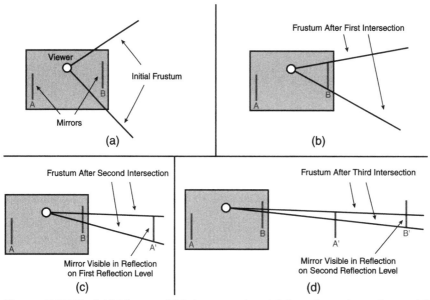

Figure 7.27 The initial frustum (a) is intersected to tightly enclose mirror B's portal (b), and the scene reflected in mirror B is rendered. Next is rendered the scene reflected in mirror A reflected in mirror B (c). The frustum is further intersected to contain as small a volume as possible. Finally, the scene reflected in three consecutive mirrors—B, A, B— is rendered (d).

As you can see, frustum intersection will be a very common operation in this algorithm. You will perform it every time you hit a mirror portal, because each successive portal can potentially narrow the visible space volume. But how do you actually calculate a frustum intersection? Note that an ideal geometrically intersected frustum would consist of the sum of all clipping planes from two input frustums. However, if you did this, the frustum would have more and more clipping planes with each successive mirror visited, which in most cases would result in inefficient culling. What you do instead is to calculate an approximate frustum using some simple heuristic approach that will prevent the total number of clipping planes from growing larger than six (initially: near, far, top, bottom, left and right). Of course, such an approximation results in the frustum enclosing more scene geometry than what would be optimal, but in most cases the difference compared to the optimal solution would be negligible. The following pseudocode shows one way to do it:

```
// return new frustum, being intersection of frustums a and b
Frustum intersect(Frustum a, Frustum b) {
  // create initial frustum from a
  Frustum result = a;
  // for each frustum plane see if it can be effectively replaced
  // by any of the frustum's b clipping plane
  for (int i = 0; i < result.planes.size(); i++)
    for (int j = 0; j < b.planes.size(); j++)
      // the "is better than" test tells whether one clipping plane
      // is likely to cull away more scene geometry than the other one;
      // see demo source code for details
      if (b.planes[j] "is better than" result.planes[i])
        result.planes[i] = b.planes[j];
  return result;
}
```

As mentioned, this implementation could be improved at the cost of complexity, but as demonstrated in the demo written especially for this section, a similar approach can be very efficient and behaves well in scenes with multiple mirrors.

Recursive Scissor Rectangle Intersection

By optimizing frustum culling, you are minimizing the amount of geometry being sent through OpenGL to the GPU. To further optimize the rendering of triangles already sent to the GPU, you use the scissor test. Setting the scissor test through OpenGL will automatically cull away pixels from outside a specified rectangle. In this case, the scissor rectangle will be calculated by projecting the mirror portal, represented as a quad, onto screen space. After having projected all four vertices of the mirror portal, you can easily calculate its bounding rectangle, which will serve as the scissor test rectangle.

As you start rendering, you set the bounding rectangle to contain the whole viewport, and then, analogically to recursive frustum tests, you calculate a new scissor rectangle as an intersection between successive mirror portals' bounding rectangles. Since the intersection of two rectangles is very simple to calculate (it always gives a rectangle or a point or is empty), the scissor test region will never grow larger and in most practical situations will decrease significantly with each successive reflection, thus effectively reducing fill rate. Once the scissor rectangle becomes empty, there's no need to recur any mirror deeper because no geometry is visible in its reflection. Figure 7.28 presents the benefits of this simple, very powerful optimization.

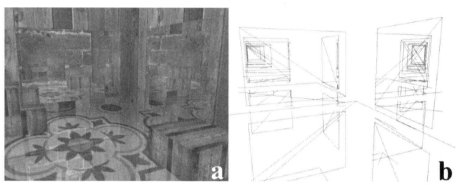

Figure 7.28 When scissor tests are applied to a normally rendered scene (a), only portals of visible mirrors are rendered (b); fill rate is thus significantly decreased, and performance increases up to several times.

Implementation: Frustum Class

Since the two key optimizations I've described are always performed together, they will be handled by a single, somewhat extended, Frustum class representing all aspects of what geometry is potentially visible—either directly or reflected in some mirror.

```
class Frustum {
  public:
    Frustum(const Camera* camera); // creates frustum from given camera
    void transform(const Matrix4x4& transformation); // transforms frustum
    bool intersect(const Mirror* mirror); // performs intersection
    bool isVisible(const BoundingBox& box) const; // tests box visibility
    bool isFrontFacing(const Plane& plane) const;// tests plane's front-facing
  protected:
    Vector3 Origin; // viewer's origin
    Set<Plane> ClippingPlanes; // frustum clipping planes
    Rectangle BoundingRectangle; // bounding rectangle used for scissor test
};
```

Executing transform() transforms the viewer's origin and all clipping planes using the given transformation (in this case it's always a reflection transformation). The intersect() function performs two intersections: the first is the approximate geometrical intersection with a frustum built from the given mirror's portal, and the second is the bounding rectangles' intersection used for the scissor test. If any of these intersections turns out to be empty, intersect() returns false, which indicates that no geometry is visible in the given mirror. The isVisible() function is a standard frustum test against a bounding box, and isFrontFacing() tells whether a given plane is facing toward the viewer's origin (Origin attribute).

Implementation: Renderer Class

In the demo source code, the class that is responsible for rendering the whole scene is Renderer. To explain the main idea behind the multilevel reflection algorithm, I'm going to provide an overview of three of Renderer's most important class methods.

renderScene()

This method is called once per frame to render the scene as seen from a given camera. At first, the OpenGL modelview transformation is set, and then, starting from reflection level 0, the rendering of the scene begins. An initial frustum (passed as the second parameter to renderReflectionLevel()) is constructed from the given camera; the initial scissor test rectangle is set to the dimensions of the current viewport.

```
void Renderer::renderScene(Camera* camera) {
  glEnable(GL_STENCIL_TEST); // enable stencil test
  camera->setView(); // set position and angles
  // render starting from 0'th reflection level (i.e. visible directly)
  renderReflectionLevel(0 /*level*/, Frustum(camera), NULL /*no mirror*/);
}
```

renderReflectionLevel()

This method renders the scene enclosed by the given frustum that is visible as a reflection in the given mirror. The first parameter, level, is the current reflection level, where 0 corresponds to geometry seen directly, 1 to geometry reflected once in some mirror, and so on.

```
void Renderer::renderReflectionLevel(int level, const Frustum& frustum,
                                     const Mirror* mirror) {
  if (level < MaxReflectionLevel) {
    // cull visible mirrors and render scene reflected in each one of them
    Set<Mirror*> visibleMirrors;
    Scene->cullVisibleMirrors(frustum, visibleMirrors);
    for (int i = 0; i < visibleMirrors.size(); i++)
      if (visibleMirrors[i] != mirror) // except for current mirror
        renderMirror(visibleMirrors[i], level, frustum, mirror);
  }
  // apply scissor test
  const Rectangle& r = frustum.getBoundingRectangle();
  glScissor(r.left(), r.top(), r.width(), r.height());
```

```
// for level > 0: set stencil test and mirror clipping plane
if (level > 0) {
  glStencilFunc(GL_EQUAL, level, ~0);// pass only when stencil equals level
  glStencilOp(GL_KEEP, GL_KEEP, GL_KEEP); // don't modify stencil buffer
  glEnable(GL_CLIP_PLANE0); // Enable clipping plane 0
  glClipPlane(GL_CLIP_PLANE0, mirror->getPlane()); // Set clipping plane
} else {
  glDisable(GL_STENCIL_TEST); // disable stencil test (no mirror)
  glDisable(GL_CLIP_PLANE0); // disable clipping plane 0 (no mirror)
}
// enable depth and color writes; set appropriate face culling
glDepthMask(GL_TRUE);
glColorMask(GL_TRUE, GL_TRUE, GL_TRUE, GL_TRUE);
glCullFace((level % 2 == 0) ? GL_FRONT : GL_BACK);

// cull (into VisibleMeshes Renderer's attribute) and render visible meshes
Scene->cullVisibleMeshes(frustum, VisibleMeshes);
for (int j = 0; j < VisibleMeshes.size(); j++)
  VisibleMeshes[j].render();
VisibleMeshes.clear();
}
```

At first a simple check as to whether to continue or stop recursive rendering is performed, and then, if the maximum reflection level hasn't been reached yet, visible mirrors are culled and rendered using renderMirror(). After returning from recursive rendering calls, the appropriate scissor rectangle is set and the stencil test is set to pass only where the stencil values equal level. These stencil values are set previously in renderMirror() (described next). Finally, visible scene geometry is culled and rendered. During this operation, alpha-blended mirror meshes are rendered too—they are treated as regular meshes.

renderMirror()

The first parameter, mirrorToRender, is the mirror you will render the reflected scene in; the three remaining parameters are the same as in renderReflectionLevel().

```
void Renderer::renderMirror(const Mirror* mirrorToRender, int level,
                const Frustum& frustum, const Mirror* mirror) {
  // test if mirror's plane is facing toward viewer
  if (!frustum.isFrontFacing( currentMirror->getPlane() )) return;

  // copy current frustum and intersect it with mirror portal's frustum
  Frustum newFrustum = frustum;
  if (!newFrustum.intersect( mirrorToRender )) return;
```

First, you make sure that the mirror is facing the viewer (using the isFrontFacing() method of the Frustum class); otherwise, it wouldn't be visible at all. Then you construct an approximate frustum intersection and make sure that the intersection is not empty. Remember that intersect() performs the intersection of bounding scissor rectangles, too. If the scissor rectangle is empty, there's no need to render the reflection either.

```
... // set scissor test, mirror clipping plane and face culling
```

The scissor test, mirror clipping, and face culling are then set (the same way as in renderReflectionLevel()) and you can start filling the stencil buffer with appropriate values:

```
// increment stencil values over mirror surface:
glStencilFunc(GL_EQUAL, level, ~0); // only where stencil equals level
glStencilOp(GL_KEEP, GL_KEEP, GL_INCR); // stencil operation is increase
glDepthFunc(GL_LESS); // set default depth function
glDepthMask(GL_FALSE); // disable depth writes
glColorMask(0, 0, 0, 0); // disable color writes
mirrorToRender->getMesh()->render(); // render mirror surface polygons
```

These operations make the stencil-buffer values increase by 1 over the mirror surface wherever the depth test passes. For optimization reasons, depth and color writes are disabled. Appropriate face culling is also set. After rendering the mirror polygons, pixels on the mirror surface have a stencil value equal to level.

Because some geometry might have already been rendered to pixels tagged during the stencil pass, we need to clear the depth buffer for all these pixels before rendering the reflected scene. This is done as follows:

```
// clear depth values over mirror surface to maximum:
glStencilFunc(GL_EQUAL, level + 1, ~0);// only where stencil equals level + 1
glStencilOp(GL_KEEP, GL_KEEP, GL_KEEP); // don't change stencil buffer
glDepthMask(GL_TRUE); // enable depth writes
glDepthRange(1, 1); // set depth range to always output maximal depth
glDepthFunc(GL_ALWAYS); // disable depth test
mirrorToRender->getMesh()->render(); // render mirror surface polygons
glDepthRange(0, 1); // set back default depth range
glDepthFunc(GL_LESS); // set back default depth function
```

In the above code, maximal depth values are written for all mirror pixels simply by rendering the mirror surface with the depth range set to always output the furthest possible value. Thanks to the stencil test, only required pixels are updated—the ones where stencil values equal level + 1. Now let's deal with reflection transformations.

```
// construct reflection transformation for mirror's plane:
Matrix4x4 matrix;
matrix.buildReflectionTransformation( mirrorToRender->getPlane() );
```

```
newFrustum.transform(matrix);

// render reflected scene on level + 1 reflection level:
glPushMatrix(); // push current modelview matrix onto the stack
glMultMatrixf(matrix); // apply reflection transformation
renderReflectionLevel(level + 1, newFrustum, mirrorToRender); // render
glPopMatrix(); // pop modelview matrix from the top of the stack
... // set back scissor test, mirror clipping plane and face culling
```

First, the reflection matrix is constructed based on the mirror's surface plane. It is then used to transform both our frustum and the modelview matrix. Recursive rendering of the reflected scene is enclosed by `glPushMatrix()` and `glPopMatrix()`, so the previous modelview transformation can easily be restored after rendering.

Finally, after rendering the reflected scene, stencil values are decreased and appropriate depth values are written to the z-buffer on the mirror's surface.

```
// decrement stencil values and fill z-buffer over mirror surface:
glStencilFunc(GL_EQUAL, level + 1, ~0);// only where stencil equals level + 1
glStencilOp(GL_KEEP, GL_KEEP, GL_DECR); // stencil operation is decreased
glDepthFunc(GL_ALWAYS); // disable depth test
glDepthMask(GL_TRUE); // enable depth writes
glColorMask(0, 0, 0, 0); // disable color writes
mirrorToRender->getMesh()->render(); // render Mirror surface polygons
glDepthFunc(GL_LESS); // set back default depth function
} // End of renderMirror
```

You're finished rendering the mirror now. As you can see, you had to do three additional drawing passes over the mirror surface. One more thing to note is that all of them should be performed with expensive OpenGL states such as texturing, vertex and fragment shaders, and vertex normals disabled, as they would only slow things down.

Rendering Mirror Surface

After rendering the reflected scene in a given mirror, and when appropriate depth values have been written for its surface, you alpha blend the mirror texture to give it a more realistic look. To do this, disable depth writes and set the depth function to GL_EQUAL. To blend the mirror texture, use a typical blending mode. The alpha color component value is the mirror's specular factor. The following code sets the needed states:

```
glEnable(GL_BLEND); // enable blending
glColor4f(1, 1, 1, mirror->getSpecular()); // set alpha value
glBlendFunc(GL_ONE_MINUS_SRC_ALPHA, GL_SRC_ALPHA); // set blend function

glDepthMask(GL_FALSE); // disable depth writes
glDepthFunc(GL_EQUAL); // set depth function to pass when depth is equal
```

Handling Stencil Shadow Volumes

As you can see, the method I've presented relies heavily on stencil-buffer usage. The popular and widely used shadow-volume method (described later in this chapter) uses the stencil buffer as well. Since there's only one stencil buffer, an obvious problem appears if you want to have both effects running at the same time.

Luckily, there is a very simple and reasonable solution to this problem. Thanks to stencil-mask usage (set through the third parameter of `glStencilFunc()`), you can easily partition the stencil buffer's bits into two parts, for example, using the five lowest bits for shadow volumes and the remaining three for recursive reflections. The mask used for shadow volumes would then equal (2 ^ 5 − 1) (00011111 in binary), and for reflections (2 ^ 3 − 1) * (2 ^ 5) (11100000 in binary). This partitioning can be adjusted according to the maximum desired reflection level or the shadow complexity. The good thing about this solution is that it doesn't require any additional implementation.

Limiting Maximum Reflection Level

One way to limit the maximum reflection level, mainly in cases when very many reflection levels are visible, is to simply not allow for deeper recursion than some constant value, such as 5. On the other hand, when a mirror's specular factor is very low (the mirror surface absorbs a lot of light), it might become practical to introduce another maximum reflection level limitation based on successive mirrors' cumulative opaqueness factor. If during the recursive rendering path this opaqueness factor exceeds a minimum specified constant value (let's call it *minimal opaqueness*), recursion stops. In detail:

- Start rendering with the opaqueness value set to 0.

- As you visit a mirror with a specular factor equal to x (a value between 0 and 1), you calculate a new opaqueness factor as follows:
  opaqueness := opaqueness + (1 − opaqueness) * (1 − x)
  and then pass this value along as part of the recursion.

- When the opaqueness value exceeds our constant limit (minimal opaqueness), no deeper reflections will be rendered. Note that the higher you set this limit, the deeper reflections will be. In practice, a value of 0.90 should be good enough. Figure 7.29 shows a comparison of different mirror specular factors for recursion limiting and alpha-blending a mirror surface.

Even using all the described optimizations, you still need to be careful with recursive reflections. Obviously, the amount of geometry rendered depends greatly on the viewer's position and his viewing angle. Even slight movement with regard to a reflective surface can drastically increase the total amount of potentially visible geometry. An additional optimization to consider is to limit recursion depth of reflections dynamically based on the current frame rate—the higher the frame rate, the deeper reflection recursion would be allowed.

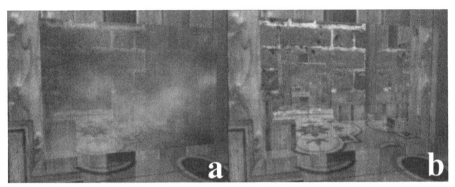

Figure 7.29 With the mirror specular set to 0.30, only two reflection levels are visible (a). With mirror specular set to 0.83, 13 levels of reflections are visible (b). (The minimal opaqueness factor in both cases was set to 0.90.)

Summary and Demo

I have described a robust solution for rendering planar multilevel reflections using several techniques. Their combination, which results in a rendering algorithm that is quite complex, was needed for both correctness and efficiency.

Almost all the techniques described were implemented in a sample application designed especially to test the most critical efficiency issues. You can switch multiple optimizations on and off interactively to see the difference in either the frame rate or amount of geometry culled. Note that, since the demo map is very simple, rendering is rarely geometry limited. Table 7.2 shows results from testing the demo using an NVIDIA GeForce 6600 graphic card and an AMD Athlon 2600+ processor, and Figure 7.30 shows the final results.

Table 7.2 Benchmarking Results

Optimizations	FPS	Culled mesh count
All disabled	30	1,665
Only frustum test enabled (*)	43	498
Only scissor test enabled	115	1,665
All enabled	149	498
All enabled except for mirror clipping (**)	166	498

*A small FPS increase is due to demo being mainly fill rate limited, so the scissor test gives a much bigger boost in speed; note, however, the big mesh count decrease with the frustum test enabled.

**Mirror clipping using an additional OpenGL clipping plane slowed down rendering slightly; disabling this feature causes rarely visible (in this specific demo) artifacts. All four remaining tests were done with mirror clipping enabled.

All tests were done with the maximum reflection level set to 10 and a minimal opaqueness of 0.90.

Figure 7.30 Screenshot from demo program.

References

Diefenbach, Paul, and Norman Badler, "Pipeline rendering: Interactive Refractions, Reflections, and Shadows." **ftp://ftp.cis.upenn.edu/pub/diefenba/displays.ps.Z**.

Kilgard, Mark J. (NVIDIA). "Improving Shadows and Reflections via the Stencil Buffer." **http://developer.nvidia.com/object/Stencil_Buffer_Tutorial.html**.

OpenGL Technical FAQ, 9 Transformations, 9.170, "How do I render a mirror?" **http://www.opengl.org/resources/faq/technical/transformations.htm**.

Shadows

Dave Astle

Look around you right now. Chances are, there are shadows all over the place. Because shadows are a common part of the world you see around you, shadows in your games will add a greater degree of realism. In addition, they serve a role in establishing spatial relationships between objects, further enhancing the illusion of 3D. Over the years, numerous techniques have been developed to create realistic-looking shadows in real time.

Creating a shadow for a sphere floating over a flat plane with a single light source is conceptually fairly easy; you can simply determine which region of the plane is blocked from the view of the light by the sphere. But what if the surface on which the shadow is being cast is not flat? What if, instead of a sphere or other simple geometric object, you have an irregularly shaped object that casts shadows upon portions of itself? What about multiple objects in the scene that can cast shadows on each other? What about multiple light sources? Then there is the issue of hard shadows versus soft shadows. Hard shadows are of (relatively) uniform darkness with a distinct edge. Soft shadows, on the other hand, have a soft edge and get gradually darker as you move toward the center. Hard shadows result from a single fairly focused light source, while soft shadows are the result of multiple light sources, area light sources, and/or ambient light. Both exist in nature, but soft shadows require more work (with most methods) than do hard shadows.

As you can see, modeling of shadows is fairly complex, which is why there are so many ways to do it. Most methods don't correctly address all the issues we've just mentioned, although a few cover the majority of them. There are, however, only a handful of methods that result in a realistic-looking shadow and that also can be rendered at interactive speeds; those are the techniques covered here.

Static Shadows

This approach avoids altogether the issue of having to calculate shadows in real time. Instead, the shadows are calculated in advance, possibly using highly realistic shadowing algorithms, and then added to the scene at run time, usually as a texture. The shadow may be as simple as a circular shape for a character or a rectangular shape for a car, or it may be a more complex shape that is projectively textured onto nonplanar geometry.

This class of methods tends to be the cheapest, and it is still used by many games, especially on platforms with limited processing power, such as cell phones. The shadows may not look very realistic, but in many cases they look good enough. Because using static shadows is really just a matter of manipulating your game data rather than doing anything programmatically, I won't cover the technique in further detail here.

Projective Shadows

Projective shadows provide a means to quickly cast shadows onto a plane, with very good-looking results. The technique does not require direct hardware support, and it is simple to implement, so it can be a viable solution in many situations. The idea behind the algorithm is to project the *occluder* (object casting the shadow) onto a plane from the perspective of the light. This has the effect of flattening the object, similar to the way objects are flattened onto your 2D screen from the perspective of the viewer. All you have to do is draw the flattened object in a dark color, and you have a shadow!

The Shadow-Projection Matrix

Now that you know the basic concept, let's look at the details of how to implement projective shadows. First of all, you'll need a matrix that performs the projection. The matrix will depend on the position of the light source and the plane onto which you're projecting. Rather than going through the complete matrix derivation, let's just look at the result:

$$
\begin{bmatrix}
dot - lightPos[0]^* \; plane.a & -lightPos[1]^* \; plane.a & -lightPos[2]^* \; plane.a & -lightPos[3]^* \; plane.a \\
-lightPos[0]^* \; plane.b & dot - lightPos[1]^* \; plane.b & -lightPos[2]^* \; plane.b & -lightPos[3]^* \; plane.b \\
-lightPos[0]^* \; plane.c & -lightPos[1]^* \; plane.c & dot - lightPos[2]^* \; plane.c & -lightPos[3]^* \; plane.c \\
-lightPos[0]^* \; plane.d & -lightPos[1]^* \; plane.d & -lightPos[2]^* \; plane.d & dot - lightPos[3]^* \; plane.d
\end{bmatrix}
$$

In this equation, `dot` is the dot `product` of `lightPos` and plane; `lightPos` is an array where elements 0, 1, and 2 correspond to the x, y, and z coordinates of the light's position, and element 3 is set to 0 or 1 depending on whether the light is directional or positional (respectively). Finally, `plane` is a structure in which a, b, c, and d come from the plane equation $Ax + By + Cz + D = 0$.

Once you've created the shadow-projection matrix, you just need to apply it to the vertices of the objects that you want to cast shadows, and the shadows will be drawn on the plane you specify. Unless you take additional steps, however, what gets drawn on the plane will look like a flattened version of the object and not like a shadow at all.

Fixing this problem is pretty easy. You just need to draw the shadow using black, which can be done by disabling lighting and textures and setting the current color to black before drawing the object. For better-looking results, you can alpha blend the shadow geometry with the surface on which it's being cast.

Handling Problems with the Depth Buffer

Another problem creeps up in that the shadow will be coplanar with the surface it is on. Although that is your intent, it creates a problem with the depth buffer. Because you can't represent depth values with infinite precision, the shadow won't always have depth values exactly equal to those of the surface. Sometimes they'll be closer, and other times they'll be farther away, and the end result is that the shadow can have holes in it. There are a few solutions to this, including using polygon offsets, but the solution I'll use here is to simply disable the depth test while drawing the shadow. Then you just have to be sure to draw the shadow before anything that might appear in front of it (otherwise, the shadow will appear in front of objects that it shouldn't).

Restricting the Shadow with the Stencil Buffer

Finally, if the surface on which you're drawing the shadow isn't infinite, you should restrict the shadow so that is not drawn outside this surface. As with reflections, this can be accomplished by using the stencil buffer. Using the stencil buffer allows you to defeat another problem that occurs when using blending: Unless the object casting a shadow is convex, there will be some pixels on the surface that have shadows drawn on them more than once. The blending will cause these spots to appear darker. For a nice even shadow, each pixel should be drawn exactly once. To do this, you just have to change the value in the stencil buffer whenever the stencil test passes as you're drawing the shadow.

The entire process can be summarized in the following steps:

1. Use the shadowed surface to set the stencil buffer, and limit the rendering of the shadow to this area only.
2. Create a shadow-projection matrix using the position of the light and plane equation, and multiply it by the modelview matrix.
3. Disable lighting and texture mapping, and set the current color to black.
4. Disable the depth test.
5. Enable blending.
6. Draw the occluder.

After you're done, be sure to set lighting, texture mapping, the depth test, and blending to their original states. One of the sample programs on the book's website shows this process in action, including the code corresponding to the preceding steps.

Handling Multiple Light Sources and Multiple Planar Surfaces

Thus far, you've assumed a single light source and a single planar surface. If you want more than one light source, you can just repeat the preceding process for each one of them. You can do the same for each surface, and even use this approach to create complex surfaces by repeating the process for each polygon, just as with reflections. Of course, the cost of doing this will soon become prohibitive. Overall, you will have to make one pass through your geometry per light per surface, which adds up quickly, so if your game requires shadows cast on nonplanar surfaces using multiple light sources, you should consider other techniques instead.

Problems with Projective Shadows

Projective shadows look good, but they aren't perfect. First of all, they don't easily allow concave objects to cast shadows on themselves, or objects to cast shadows on each other, unless you treat every polygon in your scene as a shadowed surface—which isn't practical at all. Second, they produce hard shadows. You can create soft shadows with projective shadows by moving the light source slightly as you make multiple passes (a process known as *jittering*) and blending the results, but the overhead from doing this can be significant. Third, because you're blending the shadow with the surface, any specular highlights on that surface in the shadowed area will still show up, which they shouldn't (how can there be a highlight in an area that's not illuminated by the light?). Despite their limitations, however, projective shadows work well in a wide variety of situations. As you can see from the sample program, they produce results that are quite satisfactory.

Shadow Volumes

Shadow volumes have been used in a number of recent games, including *Doom 3*. The advantage they offer is that they correctly shadow every surface in the scene, allowing objects to cast shadows on other objects and even to self-shadow. They also avoid the aliasing artifacts present in shadow maps, and they work well with omnidirectional lights.

The idea behind shadow volumes is that you cast lines from the light source through the edges of the objects in your world, which then define infinite volumes on the opposite sides of the objects, as illustrated in Figure 7.31. After all of your shadow volumes are defined, you just need to determine whether objects or portions of objects lie within the boundaries of one of them. That leaves you with two challenges: how to find the shadow volumes, and how to determine whether or not any given point is located within one.

Figure 7.31 A simple shadow volume.

Defining Shadow Volumes

Much of the cost involved with shadow volumes relates to determining what the volumes are. To do this, you need to find the *silhouette edge* of every object in the scene from the perspective of the light source. The silhouette edge is any edge where one adjacent polygon is front-facing and the other is back-facing. Although I won't go into implementation details, this essentially requires that you test every edge on every object in the scene to see if it qualifies. Once you have found all the silhouette edges, you take the vertices that define them and cast lines through them from the light source. You then use these lines to find points far beyond the silhouette edge, and use the four resulting points to define a quad. These quads collectively comprise enclosed shadow volumes. Usually, the volumes will be capped with additional geometry at both ends. The caps can be represented using the front- and back-facing geometry of the occluder, or by other means if you prefer.

Finding Shadowed Areas

To determine whether a point lies within a shadow volume, you conceptually cast a ray from the eye to the point and count each time you enter or leave a shadow volume. You can tell if you are entering a shadow volume if the quad you are intersecting is front-facing. If it is back-facing, you are leaving the shadow volume. All you need to do, then, is increment the count every time you intersect a front-facing shadow quad, and decrement the count when you intersect a back-facing quad. When the count is zero, you've exited as many shadow volumes as you've entered, so the object is not shadowed. Whenever the count is greater than zero, the object is shadowed.

The counting can be handled in hardware by using the stencil buffer (which is why the technique is often referred to as *stenciled shadow volumes*) by using the following steps:

1. Render the scene normally using ambient and emissive lighting.

2. Render only the shadow volumes. Because you don't actually want to see the shadow volumes as if they were objects in the scene, disable writes to the depth and color buffers, and write only to the stencil buffer. This time through, you're counting how many times a shadow volume is entered, so cull back-facing polygons and set the stencil buffer to increment every time the depth test passes.

3. Make a second pass with the shadow-volume geometry, similar to the second, but this time cull front-facing polygons and decrement the value of the stencil buffer when the depth test passes.

4. Render the scene again, this time using diffuse and specular lighting. Set the stencil test to pass only where the value in the stencil buffer is equal to 0. This will ensure that only nonshadowed areas are lit with diffuse and specular lighting.

Problems

The counting algorithm just described assumes that the viewer starts outside any shadow volumes. In a real game, it's likely that this assumption will often be invalid. A similar problem is introduced if any of the volumes are clipped by the near clipping plane.

Both of these problems are addressed by a modification to the shadow volume algorithm known as *z-fail* (as opposed to the z-pass approach just described). The modification is also known as *Carmack's Reverse* after id Software's John Carmack, who was one of the first people to discover and popularize the technique.

In the z-fail approach, steps 2 and 3 above are modified as follows, with the changes in bold:

2. ...cull **front**-facing polygons and set the stencil buffer to increment every time the depth test **fails**.

3. ...cull **back**-facing polygons, and decrement the value of the stencil buffer when the depth test **fails**.

It should now be evident why this method is referred to as z-fail.

This change takes care of the problems with near-plane clipping and the viewer being inside a shadow volume, but it introduces a different problem. If the far end of a shadow volume is clipped by the far plane, rendering artifacts can appear.

There are two solutions to this. One makes use of the vendor-specific extension NV_depth_clamp. This extension—which is currently only supported on NVIDIA hardware (GeForce 3 or better)—allows you to disable clipping at the near and far clipping planes. Instead, depth values that would have been clipped are clamped to the minimum and maximum (respectively) values of the depth range. This behavior can be enabled with glEnable(GL_DEPTH_CLAMP_NV) and disabled with glDisable(GL_DEPTH_CLAMP_NV).

extension

Extension name: NV_depth_clamp

Name string: GL_NV_depth_clamp

Tokens: GL_DEPTH_CLAMP_NV

The second and more robust solution is to extend the shadow volumes to infinity. This can be done by setting the rarely used w component of far ends of the shadow-volume geometry to zero (the same is done for the far end cap). Any OpenGL-compliant hardware will understand these values and render them correctly. However, this change alone will not prevent the far clipping plane from clipping the shadow volumes, since they may still intersect it; it has to be set to infinity as well. Doing this requires manipulation of the projection matrix. As you may recall, a perspective projection matrix is calculated as follows:

$$
\begin{bmatrix}
\dfrac{2n}{r-l} & 0 & \dfrac{r+l}{r-l} & 0 \\[2ex]
0 & \dfrac{2n}{t-b} & \dfrac{t+b}{t-b} & 0 \\[2ex]
0 & 0 & -\dfrac{f+n}{f-n} & -\dfrac{2fn}{f-n} \\[2ex]
0 & 0 & -1 & 0
\end{bmatrix}
$$

Here n and f are the near and far plane values, and l, r, t, and b are the left, right, top, and bottom. If you move the far plane infinitely far away, you just take the limit of this matrix as f goes to infinity, producing

$$
\begin{bmatrix}
\dfrac{2n}{r-l} & 0 & \dfrac{r+l}{r-l} & 0 \\[2ex]
0 & \dfrac{2n}{t-b} & \dfrac{t+b}{t-b} & 0 \\[2ex]
0 & 0 & -1 & -2n \\[2ex]
0 & 0 & -1 & 0
\end{bmatrix}
$$

Moving the far plane to infinity does incur a loss of depth-buffer precision, but the loss is small enough (on the order of 1 percent for most situations) to not be a concern.

Enhancements

extension

Extension name: ATI_separate_stencil
Name string: GL_ATI_separate_stencil
Functions: glStencilOpSeparateATI(), glStencilFuncSeparateATI()

Part of the expense associated with shadow volumes can be attributed to using multiple rendering passes. On newer hardware, the two shadow-volume passes (steps 2 and 3 described earlier) can be combined using two-sided stencil testing, which will reduce the amount of geometry sent to the graphics hardware. This feature—promoted to the core in OpenGL 2.0 and based on the EXT_stencil_two_side and ATI_separate_stencil extensions— allows you to specify the stencil function, operations, and stencil masking separately based on whether a polygon is front- or back-facing. This is done through three functions:

```
void glStencilFuncSeparate(GLenum face, GLenum func, GLint ref, GLuint mask);
void glStencilOpSeparate(GLenum face, GLenum fail, GLenum zfail, GLenum zpass);
void glStencilMaskSeparate(GLenum face, GLenum mask);
```

These functions are equivalent to glStencilFunc(), glStencilOp(), and glStencilMask(), other than the obvious addition of the face parameter, which can be GL_FRONT, GL_BACK, or GL_FRONT_AND_BACK.

In order to set up the stencil buffer to render both front- and back-facing shadow-volume geometry in a single pass using the z-fail approach, you'd use the following:

```
glDisable(GL_CULL_FACE); // no need to cull now
glStencilFuncSeparate(GL_FRONT_AND_BACK, GL_ALWAYS, 0, ~0);
glStencilOpSeparate(GL_BACK, GL_KEEP, GL_INCR_WRAP, GL_KEEP);
glStencilOpSeparate(GL_FRONT, GL_KEEP, GL_DECR_WRAP, GL_KEEP);
```

tip

Using the wrap variants of the stencil increment and decrement operations prevents stencil-buffer values from over- or under-flowing.

note

The EXT_stencil_two_side extension includes a different set of APIs from what was promoted to the core, and it's worth discussing if you're planning on supporting older hardware. Instead of using functions that explicitly set each face, it uses the idea of an *active stencil face*. The currently active stencil face is set by passing GL_FRONT or GL_BACK to glActiveStencilFaceEXT(). Subsequent calls to glStencilOp(), glStencilMask(), and glStencilFunc() affect only the active face. In order to use this, it must first be enabled using glEnable(GL_STENCIL_TEST_TWO_SIDE_EXT). When it's disabled, front and back faces are not handled separately.

Shadow Volume Disadvantages

Despite offering impressive visual results, shadow volumes have a number of noteworthy drawbacks. First, they consume a great deal of fill rate. Second, finding silhouette edges and generating the volumes can require a lot of processing power, though some of this work can be offloaded to the GPU. Since fill rate and CPU utilization are often bottlenecks in games, these factors should be carefully considered. Finally, they require that you have the occluding models' connectivity information available to find the silhouette edges, which is not a requirement of other techniques. However, because of their visual quality and the wide range of hardware support for them, shadow volumes are a viable solution for many games.

Shadow Mapping

One way to think about implementing shadows is to look at the scene from the light's perspective. Anything that the light can "see" should be lit, and everything it can't see should be in shadow. This approach is the basis for *shadow mapping*. The scene is rendered from the light's perspective, producing a depth buffer containing the details of how far each visible surface is from the light. The depth buffer is then used to create a texture, called a shadow map, depth map, or shadow buffer. The shadow map is then used when rendering the scene normally to determine whether or not a given fragment should be lit.

Generating the Shadow Map

The steps involved in creating the shadow map can be summarized as follows:

1. Set up the camera and modelview matrix to view the scene from the light's perspective.

2. Set up the projection matrix. To make the best use of the precision in the depth texture, the view frustum should fit the scene as tightly as possible.

3. Setup the viewport to match the size of the depth texture being used.

4. Disable all rendering states (texturing, lighting, etc.), disable color-buffer writes, and render the scene to the depth buffer.

5. Copy the depth buffer into a depth texture. This step can be optimized using the dynamic texturing methods described in Chapter 5.

This process only needs to be repeated when the light moves or an object in the scene moves. In a game, of course, this usually occurs every frame.

The shadow map itself is represented using the `GL_DEPTH_COMPONENT` internal format. When copying from the framebuffer to a texture using `glCopyTexImage()` or `glCopyTexSubImage()`, if the target texture is a depth texture, the operation will automatically use the depth buffer as the source, which is convenient.

Using the Shadow Map

Once you have the shadow map, you can use it to add shadows to your scene by doing the following:

1. Render the scene with only ambient lighting (and maybe a little diffuse).

2. Project the shadow map onto the scene using projective texturing.

3. Render the scene with full lighting and with the depth test set to `GL_LEQUAL`. At each fragment, test the distance of the current fragment from the light against the value in the shadow map. If it is larger, then something is between it in the light, so don't light it. If it is equal, then it is the closest fragment to the light, so it should be lit.

I'll now explain the second and third steps in detail.

Generating Texture Coordinates

When projecting the shadow map onto the scene, the goal is to produce texture coordinates that correspond to the x-, y-, and z-coordinates of the fragment in the light's clip space. This causes the s and t texture coordinates to index the depth texture in the appropriate spot, and the r texture coordinate to contain the distance from the light to the current fragment.

To produce these texture coordinates, the first step is to set up texture coordinate generation using GL_EYE_LINEAR mode. This will produce coordinates equivalent to the fragment's position in the camera's eye space. These coordinates then need to be translated to the light's clip space. This process, and the various coordinate spaces involved, is illustrated in Figure 7.32.

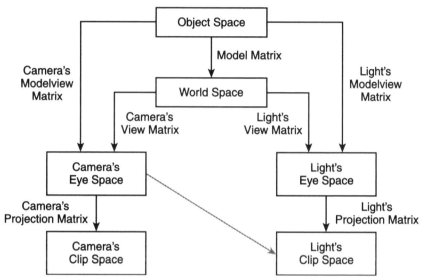

Figure 7.32 Shadow-mapping coordinate spaces. (Figure courtesy Paul Baker.)

The conversion you need to perform is shown by the diagonal arrow. As you can see, the first step is to convert back to world space, which can be done by applying the inverse of the view matrix (V_c^{-1}). You then apply the light's view matrix (V_1) followed by the light's projection matrix (P_1) to arrive in the light's clip space.

Because the resulting coordinates are in clip space, they will range from -1 to 1, but in order to use them as the s and t texture coordinates and to match the range in the depth buffer, they need to range from 0 to 1. This can be achieved by scaling and biasing the values by 0.5 using the following matrix B:

$$\begin{bmatrix} 0.5 & 0.0 & 0.0 & 0.5 \\ 0.0 & 0.5 & 0.0 & 0.5 \\ 0.0 & 0.0 & 0.5 & 0.5 \\ 0.0 & 0.0 & 0.0 & 1.0 \end{bmatrix}$$

So the texture to apply to the coordinates produced by texgen is:

$$B \times P_1 \times V_1 \times V_c^{-1}$$

This matrix can then be loaded onto the texture matrix stack. Alternatively, the texture matrix stack can be avoided altogether by loading the rows of the matrix as the eye planes used in texture-coordinate generation. The nice thing about this is that OpenGL automatically applies the inverse of the view matrix when these planes are specified. So as long as the camera view matrix is loaded into the modelview matrix when specifying the eye planes, you can skip calculating the inverse yourself.

Performing the Comparison

extension

Extension name: ARB_shadow

Name string: GL_ARB_shadow

Promoted to core: OpenGL 1.4

Tokens: GL_TEXTURE_COMPARE_MODE_ARB, GL_TEXTURE_COMPARE_MODE_ARB, GL_COMPARE_R_TO_TEXTURE_ARB

The final step in this technique is to determine whether a given fragment is shadowed or lit. This decision is based on two pieces of information: R, which is the distance to the light supplied by the r texture coordinate, and T, which is the value sampled from the shadow map at the current location. If R > T, then another fragment is closer to the light than the current fragment, so it is in shadow. Otherwise, the fragment is lit.

In the fixed-function pipeline, OpenGL will perform this comparison for you based on the texture compare mode texture parameter (which is only valid for depth textures). To perform this comparison, the following should be used when setting up the depth texture used as the shadow map:

```
glTexParameteri(GL_TEXTURE_2D, GL_TEXTURE_COMPARE_MODE,
                GL_COMPARE_R_TO_TEXTURE);
```

To disable this comparison, GL_NONE should be passed as the third parameter, in which case the depth-texture value will be directly supplied to the texture unit as the texture's color.

The comparison is performed according to the texture-comparison function, which can be set as follows:

```
glTexParameteri(GL_TEXTURE_2D, GL_TEXTURE_COMPARE_FUNC, value);
```

In this function, *value* can be any of the standard OpenGL comparison functions (e.g., GL_LESS, GL_ALWAYS). GL_LEQUAL is the default and what you'll normally use.

The result of this comparison, which I'll call D, is in the range [0, 1], with the exact value depending on the filtering mode used. For now, let's just assume nearest filtering, in which case D will be 1 if the comparison passes (e.g., with the default function, R is less than or equal to T), and 0 otherwise.

D is then provided as the "color" of the texture to the current texture unit. The way in which it is mapped to RGBA values depends on the depth-texture mode, which is set using:

```
glTexParameteri(GL_TEXTURE_2D, GL_DEPTH_TEXTURE_MODE, mode);
```

For *mode*, you can use either GL_INTENSITY (in which case the color is (D, D, D, D), GL_LUMINANCE (D, D, D, 1) or GL_ALPHA (0, 0, 0, D). You'll see why this is important in the next section.

To Light or Not to Light

At this point, you have a color value storing the results of the depth comparison. In addition, the framebuffer contains the unlit value at the current pixel, and the incoming color contains the fully lit values for the current pixel. If the comparison indicates that the current fragment is lit, the color buffer should be updated with the current color. Otherwise, the color buffer should be left as-is. In the fixed-function pipeline, there is no way to tell OpenGL to just discard the current fragment, so the most common way to get around this is to use the alpha test.

This is where the depth-texture mode comes into play. Both GL_INTENSITY and GL_ALPHA contain D in the alpha channel, so if you use one of those modes along with an appropriate texture environment (e.g., GL_MODULATE, though other combinations will work), you can set the alpha test to fail when the alpha value isn't 1. Thus, lit fragments pass, and unlit ones fail.

Various Issues

Although nearest sampling is most often used with shadow mapping, the other filtering modes can be used as well—though some hardware may revert to nearest sampling no matter what you choose. When using linear filtering or mipmapping with depth textures, instead of computing the weighted average of multiple samples, *percentage-closer filtering* will be used. Instead of averaging the depth values, the comparison is performed multiple times, and the resulting value represents the percentage of tests for which the comparison was successful. These values can be used to produce an effect similar to soft shadows along the shadow's edge.

A common artifact with shadow maps is self-shadowing, wherein the occluder shadows itself inappropriately due to floating-point precision issues. This is usually addressed by using polygon offset to slightly shift the depth values when generating the shadow map. An alternative is to cull front-facing polygons while generating the shadow map, though this requires that all occluders be composed of closed geometry.

Finally, a related extension, `ARB_shadow_ambient`, allows you to specify the texture value when the compare function fails. This is done by passing `GL_TEXTURE_COMPARE_FAIL_VALUE_ARB` and the value to `glTexParameter()`. This may allow you to render the scene geometry using a single pass. This extension is not widely supported, however, and in most cases, you'd be better off using a shader.

Shadow Mapping Using Shaders

This section has focused on the fixed-function pipeline implementation of shadow mapping, which is widely supported in hardware. This approach is viable for many situations, but more advanced techniques will require the use of shaders. Both `ARB_fragment_program` and the OpenGL Shading Language contain direct support for shadow mapping. If you're using a vertex shader, you'll have to take care of texture-coordinate generation yourself, but doing so is straightforward and generally more efficient than doing it in the fixed-function pipeline. The details of implementing shadow mapping using shaders are left as an exercise for the reader.

Shadow Mapping Advantages and Disadvantages

Shadow maps meet many of the requirements of realistic real-time shadows. They allow for self-shadowing and interobject shadows, and they work with nonplanar surfaces. They do not require preprocessing, and they benefit from hardware support.

However, shadow maps are not perfect. The biggest problem is that they tend to suffer from aliasing artifacts, producing a stair-stepping effect along the shadow's edge. This can be reduced by using high-resolution depth textures, at the cost of much greater memory usage, which isn't always practical. An alternative solution is to use *perspective shadow mapping*. This technique modifies the shadow mapping algorithm to perform the shadow-map generation and comparison in normalized device coordinates, which optimizes the depth-texture precision for areas close to the camera. This technique is described in a bonus article available on the book's website.

Finally, getting shadow mapping to work with omnidirectional lights is challenging, since depth textures aren't supported for cubemaps.

Despite these shortcomings, shadow maps are becoming increasingly common in modern games.

Other Methods

Due to space and time constraints, this section has focused on providing a survey of the primary techniques used for creating shadows in games. These methods can be improved in many ways, and even combined in hybrid approaches, to increase realism, applicability, and efficiency. Some of these improvements will be discussed in bonus articles available on the book's website.

References

Akenine-Möller, Tomas, and Eric Haines. *Real-time Rendering*, 2nd Ed. Natick, MA: A. K. Peters, 2002.

Baker, Paul. Shadow Mapping: Casting Curved Shadows on Curved Surfaces. **http://www.paulsprojects.net/tutorials/smt/smt.html**.

Everitt, Cass, and Mark Kilgard. Practical and Robust Stenciled Shadow Volumes for Hardware-Accelerated Rendering. **http://developer.nvidia.com**. March 2002.

McReynolds, Tom, and David Blythe. *Advanced Graphics Programming Using OpenGL*. San Francisco: Morgan-Kaufmann, 2005.

Summary

In this chapter, you learned about a number of ways to add eye candy and realism to your game. You learned how to use billboarding to approximately represent complex 3D objects at a fraction of the cost. You learned how particle systems can be used to create a wide variety of effects, and how to improve them using scripting and taking advantage of the hardware. You learned about creating a glow effect using image-space techniques. You learned how to create fast planar reflections and refractions, and how to robustly model multilevel reflections. Finally, you saw several alternatives to adding real-time shadows to your game.

You don't need to use all these techniques in your games, and you definitely don't want to overdo it by throwing every possible special effect in. That said, judicious use of these and other special effects can greatly add to the realism and make the game much more interesting.

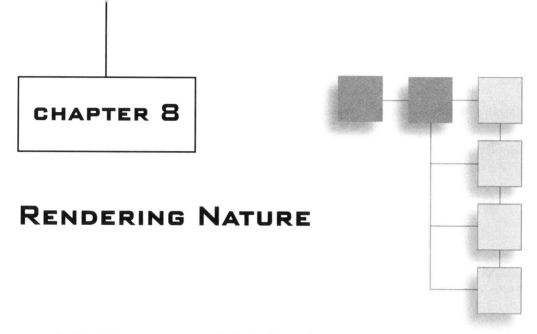

CHAPTER 8

RENDERING NATURE

The first 3D games were mostly limited to indoor environments, because modeling outdoor environments realistically was too complex to be practical. As hardware has evolved, many games have taken advantage of the variety offered by outdoor settings. The next three chapters are dedicated to techniques that you will find useful in modeling realistic outdoor scenes in real time. This chapter will focus on a number of techniques for modeling various aspects of nature. Skies and terrain are large enough topics to earn chapters of their own.

Specifically, in this chapter you'll learn about:

- Rendering water
- Plants and vegetation
- Procedural foliage generation
- Rendering fur

Rendering Water

Angus Dorbie

Water represents a challenge for typical real-time rendering methods because the optical cues our visual system interprets as a wet surface are not readily created in typical shading systems. To shade the surface of water (i.e., the air-water interface) requires an understanding of light interaction at that surface, and with that simple understanding, the game programmer can quickly implement a shading algorithm that can produce impressive realism.

There are two aspects to representing water in a 3D environment; one is the shape and motion of the water, and the other is the visual appearance of the water surface. In this section I'll focus on the shading of the water surface, but I want to emphasize that water's appearance is heavily influenced by the geometry of its surface, so we cannot entirely ignore shape and motion when demonstrating a shading algorithm.

What Makes Water Look Like Water?

When light passes through a material boundary like the air-water interface, it changes speed, and because light is a wave, the change in speed causes a change in the angle of the light. This effect is known as *refraction*. This change in speed and angle varies according to the frequency of the light, but it is characterized by the refractive index of the materials involved for each light frequency. This can be determined using Snell's law and the refractive index (n) for the materials involved, as illustrated in Figure 8.1.

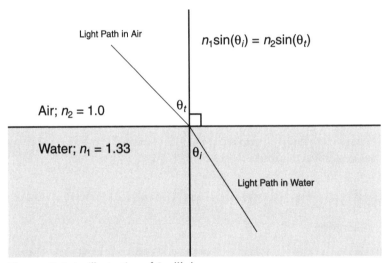

Light Path in Air

$$n_1 \sin(\theta_i) = n_2 \sin(\theta_t)$$

Air; $n_2 = 1.0$

θ_t

Water; $n_1 = 1.33$

θ_i

Light Path in Water

Figure 8.1 An illustration of Snell's law.

As shown, the refractive index for water is about 1.333 (depending on secondary factors like salinity and temperature). Differences in the refractive index of water at different frequencies that might result in chromatic aberration effects in caustics can be ignored since these are not significant for our purposes and are not the focus of our interest in this section. The refractive index of air depends on pressure and frequency but is pretty close to 1.0, and that will do as an approximation. Using the equation in Figure 8.1 you can plot the relationship of the angles, as the graph in Figure 8.2 illustrates.

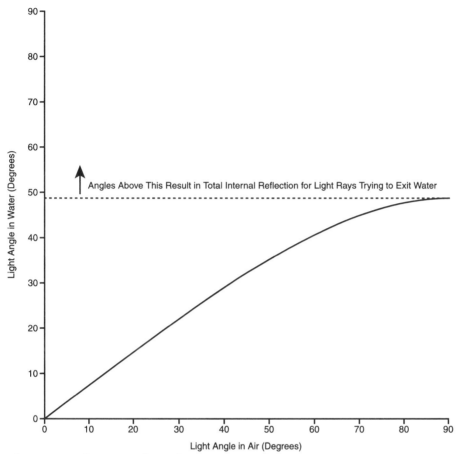

Figure 8.2 Refraction angles at the air-water interface.

This relationship is significant even when not modeling the geometric effect of refraction. When viewing a surface from the air, the light the viewer sees from beneath the water comes from the refracted viewing vector angle. To compute the light contribution from this vector, you must know the angle at which the light was incident beneath the water surface, not merely the viewing angle with the surface.

As you can see from the graph, beyond a certain angle there is no exit solution for light leaving the water. This produces an effect called *total internal reflection* where no light exits the water beyond this angle. This *critical angle* for a water-air boundary is 48.6 degrees. The total internal reflection effect is what makes water appear like a mirrored surface from beneath at a broad range of viewing angles. (It is also the principle that fiber-optic cables exploit to transmit light efficiently through a series of internal reflections in a flexible cable.)

The light from a liquid water surface is dominated by two contributions: light reflected from the surface of the water, and light transmitted (refracted) from beneath the water surface to the viewer, as shown in Figure 8.3.

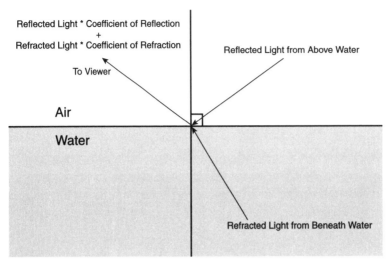

Figure 8.3 Refracted and reflected light.

The coefficients for the contributions from each of these terms are described by Fresnel's equations, which use the refractive index of the materials to determine the amount of light reflected and refracted at the surface. The Fresnel effect explains that the amount of light refracted at a surface and the amount of light reflected varies with the angle of incidence of the light. When rendering water, you know the angle of reflected light reaching the viewer because it equals the viewing angle incidence with the surface normal. You can also use Snell's equations to calculate the refracted angle as plotted in the Figure 8.2 graph. The equations themselves are slightly more complex than our purposes require because inherently they describe the different behaviors of polarized light, which reflects and refracts differently at the surface. Since the human eye cannot see the polarization of light, we are not interested in this effect, but we must at least consider it while developing a shading algorithm. Ultimately, you will average the coefficients and assume that the light is unpolarized. It is worth noting that you could accurately simulate viewing water with and without polarized sunglasses simply by treating the parallel and orthogonal polarized orientations independently.

Fresnel's Equations

The equations used to calculate the coefficients for reflection and refraction contributions are presented here. Note that depending on which media you're going from and to, you must switch incident and refracted angles and the refraction indices. The equations are presented here in multiple forms that may be useful when using vector dot products to calculate the coefficients in a shader:

$$R_s = \left(\frac{\sin(\theta_i - \theta_t)}{\sin(\theta_i + \theta_t)}\right)^2 = \left(\frac{n1\ \cos(\theta_i) - n2\ \cos(\theta_t)}{n1\ \cos(\theta_i) + n2\ \cos(\theta_t)}\right)^2$$

$$R_p = \left(\frac{\tan(\theta_i - \theta_t)}{\tan(\theta_i + \theta_t)}\right)^2 = \left(\frac{n2\ \cos(\theta_i) - n1\ \cos(\theta_t)}{n2\ \cos(\theta_i) + n1\ \cos(\theta_t)}\right)^2$$

These equations represent the two polarized orientations for the reflected light from a surface using the refractive index and the angles of the incident and the transmitted light. The transmission coefficients are then simply calculated as the remaining light by subtracting the refracted coefficients from 1.0:

$$T_s = 1 - R_s$$
$$T_p = 1 - R_p$$

As already stated, you can ignore polarization by simply averaging the coefficients for the two polarized orientations:

$$R = (R_s + R_p)/2$$
$$T = 1 - R$$

You can plot the refraction and reflection coefficients against the viewing angle to help visualize the results these equations produce. It is very important to realize that the two terms you are interested in are reflected light from above the surface and transmitted (refracted) light from below the surface. The transmitted (refracted) light from above the surface and the reflected light from below the surface do not reach the viewer directly and are ignored in your rendering, although they may be considered, as illumination of underwater surfaces in a very sophisticated system. The graph in Figure 8.4 shows the relationship between the angle of underwater light incident to the water boundary and the coefficient of reflection, which determines how much of that light is reflected away from the viewer. Subtracting this value from 1.0 leaves you with the refraction coefficient. Again you see the critical angle beyond which all light is reflected beneath the surface.

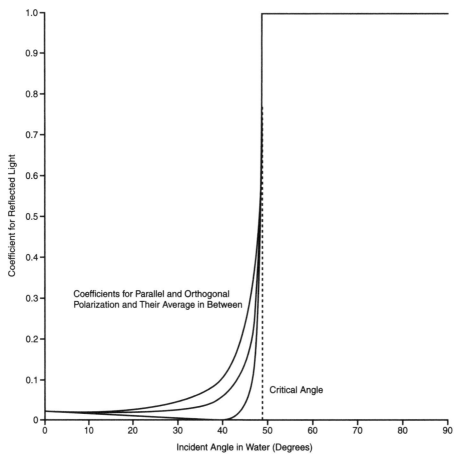

Figure 8.4 Fresnel coefficients for reflected underwater light.

Although this plot is informative, it is plotted against the angle of light incidence under the water, not the angle of viewing incidence above. For the purposes of viewing water from above the surface, you must plot these coefficients against the angle of viewing incidence. It turns out that if you plot these values against the refracted angle of viewing incidence, they match the reflection coefficients exactly for reflected light above the surface. The results are plotted on the graph in Figure 8.5.

You can see that the critical angle does not appear on this graph since the viewer is in the less dense medium and the rays always have a refraction solution into the water. In fact, the critical angle for underwater light corresponds to the 90-degree point on this new graph for angles above the surface.

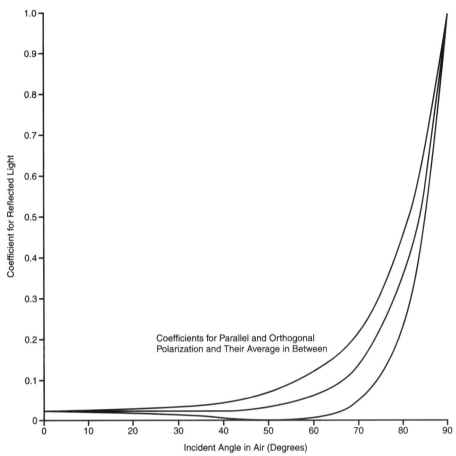

Figure 8.5 Fresnel coefficients for reflected light by viewing angle above water.

Plotting the unpolarized reflection coefficients for reflected and refracted angles against the incident viewing angle gives you the graph in Figure 8.6. It should be noted that this assumes that incident light is unpolarized and ignores the polarization of the reflected and refracted light.

For most water surfaces, the Fresnel effect alone is by far the dominant shading effect, especially when the body of water has no distinct features beneath the surface to be refracted, as would be the case with a muddy river or over the deep ocean, where the refracted term isn't greatly affected by the geometric distortion of the refraction effect. The geometric displacement of the refracted term can be a time-consuming graphics effect, and if it is not deemed significant (even when underwater detail is visible), it may be better to implement the simpler, nonrefracted effect.

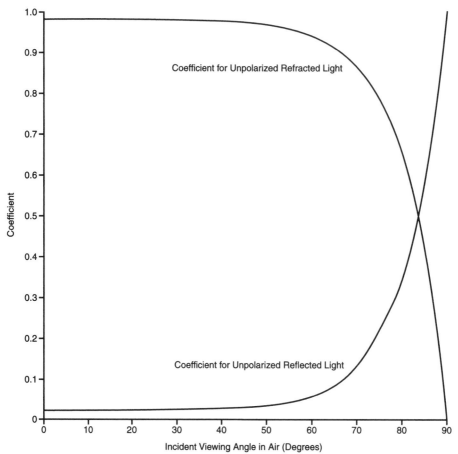

Figure 8.6 Fresnel coefficients for reflected and refracted light towards viewer.

There are many ways to render water now that you know what is required. The important concept to grasp here is that you have two terms —the reflection and the refraction terms—and two coefficients to modulate these terms. These values are easily calculated using the refractive index of water and the equations presented. You may use constant colors to represent the refraction and reflection values, or for increased realism, render accurate reflections and refractions using the methods presented in other chapters of this book and modulate those colors by the Fresnel coefficients to produce realistic-looking water.

Implementation and Results

Using the formulas presented, you can produce code using simple trigonometric operations to compute the coefficients used to modulate refraction and refraction terms. You can place similar algorithms in a vertex shader or fragment shader. Alternatively, you can use a texture lookup table (LUT) for use in a fragment shader to modulate contributions based on the vector dot products of the angles of incidence and refraction. With the latest hardware, you could even use a LUT in a vertex shader to generate the coefficients, although it may be some time before that is an efficient option.

Here is an example of the C++ code that the demo uses to calculate the Fresnel coefficients and apply the results to the per-vertex color attributes on a mesh representing the water surface. Note that for other materials, such as glass, you only need to alter the refraction index of 1.333 wherever it appears in this code to that of the desired material.

```
// calculate the incidence and refraction angles
incident_angle = acosf(view_vec.DotProduct(normal_vec));
refract_angle = asinf(sinf(incident_angle)/1.333f);

// calculate the Fresnel coefficients for both polarization orientations
coef_Rs = powf( (sinf(incident_angle-refract_angle) /
sinf(incident_angle+refract_angle)), 2.0f);
coef_Rp = powf( (1.333f*cosf(incident_angle) - cosf(refract_angle) ) /
              (1.333f*cosf(incident_angle) + cosf(refract_angle) ), 2.0f);

// apply the average of the polarization coefficients to the alpha channel
vertex_color[alpha] = (coef_Rs + coef_Rp) *0.5f;
```

As you can see, only the per-vertex alpha of the water mesh is assigned the reflection coefficient. The mesh can then be textured with a cubemap, or it can just use a simple vertex sky color to mix this color with the underwater surface already on the screen. Because the refraction coefficient is 1.0 minus the reflection coefficient, a common fragment-blending operation is sufficient to correctly combine reflection and refraction terms if the underwater image is already in the destination color buffer. The water surface is transparent and may self-occlude in some views with the usual z-buffer transparency issues. You can avoid this by first drawing the water surface to the depth buffer only, then drawing it to the color buffer so that depth fragments are occluded even when transparent. The demo does this using a simple color mask. The final rendering code therefore looks something like this:

```
glColorMask(GL_FALSE, GL_FALSE, GL_FALSE, GL_FALSE);

glDrawElements(...);

glColorMask(GL_TRUE, GL_TRUE, GL_TRUE, GL_TRUE);
glBlendFunc(GL_SRC_ALPHA, GL_ONE_MINUS_SRC_ALPHA);
glEnable(GL_BLEND);
```

```
glDrawElements(...);
```

```
glDisable(GL_BLEND);
```

As you can see in Figure 8.7, the results produced using a simple sky color combined with the water color are quite compelling for such a rudimentary per-vertex calculation and alpha-blending technique.

Figure 8.7 Screenshot from a simple approach using per-vertex water and sky colors.

Reflected and Refracted Vector Shading

Simply rendering the coefficient modulating a constant sky color is one approach, but for better results, you can use a reflection rendering to shade the reflected water surface vector. So instead of merely modulating a constant color, the coefficient modulates the color of the reflection, from either a rendered image, a cubemap, or several rendered images that form a cubemap. Supplying the color values from a reflection map and supplying the Fresnel coefficient of reflection in the alpha value will get you the desired realistic water reflection results. This is simple using a vertex or fragment shader. Even without shaders you could write the reflection coefficient to the destination alpha buffer using the z-buffer fill pass (you already fill z to avoid self-occlusion problems with transparency for large waves) and use this to weight the reflection and destination color contribution in a subsequent reflection-map pass. This should allow a very simple combination of the two algorithms without modification, albeit with the requirement that the framebuffer supports destination alpha. Obviously, you have several choices when modulating the reflection coefficient with the reflection color calculation, and the choice you make will probably depend on the range of hardware you are required to support.

For the refraction vector, you might assume that simply coloring using the color of the underwater surface is sufficient, and that would be an acceptable solution for some scenarios where the water is absolutely clear, but water is rarely clear. Some recent games achieve compelling water rendering by combining the realistic reflection of the environment with convincing colored attenuation of the underwater refraction vector. In simple terms you can think of this as an underwater fogging effect, using the color of the water as the fog color. If you implement a sufficiently general system you can support water with varying color and turbidity. The way to support underwater attenuation is therefore to calculate the distance the refraction ray has traveled through the water and fog it accordingly. This will depend heavily on the angle of the ray and the depth of the water. The choice of whether to use simple linear fog, the more complex exponential fog, or something even more complex that includes the participation of light through the medium is really up to you. Because this kind of fog is not based on distance from the eye—rather, it is based on distance through the water, where the water is approximately a horizontal plane—you need some means of specifying fog at each location on the submerged surface. There are ways to do this, such as secondary color or multiple passes. In this case, an ideal way to implement this feature is to use the fog coordinate extension (EXT_fog_coordinate). The mathematics to approximate the correct underwater distance use the assumption that the water surface is approximately flat for the purposes of fog calculation and does not account for the refraction vector, which would affect the results slightly. It involves simply dividing the depth of each vertex underwater by the cosine of the angle of the viewing vector for that vertex (or the dot product of view and up vectors). Here is the pseudocode showing the required underwater distance calculation for underwater vertices:

```
vertex_fog_distance = vertex_depth/normalized_view_vector.DotProduct(up_vector);
```

The results (shown in Figure 8.8) are really best appreciated in a dynamic situation, since a single screenshot does not show the dynamic subtlety of accurate underwater attenuation calculations.

Figure 8.8 Adding a fogging effect.

An alternative to the fog coordinate extension is the use of vertex-based alpha or color and either multi-pass rendering or texture combiners to produce the desired results. You could even combine depth-based attenuation with range-based fog as a simple way to produce convincing underwater fog without the need to resort to per-vertex calculations each frame, since depth and range do not vary for static geometry. This can be useful because the individual parameters may be tweaked to simulate increasing turbidity with increasing depth in the water. The results of this type of fog calculation are shown in Figure 8.9.

Figure 8.9 Depth-based attenuation and range-based fog.

Clipping and Submerging

Because the solution implemented here renders the underwater scene fogged correctly and then renders the water surface with appropriate Fresnel coefficient modulation, clipping with the water surface happens accurately and naturally when the clip plane intersects the water surface. No adjustment of the algorithm is required unless you decide to submerge the eye, in which case you would simply subtract the eye depth from the vertex depth in the fog calculation (taking the absolute value of the result). The results of the near clip plane intersecting the water surface are shown in Figure 8.10. The appearance is physically accurate for a scenario like a diving mask submerging beneath the waves. Note that when refraction image perturbation is added, the view through the water surface would be correctly refracted and the view beneath the surface would not be refracted, which is just as it should be.

Polarization

As mentioned earlier, this approach to rendering water can trivially support the simulation of the polarization of light at the surface because it intrinsically calculates separate coefficients. You are therefore able to simulate a polarization filter of any orientation by combining these independent coefficients in different ways. In a game, this could be useful to realistically support polarized sunglasses a player might wear. The demo simulates this by replacing

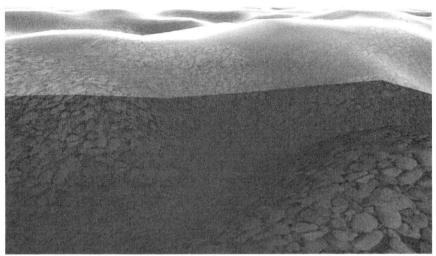

Figure 8.10 Water rendered from a submerged perspective.

```
vertex_color[alpha] = (coef_Rs + coef_Rp) *0.5f;
```

with

```
vertex_color[alpha] = coef_Rp;
```

This simulates a horizontal polarization filter that would be typical of polarized sunglasses. Although technically the brightness of everything drawn in the scene should subsequently be multiplied by 0.5, that would look too dark. So some adaptation is assumed here and the full brightness term remains. An HDR rendering algorithm and multiplying the scene brightness by 0.5 before the final transfer function would be the best way to support this effect correctly, but the vertex colors in the demo used here simply clamp to 1.0. This approach assumes that the water surface is horizontal, which needs to be taken into consideration if rendering nonhorizontal surfaces. It is also an approximation in the case of a surface perturbed by waves. A split-screen comparison with and without polarized filtering is presented in Figure 8.11.

Hardware Acceleration of Coefficient Calculation

Moving the calculation of coefficients to the GPU for hardware acceleration should be an important goal for anyone interested in improving performance on modern hardware. In this case, after querying for your shader extension of choice, you should be able to offload the calculation of coefficients to the graphics hardware, using the techniques explained in earlier chapters on shaders. The relevant portion of an appropriate vertex shader written in the OpenGL Shading Language is presented here. The output value is a varying float that must be read by the matching fragment shader. Naturally, you need to do a few other

Figure 8.11 Polarized filtering is enabled on the left and off on the right.

things in a shader, like compute and pass the screen vertex position and then do something interesting with the coefficient in the fragment shader, but this shows the use of the eye-space vertex as the view vector and the transformed normal. You'll notice that the GLSL code is quite similar to the C code presented earlier.

```
varying float r_coefficient
...
vec3 view_vec = vec3(gl_ModelViewMatrix * gl_Vertex);
view_vec = normalize(view_vec);
vec3 water_normal = normalize(gl_NormalMatrix * gl_Normal);

float incident_angle = acos(dot(view_vec, water_normal));
float refract_angle = asin(sin(incident_angle)/1.333);

float Rs = pow(sin(incident_angle-refract_angle) /
              sin( incident_angle+refract_angle)), 2.0);
float Rp = pow( (1.333*cos(incident_angle) - cos(refract_angle) ) /
              (1.333*cos(incident_angle) + cos(refract_angle) ), 2.0);

r_coefficient =  (Rs + Rp) *0.5;
```

One approach to writing an equivalent fragment shader is to build a lookup table in a texture. One advantage of such a LUT is that only a single angle of incidence is needed to directly derive all the coefficients with a texture fetch without the need to calculate the refraction vector. If the LUT is held as a dot product of the viewing vector and surface normal, then a simple dot product and texture fetch would be all the math required for a complete implementation. Simply incrementing through your LUT with a value from 0.0 to 1.0 and taking the inverse cosine before feeding the angles through the equations already presented would be sufficient to produce this LUT for all positive angles of incidence.

Plants and Vegetation

Vladimir Repcak

Every outdoor engine must handle rendering of vegetation, mainly trees and grass. There are several algorithms describing the creation of trees mathematically with fantastic results (see the following section, "Procedural Foliage," for an example). However, their biggest problem is that such trees often have an enormous number of triangles. One nice tree (with polygonal leaves) could have 10,000 triangles or more. Obviously if you need to create a dense forest, this is not an option, because with only 100 trees in the view frustum you already have 1,000,000 polygons. It's going to take a few years before cards that can handle such enormous polygon counts become mainstream (and more importantly, they have to become a minimum requirement for games to run).

Even when cards can handle polygon counts this high, there's going to be a performance problem with animation of leaves. If one leaf has at least four triangles, that's about 2,500 individual leaves that need to be translated and rotated per tree. That's a lot of calculations (whether for CPU or GPU).

Therefore you must cheat. You can leave the tree trunk polygonal, because it usually takes only about 500 to 800 triangles to get a decent-looking tree, with several branches, that looks good even from short distances.

The biggest savings is getting rid of rendering single leaves and instead rendering groups of leaves with only two triangles. How are you going to achieve that? You simply create a transparent texture that contains many leaves. You map this texture to a simple quad and put that quad over all the branches of a tree. In my experience, good-looking tree foliage can be made with only 50 quads—that's just 100 triangles! Compare that to about 10,000 triangles in the previous case, in which all leaves were polygonal, and the savings are obvious. The results are a bit less beautiful than in the case of polygonal leaves. Still, if done right, it can look great. Remember MadOnion's 3dMark 2001 Nature Demo? That was the first popular entertainment/benchmarking software to use this technique extensively. Although the Nature demo required the graphics card to support pixel shaders (for beautiful lighting effects), the technique can be used on any graphics card starting with a pretty old NVIDIA TNT chipset.

Creation of a Tree

So how are you actually going to create a tree? Using any modeling software, you'll create a polygonal trunk first. Finding a correct texture for a trunk is easy; there are tons of wood textures all over the Web.

It's a bit harder to get the leaf texture that will be mapped over each quad. This has to be created from scratch. You'll need several single reference leaves, which can be found with a quick Web search.

Once you have the reference leaves, you can use any painting software to create a 128×256 (W×H) texture. The texture could be of any resolution, but this resolution usually works well even when viewed up close. Just bear in mind that to avoid artifacts from a stretched texture, the leaves quad should be of the same aspect ratio (i.e. twice as tall as it is wide). Rather than arranging the leaves to fully occupy the texture along all edges, I recommend creating a specific shape that is a bit similar to a single leaf. Otherwise it will look very unnatural, since you can easily spot the rectangular shape.

When saving the final texture, don't use a lossy format. You need the texture to be transparent at all texels where there are no leaves (i.e. the background of the texture). The Targa format works well for this, and it is what's used in the demo.

Now that you have the leaf texture, you can start creating the quads. Create a quad that is twice as tall as it is wide and copy it 49 times all over the tree. Place it on every branch and try to create a circle shape when viewed from front view. It is important that the quads are scattered evenly over the tree along the z-axis. Since they will be billboarded at run time, rotating around the tree would look wrong if all the quads had same z-coordinate. Thus they'll be in front of each other (as far as shape and orientation of branches allow). You'll have to make a few attempts at it before you're happy with the placement of quads, but the end result is well worth it.

Performance Optimizations

The most basic requirement for the scene to be rendered effectively is to render only those trees that are in the view frustum. I'll leave the choice of visibility algorithm to you (see Chapter 12, "Scene Management," for a discussion of some of the possibilities).

The way you approach performance optimization depends on the contents of the scene in your application. Can you see the trees far off in the distance over a high hill? Render them as billboards —that is, as only two triangles. Animation of single leaves isn't visible from this distance anyway, so just keep several different static versions of the billboarded tree in a memory and, depending on the distance from the viewer, choose the most appropriate version to render.

At some distance you'll have to switch to rendering of the full tree with leaf animation or it will be apparent that you're cheating. Starting from this distance and moving closer to the viewer, you can apply several methods to make rendering faster. The first method is to use only lower-resolution textures for more distant trees. After all, with a tree that is 100 pixels high on screen, you can't tell whether it uses a 128×256 texture or 32×64 texture. This should save some texture memory bandwidth. Again find the distance at which it is apparent that the resolution is unsatisfactory. Repeat this three times for textures of dimensions 128×256, 64×128, and 32×64. A texture smaller than 32×64 shouldn't be necessary unless you are severely texture memory bandwidth-limited or are trying to support very old hardware (like TNT-class cards).

If you have enough art resources, get the trees in different levels of detail (LOD). If the tree is in the distance, you can't tell whether it has 100 quads or only 50 quads or even fewer (depending on the distance from viewer). Just change the meshes depending on the distance from viewer and how many different LODs you have.

Animation of leaves is another important feature that needs optimization. You have two choices: either do it on the CPU or do it on the GPU. The easier choice is obviously the CPU. You compute the rotation matrix for each quad on the CPU and render each quad separately. However, rendering each leaf separately (only two triangles per rendering call) is horribly inefficient. Unfortunately, you have no other choice, since each quad has a different position inside the tree and each one is being rotated differently. Inevitably, performance is CPU-limited because with 100 trees of 50 quads each, you are making 5,000 rendering calls resulting in only 10,000 triangles.

Therefore it's best to do the animation on the GPU, because it's not doing anything meaningful while you're sending it two triangles 5,000 times. Ideally, you'd render all 50 quads with a single rendering call. This would mean giving the card complete data regarding the rotation status and a translation matrix for each quad; the card would then calculate all respective rotation and translation matrices for the whole tree. I'll leave programming such a shader as an exercise for you.

Visual Enhancements

There are many things that can be done to make the trees look better. First and foremost, you should have several different leaf textures to achieve more variation.

Even a single additional leaf texture can make a tree look much better. Trees with four unique leaf textures are usually beautiful. This can consume quite a lot of art resources, since creating four different leaf textures and matching them together correctly (whether from a color or shape standpoint) is a time-consuming task. However, the final results are definitely worth it.

You can create different trees (even with same texture) that will add to scene realism because they reduce your repeat count. Just creating two more trees with different size and quad placement will look much better!

Another enhancement lies in variation of quad size. In the Nature demo in 3dmark 2001, the trees had leaf quads of different sizes all over. Just don't make the quads very small or they won't match well with the rest of the tree. Variations on the order of 30 to 40 percent are usually enough to make the tree look more realistic. If you put a different texture on smaller quads, it will be even better, because otherwise it's possible to see that those smaller quads are just a version of other bigger quads. Obviously, this puts greater burden on your art resources. But even without specific textures for the smaller quads, this enhancement alone is worth the trouble and adds a lot to final realism.

Probably the biggest visual enhancement is raising the number of quads. Obviously, if you do this, you have to make the quads smaller, or the tree will be very dense and look incorrect. It's also very probable that your current leaf texture will have to be changed ; otherwise, the leaves will be very small. Your eyes are very good at telling you that something isn't right and that it's time to update your leaf texture. Generally, the more quads there are, the better the results (and the longer it takes to place these quads correctly on a tree mesh). As always, you must decide on your minimum target hardware and performance objectives. Some applications (e.g., screensavers) can afford to have low a frame rate (less than 30 fps) because the camera is slower. Even games with a third-person camera (e.g., RPGs where camera is mostly static during combat scenes) are playable at lower frame rates. However, if you're making a game with a first-person camera, 30 frames will be very unpleasant when making fast turns.

You can make a huge visual change if you create an additional texture to be blended with the original leaf texture using multitexturing. This texture contains several transitions between different colors typical for leaves (see the file Transitions.jpg in the data subdirectory of the included demo). It's enough to have 16 different color transitions (4×4). You create additional texture coordinates for each quad and, during tree rendering, just enable this texture. You could create this additional set of texture coordinates manually inside your modeling software. However, random coordinates give great results since the purpose of this additional texture is to create the illusion that you have a colorful tree with many different textures when in fact you have only one leaf texture. Of course, the coordinates are not totally random; only the position of the colored rectangle is calculated randomly. Since you have 16 different colored rectangles inside this texture, there are only 16 different combinations of the texture coordinates.

Summary

Creating realistic trees is mostly an artistic problem, because you have to create nice leaf textures and make them match as part of the tree. Correct placement of the quads has a direct effect on final realism.

However, if your scene contains hundreds of trees with animated leaves, rendering it at interactive frame rates is also a programming challenge. This section has discussed several key aspects of rendering realistic trees, including optimizations. The implementation details of the demo were excluded for clarity reasons, but an abundance of comments is included with the source code, so it should be self-explanatory.

Procedural Foliage

Baldur Karlsson

As games have become more complex and more graphically intensive, the amount of data in the form of models and textures has increased very rapidly. Not only does this mean large storage requirements for games, but also it means more artists have to work longer to create the game art. One solution to this is to generate data on-the-fly. This would mean there would be no data read from disk; there would simply be an algorithm that describes how to generate all the model data.

Although this approach won't work for many models, it does for those that follow predictable shapes and patterns. This includes simple geometric shapes such as cubes, but also more complex things such as trees and plants. This section will show you how to generate trees in code.

Tree Generation

Trees can be generated because they follow simple patterns. To see these patterns, take a look at the tree shown in Figure 8.12. Note that the trunk splits into branches, the branches split into other smaller branches, then again into smaller branches, all the way down to twigs. This sort of self-similar pattern is called a fractal and is very useful in generating trees.

To see how this fractal works, grab a piece of paper and a pen. The first step is just to draw a vertical line. Then draw two lines slightly smaller, sticking out in a V shape above the first vertical line. Now draw four lines— slightly smaller again, each in two Vs from the last two lines. Finally, draw another eight from the last four lines in the same pattern. You should see something like Figure 8.13.

It's clear that, although not frighteningly realistic, the basic structure of a tree is there. Further refinement of the algorithm to include randomness, a three-dimensional shape, and more intricate parameters will produce a much more accurate tree representation. Fractals can also be used in other procedurally generated content, fractal-based terrain being quite common.

In addition to showing you the final tree algorithm, I'll step you through the creation process that I followed because that will make it a lot easier to extend the function shown here. You should follow the same process (although I encourage you to try things and experiment) to see how the algorithm grows.

Figure 8.12 A photograph of a typical tree.

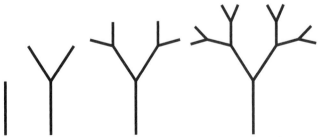

Figure 8.13 Line drawing of a tree representing fractal generation.

The Algorithm

The general idea is that we start with the simple fractal described above and refine it further and further. There is no specific way or order to add things—the best idea is to keep referring to photographs of different types of trees and see how they vary from your generated images. You may find that your mental image of a tree doesn't always match reality. Bear in mind that a lot is determined by the textures—the shapes of trees vary less than you might think.

The first step is to write the code that generates the fractal that serves as the core of the tree-generation process. You'll start with an abstract 2D tree shape and refine it from there. It will take a number of parameters to control the fractal.

Once you have the basic fractal and a set of parameters defined, the algorithm simply becomes a matter of tweaking the fractal and parameters until you get the results you want. I'd recommend modifying only a single parameter at a time so you can get a feel for how each one affects the tree-generation process.

I've provided a demo on the book's website to get you started, and the remainder of this section will use it as an example. It uses a recursive function to implement the fractal, with several constant parameters that can be modified until you get the results you want.

In order to efficiently represent the tree in a vertex array, I keep track of the current model-view matrix and perform transformations myself. So although the model is generated hierarchically, all coordinates are defined in the same local space.

For storing the data as I'm generating it, I use a Branch structure, which stores the parameters and has pointers to the child branches. I then also store the bare geometry in a line structure, holding just the vertices. This is then used later when I make a second pass through to generate the geometry.

Let's take a look at the parameters I used and then the code that implements the fractal.

Parameters

The parameters at this stage are as follows: maximum level, angle, angle random factor, branch length, and branch length modifier. The point of these parameters is just to allow you to change the shape and layout of the tree, and they don't have to be complex to do so. Having lots of parameters gives you more flexibility over the type of tree generated.

The *maximum level* parameter is simply the maximum recursion depth. You might want to add a more complex condition, such as polygon counts or processing time, but for most code it is sufficient to simply check how many levels of recursion there have been. I've found that a level of five gives fairly nice detail, but you may want to reduce this if you need to lower the triangle count.

The *angle* parameter refers to the angle between the vertical branch and the left and right branches that split off from it. The angle parameter is a constant as it is passed between functions. This, however, will produce very linear geometrical tree shapes, which isn't always what is wanted. To produce more natural-looking trees, you need to modify the angle parameter between recurses down (or, more intuitively, up) the tree. There are a lot of ways you can do this, but I've taken the simplest route and defined a second parameter *angle random factor*. This is the number of degrees by which the angle can change between levels. For example, with an angle random factor of 10 and a beginning angle of 30, the next level will be 20 to 40, the next 10 to 50, and so on.

The *length* parameter is simply the length of each branch. I also define a *length modifier*, which is a value by which the length is multiplied each level. I've chosen an initial length of 1.0 and a modifier of 0.9. This means the first level is 1.0, the next is 0.9, the next is 0.81, and so on, and the result is that the branches get progressively shorter as you go up the tree. Later when I define the width of each branch, that value is tied linearly to this value, so branches also get thinner as you look up the tree.

Take a chance at this point to play around with different combinations of the parameters. You should see how different settings can produce different types of trees. In tandem with the proper textures, you can generate any trees you need with this single algorithm.

Some Code

Let's take a look at some code for the recursive function now:

```
TreeRecurse(Branch *CurrentBranch, // a pointer to the branch to fill with data
            Matrix ModelMatrix, int level, int maxlevel, float angle,
            float anglemod, float anglerand, float length, float lengthmod)
```

The parameters are the ones described in the previous section.

```
  if(level >= maxlevel)
    return;


  CurrentBranch->length = length;
  CurrentBranch->theta = angle;
```

As you can see, the recursion ends once it has gone too many levels deep. Next, the function simply takes the parameters relevant to this branch and saves them. Note that you don't make any angle modifications to the current branch. You'll do this later, for the children.

```
  Matrix NewModelMatrix;
  NewModelMatrix.identity();
  NewModelMatrix.translate(0.0f, CurrentBranch->start, 0.0f);
  NewModelMatrix.rotate(DEGTORAD(CurrentBranch->theta), 0.0f, 0.0f);

  CurrentBranch->matrix = ModelMatrix = ModelMatrix * NewModelMatrix;
```

This is where the current rotations and transformations are taken into account. You also store the model matrix both in the current branch and the `ModelMatrix` parameter so that you can pass the new one to the children. The `start` parameter is something set by the parent (or in the case of the trunk, the calling function outside the recursion) and it just defines how far to translate to get to the top of the parent branch. In the trunk's specific case, this will be 0.

```
Line line;
line.s = CurrentBranch->matrix * Vector(0.0f, 0.0f, 0.0f);
line.e = CurrentBranch->matrix * Vector(0.0f, CurrentBranch->length, 0.0f);
line.l = level;
line.len = CurrentBranch->length;
lines.add(line);
```

This uses the current matrix to transform a single vertical line. It then stores the line data so that when generating the geometry, you'll have all the lines available.

```
if(level < maxlevel-1)
{
  CurrentBranch->middle = new Branch;
  CurrentBranch->middle->start = CurrentBranch->length;
  TreeRecurse(CurrentBranch->middle, ModelMatrix, level+1, maxlevel,
              0.0f + RAND(-anglerand, anglerand), anglemod, anglerand,
              length*lengthmod, lengthmod);

  CurrentBranch->left = new Branch;
  CurrentBranch->left->start = CurrentBranch->length;
  TreeRecurse(CurrentBranch->left, ModelMatrix, level+1, maxlevel,
              anglemod + RAND(-anglerand, anglerand), anglemod, anglerand,
              length*lengthmod, lengthmod);

  CurrentBranch->right = new Branch;
  CurrentBranch->right->start = CurrentBranch->length;

  TreeRecurse(CurrentBranch->right, ModelMatrix, level+1, maxlevel,
              -anglemod + RAND(-anglerand, anglerand), anglemod, anglerand,
              length*lengthmod, lengthmod);
}
```

note

RAND is a macro that returns a random value between the two parameters.

This step creates new `Branches` for the three directions, left, middle and right—provided it's not on the last level. Checking that makes sure you don't allocate space that you don't need if the next recursion call will just return immediately. You set up the start positions as the top of the current branch. You pass in incremented levels and updated lengths. For the left and right branches, you give them updated angles, too. This means that the next run through the recursive function will be able to create the next level of branches.

That's all there is to the code to produce a 2D tree, but we're not quite done yet. It would be nice if you could generate 3D trees, and there is one additional change I will make.

You might notice at this stage that the tree, although more random, still seems quite geometrical. The reason for this is that at every point where two branches meet, there's a split of exactly three branches. If you look again at a real tree, the branches don't necessarily split in the same place.

Luckily, this is really easy to account for. All you need to do is modify the `start` parameter so that it doesn't always start at the current branch's length:

```
CurrentBranch->left->start = CurrentBranch->length * RAND(0.5f, 1.0f);
```

That would start the left branch somewhere in the upper half of the current branch, which works fine. Depending on the type of tree, you might want to use a different method. One thing to note, however, is that you don't want to do this on the middle branch. Since the middle branch is really a continuation of the current branch as it thins out, you want it to continue at the end of the current branch.

The Third Dimension

The final modification I'm going to make is to add in a second angle rotation, this time around the y-axis. This is all you need to do to make the tree 3D. It works because it twists every branch around the y-axis, and these rotations are recursive. You can try it for yourself. All you need to do is add in another parameter: `twist`. I used the same `anglerand` to save parameters, but you can create another. Then you simply add that rotation before the current rotation. This is important so that the twisting works correctly. With that change, the matrix code looks something like this:

```
Matrix NewModelMatrix;
NewModelMatrix.identity();
NewModelMatrix.translate(0.0f, CurrentBranch->start, 0.0f);
NewModelMatrix.rotate(0.0f, DEGTORAD(CurrentBranch->alpha), 0.0f);
NewModelMatrix.rotate(DEGTORAD(CurrentBranch->theta), 0.0f, 0.0f);

CurrentBranch->matrix = ModelMatrix = ModelMatrix * NewModelMatrix;
```

Again, you should try out the code now to get a feel for how to change the parameters, and how they change the generated tree. A sample screen shot is shown in Figure 8.14.

Figure 8.14 Screenshot of the tree generated so far.

Generating Geometry

Although I now have the correct structure for a tree, it still doesn't look realistic. The reason for this, obviously, is that the branches and twigs are all the same size, because I'm just drawing lines. I'm also going to add in leaves for that final touch.

For the geometry, you'll simply generate a cylinder for each of the branches and draw it aligned so that its central axis lies along the branch line. Leaf placement is even easier. You determine a couple of points on each branch where you place leaves and decide which way they will face.

Let's start with the cylinders for branches. As I explained above, you just need to write a function that will generate a cylinder and draw it between two points specified.

One quite effective but easily implemented addition to add a little more detail to the tree is to use more than just a single cylinder for each branch. To do this, you first decide how many segments you want. In the demo, I use three segments for the first three levels, and one for each level after that. After three levels, the branches are too small and obscured to benefit from the extra polygons for detail.

The general algorithm for drawing a branch out of a line goes something like this:

```
for(every branch segment)
{
  Get a Direction vector for the branch
  Calculate the start and end of the branch
  Get a local coordinate system with the y-axis pointing along the branch line

  Draw a cylinder along the y-axis
}
```

I'm assuming that the number of the segments is calculated in the initialization code. In addition, you'll need to work out a vector offset from the line of the branch. It's up to you how you calculate this. I just took a simple random offset at values that worked out to be the right scale. You can use a more sophisticated method if you like.

Getting the direction vector is easy. You take the line's start and end points (ignoring segments) and get the direction vector between them. You then get the position vectors of the start and end of the branch. This is a little more complicated because you need to figure out what the start and end are, depending on the segment. The first and last segments use the start and end of the line—you don't want to offset these. The points in the middle get offset. This means that for three segments, you only need two offsets—one for the second point and one for the third. You also need to be careful that the separate cylinders connect. If there are gaps, they will show and destroy the illusion of the tree.

Once you have the start and end position, you need to get a local coordinate system. This means getting i, j, and k vectors (unit vectors along the x-, y-, and z-axes). Once you have these vectors, when you generate the cylinder geometry, you use them instead of just the normal i, j, k vectors to get our cylinder aligned along the y-axis.

The method for doing this relies on the fact that if you take the cylinder and rotate it around its central axis, it'll still be the same cylinder (more or less). This means you can align our coordinate system around the world y-axis, with no ill effects. Let me elaborate.

First, you only have one vector so far—the direction vector. This will be the y-axis. We know that the x- and z-axes are 90 degrees from each other, and both are 90 degrees from the y-axis. However, try this yourself: imagine you have an arbitrary coordinate system. You can use your hands to represent the three perpendicular axes with your thumb, forefinger and middle finger. Now, imagine that your thumb is the y-axis. Rotate your hand around the y-axis. You'll see that even though the axes remain perpendicular, there are an infinite number of potential axes that fit. This means we need an extra constraint.

All you do is say that the y- and z-axes that we're calculating lay in the same plane as the world y axis. Now there's only one possible set of axes. Here's how you actually calculate the axes:

1. Take the cross product of the direction vector and the world y-axis (unless these are identical; see step 2). This will produce a vector at 90 degrees to both of them—the i vector. Although there are two vectors that are at 90 degrees, all they do is flip the cylinder across the x-axis. This produces no effect because the cylinder is symmetrical.

2. If the direction vector is identical to the world y-axis, you simply set the right vector to $(1, 0, 0)$.

3. Now all you need to find is the k vector (the j vector is the direction vector). You do this simply by taking the cross product of the i and j vectors. Again, it doesn't matter that there are two possible solutions, the cylinder is symmetrical.

Figure 8.15 should help in understanding this process.

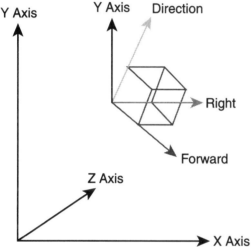

Figure 8.15 Establishing a basis for the cylinder.

Make sure these vectors are normalized, or they could produce strange problems when generating the cylinder later.

Finally, you need to generate the cylinder using the start, end, and i, j, and k vectors. There are a couple of little twists you need to consider. First, the radius of each branch needs to get smaller from its base (which is equal to the top of its parent) to its children (where it is equal to the base of the children). To do this, just calculate the radius based on the branch length. Second, you need to generate texture coordinates, but these just come from the loop variable as you'll see in a moment.

I'm using a loop to generate the cylinder in a triangle strip. I have a loop variable that increments from 0 to 2π, and I generate two vertices at each location, one at the base and one at the top. When I string these all together, it ends up as the triangle strip. Let's look at the code:

```
glBegin(GL_TRIANGLE_STRIP);
float lim = 2*PI, inc = 2*PI/segs;
float botrad = bottomrad * (1.0f-float(currentseg)/float(line.segs)) +
                 toprad * (float(currentseg)/float(line.segs));
float tprad = bottomrad * (1.0f-float(currentseg+1)/float(line.segs)) +
                 toprad * (float(currentseg+1)/float(line.segs));
for(float r=0.0f; r <= lim; r += inc)
{
  Vector pnt = start + right * cosf(r) * botrad + forward * sinf(r) * botrad;
  glTexCoord2f(r/lim, 0.0f);
  glVertex3f(pnt.x, pnt.y, pnt.z);

  pnt = end + (right * cosf(r) * tprad + forward * sinf(r) * tprad);
  glTexCoord2f(r/lim, 1.0f);
  glVertex3f(pnt.x, pnt.y, pnt.z);
}
glEnd();
```

Some variables that are passed in here might not be self-explanatory. First, `currentseg` is the current segment of the line that you're rendering. It will be 0 if there is only one segment, 1 if it is the second segment, and so on. The `line.segs` variable is the total number of segments, and `segs` is a variable passed into the branch drawing function, indicating how many segments around the y-axis you want—the higher this variable, the more accurate the cylinder, but the more polygons used. You don't generally want to reduce this below 3 because then the cylinder is a flat quad and doesn't look right. For trunks and major branches, you want a higher value. I use a function that is 5 for the first level, 4 for the second, then 3 for the rest. Increasing this will give you more detail at the expense of performance.

You start by declaring some variables outside of the loop. You precalculate the limit because you'll use this several times in the function. The same goes for the increment. You calculate `botrad` and `tprad`, which are the radii at the top and bottom of the cylinder, by doing a weighted average of the top and bottom radii of the overall line, based on the segment you're in. If there's only one segment, this works out to the bottom and top radii. If there's more than one, there's a linear change between the bottom and the top of the trunk. This is just straight linear interpolation between the two radii.

Then you start the main loop. This loops from 0 to 2π, incrementing in steps of 2π/segs. This means that there will be `segs` sides generated. The loop variable is then the angle that you're going to offset the points by. For each point, you need to figure out the coordinates of the top and bottom point at angle r. With a little trigonometry, this is easy enough. You get the x-coordinate through `cos(r)` and the z- coordinate through `sin(r)` (remember, you're aligning the cylinder along the y-axis, so the x- and z-axes contain our circle). This means we get a nice circle in the xz-plane. If we offset this by our start and end vectors, we get the circles at the top and bottom. Then we multiply by the top and bottom radii to get them the right size. However, we don't want the vertices in the xz-plane, we want them in the ik plane that we calculated. This is really easy though. All we do is multiply the x-coordinate by i and the z-coordinate by k. To calculate the v texture coordinate, we just use 0 for the bottom circle and 1 for the top. For the u-coordinate, we calculate it so that the texture wraps exactly once around the object. To do this, we divide r by lim so that it scales from 0 to 1 linearly.

That's it! You'll now draw your cylinders instead of blank lines. The more astute among you will realize that when two branches join, there will be gaps between them because we don't define any "glue" geometry between the two. This would be a bit harder to generate, but you're free to add this to your code. Unless you have close-ups on the tree joints though, you won't notice the gaps. If this is an issue, you can try drawing extra geometry or moving the branches so that they overlap more. Another problem is that although branches do generally start inside their parent, if the parent is twisted and deformed as shown above, then a segment could move away from a child. In this case the child would show up as floating in midair.

Our tree looks pretty good at this point. As before, I strongly encourage you to play around a bit with different settings, different ideas. Anything and everything should be tried at least once. You never know what might make the tree look a bit better, and it's all these little things that improve it.

However, we have one last thing to cover here before we can consider the tree finished. Unless it's the height of winter, most trees have leaves. Luckily, that's what the next section is about.

Leaf Placement

There are many different ways you can place leaves. If you wanted, you could just pick random locations and random directions. However, this doesn't look realistic, since most trees have some sort of order to them. Depending on the type of tree, you might want to have a little randomness, but generally leaves should point the same way as the branch or be perpendicular to the branch.

The demo uses a little randomness, but generally the leaves point down. This gives a realistic feel because it seems like they are being pulled down by gravity. I also placed the leaves somewhere between 30 and 100 percent of the way up the branch, and only on branches two or more levels deep. I created two leaves per branch to try to give some density to the tree. The direction is the average of a random vector and $(0, -1, 0)$.

You need to do a little bit of calculation to get the leaf's vertices because you only have a point and a line, and that's only good for a line. Luckily, you know how to solve this problem, because you just did the same thing for cylinders! You just go through the same process, but generate a square instead. Take a look at the sample code if you're unsure how to do this.

Figure 8.16 shows a screenshot of what the demo looks like at this point. The next sections will take the tree code and show some issues you might encounter when implementing it in your game.

Figure 8.16 Adding leaves to the generated tree.

Level of Detail

Let's take a look at a single tree. Starting with the settings used in the included demo, I'll calculate how many triangles are being drawn. I'm skipping the calculations for clarity, but I have 6 levels with an increasing number of branches on each one. Although the later levels reduce in complexity (fewer segments vertically and horizontally), I still end up with 2,370 triangles. With 1,440 triangles for the leaves, this means 3,810 triangles in total for the tree.

Now, in the demo I used display lists because it's a good balance between clarity and speed. With vertex buffer objects you'd probably get better performance. Even so, that is a fair number of triangles to be rendering for a single tree. You'd have to tone down the settings if you were aiming for a lower-end system.

Imagine, then, drawing a forest. Let's say you have 100 trees on screen at once with frustum culling. That's 381,000 triangles just for the trees. Even with some good culling, that's still a fair number of triangles to render just for trees —and you still have to render the rest of your scene.

This is where level of detail comes in handy. It reduces the number of polygons you actually need to render. There are pretty sophisticated techniques that can decide, based on distance and other factors, how many triangles can be safely dropped without causing significant artifacts. However, I'm going to take a slightly different, but still useful, route. Other methods can be added to the one described here with no problems.

All you do is render the tree as eight directional sprites and substitute the full 3D tree for the closest sprite available. To do this, you orient the camera at eight different points around the tree and render the tree to a texture. Then you use those textures later when rendering the tree at great distances. You've already seen this basic idea in the billboarding section in Chapter 7, "Special Effects."

note

The change to a sprite will be obvious if you are far away from the tree with nothing to obscure your vision. This also doesn't work if you leave the ground level, because the textures stored are from ground level. The way you will be doing the billboarding, it will be clear that the trees are fake when seen from above, because they will show up as flat quads. Some of the suggestions discussed in Chapter 7 may help here.

One problem is getting the tree in view. You need to make sure that you keep the camera at a fixed distance and angle from the tree and only rotate it around the y-axis, but you also need to make sure that the tree is completely within the view at all times and has no wasted space. Although you could calculate exactly how to do this, I've taken the easy way out and simply found some values that work and used them. This means that you'll need to adjust them yourself if you change the tree, or you can write some code that works them out for you.

What I did was write a function that takes the current sprite number, rotates the tree around the y-axis, renders the tree and then copies the current screen buffer straight to a texture. Before calling this function, I set the viewport to 512×512.

In the drawing function, I have a test to see if the tree is far enough away. If it is, then I draw the texture on a billboarded quad. I chose this quad by simply taking the vector from the tree's position to the camera's position and finding the angle between it and the tree's z-axis.

You save a lot of polygons using this method, because each tree drawn as a sprite goes from 3,810 triangles to 2. The trade-off is a longer load-up time as you render all those textures. This can be quite significant if you have a lot of trees. The solution I came up with for the demo is to generate 10 trees, and then create 10 random copies of them in the forest of 100 trees. It's not obvious that the trees repeat, and it saves on generation time as well as memory usage. In Figure 8.17 two trees are side by side. The tree on the right is further away, and rendered using the sprite method. The left tree is closer and rendered in full 3D. Also worth noting is that the demo included isn't perfect, and it is noticeable when the billboard changes to a 3D rendering, and vice versa. Further tweaking of the code will easily fix this problem.

Figure 8.17 One real tree and one billboarded tree.

Placement of Trees

Let's say you have a terrain that you want to populate with trees, perhaps with an odd clump of trees here and there, as well as forests and clearings. It's not possible to get this just by randomly placing trees across your terrain. The trees won't look "natural" over any large area. What you want is some way of modeling the natural placing of trees, largely into clumps with clearings and spacing between them. You can do this using a common technique called Perlin noise. Describing the technique is beyond the scope of this book, so I'll assume that you've implemented a Perlin noise function and can act on the data it returns. There is a sample implementation with the included demo.

A typical Perlin-noise map is shown in Figure 8.18 along with the "filtered" version produced by our code. You will notice that the contrast is extremely high on the filtered version. The filtered version retains the large patterns represented in the noise map without including the little gradations. This means you can simplify your noise code by reducing the number of octaves you use.

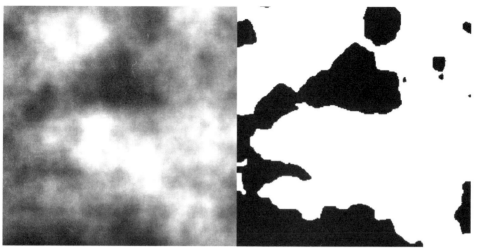

Figure 8.18 Perlin-noise map (left) and highly contrasted version used for tree placement (right).

The code to filter the map is:

```
for every pixel
  if pixel is over the threshold
    pixel = white
  if pixel is equal to or under
    pixel = black
```

A good value for the threshold will be about 0.4 to 0.5. A higher value will mean fewer white patches and more black, and vice versa. The noise generated, when filtered, can be viewed as a map of where the trees should be placed. Depending on your threshold and how many trees you want, this can be black or white. In the example, I chose white, as it produces a nice mapping of the trees.

All that's left is to look at some implementation details on how to actually place trees using this filtered map. You begin by imagining an array of points covering your landscape. Make them as dense as you want them to be. Then you just loop through the points, finding the associated pixel on your noise texture map. The noise map should entirely encompass your terrain. Then you just place a tree there if the point is white.

One easy addition you can make to this is randomly offsetting the trees. You'll notice that without a random offset, the trees are very rigid and in straight lines, like an orchard. A good rule of thumb is to move trees half the closest distance between them. That way they will never overlap.

Implementation Notes and Suggestions

You should note that the generation algorithm isn't perfect. If you feel that you can modify it in a way that improves it, do so. When developing it, I went through several complete rewrites, and if I continued working, I'd probably go through several more.

My advice after or during reading this section is to implement it yourself, from scratch, rather than modifying or copying the demo. That will give you insight into the way the algorithm works that you just can't get without doing it yourself.

Leaves will generally be quads with alpha textures on them. This means you need to deal with a common issue with transparent objects—sorting. You will need to sort your leaves according to their distance for the camera. For more information on this, see the included demo.

You'll also notice if you play around with the demo that there is visible popping, both as trees move from one billboard to another, and as trees move from billboarding to full 3D. You can solve this by slightly changing the way the billboards are rendered. The basic principle is that instead of rendering them at startup, you render them as they are needed. This means that you render a new billboard whenever a tree goes from 3D to billboard or when the user moves around the tree. This has the advantage of requiring less memory, and providing a more accurate simulation—you can view the trees from any angle, and popping should be unnoticeable. It is however too complex to detail here.

References

http://freespace.virgin.net/hugo.elias/models/m_perlin.htm. Hugo Elias's site explaining how to generate Perlin noise. An excellent tutorial on how to create the noise maps.

http://www.vterrain.org/. The virtual terrain project, a site dedicated to all things procedural. Contains many excellent articles and lots of links and ideas for more procedural content generation.

Fur Rendering

Lukas Heise

There are many different ways of rendering fur. One technique uses lines that are randomly placed on a polygon, and another uses parallax mapping to achieve the visual appearance of fur.

In this book, I decided to use a technique that I believe gives the best results in speed, implementation difficulty, and visual appearance. The technique involves adding layers of polygons on top of each other, as well as binding an alpha-blended noise texture to the polygons, creating the illusion of straws. I will refer to these layers of polygons as the shell.

To further improve the visual effect around the silhouette of our model, I will render polygons around each polygon on the model. These polygons, called fins, will be perpendicular to the normal vector of the polygon. These elements are illustrated in Figures 8.19 to 8.21.

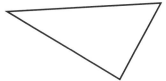

Figure 8.19 A polygon from the model.

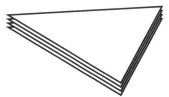

Figure 8.20 Layers of polygons (the shell).

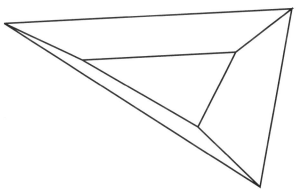

Figure 8.21 The model's polygon surrounded by fin polygons.

Generating the Textures

You begin by generating the textures that you will be using when rendering the fur. The fin texture is simple to create. All you need to do is to draw some straws into the texture's alpha channel. Figure 8.22 is an example of a fin texture.

Generating the shell texture is somewhat more difficult. You need to create a noise texture for each of the shell's polygons. For each of the layers, you will reuse the texture from the previous layer and add more noise to it. Here is the code for generating the shell textures.

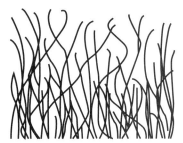

Figure 8.22 A 128×128 fin texture.

```
unsigned int* generateShellTextures(int layer_count, int size, int density)
{
  unsigned int* textures = new unsigned int[layer_count];
  unsigned char* data = new unsigned char[size * size];

  ZeroMemory(data, size * size);

  glGenTextures(layer_count, textures);

  for (int i = layer_count - 1; i >= 0; i--)
  {
    for (int j = 0; j < density; j++)
      data[rand() % (size * size)] = 255;

    glBindTexture(GL_TEXTURE_2D, textures[i]);
    glPixelStorei(GL_UNPACK_ALIGNMENT, 1);
    glTexParameteri(GL_TEXTURE_2D, GL_TEXTURE_WRAP_S, GL_REPEAT);
    glTexParameteri(GL_TEXTURE_2D, GL_TEXTURE_WRAP_T, GL_REPEAT);
    glTexParameteri(GL_TEXTURE_2D, GL_TEXTURE_MAG_FILTER, GL_LINEAR);
    glTexParameteri(GL_TEXTURE_2D, GL_TEXTURE_MIN_FILTER, GL_LINEAR);
    glTexEnvi(GL_TEXTURE_ENV, GL_TEXTURE_ENV_MODE, GL_MODULATE);
    glTexImage2D(GL_TEXTURE_2D, 0, GL_ALPHA4, size, size, 0, GL_ALPHA,
                 GL_UNSIGNED_BYTE, data);
  }

  delete [] data;
  return textures;
}
```

The code is mostly self-explanatory. It creates layer_count number of textures (14 layers or more works well), each having more noise (density parameter) than the previous texture. A reasonable value for density is 700.

Creating the Shell

For each polygon in the model, you will create a number of shell polygons. Let's assume that the model consists of triangles. For each triangle you need the following data:

- The three points that define the triangle (P_1, P_2, P_3)
- The vertex normal vectors of the triangle (N_1, N_2, N_3)
- The texture coordinates of the triangle (T_1, T_2, T_3)

You will use the following data to manipulate the look of the shell:

- How many layers the shell should have (`layer_count` ; reasonable value = 14)
- How high the fur should be, or in other words, the distance from the first layer to the last (`fur_length` ; reasonable value = 0.75)
- How much the noise texture should repeat itself (`fur_scale` ; reasonable value = 0.12)

The pseudocode below shows how to generate and render the fur's shell.

```
Bind model's colormap texture to texture unit 1
For each layer_count : A
  Bind shell texture number A to texture unit 0
  Z = (fur_length / layer_count) * A
  C = 0.25 + 0.75 * (A / layer_count)
  glColor4f(C,C,C,1)

  glBegin(GL_TRIANGLES)
  For each polygon in model : B
    F = get_face(B)

    V1 = F.P2 - F.P1
    L1 = length(V1)
    V1 = V1 / L1

    V2 = F.P3 - F.P1
    L2 = length(V2)
    V2 = V2 / L2

    D = dot_product(V1,V2)

    // first point in the triangle
    glMultiTexCoord2fARB(GL_TEXTURE0_ARB, 0, 0)
    glMultiTexCoord2fARB(GL_TEXTURE1_ARB, F.T1.x, F.T1.y)
```

```
    glNormal3f(F.N1.x, F.N1.y, F.N2.z)
    glVertex3f(F.P1.x + Z * F.N1.x, F.P1.y + Z * F.N1.y, F.P1.y + Z * F.N1.z)

    // second point in the triangle
    glMultiTexCoord2fARB(GL_TEXTURE0_ARB, fur_scale * L1, 0)
    glMultiTexCoord2fARB(GL_TEXTURE1_ARB, F.T2.x, F.T2.y)
    glNormal3f(F.N2.x, F.N2.y, F.N2.z)
    glVertex3f(F.P2.x + Z * F.N2.x, F.P2.y + Z * F.N2.y, F.P2.z + Z * F.N2.z)

    // third point in our triangle
    glMultiTexCoord2fARB(GL_TEXTURE0_ARB, fur_scale * L2 * D,
                         fur_scale * L2 * sin(acos(D)))
    glMultiTexCoord2fARB(GL_TEXTURE1_ARB, F.T3.x, F.T3.y)
    glNormal3f(F.N3.x, F.N3.y, F.N3.z)
    glVertex3f(F.P3.x + Z * F.N3.x, F.P3.y + Z * F.N3.y, F.P3.z + Z * F.N3.z)
  End For
  glEnd()
End For
```

Naturally, if your model is static, you can put this in a display list or vertex array. Doing all these calculations every time you render your model is simply a huge waste of CPU power.

Creating the Fins

When generating the fins, you use the same input data from the model that you used when you generated the shell. For each polygon you will use the points that define the polygon, its vertex normal vectors, and its texture coordinates. For each polygon in the model you will create a quad for each side on the polygon.

The pseudocode below shows how this is done for polygons that are triangles.

```
fin_length = fur_length * 2.5
Bind models colormap texture to texture unit 1
Bind the fin texture to texture unit 0
glBegin(GL_QUADS)
For each polygon in model : A
  F = get_face(A)

  // first quad
  Z = fur_scale * length(F.P1 - F.P2)
  glColor4f(0.25, 0.25, 0.25, 0.5)
  glNormal3f(F.N1.x, F.N1.y, F.N1.z)
  glMultiTexCoord2fARB(GL_TEXTURE0_ARB, 0, 1)
```

```
glMultiTexCoord2fARB(GL_TEXTURE1_ARB, F.T1.x, F.T1.y)
glVertex3f(F.P1.x, F.P1.y, F.P1.z)
glColor4f(1.0, 1.0, 1.0, 0.5)
glMultiTexCoord2fARB(GL_TEXTURE0_ARB, 0, 0)
glMultiTexCoord2fARB(GL_TEXTURE1_ARB, F.T1.x, F.T1.y)
glVertex3f(F.P1.x + fin_length * fur_length * F.N1.x,
           F.P1.y + fin_length * fur_length * F.N1.y,
           F.P1.z + fin_length * fur_length * F.N1.z)
glNormal3f(F.N2.x, F.N2.y, F.N3.z)
glMultiTexCoord2fARB(GL_TEXTURE0_ARB, Z, 0)
glMultiTexCoord2fARB(GL_TEXTURE1_ARB, F.T2.x, F.T2.y)
glVertex3f(F.P2.x + fin_length * fur_length * F.N2.x,
           F.P2.y + fin_length * fur_length * F.N2.y,
           F.P2.z + fin_length * fur_length * F.N2.z)
glColor4f(0.25, 0.25, 0.25, 0.5)
glMultiTexCoord2fARB(GL_TEXTURE0_ARB, Z, 1)
glMultiTexCoord2fARB(GL_TEXTURE1_ARB, F.T2.x, F.T2.y)
glVertex3f(F.P2.x, F.P2.y, F.P2.z)

// second quad
Z = fur_scale * length(F.P3 - F.P1)
glColor4f(0.25, 0.25, 0.25, 0.5)
glNormal3f(F.N3.x, F.N3.y, F.N3.z)
glMultiTexCoord2fARB(GL_TEXTURE0_ARB, 0, 1)
glMultiTexCoord2fARB(GL_TEXTURE1_ARB, F.T3.x, F.T3.y)
glVertex3f(F.P3.x, F.P3.y, F.P3.z)
glColor4f(1.0, 1.0, 1.0, 0.5)
glMultiTexCoord2fARB(GL_TEXTURE0_ARB, 0, 0)
glMultiTexCoord2fARB(GL_TEXTURE1_ARB, F.T3.x, F.T3.y)
glVertex3f(F.P3.x + fin_length * fur_length * F.N3.x,
           F.P3.y + fin_length * fur_length * F.N3.y,
           F.P3.z + fin_length * fur_length * F.N3.z)
glNormal3f(F.N1.x, F.N1.y, F.N1.z)
glMultiTexCoord2fARB(GL_TEXTURE0_ARB, Z, 0)
glMultiTexCoord2fARB(GL_TEXTURE1_ARB, F.T1.x, F.T1.y)
glVertex3f(F.P1.x + fin_length * fur_length * F.N1.x,
           F.P1.y + fin_length * fur_length * F.N1.y,
           F.P1.z + fin_length * fur_length * F.N1.z)
glColor4f(0.25, 0.25, 0.25, 0.5)
glMultiTexCoord2fARB(GL_TEXTURE0_ARB, Z, 1)
glMultiTexCoord2fARB(GL_TEXTURE1_ARB, F.T1.x, F.T1.y)
glVertex3f(F.P1.x, F.P1.y, F.P1.z)
```

```
  // third quad
  Z = fur_scale * length(F.P3 - F.P2)
  glColor4f(0.25, 0.25, 0.25, 0.5)
  glNormal3f(F.N3.x, F.N3.y, F.N3.z)
  glMultiTexCoord2fARB(GL_TEXTURE0_ARB, 0, 1)
  glMultiTexCoord2fARB(GL_TEXTURE1_ARB, F.T3.x, F.T3.y)
  glVertex3f(F.P3.x, F.P3.y, F.P3.z)
  glColor4f(1.0, 1.0, 1.0, 0.5)
  glMultiTexCoord2fARB(GL_TEXTURE0_ARB, 0, 0)
  glMultiTexCoord2fARB(GL_TEXTURE1_ARB, F.T3.x, F.T3.y)
  glVertex3f(F.P3.x + fin_length * fur_length * F.N3.x,
             F.P3.y + fin_length * fur_length * F.N3.y,
             F.P3.z + fin_length * fur_length * F.N3.z)
  glNormal3f(F.N2.x, F.N2.y, F.N2.z)
  glMultiTexCoord2fARB(GL_TEXTURE0_ARB, Z, 0)
  glMultiTexCoord2fARB(GL_TEXTURE1_ARB, F.T2.x, F.T2.y)
  glVertex3f(F.P2.x + fin_length * fur_length * F.N2.x,
             F.P2.y + fin_length * fur_length * F.N2.y,
             F.P2.z + fin_length * fur_length * F.N2.z)
  glColor4f(0.25, 0.25, 0.25, 0.5)
  glMultiTexCoord2fARB(GL_TEXTURE0_ARB, Z, 1)
  glMultiTexCoord2fARB(GL_TEXTURE1_ARB, F.T2.x, F.T2.y)
  glVertex3f(F.P2.x, F.P2.y, F.P2.z)
End for
glEnd()
```

Putting It All Together

Now that you know how to render fins and shells, you are ready to render the model with fur. Below is pseudocode on how this is performed.

```
RenderModel()

glEnable(GL_BLEND)
glBlendFunc(GL_SRC_ALPHA,GL_ONE_MINUS_SRC_ALPHA)

glDisable(GL_CULL_FACE)
glDepthMask(GL_FALSE)

RenderFins()
```

```
glDepthMask(GL_TRUE)
glEnable(GL_CULL_FACE)

RenderShells()

glDisable(GL_BLEND)
```

Finally, I would comment on the rendering cost for this method of fur rendering. This method is pretty expensive. First, you create three quads for each triangle in your model. Second, you create a number of triangles for each triangle in your model. On top of this, you enable blending, which can be expensive. However, my tests showed that the biggest bottleneck is in the texture coordinates of the shell. Repeating the texture too much over the polygons can seriously lower the frame rate. Keep this in mind and use a reasonable `fur_scale` value.

References

Ilmola, Markus. Fur Demo. **http://nehe.gamedev.net**, Downloads: F.

Summary

Although this chapter has not provided comprehensive coverage of every natural effect you might like to render, it has addressed several of the most significant and common techniques. Almost every outdoor environment includes water and various forms of plants and vegetation, and the ability to model fur will allow you to represent animals much more realistically.

In the next two chapters, you'll continue your exploration of nature with the important topics of sky and terrain rendering.

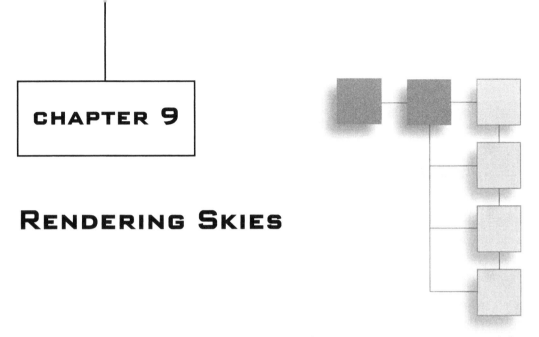

CHAPTER 9

RENDERING SKIES

Many games these days take advantage of outdoor environments. One of the most important elements in creating convincing outdoor scenes is having good-looking skies. Many techniques have been used to render skies; these range from fairly simple approaches to physically based models that try to represent skies as accurately as possible.

In this chapter, you'll learn about the following techniques for adding realistic-looking skies to your games:

- Skyplanes
- Skyboxes
- Skydomes
- Cloud generation and rendering

Skyplanes

Dimi Christopoulos

The most basic sky simulation is done using planes. It's the easiest technique to set up and texture but might need adjustments to look right. In its simplest form it is just a plane that is textured using a small tiling texture or one big texture map and placed to cover the world scene. The problem with using this simplistic approach, as illustrated in Figure 9.1, is that the end of the plane is noticeable because it does not cover the horizon.

Figure 9.1 The edge of the skyplane can be seen breaking the illusion.

In general, skyplane techniques do not enclose the camera completely; therefore they should be used with environments where the ground, mountains, objects, or something else covers the portion of the background that is not filled. An alternative that alleviates the problem of filling the horizon is using a curved plane. Initially the plane is divided into triangles and the corners are pulled down, producing a shape that resembles a parachute, as shown in Figure 9.2.

The main geometrical attributes that can be specified when creating such a skyplane are

1. The resolution (division into triangle rows) of the plane. The more divisions, the smoother the representation and the higher the triangle count.
2. The radius of the circle completely enclosing the skyplane (see Figure 9.3).
3. The height of the peak of the skyplane (see Figure 9.4).
4. The repetitions of the texture mapped onto the plane.

The final plane will consist of vertices and indices that index into the vertex array and create triangle strips. Their number depends on the number of divisions specified. Each division gives four vertices, two triangles, and six indices, and divides the plane evenly.

```
NumVertices = (Division+1)*(Division+1)
NumIndices = (Division*Division)*2*3
```

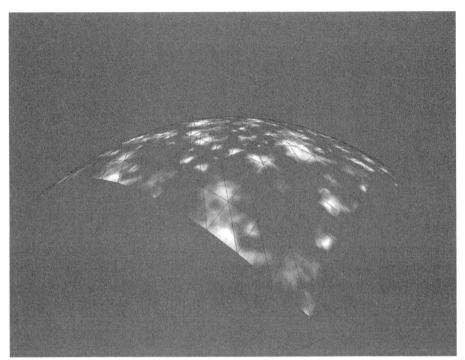

Figure 9.2 Geometry of a curved skyplane.

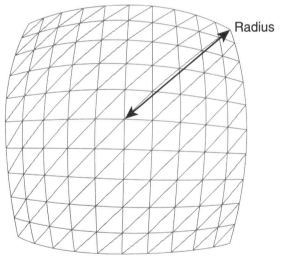

Figure 9.3 The radius of the skyplane.

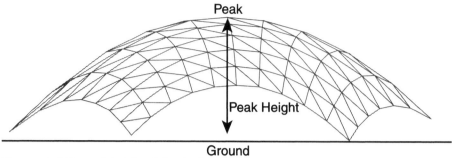

Figure 9.4 The peak height of the skyplane.

The radius of the circle and the peak height define its extent and curvature. Knowing the radius of the plane, the size of its sides can be computed using the Pythagorean theorem, assuming the plane has equal sides.

$$plane\_size = \sqrt{\frac{(2 * radius)^2}{2}}$$

Creating the Geometry

The following code illustrates the vertex and texture-coordinate generation, which is computed for every division horizontally and vertically inside a loop.

```
float plane_size = (float) sqrt((((2.0f*Radius)*(2.0f*Radius))*0.5);
float delta = plane_size/(float)divs;
float tex_delta = 1.0f/(float)divs;

for (int i=0;i <= divs;i++)
{
  for (int j=0; j <= divs; j++)
  {
    x_dist = (-0.5f * plane_size) + ((float)j*delta);
    z_dist = (-0.5f * plane_size) + ((float)i*delta);

    x_height = (x_dist*x_dist);
    z_height = (z_dist*z_dist);
    height = (x_height + z_height)/radius_squared;

    SV.x = x_dist;
    SV.y = (1.f - height) * PeakHeight;
    SV.z = z_dist;

    // Calculate the texture coordinates
```

```
    SV.u = hTile*((float)j * tex_delta);
    SV.v = vTile*((float)i * tex_delta);

    PlaneVertices[i*(divs+1)+j] = SV;
  }
}


// Calculate the indices
int index = 0;
for (int i=0; i < divs;i++)
{
  for (int j=0; j < divs; j++)
  {
    int startvert = (i*(divs+1) + j);
    // tri 1
    Indices[index++] = startvert;
    Indices[index++] = startvert+1;
    Indices[index++] = startvert+divs+1;

    // tri 2
    Indices[index++] = startvert+1;
    Indices[index++] = startvert+divs+2;
    Indices[index++] = startvert+divs+1;
  }
}
```

Here, x_dist and z_dist compute the points on the plane. Their values fall in the range [−plane_size/2, plane_size/2]. The center of the plane is the origin, and delta and tex_delta are computed incremental values used for vertex and texture-coordinate generation. To get the height of each vertex, the distance from the center is calculated and divided by the radius. This division produces a value between 1 and 0, which is inverted and multiplied by the specified peak height to produce the final height.

```
SV.y = (1.f - height) * PeakHeight;
```

Calculating texture coordinates is straightforward. The current division is multiplied by tex_delta to produce a coordinate in the range [0, 1] and by hTile and vTile, which specify the texture repetition over the plane.

```
SV.u = hTile*((float)j * tex_delta);
SV.v = vTile*((float)i * tex_delta);
```

Rendering

When rendering the skyplane, remember to disable states that are not needed, such as lighting and fog. Depth testing can be disabled since the cloud cover should always be drawn first. Disabling the depth buffer (via `glDepthMask()`) for sky rendering is important; it ensures that no intersection will occur even with objects that might be higher than the cloud layer and that the skyplane will stay in the background. To blend the skyplane with the background when it has transparency (for example, for clouds), OpenGL blending has to be enabled. The blending functions that are generally used for skyplanes are `glBlendFunc(GL_SRC_ALPHA, GL_ONE_MINUS_SRC_ALPHA)` or `glBlendFunc(GL_ONE, GL_ONE)`. Once all of this is set up, rendering the skyplane is straightforward:

```
glBegin(GL_TRIANGLES);
for (int i=0; i < NumIndices; i++)
{
  glTexCoord2f(PlaneVertices[Indices[i]].u, PlaneVertices[Indices[i]].v);
  glVertex3f(PlaneVertices[Indices[i]].x, PlaneVertices[Indices[i]].y,
            PlaneVertices[Indices[i]].z);
}
glEnd();
```

Fading

Although the radius, height, and division of the plane can be customized to cover the underlying world to avoid the horizon problem, the plane might still look unnatural if there are no objects or mountains, because it is missing the effect of fading into the distance. The clouds seem to disappear vertically below the ground, as shown in Figure 9.5.

An alternative for smooth transitions is to enable blending and specify an alpha value for each vertex. Vertices that are further away get a lower alpha value and fade to totally transparent, ensuring a smooth transition into the horizon, as shown in Figure 9.6.

The code below shows how this can be incorporated into the existing code.

```
for (int i=0;i <= divs;i++)
{
  for (int j=0; j <= divs; j++)
  {
    ... Calculate the geometry and texture coordinates as shown above
    // Calculate alpha value of vertex
    SV.alpha = (x_height + z_height)/ alpharadius_squared;
    SV.alpha = 1 - SV.alpha;
     if (SV.alpha < 0.f )
       SV.alpha = 0.f;
```

Figure 9.5 The clouds disappear vertically behind the horizon.

Figure 9.6 The skyplane transitions smoothly into the background.

```
   ... Calculate the texture coordinates as shown above
   PlaneVertices[i*(divs+1)+j] = SV;
 }
}
```

The code divides the distance from the center of each vertex by the radius specified for transparency. All vertices beyond this radius are totally transparent, and as vertices get closer, the alpha value is increased. The transparency radius can therefore not be greater than the radius of the plane. Optionally an exponential function can be used to adjust how the alpha value is computed for each vertex. Normally the transition to transparency is linear from the center to the outer edge of the plane. Using an exponential function makes the transition more steep, allowing for more interesting or natural transitions according to the environment:

```
if (exponentialFadeout)
    SV.alpha = SV.alpha * SV.alpha * SV.alpha;
```

Texture Animation

Skyplanes can be used to simulate a static cloud layer, but they can also be enhanced with animation. The most commonly used technique for animation in skyplanes is texture animation. Texture animation can be used to simulate moving clouds. Using the texture matrix, the textures of an object can be animated by translating, rotating, or even scaling their mapping on the surface. The following code illustrates how to use texture animation with the skyplane (in this case, by translation):

```
glMatrixMode(GL_TEXTURE);
glPushMatrix();
glTranslatef(ttrans[0], ttrans[1], 0.);
RenderSkyPlane();
glPopMatrix();
glMatrixMode(GL_MODELVIEW);
```

The translation is specified by ttrans[0] and ttrans[1], which are incremented inside the main loop every frame, making the cloud texture move. RenderSky() renders the skyplane as usual, using the default texture coordinates. The glPushMatrix() and glPopMatrix() commands before and after the object is drawn ensure that the texture matrix is reset for the following objects. Remember to set the matrix mode back to its original state (probably GL_MODELVIEW) after the object on which the texture translation should be applied is drawn.

Faking Volumetric Clouds

The quality and realism of the clouds using any approach depends on the quality of the textures used. Since what is essentially shown is a plane with a texture, it's up to the texture image to add any depth and shading in order to suggest clouds with volume.

An easy technique for suggesting volume using skyplanes is to draw many layers with the same or different textures and blend them together. This creates the illusion of volume and adds depth to the final image, although raising the triangle count, because multiple layers have to be drawn. Figure 9.7 illustrates this.

Figure 9.7 Volumetric clouds.

In the existing code this technique can be realized by drawing multiple skyplanes, each offset by a small amount on the y-axis (up). Because depth testing is disabled, z-fighting is not a problem. Remember to enable blending and use an appropriate blend function.

Skyboxes

Dimi Christopoulos

Using skyboxes is an old technique that suggests a larger environment "out there," just beyond the player's reach. When executed correctly, a skybox creates an almost perfect illusion of the environment and heightens the beauty and sense of immersion. Distant scenery is rendered onto six textures, which are applied to the sides of a cube, as shown in Figure 9.8. The camera is placed at the center of the cube; its distance to the walls of the cube should be kept constant. In essence this means that it can rotate freely but never be able to reach the walls, making the images of the cube appear very far away.

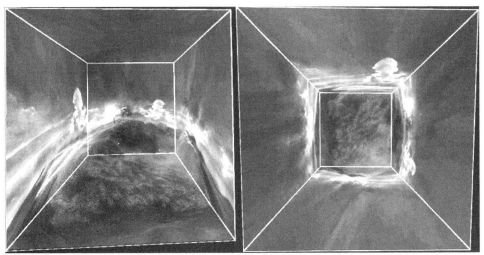

Figure 9.8 Back and top views of a skybox from far away. The user is in the center.

Rendering

The simplest technique for rendering a skybox is to render an ordinary textured cube aligned with the world axis and place the camera in the center. The skybox should be the first thing rendered. That means you don't need to clear color buffer, since the skybox always covers the whole screen. Depth writing and testing should be also disabled to reduce the number of calculations performed, because nothing is ever going to intersect with the skybox. Fog, lighting, and other operations that could alter the final image should also be disabled. The skybox images should be rendered without atmospheric effects. The size of the skybox does not matter as long as it falls within the view frustum. The dimensions should be chosen so that the farthest points (the corners) are closer to the camera than the far clipping plane. The equation below can be used to compute the maximum width of the box (zfar is the distance of the far clipping plane).

$$width \leq \frac{2\sqrt{3}}{3}\, zfar$$

The dimensions of the cube do not have to be identical; the height can be shorter than the width, as long as it looks better or is closer to the effect needed. The steps for rendering are the following:

1. Clear the depth buffer.
2. Disable depth test.
3. Disable depth writes.
4. Disable fog and lighting.
5. Render the box.
6. Enable depth test and writes.
7. Enable lighting and fog.
8. Draw the rest of scene.

Problems at Skybox Edges

Although rendering skyboxes seems quite straightforward, problems, such as those shown in Figure 9.9, can arise because of the texture filtering applied when the texture images are bigger or smaller than the screen resolution.

Figure 9.9 This skybox has problematic seams at the edges.

In cases such as Figure 9.9, the filtering process produces seams at the edges of the box, which effectively destroys the illusion. The problem is caused by the linear interpolation of texels—set using the GL_LINEAR texture filter—to get pixel values. A pixel color is determined by taking the two or four closest texels and calculating an average color.

The option to disable the interpolation and always use the nearest texel (which is done using GL_NEAREST) solves the edge problem. But this can produce awfully blocky and shimmering textures, especially if the texture size does not match the screen resolution.

The reason interpolation causes problems at the edge of a texture is improper texture wrapping. Pixels at the skybox edges do not have neighboring texels on all sides. The default behavior is to use the texel at the opposite edge (GL_REPEAT). Although this works for textures that can be tiled, it is not suitable for skybox textures when neighboring textures cannot be tiled. OpenGL also has a clamping mode (GL_CLAMP), which introduces a different behavior and interpolates the texels at the edge with a specified color. Unfortunately, this technique also introduces artifacts at the edges because of the interpolation of the edges with the border color, which darkens, brightens, or otherwise causes different coloration at the edge texels, depending on the border color used. As an example, setting the border color to black produces dark edges.

note

On Nvidia hardware, GL_CLAMP has the same result as GL_CLAMP_TO_EDGE, which, as we will see next, fixes the edge problem. This behavior is unfortunately not OpenGL-specification compliant and does not produce the same results on systems with other graphics cards.

Fixing the Edge Problem

The easy solution for proper clamping when rendering skyboxes was introduced in OpenGL version 1.2 with the GL_CLAMP_TO_EDGE clamp mode. This mode does not include edge texels when interpolating, and thus avoids the seam artifact.

extension

Extension name: EXT_texture_edge_clamp

Name string: GL_EXT_texture_edge_clamp

Promoted to core: OpenGL 1.2

Tokens: GL_CLAMP_TO_EDGE_EXT

Fixing the Seams without Extensions

You can overcome seam artifacts at skybox edges without using GL_CLAMP_TO_EDGE by including a one-pixel border within each texture and adjusting the UV-coordinates so that, instead of falling in the range [0, 1], they are half a texel less on either side. If, for example, the texture is 256×256, then the UV-coordinates would range from 1/256 to 255/256. Therefore, this method depends on the size of the texture and requires some extra work generating the textures. Also, if mipmapping is used, the above offsets are correct for mip level 0, but for higher levels, texel offsets of 2, 4, 8, and so on are needed. Fortunately, you almost never have to worry about this for skyboxes because usually the sky textures occupy more texels onscreen then the actual texture size, so they always use mip level 0.

Positioning the Skybox

When the skybox is positioned correctly, the user will never be able to reach its ends. Therefore, the box has to follow the camera to keep the distance from its walls constant. This can be done explicitly if our camera model is advanced enough to provide rotation and translation values to transform the skybox. Alternatively, the OpenGL modelview matrix can be used for making the skybox follow the camera, which is the approach described here.

After the camera transformations are applied, the modelview matrix is read back and the translation part of the matrix (entries 12, 13, and 14) is set to (0, 0, 0). The matrix is then uploaded to the OpenGL matrix stack. The specific steps are shown in the following pseudocode:

```
gluLookAt(…);                              //Apply camera transformations
glPushMatrix();                            //Push modelview matrix
glGetFloatv(GL_MODELVIEW_MATRIX, mat);     //Get the modelview matrix
mat[12] = mat[13] = mat[14] = 0.f;         //Set translation part to (0,0,0)
glLoadMatrixf(mat);                        //Push modelview matrix back to stack
DrawSkyBox();                              //Draw skybox
glPopMatrix();                             //Pop the matrix stack
// Draw rest of scene
```

If your skybox is big enough and encloses the entire scene, or if the user is static, there might be no need to make it follow the user. In that case, just render the skybox as you would any other object.

Creating Skybox Textures

There are various methods for creating skybox textures using different packages. Bell and SkyPaint (referenced at the end of this section) describe methods using common tools like 3ds max and Bryce or even painting them by hand. There is also a tool called Terragen (shown in Figure 9.10) that produces nice skyboxes and is easy to learn. The general procedure to create the textures needed is the same for every package.

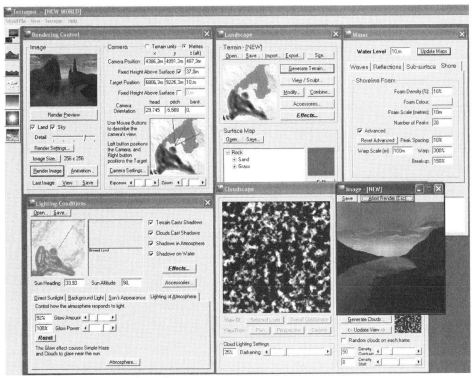

Figure 9.10 Screenshot from the Terragen program.

1. Model the scene.

2. Set up the camera.

3. Set the Field of View to 90 degrees.

4. Render six images using different pitch (rotation along x-axis) and heading (rotation along y-axis).

Table 9.1 lists the settings to use to produce each image.

Table 9.1 Settings for Skybox-Texture Creation

Image	Pitch	Heading
Front	0	0
Right	0	90
Back	0	180
Left	0	270
Top	90	0
Bottom	270	0

The texture size used should ideally be one texel for each pixel. The following equation computes the ideal texture resolution for a specified screen resolution and field of view (FOV).

$$image\_width = \frac{screen\_resolution}{\tan(\frac{FOV}{2})}$$

Skybox-texture creation using Terragen will be briefly explained. Please consult the documentation about how to create a world, as only this discussion is limited to describing the image-export process.

When done creating a world in Terragen, perform the following steps to make the texture available for your skybox:

1. Move your camera to the desired position.

2. Disable the Fixed Height Above Surface switch.

3. Set Detail to maximum.

4. In the Camera Settings dialog, set Zoom Magnification to 1.

5. Set Image Size.

6. Render six images and store them using the Render Image button, changing the Pitch and Head fields according to the values in Table 9.1, or use the export script supplied on this book's website, which outputs six images automatically.

To execute a script go to Terragen->Execute Script and specify the script file. The images will be exported into the same directory in bmp format. Rename the images and convert them to your image format. Figure 9.11 shows six skybox textures generated by Terragen.

Figure 9.11 Example view of six skybox images and their interconnection as produced by Terragen.

Multilayered Skyboxes

Skyboxes can be extended by adding more parallax detail using multiple layers and animation. These techniques can be used to effectively enhance a static background. You could use a three-layer skybox, for example, comprising an outer layer with a static background (such as stars or a sunset atmosphere), an the innermost layer containing local details (such as mountains), and a middle layer featuring clouds. Multilayer skyboxes can be implemented by rendering different-size skyboxes and blending them together using either alpha masking or a specific blending function. Figure 9.12 illustrates this concept.

Skybox Animation

To implement animation, texture translation on skyplanes, as explained in the previous section on skyplanes, can be used, especially for moving clouds. Mixing skyplanes with skyboxes introduces problems: either artifacts are created where the skyplane intersects the outermost layer of the skybox, or the skyplane's edges are visible when the plane ends inside the skybox. To avoid the intersection artifact, the depth buffer can be used. If you draw the animated skyplane into the depth buffer and before drawing the innermost

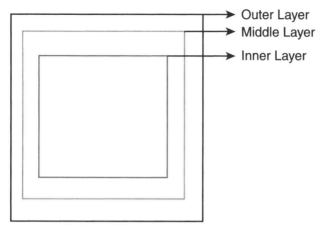

Figure 9.12 A possible scheme for a multilayered skybox.

skybox layer, the skyplane will never interfere with, intersect, or hide a skybox. The clouds will look as if they disappear behind the local details contained in the innermost skybox. This procedure involves the following steps:

1. Draw outer skybox layers.
2. Disable depth writing (glDepthMask(GL_FALSE)).
3. Draw skyplane.
4. Enable depth writing (glDepthMask(GL_TRUE)).
5. Draw inner skybox layers.

This method does not work in environments where you can see the horizon. In those cases, you must use the special techniques described earlier in the "Skyplanes" section.

Figures 9.13 and 9.14 show screenshots from the skybox demo included on this book's website. These feature simple and multilayered animated skyboxes on an alien landscape.

References

Terragen. **http://www.planetside.co.uk/terragen/**.

Bell, Gavin, "Creating Backgrounds for 3D Games," **http://www.gamasutra.com/features/19981023/bell_01.htm**.

SkyPaint. **http://www.skypaint.com/**

Figure 9.13 Simple multilayered skybox.

Figure 9.14 Animated skyboxes using different blending functions to blend in the middle layer.

Skydomes

Andrei Stoian and Dimi Christopoulos

When you're deciding which sky-rendering method to use, it's important to understand the advantages and disadvantages of each so you can choose the one that's best for your project. An indoor game will not need a realistic sky, so a skybox will do, but for rendering outdoor environments, a good sky algorithm is critical to getting quality images. For such outdoor environments, a skydome is a good tool. Here are some of the advantages of the skydome:

- It produces realistic colors easily, which allows you to show transitions between night and day.
- It works well with advanced coloring algorithms such as simulating atmospheric scattering.
- If textured, it requires only one texture, as opposed to the six needed for a skybox, which means the resolution of the texture can be quite large.
- It allows the fog color to be computed easily, allowing a seamless transition in coloring from terrain to sky.

The skydome's advantages make it an easy-to-use method when you need a dynamic sky or when you want to use a high-resolution sky texture, which especially suits outdoor environments like those found in many third-person role-playing games, where day-night transitions and sky effects are important. When using a dynamic sky method, you often must compute the angle between a specific vertex of the dome and the sun, for which the polar coordinates used to construct the dome are useful.

Some of the drawbacks of skydomes are:

- They require more polygons than skyboxes.
- Textures for skydomes can be harder to create or obtain.
- They only show the sky above to the horizon and not below it, as skyboxes do.

Let's examine the number of polygons the skydome will need. If the dome is split up into N slices and M sides, then it will have $2N(M + 1)$ vertices and 2MN triangles. For a high-quality, well-tessellated dome, values for N and M of 32 and 48, respectively, give us around 3,000 triangles. When programming for a modern PC or console platform, 3,000 triangles is a very low number, but if the application is to be run on a mobile device, a number that high might cause problems. The number of slices and sides can be tweaked for optimum performance, and the whole skydome vertex array can be stored in video memory, increasing performance. The fill-rate hit is about the same as that of the skydome, so either method will give the same fill-rate-related speed decrease.

As mentioned, textures for a skydome are harder to find or create. A number of skydome textures are available free online, and there are several commercial options for high-resolution textures; some of each are listed in the references at the end of this section. If you want to create a texture yourself, you can do so in a few easy steps with freely available tools, as described in the following section. The method presented can produce high-quality photorealistic skies, given enough processing time and some artistic inclination.

Before we get into dome-texture creation, a word about the third disadvantage listed above. There are two ways to address the problem of the skydome's inability to show the sky below the horizon. First, when you're working with a dome with vertex colors, you can obtain the color at the horizon, which then clears the screen and becomes the fog color, thus giving the impression of a transition between the terrain and the sky. Some dynamic methods use atmospheric scattering to compute this color, which gives even better results. A second option is to add a disk at the base of the dome to close it and color its edges to match the horizon.

Generating the Dome

A skydome could be essentially described as a half-sphere. Figure 9.15 shows a skydome in wireframe. To render a half-sphere, you first need to compute the points (vertices) used to create it.

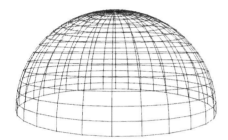

Figure 9.15 Geometry of a skydome.

The following equations can be used to define a sphere at the center of the Cartesian coordinate system with radius r.

$$x^2 + y^2 + z^2 = r^2$$

$$f(p) = x^2 + y^2 + z^2 - r^2$$

Each point p can be computed analyzing this equation. However, working with this representation can be very involved; therefore we use polar coordinates to describe the sphere. In polar coordinates each point is computed by specifying two angles, Θ (theta) and Φ (phi), which represent the longitudes and latitudes of a sphere. Essentially Φ is the angle between the vertex and the y-axis and Θ is the angle between the projection of a vertex on the xz-plane and the x-axis. Figure 9.16 illustrates this more clearly.

Computing the Vertices

Computing the x, y, and z Cartesian coordinates from these polar coordinates can be accomplished using the equations below.

$$x = r * \cos(\theta) * \cos(\phi)$$

$$y = r * \sin(\phi)$$

$$z = r * \sin(\theta) * \cos(\phi)$$

Θ ranges from 0 to 2π radians or 0 to 360 degrees, and Φ from 0 to $\pi/2$ radians or 0 to 90 degrees. Now that we know how to compute any specific point on a half sphere, we must specify the precision or interval with which the points will be computed. For this, the sphere will be cut horizontally (from top to bottom) into *slices*, each of which represents a ring of

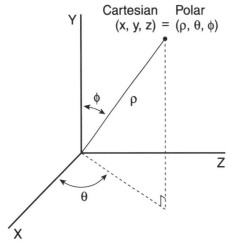

Figure 9.16 A vertex's Θ (theta) and Φ (phi) polar coordinates.

vertices. The number of vertices in each ring is specified by the number of *sides* by which the ring will be divided. The number of vertices of a slice is (sides + 1) and not just equal to the number of sides, because the first and last point, although the same, have to be specified separately for rendering. Similarly, the number of rings for a half dome is (slices + 1) because the top of the dome also has to be rendered as a ring although all of its vertices will be the same point. Therefore the total number of vertices needed for rendering the dome as a vertex array is:

```
NumVertices = (Slices +1) * (Sides +1)
```

Once we know the number of slices and sides, we can compute the intervals ΔΘ, ΔΦ in the Θ and Φ angles at which to compute our points.

ΔΘ : 2π/sides

ΔΦ : (π/2)/slices

The vertices are computed in two nested loops, as the following code excerpt shows.

```
// Allocate space
VertexBuffer = new Vector3[(Slices + 1) * (Sides + 1)];

// Calculate ΔΘ
float polyAng = 2.0f * PI / Sides;
for (j = 0; j <= Slices; j++)
{
  // Calculate ΔΦ
  ang = j * ( (PI / 2) / Slices );
```

```
  for (i = 0; i <= Sides; i++)
  {
    // Calculate Cartesian coordinates
    vx = cos(i * polyAng) * cos(ang);
    vy = dampening_factor * sin(ang);
    vz = sin(i * polyAng) * cos(ang);

    VertexBuffer[j * (Sides + 1) + i].x = vx * SkyRadius;
    VertexBuffer[j * (Sides + 1) + i].z = vz * SkyRadius;
    VertexBuffer[j * (Sides + 1) + i].y = vy * SkyRadius;
  }
}
```

The angles are computed in radians (note that the sin() and cos() functions work with radians only and not degrees). $\Delta\Theta$ is stored in the polyAng variable and $\Delta\Phi$ is computed inside the loop and stored in the ang variable. Each of these values is multiplied by the loop counters i and j to calculate the final angle and the Cartesian coordinates. VertexBuffer[] is a vector array that stores the coordinates and allocates enough memory for NumVertices, as calculated earlier.

When generating the geometry, dampening of the dome in the y-axis produces an elliptical dome that might be useful in certain situations, since it is not as high and more vertices can be seen. Dampening is specified by a factor (dampening_factor in the code listing above), which is multiplied by the y-coordinate, scaling it accordingly. The factor can be between 0 and 1. A value of 1 leaves everything unchanged, whereas a value of 0.5 produces a dome with half the height.

Creating and Rendering the Triangles

Indices are calculated after the coordinates, and they are used to form triangles pointing into VertexBuffer[]. The optimal form to render a dome is using triangle strips. Thus we will create as many triangle strips as there are slices, and each strip will form triangles between two vertex rings.

```
IndexBuffer = new unsigned short [Slices * (Sides + 1) * 2];

for (j = 1; j <= Slices; j++)
{
  for (i = 0; i <= Sides; i++)
  {
    IndexBuffer[ind++] =  j       * (Sides + 1) + i;
    IndexBuffer[ind++] = (j - 1) * (Sides + 1) + i;
  }
}
```

Rendering is straightforward once the vertex arrays and index arrays are passed into OpenGL.

```
glEnableClientState(GL_VERTEX_ARRAY);
glVertexPointer(3, GL_FLOAT, 0, &VertexBuffer[0]);
for (i = 0; i < NumSlices; i++)
{
  glDrawElements(GL_TRIANGLE_STRIP, (NumSides + 1) * 2, GL_UNSIGNED_SHORT,
                 &IndexBuffer[i * (NumSides + 1) * 2]);
}
glDisableClientState(GL_VERTEX_ARRAY);
```

Mapping a Sky Image onto the Dome

We have generated a dome and can display it either as wireframe or using a uniform color. To finish the simulation, we have to add a sky texture. The easiest way to do this is by planar texture mapping the image from above onto the xz-plane. Unfortunately, this method produces heavy artifacts and stretching at the base of the dome, and it is rarely used for texturing a 180-degree dome. Instead, spherical texture mapping is the method of choice. In spherical texture mapping, a rectangular texture is projected onto the sphere, covering its surface. The UV-coordinates can be computed from the vertices using the following sphere-mapping equations.

$$\theta = \arcsin \frac{z}{\sqrt{x^2 + z^2}} \, , \, \varphi = \arcsin \frac{y}{\sqrt{x^2 + y^2 + z^2}}$$

$$U = \frac{1}{2} + \frac{\theta}{2\pi} \, , \, V = \frac{1}{2} + \frac{\varphi}{\frac{\pi}{2}}$$

Fortunately, these equations don't have to be evaluated because we are constructing the dome ourselves. We already know the polar angles v (theta) and Φ (phi) and can compute the texture coordinates in the loop that we compute the vertex coordinates in (shown in the "Computing the Vertices" section above). First, the following line must be added to allocate space for the texture coordinates:

```
TexCoordBuffer = new Vector2[(Slices + 1) * (Sides + 1)];
```

The number of texture coordinates is equal to the number of vertices since each vertex has one texture coordinate. Second, the texture coordinates must be computed. Figure 9.17 illustrates how this is done.

Every vertex of the sphere is mapped onto the image according to which side and slice it belongs to. Two lines are added to the innermost loop, in which the counters i and j are divided by the respective sides and slices to produce UV-coordinates in the range [0, 1]:

```
TexCoordBuffer[j * (Sides + 1) + i].u = (float)(i) / (float)(Sides);
TexCoordBuffer[j * (Sides + 1) + i].v = (float)(j) / (float)(Slices);
```

Figure 9.17 The distribution of texture-sphere-mapping texture coordinates over the actual image for a dome with 7 slices and 15 sides.

Rendering the Skydome

Before rendering the dome with a texture map applied, the TexCoordBuffer[] has to be passed as an element array using glDrawElements(). As with skyplanes and skyboxes, you should disable any unnecessary pipeline operations such as fog, lighting, and depth testing.

```
glEnableClientState(GL_VERTEX_ARRAY);
glEnableClientState(GL_TEXTURE_COORD_ARRAY);

glVertexPointer(3, GL_FLOAT, 0, &VertexBuffer[0]);
glTexCoordPointer(2, GL_FLOAT, 0, &TexCoordBuffer[0]);

for (i = 0; i < NumSlices; i++)
{
  glDrawElements(GL_TRIANGLE_STRIP, (NumSides + 1) * 2, GL_UNSIGNED_SHORT,
                 &IndexBuffer[i * (NumSides + 1) * 2]);
}
glDisableClientState(GL_VERTEX_ARRAY);
glDisableClientState(GL_TEXTURE_COORD_ARRAY);
```

Figures 9.18 and 9.19 show screenshots from the skydome demo included on this book's website. By replacing the texture, different environments can be simulated.

Figure 9.18 Screenshots from the demo, using the textured skydome.

Figure 9.19 The skydome from above, with a dampening factor of 0.5.

Making Skydome Textures from Cubemaps

A skydome texture represents a 360-degree equirectangular projection of the sky, one that maps a spherical surface surrounding the camera onto a plane. This type of projection shows great distortion at the poles (since this case deals with a dome, a single pole is present) and very little distortion at the equator. This is exactly what a skydome needs, since at its zenith the triangles comprising the structure are very small and close together compared to the ones at the horizon. Using this equirectangular projection also allows very simple texture mapping, by assigning texture coordinates based on latitude and longitude on the dome. Luckily, a skydome texture can be easily made with freely available tools. The process, which is illustrated in Figure 9.20, requires the following steps:

1. Create six textures that map onto a skybox (this process was described in the "Skyboxes" section earlier).

2. Using a 180-degree fisheye camera pointing straight up, render a square image (see Figure 9.21).

3. Unwrap the result to an equirectangular image.

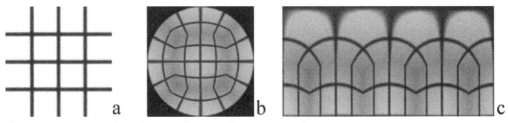

Figure 9.20 Conversion of texture from a cubemap to a sphere map.

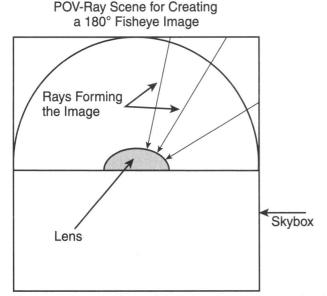

Figure 9.21 A 180-degree fisheye lens pointing up into the skybox.

The images shown give an idea of the transformations that occur to the original skybox textures. Figure 9.20a shows the original image, which is mapped, in our case, to all the sides of the box. To generate the fisheye image we construct a scene in POV-Ray, a free raytracer, that consists of:

1. A skybox mapped with the cubemap. The skybox extends from $(-x, -x, -x)$ to (x, x, x). We chose a value of 2 for x.

2. A 180° fisheye camera pointed up, located in the middle of the skybox.

Using anti-aliasing and texture clamping will remove any artifacts on the edges of the box where the faces meet. Using a script provided with the demos for this chapter, the process can be easily replicated; you only need to get textures for the box. The rendering can be done to arbitrary resolution, but a power of two size for both width and height is recommended for compatibility with graphics hardware. After the rendering is done we end up with a texture looking something like Figure 9.20b. We need to unwrap this texture to create the final image, which will be mapped onto the dome. This can be accomplished with ease in The GIMP, another free utility. The steps, in order, are:

1. Load the texture.

2. In the main menu, go to Filter, then Distort, and choose Polar Coords. Uncheck the To Polar box. Apply the filter.

3. Rescale to half the height since it is vertically stretched (choose Image size in the Image menu).

Sphere maps can also be found on the Internet for free or for purchase. TurboSquid, MarlinStudio, and 1000skies may be of interest. SkyPaint has a tool for automatically converting cube maps to sphere maps. LithUnwrap also has usable freeware tools for generating sphere maps from cubemaps and creating equirectangular textures, as we did in this section using The GIMP.

Using Color Tables for Skydome Simulation

A simple method of applying colors to the dome's vertices is to use a lookup table. Provided we have a realistic lookup table, this is a quick way to get a nice look for the sky that doesn't require much computational power or work on the programmer's part. The table can be read from an image file, where each pixel represents the color at a specific point in time and latitude on the skydome. Thus the x-dimension on the image will represent time, and the y-dimension, latitude. After loading the image, we will create a 2D color array in which to store the color values, which will be applied to the dome. Since the number of sides and slices of the dome may not be equal to the number of pixels in the x and y dimensions respectively, we will use interpolation, which is very similar to the way texturing is done. Each vertex is considered individually, and in the first step, the four closest values in the table are determined. On the x-axis, representing time, which is a floating-point value from 0 to 24:

```
float fX = TimeofDay / 24.0f * Width;
int iX = fX;
int iXn = (iX >= Width - 1 ? iX : iX + 1);
```

iX gives the index of the closest previous color and iXn of the next color, while fX gives the floating point value on the x-axis the vertex is at. We do the same process on the y-axis, taking care not to get indexes out of the bounds of the table.

```
float fY = Theta / (PI / 2) * Height;
int iY = fY;
if (iY >= Height) iY = Height - 1;
int iYn = (iY >= Height - 1 ? iY : iY + 1);
```

Theta contains the latitude on the dome, ranging from 0 at the bottom to PI/2 at the top. Knowing the dimensions of the table, we can extract the colors from the tables using these indexes,. These constitute a square and the variables are named appropriately with (0,0) being the bottom left corner and (1,1) the top right corner. ColorTable[] holds the image data loaded from a file.

```
Color4 Col00 = ColorTable[iY * Width + iX];
Color4 Col01 = ColorTable[iY * Width + iXn];
Color4 Col11 = ColorTable[iYn * Width + iXn];
Color4 Col10 = ColorTable[iYn * Width + iX];
```

Finally, we can do bilinear interpolation: first the values in the z-dimension are interpolated—Col00 with Col01 and Col10 with Col11.

```
float hf = fX - iX;
Color4 Horiz0 = Col00 * (1.0f - hf) + Col01 * hf;
Color4 Horiz1 = Col10 * (1.0f - hf) + Col11 * hf;
```

Now these two colors are interpolated on the y-axis, and the result is stored in the pointer provided:

```
float vf = fY - iY;
*ptr = Horiz0 * (1.0f - vf) + Horiz1 * vf;
```

The function below shows how to compute a specific color value for a vertex based on the color tables.

```
void GetColor(float TimeofDay, float Phi, float Theta, Color4* ptr)
{
  float fX = TimeofDay / 24.0f * Width;
  int iX = fX;
  int iXn = (iX >= Width - 1 ? iX : iX + 1);
  float fY = Theta / (PI / 2) * Height;
  int iY = fY;
  if (iY >= Height) iY = Height - 1;
  int iYn = (iY >= Height - 1 ? iY : iY + 1);

  Color4 Col00 = ColorTable[iY * Width + iX];
```

```
  Color4 Col01 = ColorTable[iY * Width + iXn];
  Color4 Col11 = ColorTable[iYn * Width + iXn];
  Color4 Col10 = ColorTable[iYn * Width + iX];

  float hf = fX - iX;
  Color4 Horiz0 = Col00 * (1.0f - hf) + Col01 * hf;
  Color4 Horiz1 = Col10 * (1.0f - hf) + Col11 * hf;
  float vf = fY - iY;
  *ptr = Horiz0 * (1.0f - vf) + Horiz1 * vf;
}
```

Before the dome is rendered, the ColorBuffer[] has to be passed as an element array by using glDrawElements().The color buffer has to be updated whenever the time of day changes.

```
float halfPI = PI / 2;
float SliceAng = (PI / 2) / NumSlices;
float SideAng = (PI * 2) / NumSides;
float theta, phi;

Color4* ColorPtr = ColorBuffer;
for (ind = 0; ind <= NumSlices; ind++)
{
  for (num = 0; num <= NumSides; num++)
  {
    theta = halfPI - SliceAng * ind;
    phi = num * SideAng;
    GetColor(TimeofDay , phi, halfPI - theta, ColorPtr);
    ColorPtr++;
  }
}
void CSkyDome::RenderDome()
{
  glEnableClientState(GL_VERTEX_ARRAY);
  glEnableClientState(GL_COLOR_ARRAY);
  glVertexPointer(3, GL_FLOAT, 0, &VertexBuffer[0]);
  glColorPointer(4, GL_FLOAT, 0, &ColorBuffer[0]);
  for (i = 0; i < NumSlices; i++)
  {
    glDrawElements(GL_TRIANGLE_STRIP, (NumSides + 1) * 2, GL_UNSIGNED_SHORT,
                   &IndexBuffer[i * (NumSides + 1) * 2]);
  }
  glDisableClientState(GL_VERTEX_ARRAY);
  glDisableClientState(GL_COLOR_ARRAY);
}
```

Using Sky Maps for Skydome Simulation

The sky-map technique combines the color-table and dome-texturing methods. Instead of using a color table to color the vertices of a dome, sky maps are colored using a stripe of a 2D texture. The advantages of using texturing instead of a color table are that texturing is not dependent on the number of vertices (fewer vertices does not mean coarser interpolation), the textures can be created in any paint program, and no additional color buffer (or other special setup) is needed, leading to simpler implementation. This method is based on the white paper by Jesus Alonso Abad.

As stated earlier, the dome will get its colors from the texture, but instead of mapping the whole texture map onto the dome as in the dome-texturing section, only one 1-pixel-wide stripe is mapped vertically onto the dome. A 32×32 texture, for example, would yield 32 vertical stripes 32 pixels long. Each of these stripes represent a specific time of day. For example, stripe 0 is usually mapped to 6 am, strip 16 is 6 pm and stripe 24 is 12 am midnight. The Figure 9.22 shows how a skymap texture looks and is encoded. U and V are the texture coordinates and T is the time of day starting from 6 am in the morning.

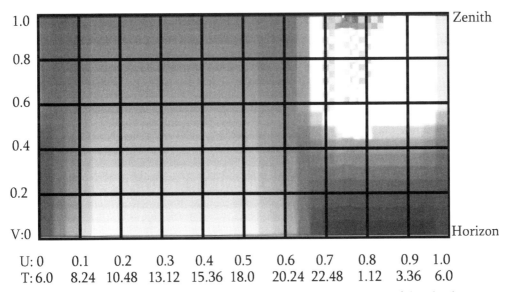

U: 0	0.1	0.2	0.3	0.4	0.5	0.6	0.7	0.8	0.9	1.0
T: 6.0	8.24	10.48	13.12	15.36	18.0	20.24	22.48	1.12	3.36	6.0

Figure 9.22 How a texture stripe is applied on the dome depending on time of day. The dome consists of 5 slices and 10 sides.

Applying a stripe to the dome is easy. Once the texture is defined, the UV texture coordinates of a vertex have to be calculated depending on the time of day. U represents the time of day and changes in real time for every vertex to simulate a day cycle; all vertices have the same U-coordinate. V represents the slices from which a dome is constructed and remains constant for every vertex through the whole day cycle. Only vertices that are in the same slice have the same V-coordinate. The time of day can be specified in hours or can be computed from the Θ (SunTheta) angle of the sun. Based on a 24-hour-day cycle, the equation that computes the U and V values for a specific vertex is:

```
TimeofDay = SunTheta * 24 * 60 / 360
U = (TimeofDay) * (1.0 / 24)
V = Slice * (1.0 / NumberofSlices)
```

The above equation results in a value between 0 and 1 for a specific time of day expressed in hours. As can be seen, U depends only on the time of day, and V, only on the slice number it is on. The color of the day cycle is encoded into the texture; thus, by changing the colors of the texture, different color cycles can be created. The code below shows the texture-coordinate calculation for a specific time of day. Note that the TexCoordBuffer[] has to be refreshed if the time of day has changed, because new U values have to be calculated. Also note that the skymap texture can also have alpha, which allows you to make certain regions transparent at night to let the stars or moon be visible.

```
u = TimeofDay*(1.f/24.f);
for (j = 0; j <= Slices; j++)
{
  for (i = 0; i <= Sides; i++)
  {
    TexCoordBuffer[j * (Sides + 1) + i].x = u;
    TexCoordBuffer[j * (Sides + 1) + i].y = (float)(j) / (float)(Slices);
  }
}
```

The sky map is rendered the same way as the static-sky-image approach, but the texture coordinates have to be recomputed and TexCoordBuffer[] updated as shown above as soon as the time of day changes.

The figures below show screenshots from the animated-dome-texturing-demo that simulates time of day, included on this book's website.

Figure 9.23 Screenshots from the demo simulating sunset and midday sky colors, and the skymap used.

Physically Based Sky Color Computation

Outdoor scenes are becoming more feasible and common. We present an inexpensive analytic model based on "A Practical Analytic Daylight," by A. Preetham, P. Shirley, and B. Smits, that approximates the full spectrum of daylight for various conditions. Instead of using preconstructed textures or color tables to simulate the sky on a dome, computational methods based on equations are used to compute the color at each vertex of the dome. Such analytical methods have the advantages of low memory consumption, procedural color generation, high-quality physically based pictures, no need for third-party plug-ins, and ease of use once implemented. To implement such a color model, a basic understanding of how the colors in our atmosphere at any given hour are created, is needed. The light that comes from the sun is scattered in the atmosphere, resulting in the sky-color variations from the pale red of dawn to the blue of midday and back again. The color depends not only on the time of day, but also on other factors such as weather, pollution, and atmospheric conditions. If atmospheric scattering were not present, we would look at a black sky.

The two most common forms of scattering are Rayleigh and Mie. Rayleigh scattering is caused by small molecules and scatters light more at shorter wavelengths (blue first, then green, then red). The sky during the day is blue because blue light is scattered more and reaches the eye. The sky turns yellow, orange, and red at sunset because the sunlight travels a longer distance through the atmosphere when the sun is at the horizon; almost all of the blue and green is scattered before the light reaches the eye, leaving reddish colors. Mie scattering is caused by larger particles in the air called aerosols (dust, pollution, etc.) and scatters all wavelengths. On a hazy day, Mie scattering is what causes the sky to look gray and the sun to have a white halo around it.

The input data for computing the final sky color will be the sun position and the weather conditions using this simplified equation:

```
Sky (sun position, weather conditions) -> sky color -> RGB color
```

The sun position is calculated from latitude, longitude, time, and date, and is specified in polar coordinates theta (Θ) and phi (Φ). Weather conditions are represented by a factor called *Turbidity*. Turbidity shows the fraction of scattering due to haze aerosols (smoke, dust, smog) and describes Mie scattering. In essence it's a measure of haze density in the atmosphere; a value of 2.0 describes a clear sky, and a value of 6.0, a mistier atmosphere. Although it's a simplification of the parameters that actually describe weather conditions, it is preferred because of its practical use not just for real-time applications but also by atmospheric scientists. Rayleigh scattering is described by equations and simulation tables and is computed based on the Turbidity value, as will be shown later. Weather and atmospheric equations and models as proposed by Nishita et al. have nested integrals that are impossible to solve in real time. Therefore, real-time models such as the one we will implement (Preetham et al.) are based on assumptions that simplify the derivations. The user is assumed to be near the ground, precalculated tables for certain quantities will be used, only secondary and primary scattering is taken into account, and simpler weather parameters are used. Figure 9.24 shows the approach of the analytical-sky-color-computation model based on domes. The user is placed in the center, and the amount of light that passes through a vertex before it reaches the eyes and after it has been scattered in the atmosphere is calculated and stored.

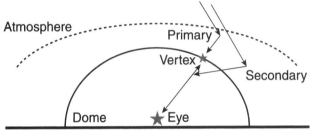

Figure 9.24 The primary and secondary scattering as the light passes the atmosphere determines the vertex color.

Computing the Sky Color

For computing the color at a specific vertex of the dome, the coordinates and position of the sun are used to compute the angles needed, as Figure 9.25 shows. The angles of interest are:

- **Theta** (Θ). It is the angle of the y-axis of the dome and the vector from the center of the dome to the specific vertex (longitude).
- **ThetaS** (Θs). The angle between the y-axis of the dome and the vector of the sun. This is also known because the sun coordinates are usually computed in polar coordinates (theta, phi).
- **PhiS** (Φs). The phi angle in polar coordinates of the sun. It's the angle between the x-axis and the projected onto the ground sun vector.
- **Gamma** (Γ). The angle between the sun vector and the vector from the center of the dome to the vertex.

These angles will be used by a model to compute the final vertex color using luminance (Y) and chromaticity values (xy). Luminance is the perceived brightness, or grayscale level, of a color. Luminance and chromaticity values together fully define a perceived color. Colors, which are expressed this way, are said to be in the CIE Yxy color space. We will see later how to convert such a value into the familiar RGB color space.

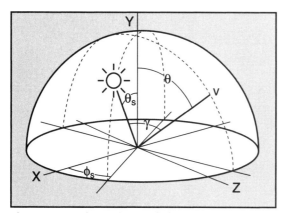

Figure 9.25 The angles needed in the skydome.

Perez et al. have developed a sky-luminance-distribution model, which needs the luminance at the zenith (Yz) (maximum luminance value of dome) and five other parameters, each having a specific physical effect on the atmosphere. The parameters relate to darkening or brightening of the horizon (A), the luminance gradient near the horizon (B), the relative intensity of the circumsolar region (C), the width of the circumsolar region (D), and relative backscattered light (E). The Perez equation for the luminance distribution is

$$F(\theta, \gamma) = (1 + Ae^{B/\cos\theta})(1 + Ce^{D\gamma} + W\cos^2\gamma)(0)$$

where A, B, C, D, and E are the coefficients of the parameters described above, and Γ and Θ are the angles shown in Figure 9.25. The final luminance value (Y) for a vertex is given by

$$Y_p = Y_z \frac{F(\theta, \gamma)}{F(0, \theta_s)} \quad (1)$$

Yz is the zenith luminance, $F(\Theta, \Gamma)$ is the result of the Perez equation (0) using the computed theta and gamma angles of a vertex as parameters, and $F(0, \Theta s)$ is the Perez equation (0) with a theta value of zero and the theta of the sun as parameters. $F(0, \Theta s)$ produces the maximum value for the specified sun position, and it therefore divides $F(\Theta, \Gamma)$ to produce a value in the range [0, 1] to scale the zenith luminance. The Perez equations use specific coefficients (AY, BY, CY, DY, EY) to compute luminance values. Fortunately, values for the (Yz) zenith luminance and (AY, BY, CY, DY, EY) coefficients have already been computed for our earth by atmosphere researchers, and Preetham et al. provides tables and equations to compute them.

Computing the luminance (Y) at a specific vertex is not enough to specify a color; the chromaticity values (x, y) have also to be computed to provide a full-color representation in (Yxy) color space. The chromaticity values for a vertex are computed in a similar fashion as the luminance value for this vertex. The zenith chromaticity (xz, yz) (maximum chromaticity values) and the Perez equation with different (A, B, C, D, E) coefficients will be used to compute the final values similar to (1).

$$x = xz \frac{F(\theta, \gamma)}{F(0, \theta_s)} \quad \text{and} \quad y = yz \frac{F(\theta, \gamma)}{F(0, \theta_s)} \quad (2)$$

Again, xz, yz are the zenith chromaticity values, and the Perez equations $F(\Theta, \Gamma)$, $F(0, \Theta s)$ are the same as in (1) but with different coefficient parameters (Ax, Bx, Cx, Dx, Ex) and (Ay, By, Cy, Dy, Ey) to compute chromaticity values. As mentioned, values for the (xz, yz) zenith chromaticity values and (Ax, Bx, Cx, Dx, Ex) or (Ay, By, Cy, Dy, Ey) coefficients have already been computed for our earth by atmosphere researchers and Preetham et al. provide tables and equations to compute them. The code below shows the C++ implementation for computing the luminance (Y) and chromaticity (x,y) values.

```
float CSkyColor::PerezFunction_x (float cosTheta, float cosGamma, float gamma)
{
    float val1 = ( 1 + Ax * exp(Bx / cosTheta ) ) *
                 ( 1 + Cx * exp(Dx * gamma) + Ex * SQR(cosGamma) );
    float val2 = ( 1 + Ax * exp(Bx) ) *
                 ( 1 + Cx * exp(Dx * suntheta) + Ex * SQR(cosSTheta) );
    return val1 / val2;
}


float CSkyColor::PerezFunction_y(float cosTheta, float cosGamma, float gamma)
{
    float val1 = ( 1 + Ay * exp(By / cosTheta) ) *
                 ( 1 + Cy * exp(Dy * gamma    ) + Ey * SQR(cosGamma  )  );
    float val2 = ( 1 + Ay * exp(By           ) ) *
                 ( 1 + Cy * exp(Dy * suntheta) + Ey * SQR(cosSTheta) );
    return val1 / val2;
}


float CSkyColor::PerezFunction_Y(float cosTheta, float cosGamma, float gamma)
{
    float val1 = ( 1 + AY * exp(BY / cosTheta) ) *
                 ( 1 + CY * exp(DY * gamma    ) + EY * SQR(cosGamma) );
    float val2 = ( 1 + AY * exp(BY           ) ) *
                 ( 1 + CY * exp(DY * suntheta) + EY * SQR(cosSTheta) );
    return val1 / val2;
}
```

```
void CSkyColor::GetVertexColor(float theta, float phi, float sunphi, Color4* color)
{
  float x, y, Y;
  float cosTheta, cosGamma, cosSTheta;

  float gamma = Angle(theta, phi, suntheta, sunphi);

  // Error check for theta bigger than 90 degrees.
  if (fabs(th - (PI / 2)) < 0.001f)
    cosTheta = 0.00001f;
  else
    cosTheta = cos(th);

  cosGamma = cos(gm);
  cosSTheta = cos(suntheta);

  x = xz * PerezFunction_x(cosTheta, cosGamma, gm);
  y = yz * PerezFunction_y(cosTheta, cosGamma, gm);
  Y = Yz * PerezFunction_Y(cosTheta, cosGamma, gm);

  Color3 rgb;
  ToRGB(x, y, Y, &rgb);

  color->R = rgb.R;
  color->G = rgb.G;
  color->B = rgb.B;
  color->A = 1.0f;
}
```

The functions `PerezFunction_[x,y,Y]()` compute the scaling factor $F(\Theta, \Gamma)/F(0, \Theta s)$ of equations (1) and (2) and use the respective coefficients (Ax, Bx, Cx, Dx, Ex), (Ay, By, Cy, Dy, Ey), and (AY, BY, CY, DY, EY). `GetVertexColor()` computes the color for a specific vertex, taking as input its theta and phi polar coordinates and the `sunphi` and `suntheta` polar coordinates of the sun (the variable `suntheta` is defined as a global). First the `gamma` (Γ) angle is computed by function `Angle()`, then the cosine value of `gamma` and `suntheta` are precomputed for speedup and passed to the Perez functions to compute the final Yxy value. The Yxy value is then transformed to RGB color by `ToRGB()`. Note that theta values for vertices greater than 90 degrees (below the horizon) are clamped to 90 degrees because they would produce undefined results.

Calculating the Missing Parameters

The only information that is missing right now is how to compute these Yz (zenith luminance), xz, yz (zenith chromaticity values), and (Ax, Bx, Cx ,Dx, Ex), (Ay, By, Cy, Dy, Ey), and (AY, BY, CY, DY, EY) coefficients. To compute these values, precomputed simulation matrices will be used which will be multiplied by Θs suntheta, and the Turbidity value. This means that these parameters are based upon the sun position and Turbidity and have to be recalculated only if one of these changes. Fortunately these precomputed matrices have already been constructed by Preetham et al. and are based on a detailed multiscattering model by Nishita et al. The simulation was run for combinations of 12 sun positions, 5 turbidity values between 2 and 6, and 343 viewing positions, resulting in 600 CPU hours. These results were then fitted to a parametric representation to produce the final tables and equations. The tables and equations are given below, and the SetInfo() functions compute these in code taking as input parameters the sun position (suntheta) and the Turbidity value.

Coefficients:

$$
\begin{bmatrix} AY \\ BY \\ CY \\ DY \\ EY \end{bmatrix} = \begin{bmatrix} 0.1787 & -1.4630 \\ -0.3554 & 0.4275 \\ -0.0227 & 5.3251 \\ 0.1206 & -2.5771 \\ -0.0670 & 0.3703 \end{bmatrix} \begin{bmatrix} T \\ 1 \end{bmatrix}
\quad
\begin{bmatrix} Ax \\ Bx \\ Cx \\ Dx \\ Ex \end{bmatrix} = \begin{bmatrix} -0.0193 & -0.2592 \\ -0.0665 & 0.0008 \\ -0.0004 & 0.2125 \\ -0.0641 & -0.8989 \\ -0.0033 & 0.0452 \end{bmatrix} \begin{bmatrix} T \\ 1 \end{bmatrix}
\quad
\begin{bmatrix} Ay \\ By \\ Cy \\ Dy \\ Ey \end{bmatrix} = \begin{bmatrix} -0.0167 & -0.2608 \\ -0.0950 & 0.0092 \\ -0.0079 & 0.2102 \\ -0.0441 & -1.6537 \\ -0.0109 & 0.0529 \end{bmatrix} \begin{bmatrix} T \\ 1 \end{bmatrix}
$$

Zenith y:

$$
Yz = (0.4.0453 * T - 4.9710)\ \tan X - 0.2155 * T + 2.4192 \text{ where } X = \left(\frac{4}{9} - \frac{T}{120}\right)(\pi - 2\theta_2)
$$

Zenith x:

$$
xz = \begin{bmatrix} T^2 & T & 1 \end{bmatrix} \begin{bmatrix} 0.00166 & -0.00375 & 0.00209 & 0 \\ -0.02903 & 0.06377 & -0.03202 & 0.00394 \\ 0.11693 & -0.21196 & 0.06052 & 0.25886 \end{bmatrix} \begin{bmatrix} \theta_s^3 \\ \theta_s^2 \\ \theta_s \\ 1 \end{bmatrix}
$$

Zenith y:

$$
yz = \begin{bmatrix} T^2 & T & 1 \end{bmatrix} \begin{bmatrix} 0.00275 & -0.00610 & 0.00317 & 0 \\ -0.04214 & 0.08970 & -0.04153 & 0.00516 \\ 0.15346 & -0.26756 & 0.06670 & 0.26688 \end{bmatrix} \begin{bmatrix} \theta_s^3 \\ \theta_s^2 \\ \theta_s \\ 1 \end{bmatrix}
$$

Converting Yxy Colors to RGB

There are various methods for defining color. A computer will define a color in terms of the excitations of red, green, and blue phosphors on the CRT (cathode ray tube) faceplate (RGB color space). A printing press defines a color in terms of the reflectance and absorbency of cyan, magenta, yellow, and black inks on the paper (CMYK color space). There are also color spaces like HSV, XYZ, Yxy, and others that are used more in science and research. The two previously mentioned color spaces, RGB and CMYK, are device dependent. A pixel value of for example, RGB = 255, 255, 255 (white) on one particular computer monitor may not look the same on another monitor, as the red, green, and blue phosphors of the other display may be slightly different. For color to be reproduced in a predictable manner across different devices and materials, it has to be described in a way that is independent of the specific behavior of the mechanisms and materials used to produce it. Therefore the scientific organization CIE (Commission Internationale de l'Eclairage) has defined a system that classifies color according to the human visual system, and makes other color spaces subsets of this perceptual space. This system is therefore device independent, at least to humans. Also among these color spaces are the previously mentioned HSV, XYZ, and the Yxy color spaces, the last of which is used by our simulation model.

To convert between CIE Yxy based colors to device-dependent RGB colors that are used in computer graphics, the colors have to be converted to the XYZ color space, and then a transformation matrix [sRGB] is necessary to map CIE XYZ values to monitor RGB values. Unfortunately, the RGB color space is a subset of the Yxy color space, and some Yxy colors produce RGB values out of range with negative components or components over 1. Therefore clamping of the computed RGB values is required.

High Dynamic Range Rendering

Clamping the computed RGB values avoids artifacts, but often the colors computed are too bright or too dark. This is again because the RGB color space is a subset of Yxy and the conversion maps a lot of Yxy triplets to white or black since no corresponding RGB color exists. High Dynamic Range (HDR) rendering can improve the mapping of these colors to more visible RGB colors. It is accomplished by multiplying the color by an exposure equation: $1.0 - \exp(fExposure \times color)$. The *fExposure* constant works like the aperture of the camera. A low constant lets less light in and a higher constant allows more light to pass, thus enabling the image to avoid getting too dark or bright. In our source code, we use a clamping constant of 1.0/15000; changing this constant produces different effects in the sky color. The following function illustrates how the conversion, HDR rendering, and clamping is performed.

```
void CSkyColor::ToRGB(float x, float y, float Y, Color3* rgb)
{
  float fX, fY, fZ;
```

```
// Conversion from Yxy to XYZ color space
fY = Y;
fX = x / y * Y;
fZ = ((1.0f - x - y) / y) * Y;

// Conversion from XYZ to RGB color space by multiplying with a matrix
float r, g, b;
r =  3.240479f * fX - 1.537150f * fY - 0.498535f * fZ;
g = -0.969256f * fX + 1.875991f * fY + 0.041556f * fZ;
b =  0.055648f * fX - 0.204043f * fY + 1.057311f * fZ;

// High Dynamic Range Conversion
float expo = -(1.0f / 15000.0f);
r = 1.0f - exp(expo * r);
g = 1.0f - exp(expo * g);
b = 1.0f - exp(expo * b);

// Clamping to avoid values out of bounds
if (r < 0.0f) r = 0.0f; if (g < 0.0f) g = 0.0f;
if (b < 0.0f) b = 0.0f; if (r > 1.0f) r = 1.0f;
if (g > 1.0f) g = 1.0f; if (b > 1.0f) b = 1.0f;

    rgb->R = r; rgb->G = g; rgb->B = b;
}
```

The conversion from the Yxy to the XYZ color space is performed first.

```
fY = Y;
fX = x / y * Y;
fZ = ((1.0f - x - y) / y) * Y;
```

Then the color is transformed to RGB by multiplying these values with a conversion matrix.

```
r =  3.240479f * fX - 1.537150f * fY - 0.498535f * fZ;
g = -0.969256f * fX + 1.875991f * fY + 0.041556f * fZ;
b =  0.055648f * fX - 0.204043f * fY + 1.057311f * fZ;
```

Afterward, High Dynamic Range rendering is performed and the results are clamped.

```
float expo = -(1.0f / 15000.0f);
r = 1.0f - exp(expo * r);
g = 1.0f - exp(expo * g);
b = 1.0f - exp(expo * b);
```

```
// Clamping to avoid values out of bounds
if (r < 0.0f) r = 0.0f; if (g < 0.0f) g = 0.0f;
if (b < 0.0f) b = 0.0f; if (r > 1.0f) r = 1.0f;
if (g > 1.0f) g = 1.0f; if (b > 1.0f) b = 1.0f;
```

Rendering the Dome

Rendering is performed as shown in the skydome-color-table approach, but during the update, the vertex color is computed by calling GetVertexColor() rather than being taken from a table. The following code shows how the update of the color buffer is performed per frame.

```
Color4* ColorPtr = ColorBuffer;

SetInfo(SunTheta, Turbidity);

for (ind = 0; ind <= NumSlices; ind++)
{
  for (num = 0; num <= NumSides; num++)
  {
    theta = halfPI - SliceAng * ind;
    phi = num * SideAng;
    GetVertexColor(theta, phi, SunPhi, ColorPtr);
    ColorPtr++;
  }
}
```

Initially SetInfo() is called to compute the Yz, xz, and yz zenith values and the coefficients (A, B, C, D, E) needed for the Perez functions. This function is called per frame because the Turbidity or SunTheta position could have changed. Inside the nested loop, the color values for each vertex are computed by passing its polar coordinates (theta, phi) and the SunTheta position. Remember to enable the OpenGL smooth shading option to let the vertex colors interpolate smoothly.

Figures 9.26 and 9.27 show screenshots from the skylight demo included on this book's website featuring a sunset and a midday-sky light simulation.

note

This model only computes values for daylight correctly and is not suitable for night color computation (when sunTheta is greater than 90 degrees). If a full day cycle is needed, it is suggested to fade the colors of the skydome to a constant color (dark blue or black) when the sun sets. Adding alpha transparency to these colors during nightfall also enables the blending with sky elements such as stars and moon, which are rendered outside of the dome.

Figure 9.26 Screenshots from the demo, simulating sunset and midday sky colors. Turbidity 2.0.

Figure 9.27 Screenshot from the demo, simulating sunset sky colors. Turbidity 4.0.

Getting the Color at the Horizon

When rendering a sky and terrain, one usually finds that there is too high a contrast between the far end of the view volume, where the world is clipped, and the sky, which is located virtually much farther away. To fix this unappealing artifact, fog is usually used, but choosing a good fog color is essential. When using a skydome, getting this color is quite easy because we can find the vertices right in front of the camera and interpolate the colors.

First of all, to find these vertices, we need to know the angle at which the camera points in the XZ plane (which constitutes the base of the dome). This angle is simply the arctangent of the ratio of the z and x components of the view vector. Even better, the C math library provides the atan2() function that gives this angle exactly in the $[-\pi, \pi]$ range, which is then mapped to the $[0, 2\pi]$ range.

Now, converting theta to degrees, get the index of the vertex at theta degrees, knowing that each side of the dome spans a number of degrees equal to 360 divided by the number of sides. If the skydome is built from the horizon up, the colors at the horizon will be in the first row of the color buffer:

```
float ang = atan2(CameraView.z, CameraView.x);
if (ang < 0) ang = 2 * PI + ang;
int ri = (ang / (2 * PI)) * NumSides;
return Color3(ColorBuffer[ri].R, ColorBuffer[ri].G, ColorBuffer[ri].B);
```

Planetary Elements

A simple colored skydome gives a rather dull image of the sky, even using realistic color calculation algorithms. To achieve a more appealing image of the sky, we can add elements such as the sun, the moon, stars, and clouds. (Clouds are a rather complex topic that will be dealt with separately.) First of all, to determine the position of an element on the dome we use two angles: latitude and longitude. There are also two astronomical variables that are very similar to these and are used in some papers: declination and right ascension, respectively. Knowing the latitude and longitude and the radius of the dome (used to avoid Z problems with having a too-small dome), we can compute a 3D point:

```
x = cos(latitude) * cos(longitude) * radius
y = sin(latitude) * radius
z = cos(latitude) * sin(longitude) * radius
```

A good way to represent the stars is by using OpenGL point primitives. Some stars are dimmer and some are brighter, features that depend on the nature of the stars themselves. To simulate this we can use alpha blending, fading the stars depending on their magnitude (an arbitrary unit for brightness). On the other hand, some stars are very bright in the night sky (they have a very low magnitude), and for these a simple point is not enough. A small billboard with a star halo image alpha blended onto the back buffer using additive blending colored with the star's color can add some detail. To generate star positions you can use two methods: a star catalog—the "Bright Star Catalog" (BSC)—which contains accurate positions for the stars, or a random position and magnitude generator. To generate the positions, we randomly choose two angles from 0 to 2PI (longitude) and from 0 to PI/2 for the latitude and a floating-point value for the brightness.

```
for (i = 0; i < NumStars; i++)
{
    st = (rand() % 90) / 180.0f * PI;
    sp = (rand() % 360) / 180.0f * PI;
    Stars[i].x = cos(sp) * cos(st) * SkyRadius;

    Stars[i].y = sin(st) * SkyRadius;
    Stars[i].z = sin(sp) * cos(st) * SkyRadius;

    c = (rand() % 256) / 255.0f;
    StarColors[i] = Color4(c, c, c, c);
}
```

We store these values in an array, and we render them first, before the dome, using a call to draw vertex arrays with no texture but with color.

```
glEnableClientState(GL_VERTEX_ARRAY);
glEnableClientState(GL_COLOR_ARRAY);
glVertexPointer(3, GL_FLOAT, 0, Stars);
glColorPointer(4, GL_FLOAT, 0, StarColors);
glDrawArrays(GL_POINTS, 0, NumStars);
glDisableClientState(GL_VERTEX_ARRAY);
glDisableClientState(GL_COLOR_ARRAY);
```

As mentioned, the dome is only rendered after the stars, using transparent alpha blending (GL_SRC_ALPHA, GL_ONE_MINUS_SRC_ALPHA) to achieve a transition from night to day. The alpha values for each vertex can be obtained from a table. The code for rendering the dome is only augmented with:

```
glEnable(GL_BLEND);
glBlendFunc(GL_SRC_ALPHA, GL_ONE_MINUS_SRC_ALPHA);
// Draw everything here
glDisable(GL_BLEND);
```

After the dome is drawn, we can render the sun and the moon. We will generate a billboard for each of them, using their positions in the sky. There are realistic ways of calculating these positions, which are rather complex and based on many astronomical units. The demo contains implementations of algorithms for calculating the positions for the sun and the moon, but explaining them is beyond the scope of this book. Generating the billboards can be done by extracting the up and right vectors from the modelview matrix and using the center point of each object.

```
Vector3 MoonPos(sin(MoonTheta) * cos(MoonPhi) * SkyRadius,
                cos(MoonTheta) * SkyRadius,
                sin(MoonTheta) * sin(MoonPhi) * SkyRadius);
glGetFloatv(GL_MODELVIEW_MATRIX, mat);
Vector3 vx(mat[0], mat[4], mat[8] );
Vector3 vy(mat[1], mat[5], mat[9] );
//render a quad using these up, right, and center vectors
```

Next, after choosing some size for these elements and armed with good-looking textures, we can render the sun and the moon. For the sun, we use additive blending since it is a powerful light source saturating the colors in the atmosphere around it. An additional glow (a circular fade pattern) can be added for extra brightening. For the moon, we use transparent blending to simulate its being behind the atmosphere and an optional glow on clear nights.

Conclusion

As seen in this section, analytic models can be used successfully for computing sky color in real time. The methods used are based on well-established research and constructed simulations. Adjusting the Turbidity, fExposure (HDR) values, and the position of the sun can produce breathtaking sky simulations without touching any modeling or texturing tool. Enhancing the world with real-time sky simulations enhances the immersion and physical simulation of any 3D world.

References

Abad, Jesus Alonso. "A Simple Model for Fast, Realistic Sky Dome Color Rendering." **http://www.geocities.com/ngdash/whitepapers/skydomecolor.html** (accessed July 2005).

LithUnwrap. **http://www.geocities.com/lithunwrap/** (accessed July 2005).

Marlin Studios. Offers Panoramica Land & Sky for $250. **http://www.marlinstudios.com/products/pano/pano.htm** (accessed July 2005).

Nishita, T., Y. Dobashi, K. Kaneda, and H. Yamashita. "Display Method of the Sky Color Taking into Account Multiple Scattering." In *Pacific Graphics '96* (1996): 117–32.

Preetham, A., P. Shirley, and B. Smits. "A Practical Analytic Daylight." October 1999. **http://www.cs.utah.edu/vissim/papers/sunsky/**.

RGB. **http://www.sRGB.com/**.

SkyPaint. **http://www.skypaint.com/** (accessed July 2005).

1000skies. Sells textures for $25 to $50.
http://www.1000skies.com/fullpanos/index.htm (accessed July 2005).

TurboSquid. Sky textures are available from this site for $5 each.
**http://www.turbosquid.com/HTMLClient/FullPreview/FullPreview.cfm/ID/211718/
Action/FullPreview** (accessed July 2005).

Clouds

Jesse Laeuchli

Clouds are one of the most difficult things to render well in computer graphics, because everyone has seen many clouds and can immediately tell if they do not look right. Clouds have no regular defined shape, but have many random properties as well as some ordered ones. This property of randomness and order, which at first seems to provide the most difficulties, in fact lends itself well to fractal modeling.

Noise

The first step toward developing a fractal that can be used to model clouds is to develop a pink-noise function. Pink noise is a function that is not totally random like white noise (television static is a classic example of white noise) but not totally ordered either. A noise function can be any dimension, but one-, two-, three-, and four-dimensional functions are the most common and useful. The most famous noise function is Perlin's noise function, and that is what will be examined here.

Noise functions all work by taking white noise and smoothing it in some way so that it is less random. Perlin's noise function works by taking an integer lattice of any dimension, randomly indexing into the vector table at each lattice point, and then using a curve function to interpolate between the vectors on the lattice based on the point in space at which the function is called. The function contains two precomputed tables—one a list of random integers, the other a set of vectors—that are specifically chosen to avoid the appearance of clumping. The code for the 3D Perlin noise function is

```
double noise(double x, double y, double z)
{
  int X = (int)floor(x) & 255,    // FIND UNIT CUBE THAT
  Y = (int)floor(y) & 255,        // CONTAINS POINT.
  Z = (int)floor(z) & 255;

  x -= floor(x);                  // FIND RELATIVE X,Y,Z
  y -= floor(y);                  // OF POINT IN CUBE.
  z -= floor(z);
```

```
double u = fade(x),              // COMPUTE FADE CURVES
       v = fade(y),              // FOR EACH OF X,Y,Z.
       w = fade(z);
int A = p[X  ]+Y, AA = p[A]+Z, AB = p[A+1]+Z,   // HASH COORDINATES OF
    B = p[X+1]+Y, BA = p[B]+Z, BB = p[B+1]+Z;   // THE 8 CUBE CORNERS,

return lerp(w, lerp(v, lerp(u, grad(p[AA  ], x  , y  , z ), // AND ADD
                           grad(p[BA  ], x-1, y  , z  )),       // BLENDED
                   lerp(u, grad(p[AB  ], x  , y-1, z   ),       // RESULTS
                           grad(p[BB  ], x-1, y-1, z   ))),      // FROM  8
               lerp(v, lerp(u, grad(p[AA+1], x  , y  , z-1 ),  // CORNERS
                           grad(p[BA+1], x-1, y  , z-1 )),       // OF CUBE
                   lerp(u, grad(p[AB+1], x  , y-1, z-1 ),
                           grad(p[BB+1], x-1, y-1, z-1 ))));
}
```

Here grad() is a function that uses a hash table to generate a random vector to be interpolated, and fade() is a high-order polynomial used to interpolate more smoothly. The function starts off by finding the closet integer values and the fractional values of the current position. Then it generates a random value for each point of the cube, and passes this on for further randomization in the grad() function. The calls to grad() return random vectors, which are then interpolated until a final noise value is obtained.

The graph of this function does not resemble clouds very closely. However, by using this function as the building block for a fractal, a function can be produced that looks very cloudlike. The fractal is known as an *fBm* fractal and is produced by taking noises of increasing higher frequencies, scaling them, and then summing them together as below:

$$noise(x, y, z) + 1/2 * noise(2 * x, 2 * y, 2 * z) + 1/4 * noise(4 * x, 4 * y, 4 * z) + \ldots$$

At some point the additional detail contributed by the higher frequencies is no longer noticeable, so after enough frequencies of noise have been added, the rest can be dropped. Exactly how many are needed is determined by the resolution at which the fractal will be displayed. This can be determined visually or by using the Nyquist limit. This fractal can be implemented with any dimension of noise function, but again, one-, two-, three-, and four-dimensional functions are the most common.

Using the Fractal

This fractal can be used to display a very convincing cloud representation. The simplest way, which will be described here, is to have a white texture on a blue background, and then interpret the fractal as an alpha map. The third dimension of the texture can be interpreted as time, so the clouds can be animated. Below is the code for the rendering and updating of the cloud texture

```
double fBm(double x, double y, double z)
{
  return noise(x,y,z)+2*noise(.5*x,.5*y,.5*z)+4*noise(.25*x,.25*y,.25*z)+
          16*noise(.125*x,.125*y,.125*z);
}


void Setup()   //Called by the timer to update the clouds
{
  for(int x=0;x<128;x++)
    for(int y=0;y<128;y++)
    {
      float cloud=fBm(((float)x)/5+Time,(float(y))/5+Time,Time*2)/20;
      TexData[x][y][0]=1;
      TexData[x][y][1]=1;
      TexData[x][y][2]=1;
      TexData[x][y][3]=cloud;
    }

  glEnable(GL_TEXTURE_2D);
  glGenTextures(1,&Texture1);
  glBindTexture(GL_TEXTURE_2D, Texture1);
  glTexImage2D(GL_TEXTURE_2D, 0, GL_RGBA, 128, 128, 0, GL_RGBA, GL_FLOAT,
                  TexData);
  glTexParameteri(GL_TEXTURE_2D,GL_TEXTURE_MIN_FILTER,GL_LINEAR);
  glTexParameteri(GL_TEXTURE_2D,GL_TEXTURE_MAG_FILTER,GL_LINEAR);
}
```

The disadvantage of this method is that recomputing the texture and uploading it to the graphics card can be very expensive. A solution to this is to offload the work to the GPU. This can be done using fragment shaders. However, current graphics cards do not provide a hardware implementation of Perlin noise with which to implement the fBm fractal. There are two ways to implement it. The first is to implement the noise function in a fragment shader. While this provides the most flexible implementation, it takes up many of the limited instruction slots available, and is very computationally expensive. A method that works better with most hardware is to generate beforehand a large body of noise, save it as a texture, and then using this texture as the noise function in the fragment shader, create an fBm fractal. The disadvantage of this method is that it requires the use of a 3D texture, which requires a significant amount of texture memory. Also, no hardware currently supports 4D textures. Thus any shader that requires four-dimensional noise cannot use this method.

When generating the noise texture, it is important to make sure that the texture tiles; otherwise, there will be sharp breaks in the resultant cloud texture where the fractal uses data from the edge of the noise function. To make sure the texture tiles, we compute the weighted average of the function at each point as below:

```
double tilednoise(double x,double y,double z)
{
  float noisev=
    (noise(x, y,z) * (6.4 - x) * (6.4 - y) * (6.4-z)+
      noise(x - 6.4, y,z) * (x) * (6.4 - y) * (6.4-z)+
      noise(x - 6.4, y - 6.4,z) * (x) * (y) * (6.4-z)+
      noise(x, y - 6.4,z) * (6.4 - x) * (y) * (6.4-z)+
      noise(x, y,z-6.4) * (6.4 - x) * (6.4 - y) * (z)+
      noise(x - 6.4, y,z-6.4) * (x) * (6.4 - y) * (z)+
      noise(x - 6.4, y - 6.4,z-6.4) * (x) * (y) * (z)+
      noise(x, y - 6.4,z-6.4) * (6.4 - x) * (y) * (z))
    /(6.4*6.4*6.4);
  return noisev;
}
```

This looks confusing, but is actually a simple application of the linear interpolation equation A*B + (1-A)*C, extended to more dimensions and parameters. B and C are simply functions instead of constants, and the function repeats at intervals longer than one.

This weighted-average function is then used to create a 3D noise texture as below:

```
for(int x=0;x<64;x++)
{
  for(int y=0;y<64;y++)
  {
    for(int z=0;z<64;z++)
    {
      progress++;
      if(progress%28000==0)
        cout<<"."<<flush;//Progress bar

      float paramx=x*.1;//Perlin noise is zero at integer lattices
      float paramy=y*.1;
      float paramz=z*.1;

      TexData[x][y][z][3]=tilednoise(paramx,paramy,paramz);
    }
  }
}
```

Using the 3D Texture

After the 3D texture has been created, using it to form a fragment program to create a fBm fractal is simple:

```
uniform sampler3D tex;
uniform float time;

void main()
{
  vec3 input=(gl_TexCoord[0].xyz*2.0)+(time,time,time*2.0);
  vec4 color=(texture3D(tex,input)+2.0*texture3D(tex,input*.5)+
              4.0*texture3D(tex,input*.25)+16.0*texture3D(tex,input*.125));
  gl_FragColor.xyz=vec3(1,1,1);
  gl_FragColor.w = color/4;//Scale results
}
```

The fractal is built up by four calls to the noise texture at different frequencies, which are then added together. The texture is animated by shifting the texture coordinates using the time variable set in the host program. The z-axis coordinate is treated as time here and is used to animate the clouds. Finally, the fractal is interpreted as an alpha value. Setting the output color to pure white creates white, fluffy-looking clouds. Modifying this value can create clouds that look stormier. In this shader, only the alpha value of the texture is used, so the other three channels should be used for other things, like lighting information.

The assembly code for this program is also fairly simple, and is shown below:

```
PARAM c[3] = { { 2, 0.5, 0.25, 4 },
               program.local[1],
               { 0.125, 16, 1 } };

TEMP R0;
TEMP R1;
TEMP RC;
TEMP HC;
#Scale the texture coordinates
MOVR  R0.w, c[0].x;
MULR  R0.xyz, fragment.texcoord[0], c[0].x;
MULR  R0.w, c[1].x, R0;
MOVR  result.color.xyz, c[2].z;
#Create Fractal
ADDR  R0.yzw, R0.xxyz, R0.w;
MULR  R1.xyz, R0.yzww, c[0].y;
TEX   R0.x, R1, texture[0], 3D;
MULR  R1.xyz, R0.yzww, c[0].z;
```

```
MULR   R1.w, R0.x, c[0].x;
TEX    R1.x, R1, texture[0], 3D;
MULR   R1.x, R1, c[0].w;
TEX    R0.x, R0.yzww, texture[0], 3D;
ADDR   R1.w, R0.x, R1;
MULR   R0.xyz, R0.yzww, c[2].x;
TEX    R0.x, R0, texture[0], 3D;
MULR   R0.x, R0, c[2].y;
ADDR   R0.w, R1, R1.x;
ADDR   R0.x, R0.w, R0;
#Scale Results
RCPR   R0.y, c[0].w;
MULR   result.color.w, R0.x, R0.y;
END
```

The first part of the shader scales the texture coordinates and then sets the RGB output color to one. In the next section the fractal is built up by adding the results together with ADDR, scaling the texture coordinates with MULR, and then accessing the texture with TEX. Finally, results are scaled by multiplying with the reciprocal of 4, and then written to the output register.

Spherical Implicit Equations

If all three parameters of the fractal are interpreted in space, then the function can be used as the input to a spherical implicit equation. An implicit equation is an equation defined as an algebraic relation for which it is not generally possible to solve with respect of its individual terms. If the equation

$$\sqrt{((x - .5) * (x - .5) + (y - .5) * (y - .5) + (z - .5) * (z - .5))}$$

is graphed, it resembles a sphere. Adding fBm inputs to the x-, y-, and z-coordinates results in a cloudlike structure. A further added improvement is that the result is blended with turbulence (noise scaled to the [0, 1] range). This can be used to control the wispiness of the clouds.

The spherical implicit equation is not the only one that can be used. Furthermore, implict primitives can be blended using linear or other forms of interpolation (see Ebert for more information) to provide control over the cloud shapes.

Implementation with Volume Rendering in OpenGL

OpenGL provides no built-in support for volume rendering, so to use this method, a simple volume renderer needs to be implemented. The method shown in the sample application works by drawing alpha-blended quads parallel to the viewer, with each quad having a slightly increased third texture coordinate. Camera rotations are applied to the texture matrix instead of the modelview matrix. The fragment program is then bound to each of the quads, with the texture coordinates being taken as the input parameters for the implicit function. The more quads used, the closer this method comes to evaluating the equation at every pixel, and so visual quality increases as more quads are used, but performance suffers as the fragment shader has to be run more times, and more fragments have to be alpha-blended. The code for this is shown below.

```
glBlendFunc(GL_SRC_ALPHA, GL_ONE_MINUS_SRC_ALPHA);
glBindTexture(GL_TEXTURE_2D, Texture1);
glBegin(GL_QUADS);
for(int i=0;i<50;i++)
{
  glTexCoord3f(0,0,i*.025);
  glVertex3f(0,0,-i*.01);
  glTexCoord3f(0,1,i*.025);
  glVertex3f(0,1,-i*.01);
  glTexCoord3f(1,1,i*.025);
  glVertex3f(1,1,-i*.01);
  glTexCoord3f(1,0,i*.052);
  glVertex3f(1,0,-i*.01);
}
glEnd();
```

The fragment shader for the clouds:

```
vec3 input=gl_TexCoord[0].xyz;
vec4 perturb=texture3D(tex, input)+(.5*texture3D(tex, 2.0*input))+
                (.25*texture3D(tex, 4.0*input))+(.125*texture3D(tex, 8.0*input));
vec4 turbperturb=(texture3D(tex, input)*.5)+vec4(.5,.5,.5,.5);
input+=(perturb.www)/ScaleNoise;
float color=sqrt((input.z-.5)*(input.z-.5)+(input.y-.5)*(input.y-.5)+
                (input.x-.5)*(input.x-.5));
float cloud=mix(color,turbperturb.w,LerpConst);
cloud=1.0-cloud*2.0;

if(cloud>.01)
{
  cloud=pow(cloud,1.45); //Increases wispiness
}

gl_FragColor.xyz=vec3(1,1,1);
gl_FragColor.w=cloud;
```

The parameter ScaleNoise controls how much noise is added to the implicit function. Increasing the value of ScaleNoise will result in the implicit function being closer to the original sphere; decreasing it will increase the randomness of the cloud.

This shader uses only one channel of the noise texture. By storing the partial derivative with respect to x, y, and z in the RGB channels, we can simulate lighting, as the normal of an implicit function is its gradient. As the analytical derivative of noise can be difficult to find, the example program instead computes it numerically, as follows:

```
for(int x=0;x<64;x++)
{
  for(int y=0;y<64;y++)
  {
    for(int z=0;z<64;z++)
    {
      progress++;
      if(progress%18000==0)
        cout<<"."<<flush;

      float paramx=x*.1;
      float paramy=y*.1;
      float paramz=z*.1;

      TexData[x][y][z][0]=(tilednoise(paramx+.1,paramy,paramz)-
        tilednoise(paramx,paramy,paramz))/.1;
      TexData[x][y][z][1]=(tilednoise(paramx,paramy+.1,paramz)-
        tilednoise(paramx,paramy,paramz))/.1;
      TexData[x][y][z][2]=(tilednoise(paramx,paramy,paramz+.1)-
        tilednoise(paramx,paramy,paramz))/.1;
      TexData[x][y][z][3]=tilednoise(paramx,paramy,paramz);
    }
  }
}
```

To the fragment shader we then add a light normal, and normalize our cloud normals as follows:

```
vec3 lightpos=vec3(1.0,1.0,-0.5);
lightpos=normalize(lightpos);
vec3 normal=perturb.xyz*inversesqrt(dot(perturb.xyz,perturb.xyz));
float shaded=dot((.5*normal)+.5,lightpos);
```

This is not a perfectly accurate lighting model. It does not take into account the interpolation between the turbulence and the cloud structure, nor the complex physics of real cloud lighting.

The assembly code for this is as follows:

```
PARAM c[4] = { { 2, 0.5, 4, 0.25 },
               { 8, 0.125, 1.75, 0.8 },
               { 1, 0.0099999, 1.45 },
               { 0.66666, -0.33333 } };
TEMP R0;
TEMP R1;
TEMP R2;
TEMP R3;
TEMP RC;
TEMP HC;


#Fractal
MULR  R0.xyz, fragment.texcoord[0], c[0].x;
TEX   R0, R0, texture[0], 3D;
MULR  R1, R0, c[0].y;
TEX   R0, fragment.texcoord[0], texture[0], 3D;
ADDR  R1, R0, R1;
MULR  R2.xyz, fragment.texcoord[0], c[0].z;
RCPR  R0.x, c[1].z;
TEX   R2, R2, texture[0], 3D;
MULR  R2, R2, c[0].w;
MULR  R3.xyz, fragment.texcoord[0], c[1].x;


#Turbulence
TEX   R3, R3, texture[0], 3D;
ADDR  R1, R1, R2;
MULR  R2, R3, c[1].y;
ADDR  R1, R1, R2;
MULR  R0.xyz, R1.w, R0.x;


#Set up the implicit function
ADDR  R0.y, fragment.texcoord[0], R0;
ADDR  R2.x, fragment.texcoord[0].z, R0.z;
ADDR  R1.w, R0.y, -c[0].y;
ADDR  R0.x, fragment.texcoord[0], R0;
ADDR  R2.w, R2.x, -c[0].y;
MULR  R2.x, R2.w, R2.w;
MULR  R2.w, R1, R1;
ADDR  R2.x, R2, R2.w;
ADDR  R2.w, R0.x, -c[0].y;
MULR  R0.x, R2.w, R2.w;
```

```
ADDR   R0.x, R2, R0;
RSQR   R0.x, R0.x;
MULR   R0.y, R0.w, c[0];
RCPR   R0.x, R0.x;
ADDR   R0.y, R0, -R0.x;
ADDR   R0.y, R0, c[0];
MULR   R0.y, R0, c[1].w;
ADDR   R0.x, R0, R0.y;
MULR   R0.x, R0, c[0];
ADDR   R1.w, -R0.x, c[2].x;
DP3R   R0.x, R1, R1;
RSQR   R0.x, R0.x;
MULR   R0.xyz, R1, R0.x;

#See how transparent the cloud is; if it is under a certain threshold,
#raise it to a power of 1.45. This increases cloud "wispiness"
SGTRC  HC.w, R1, c[2].y;
MULR   R0.xyz, R0, c[0].y;
MOVR   R0.w, R1;
POWR   R0.w(GT), R1.w, c[2].z;

#Finish lighting clouds, and move results to output register
ADDR   R0.xyz, R0, c[0].y;
MOVR   result.color.w, R0;
DP3R   result.color.xyz, R0, c[3].xxyw;
END
```

Improvements

There are further modifications that can be made to increase the performance and quality of cloud rendering, the details of which are quite advanced, and outside the scope of this book. First, the cloud does not need to be rerendered every frame, especially if the user's point of view is changing slowly. A better method is to create a billboard for each cloud, render the cloud to texture, and then use texture on the billboard. Once the user's view moves enough to make a difference, the cloud can be rerendered to texture from the new point of view and reapplied to the billboard. A further important improvement is to more accurately simulate the cloud's lighting. Clouds are difficult to light, because a simple model does not realisticly simulate how clouds absorb light and reflect it internally. A lighting model is covered in detail in Harris's article on cloud rendering. In addition, Andrei Stoian has written an article titled "Real-Time Realistic Cloud Rendering and Lighting" that provides excellent supplementary information on this topic. It is available online at **http://www.gamedev.net/columns/hardcore/cloudrendering/**.

References

Ebert, David S., et al. "Volumetric Cloud Modeling with Implicit Surfaces." In *Texturing and Modeling: A Procedural Approach*, 3rd ed., 263–86, Morgan Kaufmann, 2002.

Harris, Mark. "Real-time cloud rendering." **http://www.markmark.net/clouds/**.

Perlin, Ken. "Improved Noise Reference Implementation."
http://mrl.nyu.edu/~perlin/noise/.

Summary

You've now learned about how to represent skies using skyplanes, skyboxes, and skydomes, and even combinations of these methods. You've learned about various methods for coloring and texturing your skies, and you've seen how clouds can be generated for an additional degree of realism.

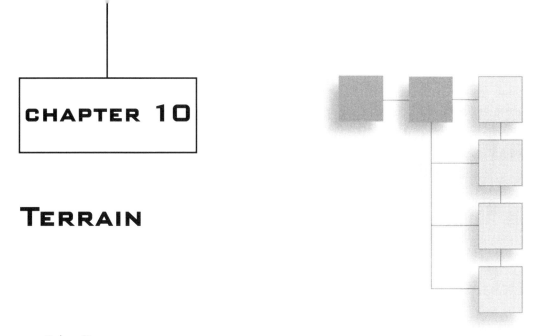

CHAPTER 10

TERRAIN

Brian Story

errains, from the vector-based landscapes in Battlezone to the amazing landscapes in Far Cry, are generally a requirement for any game taking place outdoors. Your terrain could be a lush forest with streams winding through perpetual valleys. It could be a chain of islands swimming in the middle of an expansive ocean. It could be an oasis hiding among endless sand dunes. It could even be a flat cityscape cut out of the side of a mountain. No matter what setting you use, without the terrain, your buildings and characters will float in space.

Scale-wise, it doesn't get much bigger than "the ground." While RPGs tend to have wide, expansive landscapes, even an FPS can have large sections of terrain. The terrain could easily become the largest 3D object in your project, yet to the player it's little more than something to stand on. For the developer, rendering the terrain becomes the daunting task of keeping a piece of geometry that adds little to gameplay from taking the most time to render. Just keeping your terrain engine running in real time can be a difficult task.

To be effective, a terrain needs to meet a number of requirements, many of which can contradict each other. A terrain should appear to be continuous to the player, yet the mesh should be simplified or culled where possible to reduce the load on the graphics card. Some games draw a terrain just beyond the point a player can reach and then use a terrain drawn onto a skybox to simulate hills or mountains in the distance. The terrain should appear realistic to the setting for the game, yet this can be taxing on the video card, and a balance needs to be maintained. Detail textures are often used close to the camera, allowing the areas farther off to be rendered more quickly. The terrain should appear static, even if a level-of-detail (LOD) algorithm is used. There are methods for slowly moving vertices into place when the LOD changes, rather than letting the new geometry suddenly appear, or "pop," into place.

In this chapter, you'll learn about the most important concepts involved with efficiently rendering realistic terrain. The topics you'll learn about include:

- Heightmaps
- Terrain generation
- Terrain rendering
- Terrain texturing

Heightmaps

The first thing needed for terrain rendering is a representation of the terrain's shape. While there are a number of structures that can do this, the most widely used is the heightmap, which will be covered here. Others include NURBS, which can be manipulated through a number of control points, and voxels, which allow for overhangs and caves.

Heightmaps have their drawbacks. For any point on the xz-plane, there can only be one height. This means that landforms like overhangs or caves can't be represented by the heightmap alone and often require a separate model. Heightmaps also take a large amount of memory, as each height must be represented. On the other hand, heightmaps lend themselves to the creation of regular meshes easily. It's also easy to determine the height at any given location, which is useful for collisions against the terrain as well as laying dynamic shadows onto the terrain.

A heightmap is represented by a two-dimensional grid of heights as can be seen in Figure 10.1. This grid of heights is best stored using a two-dimensional array of floating-point values, where for any point {x, y, z}, x and z are the indexes into the array, and the value of the array is the y value:

```
vector p;
p.x = 2;
p.z = 2;
p.y = Heights[p.x][p.z];
```

Because of this, x and y will increase in equal steps while y will fluctuate up and down. When viewed from above, as in Figure 10.2, the mesh will look uniform. This will help when calculating normals and texture coordinates.

Some compilers have problems creating static arrays over a certain size, so it's best to create this array dynamically:

Int Heights[5][5] = {{0, 0, 1, 1, 2},
　　　　　　　　 {0, 1, 2, 2, 3},
　　　　　　　　 {0, 1, 3, 2, 3},
　　　　　　　　 {0, 1, 2, 1, 2},
　　　　　　　　 {0, 0, 1, 1, 1}}

0	0	1	1	2
0	1	2	2	3
0	1	3	2	3
0	1	2	1	2
0	0	1	1	1

Figure 10.1 A heightmap stored in a multidimensional array on the left and the corresponding heightmap on the right.

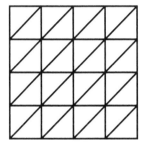

Figure 10.2 The terrain mesh as seen from above.

```
int Height = 1025;
int Width = 1025;

float **heights;
heights = new float*[Width];
for (int x = 0; x < Width; x++)
{
  heights[x] = new float[Height];
}
```

As with all dynamic memory, you are responsible for freeing it once you're finished with it:

```
int Width = 1025;

for (int x = 0; x < Width; x++)
{
  delete [] heights[x];
}

delete [] heights;
heights = NULL;
```

Terrain Generation

There are a number of different algorithms you can use to fill in your array of heights, and each creates a different appearance. Some will have larger, steeper mountains while others will create low rolling hills. Some add very minute detail while others are smooth. There are also a number of ways to manipulate this data once it is created and during creation to add different landforms like rivers, lakes, or mountains.

The creation of heightmaps is an art, and there are many variables you can tweak to get the results you're looking for. No one set of variables will work for every situation, so you should play with the variables in the following sections until you find something that you like. There are a number of different steps that you can take to adjust your heightmap, and they can be taken in almost any order. The steps outlined below are as follows:

- Initial creation
- Smoothing
- Scaling
- Adjusting

Initial Creation

There are a number of common methods available for heightmap creation. I'll cover the three most common, and then describe how they can be modified to add things like islands and rivers.

Midpoint Displacement

Midpoint displacement, also known as the *diamond square method*, is a subdivision algorithm that starts out adding larger details to the terrain and creates smaller, more intricate detail as it subdivides the heightmap. (See the "Midpoint Displacement" chapter of *Game Programming Gems*, listed at the end of this chapter.) Because of the subdivision process, it's best to have a heightmap size that is a power of two plus one.

Midpoint displacement has two steps, the diamond step and the square step, and uses an ever decreasing random displacement, which we'll call d. d represents a range of random numbers rather than a single number, so the actual displacement value would be in the set $[0-d]$.

The diamond step starts by getting the corner points of a square. The heights at these corners are averaged and assigned to the center point of the square. This center point is then displaced by d, by either adding or subtracting d from the center value. Adding this center point creates four diamonds in the heightmap.

The square step creates values for the center points of the new diamonds created by the diamond step, creating four more squares. The values at the four points making up a diamond are averaged, and then displaced by d. This value is assigned to the center point. Once this step is performed for each diamond, it creates four more squares.

Figure 10.3 illustrates these steps.

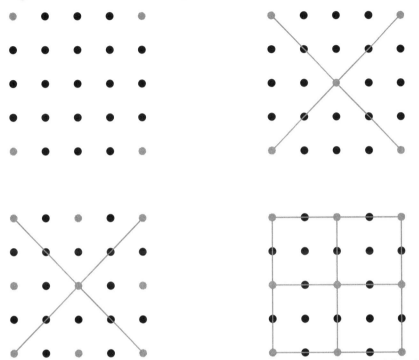

Figure 10.3 Upper left: The four corners of a square are averaged. Upper right: The center point is assigned this average and displayed. Lower left: The corners of the four new diamonds (only half shown here) are averaged. Lower right: The center of the diamonds are set to the average and displaced, creating four new squares.

These two steps are repeated for the newly formed squares and diamonds until the heightmap is completely filled, with *d* being reduced each time. Before starting, the corner values need to be initialized with values. Different values will create different types of heightmaps. Another thing to note about this method: You can initialize points in the heightmap before running midpoint displacement, and height values will be assigned for the points surrounding the initialized points. This works well for predefined structures like roads or for tiling heightmaps by copying the edge of a finished heightmap onto the edge of a heightmap that hasn't been created yet.

Fault Lines

Fault-line heightmap generation is quite simple (see the "Fault Formation" chapter of *Game Programming Gems*). A line is drawn from one edge of the heightmap to the other. The values on one side of the line are raised, while the values on the other side are lowered.

One way of doing this is by selecting two random points, (x1, z1) and (x2, z2), from within the height array to create the line.

```
float x1, z1;
float x2, z2;

x1 = rand() % Width;
x2 = rand() % Width;
z1 = rand() % Height;
z2 = rand() % Height;
```

You can then traverse the array, and for each point (xn, zn) in the array, calculate the y component of the cross product between the vector created by the line (x2−x1, z2−z1) and a vector created by one endpoint of the line and the point whose height is to be calculated (x2−xn, z2−zn). This y component will be positive on one side of the line and negative on the other side of the line.

```
vector a;
a.x = x2 - x1;
a.z = z2 - z1;

for (int z = 0; z < Height; z++)
{
  for (int x = 0; x < Width; x++)
  {
    vector b;
    b.x = x2 - x;
    b.z = z2 - z;

    if ((a.z * b.x) - (a.x * b.z) > 0)
    {
      heights[x][z] = heights[x][z] - 1;
    }
    else
    {
      heights[x][z] = heights[x][z] + 1;
    }
  }
}
```

This process is continued until the desired effect is achieved, producing results similar to those shown in Figure 10.4. Fault line generation often produces a noisy terrain, which can be adjusted using one of the methods described below.

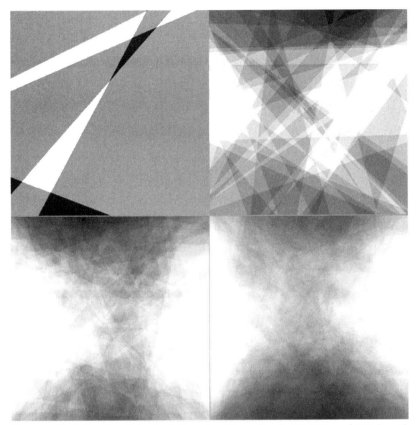

Figure 10.4 Results of the fault-line algorithm after 5, 50, 150, and 500 iterations.

Hill Algorithm

The *hill algorithm* raises a number of hills up out of the heightmap (see Bob Nystrom's Terrain Generation Tutorial). The shape of the hills can vary from perfect hemispheres, which build low rolling hills, to something more parabolic, which will build taller, thinner peaks.

```
First, we calculate a random radius.
float randMin = 5.0f;
float randMax = 50.0f;

float radius = (rand() % (randMax + randMin)) - randMin;
```

Next, we choose a center point. While the most obvious choice is to pick a center that always falls on the heightmap itself, that would cause the heights at the edges of the heightmap to be lower than those at the center of the heightmap. Instead, we find a random center where the hill will still affect the heightmap. That means we want to find an x value in the range of $-$radius $<$ x $<$ Width $+$ radius and a z value of $-$radius $<$ z $<$ Height $+$ radius.

```
float centerX = (rand() % (Width + (2 * radius))) - radius;
float centerZ = (rand() % (Height + (2 * radius))) - radius;
```

Now that we have a center and a radius, we can start to raise our hill. First we need to find out where the hill lies on the heightmap. We'll loop through the heights on the heightmap that are radius distance from the center point in all four directions, making sure we stay within the extent of the heightmap itself.

```
int left = centerX - radius;
if (left < 0)
  left = 0;

int right = centerX + radius;
if (right > Width-1)
  right = Width-1;

int top = centerZ - radius;
if (top < 0)
  top = 0;

int bottom = centerZ + radius;
if (bottom > Height-1)
  bottom = Height-1;
```

To raise the hill, we first need to know the formula for a sphere. The formula for a sphere is:

$$(x2 - x1)^2 + (y2 - y1)^2 + (z2 - z1)^2 = r^2$$

where r is the radius, (x1, y1, z1) is the center point, and (x2, y2, z2) is the point we are calculating the height for. We will already know x2 and z2, so we want to solve this equation for y2. When we solve this for y2, we get:

$$y2 = \sqrt{r^2 - (x2 - x1)^2 - (z2 - z1)^2} + y1$$

Now we can calculate the new heights. We need to ignore any negative values we get, which will be the values that are outside of the hemisphere we're raising. These values will fall in the corners of the bounding box we calculated above.

```
float radiusSquared = radius * radius;

for (int z = top; z <= bottom; z++)
{
  for (int x = left; x <= right; x++)
  {
    float xValue = (x - centerX) * (x - centerX);
    float zValue = (z - centerZ) * (z - centerZ);
```

```
    float height = sqrt(radiusSquared - xValue - zValue);

    if (height > 0)
    {
      heights[x][z] = heights[x][z] + height;
    }
  }
}
```

How many hills you raise will depend on how you want your terrain to look. I've had good results from 300 hills with radii between 5 and 50.

Landmass Considerations

The methods we've looked at so far in this chapter will produce a series of hills or mountains, but what about other landscape features? One way to create things like islands, lakes, and rivers is to adjust the previous methods slightly.

Building islands is quite easy using the hill method. For each island you want to create, you need a point for the center of the island and an average radius for the size of the island. When adding hills to the terrain, only add those hills that will fall within the bounds of one of the islands. Lakes can be made in the opposite way. Create a center point and radius for each lake and only add hills that lie outside the bounds of the lakes.

Rivers are more complicated, and there isn't a clear-cut way to create them. One method is to partially create the initial terrain that will act as a rough lay of the land. Then select a start and end point for the river. The starting point should be somewhere in the highest half of the range of heights, while the end point should be somewhere in the lower third. A path-finding algorithm like A* can then be used to find the best path for the river. The rest of the heightmap can then be created that avoids raising the heights within X distance from the river. X will become the size of the flood plane, and as X increases, the flood plain of the river grows. Once the heightmap is created, the riverbed can be cut out of the terrain by subtracting a hill at each point along the river using the method in the hill algorithm, except subtracting rather than adding heights.

Smoothing

Many of these initial creation methods create terrains that are too bumpy or have very steep peaks. These can be smoothed out by running a smoothing filter over the terrain. The filter can be run a number of times until the desired result is achieved.

For each point in the terrain, we want to average the height with the surrounding heights. An average can be taken from just the points directly on the four sides of the point, or include the four corners as well. This will lower the terrain as it smoothes and remove detail.

```
for (z = 0; z < Height; z++)
{
  for (x = 0; x < Width; x++)
  {
    float sum = heights[x][z];
    int numValues = 1;

    if (x > 0)
    {
      sum += heights[x-1][z];
      numValues++;
    }

    if (x < Width-1)
    {
      sum += heights[x+1][z];
      numValues++;
    }

    if (z > 0)
    {
      sum += heights[x][z-1];
      numValues++;
    }

    if (z < Height-1)
    {
      sum += height[x][z+1];
      numValues++;
    }

    heights[x][z] = sum/numValues;
  }
}
```

Scaling

Sometimes the terrain needs to be scaled to fall within a certain range. To do this, we first need to find the current range.

```
float min = heights[0][0];
float max = heights[0][0];
```

```
for (int z = 0; z < Height; z++)
{
  for (int x = 0; x < Width; x++)
  {
    if (heights[x][z] > max)
      max = heights[x][z];
    if (heights[x][z] < min)
      min = heights[x][z];
  }
}
```

Once we know the current range, we can scale the terrain to the new range by scaling the terrain to be between 0 and 1, and then multiplying it by the new range.

```
// The maximum value for our new height range.
// 255 works well for saving the heightmap as a bitmap.
float scaleValue = 255;

for (int z = 0; z < Height; z++)
{
  for (int x = 0; x < Width; x++)
  {
    heights[x][z] =( heights[x][z] - min) / (max - min) * scaleValue;
  }
}
```

Adjusting

When the heightmap is created, the heights should be evenly distributed between the minimum height and the maximum height. If the distribution favored the lower values, the peaks would stay as tall, but the rest of the heights would be lowered, giving the appearance of taller peaks and wider valleys. This can be done by scaling the heights to be between 0 and 1 and squaring or cubing them. This accentuates the features of a heightmap.

Terrain Rendering

Over the years, many people have researched various methods of rendering terrain, producing a number of innovative techniques. Traditionally, many of these approaches required considerable processing on the CPU, but as GPUs have become more powerful and programmable, GPU-oriented techniques have gained favor. Since I don't have space to comprehensively cover terrain-rendering methods here, I'll focus on techniques that can leverage the GPU more effectively.

You'll first learn about the brute force approach, which, while not terribly efficient, provides a foundation for other techniques. You'll then learn how to improve this with frustum culling. Finally, you'll learn about the more advanced chunked LOD method.

Brute Force

Brute force methods render every polygon with little to no spatial partitioning and no mesh simplification. Because every polygon is rendered, it's the easiest to write, yet it uses the most resources.

A brute force heightmap will have (Height−1) * (Width*2) polygons, which are arranged in a grid with equal spacing between the x coordinates and the z coordinates. Because of this, triangle strips are a logical choice.

Creating the Vertex Array

Our vertex array will contain not only the vertex positions, but also normals calculated for each vertex using the average of the surrounding faces, texture coordinates, and colors that will be used later to blend numerous textures together. Later, if lightmap textures and detail textures are used, coordinates for them may be added.

To make accessing the array easier now while creating the array and in the future when binding the array, we'll create offsets for each of these values.

```
int arraySize = sizeof(GLfloat) * Height * Width * 9;


glBindBuffer(GL_ARRAY_BUFFER, bufferVertList);
glBufferData(GL_ARRAY_BUFFER, arraySize, NULL, GL_STATIC_DRAW);


int normalOffset = Width * Height * 3;
int textureOffset = Width * Height * 6;
int colorOffset = Width * height * 8;
```

Position

The vertex position is easy. The x and z array indices are also the x- and z-coordinates. The value of the array at the x and z indicies is the y-coordinate.

```
GLfloat *vertBuff = (GLfloat *)glMapBuffer(GL_ARRAY_BUFFER, GL_WRITE_ONLY);
int count = 0;
for (int z = 0; z < Height; z++)
{
  for (int x = 0; x < Width; x++)
  {
    vertBuff[count++] = x;
    vertBuff[count++] = heights[x][z];
```

```
        vertBuff[count++] = z;
    }
}

glUnmapBuffer(GL_ARRAY_BUFFER);
```

Normals

To find the vertex normal, you must first find the normals for all faces that the vertex belongs to. When using triangle strips, each vertex will be associated with six faces. The normal for each face is calculated, and then all six face normals are added together and normalized to create the vertex normal, as illustrated in Figure 10.5.

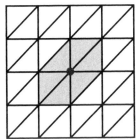

Figure 10.5 The normals for the highlighted polygons are added together and normalized to get the normal for the highlighted vertex.

```
// First we need a normalize function.
void normalize(vector &v)
{
    float length = sqrt((v.x * v.x) + (v.y * v.y) + (v.z * v.z));
    v.x /= length;
    v.y /= length;
    v.z /= length;
}


// Then we need a function to create a cross product.
vector cross(vector a; vector b)
{
    vector result;

    result.x = a.y * b.z - a.z * b.y;
    result.y = a.z * b.x - a.x * b.z;
    result.z = a.x * b.y - a.y * b.x;

    return result;
}
```

```
// And finally a function to add two vectors.
vector add(vector a, vector b)
{
  vector result;

  result.x = a.x + b.x;
  result.y = a.y + b.y;
  result.z = a.z + b.z;

  return result;
}


// Now to create our vertex normals.
// One optimization that could be made is to precalculate the face normals.
GLfloat *vertBuff = (GLfloat *)glMapBuffer(GL_ARRAY_BUFFER,GL_WRITE_ONLY);
int count = normalOffset;
for (int z = 0; z < Height; z++)
{
  for (int x = 0; x < Width; x++)
  {
    vector a;
    vector b;
    vector crossProduct;
    vector normal;

    normal.x = 0;
    normal.y = 0;
    normal.z = 0;

    // Face A
    a.x = 0;   a.z = -1;  a.y = heights[x][z-1] - heights[x][y];
    b.x = -1;  b.z = 0;   b.y = heights[x-1][z] - heights[x][y];

    crossProduct = cross(a, b);
    normalize(crossProduct);
    normal = add(normal, crossProduct);

    // Face B
    a.x = -1;  a.z = 0;  a.y = heights[x-1][z] - heights[x][y];
    b.x = -1;  b.z = 1;  b.y = heights[x-1][z+1] - heights[x][y];
```

```
crossProduct = cross(a, b);
normalize(crossProduct);
normal = add(normal, crossProduct);

// Face C
a.x = -1;  a.z = 1;  a.y = heights[x-1][z+1] - heights[x][y];
b.x = 0;   b.z = 1;  b.y = heights[x][z+1] - heights[x][y];

crossProduct = cross(a, b);
normalize(crossProduct);
normal = add(normal, crossProduct);

// Face D
a.x = 0;  a.z = 1;  a.y = heights[x][z+1] - heights[x][y];
b.x = 1;  b.z = 0;  b.y = heights[x+1][z] - heights[x][y];

crossProduct = cross(a, b);
normalize(crossProduct);
normal = add(normal, crossProduct);

// Face E
a.x = 1;  a.z = 0;   a.y = heights[x+1][z] - heights[x][y];
b.x = 1;  b.z = -1;  b.y = heights[x+1][z-1] - heights[x][y];

crossProduct = cross(a, b);
normalize(crossProduct);
normal = add(normal, crossProduct);

// Face F
a.x = 1;  a.z = -1;  a.y = heights[x+1][z-1] - heights[x][y];
b.x = 0;  b.z = -1;  b.y = heights[x][z-1] - heights[x][y];

crossProduct = cross(a, b);
normalize(crossProduct);
normal = add(normal, crossProduct);

normalize(normal);
```

```
    vertBuff[count++] = normal.x;
    vertBuff[count++] = normal.y;
    vertBuff[count++] = normal.z;
  }
}


glUnmapBuffer(GL_ARRAY_BUFFER);
```

Texture Coordinates

A number of different texturing methods will be explored later in the chapter, and the number of times the textures will be tiled over the terrain will change depending on the method used. It would be nice to be able to change the tile amount easily later, so we'll add that functionality here.

```
// Tile each texture 20 X 20 times over the terrain.
int tileAmount = 20;
```

The easiest way to avoid wrapping artifacts when tiling a texture over a terrain is to make sure the texture repeats. This allows us to extend the texture coordinates past 1. This can be done through the following code when loading textures:

```
glTexParameteri(GL_TEXTURE_2D, GL_TEXTURE_WRAP_S, GL_REPEAT);
glTexParameteri(GL_TEXTURE_2D, GL_TEXTURE_WRAP_T, GL_REPEAT);
```

Because textures start to wrap at the texture coordinate of 1, we know that the coordinates we calculate will fall between 0 and *tileAmount*. We can find out the difference from one point to the next by dividing *tileAmount* by the width and height of the terrain, and can find the texture coordinate for any point on the heightmap by multiplying the difference by the x and z values of the point.

```
float tileStepX = tileAmount/(float)Width;
float tileStepZ = tileAmount/(float)Height;

GLfloat *vertBuff = (GLfloat *)glMapBuffer(GL_ARRAY_BUFFER, GL_WRITE_ONLY);
int count = textureOffset;
for (int z = 0; z < Height; z++)
{
  for (int x = 0; x < width; x++)
  {
    vertBuff[count++] = x * tileStepX;
    vertBuff[count++] = z * tileStepZ;
  }
}


glUnmapBuffer(GL_ARRAY_BUFFER);
```

Colors

Later in the chapter, colors will be used to hold blending information for texture combiners. Until then, we can use them to color the terrain and then lay a detail texture over the top. This will leave much to be desired, but it's better than looking at a white terrain. Much like we'll do with textures later, I'm going to blend two colors together based on height and then add a third color for the steep slopes. First we need to choose some colors. I'll be using a green, brown, and gray.

```
struct ubyteColor
{
    GLubyte r, g, b, a;
};

ubyteColor color1;
color1.r = 0;
color1.g = 128;
color1.b = 0;

ubyteColor color2;
color2.r = 128;
color2.g = 100;
color2.b = 0;

ubyteColor color3;
color3.r = 192;
color3.g = 192;
color3.b = 192;
```

We start out similar to the way we started with vertex position, normals, and texture coordinates, by mapping our vertex array and looping through the height values.

```
GLfloat *vertBuff = (GLfloat *)glMapBuffer(GL_ARRAY_BUFFER, GL_WRITE_ONLY);
int count = colorOffset;
for (int z = 0; z < Height; z++)
{
    for (int x = 0; x < width; x++)
    {
```

To blend our three colors together, we'll use the standard alpha blending function

```
result = alpha * sourceColor + (1 - alpha) * destinationColor;
```

where `alpha` is a number between 0 and 1. When `alpha` is 0, the result color will be the same as `destinationColor`, and when `alpha` is 1 the result will be `sourceColor`. The actual numbers you use to create the alpha value will depend on the way you construct your heightmap. I used the smoothing algorithm a number of times and then squared the values. This means that the majority of my height values are small. I'd like the first quarter of height values to be green, and then blend to brown over the next quarter. That will leave the top half brown. Because the majority of the height values will be on the bottom, the majority of the color will still be green.

```
// min and max should be known if the heightmap has been scaled.  If not,
//step through the terrain and calculate them before entering the loop.
float range = max - min;
float quarter = range / 4.0f;
```

First we subtract the height we want to start blending at from the current height. This effectively lowers the heights that won't be blended to below 0. We then clamp this value to 0, since alpha values need to be in the range of 0 to 1. Remember, an alpha of 0 causes no blending to occur, which is what we want for these values.

```
float alpha = max(0, heights[x][z] - quarter);
```

We then want to divide this by the difference between our blending starting point and our blending ending point. This will give us a range between 0 and 1 where we want the blending to occur, and a range over 1 where we want the blending to stop. We must then clamp this value to 1.

```
alpha = min(1, alpha / quarter);

ubyteColor result;
result.r = alpha * color2.r + (1 - alpha) * color1.r;
result.g = alpha * color2.g + (1 - alpha) * color1.g;
result.b = alpha * color2.b + (1 - alpha) * color1.b;
```

For the next blend, we want to add gray to the places that are steep. Faces, like planes, don't have slopes, but they do have normals that represent their orientation, and the normals are already in the range of 0 and 1. A plane that is perfectly horizontal will have a normal with a y-coordinate of 1. A plane that is perfectly vertical will have a normal with a y-coordinate of 0. We shouldn't have any y coordinates that are negative since we have no faces that face down. We'll use 1 − normal.y as our alpha value. Instead of recalculating the normal, let's use the value we already found. Don't forget to change the second parameter of glMapBuffer() to GL_READ_WRITE.

```
alpha = 1 - vertBuff[normalOffset + (count - colorOffset)];

result.r = alpha * color3.r + (1 - alpha) * result.r;
result.g = alpha * color3.g + (1 - alpha) * result.g;
result.b = alpha * color3.b + (1 - alpha) * result.b;
```

Our color values are saved as unsigned bytes, while our vertex array is an array of floating point numbers. We need to convert our array so we can save byte values.

```
    GLubyte *byteBuff = (GLubyte *)&vertBuff[count++];

    byteBuff[0] = result.r;
    byteBuff[1] = result.g;
    byteBuff[2] = result.b;
    byteBuff[3] = 255;
  }
}


glUnmapBuffer(GL_ARRAY_BUFFER);
```

Creating the Index Array

Now that we have the vertex array, all we need is the index array, and creating that is easy when using triangle strips. All we need to do is step through all but the last row of height values, and add the index for that vertex and the vertex below it.

To continue the strip onto the next row, we'll use two *degenerate triangles* per row. A degenerate triangle, shown in Figure 10.6, is a triangle that has two vertices that are the same. Since a triangle needs to have three different vertices, OpenGL won't draw the triangle except as a line in wireframe mode. To add these degenerate triangles, we need to repeat the very last vertex of a row (excluding the last row), and the very first vertex of a row (excluding the first row).

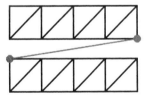

Figure 10.6 When drawing with triangle strips, the highlighted vertices are repeated to move to the next strip without drawing any geometry.

For each row, we will be adding two times the width number of vertices plus the two degenerates, except for the first and last rows, which have one each. This means that, in total, we will have (Height − 1) * (Width * 2 + 2) − 2 indices in our index array.

```
int length = ((Height-1) * (Width*2+2))-2;

// Create our buffer objects.
glBindBuffer(GL_ELEMENT_ARRAY_BUFFER, bufferTriList);
glBufferData(GL_ELEMENT_ARRAY_BUFFER, sizeof(GLuint) * length,
```

```
                   NULL, GL_STATIC_DRAW);

// Bind the buffer.
GLuint *triBuff = (GLuint *)glMapBuffer(GL_ELEMENT_ARRAY_BUFFER, GL_WRITE_ONLY);

// Create index array.
currentIndex = 0;
for (z = 0; z < Height-1; z++)
{
  for (int x = 0; x < Width; x++)
  {
    if (x == 0 && z != 0)
      triBuff[currentIndex++] = x + (z * Width);

    triBuff[currentIndex++] = x + (z * Width);
    triBuff[currentIndex++] = x + ((z+1) * Width);

    if (x == Width-1 && z != Height-2)
      triBuff[currentIndex++] = x + ((z+1) * Width);
  }
}
glUnmapBuffer(GL_ELEMENT_ARRAY_BUFFER);
```

Rendering the Mesh

At this point, you should be able to render your mesh. If done right, it should look something like the Figure 10.7. For this screenshot, I used a heightmap 1024×1024 in size. The hill algorithm was run, building 2000 hills. A riverbed was added after 500 hills, the smooth filter was run forty times, and the values were squared. A detail texture was added and tiled eighty by eighty times over the terrain.

Figure 10.7 An example of the terrain rendered with a detail texture.

Rendering involves binding your vertex and index buffers, setting the vertex, normal, color, and texture coordinate pointers to the correct offsets (which we calculated above), and then calling glDrawElements().

```
glBindBuffer(GL_ARRAY_BUFFER, bufferVertList);

glVertexpointer(3, GL_FLOAT, 0, (float *)NULL + vertOffset);
glNormalPointer(GL_FLOAT, 0, (float *)NULL + normalOffset);
glColorPointer(4, GL_UNSIGNED_BYTE, 0, (float *)NULL + colorOffset);
glTexCoordPointer(2, GL_FLOAT, 0, (float *)NULL + textureOffset);

glBindBuffer(GL_ELEMENT_ARRAY_BUFFER, bufferTriList);

int length = ((Height-1) * (Width*2+2))-2;
glDrawElements(GL_TRIANGLE_STRIP, length, GL_UNSIGNED_INT, 0);
```

Frustum Culling

While the brute force method combined with buffer arrays is very bandwidth efficient, it renders far too many polygons to really be useful. We can fix this by culling out those that fall outside of the view frustum.

Culling each polygon would add a decent amount of CPU overhead and would remove all the bus efficiency due to the index array being rebuilt each frame. Instead, we'll divide the heightmap into a number of sections and create bounding volumes around each one.

The size of each section should be small enough so the majority of the heightmap is culled out, yet large enough to maintain some efficiency. The edges of each section will have to be shared by adjacent sections to keep the mesh from having holes at section boundaries. We'll want to pick a size that divides the width and height of the heightmap equally and then add one to account for the shared vertex. For a 1024×1024 heightmap, 33×33 works well.

We'll use axis-aligned bounding boxes (AABB) for our bounding volumes. Spheres are faster, but they are also larger and will create overdraw. If you find you have artifacts from using AABBs, try converting to a sphere. For AABBs, we only need to keep track of two points, one for the maximum x-, y-, and z-coordinates, and one for the minimum x-, y-, and z-coordinates. We can then create a bounding box from these values and cull using the eight corners. You can see bounding boxes assigned to the terrain in Figure 10.8.

Figure 10.8 Bounding boxes drawn around each section of terrain.

First, for each chunk of our terrain, we need a data type containing the index array and bounding information:

```
struct chunk
{
  Gluint bufferTriList;
  vector max;
  vector min;
};
```

Next, we need an array of chunks to represent our terrain. Remember, we need the edges of each chunk to overlap, so one has to be subtracted from both the chunk width and the chunk height when calculating the array size.

```
chunk **chunkArray = new chunk*[Width/(ChunkWidth-1)];
for (int x = 0; x < Width/(ChunkWidth-1); x++)
  chunkArray[x] = new chunk[Height/(ChunkHeight-1)];
```

And, finally, we need to adjust our code to build the index arrays. We need to loop through our new chunk array, moving the creation of the index array and building the index array inside of this loop. The size of the new index arrays will now be $((\text{ChunkHeight} - 1) * (\text{ChunkWidth} * 2 + 2)) - 2$.

When filling in the index array, we no longer want to loop through every height, but only those heights that fall inside our chunk. To calculate the starting width and height, we multiply the chunk array index by the chunk's width and height minus one. The chunk width and height are added to that to find the ending points.

```
int startx = chunkX * (ChunkWidth - 1);
int startz = chunkZ * (ChunkHeight - 1);

// Initialize our bounding values.
chunkArray[chunkX][chunkZ].min.x = startx;
chunkArray[chunkX][chunkZ].min.y = heights[startx][startz];
chunkArray[chunkX][chunkZ].min.z = startz;

chunkArray[chunkX][chunkZ].max.x = startx;
chunkArray[chunkX][chunkZ].max.Y = heights[startx][startz];
chunkArray[chunkX][chunkZ].max.Z = startz;

int currentIndex = 0;

for (int z = startz; z < startz + ChunkHeight; z++)
{
  for (int x = startx; x < startx + ChunkWidth; x++)
  {
    // Adjust our bounding values
    if (z > chunkArray[chunkX][chunkZ].max.z)
```

```
    chunkArray[chunkX][chunkZ].max.z = z;
  if (z < chunkArray[chunkX][chunkZ].min.z)
    chunkArray[chunkX][chunkZ].min.z = z;
  if (x > chunkArray[chunkX][chunkZ].maxx)
    chunkArray[chunkX][chunkZ].max.x = x;
  if (x < chunkArray[chunkX][chunkZ].min.z)
    chunkArray[chunkX][chunkZ].min.z = x;
  if (heights[x][z] > chunkArray[chunkX][chunkZ].max.y)
    chunkArray[chunkX][chunkZ].max.y = heights[x][z];
  if (heights[x][z] < chunkArray[chunkX][chunkZ].min.y)
    chunkArray[chunkX][chunkZ].min.y = heights[x][z];


  // Create the index array.
  if (x == startx && z != startz)
    triBuff[currentIndex++] = x + (z * Width);


  triBuff[currentIndex++] = x + (z * Width);
  triBuff[currentIndex++] = x + ((z+1) * Width);


  if (x == (startx + ChunkWidth)-1 && z != (startz + ChunkHeight)-2)
    triBuff[currentIndex++] = x + ((z+1) * Width);
  }
}
```

To render, loop through the array and check to see if the points of the bounding box are in the frustum. If they are, draw that section of the terrain.

```
for (int z = 0; z < Height / (ChunkHeight-1); z++)
{
  for (int x = 0; x < Width / (ChunkWidth -1); x++)
  {

    int maxX = chunkArray[x][z].maxX;
    int maxY = chunkArray[x][z].maxY;
    int maxZ = chunkArray[x][z].maxZ;
    int minX = chunkArray[x][z].minX;
    int minY = chunkArray[x][z].minY;
    int minZ = chunkArray[x][z].minZ;


    if (!frustum->pointInFrustum(maxX, maxY, maxZ) &&
        !frustum->pointInFrustum(minX, maxY, minZ) &&
        !frustum->pointInFrustum(minX, maxY, maxZ) &&
        !frustum->pointInFrustum(maxX, maxY, minZ) &&
```

```
      !frustum->pointInFrustum(maxX, minY, maxZ) &&
      !frustum->pointInFrustum(minX, minY, minZ) &&
      !frustum->pointInFrustum(minX, minY, maxZ) &&
      !frustum->pointInFrustum(maxX, minY, minZ))
    continue;

  glBindBuffer(GL_ELEMENT_ARRAY_BUFFER, chunkArray[x][z].bufferTriList);
  glDrawElements(GL_TRIANGLE_STRIP, numElements, GL_UNSIGNED_INT, 0);
  }
}
```

Chunked LOD

Chunked LOD is a level-of-detail algorithm that combines a simplified mesh with a quadtree (see Thatcher Ulrich's website for more information). It uses a view-independent progressive mesh (VIPM) technique to simplify the mesh a number of times using different amounts of error. The quadtree is then used to decide which simplified mesh to display (more on this later). The closer to the camera, the more detailed the mesh.

This technique, while simplifying the mesh and increasing our frame rate, will cause two problems that we must fix: cracks between meshes, and popping of geometry.

Since the simplified mesh will be irregular, points on the borders of adjacent meshes won't line up. This will cause cracks between the meshes, and the terrain will no longer look continuous. We can fix this by drawing a skirt around the mesh. A skirt is a vertical piece of geometry that runs along the outside of the mesh. The top of the skirt follows the heights along the edges of the mesh. The bottom falls below the adjacent mesh. The cracks are usually small close to the camera, so these skirts are hardly noticeable.

The second problem involves the transition from one LOD to another. As more polys are added, the shape of the terrain changes. Geometry will appear to pop in and out of view as the camera moves. This can be fixed by slowly transitioning between the two height values rather than having a sudden change.

Mesh Simplification: A VIPM approach

A view-independent progressive mesh is a mesh that is simplified based on the properties of the mesh and not the position of the viewer. It can also be simplified to differing degrees, depending on the amount of error allowed. We will be using a quadtree (see Thatcher Ulrich's article, listed at the end of the chapter, on the Gamasutra website) to achieve this, and that means our heightmap's width and height will need to be a power of two plus one.

Each node of our quadtree will contain a triangle fan with a vertex in the center, one at each of the four corners, and an optional one at each of the sides. The height values at each point that falls inside the node are compared with the height value created by the triangle fan at that point. If the difference is too great, the corresponding child node is created and subdivided. In order to remove cracks, the creation of a child node may cause the surrounding nodes to create additional node children. There can never be more than one level difference between adjacent nodes.

Keeping Track of Our Mesh

Each node will have to be self-contained and use no other information to build its piece of the mesh. When all meshes from the bottommost layers are combined, they create the final mesh. Each node will have to keep track of where on the terrain it resides. To do this we will need four integers; one each for the top, bottom, left, and right extents. We'll also need to hold the mesh data. For this, we'll need a center point, an array of four corner points, an array of four side points, and an array of four Boolean values that indicate whether or not the side points are used. A side point is only used if the node has children, or an adjacent node has children.

```
// Quadtree Node
struct quadNode
{
  int top, left, right, bottom; // Bounds of this node.
  vector center;                // Center point.
  vector corner[4];             // Corner vectors.
  bool activeSide[4];           // Sides that are active.
  vector side[4];               // Side vectors.
  quadNode* children[4];        // Children nodes.
  quadNode *parent;             // parent node.
  int level;                    // How deep this node is.
};
```

Figure 10.9 shows the orientation of the corners, sides, and children as they are stored in the array. This ordering will allow us to easily create our triangle fan later.

Creating the Mesh

Creating the mesh is quite simple in concept. We create a recursive function that does one simple thing: it decides if any of the children nodes need to be created. If so, it creates them and sends them to the recursive function to be processed as well.

So how does this create a mesh? If a node has no children, it creates a triangle fan of four triangles. When a child is created, that corner vertex is no longer used, and two side vertices are activated. A node with a single child will still have four triangles, but will lose a triangle for each additional child. Figure 10.10 illustrates this.

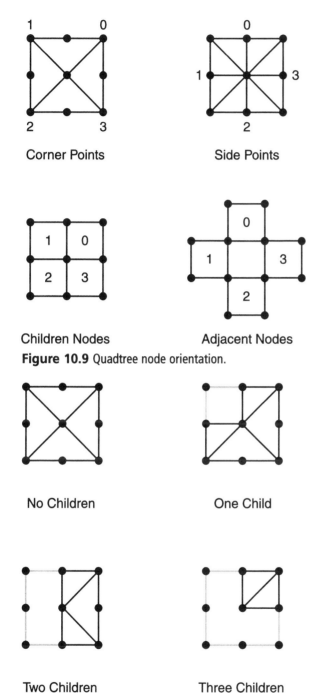

Corner Points   Side Points

Children Nodes   Adjacent Nodes

Figure 10.9 Quadtree node orientation.

No Children   One Child

Two Children   Three Children

Figure 10.10 Mesh drawn for a node with zero, one, two, and three children.

Adding children is where the process starts to get tricky. When you have a mesh where all nodes are at the same level, all the vertices line up fine. When a node from a lower level is introduced, vertices start showing up in the middle of polygons, and cracks are formed. To fix this, we activate side vertices not only for the parent node, but also for the adjacent parent nodes that are affected by this new child. If the child node then creates its own child, and adjacent nodes don't exist, we must create adjacent nodes to keep the mesh from forming cracks. Figure 10.11 should make this clearer.

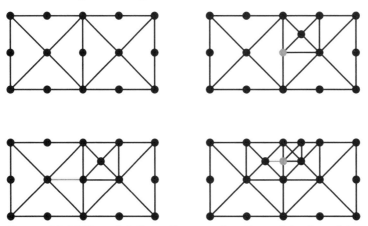

Figure 10.11 Upper left: Two adjacent nodes. Upper right: One of the nodes with a child node, causing a crack. Lower left: A side vertex is activated to remove the crack. Lower right: A child is created in the left node to fix a crack caused by a child of a child node on the right.

We'll start with a function to initialize a node. This function will take the node to be initialized as a parameter. The node should already have its parent set.

```
void initNode(quadNode *node)
{
  // A node's level is one more than its parent's level.
  node->level = node->parent->level + 1;

  // Set the node's children to NULL and deactivate its sides.
  for (int i = 0; i < 4; i++)
  {
    node->children[i] = NULL;
    node->activeSide[i] = false;
  }
```

To initialize the rest of the variables, we'll need to know the width of the node. We can find the width of the node by finding the difference between one of the parents' corners and one of its adjacent sides, plus one. Because we want the midpoint between these two points, we'll be using width minus one in our calculations rather than width (if width is 513, the endpoints are 0 and 512. The midpoint between them is 512/2, or 128, rather than 513/2, or 128.5). We'll need a special case for the root node, as it will have no parent.

```
int nodeWidth = Width;
if (node != root)
nodeWidth = node->parent->corner[0].x - node->parent->side[0].x + 1;
```

We'll also need to know at least one point in our node to base the other points off of. We can figure this out by finding which child we are working with and where our upper left-hand corner is, based on the parent's data.

```
vector upperLeft;
if (node == root)
{
  upperLeft.x = 0;
  upperleft.z = 0;
  upperLeft.y = heights[0][0];
}
else
{
  if (node == node->parent->children[0])
    upperLeft = node->parent->side[0];

  if (node == node->parent->children[1])
    upperLeft = node->parent->corner[1];

  if (node == node->parent->children[2])
    upperLeft = node->parent->side[1];

  if (node == node->parent->children[3])
    upperLeft = node->parent->center;
}
```

We can now finish off the function by calculating the corner vectors, side vectors, and center vector.

```
// Initialize corners.
node->corner[0].x = upperLeft.x + (nodeWidth-1);
node->corner[0].z = upperLeft.z;
node->corner[0].y = data[node->corner[0].x][node->corner[0].z].y;

node->corner[1].x = upperLeft.x;
node->corner[1].z = upperLeft.z;
node->corner[1].y = data[node->corner[1].x][node->corner[1].z].y;
```

```
    node->corner[2].x = upperLeft.x;
    node->corner[2].z = upperLeft.z + (nodeWidth-1);
    node->corner[2].y = data[node->corner[2].x][node->corner[2].z].y;

    node->corner[3].x = upperLeft.x + (nodeWidth-1);
    node->corner[3].z = upperLeft.z + (nodeWidth-1);
    node->corner[3].y = data[node->corner[3].x][node->corner[3].z].y;

    // Initialize sides.
    node->side[0].x = upperLeft.x + ((nodeWidth-1)/2);
    node->side[0].z = upperLeft.z;
    node->side[0].y = data[node->side[0].x][node->side[0].z].y;

    node->side[1].x = upperLeft.x;
    node->side[1].z = upperLeft.z + ((nodeWidth-1)/2);
    node->side[1].y = data[node->side[1].x][node->side[1].z].y;

    node->side[2].x = upperLeft.x + ((nodeWidth-1)/2);
    node->side[2].z = upperLeft.z + (nodeWidth-1);
    node->side[2].y = data[node->side[2].x][node->side[2].z].y;

    node->side[3].x = upperLeft.x + (nodeWidth-1);
    node->side[3].z = upperLeft.z + ((nodeWidth-1)/2);
    node->side[3].y = data[node->side[3].x][node->side[3].z].y;

    // Initialize center.
    node->center.x = upperLeft.x + ((nodeWidth-1)/2);
    node->center.z = upperLeft.z + ((nodeWidth-1)/2);
    node->center.y = data[node->center.x][node->center.z].y;
}
```

Next we'll need a function to activate a child node. This function will initialize a child node, activate the parent's side vertices, and activate adjacent children if needed. The function will take the parent node and the index for the child to be created as parameters.

```
void activateChild(quadNode *node, int child)
{
    // Check to see if the child already exists.
    if (node->children[child] != NULL)
        return;

    // Create and initialize the child.
    node->children[child] = new quadNode;
```

```
node->children[child]->parent = node;

initNode(node->children[child]);
```

Now that the child has been created, we activate the parent node's side vertices. Because of the way the sides are numbered, we want to activate side[child] and side[child - 1], making sure that we wrap around to side 3 in case child - 1 is negative.

```
node->activeSide[child] = true;
if (child-1 < 0)
  node->activeSide[3];
else
  node->activeSide[child-1];
```

After activating the parent node's sides, we want to activate the corresponding sides of the adjacent nodes. For any one child, there will be two parent sides. We'll want to activate sides for adjacent node child and adjacent node child - 1. Once we find the adjacent node, we'll want to activate the side that is adjacent to the original node. For adjacent node child we'll want to activate side[child + 2] and for adjacent node child - 1, we'll want to activate side[child + 1].

```
quadNode *adjacent = findAdjacent(node, child);
if (adjacent != NULL)
{
  // (child+2) % 4 will add two to child and keep the value between 0 and 4.
  tmp->activeSide[(child+2) % 4] = true;
}

if (child -1 < 0)
{
  adjacent = findAdjacent(node, 3);
  if (adjacent != NULL)
    tmp->activeSide[1] = true;
}
else
{
  adjacent = findAdjacent(node, child-1);
  if (adjacent != NULL)
    tmp->activeSide[child+1] = true;
}
}
```

FindAdjacent() is a simple function that searches the tree for the adjacent node. If the tree doesn't expand down far enough, it creates nodes until it reaches the adjacent node. Once the adjacent node is found, it is returned.

```
quadNode *findAdjacent(quadNode *node, int direction)
{
```

Adjacent nodes should have two vertices in common and be of the same width. We'll use one of the vertices and the width to decide when we've found the correct adjacent node. Before we do this, we must first decide if there will be an adjacent node at all. Nodes along the edge of the heightmap won't have one.

```
if ((direction == 0 && node->corner[1].z == 0) ||
    (direction == 1 && node->corner[1].x == 0) ||
    (direction == 2 && node->corner[3].z ==  Height-1) ||
    (direction == 3 && node->corner[3].x == Width-1))
{
   return NULL;
}
```

Next, we'll create the variables used to decide whether we have found our adjacent node. First we find the width of our node, and then we find which corner vertices we are going to use. For the original node, we'll use corner[direction] and for the adjacent node, we'll use corner[direction − 1].

```
int nodeLength = node->corner[0].x - node->corner[1].x;
int cornerA = direction;
int cornerB = direction -1;
if (cornerB < 0)
   cornerB = 3;
```

To find the adjacent node, we'll start with the root node. After checking to see if the root node is our adjacent node (it won't be), we'll figure out which of the root's children will hold the root node. We'll then repeat these two steps with the child node. We'll continue this process until we find the adjacent node. To decide which of the children will contain the root node, we'll need the upper left-hand corner of our adjacent node. This can easily be determined from the information in our original node.

```
// Variables to hold the upper left hand x and z coordinates.
int ulx, ulz;

if (direction == 0)
{
   ulx = node->corner[1].x;
   ulz = node->corner[1].z - nodeLength;
}
if (direction == 1)
{
   ulx = node->corner[1].x - nodeLength;
```

```
    ulz = node->corner[1].z;
  }
  if (direction == 2)
  {
    ulx = node->corner[2].x;
    ulz = node->corner[2].z;
  }
  if (direction == 3)
  {
    ulx = node->corner[0].x;
    ulz = node->corner[0].z;
  }
```

Now we loop through and find our adjacent node, creating nodes when needed.

```
// Start at the root node and work our way down.
quadNode *tmpNode = root;

// While the lengths aren't equal or they don't have the correct common vertex
while (nodeLength != (tmpNode->corner[0].x - tmpNode->corner[1].x) ||
       !vectorEqual(node->corner[cornerA], tmpNode->corner[cornerB]))
{
  int active = 0;

  // Find out which child of tmpNode we need to check next.
  // The first if decides if it's on the left or right, and the second
  // if decides if it's top or bottom.
  if (ulx < tmpNode->center.x)
  {
    if (ulz < tmpNode->center.z)
      active = 1;
    else
      active = 2;
  }
  else
  {
    if (ulz < tmpNode->center.z)
      active = 0;
    else
      active = 3;
  }

  // If the child doesn't exist, create it.
```

522   Chapter 10 ▪ Terrain

```
      if (tmpNode->children[active] == NULL)
        activateChild(tmpNode, active);

    tmpNode = tmpNode->children[active];
  }


  return tmpNode;
}
```

The final part of the process is the function that starts it all off. This function is recursive and takes a single node as a parameter. It decides if child nodes need to be created. If a child node is to be created, it activates the child and calls itself, passing the child as the parameter. The process is started by calling the function and passing in the root node.

```
void createMesh(quadNode *node)
{
```

The smallest possible node that can still create a piece of the mesh is three by three. If the current node is already three by three, we can't do anything with it, and should return NULL.

```
    if (node->corner[0].x - node->corner[1].x <= 3)
      return;
```

Now we must decide which children should be subdivided. We do this by finding the maximum amount of difference between the actual heights and the heights created by the current mesh for the range of heights each child would occupy. If this value is greater than an already-determined maximum, we create that child.

note

If we were to change this section to subdivide based on the distance away from the viewer, we would have a view-dependent progressive mesh, which would be yet another way of rendering a terrain. This method produces a good frame rate, but is heavy on the CPU.

We will create a separate function to find the difference between the mesh and the actual height values. This function will take the node and child node we are calculating for as parameters. If it is determined a child must be created, the child is activated and then sent to this function.

```
    for (int child = 0; child < 4; child++)
    {
      if (findDifference(node, child) > maxDifference)
      {
        activateChild(node, child);
        createMesh(node->children[child]);
```

```
      }
   }
}
```

First `findDifference()` will need to pick a range of points to check, and then it will loop through them. For each point, it will need to determine which polygon it is inside, and then use the equation of a plane to find the height at that point.

First, we find the range of points we need to search through. We can do this by finding the upper left-hand corner of the child, and the lower right-hand corner of the child.

```
float findDifference(quadNode *node, int child)
{
  vector upperLeft, lowerRight;

  if (child == 0)
  {
    upperLeft = node->side[0];
    lowerRight = node->side[3];
  }
  if (child == 1)
  {
    upperLeft = node->corner[1];
    lowerRight = node->center;
  }
  if (child == 2)
  {
    upperLeft = node->side[1];
    lowerRight = node->side[2];
  }
  if (child == 3)
  {
    upperLeft = node->center;
    lowerRight = node->corner[3];
  }
```

There will always be two triangles that are inside of the area affected by a child. Two of the points are always the same; the center point of the node, and the corner point with the same index as the child. The other two points, one for each triangle, depend on which of the node's sides are active. For the first triangle, we'll want to use either corner[child − 1] or side[child − 1]. For the other, we'll use either corner[child + 1] or side[child].

```
  vector tri1[3];
  vector tri2[3];
```

```
// Make sure child+1 and child-1 wrap.
int childMinusOne = child-1;
if (childMinusOne < 0)
  childMinusOne = 0;

int childPlusOne = child+1;
if (childPlusOne > 3)
  childPlusOne = 0;

// Find the points for triangle A.
tri1[0] = node->center;
if (node->activeSide[childMinusOne])
  tri1[1] = node->side[childMinusOne];
else
  tri1[1] = node->corner[childMinusOne];
tri1[2] = node->corner[child];

// Find the points for triangle B.
tri2[0] = node->center;
tri2[1] = node->corner[child];
if (node->activeSide[child])
  tri2[2] = node->side[child];
else
  tri2[2] = node->corner[childPlusOne];
```

To find the height of a point inside a polygon, we're going to use the plane formula. Before we can do that, we'll need to create some variables. Any three points, like the three in a triangle, will form a plane, and this plane is defined as

$$ax + by + cz + d = 0$$

where (x, y, z) is a point on the plane, (a, b, c) is a normal to the plane, and d is defined as

$$d = -ax - by - cz$$

where (a, b, c) is the normal, and (x, y, z) is the point where the normal is calculated. We'll precalculate a, b, c, and d. Once we have these vectors, we can plug them in to the equation to find the value of y for any x, z pair. When we solve the formula for y, we get

$$y = (-d - ax - cz)/b$$

We first find (a1, b1, c1) and (a2, b2, c2) by calculating the cross product between two vectors in our triangles.

```
float a1 = ((tri1[1].y - tri1[0].y) * (tri1[2].z - tri1[0].z)) -
           ((tri1[1].z - tri1[0].z) * (tri1[2].y - tri1[0].y));

float b1 = ((tri1[1].z - tri1[0].z) * (tri1[2].x - tri1[0].x)) -
           ((tri1[1].x - tri1[0].x) * (tri1[2].z - tri1[0].z));

float c1 = ((tri1[1].x - tri1[0].x) * (tri1[2].y - tri1[0].y)) -
           ((tri1[1].y - tri1[0].y) * (tri1[2].x - tri1[0].x));

float d1 = (-a1 * tri1[0].x) - (b1 * tri1[0].y) - (c1 * tri1[0].z);
```

The same must be done with the second triangle, calculating (a2, b2, c3) and d2. We now have all our variables ready, so we can go through the points inside our children and find the maximum difference between the polygons and the actual heights.

First, we set up our loop.

```
// This variable will hold the maximum difference calculated so far.
float maxDiff = 0;

for (int z = upperLeft.z; z <= lowerRight.z; z++)
{
  for (int x = upperleft.x; x <= lowerRight.x; x++)
  {
```

You may not have noticed it, but when we created our polygons, we did it in counter-clockwise order. This means that if the point we are calculating for is inside the polygon, it will be on the left-hand side of each line segment that makes up the polygon. We already know how to find out which side of a line a point is on from the fault-line algorithm earlier in the chapter. We calculate the y component of the cross product between the vectors created by the points in our triangle and a vector created by a triangle point and the point we are calculating for. If the y component is positive for all three cross products, it's inside the triangle.

```
// Are we in triangle 1?
if (  ((tri1[1].z - tri1[0].z) * (x - tri1[0].x )) -
      ((tri1[1].x - tri1[0].x) * (z - tri1[0].z)) > 0 &&
      ((tri1[2].z - tri1[1].z) * (x - tri1[1].x )) -
      ((tri1[2].x - tri1[1].x) * (z - tri1[1].z)) > 0 &&
      ((tri1[0].z - tri1[2].z) * (x - tri1[2].x )) -
      ((tri1[0].x - tri1[2].x) * (z - tri1[2].z)) > 0)
{
  // Calculate the actual y value.
  float y = (-d1 - (a1*x) -(c1*z))/b1;
```

```
          // Set maxDiff if the difference is greater.
          if (maxDiff < (abs(y - heights[x][z])))
            maxDiff = abs(y - heights[x][z]);
      }
      // If not, we must be in triangle 2.
      else
      {
          // Calculate the actual y value.
          float y = (-d2 - (a2*x) -(c2*z))/b2;

          // Set maxDiff if the difference is greater
          if (maxDiff < (abs(y - heights[x][z])))
            maxDiff = abs(y - heights[x][z]);
      }
    }
  }
  // Finally we return maxDiff.
  return maxDiff;
}
```

Drawing the Mesh

With our mesh created, we now have a number of nodes that have either four children, four polygons, or a number of each. We can draw the complete mesh by starting at the root node and working our way down, drawing any polygons that we come across. Each of the four quadrants in a node can have either a child or a part of the mesh, but not both.

We can build the mesh by using a triangle fan. We'll first draw the center point and then work around the node counterclockwise. For each of the four quadrants, we first check to see if the child exists. If it doesn't, we draw corner[child], building a mesh through that quadrant. We then check to see if activeSide[child] is true. If it is, we also draw that. We must then check to see if the next child exists. If it does exist, and we continue around the node as we were, part of the mesh will be drawn in that quadrant. We need to make sure this area is skipped by repeating the center vertex.

```
// We start with a recursive function.
void renderQuad(quadNode *node)
{
  if (node == NULL)
    return;

  // If this node has four children, it doesn't need to be rendered.
  if (node->children[0] != NULL || node->children[1] != NULL ||
      node->children[2] != NULL || node->children[3] != NULL)
```

```
  {
    // Start with the center point.
    glBegin(GL_TRIANGLE_FAN);
    glVertex3f(node->center.x, node->center.y, node->center.z);

    // Loop through all four children, adding vertices as needed.
    for (int i = 0; i < 4; i++)
    {
      // Add the corner vertex if the child doesn't exist.
      if (!node->children[i])
        glVertex3f(node->corner[i].x, node->corner[i].y, node->corner[i].z);

      // If the side is active, also add that.
      if (node->activeSide[i])
        glVertex3f(node->side[i].x, node->side[i].y, node->side[i].z);

      // If the next child exists, make sure we skip it by
      // adding the center point again.
      int next = i+1;
      if (next > 3)
        next = 0;

      if (node->children[next])
        glVertex3f(node->center.x, node->center.y, node->center.z);
    }

    // Make sure we finish the last triangle if the first child exists.
    if (!node->children[0])
      glVertex3f(node->corner[0].x, node->corner[0].y, node->corner[0].z);
    glEnd();
  }

  // Render this node's children.
  for (int i = 0; i < 4; i++)
    renderQuad(node->children[i]);
}
```

Don't forget to also add your texture coordinates, normals, and colors.

Creating a Vertex Buffer from the Mesh

The mesh won't change from frame to frame, so walking the quadtree and creating the mesh each frame is a waste of time. Besides, we're going to want to save the mesh to file eventually so we can use it with the chunked LOD method, and it should be optimized a bit first. Instead, we'll create a vertex array, making sure each vertex is used only once, and an index array. Because the mesh is irregular, we'll create an index array of triangles rather than triangle strips.

The first thing we need to do is decide which vertices are being used and assign a unique index to each. We'll temporarily hold this index data in a new multidimensional array, the same size as the heightmap. This will also preserve the orientation of each vertex, which will come in handy later. Once this new array is created and each value initialized to −1, we find all the used vertices. The function to do this looks exactly like the function to draw the mesh, but instead of the call to glVertex(), we set the index of that vertex, increasing the index by one for each vertex that is used. Remember, a vertex may be used several times, so if the current index isn't −1, continue on to the next vertex.

Now each used vertex should be accounted for and have its own index. We also know the number of used vertices, which should be the last index used plus one. We can create our vertex array by taking the number of vertices and multiplying the number of components each vertex will use. If each vertex gets a normal, texture coordinate, and color, we have nine components. Filling the vertex array is similar to the brute force method. The only difference is that we must check to see if each vertex is used, and then use that index when setting our variables. The index into the buffer for each element will be the precalculated offset plus the index multiplied by the number of components for that element. For example, the code to set the vertex position would look like this:

```
int vertOffset = 0;
for (int z = 0; z < Height; z++)
{
  for (int x = 0; x < Width; x++)
  {
    if (indextList[x][z] > -1)
    {
      int index = indexList[x][z];

      vertBuffer[vertOffset+(index*3)+0] = x;
      vertBuffer[vertOffset+(index*3)+1] = heights[x][z];
      vertBuffer[vertOffset+(index*3)+2] = z;
    }
  }
}
```

To create the index list, we must first know how many triangles we have. We do this by traversing through our quadtree, and for each node, we count the number of triangles in its mesh. As stated earlier, a node with zero children or one child will have four triangles, a node with two children will have three triangles, and a node with four children will have no triangles.

Once we know how many triangles we have, we can start to create the index list. The index list will be three times as long as the number of triangles. We create this list by traversing the quadtree again.

We loop through each of the children, where there are four possible outcomes: child[i] and child[i + 1] exist, and no triangles have to be built; child[i] and child[i + 1] don't exist and a triangle needs to be built; child[i] doesn't exist and side[i] is active and a triangle needs to be built; or child[i + 1] doesn't exist and side[i] is active and a triangle needs to be built.

```
for (int i = 0; i < 4; i++)
{
  if (!node->children[i] && node->activeSide[i])
    // Build Triangle center, corner[i], side[i]
  else if (!node->children[i] && !node->children[i+1])
    // Build Triangle center, corner[i], corner[i+1]

  if (node->activeSide[i] && !node->children[i+1])
  // Build Triangle center, side[i], corner[i+1]
}
```

Fixing Cracks with Skirts

We haven't experienced cracks yet, but in the next section, when we put two or more of these meshes together, we will. Since we have preserved the orientation of our mesh before we put it into a vertex array, this step should be easy. This step would be quite a chore if we had just loaded the vertex and index arrays from a file, as we will do later.

First, we need to know how many vertices we will have in our skirt. We can find this by counting the number of vertices that are on the edge of the mesh. Anything with an x value of 0 or Width − 1, and a z value of 0 or Height − 1 will be in our skirts vertex array. The number of vertices in the array will be this count times two: one for the vertex at (x, y, z), and one for the vertex at (x, 0, z).

Once we have our count, we traverse along the edges again, except this time we add our vertices. Each time we find a vertex that is used, we add that vertex to our array along with a vertex at the same x and z position with a height of 0, placing it directly under the first one. Make sure that the normal and color for this second vertex matches the one above it, and that the texture coordinates reflect the distance between the two vertices. The skirt won't blend in if it doesn't share normals and colors with the original vertex.

Creating the index array is much easier. We can do this by starting in one corner and building a triangle strip around the outside of the mesh. The vertices should already be in the correct order.

These skirts may be quite visible, depending on the terrain. If you don't mind adding a few polygons, you can reduce the visible area of the skirts by making sure that the sides on the outside edge of the mesh are active. This adds extra vertices along the edge to possibly match up. Alternatively, you can also make sure adjacent nodes of adjacent chunks match up as in the LOD algorithm. This will also reduce the amount of skirt that is visible.

Chunked LOD Implementation

When using chunked LOD, the terrain consists of a number of square chunks, arranged end to end, over the terrain like the brute force frustum culling example. Each chunk is rendered using a quadtree where the root node contains a VIPM mesh created with a large amount of error. Each child node contains a mesh one quarter the size of the parent mesh with less error. Children are created until the error equals 0. When we draw the terrain, we draw based on distance, so the mesh closest to the viewer is rendered using the lowest level of the quadtree, giving the highest detail. The farther away from the viewer, the higher the quadtree level used to render the terrain. We will also add a bounding box to each node so we can cull out unseen nodes.

Creating a Chunk

To create a chunk, we first create a quadtree to hold the meshes. Each node uses our VIPM implementation to obtain a mesh, decreasing the amount of error for each level in the quadtree. We can do this by using an error of (maxError − quadtreeLevel * step), where step is the error difference between levels, and maxError is evenly divisible by step. The mesh will start with maxError at the root node and work its way down, reducing each level by step until it reaches 0. The total number of levels will be (maxError/step) + 1. Each node will also need to obtain a skirt mesh for its terrain mesh. Once the meshes are in the node, we calculate two points to use as a bounding box the same way we did in the brute force example.

Modifying the LOD Implementation

Our VIPM implementation currently creates a mesh for the whole terrain. That's perfect for the root node, but we need it to create pieces of the full mesh for the other children. We'll need to change the implementation a bit so we can give it a range, and have it create a mesh just for that range. We can do this by keeping track of four variables; chunkWidth, chunkHeight, chunkLeft, and chunkTop. We also need to change initNode and findAdjacent to use these variables.

Saving and Loading Chunks

Once our chunk quadtree is created, it should be holding a vertex and index array for the mesh, and a vertex and index array for the skirt. We also want to store the size of each array and two points for our bounding box. Since we'll be using many chunks for our terrain, we don't want to have to wait for them to be created each time we run the program. We need saving and loading functions.

A chunk can be saved by creating a recursive function that saves a single node and then is called for the node's children. As long as the load function is structured the same way as the save function, everything should load properly. For each node, we'll first save the bounding-box points. We'll then save the array size and the array values for each of the arrays in the node. When loading, we'll load in the same order, using the array size to determine how much data needs to be loaded for each array.

The Popping Problem

When the viewer moves, the distance between nodes changes, and different meshes are drawn. When this happens, the shape of the terrain itself changes, as detail is added and removed. This is quite noticeable and very sudden. We want our geometry to change, but we'd like it to be more gradual.

Instead of switching meshes as a new node is used, we're going to slowly move the mesh's vertices into place. When a node is first set to a lower level, we'll display the mesh's vertices in the same position as the parent mesh. As the node gets closer to the viewer, the vertices will gradually move closer to their correct position. This is called *geomorphing*. To do this, we need to know how close the player is to the node, and the position of each vertex in the parent mesh.

Adding Morphing Data

For each vertex in our vertex array, we'll need to hold an extra piece of data: the difference between the current y-coordinate and the y-coordinate of the point on the parent mesh. To do this, we'll need to be able to find the height of any (x, z) point on the parent mesh. This is very similar to our find difference function. We just need to add code to figure out which node the point lies in. Once we have our new function, we create our new array of Δy values by sending each vertex in the vertex array to this function and subtracting the current y value. We also need to add this data to our skirt list, but we only need it for the top vertex. The bottom doesn't need to move. We'll need to fill the bottom values with a delta of 0.

Geomorphing

To morph our vertices, we'll multiply our Δy value by a number between 0 and 1. This multiplication value will be 0 at the distance where the parent node splits, 1 at the distance where the current node splits, and interpolated between 0 and 1 for the distances between. This can be found by subtracting the distance where the current node splits from both the current distance to the node and the distance to the parent node. The resulting current distance is divided by the parent distance and clamped to be between 0 and 1.

```
float parentSplits;    // Distance where parent node splits.
float currentSplits;   // Distance where current node splits.
float distance;        // Distance to current node.

float multFactor = max(0, min(1, (distance - currentSplits) /
                                  (parentSplits - currentSplits)));
```

This multiplication value will be used for the whole node, so it can be calculated once before drawing. To move the vertices, we can use a vertex shader. The Δy value can be sent as an attribute to the shader along with the other pieces of the vertex array. The multiplication factor can be sent as a uniform variable before the mesh is drawn. Inside the shader, the y position of each vertex is adjusted by adding the Δy value multiplied by the multiplication factor.

Using More Than One Chunk

In some games, the terrain from a single chunk won't be large enough, so a number of chunks will need to be used. For larger games that take place outside, like multiplayer RPGs, hundreds or thousands of chunks may be used.

With our current heightmap generation techniques, two chunks placed next to each other will create quite a mess. The two sets of meshes won't line up. A mountain will suddenly fall off into a valley. Rivers will stop suddenly. Large sections of skirt will show, creating walls around chunks. We need to find a way to create one large, continuous terrain.

One obvious solution is to use a giant heightmap. This heightmap can take a long time to generate, but sections of it will definitely piece together nicely. Another solution is to create a heightmap that tiles with itself. This can be done by smoothing each edge with the opposite edge during the smoothing process. This creates decent results when it's important that a terrain exists, but the fine details aren't important, like in flight simulators. When the terrain becomes a crucial part of the game, you don't want terrain features to repeat. Another option is to create different sections of terrain and use adjacent heightmap values during the smoothing and scaling process.

Determining Which Chunks Are Needed Now

With a single chunk weighing in at between two and five megabytes, we couldn't possibly keep all chunks of a large terrain in system memory at one time, much less video memory. What we can do is make sure all chunks that are currently being displayed are in video memory, and all chunks that may be displayed within a certain amount of time are in system memory, ready to go into video memory.

We know that at any one time, the chunk directly under the viewer's position will most likely be displayed, and should be in video memory. Depending on the view distance, the eight chunks directly adjacent to that chunk may also be displayed, as shown in Figure

10.12. Most of today's video cards can handle nine chunks' worth of video memory, so that's where we'll put these chunks.

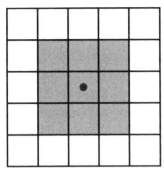

Figure 10.12 The visible chunk in the center is surrounded by other possibly visible chunks, which are kept in video memory. Chunks surrounding those nodes may be needed soon, and are kept in system memory.

When the player moves from one chunk to another, up to five chunks may need to be moved to video memory. If we take those chunks from disk and move them to video memory, there will be a definite slowdown. It would be better if we could move them from system memory into video memory. To do this, we'll need to keep an additional sixteen chunks in system memory.

When Is a Chunk No Longer Needed?

When a player moves from one corner chunk to another, we have five new chunks entering video memory, five chunks leaving video memory, nine chunks being loaded from disk, and nine chunks being removed from memory. If our chunks are 5 megs each, that's 140 megs worth of data moving around. That's a lot of memory to be moving in a single frame. If a player then moves back to the original chunk, the whole process has to be undone.

Creating a Paging System

Instead of loading and unloading chunks as the player moves, it would be nice to keep it around a little while in case the player returns to a location. Once a chunk moves out of range, we can give it a time stamp. After a set amount of time, we can free the memory, knowing that the player won't quickly be returning to that location.

We can also lighten the load when loading new chunks. If the player moves at a rate of m per second, and the chunk has a width of x, we know it will take x/m seconds before a new chunk will need to be used. If we have nine chunks to load, we have $(x/m)/9$ seconds per chunk to load the data. We can use this knowledge to spread the loading of chunks across a number of frames.

When creating a system like this, the actual numbers will depend on a number of variables that will need to be balanced to get the desired result on the desired hardware. With a shorter drawing distance, the number of chunks used will decrease along with the amount of video and system memory used. Slower movement speeds will give the program more time to page chunks in and out. A larger chunk will increase the memory requirements, but allow for more time to move chunks from system to video memory.

Terrain Texturing

Even the most inspired heightmap-creation technique and the most optimal terrain renderer will fail if the texturing is done badly. Which textures to use is an artistic choice. The only requirement is that they tile without noticeable artifacts. The most common artifacts are seams at tile edges or a noticeable pattern when the texture is tiled. You may find that you need to try a number of textures before you find any you like. You may also find that textures that work in one situation won't work in another. I went through over 50 textures while writing this chapter before finding the ones that I liked.

Texture Blending

Once a number of textures that go well together have been picked, we need to choose a method of blending them together to create our terrain's texture. For the examples here, we'll use the same method outlined in the "Colors" section of the brute force render method. Low elevations will get one texture, high elevations a second texture, and areas with a steep slope will get a third texture. I've chosen a mud texture for my low areas, a grass texture for my high areas, and a stone texture for my steep slope areas.

This is definitely not the only method that can be used. An artist could create a texture map that places different textures at different locations which are then blended together smoothly. Instead of assigning full textures, each vertex could be given a specific texture to use and then those values could be blended together. A system where areas that get lots of light get a grass texture while areas with little to no light get dirt and rock could be another method.

Creating a Single Texture

The first option when texturing our terrain is to use one large texture and stretch it over the entire terrain. The quality of the texturing increases as the texture size grows, so this produces nice results with very large texture sizes. This is much faster than doing any real-time blending, but the textures get big quickly and take some time to generate. For a rendering system like chunked LOD, where a number of chunks need to be in memory at once, this is not an option.

We first need to create a buffer for our texture. With a 1024×1024 heightmap, 2048×2048 will work well. If our textures are 512×512, they will tile four times over the width and height of the texture.

```
// Width and height of our terrain texture.
int textureWidth = 2048;
int textureHeight = 2048;

// Create a buffer to hold our texture data.
GLubyte *terrainTexture;
terrainTexture = new Glubyte[2048*1048*3];
```

For each point on our terrain texture, we need to find the corresponding points on our source textures. If we take the current x- and y-position in the texture and divide it by the width and height of the source texture, the remainder will be the pixel in the source texture we're looking for.

```
// Width and height of our source textures.
int sourceWidth = 512;
int sourceHeight = 512;

for (int z = 0; z < textureHeight; z++)
{
  for (int x = 0; x < textureWidth; x++)
  {
    // The index into our terrain texture for this pixel.
    int destIndex = (z * textureWidth * 3) + (x * 3);

    // The index into our source textures.
    int sourceX = x % sourceWidth;
    int sourceY = z % sourceHeight;
    int sourceIndex = (sourceY * sourceWidth * 3) + (sourceX * 3);
```

Once we know the offset into our source image, we can set up the three source colors that will be used to create this pixel of our terrain texture.

```
    ubyteColor color1, color2, color3;

    color1.r = sourceTexture1[sourceIndex];
    color1.g = sourceTexture1[sourceIndex+1];
    color1.b = sourceTexture1[sourceIndex+2];

    color2.r = sourceTexture2[sourceIndex];
    color2.g = sourceTexture2[sourceIndex+1];
```

```
    color2.b = sourceTexture2[sourceIndex+2];

    color3.r = sourceTexture3[sourceIndex];
    color3.g = sourceTexture3[sourceIndex+1];
    color3.b = sourceTexture3[sourceIndex+2];
```

From here it's all the same as calculating the vertex color in the brute force example. We calculate our result RGB by blending the three colors together. When calculating the alpha, remember that when looking up the height, you need to divide x by `TextureWidth/Width` and y by `TextureHeight/Height` to find the actual height at that point. Once the buffer is created, we can turn it into a texture through one of the OpenGL texture-creation functions.

An example using this approach is shown in Figure 10.13.

Figure 10.13 An example of the single-texture method.

Multitexturing

We can easily get the same effect as a large single texture without the excessive amount of memory and without spending the time to create the texture, by moving the process to the video card. As we've already seen in the brute force example, when using a detail texture, a texture will seamlessly tile over our terrain without any additional changes. Our goal is to tile three textures over the terrain, blending them together based on the terrain's height and slope at each vertex.

Using Combiners

The results using texture combiners will be similar to the above example. We'll first lay down a base texture over the whole terrain. We'll then blend in a second texture on top of that, based on the height at each vertex. The third texture will be blended in based on slope. To do this, we'll need two sets of values for each vertex: an alpha value for the first blend and an alpha value for the second.

By texturing the terrain, we are essentially coloring it. Because of this, we can use the primary color as one source for our alpha values. The terrain probably won't be alpha blending, so we can use the terrain's alpha value as our second source. When we create our vertex array, set the color values to the first alpha value we calculated in the brute force example. Set the alpha component to the second alpha value.

Now that we have our alpha values, we can start blending the two textures. For texture unit 0, we can use the function GL_REPLACE since we don't want to blend this texture with anything. We'll lose our lighting, because light is calculated before combiners, but we'll end up losing it later anyway when we blend in the other two textures. We can fix that in the next section.

For texture unit 1, we want to use the GL_INTERPOLATE function to alpha blend between the two colors. We want to blend between the previous color and the texture color, so use GL_PREVIOUS and GL_TEXTURE as sources with GL_SRC_COLOR as the operand. Last, set the third source to the primary color, which holds our alpha value.

Texture unit 2 is set up in the same way, except the GL_SRC_ALPHA operand is used instead of GL_SRC_COLOR for the third source.

Using Fragment Shaders

Moving the texturing process to a fragment shader is a straightforward process that adds a lot of flexibility. For modern video cards, blending your textures with a fragment shader will give you an additional 12 texture units that can be used for detail textures or additional source textures. When we fixed the popping problem with chunked LOD, we never addressed textures popping. This can be fixed by doing your blending calculations per fragment rather than per vertex.

Lighting and Shadows

Without lighting, our terrain looks bland, and all of the terrain features we created appear to blend together. Lighting helps the eye distinguish distances between objects, and the subtle accents lighting adds imply orientation. The eye is so used to lighting effects in everyday life that they are almost never noticed when done correctly, but they pop out when something is wrong.

Figure 10.14 An example of the combiner method.

Creating a Lightmap

Using combiners has removed our lighting effects, and we need to get them back. We can do this by blending a lightmap onto the terrain using our fourth texture unit with GL_MODULATE as our blending function. We don't want our lightmap to tile along with the other textures, so we'll need a second set of texture coordinates, and we can achieve this by using a tileAmount of 1 and repeating the terrain coordinate section of our vertex array code.

I've found that using a ratio of one texel to every two vertices gives a nice result without being too blurry. Since we are going to blend this along with three other textures, the loss of precision won't be noticed. To produce the desired lightmap, we'll need to create a texture that is half the size of the heightmap, and when we do our calculations, we'll calculate for every other height in the heightmap.

The colors in our lightmap will be generated using the same method that OpenGL uses for diffuse light. While this is not a perfect model for the sun's light, it does the job quite well, and it is fast to compute. I've had success calculating both lighting and shadows for a 512×512 lightmap in real time.

For each vertex we are calculating lighting for, we first create a vector from that point to the light source and normalize it. We then find the dot product of that vector and the normal at that vertex. We then multiply that value by the light's RGB values to get the color of the light at that vertex. We can simplify this if we assume the light color to be white.

```
// The position of the light.
vector pos;

// Normalize the position vector by dividing each component by the vector's length.
double length = sqrt(pos.x*pos.x + pos.y*pos.y + pos.z*pos.z);
pos.x = pos.x/length;
pos.y = pos.y/length;
pos.z = pos.z/length;

// We find the dot product and then multiply by the light color to find the color at a
vertex.
// This assumes we have saved the normals in a multidimensional array named normal.
lightColor = 255 * (pos.x * normal[x][z].x +
                    pos.y * normal[x][z].y +
                    pos.z * normal[x][z].z);
```

With this value saved in the lightmap and textured onto the terrain, we should have something that looks like OpenGL's lighting. To finish our lighting effect, we'll add some shadows.

Adding Shadows

Shadows are cast on an object when something falls between that object and a light source. In our case, a shadow is cast on a point when part of the surrounding terrain falls between the point and the light. While there are a number of techniques to determine if a point should be shadowed or not, most involve calculating a line between the point and the light source and checking each point on that line to see if it intersects the heightmap. This is a slow process and can't be done in real time.

In order to calculate shadows in real time, we will use horizon mapping. One drawback of horizon mapping is that the light source can only move along one plane; in this case, the xy-plane. There are some methods that can be explored further to get past this limitation at the expense of memory and time.

For each position in the heightmap, we need to record two new numbers. One will represent the highest point on the horizon in the positive x direction, and the other in the negative x direction. The actual value recorded will be the slope of a line drawn from the tallest point on the horizon to the point we are calculating for. This value can be obtained by looping through the x values to the left and the right of each point, calculating the slope for each one. The greatest slope will be the horizon value at that point. The process is then repeated in the other direction. This will create our horizon map, which only needs to be calculated once when the heightmap is created.

```
// Calculates the horizon map in one direction.
for (int z = 0; z < Height; z++)
{
  for (int x = 0; x < Width; x++)
  {
    // Loop through all values of x to the left of our current point.
    float maxSlope = 0;
    for (int i = x-1; i >= 0; i--)
    {
      // Calculate the slope.
      float slope = 0;
      slope = float(heights[i][z] - heights[x][z]) / (i - x);

      // If this slope is greater than the previous greatest, save it.
      if (slope > maxSlope)
        maxSlope = slope;
    }
    // Save our horizon information for this point.
    horizon[x][z] = maxSlope;
  }
}
```

When it's time to decide if a point needs to be shadowed or not, we calculate the slope of a line between the light source and the point's position. If this slope is greater than the horizon slope, the point isn't shadowed. If the slope is less, the horizon comes between the light source and the point. There is always ambient light, so we don't want to make shadowed areas completely black. A value around half lit works well. This value should be blended with the current lighting value at that point.

```
// The light position.
vector pos;

for (int z = 0; z < Height; z++)
{
  for (int x = 0; x < Width; x++)
  {
    float shadow = 1.0;

    // Slope is undefined if the light is directly overhead.
    if (x != pos.x)
    {
      // Calculate the slope between the point and light position.
      slope = float(pos.y - heights[x][z])/(pos.x - x);
```

```
    if (slope < horizon[x][z])
      shadow = 0.4;
  }

  // Multiply our shadow value by our lighting value.
  lightValue[x][z] *= shadow;
 }
}
```

Additionally, you can calculate a slope for the top of the light source and one for the bottom of the light source and blend from fully lit to full shadow if the horizon falls between the two values. This will give you a nice soft transition for your shadows.

Summary

The topic of terrain simulation for games could fill an entire book (in fact, several already exist), but in this chapter, you've learned about some of the most important aspects of it. You've learned about several techniques for creating terrain data, and a few approaches for rendering it. You've also learned the basics of terrain texturing. Armed with this knowledge, you're well on your way to adding good-looking, efficient terrains to your games.

References

Deloura, Mark, ed. *Game Programming Gems.*[city]: Charles River Media, 2000.

Hoffman, Naty, and Kenny Mitchell. "Methods for Dynamic Photorealistic Terrain Lighting." In *Game Programming Gems 3*, 433–43. [city]:Thomson Delmar Learning, 2002.

Nystrom, Bob. Terrain Generation Tutorial: Hill Algorithm. **http://www.robot-frog.com/3d/hills/hill.html**.

Ulrich, Thatcher. "Continuous LOD Terrain Meshing Using Adaptive Quadtrees." Gamasutra, **http://www.gamasutra.com/features/20000228/ulrich_pfv.htm** (accessed February 28, 2000).

Ulrich, Thatcher. "Rendering Massive Terrains Using Chunked Level of Detail Control." **http://tulrich.com/geekstuff/chunklod.html** (accessed April 2002).

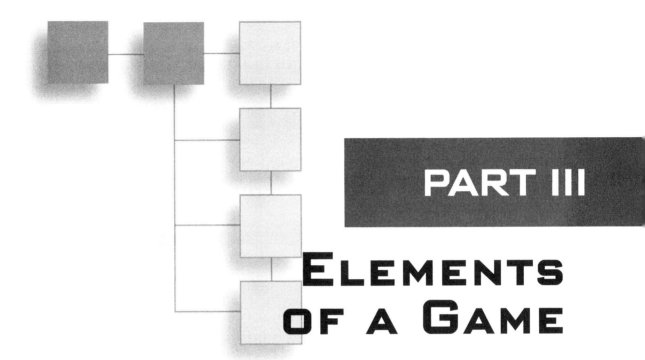

PART III

ELEMENTS
OF A GAME

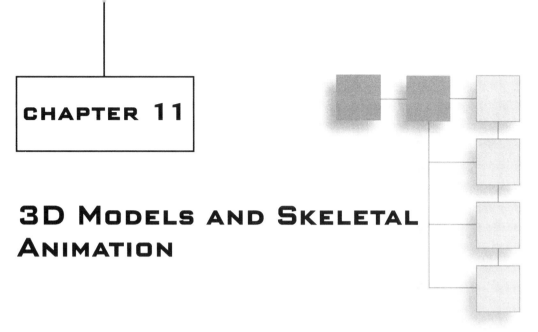

CHAPTER 11

3D Models and Skeletal Animation

Evan Pipho

Introduction

Think back to your first real 3D program. You managed to wrestle OpenGL into submission, and you put the hallmark spinning triangle or rotating cube on the screen. You may have used paper to plot out the position of each vertex and how they were joined together to make your shape of choice.

This approach works great for the basic box and other simple shapes, but imagine typing, one by one, thousands of numbers to represent your game's character. Sounds like a nightmare, doesn't it? Thankfully, you don't have to do that. You can create complex objects, from characters to weapons, in a separate program such as 3ds max, Maya, XSI, Blender, or Milkshape 3D. You can then write code to load these models from the resulting files and move and animate them within your game or application.

Types of 3D Models

There are two major subcategories of 3D models: static and animated. Static models are the simplest type of 3D model and generally contain only vertex and polygon information. Since static models by definition do not animate, they are ideal for scene elements such as trees, rocks, and furniture. Another advantage of static models is that they require less disk space and memory than their animated counterparts because they contain a minimal amount of data. This also makes working with them in your application a lot easier.

Animated models, on the other hand, are more complex, containing all the information needed to morph and animate the model. You will want to use animated models for things such as characters, monsters, vehicles, animals, or anything that moves. Despite their added complexity and memory costs, animated models are a necessity for many game elements. It would look very silly to have human characters slide across the ground without using their legs or a bird fly by without flapping its wings.

Animated models can also be broken into several categories based on the way their animation data is stored. Models that use keyframe animation store "snapshots" of the model in various positions. The position of each vertex in the model is stored for each frame of the model. Then the renderer loads the frameset and interpolates between frames to produce a smooth animation. Popular games such as those in id Software's Quake series use keyframe animation for their character and enemy models. Keyframe animation is simple and fast, but it does have some downsides. As models in games become more complex, having tens of thousands of vertices each, keyframe animation becomes undesirable for both the programmer and the artist. From the artists' side, animating 20,000 vertices one vertex at a time would take months and be extremely tedious. These giant models would also take up a tremendous amount of memory—a model with 20,000 vertices and 500 frames of animation would take up almost 120 megabytes for position data alone! Not to mention the space taken up by lighting information and other data.

The solution? Skeletal animation. Skeletal animation stores the mesh data only once, not hundreds of times like keyframe animation. Skeletal animation uses a system of "bones" to deform the mesh. Each vertex is attached to one or more bones, and as the bones move, the vertices move with them. This not only results in more realistic animation, it makes creation of animation much easier. With skeletal animation, the artist doesn't need to manually move hundreds of vertices; instead, the artist can animate the hip, knee, and foot bones, and the character's leg will move. Skeletally animated models also take much less memory; the model I theorized about in the previous paragraph might take a tiny fraction of the space if it used skeletal animation. Storing the positions and orientation of each bone per frame takes much less space than storing the entire mesh for each and every frame. Most modern 3D games use skeletal animation for their characters for these very reasons.

What You Will Learn in This Chapter

This chapter is meant to give you an overview of both static and animated models. You will learn not only the basic concepts behind both, but also how to parse and use several of the popular formats common in today's games.

I will start with the Wavefront OBJ file format, one of the most universal model formats. It is a static format, and it is easy to find example models as well as create your own. After creating a working OBJ loader, I will take a look at animated models. Because of the limitations of space and the wide availability of information, I will not go over keyframe animation. There are many sources—including the predecessor to this book—that cover keyframe animation in detail. Instead, we will go right to basic skeletal animation.

After a review of some of the basic math needed for skeletal animation, I will take a look at the Milkshape 3D (MS3D) format. This format is an excellent one to start with as it uses basic skeletal animation and the tool to create these models is very affordable, well within the reach of any game developer.

Once you have finished this chapter you should be ready to implement static models as well as a skeletal animation system in your own game. Demos and source code for all of the covered formats will be available on the website accompanying this book.

Basic Model Loading and the OBJ format

The first and most basic of the formats I will discuss in this chapter is the Wavefront Object (OBJ) format. The OBJ format is one of the most widely used 3D model types. Despite having been created by Alias|Wavefront (**http://www.alias.com**), the maker of the popular Maya 3D package, nearly every 3D modeling package can import and export the OBJ format.

Object files are in a convenient, human-readable form. You can open a file in your favorite text editor and see a list of the vertices, normals, texture coordinates, and faces.

Each line of the file contains a single vertex position, a single texture coordinate, or another small piece of the model. Parsing an OBJ file is quite easy. All you need to do is read the file one line at a time. Each line begins with an identifier that tells you what the rest of the line contains. A line starting with a v, for instance, will be a vertex position with one value each for the x, y, and z components.

Table 11.1 shows a list of the lines you need to be concerned with when loading Wavefront Object files, followed by more detailed descriptions of each type.

Table 11.1 OBJ File Identifiers

Identifier	Example	Description
#	# comment	Lines starting with a pound sign are comments; just skip over them
v	v 1.0 2.4 5.1	A vertex position; will contain three values for the x, y, and z components
vt	vt 0.1 0.6	A texture coordinate pair; will contain two values for the u- and v-axis
vn	vn 0.0 0.0 1.0	A vertex normal, contains three values that make up a normalized direction vector
f	f 1/1/2 2/3/4 5/1/2	A polygon definition (more on this later in the chapter)

Vertex Information

In each OBJ file, there are three lines that contain vertex information. Since the file doesn't tell you the *amount* of vertex information, you need to use a resizable array, such as an std::vector, to store the information as you read it in.

As mentioned, lines starting with *v* contain a vertex position. These lines contain three floating-point values representing x, y, and z. A line that starts with *vt* contains a texture coordinate: two floating-point values representing the u and v texture coordinates. A line starting with *vn* contains a vertex normal. A vertex normal has three values as well, representing a vector that has a unit length of one.

Face Information

Lines beginning with *f* contain the indices for one face of the model. Each index for the face contains between one and three values. At the very least, each face index must contain an index into the array of vertex positions. However, it may also contain an index into the array of texture coordinates, the array of vertex normals, or both.

Face indices can take several forms. A face that contains only vertex indices will be very simple: f 1 2 3. If a face contains both vertex and texture coordinates, they will be separated by slashes, like so: f 1/1 2/2 3/3. A face with vertex and normal indices will be similar to the one with texture coordinates, but with two slashes instead of one: f 1//1 2//2 3//3. Finally, a face may contain all three and will be in form f 1/1/1 2/2/2 3/3/3.

Fortunately, all faces in the file are the same style, so you do not have to worry about switching between formats. However, not all faces in an OBJ file are triangles. A face line can hold any number of indices, creating a convex polygon with any number of vertices. While this can be a tad annoying, it is very easy to convert these faces to raw triangles when you read them in.

The formula for converting a convex polygon is quite simple. The first triangle is simply the first three vertices of the face. For each additional vertex you take the first vertex of the line, the last vertex you read, and the new vertex, and this creates a new triangle. If you do this while you are loading the file, it greatly simplifies the rendering process.

There are two other things to watch out for. First, the indices in a standard OBJ file start at one, not zero. Failing to subtract one before looking up the vertex in the vertex array will cause everything to be messed up. Second, you will occasionally find a file with all negative indices. These are not corrupt files and are simply stored in a different form. To convert the negative indices into positive ones, use the following formula:

```
converted index = total vertices + negative vertex index
```

Rendering the Model

Once you have loaded the vertex and face information, you are ready to render the model. A simple rendering loop would look like this.

```
glBegin(GL_TRIANGLES);
for(int i=0; i<numFaces; i++) {
  for(int j=0; j<3; j++) {
    if(hasNormals)
      glNormalfv(&VertexNormals[NormalIndices[i*3+j]]);
    if(hasTexCoords)
      glTexcoord2fv(&TextureCoords[TexcoordIndices[i*3+j]]);
    glVertex3fv(&VertexPositions[VertexIndices[i*3+j]]);
  }
}
glEnd();
```

This code loops through the entire array of triangle indices, rendering each using normals and texture coordinates if necessary. This is the simplest way to go about rendering the file, but it is also one of the slowest. Converting the three index arrays into a single large array and using OpenGL's vertex arrays or vertex buffer objects would speed up the model's rendering loop considerably. That operation is beyond the scope of this text, but it is included in the example source code and demo.

The source code for this chapter contains an OBJ loader that not only handles vertex positions, normals, texture coordinates, and faces, but also converts the data into a format that can be used in a standard OpenGL vertex array. The demo also contains code that will read material information from the file, mapping the appropriate materials to the correct parts of the model.

The OBJ format can contain much more than what I have mentioned here. Besides material information, the files can contain curved surfaces, editor data, points, lines, and more. You can obtain a complete specification by following the links at the end of this chapter.

Skeletal Animation

The first part of the chapter dealt with a simple, static model format. Now it's time to move on to something a little more difficult. Since there are plenty of tutorials and books out there that cover the basic keyframe animation formats such as MD2, I will skip directly to skeletal animation.

tip
_____

Keyframe animation and the MD2 format were covered in one chapter of the original *OpenGL Game Programming*, and that complete chapter was included as bonus material on the CD for *Beginning OpenGL Game Programming*. In addition, many of the examples in the latter book, as well as in this book, use the MD2 format, so if you're interested, you can check out the demos to learn more.
_____

The section begins with a short introduction to skeletal animation explaining how it works and why it is superior to basic keyframe animation. This will be followed by an introduction to *quaternions*, an essential mathematical part of skeletal animation. Finally, I'll delve into the popular model format MS3D, exported from the Milkshape 3D package.

What is Skeletal Animation?

Many games today advertise "advanced skeletal animation system" or "cutting-edge skeletal animation technology," but what does this really mean? Skeletal animation is a technique where a model is represented by two parts. The first part is the mesh, or *skin*, of the model. The skin represents the surface of the model and may contain hundreds of thousands of vertices. The second part is the skeleton, a set of bones that deform the skin as they move.

Think of your own body as a 3D model. Your skin would represent the mesh of the model, while your bones and muscles would be the skeleton of the model. Just as your skin moves as you move your own skeleton, the mesh on the outside of a model moves with the bones.

This is great for animators as it allows them to animate models much faster. Rather than animating thousands of points to make the character walk, they just need to manipulate the leg bones, and the leg mesh will automatically deform.

Skeletal animation is a hierarchical system. This means that whatever happens at the beginning of the system is carried down the line to the end. For instance, if the hip and thigh are moved, the calf and foot follow, just as they do in real life. Figure 11.1 shows how moving a single *parent* bone automatically affects the bones, known as the *child* bones, later down the line.

A bone can have multiple children. For instance, the hip bone may connect to both leg bones, or the wrist may connect to multiple fingers. In these cases, the same rules apply: any transformations done to the parent will also be done to all of its children, all its children's children, and so on. Figure 11.2 shows the same action as Figure 11.1, but this time one of the joints has more than one child.

Before you deform the skin, you need to calculate the transforms for the entire skeleton. You first set the local transformation for each bone. This data is generally given to you within the model files. Then, for each bone, you need to calculate the final transformation.

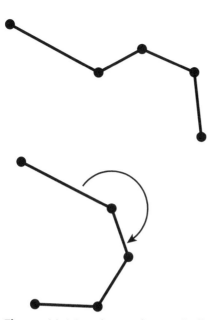

Figure 11.1 Rotating one bone will affect all the bones later in the hierarchy.

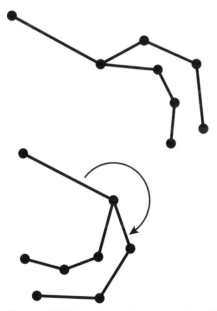

Figure 11.2 Bones can have multiple child bones.

Starting with the bone you are transforming, travel to its parent, its parent's parent and so forth until you get to the root node, a node with no parent. As you traverse the skeleton, concatenate the local transform of each bone you come to, which will result in a final transformation. The skeleton is now ready to deform the skin.

Each vertex in the skin will reference a specific bone. All you need to do is transform the vertex by the bone's final transformation, which is the one you calculated in the previous step. This will cause the mesh to deform along the bone, just as your flesh moves with your own bones.

I'll talk more about the specific mathematics later on in this chapter. Before I get to the actual model-file loading, you may need to review some important 3D math concepts. Be sure you are familiar with vectors and transformation matrices before you continue; both are essential to understanding the next part of the chapter.

You will also need a rudimentary understanding of quaternions. I have included a short review in the next section. If you are familiar with the concept of quaternions, you may skip to the next section, "Loading MS3D."

Quaternion Review

This section contains a brief synopsis of the math behind some of the most common quaternion operations and conversions. It will give you a basic understanding of quaternions, as well as enough knowledge to allow you to implement a skeletal animation system.

You will learn how to interpolate between quaternions for smooth animation, convert between matrices and quaternions, convert a set of Euler angles to a quaternion, and do mathematical operations such as multiplication, addition, and subtraction on quaternions.

What are Quaternions?

Quaternions are an extension of complex numbers first discovered by Sir William Hamilton in 1843. Quaternions are represented by four components, one real and three imaginary. On paper, quaternions are usually represented by a scalar, representing the real component, and a vector, representing the imaginary components. They can also be represented as a four-component vector where the w-component is the real component and the x, y, and z components are imaginary.

Quaternions can be used to represent a rotation in 3D space, much as three Euler angles and 3×3 matrices can. There are several reasons to use quaternions rather than matrices and Euler angles. First, it is easy to interpolate between two quaternions, allowing for smooth, constant-speed rotations. Second, Euler angles can suffer from gimbal lock, which will cause problems when attempting to rotate bones in certain directions. Last, they take up less space than matrices but can still be quickly converted back to matrices to send to OpenGL. Now, let's take a look at doing math with quaternions.

All quaternions that represent a 3D rotation must be of unit length. The length of a quaternion is calculated the same way as a four-dimensional vector. Other operations such as the dot product, normalization, and addition and subtraction are the same for quaternions as for vectors.

Addition and Subtraction

Adding and subtracting quaternions is as easy as adding or subtracting each individual component, just as you would a standard vector. There are no special rules for adding or subtracting imaginary numbers, so all four components can be treated the same. Figure 11.3 shows the process for adding and subtracting quaternions.

$$p = [w_1, x_1, y_1, z_1]$$
$$q = [w_2, x_1, y_2, z_2]$$
$$p + q = [w_1 + w_2, x_1 + x_2, y_1 + y_2, z_1 + z_2]$$

Figure 11.3 Adding and subtracting quaternions is the same as adding or subtracting vectors with four components.

Quaternion Multiplication

Multiplying two quaternions serves the same purpose as multiplying two rotation matrices: the rotations will be added together. This will be used extensively when the bone transformations are calculated. It looks a bit complicated, but it really only uses basic vector operators such as the vector dot and cross products; see Figure 11.4 for the formula. Keep in mind, just like matrices, quaternion multiplication is not commutative. The product pq is not the same as qp.

$$p = [s_1, \vec{v_1}]$$
$$q = [s_2, \vec{v_2}]$$
$$p * q = [s_1 s_2 - \vec{v_1} \circ \vec{v_2}, s_1 \vec{v_2} + s_2 \vec{v_1} + \vec{v_1} \times \vec{v_2}]$$

Figure 11.4 The formula to multiply two quaternions; s is the scalar part of the quaternion, and v is the imaginary vector part.

Inverse and Conjugate

The inverse of the quaternion is the same as the inverse of a rotation matrix; it represents the opposite rotation of the noninverted quaternion. To find the inverse, you first need the conjugate of the quaternion. The conjugate is calculated by simply negating all of the imaginary components, as shown in Figure 11.5. This conjugate is also the inverse of the quaternion, as long as the quaternion is of unit length. Since all rotation quaternions must be unit length, all you need to do to invert a rotation quaternion is find its conjugate.

$$p = [w_1, x_1, y_1, z1]$$
$$\bar{p} = [w_1, -x_1, -y_1, -z_1]$$

Figure 11.5 Calculating the conjugate and inverse of a unit quaternion.

Quaternion Conversions

As useful as quaternions are, they are not always the easiest way to represent rotations. For artists, representing orientation as a rotation around an axis, or the x, y, and z rotations of an object, is much more natural and convenient. On the programmer's side of things, OpenGL does not support quaternions naturally, only matrices. This means that you need to be able to convert between representations.

I will cover how to convert from Euler angles and axis-angle rotation representations to quaternions as well as how to convert a quaternion to a rotation matrix.

Euler Angle to Quaternion

The most common way to represent angles is via Euler angles. Euler angles allow you to specify a rotation for each of the x-, y-, and z-axes. Converting to a quaternion prevents some of the inherent problems with Euler angles such as gimbal lock. Figure 11.6 gives the Euler-to-quaternion formula.

$$Q_x = [\cos(\frac{X_{rot}}{2}), \sin(\frac{X_{rot}}{2}), 0, 0]$$

$$Q_y = [\cos(\frac{Y_{rot}}{2}), 0, \sin(\frac{X_{rot}}{2}), 0]$$

$$Q_z = [\cos(\frac{Z_{rot}}{2}), 0, 0, \sin(\frac{X_{rot}}{2})]$$

$$Q_{final} = Q_x * Q_y * Q_z$$

Figure 11.6 Converting a set of Euler angles to a quaternion.

Axis-Angle to Quaternion

Another popular way to represent rotations is to use axis-angle representation. This representation gives the amount of rotation around an arbitrary axis, represented by a unit vector. Figure 11.7 shows how to convert from axis-angle to a unit-length quaternion.

Quaternion to Matrix

Since OpenGL does not directly support quaternions, you may need to convert a quaternion back into a matrix. A quaternion directly represents a 3×3 rotation matrix and can easily be converted to one. To convert to a 4×4 matrix for OpenGL, simply use the upper-left 3×3 elements as shown in Figure 11.8.

$$q = [\cos(\frac{\theta}{2}),$$

$$axis_x * \sin(\frac{\theta}{2}),$$

$$axis_y * \sin(\frac{\theta}{2}),$$

$$axis_z * \sin(\frac{\theta}{2})]$$

Figure 11.7 Converting an axis-angle to a quaternion.

$$\begin{bmatrix} 1 - 2y^2 - 2z^2 & 2xy - 2wz & 2xz + 2wy \\ 2xy + 2wz & 1 - 2x^2 - 2z^2 & 2yz - 2wx \\ 2xz - 2wy & 2yz + 2wx & 1 - 2x^2 - 2y^2 \end{bmatrix}$$

Figure 11.8 Converting a quaternion to a 4×4 matrix.

Interpolating Quaternions

One of the biggest strengths of quaternions is that interpolation between them is easy. This is great when using skeletal animation as it allows you to generate an infinite number of intermediate frames.

There are two main types of quaternion interpolation: linear interpolation (LERP) and spherical linear interpolation (SLERP), shown in Figure 11.9.

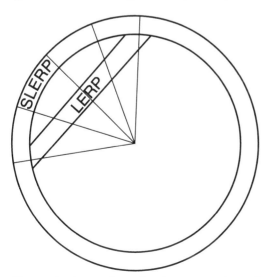

Figure 11.9 Two-dimensional representations of SLERP and LERP quaternion interpolation.

LERP interpolates along a straight line between the two rotations. While LERP is very fast and simple, it has a major drawback. Interpolating in equal steps along a straight line between rotations will look odd if the distance is large. As Figure 11.9 shows, even though the steps are the same size, the distances between steps change, causing the interpolation to appear to speed up as it nears the middle of the rotation. Figure 11.10 has the linear interpolation formula for quaternions.

$$LERP(q_0, q_1, t) = (1 - t)q_0 + tq_1$$

Figure 11.10 Linear interpolation of two quaternions.

SLERP, on the other hand, interpolates along an arc. This ensures that the rotation will happen at a constant speed and that the quaternion will stay normalized throughout the interpolation. Referring to Figure 11.9 again, you can see that SLERP interpolates much more evenly than LERP does.

SLERP does have two problems: it does not work well when the quaternions are very close together, and there are two possible paths that interpolation can take. The first is easy to fix; when the quaternions are very close together, use LERP to interpolate them rather than SLERP. As for the second problem, if you look at Figure 11.9 once again, you can see that you could go the long way around the circle as well as the short way. To combat this, you must force SLERP to take the shorter route. To do this, you calculate the dot product of the two quaternions, negating the first quaternion if the dot product is negative. Figure 11.11 has the formula for spherical linear interpolation.

$$\theta = \arccos(q_0 \cdot q_1)$$

$$SLERP(q_0, q_1, t) = \frac{(\sin((1 - t)\theta))}{(\sin(\theta))} q_0 + \frac{(\sin(t\theta))}{(\sin(\theta))} q_1$$

Figure 11.11 Spherical linear interpolation of two quaternions.

Conclusion

That was a very brief synopsis of what you will be using in the next part of the chapter. Don't worry if you are still a little confused; using quaternions is the best way to understand them. There is not room to cover any of the complex theory or history behind quaternions, so if you would like to know more, check the links at the end of the chapter.

Loading MS3D

Now you are ready to start putting some animated models on the screen! The first format I am going to cover is the MS3D format, created by the popular (and inexpensive) 3D package Milkshape 3D. Milkshape 3D is a modeling package created specifically for video games, complete with plug-ins to import and export almost every major model format. It is very reasonably priced (US$25 at the time of writing) and is great for hobbyists.

This section will detail loading and animating Milkshape 3D's native format, .MS3D. The text covers only the binary version of the file, but the demo will load the text-based format as well as the binary format.

tip

All of the data in an MS3D file is stored in little-endian (Intel) byte order.

The Header

The header for MS3D files is very simple. It contains a 10-byte identification code and a 4-byte version number. The files I am covering have an ID of "MS3D000000" and are version "4".

Vertices

Immediately following the header data is the vertex data. First there is a two-byte, unsigned integer that contains the number of vertices in the file. The vertex count is followed by the vertex data.

Vertices used in skeletal animation must contain at least one extra piece of information: the bone ID. This parameter tells the renderer what bone the vertex is connected to, allowing it to be transformed to the correct position.

```
The vertex structure for Milkshape 3D looks like this:
struct Ms3dVertex {
  unsigned char mFlags;
  float         mVertexPosition[3];
  char          mBoneId;
  unsigned char mReferenceCount;
};
```

For now, the only parts that matter are `mVertexPosition`, which contains three floating-point values, the x-, y- and z-positions of the vertex; and `mBoneID`, which contains the number of the bone the vertex is attached to, or -1 if the vertex is not attached to a bone. The `mFlags` parameter and `mReferenceCount` parameter are unimportant at this time.

Faces

Much like the vertices, the face chunk also starts with a two-byte number that gives the number of faces in the file, followed by the face data.

Unlike the OBJ file, the MS3D face data contains much more than just a set of indices. It also contains the actual vertex normals and texture coordinates along with the vertex indices. Moreover, unlike OBJ, all faces in MS3D are triangles, meaning they always contain exactly three sets of data.

The MS3D face structure looks like this:

```
struct Ms3dFace {
  unsigned short mFlags;
  unsigned short mVertexIndices[3];
  float          mVertexNormals[3][3];
  float          mTextureS[3];
  float          mTextureT[3];
  unsigned char  mSmoothingGroup;
  unsigned char  mGroupIndex;
};
```

Again, as with the vertices, the flags are not important. The `mVertexIndices` variable contains three indices into the array of vertices you just read; `mVertexNormals` contains the actual vertex normal for each corner of the triangle. Each normal is three floating-point values that create a unit vector.

The `mTextureS` and `mTextureT` arrays contain the texture coordinate pair for each vertex. The last two parameters are the smoothing group (used by the editor) and the group index, which is also unnecessary for our demo.

Groups

The reason I discarded the `mGroupIndex` variable in the face structure is because all the information you need as far as grouping goes is in the next chunk. The group chunk tells you which faces are in the same group and therefore use the same material information.

As usual, there is a two-byte number representing the number of groups, followed by the group information. Unlike the previous chunks, the group chunks are not all the same size. Each chunk only includes what is necessary; check out the group structure below.

```
struct Ms3dGroup {
  unsigned char  mFlags;
  char           mName[32];
  unsigned short mNumTriangles;
  unsigned short mTriangleIndices[mNumTriangles];
  char           mMaterialIndex;
};
```

The catch with this structure is the fourth variable, mTriangleIndices. Unlike the parameters before it, it is not a fixed-size array; it contains exactly mNumTriangles indices into the array of faces. For that reason, you will need to use some sort of dynamic array. The demo uses an std::vector. The last variable is an index into the material array, defining what texture and lighting properties the group will use.

Materials

Material information is up next. Read the two-byte number of materials followed by the material and lighting information structure below for each material.

```
struct Ms3dMaterial {
  char   mName[32];
  float mAmbient[4];
  float mDiffuse[4];
  float mSpecular[4];
  float mEmissive[4];
  float mShininess;
  float mTransparency;
  char   mMode;
  char   mTexture[128];
  char   mAlphaMap[128];
};
```

The first variable is the name of the material, an ASCII string. The next six variables define the way the mesh reacts to lighting data. The mMode variable is unused, and the last two variables contain the paths to the texture and alpha maps.

These paths are generally absolute paths, which makes them incompatible from computer to computer, so I suggest stripping the path name and only using the actual texture file-name. For instance, c:\documents\evan\texture.bmp would simply become texture.bmp.

Joints

The last thing in the file is the joint or bone information. This section is the most complicated of them all. Not only are there arrays of variable sizes, but they are arrays of other structures.

This chunk does not start off with the joint count; there is some other important animation data before that. First, there is a floating-point value that gives the number of frames per second the animations are meant to run at. Next, there are four bytes of editor information, which can be skipped. Then there is a four-byte integer that contains the number of animation frames in the file. Finally, there is the standard two-byte number of joints.

Before you read the actual joint information, you need to define another structure you will use inside the joints. The Ms3dFrame structure contains one keyframe of the animation.

```
struct Ms3dFrame {
  float mTime;
  float mData[3];
};
```

The time designates, in seconds, the amount of time into the animation that the bone should be at this position or rotation. The `mData` variable can contain either three Euler angles designating the rotation of the bone at the time, or x-, y-, and z-positions of the bone, depending on which array the frame belongs to.

The joints in the file look like this:

```
struct Ms3dJoint {
  unsigned char  mFlags;
  char           mName;
  char           mParentName;
  float          mRotation[3];
  float          mTranslation[3];
  unsigned short mNumRotationFrames;
  unsigned short mNumTranslationFrames;
  Ms3dFrame      mRotationFrames[mNumRotationFrames];
  Ms3dFrame      mTranslationFrames[mNumTranslationFrames];
};
```

Here, `mName` is the name of the bone. You need to keep this so you can match it with `mParentName` when building the hierarchy. The next two parameters contain the initial rotation and translation for the bone, and the two after that contain the number of rotation and translation frames for the bone. Following the information for each joint are the rotation and translation keyframes. These frames tell the bones what position and rotation they should be in at a given time.

This is one place where what is stored in memory differs considerably from what is stored in the file. First of all, I convert all rotations to quaternions during load time. There's no reason to keep Euler angles around; you will just waste time converting them to quaternions during rendering.

Next, I look up the parent of each bone and store an index so I do not need to look it up during rendering.

Last, I add two extra sets of rotation and translation to the joint to store the current local transformation and the current final transformation. These will be used during rendering to transform the skeletons and skin.

The new joint structures look something like this:

```
struct Ms3dRotationFrame {
  float      mTime;
  Quaternionf mRotation;
};
struct Ms3dTranslationFrame {
  float    mTime;
  Vector3f mTranslation;
};
struct Ms3dJoint {
  char                  mParentId;
  Quaternionf           mInitialRotation;
  Quaternionf           mLocalRotation;
  Quaternionf           mFinalRotation;
  Vector3f              mInitialTranslation;
  Vector3f              mLocalTranslation;
  Vector3f              mFinalTranslation;
  unsigned short        mNumRotationFrames;
  unsigned short        mNumTranslationFrames;
  Ms3dRotationFrame     mRotationFrames[mNumRotationFrames];
  Ms3dTranslationFrame mTranslationFrames[mNumTranslationFrames];
};
```

Once you have set up this new joint array, you are finally ready to render the model.

Rendering the Base Model

Now it's time to render your model. Just rendering the base model, or the model you see in the Milkshape 3D editor with animation turned off, is quite easy.

In order to keep the loading and rendering code simple, OpenGL immediate mode will be used. This method is not nearly as fast as using vertex arrays or vertex buffer objects, but it will suffice as a demonstration. For sample code on converting the code to vertex arrays, look back at the OBJ file loader.

To render the base model, you will not need to use the joints at all; only the group, material, triangle, and vertex arrays are needed. The process of rendering looks like this:

For each group

```
    Set the material as indicated by the mMaterialIndex flag
    For each index in mTriangleIndices
        Draw the triangle using the vertices texture coordinates and normals listed
        in the triangle structure
```

For the actual code, take a look at the `RenderBaseModel()` function in the MS3D model class.

Rendering the base model has limited uses, but is good for any static objects or objects that do not require any animation. It is very simple and fast and does not require any extra setup or data processing after the model has been loaded. Next up, let's animate the model.

Animating the Model

Animation adds a whole new degree of realism to your model. Moving from rendering just the base model to rendering a fully animated MS3D model isn't as hard as it looks.

Before you can begin applying the animations, there is a preprocessing step you need to do. You must first transform every vertex by the inverse of the initial translation and rotation specified by the joint. This is done by the SetupBones() function. SetupBones() takes each vertex and applies the appropriate transformation to it, storing the result in a new vertex array. You must also do this with the normals, but you only apply the inverse rotation, not the translation.

The next step is to transform the bones to a specific animation frame. The frame number is a floating-point number between 0 and the number of frames specified by the file. The nature of skeletal animation makes it possible to generate any number of frames between the keyframes in the file. The frame number 105.5, for instance, would be halfway between keyframe 105 and 106.

Next, you need to calculate the local transformations for each bone. Since each joint is different, you must do all the calculations for each bone or joint in the skeleton.

You may have noticed that each keyframe of each joint has a "time" parameter. Your job is to calculate the time of your "frame" and find the two frames it falls between.

To calculate the frame time, you need to multiply your frame number by the frames per second that was calculated during loading. This will give you the exact time in the animation sequence where your desired frame falls. To find the nearest frames, you need to iterate through the rotation and translation frames of the current joint. By comparing the keyframe time to your calculated time, you can easily find the two keyframes in translation and rotation arrays that bound your desired frame.

Now that you know the two end frames, you need to generate the actual interpolated transformations. The interpolation code takes the start and end values and a value between 0 and 1 that signifies the interpolated position. Since you already have the frames, all you need is the interpolation factor. This is calculated with the formula in Figure 11.12.

By using SLERP for rotation and LERP for the translation values along with the start, end, and calculated interpolation values, you can calculate the new transformations.

$$t_{cur} = current\ time$$

$$t_0 = time\ of\ prev\ keyframe$$

$$t_1 = time\ of\ next\ keyframe$$

$$t_{interp} = interpolation\ factor$$

$$t_{interp} = \frac{(t_{cur} - t_0)}{(t_1 - t0)}$$

Figure 11.12 Calculating the interpolation factor.

Calculating the local transformation is not the only thing you need to do for a joint. You also must calculate the "final" transformations. The final rotation is the concatenation of all the joint's parents, all the way down to the root joint.

If you take a look at the `TransformJoints()` function, you can see how all of the setup comes together to move the full skeleton into position.

With the skeleton in place, it is time to render the mesh. Rendering the transformed mesh is a little more difficult than rendering the base model. The pseudocode for rendering the mesh now looks like this:

For each group

```
    Set the material as indicated by the mMaterialIndex flag
    For each index in mTriangleIndices
        - Transform the vertices by the final rotation and translation of the
          appropriate bone.
        - Transform the normals of the triangle.
        - Draw the triangle.
```

You can see the code for this in the function `RenderFrame()`.

If you can render one transformed frame, you can animate the model. The `Animate()` function takes a start and end frame and renders the appropriate frame at the appropriate time. This makes the animation incredibly smooth. Since an infinite number of intermediate frames can be generated, the model will move smoothly and at the same speed, regardless of frame rate.

Conclusion

Skeletal animation can be a hard topic to understand, particularly when it comes to quaternions and quaternion operations. Rest assured that with a little practice, anyone can implement it. After a few tries, you will understand enough about the math and equations behind skeletal animation to enhance and expand your implementation.

You should now have enough information to implement a basic model loader, as well as a skeletal animation system. Using the information contained here and in the code repository, you can add the fluid animation of modern 3D games to your own.

References

Milkshape 3D editor, SDK, and MS3D Specification. **http://www.milkshape3d.com/**.

OBJ file-format document. **http://astronomy.swin.edu.au/~pbourke/dataformats/obj/**.

Porter, Brett. Real Soon Now. **http://rsn.gamedev.net**.

"The Matrix and Quaternions FAQ",
http://www.gamedev.net/reference/articles/article1691.asp

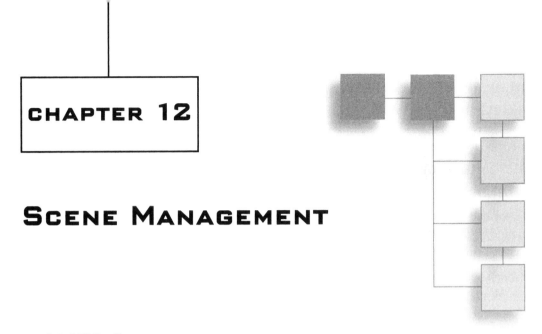

CHAPTER 12

SCENE MANAGEMENT

Wael El Oraiby

Interestingly, the largest part of the human brain is the portion that deals with visuals. Perhaps that's why our hearts jump when we see awesome graphics. The current revolution in graphics hardware allows a huge amount of realism through the use of shaders. Another silent revolution was the introduction of the much anticipated "occlusion query." Engines now can use them efficiently to perform visibility determination in real time, thus getting rid of the static aspect that characterized games for so long.

Some things need to be clear, though. While libraries such as OpenGL and DirectX deal with the low-level primitives, dealing with higher-level objects and maps requires the use of scene-management techniques, as you can see in Figure 12.1.

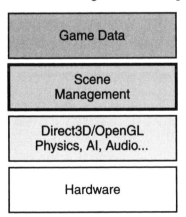

Figure 12.1 Game application layers.

I will start by introducing the elements in a game level. Later I'll explain scene management, describing the view frustum and scene graphs. Moreover, I'll talk about portal-based engines and BSP trees. I'll show how combining them will give you a powerful hybrid scene-management technique. Finally, you'll learn about other techniques, including quadtrees, octrees, and adaptive binary trees.

Elements of a Game Level

Any video game is mainly a mixture of visuals and interactions (not to ignore the music and sound). You can basically say that a game level consists of visual objects and interactive objects (solid objects, triggers, etc.).

Generally speaking, elements in a game fall into the following categories: rendering, physics or collision, audio, and logic. Each of these categories can be also divided into subcategories, and so on.

I deal here with rendering and collision elements. You should approach your work on other types of elements (such as AI) with the same kind of thinking.

Let's start with the rendering elements.

Rendering Elements

There are many kinds of rendering elements; most of them are GPU driven:

- **Static meshes.** As the name indicates, these meshes do not have any animation in them. They do, however, have a material assigned to them.
- **Moving meshes.** Moving meshes move around the scene; they represent things like an elevator or a door.
- **Morph targets.** These are multiple meshes with the same number of vertices, and the animation is a kind of interpolation between two targets.
- **Skeletal meshes.** All characters and monsters in a game are of this kind; vertices are assigned to bones, and the vertices move with the bones when the bones are animated.
- **Materials.** In the old days, materials were only texture maps; now they are a mixture of shaders and textures. Some new systems even have scripted materials, and they now extend to include collision-related data.

While optimizing the rendering process is tricky and depends heavily on the system you are working on, one thing is certain: rendering what is not seen is a waste of CPU and GPU time. So you should have a system that tells you whether it's worthwhile to render a specific object. To help you determine what is hidden and what is not you have

- **Sectors.** A kind of object collection, and they are geometric by nature. If a sector is invisible, then all the objects inside it are invisible as well.

- **Portals.** The link between two sectors. If a portal is visible, then the sectors and the portal links are both visible.

- **Occluders.** Anything that hides other objects. Objects that are totally behind occluders are not sent to the GPU to render. In the Unreal engine these are called "antiportals."

- **Potentially Visible Set (PVS).** An array marking whether a specific object or group is visible from a specific view point. Quake and almost all old indoor engines used them. They increase the frame rate enormously: in his *Graphics Programming Black Book*, Michael Abrash wrote that their use led to a dramatic increase in Quake's frame-rate.

Collision Elements

As you probably know, a game scene also consists of collision elements. Collision detection is one of the most important aspects in a game today; it is the building block for physics. It's also the most demanding when it comes to CPU horsepower (along with physics). You have to check whether objects intersect each other; for example, you must prevent players or bullets from passing through a solid wall.

Some of the collision elements are

- **Collision bounding volumes.** Object bounding volumes that the player cannot walk in. In other words, this is the solid boundary of an object. Traditionally, these were usually convex shapes such as spheres or bounding boxes; now we have the processing power to deal with any geometric shape. Remember though, that the fastest test is the test you don't do, so keep things simple.

- **Trigger volumes.** Volumes that trigger an action in a game once the player collides with them, such as traps and switches.

- **Bullets.** These usually work along with particle systems, and they usually do damage to what they hit (players, objects).

Rendering and collision objects are not the only things present in a game scene.

Miscellaneous Elements

Miscellaneous elements include AI paths, music, and sounds. Not to underestimate them, but they are outside of the scope of this book. Note that some sounds are assigned to materials—for example, when you walk on wood, a special sound must be played. As for music, it will change from location to location in a map to give a sense of immersion in the environment.

Having introduced the different elements in a game scene, it's time to dive into the true meat of the chapter.

What Is Scene Management?

For a game, there are two expensive operations affecting frame rate: rendering and physics. As mentioned earlier, when rendering, only visible objects should be sent to the GPU so that you waste no time on hidden objects, and physics depends heavily on collision detection, which itself relies on spatial location and local neighboring. In short, the faster you can obtain the potential visible object set (PVS) and the potential collision object set, the faster the game will go. Figure 12.2 illustrates this general mechanism.

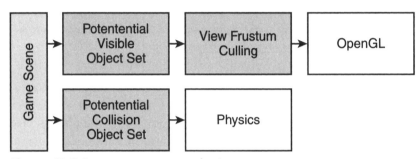

Figure 12.2 Scene-management mechanism.

Once you have obtained the PVS, you will cull it with the view frustum.

View Frustum Culling

If you've read *Beginning OpenGL Game Programming*, you've already learned about view frustum culling (VFC), so you can skip to the next section if you like. If you haven't read about it, or if you need a review, read on.

One of the oldest and simplest culling methods used since the dawn of 3D games, view frustum culling is based on the idea that you have a view frustum, and everything outside that frustum should not be rendered. To save processing power, you will not test all the object primitives (vertices or faces) to see if they lie inside or outside the viewing frustum; instead, testing the bounding sphere or the bounding box should suffice. To give a simple idea on what view frustum is, take a look at Figure 12.3.

Figure 12.3 shows a representation of the view frustum with five planes (far, top, bottom, left, and right), but the actual OpenGL view frustum has six planes (*near*, far, top, bottom, left, and right), as shown in Figure 12.4.

Since frustum culling and some of the algorithms in this chapter rely on testing a point against a plane, let's review how to do that.

Figure 12.3 The view frustum as it is in the scene (left) and what it can see (right). Notice that three objects lie totally outside the frustum (a torus and two teapots).

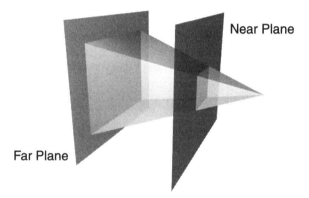

Near Plane

Far Plane

Figure 12.4 View frustum with near and far planes.

The Basics: A Point and a Plane

A plane in the space is given by the formula $Ax + By + Cz + D = 0$, where the vector (A, B, C) is the normal vector of the plane and D is the distance from the origin $(0, 0, 0)$ to the plane (Figure 12.5). Planes are used in almost everything dealing with classification: collision detection, view frustum culling, portals, neural networks, and so on.

Now, any point (x, y, z) in the space that satisfies the plane equation $(= 0)$ lies on the plane; however, what interests us is whether a point lies in front of or behind a plane. If a point lies in front, it should satisfy $Ax + By + Cz + D > 0$; if behind, $Ax + By + Cz + D < 0$. Now, given a point and a plane, you have the tool to determine where a point lies.

note

Due to floating-point precision error we tend to test against EPSILON and not 0; EPSILON is usually set to 1/32 (as in Quake).

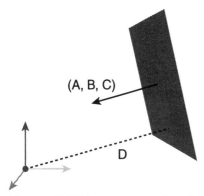

Figure 12.5 Plane representation; the yellow vector is the plane normal vector.

The code to classify a point against a plane is as follows:

```
POINT_CLASS classifyPointPlane(Vector3 v, Plane p)
{
  distance = dot(v, p.normal) + p.distance;
  if ( distance < -epsilon )
    return BEHIND;       // point is behind the plane
  else if ( distance > epsilon )
    return IN_FRONT;     // point is in front of the plane
  return ON_PLANE;       // point is on the plane
}
```

Since you can now determine the position of a point relative to a plane, you should be able to understand how to check if objects are inside a frustum.

Sphere and Frustum

The code to test whether a sphere intersects a frustum or is inside it looks like the following:

```
bool isSphereInsideFrustum(Sphere s, Frustum f)
{
  foreach plane in f.planes do {
    // compute the distance between the sphere center and the plane
    distance = dot(s.center, plane.normal) + plane.distance;
    if ( distance < - s.radius )
      return false; // outside
  }
  // we tested against all the planes, the sphere is inside
  return true;
}
```

You test the bounding sphere of an object against all the frustum planes, and then compute the distance between the sphere center and the plane. If the distance is less than the negative radius, then the sphere lies outside the frustum.

Box and Frustum

Testing a box against a frustum requires a little work:

```
bool isBoxInsideFrustum(Box b, Frustum f)
{
  foreach plane in f.planes do {

    backVertsCount = 0;

    // check the eight vertices of the bounding box against the plane
    foreach v in b.vertices do {
    distance = dot(plane.normal, v) + plane.distance;
    if (  distance < -epsilon )
      backVertsCount++;
    }

    // check if all the vertices are outside
    if ( backVertsCount == 8 )
      return false; // outside
  }

  // the box is totally or partially inside the frustum
  return true;
}
```

You check all the vertices of the bounding box against every view frustum plane. If all eight vertices are behind a plane, then the bounding box is outside the view frustum. If you test the eight vertices against all the planes and they are not totally outside, then the box is either totally or partially in, or maybe (in some very few cases, as shown in Figure 12.6) totally out. The code will get a bit complex if you want to treat all cases. Usually the above code will do fine, as you can tolerate 1 percent error.

Obtaining the PVS and potential collision object set to send to view frustum culling usually requires scene-graph mechanisms.

Scene Graphs

Because levels are made of thousands of objects, it's necessary to group objects together based on their spatial location and assemble these groups into higher-level groups, which

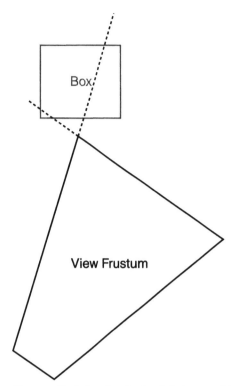

Figure 12.6 Despite the box's being outside the view frustum, the code reports it as being inside. In practice, this doesn't happen often.

are then grouped into higher-level groups, and so on. By grouping, you obtain some kind of a tree structure, and trees are usually fast since they allow you to avoid processing whole subtrees.

If you allow instancing (in which objects can be shared between tree nodes), the tree will transform into a directed acyclic graph (Figure 12.7).

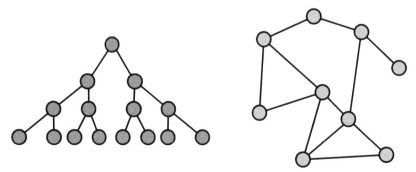

Figure 12.7 Tree scene graph (left) and directed acyclic scene graph (right).

Although most game engines use trees to represent scenes, they allow instancing. Here, I am going to use a portal-based engine. A portal engine implies the use of direct acyclic graphs, with every node in the graph being a tree itself. You'll be learning about portal-based engines in detail.

Portal-and-BSP Scene Management

Now that you have the appropriate background information, it's time to move on to the main scene-management method described in this chapter. The method is a hybrid of portal-based engines and BSP trees that takes advantage of occlusion queries for optimal performance. The following sections describe the major components of this system in detail.

Portal-Based Engines

I believe Descent was one of the first games to use a portal-based engine, in 1995. Later on, portals were used in many engines and many games. Recently, the Doom 3 engine used portals along with BSP trees in a cool way to bypass many problems. Let's take a look at how they work.

First, the world, map, or level is divided into *sectors*, which are also called *areas* or *zones*. These sectors are connected with each other using portals (thus the name *portal engine*). Figure 12.8 shows this concept. Unlike Quake and purely BSP engines, portals are often placed manually by the level designer and are not automatically generated. The level designer needs a good amount of skill to optimize the level so it runs fast.

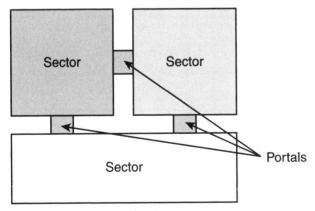

Figure 12.8 Portals and sectors.

When you walk through a portal, you are leaving one sector and entering a new one. Engines depend heavily on this information to determine which area the player is in so they can determine what to render and what to interact with.

In the old days, sectors had to be convex geometries. Some relatively recent engines still force sectors to be convex, but the method presented later in this chapter allows them to be in any shape (see Figure 12.9) as long as they are legal closed geometry (with no intersecting faces and no holes).

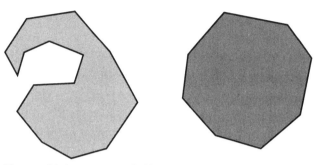

Figure 12.9 Nonconvex (left) and convex (right) shapes.

To achieve this degree of freedom in modeling sectors, I'll need to reformulate the problem.

Occluders, Portals, and Boolean Operations

One thing the level designer doesn't want to do is make the sectors one by one and assign every object in a map to a sector (building the scene graph manually). If you have 50 objects per map and only 4 sectors, this could work, but it is still considered torture. Let's try to find a work-around!

Sectors usually consist of bounding walls. These walls often act as occluders, separating and hiding the objects in the sector from the rest of the level. Why not model the occluders, then place the portals and automatically cut and decompose the level into sectors?

In order to cut by portals, you need to have legal geometry, which means no face intersects another face, and objects are closed, with no open caveats (see Figure 12.10). You can get that geometry by either modeling using Boolean or CSG (Constructive Solid Geometry) operations (e.g. add, subtract) or by taking some precautions.

Figure 12.10 Illegal geometry: a sphere with caveats (holes), a deformed cylinder with intersecting faces. Legal geometry: a torus.

As for the Boolean or CSG operations, I believe that Figure 12.11 says it all.

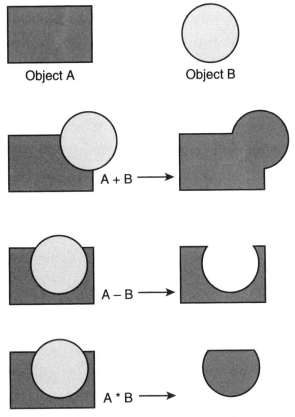

Figure 12.11 Boolean operations: union (+), subtraction (−), and intersection (*).

Boolean operations work best on solid objects. The difference between solid and hollow objects is explained in the following section.

Hollow and Solid Objects

An important level-modeling aspect in general is the notion of hollow and solid spaces. A hollow space is a space you can walk in or to. Solid spaces, on the other hand, are spaces that you cannot go through. Figure 12.12 illustrates this. A wall, for example, is a barrier between solid and hollow space. This has a deep impact on level building and modeling. A hollow object is generally represented as an object with all the face normals pointing inside, while a solid object has all face normals pointing outside. In this sense, a room is a hollow object (or empty object), while a sphere inside that room is a solid object. The space behind the walls is considered solid because you cannot walk there.

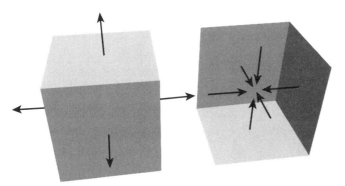

Figure 12.12 Solid (left) and hollow (right) boxes.

Putting all these ideas together, you can now build the level—or level skeleton, to be exact.

Building the Level

Once all occluder meshes are modeled, you join them together in one mesh. This mesh will be called hereafter the *occluders mesh*. Although these occluders are static, you can have dynamic ones. I'll shed more light on dynamic occluders once I deal with visibility determination. In the modeler, rename the occluders mesh OCCLUDERS_MESH since it's what the script will be looking for.

Since you are going to use Boolean operations to compile the level, portals are not allowed to be planes; they must have thickness. Usually a box with a height of 0.01m should be enough. Don't give it a thickness of more than 0.05 or it will cause trouble when you walk through the level. Give all portals the prefix PORTAL_—for example, PORTAL_GATE01— because the script will query them by that prefix. Put these portals where you think it's appropriate, remembering that portals and sectors are used to separate objects into groups. Don't use a lot of them, but remember that a huge scene without portals will perform poorly. Use them wisely!

Figure 12.13 shows the workflow process.

To build and export the map, you'll use a script that performs the following steps:

1. Search for the OCCLUDERS_MESH.
2. Invert OCCLUDERS_MESH normals (make it solid).
3. Subtract all PORTAL_*s from OCCLUDERS_MESH (CSG/Boolean).
4. Invert the normals for the resulting mesh (make it hollow).
5. Export the resulting mesh, the OCCLUDERS_MESH, and the portals to a map file.

Inversion of normals is needed to ensure that the Boolean operation works well. Remember that the occluders mesh is a hollow mesh, and Boolean operations were intended to work on solid objects.

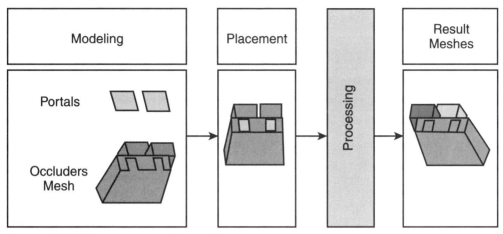

Figure 12.13 Game-scene creation workflow.

The subtraction of portals from the occluders mesh will ensure that the occluders mesh is divided into sectors; you should check that all your portals span the occluders mesh (Figure 12.14). After the subtraction you should obtain some kind of mesh that can be divided into separate objects.

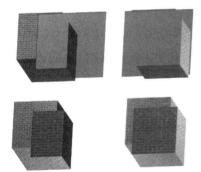

Figure 12.14 Bad (left) vs. good (right) portal placement.

The Boolean functionalities being used are available in all descent modelers, even in Blender, so porting the script to another modeler should not be a problem.

You now have the result mesh in the map file; however, it's not yet officially decomposed into distinct objects.

Decomposition into Sectors

The algorithm that does the decomposition is not very complicated to understand or to code.

First, at each vertex you need to keep the faces incident to that vertex. After that, we initialize the area that the face belongs to with a value of -1 (meaning a solid area):

```
foreach face in occludersMesh do
  face.areaId = -1;
```

Then you create a vertex list where, in each vertex, you store all faces incident to that vertex. You loop through the faces and for every vertex in that face, you add the face to the list:

```
foreach face in occludersMesh do
  foreach vertex in face do
    vertexList[vertex].facesList.push_back(face.id);
```

Moreover, you will set the area's count and ID to 0, and every time you finish an area, you increment the count.

```
areaCountAndID = 0;
foreach vertex in vertexList do
  if(vertex.visited == false){
    markVertexArea(vertex, vertexList, areaCountAndID);
      areaCountAndID++;
  }
```

As you might expect, markVertexArea is a recursive function that first marks the current vertex as visited. Next it checks to see if the faces that share that vertex have been visited. If not, it'll assign the area ID to the faces. With the area IDs assigned to every face, the occluders mesh is decomposed:

```
markVertexArea(vertex, vertexList, areaCountAndID)
{
  vertex.visited == true;

  foreach face in vertexList[vertex].facesList do
    faceList[face].area = areaCountAndID;
    foreach v in face.verts do
      if(v.visited == false)
        markVertexArea(v, vertexList, areaCountAndID)
}
```

Apart from error checking and the very relaxed pseudocode, you should be able to find your way through the C++ code.

While you now have the level (occluders mesh) decomposed into sectors, you still lack vital information: Given an object in the space (e.g., a camera, rock, bullet, player), how can you find the sector in which the object lies? For that you need the famous BSP trees.

BSP Trees: Where We Are and What We See

The BSP tree is one of the best-known geometry algorithms. We won't go through the history of BSP trees, since you can get that by reading the BSP FAQ at **http://www.gamedev.net/reference/articles/article657.asp**. The BSP FAQ also contains a fairly good, brief explanation of some basic aspects presented here; consider using it as a side reference.

BSP means Binary Spatial Partitioning. As the name indicates, a BSP tree recursively divides the space in half (Figure 12.15), thus creating a binary tree representing the space. The importance of the BSP tree lies in the fact that the geometry is decomposed into *convex spaces* (which is the reason for BSP trees in the first place). There are basically three kinds of BSP trees: *regular*, *leafy*, and *solid node* (SNBSP). Leafy and solid node BSP trees are very similar, and you can easily convert from one to the other.

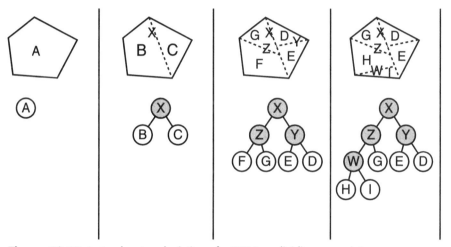

Figure 12.15 A step-by-step depiction of a BSP tree dividing space into convex spaces.

Classifying a Polygon: More Points and a Plane

Testing a point against a plane is useful, but in a game scene, you deal with polygons. Similar to points, polygons can be in front of, behind, or on the plane, but that's not all. A polygon can span a plane with some points in front and others behind. Thus, you have four cases for polygons, as shown in Figure 12.16.

The code to classify a polygon against a plane is straightforward. You just count the number of polygon vertices that are in front of, behind, or on the plane, and return the polygon class accordingly:

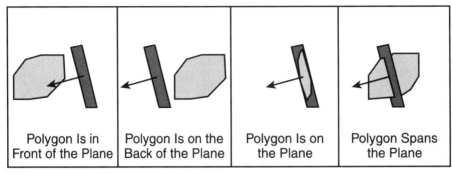

| Polygon Is in Front of the Plane | Polygon Is on the Back of the Plane | Polygon Is on the Plane | Polygon Spans the Plane |

Figure 12.16 The four plane/polygon cases.

```
classifyPolyToPlane(polygon, plane)
{
  numInFront = numOnPlane = numBehind = 0

  foreach point in polygon.points do {
    res = dot(plane.normal, point) + plane.distance
    if ( res > epsilon )
      numInFront++;
    else if ( res < -epsilon )
      numBehind++;
    else numOnPlane++;
  }

  if ( numOnPlane == polygon.points.count )
      return ON_PLANE;
  if ( numInFront > 0 && numOnBack == 0 )
    return IN_FRONT;
  if ( numInFront == 0 && numOnBack > 0 )
    return ON_BACK;
  return POLY_SPANNING;
}
```

Now that you have the building blocks, you can proceed to construct the tree.

Building the Tree

The occluders mesh is made of polygons. From this polygon soup, you extract the planes. Each polygon has at least three vertices in this order: v0, v1, v2. You can get the plane from these vertices by doing plane.normal = cross(v2 − v0, v1 − v0), where cross is the cross product of two vectors, giving you the plane normal. Then plane.dist = −dot(normal, v0) provides the plane distance from the origin (0, 0, 0).

Now you're ready to start with the basic regular BSP tree.

Regular BSP

First, you're going to pick a polygon, which will be called a *splitter*, and create three lists: on, front, and back. You will test each polygon in the scene against the splitter. There are four possible cases and corresponding actions to take:

1. Polygon in front of the splitter: push the polygon to the front list.
2. Polygon is behind the splitter: push it to the back list.
3. Polygon is on the splitter plane: push it to the on list.
4. Polygon spans the splitter plane: split the polygon into two polygons, one in front of the splitter, which goes to the front list, and one behind the splitter, which goes to the back list.

Let's see what a regular BSP tree node is made of:

```
struct RegBSPNode {
  plane        splitter;
  PolygonList on;
  RegBSPNode  front;
  RegBSPNode  back;
};
```

The basic idea behind building the tree is just to push the onList to the on struct member, create front and back nodes, and recursively call the tree builder until there are no more polygons.

```
buildRegBSP(RegBSPNode node, PolygonList polys)
{
  PolygonList onList, frontList, backList;
  Plane       splitter;

  if ( polys.empty() == false )
    splitter = polys[0];

  foreach polygon in polys do {
    polyClass = classifyPolyToPlane(poly, splitter)
    if ( polyClass == ON_PLANE )
      onList.push(polygon);
    else if ( polyClass == IN_FRONT )
      frontList.push(polygon);
    else if ( polyClass == ON_BACK )
      backList.push(polygon);
    else if ( polyClass == SPANNING )
    {
```

```
        splitPolygon(splitter, frontPoly, backPoly);
        frontList.push(frontPoly);
        backList.push(backPoly);
      }
    }

    node.splitter = splitter;
    node.on        = onList;

    buildRegBSP(node.front, frontList);
    buildRegBSP(node.back, backList);
}
```

That's the regular BSP tree and the base for all other variants. As you may have noticed, a regular BSP tree is not much help, since it was meant for rendering: it sorts the space to help rendering from back to front. It was made at a time when z-buffer-accelerated hardware didn't exist (luckily, their use is almost free now).

We want to use the tree to determine which sector we are in. Regular BSP trees don't have that feature because the onList contains polygons from different sectors. Fortunately, the two other variants provide what we need.

Leafy BSP trees and SNBSPs have the same pros and cons; the only thing that differs is the data structure (and again, conversion between the two is easy). I will only discuss SNBSP since it's the most used.

Solid Node BSP

Unlike regular BSPs, which store a list of polygons in each node, SNBSPs don't need to store polygons (as long as you don't render the tree). SNBSPs also distinguish between two types of nodes: solid nodes and regular ones. Solid nodes act as a barrier between solid and hollow spaces, and regular nodes act pretty much the same as in regular BSP (except they don't have any polygons). I'll tweak the original algorithm so instead of only knowing whether I am inside a solid or a hollow area, I can get the sector I am in. The node will thus have the following form:

```
struct SnBSPNode
{
  plane       splitPlane;
  int         area;   // sector ID

  SnBSPNode   frontNode;
  SnBSPNode   backNode;
};
```

In this form, splitPlane indicates the splitter plane, and frontNode and backNode are pointers to the front and back nodes if they exist. The only indication of whether you are in a solid or a hollow space is when you encounter a node that has either frontNode or backNode set to NULL. Usually, if the point lies in front of the leaf splitter plane and frontNode is NULL, the point resides in a hollow area. If it lies behind the plane and backNode is NULL, then the point is in a solid area. You only look at the area field when the point lies in hollow space.

Similar to the building of regular BSP trees, SNBSP requires three lists: frontList, backList and onPlane. The first portion of the code is the same as before:

```
buildSnBSP(SnBSPNode node, PolygonList polys)
{
  PolygonList onList, frontList, backList
  Plane       splitter

  splitter = polys[0].plane

  foreach polygon in polys do {
    polyClass = classifyPolyToPlane(poly, splitter)
    if ( polyClass == ON_PLANE )
      onList.push(polygon)
    else if ( polyClass == IN_FRONT )
      frontList.push(polygon)
    else if ( polyClass == ON_BACK )
      backList.push(polygon)
    else if ( polyClass == SPANNING )
    {
      splitPolygon(splitter, frontPoly, backPoly)
      frontList.push(frontPoly)
      backList.push(backPoly)
    }
  }

  node.splitter = splitter
```

However, after this point, things need to be handled a bit differently than they are for a regular BSP, since different cases need to be accounted for.

The first is when you have no front and no back faces. In this case you only have "on plane" polygons, and thus a leaf (frontNode and backNode are then set to NULL). Since the BSP decomposes the space into convex areas, all the polygons in a leaf belong to the same area:

```
if ( frontList.empty() == true && backList.empty() == true ) {
  node.area      = onList[0].area;   // same area for all
  node.frontNode = NULL;
  node.backNode  = NULL;
}
```

Next you have to treat the case where you only have front polygons. If a point lies on the back of the splitter it'll be in solid area:

```
if ( frontList.empty() == false && backList.empty() == true )
{
  node.area      = -1;        // no hollow area
  node.backNode  = NULL;
  node.frontNode = new SnBSPNode();
  buildSnBSP(node.frontNode, frontList + onList)
}
```

Finally, when both frontList and backList are not empty, you build two nodes:

```
if ( frontList.empty() == false && backList.empty() == false )
{
  node.area      = -1;
  node.frontNode = new SnBSPNode();
  node.backNode  = new SnBSPNode();
  buildSnBSP(node.frontNode, frontList + onList);
  buildSnBSP(node.backNode, backList);
}
```

Notice that onList ("on plane" polygons) is merged with frontList. You could also merge onList with backList, but not with both!

note

The only case for which frontNode is NULL is a leaf (i.e., frontNode = NULL and backNode = NULL). If you get a frontNode != NULL when backNode is NULL, then the geometry is illegal.

Finding the Best Splitter

When you built the tree, you selected the first plane as the splitter plane. This will lead to an unbalanced tree. You'll usually try to find the best splitter that would balance the sub tree by using the following heuristic function:

```
plane findBestSplitter(PolygonList polys)
{
  plane  bestSplitter;
  int    bestScore = 9999999;
```

```
int     numOn, numFront, numBack, numSpan;

foreach cmpPolygon in polys do
{
  numOn = numFront = numBack = numSpan = 0;

  foreach polygon in polys do
  {
    if(polygon != cmpPolygon)
      switch( classifyPolyToPlane(polygon, cmpPolygon.plane) )
      {
        case ON_PLANE: numOn++; break;
        case IN_FRONT: numFront++; break;
        case ON_BACK: numBack++; break;
        case SPANNING: numSpan++; break;
      }
  }

  int score = 2*numSpan + abs(numFront - numBack) + numOn;
  if ( score < bestScore )
  {
    bestScore = score;
    bestSplitter = cmpPolygon.plane;
  }
}

  return bestSplitter;
}
```

You loop through all the polygons, counting those that are on, are in front of, are on the back of, or span a candidate splitter. You try to minimize the following equation:

```
score = 2 * numSpan + abs(numFront - numBack) + numOn
```

This will balance the number of polygons that are in front of and on the back of the candidate splitter. The lower this score is, the better.

Position Determination

Everything done thus far is to help you find the sector in which a given point lies. Luckily, the SNBSP you built will give you that:

```
int findSectorID(vec3 pointPos, SnBSPNode node)
{
  pointDistance = dot(node.splitter.normal, pointPos) + node.splitter.distance;
```

```
    // in front or on the splitter plane
    if ( pointDistance >= -epsilon )
    {
      if ( node.frontNode == NULL )
        return node.area;
      else return findSectorID(pointPos, node.frontNode);
    }

    // the case where pointDistance < -epsilon (behind the plane)
    if ( node.backNode == NULL )
      return SOLID_AREA;
    return findSectorID(pointPos, node.backNode);
}
```

You first try to get the distance from the point to the node splitter plane. If the point is in front of or on the splitter plane you check to see if frontNode is NULL. If so, you are in a hollow area. Otherwise, you recursively walk the frontNode subtree. The process is similar for a point lying behind the splitter plane, but if backNode is NULL, the point is in a solid area.

Since you can now determine the sector in which a point lies, you know the two sectors each portal connects.

Building Sector/Portal Scene Graph

When you exported the portals, you actually exported the intersection between the portals and the occluders mesh. It's important that the intersection of a portal with the occluders mesh be a single mesh, so take care when placing the portals in your scene.

To find the sectors sharing a portal, you loop through all the portal vertices and find their corresponding sectors (findSectorID()). If the portal was well-placed you will end up with two sectors. If you did something wrong, the code will report it:

```
void getPortalSectors(Portal p)
{
  p.sector[0] = portal.sector[1] = -1;  // initialize to nothing
  sectorsCount = 0; // number of sectors the portal connects

  foreach vertex in p.vertices do {
    sector = findSectorID(vertex);
    switch ( sectorsCount ) {
    case 0:
      p.sector[0] = sector;
      sectorsCount++;
      break;
```

```
    case 1:
      if ( sector != p.sector[0] ) {
        p.sector[1] = sector;
        sectorCount++;
      }
      break;

    case 2:
      if ( sector != p.sector[0] && sector != p.sector[1] ) {
        report("ERROR: portal overlaps more than 2 sectors!!!");
        exit();
      }
    }
  }
  if ( sectorsCount < 2 ) {
    report("ERROR: portal has less than 2 sectors!!!");
    exit();
  }
}
```

You keep a sector counter, and you always check it to see if the portal has more than two sectors. If that happens, you know that the portal was poorly placed.

After building the data structure, you can attack the visibility determination.

Visibility Determination Using Occlusion Queries

Occlusion queries suffer from major fill-rate issues, as well as function-call overhead and wait time (if the query's results are not available when requested). The fill-rate problem can be solved using hierarchies, and the wait time can be solved by returning the query result in the next frame (see Chapter 1 for more information on occlusion queries).

What I am going to present here doesn't require a hierarchy structure. It's very simple because it benefits from the portals mechanism.

You remember the occluders mesh? Well, it is going to serve you once again. The occluders mesh contains all major occluders in the level. Since it is a low-resolution mesh (for indoor levels it usually contains at most 200 triangles), rendering it is basically free. For other dynamic occluders, you push them along with the static occluders mesh in one draw call to save CPU-GPU interface overhead (remember to transform them).

Once the occluders mesh is rendered, you take all the portals and test them against the view frustum. You will then issue occlusion queries only for the portals that pass frustum culling (usually around 15 portals will pass the VFC test). Once the query results are available, you'll know which portals are visible. Each portal connects two sectors, and both of those sectors will be visible for every visible portal. Finally, for every visible sector, you draw all the objects inside that sector.

Let's address the fill-rate issue now. The higher the screen resolution, the greater the fill-rate burn. Luckily, OpenGL gives you two functions that can help: glViewport() and glScissor(). These functions allow rendering to only a portion of the screen. The only question to be answered is how much accuracy you want. For medium accuracy you can render to half the resolution (e.g. for a 800×600 resolution, you'd render to a viewport of only 400×300), thus multiplying the fill rate by 4).

```
createFirstQueries();

// game loop
do {
  doLogic();
  doPhysics();

  // rendering
  {
    glClear();

    // set the viewport to screen size
    glViewport(screenSize);
    glScissor(screenSize);

    // enable rendering and fancy stuff
    enableWritingToScreenBuffer();
    enableWritingToDepthBuffer();
    enableFancyStuff();

    // process issued queries and render
    getQueriesResult();
    foreach portal in portalList do {
      if ( portal.isVisible == true ) {
        renderSector(portal.sector[0]);
        renderSector(portal.sector[1]);
      }
    }
    SwapBuffers();

    // now issue queries
    glClear(…);
```

```
    // set the viewport to half screen
    glViewport(screenSize / 2);
    glScissor(screenSize / 2);

    disableFancyStuff();

    // render all the occluders
    renderOccluders();

    // issue the portals queries
    disableWritingToScreenBuffer();
    disableWritingToDepthBuffer();

    foreach portal in portalList do {
      if ( isInsideFrustum(portal) == true )
        issueQuery(portal);
    }
  }
} while (endGame == false);
```

tip

According to NVIDIA's SLI developer's docs, you must not use `glViewport()` or `glScissor()` often since they break the balance between the GPUs. I do not have SLI cards to test the performance of this method, but it's my belief that if you do have two GPUs, then you won't have a fill-rate problem. In that case, there's no need to use the `glViewport()`/`glScissor()` method.

About the Code

The SNBSP tree presented here illustrates the basic idea. The code in the demo is a bit more optimized, as I used STL to reduce the complexity. All nodes and leaves are stored in `STL::vector` objects, so the node structure has indices for children (front and back). I assigned positive indices to nodes, and I used negative indices to represent the sectors (Doom 3 .proc files use a similar approach). For more information on how to use the scripts and code, refer to the file readme.html, found in the code directory.

References

Abrash, Michael. *Michael Abrash's Graphics Programming Black Book*.Scottsdale, AZ: Coriolis, 1997.

Bittner, Jiri, Michael Wimmer, Harald Piringer, and Werner Purgathofer. "Coherent Hierarchical Culling: Hardware Occlusion Queries Made Useful." *Computer Graphics Forum* (Proc. Eurographics 2004) 23, no. 3 (September 2004): 615–24.

BSP FAQ. **http://www.gamedev.net/reference/articles/article657.asp**.

Fernando, Randima, ed. GPU Gems. Upper Saddle River, NJ: Addison-Wesley, 2004.

Hammersley, Tom. BSP Trees. **http://thorkildsen.no/faqsys/docs/bsp2.txt**.

NVIDIA developers: **http://developer.nvidia.com/page/home.html**.

Pharr, Matt, ed. *GPU Gems 2*. Upper Saddle River, NJ: Addison-Wesley, 2005.

Other Scene-Management Techniques

Joel Villagrana

There are, of course, many other methods for scene management, some of which are simpler than the portal/BSP hybrid method discussed thus far, and some of which simply work better in certain situations. In this section, you'll learn about three more scene-management techniques: quadtrees, octrees, and adaptive binary trees.

Quadtrees

A quadtree is a data structure for space partitioning in 2D, and it's used in both 2D and 3D applications. A quadtree is built by constructing a square around the scene and then recursively subdividing it into four quadrants of equal size until each quadrant has some maximum number of objects in it, as shown in Figure 12.17.

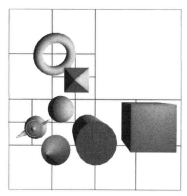

Figure 12.17 Illustration of a quadtree; the maximum allowed number of objects in a leaf is two.

The algorithm for building a quadtree is as follows:

1. Compute the bounding box for every object in the scene.

2. Compute the bounding box containing the entire scene.

    a. Divide the bounding box into four boxes (not necessarily the same size).

    b. Sort each object in the parent into one of the four boxes.

    c. Repeat until a decomposition limit is reached or the maximum count of objects in a node is reached; this node will be a leaf.

Walking the quadtree is similar to walking BSP trees. In each step, you check whether the point is inside the children's bounding rectangles, and you recurse until you find the leaf.

Quadtrees are often used to implement terrain LOD systems. Since terrains can be represented by a grid, a quadtree can be used to subdivide different parts of the grid to show more detail when it's needed. Because quadtrees are in most ways a simplification of octrees, I'll focus on the latter instead.

Octrees

Octrees extend the quadtree concept into three dimensions. They are much simpler than BSP trees, and they work well with outdoor scenes or with scenes where the objects are separated by large empty spaces.

With octrees, nodes are partitioned with three axis-aligned planes that split the node in the middle point along each axis. This creates eight children of equal size in each subdivision. Each node is represented by an axis-aligned box (AABB) and contains the geometry that lies within its volume.

The advantage of octrees is that they can provide hierarchical culling. When rendering, the axis-aligned bounding boxes of the nodes are tested for visibility against the view frustum in a recursive process starting from the root node. If a node is not visible, then all subnodes are also not visible and can be culled. This allows you to discard large portions of the scene quickly.

Building an Octree

The basic structure for an octree node includes a geometry list, an AABB, and pointers to its parent and children. You start by creating an AABB around the scene (the root node) and recursively subdividing it into eight children. The subdivision of a node stops when either a maximum depth level is reached or a minimum number of polygons are contained in a node.

Geometry is usually stored in leaf nodes only, but rather than storing the actual geometry data, leaf nodes store indices or pointers to the geometry to avoid duplicating data.

The subdivision function checks first to see if the node needs to be subdivided. If so, the eight children are created, and every triangle in the given geometry list needs to be assigned to one child; or, if it's contained in more than one child, we have a few options. One is to split the triangle and assign the resulting triangles to the appropriate nodes.

For collision-detection purposes, you might need to store pointers to neighbor nodes as well. A neighbor of a node is the node of equal size or greater that touches it. Neighbor finding is done after the tree is built, and it is usually done from bottom to top. This means you start at leaf nodes and go up one level and check the other child nodes to determine the neighbors. For every face of the AABB of a node, you would need to find another node with a face that shares the same face vertices (this face will have its normal in the opposite direction and its size will be equal or greater).

Another approach for neighbor searching, which is described in detail by Frisken and Perry (see this section's references), involves assigning a location code to each node, where each bit in the location code indicates the branching pattern at a level of the tree, so that the location code acts as a search key.

Figure 12.18 shows a simple example octree.

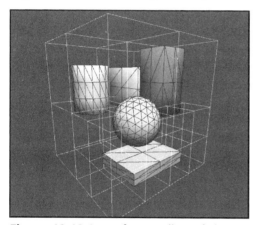

Figure 12.18 Octree for a small set of objects.

Splitting Triangles

Regardless of the spatial-partitioning structure you choose, at some point you might need to split triangles, so it's useful to see one way in which this can be done.

Given a triangle and a plane, if the plane splits the triangle you should have exactly two intersection points and at most three resulting fragments (Figure 12.19). So you test each edge, looking for the intersection points, and create the appropriate resulting triangles as shown in the following code (note that the code is not optimized):

```
enum HALFSPACE
{
  NEGATIVE = -1,
```

```
      ON_PLANE = 0,
      POSITIVE = 1
};

int SplitTriangle(Triangle tri, Plane plane, Triangle *splitTris, int *numSplit)
{
    int split=0;
    HALFSPACE side1, side2, side3;
    Vector3 v1, v2, v3;
    Vector3 intersectionPt1, intersectionPt2;

    tri.Get_Vertices(&v1, &v2, &v3);

    // Classify vertices
    side1 = ClassifyPoint(plane, v1);
    side2 = ClassifyPoint(plane, v2);
    side3 = ClassifyPoint(plane, v3);

    // If plane intersects first edge (v1 -> v2)
    if(EdgeIntersectsPlane(v1, v2, plane, &intersectionPt1))
    {
        // Find second intersection point

        // First case, v2 and v3 are not on the same side as v1
        if( (side2 != side1) && (side3 == side2) )
        {
            // Then, the other intersection point must be in the edge v1 -> v3
            if(EdgeIntersectsPlane(v1, v3, plane, &intersectionPt2))
            {
                split = 1;
                splitTris[0].setValues(v1, intersectionPt1, intersectionPt2);
                splitTris[1].setValues(intersectionPt1, v2, intersectionPt2);
                splitTris[2].setValues(intersectionPt2, v2, v3);
                *numPart = 3;
            }
        }
        // Second case, the other intersection point is v3
        else if( (side2 != side1) && (side3 == ON_PLANE) )
        {
            intersectionPt2 = v3;
            split = 1;
            partTris[0].setValues(v1, intersectionPt1, intersectionPt2);
```

```
      partTris[1].setValues(intersectionPt1, v2, intersectionPt2);
      *numPart = 2;
    }
    // Last case, the other intersection point must be in the edge v2 -> v3
    else if( (side2 != side1) && (side3 == side1) )
    {
      if(EdgeIntersectsPlane(v2, v3, plane, &intersectionPt2))
      {
        partTris[0].setValues(v1, intersectionPt1, intersectionPt2);
        partTris[1].setValues(v1, intersectionPt2, v3);
        partTris[2].setValues(intersectionPt1, v2, intersectionPt2);
        *numPart = 3;
      }
    }
  }
  // Still not found intersection point, try the other two edges...

  return split;
}
```

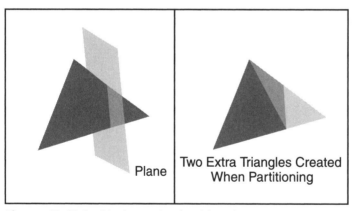

Figure 12.19 Partitioning a triangle with a plane.

Rendering an Octree

The rendering process for octrees is another recursive process that starts from the root as well. We test each node for visibility against the view frustum.

- If it's not visible, the node and all subnodes are discarded.
- If it's visible and it's a leaf node, it's rendered.
- If it's visible but it's not a leaf node, the recursive process continues on the node's children.

When building the tree, if a triangle is contained in more than one node, you have the option not to split it and to assign it to all the nodes it's contained in, but this would decrease performance because you would need to check every frame if the triangle has already been rendered. If the nodes don't share triangles, you can send all the triangles to the graphics card at once.

Loose Octrees

Another approach for avoiding splitting triangles is to use a loose octree (see Ulrich's "Loose Octrees"). Basically, the difference with loose octrees is that the size of the nodes is not fixed, but the center of the nodes is still the same. That way, the nodes will overlap, and if the size of the node is enlarged enough, the objects that would be split can now fit in only one node.

If an object doesn't fit in only one node, it will be assigned to the parent node. Therefore it's important to decide how much to enlarge the nodes. Ulrich proposes enlarging the nodes so they're at most twice the original size. If the nodes are enlarged too much, the tree could become inefficient.

Loose octrees are illustrated in Figure 12.20.

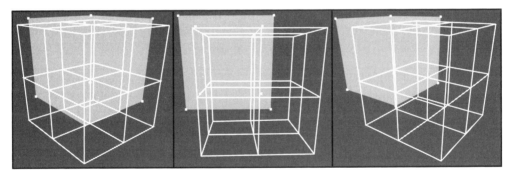

Figure 12.20 A loose octree node is larger than an original node, but it has the same center location.

Hybrid Approaches

Each scene-management approach has advantages and disadvantages. Octrees might provide hierarchical culling, but they don't provide depth sorting, which is essential to deal with transparency. Some engines, such as Ogre, implement both BSP trees and octrees, and they decide which one to use depending on the type of scene.

Depending on your specific needs, you might want to use more than one spatial-partitioning structure. For example, you can build an octree and on each node you can build a small BSP tree used for depth sorting and doing collision detection against the primitives of the node.

Adaptive Binary Trees

The final spatial subdivision topic that we'll look at is the adaptive binary tree, or ABT. The amount of documentation available on this technique is very limited. Most of the information comes from posts made by Yann Lombard on GameDev.net, so this section is a compilation of those ideas and my own experimentation.

What Is an ABT?

An ABT is another spatial data structure similar to octrees, k-d trees, and BSP trees. Like octree nodes, ABT nodes are partitioned with a plane coincident with the x-, y-, or z-axis, but instead of being partitioned into eight children, they are partitioned into only two, making the tree binary. ABTs are also similar to k-d trees in that the nodes are split with an axis-aligned plane, but k-d trees do not typically split primitives, and they use a median split scheme; that is, they always partition the node into two equal sets. ABTs use a different splitting scheme.

Geometry Management with ABTs

With ABTs, the geometry is stored in the leaf nodes only. Nonleaf nodes are used to help in doing hierarchical frustum culling when rendering. Since each primitive is unique to a leaf node, no tagging is needed; this helps with performance because the CPU does not need to check whether a primitive has already been rendered in the current frame, as would be the case if the primitive were shared among leaf nodes.

With ABTs, a geometric primitive can be a single triangle or a whole object. This is because, for ABTs, it is more convenient to deal with triangle primitives for static geometry and whole objects when it comes to dynamic geometry. You'll see the reasons for this a bit later.

As the geometry stored in a node is independent of any other geometry, you can improve rendering performance by sending the geometry directly to the GPU with a vertex array or a vertex buffer object; no additional processing is involved. You can also improve memory usage if you do not allow each leaf node to have more than 65,536 primitives; that way you can use `shorts` instead of `ints` for the array of indices.

Why Adaptive?

Unlike other fixed structures, such as the traditional octree, ABT nodes can overlap a bit. This overlapping is used to minimize primitive-splitting when creating the nodes. More importantly, the tree is adaptive because it can manage dynamic geometry at run-time.

Aren't ABTs Just AABB Trees?

Since the splitting planes used to partition space in ABTs are coincident with one of the three major axes, what you get after finishing partitioning is a set of axis-aligned bounding boxes (AABB).

You may disagree with this, but I do not consider the ABT to be just an AABB tree. Both ABTs and AABBs are three-dimensional data structures, but AABBs are *object-centric data structures* (also called bounding volume hierarchies, or BVHs), and they do not contain information on how to partition space. ABTs are *spatial data structures*, and they do partition space since that is their purpose.

In the ABT case just as in the octree case, the regions formed as a result of their partitioning scheme are AABBs. But an ABT has additional features, such as being able to deform at run time to manage dynamic geometry, which distinguish it from an AABB tree.

ABT Creation

The first step is to create an AABB around the entire scene; this will be the root node. You will then use a recursive function to subdivide the tree. This recursive function will stop either when you reach a defined subdivision depth or when the number of faces in a node is under a defined threshold. If you choose the number-of-faces criterion, a good threshold is about 3,000 to 5,000 faces per leaf node.

Node Subdivision

At each recursive step, the node gets divided into two children with a plane perpendicular to one of the three major axes. The pseudocode for each recursive call will be as follows (note I chose to use the number-of-faces criterion to stop the subdivision):

```
/* subdivides node n into two children if the number of faces in geometry g is
   not under threshold t; otherwise it stops the subdivision process on this
   node, sets the node as a leaf node, and assigns the geometry to it. */
SubdivideNode (n, g, t)
Begin
   If number of faces in geometry g is under threshold t then
      Set leafnode = true
      Assign geometry to node
   Else:
      Choose best splitting plane
         Evaluate the set of functions on candidate planes of this node
         Choose the plane with the lowest score
      Subdivide node
         Create two new nodes
         Assign each node its corresponding geometry that does not need to be
         split.
         Overgrow nodes to minimize splitting and split the needed geometry.

      Call recursive function to subdivide children
         Set leafnode = false
```

```
            Set geometrylist = null
            SubdivideNode(child1, geometry1, t)
            SubdivideNode(child2, geometry2, t)
End
```

Choosing the Splitting Plane

The most interesting part of building the ABT is choosing the splitting plane. The splitting plane is perpendicular to the x-, y-, or z-axis, but the splitting position is not fixed, which means it will vary from node to node depending on the geometry it contains.

In order to choose the axis and the splitting position for a node, you will sample a set of candidate planes at random locations along each axis and evaluate the following functions on each plane:

- **Axis function.** The purpose of this function is to try to split the node along the largest axis, so you will evaluate this function for our x-, y-, and z-axes; this function will evaluate lower scores for larger axes.
  ```
  Axis_function = Dimension(thisAxis) / Dimension(largestAxis)
  ```
- **Node Volume function.** The purpose of this function is to try to get balanced volumes on the child nodes when splitting with a plane. This function will evaluate lower scores when the difference between the volumes of the nodes being created is small.
  ```
  Volume_function(plane) = abs(Dimension(child1) — Dimension(child2))
  ```
- **Face function.** The purpose of this function is to get a balanced number of faces on the child nodes when splitting with a plane. This function will evaluate lower scores when the number of faces on both sides is more or less equal
  ```
  Face_function(plane) = abs(faceschild1 — faceschild2) / numfaces
  ```
- **Splits function.** The purpose of this function is to minimize primitive-splitting. This function will evaluate lower scores when the number of faces split by a plane is minimal.
  ```
  Splits_function(plane) = numsplitfaces / numfaces
  ```

What you will try to get is the lowest possible score from these functions; the lower the score, the better the split location is, and the more balanced the tree will be. The first function depends only on the splitting plane, the other functions will be affected by the geometry and the candidate plane we choose. For example, a candidate plane can evaluate a very low score for the Node Volume function but can evaluate a high score for the Splits function.

Depending on your priorities, you should assign weights to each of these functions. The final score will be the weighted sum of the function scores:

```
Plane_score = (Axis_function * AxisFuncWeight ) +
              (Volume_function(plane) * VolumeFuncWeight) +
              (Face_function(plane) * FaceFuncWeight) +
              (Splits_function(plane) * SplitsFuncWeight)
```

Primitive-Splitting and Node Overgrowing

When you have chosen your plane, you will split the node with it to create two child nodes and assign the corresponding geometry to each one (the geometry that does not need to be split). For the geometry that needs to be split, assign each of those primitives to the node that contains the largest portion of its area. At this point you may have a large number of primitives to split. In order to minimize this splitting, you can overgrow the nodes *along the split axis*, letting them overlap a bit (note that even if the nodes overlap, you will still keep each primitive in only one node).

The basic idea of node overgrowing (Figures 12.31 and 12.32) is:

- Overgrow each child node by about five discrete steps of 1 percent.
- On each step, check if the number of primitives to split is reduced and choose the one with the fewest splits.
- Finally, split the primitives and continue the recursive subdivision.

The overgrow is allowed to be at most 5 percent of the original volume because larger volumes are more likely to intersect the viewing frustum and you could end up doing a lot of frustum checks.

Optimizing the Tree Nodes

Once you have finished the recursive subdivision, you need to recompute the AABBs of the nodes from bottom to top to ensure you have a tight AABB for each node. This is because the parent nodes may have a larger volume than the combined AABBs of their children nodes (Figure 12.33). Once you have done this, the tree will be complete.

Eliminating T-junctions

Due to the ABT splitting scheme, you can have primitives that were split once and assigned to different nodes and then were further subdivided in one of those nodes. This could result in T-junctions and visible small gaps due to rounding-off errors. After the tree is built, you need to do a T-junction removal pass.

When building the tree, you keep track of the split faces in each node, and in the removal pass, you check if they were further subdivided; if so, you need to subdivide the other connected face. This will eliminate any T-junctions.

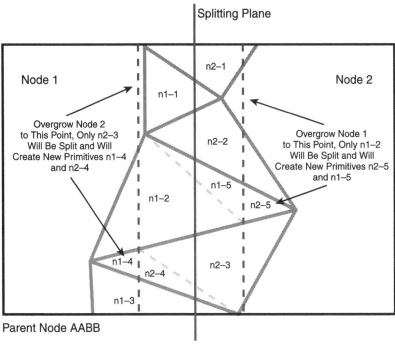

Figure 12.31 Determining how to overgrow each node.

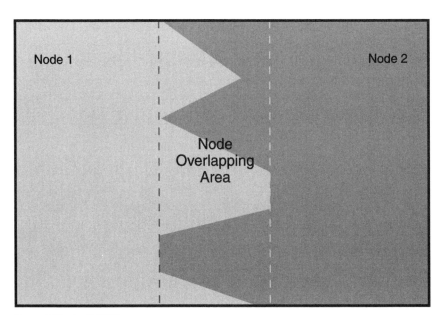

Parent Node AABB

Figure 12.32 Final geometry distribution.

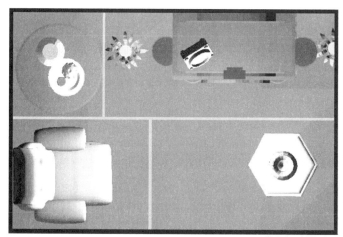

Original Nodes

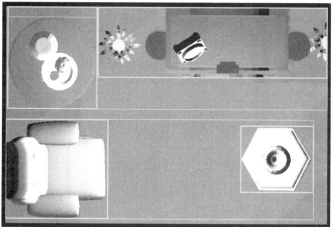

Recomputed AABBs

Figure 12.33 Tree after adjusting nodes for overgrow.

Managing Dynamic Geometry

So far you have worked the subdivision process at the mesh level. This is ideal for static geometry, but ABTs can manage dynamic geometry as well. For dynamic geometry it is better to work at the object level to avoid real-time face subdivision; in this case you will treat a whole object as a primitive.

There are two basic ways the ABT can manage dynamic geometry. The first one is just to move the object's AABB along when the object moves; if the object moves to a position where it would be split, reunify the AABBs of the affected nodes and treat them as a single node.

The second approach is to use a precomputed hierarchical object-oriented bounding box (OOBB) tree for each dynamic object. This means that you need to subdivide each dynamic object in a preprocessing stage and create an OOBB tree for it. At run-time when the object moves, instead of inserting its whole mesh in a single leaf node, you only need to insert its OOBBs in the appropriate nodes.

Structures Needed to Build an ABT

ABT construction is usually done as a preprocess because some scenes might have a large number of polygons (the custom scene for the demo has around 500,000 triangles).

Basically, you need two classes: one to represent an ABT node and one to represent the ABT itself. The ABT node class will have node-related information such as partition plane, pointers to its children and parent, and a flag to indicate whether the node is a leaf node. The ABT class will have a pointer to the root of the tree, the maximum number of triangles allowed in a node, the weights for the minimizing functions, and the methods for building the tree.

```
/*************************/
struct ABT_node_batch
{
    unsigned int textureID;
    unsigned int startFace;
    unsigned int faceCount;
};
/*************************/

class ABT_node
{
private:
    GLPlane   m_partitionPlane;                          // Partition plane
    ABT_node *m_pChild1, *m_pChild2, *m_pParent;  // Pointers to children
                                                         // and parent
    Geometry *m_pGeometry;                               // Pointer to geometry
    bool      m_bIsLeaf;                                 // Is this node a leaf?
    int       m_iBatches;                                // Number of tri batches
    STLbatchV m_batchList;                               // An STL list of batches
    //...

public:
    ABT_node();
    ~ABT_node();
};
```

```
/***************************/

class ABT
{
private:
    ABT_node *m_pRoot;                      // Pointer to root of the tree
    int   m_fMaxNodeTris;                   // Max triangles per node
    float m_fAxisScoreWeight, m_fVolumeScoreWeight;// Weights for the minimizing
    float m_fFaceScoreWeight, m_SplitsScoreWeight; // functions...
public:
    ABT(Geometry *pSceneGeometry, int maxNodeTris,
        float axisScWeight, float volumeScWeight,
        float faceScWeight, float splitsScWeight);
    ~ABT();
    int BuildABT(Geometry *m_pGeometry);
    int SubdivideNode(ABT_node *node, Geometry *m_pGeometry);
    int ComputeAABBforNode(ABT_node *node, AABB *aabb);
    void GenerateCandidatePlanes(GLPlane planes[]);
    //...
};
```

Rendering the ABT

Rendering an ABT is pretty simple; you start a recursive visibility test process at the root. You need to test both child nodes' AABBs against the viewing frustum; if a node is visible, continue the recursive testing on that branch; otherwise, stop testing. If a leaf node is reached on the recursive testing, render it.

As you saw before, since each primitive is guaranteed to be in only one leaf node, you can build a vertex array/buffer for each leaf node for fast rendering. The slight disadvantage with this approach is that textures have not been taken into account; the geometry on each node might have quite a few different textures or shaders associated with it.

Since texture and shader state changes are very expensive, if the level has a high polygon count, you can modify the rendering approach to cater to this situation. When rendering a leaf node, instead of sending the geometry to the GPU as-is, you add the geometry to a list of visible primitives. Once all visible leaf nodes' geometry has been added to the list of visible primitives, you sort the list by texture or shader ID and render all primitives sharing the same texture or shader at once.

Figure 12.34 shows a small section of the eTown scene ABT from the demo.

Figure 12.34 A screenshot from the ABT demo.

ABT References

Lombard, Yann, BSP Usefulness.
http://www.gamedev.net/community/forums/topic.asp?topic_id=130479.

Lombard, Yann. Combining Octrees and BSP Trees [...] Is It possible?
http://www.gamedev.net/community/forums/topic.asp?topic_id=123169.

Lombard, Yann. Octree Questions.
http://www.gamedev.net/community/forums/topic.asp?topic_id=138216.

Lombard, Yann, and Michael K. ABTs and the Possibility of Multiple Division Planes.
http://www.gamedev.net/community/forums/topic.asp?topic_id=133512.

Lombard, Yann, and Colt McAnlis. ABT Questions: Construction and Use.
http://www.gamedev.net/community/forums/topic.asp?topic_id=163240.

Lombard, Yann, Anthony Whitaker, and Christer Ericson. KD-Tree Nodes in 4 Bytes.
http://www.gamedev.net/community/forums/topic.asp?topic_id=295063.

Summary

Properly managing the objects that make up your scene is a vital part of attaining good performance. In this chapter, you've learned about a number of techniques—including portals, BSP trees, quadtrees, octrees, and adaptive binary trees—that have been used successfully in countless games. You may find that one of these techniques suits your game perfectly, or you may come up with a hybrid approach that works even better.

References

Akenine-Moller, Tomas, and Eric Haines. *Real-Time Rendering*, 2nd ed. Natick, MD: A.K. Peters, 2002.

Ginsburg, Dan. "Octree Construction." In *Game Programming Gems*, Mark Deloura, ed., 439–43. Hingham, MA: Charles Rivers Media, 2004.

Ulrich, Thatcher. "Loose Octrees." In *Game Programming Gems*, Mark Deloura, ed., 444–53. Hingham, MA: Charles River Media, 2000.

Watt, Alan, and Fabio Policarpo. *3D Games: Real-Time Rendering and Software Technology*, vol. 1. Upper Saddle River, NJ: Addison-Wesley, 2000.

Luebke, David, Martin Reddy, Jonathan D. Cohen, Amitabh Varshney, Benjamin Watson, and Robert Huebner. *Level of Detail for 3D Graphics*. San Francisco, CA: Morgan Kauffman, 2003.

Frisken, Sarah F., and Ronald N. Perry. Simple and Efficient Traversal Methods for Quadtrees and Octrees. **http://www.merl.com/people/perry/treeTraversalJGTWithCode.pdf**.

Saunders, Rob. Games Design, Theory and Practice, Lecture 08 - Spatial Partitioning. **http://www.soi.city.ac.uk/~rob/Lecture08-8up.pdf**.

SceneManager Class Reference.
http://www.ogre3d.org/docs/manual/manual_7.html#SEC10,
http://www.ogre3d.org/docs/api/html/classOgre_1_1SceneManager.html.

INDEX

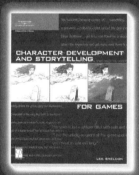